Environmental Law

ASPEN PUBLISHERS

Environmental Law
A Conceptual and Pragmatic Approach

David M. Driesen
Angela S. Cooney Professor
Syracuse University College of Law

Robert W. Adler
Associate Dean for Academic Affairs
James I. Farr Chair and Professor of Law
University of Utah, S.J. Quinney College of Law

Wolters Kluwer
Law & Business

AUSTIN   BOSTON   CHICAGO   NEW YORK   THE NETHERLANDS

ISBN 978-0-7355-6182-3

Library of Congress Cataloging-in-Publication Data

Driesen, David M.
    Environmental law : a conceptual and pragmatic approach / David M. Driesen . . . [et al.].
       p. cm.
    Includes bibliographical references and index.
    ISBN 978-0-7355-6182-3
    1. Environmental law—United States. 2. Environmental protection—United States. 3. Liability for environmental damages—United States. I. Title.

KF3775.D75 2007
344.7304'6—dc22   2007015008

About Wolters Kluwer Law & Business

Wolters Kluwer Law & Business is a leading provider of research information and workflow solutions in key specialty areas. The strengths of the individual brands of Aspen Publishers, CCH, Kluwer Law International and Loislaw are aligned within Wolters Kluwer Law & Business to provide comprehensive, in-depth solutions and expert-authored content for the legal, professional and education markets.

CCH was founded in 1913 and has served more than four generations of business professionals and their clients. The CCH products in the Wolters Kluwer Law & Business group are highly regarded electronic and print resources for legal, securities, antitrust and trade regulation, government contracting, banking, pension, payroll, employment and labor, and healthcare reimbursement and compliance professionals.

Aspen Publishers is a leading information provider for attorneys, business professionals and law students. Written by preeminent authorities, Aspen products offer analytical and practical information in a range of specialty practice areas from securities law and intellectual property to mergers and acquisitions and pension/benefits. Aspen's trusted legal education resources provide professors and students with high-quality, up-to-date and effective resources for successful instruction and study in all areas of the law.

Kluwer Law International supplies the global business community with comprehensive English-language international legal information. Legal practitioners, corporate counsel and business executives around the world rely on the Kluwer Law International journals, loose-leafs, books and electronic products for authoritative information in many areas of international legal practice.

Loislaw is a premier provider of digitized legal content to small law firm practitioners of various specializations. Loislaw provides attorneys with the ability to quickly and efficiently find the necessary legal information they need, when and where they need it, by facilitating access to primary law as well as state-specific law, records, forms and treatises.

Wolters Kluwer Law & Business, a unit of Wolters Kluwer, is headquartered in New York and Riverwoods, Illinois. Wolters Kluwer is a leading multinational publisher and information services company.

To our parents, George and Sue Driesen and the late David and Juanita Adler.

Summary of Contents

Contents

PART II
Goals for Particular Regulations

PART III
The Means of Environmental Protection

PART IV
Allocation of Responsibility

Preface

This book teaches the principal concepts that underlie environmental law. The book's structure reflects this emphasis, as it offers chapters on key concepts, such as technology-based standard setting, economic incentives, and citizen enforcement. This approach takes advantage of some of the commonalities that bind environmental law together in order to provide a coherent introduction to environmental law.

While we weave detailed information about particular environmental statutes into the text, we single out for special emphasis details that help illustrate key concepts. This approach recognizes that it is not possible to teach all of environmental law, or even all of one of the more comprehensive statutes, in a single introductory environmental law course. This means that textbooks must reflect some selection principle or risk presenting environmental law as an incoherent mass of meaningless detail. We have employed a principle of choosing the materials that best illustrate the concepts most central to environmental policy and practice.

We also employ problems to give students practice in applying the law illustrating key concepts to concrete facts. Most of the problems focus on a single chemical, PFOA, which is widely used in Teflon cookware, Gore-Tex jackets, and a host of other applications. By using this example in many different chapters, we help students see how many statutes and concepts can often address a single problem. Also, by using a common problem throughout the book, we hope to increase the depth of students' understanding and free them to devote most of their energy to learning the law.

No environmental law course can hope to teach practitioners all of the law they might need to know. But such a course can orient students, so that they know important aspects of the law and are well prepared to deeply understand new material, even material that is not part of the law today. We hope this book provides a coherent introduction to this complex field.

April 2007   David M. Driesen
                                                             Robert W. Adler

Acknowledgments

The authors want to express their great appreciation to Aspen's Richard Mixter, who supported this book from the time it was a mere possibility, and Eric Holt, our editor. We benefitted from thoughtful comments from Douglas Kysar, Amy Sinden, Amy Wildermuth, and anonymous reviewers of the text.

David Driesen would also like to thank George Aposporos for getting his book writing off to a great start by providing wonderful companionship and a great setting to get underway. Syracuse University colleague Robin Malloy helped him see the potential scholarly value of a textbook. He's grateful to Syracuse University College of Law (SUCOL) Dean Hannah Arterian for a research leave and other crucial support for the book. SUCOL and University of Michigan library staffs provided wonderful help in assembling materials, and Wendy Scott and Josh Gillette helped out with copyright permissions. Josh and several other students in his Fall 2005 Environmental Law class provided thoughtful comments on the book during his first experience teaching from the draft. He also thanks Rodney Richardson, Lauren Montforte, and Melina Williams for research assistance and Sheila Welch and Kimberley Latta for editorial assistance.

Bob Adler also wants to thank Sandra Fatt for editorial and other assistance, and Kirsten Uchitel for research assistance—including her tremendous efforts to identify and collect primary source materials on PFOA. The students in his Fall 2005 Environmental Law class served as guinea pigs by studying from the first draft of the book, and several of those students provided useful comments about everything from typos to improvements to questions and problems to case selection. The staff of the S.J. Quinney Law Library at the University of Utah provided their usual high level of service, and the College of Law's IT staff helped to solve a number of technical problems.

The authors would like to acknowledge the permission of the authors, publishers, and copyright holders of the following publications for permission to reproduce excerpts herein:

Ackerman, Bruce A., and Richard B. Stewart, Comment: Reforming Environmental Law, 37 Stanford Law Review (1985). Reprinted by permission.

Baxter, William F., People or Penguins: The Case for Optimal Pollution (1974). Reprinted by permission of Columbia University Press.

Bodansky, Daniel M., The United Nations Framework Convention on Climate Change: A Commentary, 18 Yale Journal of International Law 451 (1993). Reprinted by permission.

Botts, Lee, and Paul R. Muldoon, Evolution of the Great Lakes Water Quality Agreement (2005). Reprinted by permission of Michigan State University Press.

Bullard, Robert D., The Quest for Environmental Justice, Human Rights, and the Politics of Pollution. Copyright © by Sierra Club Books. Reprinted by permission.

Caldwell, Lynton K., The National Environmental Policy Act: An Agenda for the Future (1998). Reprinted by permission of Indiana University Press.

Carson, Rachel L., from Silent Spring, Houghton Mifflin, Boston, 1962. Copyright © 1962 by Rachel L. Carson. Copyright © renewed 1984 by Roger Christie. Used by permission of Frances Collin, Trustee u-w-o Rachel L. Carson.

Coase, Ronald H., The Problem of Social Cost, 3 Journal of Law and Economics 1 (1960). Copyright © 1960 by The University of Chicago. Reprinted by permission.

Daly, Herman E., Sustainable Growth: An Impossibility Theorem, in Valuing Earth (Herman E. Daly and Kenneth N. Townsend eds. 1992, The MIT Press). This essay originally appeared in the journal Development, 1990, nos. 3/4, 45-47. Copyright © by Palgrave Macmillan. Reprinted by permission of Palgrave Macmillan.

Dwyer, John P., The Pathology of Symbolic Legislation, Ecology Law Quarterly, Vol. 17, No. 2 (1990). Copyright © 1990 by the Regents of the University of California. Reprinted by permission of the Regents of the University of California.

Hardin, Garrett, The Tragedy of the Commons, 162 Science 1243-1248 (1968). Copyright © 1968 AAAS. Reprinted by permission.

Krier, James E., The Irrational National Air Quality Standards: Macro- and Micro-Mistakes, 22 U.C.L.A. Law Review 323 (1974-1975). Reprinted by permission.

Lazarus, Richard J., Restoring What's Environmental about Environmental Law in the Supreme Court, 47 U.C.L.A. Law Review 703 (2000). Reprinted by permission.

Leopold, Aldo, Sand County Almanac, Oxford University Press ed. 1966. Reprinted by permission of Oxford University Press, Inc.

Princen, Thomas, and Matthias Finger, Environmental NGOs in World Politics: Linking the Local and the Global (1994). Reprinted by permission of Routledge.

Rechtschaffen, Clifford L., Deterrence vs. Cooperation and the Evolving Theory of Environmental Enforcement, 71 Southern California Law Review 1181-1271 (1998). Reprinted with the permission of the Southern California Law Review.

Reitze, Arnold W. Jr., Air Quality Protection Using State Implementation Plans—Thirty-Seven Years of Increasing Complexity, 15 Villanova Environmental Law Journal 209 (2004). Reprinted by permission.

Salzman, James, and J.B. Ruhl, Currencies and the Commodification of Environmental Law, 53 Stanford Law Review 607-694 (2000). Reprinted by permission.

Stewart, Richard B., Regulation, Innovation, and Administrative Law: A Conceptual Framework, 69 California Law Review 5 (1981). Copyright © 1981 by the California Law Review, Inc. Reprinted by permission of the California Law Review.

Swift, Byron, Command Without Control: Why Cap-and-Trade Should Replace Rate Standards for Regional Pollutants, 31 Envtl. L. Rep. (Envtl. L.Inst.) 10330 (2001). Reprinted by permission of the Environmental Law Institute.

Weiss, Edith B., and Harold Jacobsen, eds., Engaging Countries: Strengthening Compliance with International Environmental Accords (1998). Reprinted by permission of The MIT Press.

Environmental Law

INTRODUCTION

This book offers a conceptual and pragmatic approach to environmental law. It reflects a conviction that a set of core concepts lies behind the mass of details found in environmental statutes, cases, and regulations, and that learning these concepts prepares students to master and make sense of the details they will encounter in practice. Mastery of these concepts also prepares students, including students who will not practice environmental law, to participate in the formulation of environmental policy as citizens. Accordingly, this book employs a conceptual organization, with sections of the book devoted to studying criteria for setting standards, the means of meeting environmental goals, the distribution of authority and responsibility among actors, and the means of enforcing standards. It does not employ the statute-by-statute organization found in most textbooks. We hope that this conceptual organization will make it easier for you to grasp the meaning of the materials that you study, rather than to think of environmental law as simply a mass of meaningless detail.

This book does, however, provide a lot of information about individual statutes and how they operate. Because the field has become too vast to offer a comprehensive introduction to natural resources law and pollution control law in one course, we include materials on the major pollution control statutes and the two statutes in other areas most often included in general environmental law courses, the Endangered Species Act and the National Environmental Policy Act. All books involve decisions about which parts of statutes to include, because no course can cover even the pollution control statutes comprehensively in a one-semester course. This book includes those materials that best emphasize the major policy issues and concepts that animate environmental law. We orient students to the universe of environmental statutes early on, in a chapter (Chapter 4) on the goals of environmental law, where we introduce students to the central goals of the major environmental statutes. Subsequent chapters provide practice in mastering some of the complexities in these statutes, but focus on those details that help them make sense of core concepts that they should master. The materials on allocation of responsibility in Chapters 12 and 13 explain how Congress has combined these concepts to create statutory schemes, thereby providing a good overview of several major statutes.

We present edited cases to illustrate the core concepts without leaving out important contextual information. We then use notes and questions to further develop students' understanding of the core concepts and how lawyers and agency officials use them in practice. Most chapters include a problem designed to allow students to integrate the concepts taught. Some of these problems also provide practice in applying detailed statutory provisions to complex regulatory questions, a skill students must master to practice in the field.

The book begins with four chapters devoted to providing basic background. The first of these chapters presents an overview of environmental problems to help students appreciate the challenges confronting environmental law. The second of these introductory chapters provides an overview of the common law, asking why policy makers turned to statutory solutions in the 1970s. The third introductory chapter discusses the idea of statutory schemes, the role of administrative agencies and judicial review, and the continuing role of the common law in this "age of statutes." The final introductory chapter introduces students to the goals of environmental law, and some of the theories that underlie them.

The book's second part addresses decisions about the stringency of regulations that often determines how much clean-up is accomplished. It includes chapters on the criteria that most frequently govern decisions about the stringency of regulatory standards, namely effects-based (or health- and environment-based), technology-based, and cost-benefit-based criteria.

The third part addresses the means of environmental protection. This part's first chapter (Chapter 8) addresses traditional regulation, which some commentators refer to as command-and-control regulation. The second chapter (Chapter 9) discusses market-based alternatives. The third chapter (Chapter 10) discusses information-based approaches, including the role of the National Environmental Policy Act and the Toxic Substances Control Act in generating information. The fourth chapter (Chapter 11) discusses pollution prevention and recycling. We provide material on the Resource Conservation and Recovery Act here, because policy regarding recycling has played such an important role in that statute.

The book's fourth part addresses the problem of distributing responsibility, both for clean-up and for making the decisions designed to spur clean-up. It begins with a chapter (Chapter 12) on the distribution of responsibility for clean-up under the Superfund statute. The next chapter (Chapter 13) addresses the distribution of responsibilities among governmental units. Both chapters show how Congress has used the concepts that we highlight in this book to create statutory schemes.

The book closes with an enforcement part. After a general introduction to enforcement philosophy, it addresses both government and citizen enforcement of environmental statutes.

We believe that this book offers a coherent education in environmental law that will provide a solid foundation for subsequent work. It requires attention to detail, but offers a framework for understanding what this area of law is about.

I

The Nature and Evolution of Environmental Law

What *is* environmental law? How does it differ from other kinds of law, and why? To some, it is simply a vast, somewhat disjointed collection of relatively recent environmental statutes, regulations, policies, cases, and other documents written to address an array of threats to human health and environmental quality caused by our modern economy and lifestyle. This view, although accurate as far as it goes, misses a lot, and makes the field hard to study. It misses the much longer history of common law and other approaches to environmental protection that pre-dated, and, to some degree, informed the era of environmental statutes and regulations. By approaching environmental law merely as a collection of separate statutes, regulations, and interpretive cases, the field becomes just another application of general administrative law. More importantly, approaching environmental law as a series of discrete statutes obscures the cohesion that becomes evident by taking a more holistic view, in which broader themes become apparent.

Under the narrow view, environmental law is a very new field. Of course, this is true in the sense that we only began to adopt comprehensive statutory approaches to environmental protection in the 1960s. Efforts to protect people and property from environmental harm, however, date back to the early days of English common law. *See* A.S. WISDOM, THE LAW ON THE POLLUTION OF WATERS 3 (Shaw & Sons Ltd., London, 1956).

To the extent that "environmental" issues involve efforts to allocate various resources among competing users—including public, shared resources, such as clean air, as well as more traditional "natural resources" like coal or water—environmental law has roots in property law. Likewise, if environmental issues involve efforts to prevent one person's activity from causing inappropriate harm to other people or environmental resources, or to compensate for that harm, environmental law has precedents in the law of torts. Some of those themes also persist in modern environmental statutes. Other somewhat more obscure common law doctrines have been resurrected over the past several decades to protect environmental values. *See, e.g.,* Joseph Sax, *The Public Trust Doctrine in Natural Resource Law: Effective Judicial Intervention,* 68 Mich. L. Rev. 471 (1970) (arguing for resurrection and expansion of public trust doctrine to protect environmental resources); National Audubon Society v. Superior Court, 658 P.2d 709 (Cal. 1983) (applying public trust doctrine to protect Mono Lake and associated wildlife resources from water depletions).

The very fact that we now have so many complex environmental statutes indicates that Congress and others believed that common law approaches did not adequately address modern environmental problems. *See, e.g.,* RACHEL CARSON, SILENT SPRING (1962) (urging increased attention to the problem of contamination by pesticides and other toxic pollutants, and leading eventually to passage of remedial federal legislation). In some of these laws, Congress borrowed principles from existing common law approaches, or modified them to fit new circumstances and the contours of an administrative regulatory system. In others, Congress adopted entirely new approaches to environmental protection.

In this opening part of the book, our goal is to orient you to a conceptual approach to environmental law by addressing three questions. First, what is the nature of environmental problems, and what particular challenges do they pose for the law? Second, how did the common law respond to those challenges, and to what degree and in what ways did those approaches succeed or fail? Third, in what major ways does the modern statutory and regulatory system complement, supplement, or supplant common law approaches, and why? These questions are addressed in the first three chapters of this book, respectively.

1

The Nature of Environmental Problems

What are the problems with which environmental law must wrestle? Billows of black smoke emanating from factory smokestacks? Torrents of noxious brew spewing from pipes into our otherwise pristine rivers? Rusty barrels of hazardous waste laying half buried in abandoned lots, leaking into ground water and causing clusters of cancer cases in adjacent communities? Certainly these kinds of problems remain, in some places and to some degree. Much more varied, often subtle, and frequently complex forms of environmental degradation also present key challenges for environmental law. We have addressed some of the most obvious forms of pollution through common law or statutory remedies. Others remain, but linkages between ongoing pollution and the kinds of harm for which legal solutions are appropriate may be less clear. Big players, such as petrochemical plants and public sewage treatment facilities, continue to pose problems, but the range of "polluters" is much larger. Indeed, all of us pollute in some ways. Significant issues of chemical contamination continue unabated, but environmental harm is caused by a litany of less obvious activities as well, from residential development to seemingly "green" golf courses. *See Golf Contaminates Environment*, Golf Course News, March 2003.

This chapter has two basic purposes. First, we provide a brief summary of the kinds of environmental problems that modern environmental law addresses. Any effort to "summarize" the nature of environmental problems is necessarily incomplete, as many volumes have been written even about individual kinds of environmental harm. Rather, our goal is to provide enough information to give you a feel for the range, complexity, and severity of various forms of environmental harm so that you can understand why this field is so important, and the basic nature of the challenges addressed by environmental law.

Second, we want to use this information as a platform from which to explore the various ways in which environmental problems present particular kinds of legal challenges. These are the issues that largely characterize environmental law, as distinct from other kinds of issues and disputes with which lawyers must grapple. This will guide our journey through the maze of laws, regulations, and cases, and help you to understand what some of the theories and methods that underpin environmental law seek to accomplish, and how.

A note about nomenclature and distinctions is in order before we begin. In this chapter, we use the term "environmental problems" somewhat broadly, to encompass pollution, overuse of natural resources, and ecosystem degradation. These issues are often closely related. The more resources we use, for example, the more waste we are likely to generate. Similarly, when we pollute more, and when we disturb land through various kinds of development, we will likely cause more significant changes to natural ecosystems. Regardless of the breadth of a particular course, it is useful to explore all three general categories of environmental harm briefly before we begin to evaluate various legal responses and solutions to those problems.

As you read the following information, take note of the characteristics of environmental problems that poses particular challenges for the law. What is "unique" or different about these issues, compared to those addressed by other areas of law?

A. POLLUTION

When we extract resources, and use them to make things, we often produce either products or by-products that contain substances that may harm human health or the environment. Harmful substances may be released into the air, water, or onto the land because we no longer want or need them, and because discarding them is cheaper or easier than reducing or eliminating the pollution. We categorize all of these issues in the general category of "pollution."[1]

1. Air Pollution

The following is based in part on a summary of data and analysis of air pollution trends produced by the U.S. Environmental Protection Agency (EPA) over a period of more than 30 years.[2] According to these estimates, the air pollution "glass" is half empty and half full.

---

1. The Clean Water Act includes an even more comprehensive definition of "pollution" as "the man-made or man-induced, alteration of the chemical, physical, biological, and radiological integrity of water." 33 U.S.C. §1362(19). This broader concept is addressed in Chapter 4.

2. These data are from EPA, Air Emissions Trends — Continued Progress Through 2003, http://www.epa.gov/airtrends/. Information on trends in emissions of particular pollutants is also available at this site.

The bad news is that EPA estimates that about 160 million tons of air pollutants are emitted into the atmosphere in the United States every year. The good news is that significant progress has been made in the more than three decades since Congress passed the 1970 Clean Air Act (CAA). During that time, total emissions of the six major air pollutants have declined by 51 percent. To put those improvements in further perspective, EPA notes that during the same period gross domestic product increased by 176 percent, total vehicle miles traveled increased 155 percent, energy consumption increased 45 percent, and the U.S. population grew by 39 percent. Thus, total air emissions decreased markedly in spite of the fact that there are more of us, and that most of us travel more and consume more of the goods and resources that contribute to air pollution.

As with almost all environmental data, some caution is in order when evaluating these statistics. It is not easy to estimate total air emissions accurately on a nationwide basis, given the large diversity of air pollution sources. Those sources include major "stationary sources" such as factories, power plants, and incinerators. Even for this fixed, relatively easy to identify category of sources, emissions estimates can be challenging because old facilities are retired and new ones built, production levels and other factors vary over time, and technical limitations prevent reliable monitoring of some of their emissions. (Pollution monitoring issues are addressed in Chapter 14.) However, air pollution also comes from a wide range and much larger number of smaller but cumulatively significant sources, called "area sources," such as auto paint shops and dry cleaners. Significant air pollution is emitted from the hundreds of millions of fossil-fuel powered vehicles ("mobile sources") that most of us drive, both on- and off-road. One of the major challenges in air pollution law and policy is how to address pollution from such a substantial and diverse number of emissions sources. Emissions estimates are also complicated by changes over time in the emissions we "count" as part of the analysis, and in the methods of analysis.[3] One key skill for environmental lawyers is to think critically about sources of information, and more importantly, the likely limitations in that information.

EPA has issued national air quality standards (addressed further in Chapter 5) for six ubiquitous air pollutants, known as "criteria pollutants": particulate matter, carbon monoxide, nitrogen oxides, sulfur dioxide, lead, and ozone (which is formed in the lower atmosphere by the interaction of various "precursor" pollutants and sunlight).[4] These pollutants cause a wide range of adverse health and environmental effects, as shown in Table 1-1.

---

3. Over the reported period, EPA changed its methods for estimating various emissions several times, for different pollutants. This makes it somewhat challenging to compare EPA's estimates over the decades. Likewise, during various periods EPA either counted, or did not count, certain sources of emissions, such as nitrous oxide emissions from fires.

4. *See* http://www.epa.gov/air/urbanair/6poll.html for more information about each of these pollutants and their effects.

TABLE 1-1
Effects of criteria air pollutants

Pollutant	Effects
Particulate matter	Associated with tens of thousands of annual deaths. Coughing and painful or difficult breathing. Increased risk of respiratory infections. Causes or exacerbates respiratory illnesses such as asthma and chronic bronchitis, and can make heart attacks and strokes more likely. Reduces visibility, adds excess nutrients to water bodies and soil, acidifies lakes and streams, and causes damage to forests and crops.
Lead	Causes harm to various parts of the body, including the kidneys, liver, nervous system, and the brain. Brain and central nervous system impacts include lower IQ, reduced attention spans and other behavioral disorders, and effects on growth, language abilities, and learning. Lead in the environment can also harm fish and wildlife.
Ozone	Irritates and inflames the lungs, causing wheezing, coughing, and painful and difficult breathing. Can lead to permanent lung damage, exacerbation of other respiratory conditions such as asthma, higher rates of pneumonia and bronchitis. Harms crops and other plants.
Carbon monoxide	Causes chest pain and adverse cardiovascular effects, especially to persons with existing heart conditions. It also harms the central nervous system, with effects on vision, attention span, and impaired learning and manual dexterity.
Nitrous oxides	Contributes to ozone formation, and to acid rain that impairs lakes, streams, and forests, and damages cars and buildings. Nitric acid in the atmosphere can impair breathing and cause lung damage, reduce visibility, and add excess nutrients to large water bodies.
Sulfur oxides	Impair breathing, especially for those with asthma, other forms of respiratory illness, and heart disease. They also reduce visibility, contribute to acid rain, and damage plants and buildings.

In addition to these large volume pollutants, toxic air pollutants emitted in smaller quantities can cause cancer, reproductive problems, birth defects, and other adverse health and environmental effects. *See* 42 U.S.C. §7412(b)(1) (long list of hazardous air pollutants identified by Congress).

Despite the apparent improvements noted above, air pollution in the United States continues to contribute to significant human health and other problems. According to EPA, at least 100 million people in the United States suffer from air-pollution-related health effects, including premature deaths, as well as illnesses from diseases such as asthma, emphysema, upper respiratory infections, and other pulmonary disorders. Air pollution also damages property, such as buildings and crops, and environmental resources, such as forests and lakes.

Finally, some air pollutants have more global impacts, contributing to depletion of the stratospheric ozone layer which protects us from solar radiation, and to global warming.[5] Carbon dioxide from fossil fuel combustion, along with other artificially-produced gases, build up in the atmosphere to cause what is called the "greenhouse effect." Even small increases in the concentration of these gases in the atmosphere traps more solar energy within the atmosphere, leading to a gradual rise in the earth's average mean surface temperature. See NATIONAL OCEANIC AND ATMOSPHERIC ADMINISTRATION, REPORT TO THE NATION, OUR CHANGING CLIMATE (1997). Over the past 250 years, the concentration of carbon dioxide in the Earth's atmosphere increased by over one third, and in the past century, global temperature has increased by 0.6°C.

The implications of these changes are not fully understood, but could be dramatic. Already, for example, warmer ocean temperatures appear to have killed off portions of the world's coral reefs. Other observed effects of increased global temperatures are permanent loss of glaciers and ice sheets, thawing of permafrost, shifts in growing seasons, migration of plant and animal populations, and declining plant and animal populations in some regions. It is widely believed that ongoing climate change has and will continue to result in rising sea levels and increasing sea temperatures, shifting precipitation patterns, increased risk of forest fire, increased severity of droughts and desertification, increased severity and frequency of storms, floods, landslides, mudslides and avalanches, shifting patterns in the spread of pests and disease among plants, animals and humans, continued significant habitat loss for fish and wildlife, and increasing species extinction and overall decline in global biodiversity.[6] Climate also raises serious potential issues of global economic and environmental equity, with serious political implications. For example, low-lying and arctic countries, some of which face serious economic challenges, may bear a higher share of the risk from rising ocean levels. Some Inuit villagers in the Arctic have already been displaced by rising seas, and are demanding compensation.

2. Water Pollution

Water pollution similarly results from a surprisingly wide range and large number of sources. The stereotypical water polluter is a large factory spewing

---

5. Ozone is a deleterious pollutant at lower levels (the "troposphere") where it is a respiratory irritant, but is an important part of our protective atmosphere at much higher elevations.

6. See Climate Change 2001: Impacts, Adaptation and Vulnerability, Contribution of Working Group II to the Third Assessment Report of the Intergovernmental Panel on Climate Change (February 2001). For more in-depth discussion and analysis of climate change, see TIM FLANNERY, THE WEATHER MAKERS: HOW MAN IS CHANGING THE CLIMATE AND WHAT IT MEANS FOR LIFE ON EARTH (2005); ELIZABETH KOLBERT, FIELD NOTES FROM A CATASTROPHE (2006); and EUGENE LINDEN, THE WINDS OF CHANGE: CLIMATE, WEATHER, AND THE DESTRUCTION OF CIVILIZATIONS (2006).

a noxious brew of chemicals into an otherwise pristine river. And while industrial pollution remains a problem for U.S. waterways, pollutants find their way into rivers, lakes and other waters from many other sources that are more closely connected with the everyday lives of most citizens. Most obviously, every time we flush the toilet or wash household chemicals down the drain we send wastes into the public sewer system. Safe collection, treatment and disposal of municipal sewage has been one of our largest, and most expensive, water pollution challenges.

Perhaps less obvious is the pollution that reaches our waterways from virtually every human activity that changes the character of land. Because this form of pollution usually stems from precipitation and runoff from large areas, rather than discrete pipes or ditches, it is known as "nonpoint source pollution," or more descriptively, as polluted runoff.[7] Soil tilled on farms is exposed to wind and rain, and can erode in large quantities into adjacent waters. (This both wastes valuable soil as a natural resource and pollutes waterways.) Fertilizers and pesticides used to grow crops add to the broad scope of agricultural pollution. But while agricultural runoff is the largest single source of polluted runoff, virtually every land-altering activity adds its own mix of pollutants. Land disturbed by construction, grazing, logging, and mining contributes sediment and other pollutants, particularly after intensive rainfall. An even wider range of pollutants runs off of built and paved surfaces (roads, buildings, parking lots), because of the wide range of chemicals and other pollutants that collect there. These pollutants include oil and other fluids from motor vehicles; metals, paints, and other materials that wear off of structures; stored or spilled industrial or construction chemicals; and organic waste from a wide variety of sources (including pet wastes). Much like mobile and area source air pollution, nonpoint source water pollution poses a serious challenge due to the sheer volume and diversity of sources.

As with the air pollution picture, U.S. water pollution control efforts over the past several decades involve a mixture of success and failure. Although major problems remain, available evidence shows significant progress in reducing discharges of pollutants to U.S. waters over the past thirty years, in large part due to requirements imposed in the Clean Water Act (CWA).

In 1972, despite decades of significant federal, state, and local investment in public sewage treatment infrastructure, domestic sewage remained one of the major unaddressed sources of water pollution. By 1996, modern public sewage treatment plants served approximately 73 percent of the U.S. population. Lest this fact lull us into complacency, however, we have still not solved this aspect of water pollution control. According to EPA's most recent analysis, the nation faces estimated public sewerage needs of almost $140 billion by 2016, for new plants, collection systems, and efforts to control sewer system

---

7. The precise legal distinction between "point source" and "nonpoint source" pollution is more complex, and is addressed in Chapter 13.

overflows.[8] Similarly, from 1972 through the early 1990s, U.S. industry invested over $57 billion in water pollution control. This resulted in reductions of millions of tons of conventional pollutants and over a billion pounds of toxic pollutants[9] per year. As is true for municipal sewage, however, significant releases of industrial pollutants into U.S. waterways continue. In 2000, for example, U.S. industries reported releases of almost 261 million pounds of toxic pollutants to surface waters.[10]

Despite progress in reducing the discharge of pollutants from municipal and industrial point sources, trends in ambient water quality, *i.e.*, in the "chemical integrity" of U.S. waters, remain ambiguous and inconsistent. This is due in part to the ongoing releases of point source pollutants discussed above, and in large part to the runoff of pollutants from nonpoint sources. Large numbers of urban watersheds remain chemically impaired due to pathogens, phosphorus, insecticides, herbicides, and toxics from municipal and industrial sources; and many rural watersheds remain chemically impaired due to nutrients, sediment, and agricultural chemicals.[11] Long-term water quality trends can be difficult to assess due to gaps in data, differences in methods of data collection and analysis, and other factors, although methods and information have improved in recent years.[12] Available evidence, however, indicates that the nationwide reduction in releases of pollutants from point sources has not translated universally to improved ambient water quality. Where consistent, long-term water quality data is available, more often than not they show *no clear trends* in ambient water quality. Improvements are evident largely in areas where pollution comes predominantly from point sources, but water quality has remained steady or declined in areas where nonpoint sources predominate.

The evidence of ongoing impairment of chemical water quality in some areas, in turn, translates to documented harm to human health and aquatic ecosystems. Over a third of the nation's rivers and almost half of its lakes do not have sufficiently high water quality to protect uses such as drinking water, swimming, and fishing, in whole or in part, due to a combination of chemical

8. U.S. Environmental Protection Agency, 1996 Clean Water Needs Survey, available at http://www.epa.gov/owm/uc.htm (visited June 18, 2001). The expected 2002 Needs Survey report has not been issued.

9. "Conventional" pollutants include biological oxygen demand, suspended solids, fecal coliform, and pH. 33 U.S.C. §1314(a)(4). The toxic "priority pollutants" were identified in a 1976 Consent Decree between EPA and national environmental groups, which was later ratified by Congress. *See* 33 U.S.C. §1311(b)(2)(C).

10. U.S. Environmental Protection Agency, TRI 2000 Data Release, http://www.epa.gov/tri/tridata/tri00/index.htm (released May 23, 2002).

11. *See* U.S. Department of the Interior, U.S. Geological Survey, Selected Findings and Current Perspectives on Urban and Agricultural Water Quality by the National Water-Quality Assessment Program (USGS Fact Sheet FS-047-01, April 2001).

12. *See* Richard B. Alexander, et al., *Data from Selected U.S. Geological Survey National Stream Water Quality Monitoring Networks*, 34 Water Resources Res. 2401 (1998).

pollution and other factors.[13] For example, the states and EPA issued over 2,500 fish and wildlife consumption advisories in 1998, and more than 2,800 in the year 2000, due to toxics and other contaminants in waterways (mercury, PCBs, chlordane, dioxins, DDT residues), reflecting a steady increase since 1993. (The apparent increasing trend may be due in part to better monitoring and reporting.)[14] Similarly, states and localities issued at least 13,410 beach closings or advisories in 2001, some due to heavy rainfall but most due to pathogens and other contaminants, a 19 percent jump over the previous year and over twice as many as in 1999 (again, in part due to improved testing and reporting).[15]

3. Solid and Hazardous Wastes

In the business of modern life we produce a lot of garbage, especially in the United States. U.S. citizens, businesses, and institutions generated over 229 million tons of "municipal solid waste" in 2001, an average of 4.4 pounds per person per day (up significantly from an estimated 2.7 pounds in 1960).[16] While not as dangerous in small amounts as the "hazardous waste" discussed below, municipal waste still poses serious environmental problems if it is not handled safely. In the past, we sent much of our municipal garbage to open dumps, which contaminated land and water and posed public health hazards from pathogens. Other waste we burned in unregulated incinerators, causing air pollution, and still more we simply dumped into the ocean or other large water bodies. Moreover, not all of our household waste is ordinary "garbage." Household hazardous waste includes a wide range of chemicals that can be every bit as toxic as industrial "hazardous wastes." For example, hazardous ingredients are commonly found in oven cleaners, toilet cleaners, laundry bleach, lawn insecticides, indoor pesticides, mouse and rat poisons, paint thinners, turpentine, oil and enamel-based paints, wood stains and finishes,

13. U.S. ENVIRONMENTAL PROTECTION AGENCY, NATIONAL WATER QUALITY INVENTORY, 2000 REPORT TO CONGRESS (EPA841-R-02-001, August 2002) (2000 NATIONAL WATER QUALITY INVENTORY).

14. *See* U.S. ENVIRONMENTAL PROTECTION AGENCY, NATIONAL WATER QUALITY INVENTORY, 1998 REPORT TO CONGRESS 191-221 (EPA841-R-00-001, June 2002) (1998 NATIONAL WATER QUALITY INVENTORY); 2000 NATIONAL WATER QUALITY INVENTORY, *supra* note 13, at ES-4. *See also* U.S. Environmental Protection Agency, National Listing of Fish and Wildlife Consumption Advisories, http://fish.rti.org/; http://www.epa.gov/ost/fish; and U.S. Environmental Protection Agency, Fact Sheet, Update: National Listing of Fish and Wildlife Advisories, EPA-823-F-01-010 (April 2001).

15. *See* NATURAL RESOURCES DEFENSE COUNCIL, TESTING THE WATERS 2002: A GUIDE TO WATER QUALITY AT VACATION BEACHES, available at http://www.nrdc.org/water/oceans/ttw/titnx.asp.

16. This information is available at http://www.epa.gov/epaoswer/non-hw/muncpl/facts.htm.

fluorescent lightbulbs, batteries and several automotive products.[17] While each of us may generate only a small amount of this waste, collectively we produce over one and a half million tons of household hazardous waste a year.

Under federal law, we have taken several steps to handle this huge solid waste burden more carefully. First, by encouraging material reuse and recycling, we try to reduce the amount of waste material that must be disposed of. (At the same time, by reusing and recycling these materials, we reduce the amount of virgin natural resources used for new products.) We recycled 68 million tons of municipal solid waste in the United States in 2001, double the amount recycled just a decade earlier, and more than a ten-fold increase from 1960. Second, we have prohibited unsafe open dumping of garbage, and require states to regulate the design and operation of landfills and incinerators, to reduce adverse environmental impacts from those practices. Nonetheless, the safe disposal of the remaining 70 percent of municipal solid waste every year presents a huge ongoing challenge. Properly designed and operated sanitary landfills require a considerable amount of space, which is particularly problematic in crowded urban areas. Moreover, both landfills and incinerators now must meet strict siting requirements, further limiting the number of available locations for these activities. Landfills, for example, cannot be placed in wetlands or flood plains where groundwater contamination is likely, and incinerators must be situated where they will not cause or exacerbate air pollution health problems.

The amount of waste we each generate to sustain our modern lifestyle is not limited to the bags of garbage we take to the curb every week. Virtually everything we produce creates industrial waste, only some of which is released as air and water pollution. The rest is treated as solid waste, *i.e.*, disposed of on land, in storage pits or lagoons, injected into underground wells, or incinerated. Ironically, the pollution control methods developed to stem air and water pollution concentrated many of those wastes into municipal and industrial sludge or other forms of solid waste that now must be addressed in some other way to prevent environmental harm. As with municipal waste, federal law encourages material reuse and recycling to reduce our industrial waste burden as much as possible. Nevertheless, the United States produces huge volumes of industrial wastes every year.[18]

17. See http://www.epa.gov/msw/hhw-list.htm for further information on household hazardous waste items, and http://www.epa.gov/msw/hhw.htm for further information on disposal issues and figures related to household hazardous waste.

18. In 1988, EPA estimated that 11 billion tons of non-hazardous industrial and municipal waste were generated in the United States per year. EPA, OFFICE OF SOLID WASTE AND EMERGENCY RESPONSE, REPORT TO CONGRESS: SOLID WASTE DISPOSAL IN THE UNITED STATES (Vols. I-III), EPA/530-SW-88-011B (October 1988). EPA's Industrial Waste Management web page states that "American industrial facilities generate and dispose of approximately 76 billion tons of industrial solid waste each year." http://www.epa.gov/epaoswer/non-hw/industd/index.htm (also using 1988 data).

Some industrial waste is no more dangerous than municipal waste, and can be disposed of safely in well-designed and located landfills. Other kinds of industrial waste are generated in smaller volumes but have far greater potential for harm due to their inherent toxicity and other properties. According to data reported to EPA,[19] over 19,000 facilities generated at least 41 million tons of legally-defined hazardous waste in the United States in 2001.[20] These wastes cannot safely be disposed of through methods used for other kinds of solid waste without prior treatment, unless more carefully constructed and operated facilities are used.

The nation awoke with a start to the legacy of our past inattention to hazardous waste disposal as hazardous waste nightmares surfaced in the 1960s and 1970s. The most notorious example was the "Love Canal" site in Tonawanda, New York, in which huge volumes of highly toxic wastes had been dumped for many years in an area later developed as a typical American suburb (complete with homes, schools, and playgrounds later found to be contaminated). *See* ADELIN GORDON LEVINE, LOVE CANAL: SCIENCE, POLITICS AND PEOPLE (1982). In this and in many other locations around the country, controversy continues about how many people were exposed to what kinds of wastes, and how much increased health and environmental risk resulted from that exposure. In some cases, evidence exists of "cancer clusters" and other concentrations of illness in the vicinity of hazardous waste sites. But a range of contaminants from other sources, routine chemical use and exposure (addressed in the following subsection), smoking and diet, and a wide range of other variables complicate our ability to determine clear cause-and-effect relationships.

Nevertheless, the problem of haphazard past hazardous waste disposal practices remains a major national problem now addressed by the federal Superfund program, which establishes a system of identifying and ranking large hazardous waste sites, cleaning them up or minimizing their risks, and allocating responsibility for cleanup among responsible parties (if they can be located or even still exist). As of April 28, 2005, the list of Superfund sites around the country[21] included 1,244 active sites, with 64 more proposed. (This list does not include the thousands of other hazardous waste disposal sites around the country that do not meet the criteria for the Superfund program.) On EPA's website, you can locate listed Superfund sites in your state.[22] While EPA, state agencies, and private parties have taken actions to reduce risks or to clean up

---

19. EPA, THE NATIONAL BIENNIAL RCRA HAZARDOUS WASTE REPORT (BASED ON 2001 DATA) (EPA 530-R-03-007, July 2003).

20. This statistic is conservative for several reasons. First, the legal definition of what "solid waste" is also "hazardous waste" is complex and often uncertain. Second, the data reported above includes only "large quantity generators," typically only those facilities that generate more than 1,000 kg (1.1 tons) of hazardous waste in any one month. Small quantity generators (generators who produce more than 100 kg but less than 1,000 kg of hazardous waste in any month), taken together, may add significantly to this amount.

21. *See* http://www.epa.gov/superfund/sites/query/queryhtm/npltotal.htm.

22. http://www.epa.gov/superfund/sites/npl/npl.htm.

many sites,[23] the problem of solving past improper waste disposal practices remains serious.

4. Toxic Chemicals

Not all of the chemicals and other materials that pose hazards to human health and to the environment are "pollutants" or "wastes," although they can become so if stored, used or transported improperly. Depending on the substances, some chemicals can pose human health and environmental risks even when used as intended, due to their toxicity, persistence in the environment or in our bodies, combinations with other chemicals, and other factors.

The growth of chemicals used in modern life has been astonishing.[24] As of 1976, an estimated 60,000 chemicals were used in the United States, most of which were developed and manufactured absent any testing or other regulatory requirements to determine potential harm to human users or to the environment. Moreover, an estimated 1,000 new chemicals enter the market every year. The sheer volume of chemicals used has grown rapidly as well. Between 1966 and 1994, the production of synthetic organic chemicals alone grew from 40 to 149 million tons per year. Agricultural pesticide use in the United States increased as well, from about 400 million pounds a year in the mid-1960s to over 800 million pounds annually by 1985.[25] When we tally all uses of insecticides, herbicides, and fungicides, for activities ranging from water disinfection to crop protection to lawn and garden maintenance, approximately 4 billion tons of pesticide products were used annually in the United States by 1997.

Determining what health and environmental risks this huge array of chemicals may present is a daunting and uncertain task. If a human subpopulation experiences an increase in cancer, or if birds in a local lake begin to develop abnormalities or have trouble reproducing, how do we know where to fix blame, given the wide range of potential causes? Even if one or more chemicals appears to be implicated, how can we determine what levels of exposure pose what degree of risk? We do know that many chemicals, including some that provide useful services to society, can cause cancer or other health risks, including birth defects and other developmental harm to fetuses and infants, and genetic changes that may affect future generations. More recent evidence suggests that many chemicals affect our endocrine (hormone) systems, with changes in reproductive health and other impacts on our children.

23. EPA reports that over 6,400 actions have been taken to reduce public health and environmental risks at Superfund sites, and that cleanups have been completed at 757 sites. *See* http://www.epa.gov/superfund/action/20years/preface.htm.

24. Data in this section are taken from Lynn R. Goldman, *Toxic Chemicals and Pesticides*, in STUMBLING TOWARD SUSTAINABILITY (JOHN DERNBACH, ed. 2002).

25. Nonagricultural use of pesticides, on the other hand, decreased by a third between 1970 and 1990.

See THEO COLBORN, DIANNE DUMANOSKI, AND JOHN PETERSON MYERS, OUR STOLEN FUTURE (1996). Certain chemicals persist for long times within the global ecosystem, posing similar risks to fish and wildlife populations worldwide. Even in the remote arctic, we find persistent toxic chemicals in the fat of seals and polar bears.[26]

As you might imagine, regulation of environmental risks from chemicals that otherwise provide useful services to society presents somewhat different challenges from those discussed above with respect to pollutants and waste products. We can reduce risks from production process wastes (known as "residuals") without necessarily foregoing the good or service produced, by changing production methods or materials, by installing pollution controls at the end of the process, or both. We neither want nor need the residual itself, but rather the good or service provided. A different set of choices is suggested when a risk is inherent in the useful product itself. We can simply decide that the benefits from the product outweigh its risks, or vice versa. We can determine whether those risks can be reduced to acceptable levels by changing the way in which we use that product (safe handling requirements, quantity restrictions, place restrictions, etc.). Or, we can phase out the use of a particularly dangerous chemical if viable substitutes are found.

B. OVERUSE OF NATURAL RESOURCES

By virtually any measure, we Americans are profligate in our use of resources. *See* THOMAS PRINCEN, MICHAEL F. MANIATES, AND KEN CONCA, EDS., CONFRONTING CONSUMPTION (2002); ALAN DURNING, HOW MUCH IS ENOUGH: THE CONSUMER SOCIETY AND THE FUTURE OF THE EARTH (Worldwatch Environmental Alert Series 1992). As of 1990, it took over 50 kilograms (110 pounds) of raw materials per person per day (not including water) to support the lifestyle of the average American, and that amount increased by another 10 percent by the turn of the century.[27] Over the course of the Twentieth Century, raw material extraction and use in the United States increased at an astonishing rate, from less than 100 million metric tons to nearly 3 billion metric tons, growing more than twice as fast as population over the same period.

Natural resource use is the flip side of pollution, because the more resources we use, the more waste and other forms of pollution we are likely to generate. Moreover, we cause additional environmental harm when we extract (dig, drill, mine) resources, transport them to where they will be used, and convert them into usable products. Finally, with respect to some resources, our

---

26. *See* WORLD WILDLIFE FUND, THE TIP OF THE ICEBERG, CHEMICAL CONTAMINATION IN THE ARCTIC (2005).

27. Statistics in this paragraph come from Amit Kapur and Thomas E. Graedel, *Production and Consumption of Materials, in* STUMBLING TOWARD SUSTAINABILITY, *supra* note 24, at 63.

current rate of use exceeds sustainable levels. This trend is particularly troubling for materials and other resources that are not renewable, *i.e.*, whose supplies are not continuously re-generated by natural processes, such as fossil fuels (such as coal and oil). Even renewable resources, such as trees, however, are depleted if we use them faster than they are naturally or artificially replaced.

Americans are especially notorious for our use of energy, particularly nonrenewable fossil fuels, emissions from which also contribute significantly to the threat of global warming (discussed above). Recent trends in energy use are not encouraging. Total energy use in the United States jumped 20 percent from 1992 to 2000, and energy-related emissions of carbon dioxide (the major gas contributing to global warming) increased by 10 percent during the same period.[28] Increased energy use stems both from our increasing population and from our love affairs with energy-consuming devices, from cars to computers, and our desire that these products themselves become more powerful. This persistent growth in energy demand, in turn, prompts proposals to drill for more oil and gas (in places like the Arctic National Wildlife Refuge in Alaska and other wilderness areas in the West), dig more coal, build more dams, or seek alternative sources of energy or ways to use existing energy more efficiently. Recently, policy makers have showed renewed interest in nuclear power, which currently generates about 20 percent of our electric power, but which has seen no new plant construction for over a quarter century.

Water is perhaps our most basic natural resource. Total water supplies in the United States are abundant, especially relative to many other countries. But we do not always have clean, fresh water where and when we want it. Some regions of the United States have abundant supplies, while others are more arid. In some areas, water is plentiful during wet seasons of the year but not others, or in wet periods but not during droughts.[29] Americans also *use* considerably more water than do people in most other countries. Per capita water use in the United States is higher, in most cases significantly, than in all but five relatively small countries.[30]

Many areas of the country, historically in the West but increasingly in the eastern states as well, face serious periodic water shortages during times of drought, especially given rapid urban growth and competition with agriculture and other traditional water users. In most western states, surface water resources are already fully allocated to specified uses, but population growth continues.[31] In some regions, such as the Ogalalla aquifer in the high plains region, fresh water is being withdrawn from groundwater at rates significantly higher than the rate of natural renewal. Obviously, this practice of "mining"

28. Lynn Price and Mark D. Levine, *Production and Consumption of Energy, in* Stumbling Toward Sustainability, *supra* note 24, at 79, 86.

29. Information in this paragraph is taken from Robert W. Adler, *Fresh Water, in* Stumbling Toward Sustainability, *supra* note 24, at 215-216.

30. Peter H. Gleick, The World's Water 2000-2001, at 205-211.

31. *See* Western Water Policy Review Advisory Commission, Water in the West: The Challenge for the Next Century 3-6 (1998).

groundwater cannot be sustained indefinitely.[32] On a more positive note, however, while U.S. water use grew steadily throughout most of the 20th Century, on both an absolute and per capita basis, both total water withdrawals and per capita consumptive use have actually declined since 1980,[33] reflecting some improvements in water use efficiency.

Dwindling agricultural and other productive land resources are also a concern in many parts of the country. According to the National Resources Inventory[34] prepared by the Natural Resources Conservation Service, a branch of the U.S. Department of Agriculture, between 1982 and 2001 about 34 million acres — roughly the size of Illinois — was converted to development. Almost half of this land was formerly forested, about a fifth was crop land, and another 16 percent was pasture. Increasingly, lands identified as "prime farmland" are the targets of this development. Thus, during this period the nation lost about 12 percent of its total crop land. Americans also continue to cut forests at a rapid pace, although reforestation efforts have increased, and reliable information on the health of our forest base is scarce.[35] According to the National Report on Forest Resources prepared by the U.S. Forest Service,[36] while the amount of forested land in the United States has dropped by more than 20 percent since the time of European settlement, total forested acreage has remained relatively constant since about 1920 (between 700-800 million acres). That statistic about net acreage is somewhat misleading, however, because considerable amounts of old growth forest have been cut and replaced with newer forests. We cut timber on about 10 million acres of that land each year, about 38 percent by clear cutting.

C.   ECOSYSTEM DEGRADATION

Very often the law of pollution, with its attention to toxic and other chemicals, focuses heavily on human health issues. Much environmental law, however, also addresses the destruction, alteration, or degradation of the

---

32. *See* ROBERT GLENNON, WATER FOLLIES (Island Press 2002).

33. *See* WAYNE SOLLEY ET AL., ESTIMATED WATER USE IN THE UNITED STATES 1995 at 1 (U.S. Geological Survey Circular No. 1200). Offstream water use continued to grow between 1950 and 1980; that same use dropped between 1980 and 1985 and has remained approximately level since then, despite continuing growth in the U.S. population. *Id.* at 63.

34. These data are reported as follows: Development: http://www.nrcs.usda. gov/technical/land/nri01/nri01dev.html. Erosion: http://www.nrcs.usda.gov/technical/ land/nri01/nri01eros.html. Land use: http://www.nrcs.usda.gov/technical/land/nri01/ nri01lu.html.

35. *See* Robert L. Fischman, *Forestry, in* STUMBLING TOWARD SUSTAINABILITY, *supra* note 24, at 327, 329.

36. W. Brad Smith,; Patrick D. Miles,; John S. Vissage,; and Scott A. Pugh. Forest Resources of the United States 2002 (U.S. Forest Service, General Technical Report NC-241, 2004).

ecosystems on which human and other life depends. To some extent, humans have always altered the natural world — at least since the beginning of recorded history, and probably long before then.[37] In the modern industrial world, we accelerated such changes with unprecedented magnitude and speed. This degree of change presents a different kind of challenge for environmental law.

Aquatic ecosystems present one of the most dramatic examples of the degree to which humans have changed the natural world at the expense of ecosystem health. Waterfront areas were among the first to be developed in the Old World, because proximity to water served a multitude of purposes, including navigation, irrigation, industry, defense, and culinary uses. Relatively flat, fertile floodplain lands were easier to build on and more productive to farm. Similarly, from the earliest days of the American Republic, waterways were critical for transportation and trade, settlement, fishing, farming, and defense.[38]

To promote these uses, America's waters have been dammed, channelized, dewatered, levied, and riprapped, and farms and communities have been developed right up to the water's edge, at the expense of natural floodplain, wetland, and riparian habitats. These changes caused severe accompanying degradation of our aquatic resources.[39] According to the Federal Emergency Management Agency, floodplain development has destroyed about one-half of the natural woody riparian habitat in the contiguous states. Dams have caused the inundation of over 600,000 stream miles, and diversions from those structures seriously alter natural stream flows and habitats. The U.S. Fish and Wildlife Service reports that over one-half of the wetlands in the coterminous states have been lost; and while the rate of wetlands destruction has slowed, we continue to lose about 60 thousand acres a year. This is significant because functioning wetlands serve as natural filters for pollutants, greatly reduce the potential impacts of flooding, and provide invaluable habitat for plants, fish and wildlife.[40]

This development on or near waterways led to a serious decline in freshwater aquatic biodiversity in the United States. According to a comprehensive national survey conducted by The Nature Conservancy, "animals that depend on freshwater habitat — mussels, crayfishes, fishes, and amphibians — are in the

---

37. *See, e.g.*, DONALD WORSTER, RIVERS OF EMPIRE, WATER, ARIDITY AND THE GROWTH OF THE AMERICAN WEST (1985) (describing ecosystem-altering deforestation by American Indians many centuries ago).

38. *See* Charles F. Wilkinson, *The Headwaters of the Public Trust: Some Thoughts on the Sources and Scope of the Traditional Doctrine*, 19 Envtl. L. 425, 431-35 (1989) (describing the importance of waterways in the early United States).

39. *See* ROBIN A. ABELL ET AL., FRESHWATER ECOREGIONS OF NORTH AMERICA: A CONSERVATION ASSESSMENT (2000); Robert W. Adler, *The Two Lost Books in the Water Quality Trilogy: The Elusive Objectives of Physical and Biological Integrity*, 33 Envtl. L. 29, 71 (2003) (evidence from state bioassessment programs that stressors other than pollutants are responsible for more damage to aquatic ecosystem integrity).

40. EPA, Functions and Values of Wetlands (EPA 843-F-01-002c, September 2001).

worst condition overall."[41] Approximately 10 percent of bird, mammal, and reptile species are threatened or endangered, compared to about 30 percent for amphibians and fishes, and an alarming 60 to 70 percent for freshwater crayfishes and mussels. The World Wildlife Fund-U.S. concluded that sufficient numbers of aquatic species are affected that entire "faunal assemblages are in a precarious state." Likewise, a recent assessment of riparian area health published by a committee of the National Research Council[42] reported widespread impairment of riparian habitats, along with accompanying impacts to water quality and aquatic ecosystem health.

Aquatic ecosystems are not alone in this regard. The U.S. Fish and Wildlife Service and the National Marine Fisheries Service have listed over 1,300 species as threatened or endangered (or some combination, depending on location) under the Endangered Species Act (ESA).[43] But most experts agree that these agencies have formally listed only a fraction of imperiled species under the ESA. As with aquatic ecosystems, most of this lost biodiversity stems from extensive habitat loss and degradation. Over the past two centuries, we plowed most of the extensive grassland prairies that once covered large portions of the continent. Likewise, while raw acreage of land covered by forests has remained relatively constant since the 1930s (following the initial decline from pre-Colonial times), most of the natural, planted substitutes have replaced ecologically-rich old growth forest. These planted forests generally consist of much less diverse and less healthy monocultures. In the West, grazing lands once covered with a diverse assemblage of resilient natural grasses and shrubs have either been denuded, or replaced with vast swaths of cheat grass and other exotic or invasive species.[44]

Exotic (non-native, or "alien") species, in fact, are one of our most pervasive, potentially destructive, and least appreciated forms of ecosystem alteration.[45] Invasive plants infest an estimated 100 million acres in the United States, and are spreading to another three million acres a year. According to the National Invasive Species Information Center, human action is the primary culprit in the proliferation of non-native species in the United States.[46] Exotic species sometimes are introduced intentionally (for example, as ornamental plants) but spread well beyond their intended domesticated areas. In other cases, they are introduced accidentally, for example, in the ballast water or cargo holds of ships.

41. BRUCE A. STEIN & STEPHANIE R. Flack, 1997 SPECIES REPORT CARD: THE STATE OF U.S. PLANTS AND ANIMALS.

42. NATIONAL RESEARCH COUNCIL, RIPARIAN AREAS: FUNCTIONS AND STRATEGIES FOR MANAGEMENT 8-13 (2002).

43. 16 U.S.C. §1531 et seq.

44. With respect to the grazing issue, see DEBORA L. DONAHUE, THE WESTERN RANGE REVISITED, REMOVING LIVESTOCK FROM PUBLIC LANDS TO CONSERVE BIODIVERSITY (1999).

45. NATIONAL INVASIVE SPECIES COUNCIL, MEETING THE INVASIVE SPECIES CHALLENGE, MANAGEMENT PLAN (2001).

46. See http://www.invasivespeciesinfo.gov/whatis.shtml.

Exotic species can cause fundamental ecosystem changes. The giant reed (*Arundo donax*) now clogs rivers in southern California, and the leafy spurge (*Euphorbia esula*) covers over 2.5 million acres of range across the Great Plains. Cheatgrass has accelerated the fire cycle in the West by a factor of 20. In a sense, this form of environmental change is more insidious than clear cut forests or dense urban smog, which are readily apparent to the untrained eye (or nose). And the problem of invasive plants continues to grow. The Biota of North America Program (BONAP) at the University of North Carolina, Chapel Hill, adds about 300 species per year to the list of the nation's flora, and only about 10 percent of those are natives. But the precise scope of the problem is not well known. Total estimates of non-native species introduced to the United States range from 5,000 to 50,000.

Invasive animal species pose similar threats to ecosystem health. The Asian long-horned beetle destroys city trees. The nutria, a South American rodent, is devastating wetland ecosystems. Other obvious examples include the West Nile virus, red fire ants, and the notorious zebra mussel. Introduced to the Great Lakes during the 1980s via discharged ballast water from ships, by 1999 zebra mussels had spread throughout much of the Mississippi River basin and northward into Canada. Collectively, exotic species cause severe ecological and economic harm. Almost half of all listed endangered species in the United States are adversely affected by invasive species. The National Invasive Species Council identified the problem as one of the most serious environmental threats of the Twenty-First Century. One group of researchers at Cornell University estimated that invasive species impose an economic cost in the United States of $137 billion per year.

Ecosystem alteration, with its serious implications for human society and other species, is not just a domestic problem. In 2005, a group of over 1,300 scientists in 95 countries prepared a comprehensive inventory and assessment of the Earth's ecosystems.[47] The conclusions are sobering. According to these scientists, virtually all of the Earth's ecosystems have been significantly transformed by human activity. Large groups of species are in danger of extinction on an unprecedented scale, with between 10 and 50 percent of species at risk, depending on the categories of species studied. Prominent experts like Paul Ehrlich and Edward O. Wilson believe that up to a quarter of all species that currently exist will be extinct by the middle of the Twenty-First Century, especially if tropical deforestation continues at current levels. *See* YVONNE BASKIN, THE WORK OF NATURE, HOW THE DIVERSITY OF LIFE SUSTAINS US 10 (1997). In the oceans, the total mass of commercially used species has plummeted by 90 percent throughout much of the world. On land, over half of our grasslands and forests have been converted to farms, and that has changed dramatically the use and release of soil, sediment, and nutrients such as nitrogen and phosphorous in the terrestrial and aquatic environments. Water withdrawals

---

47. MILLENNIUM ECOSYSTEM ASSESSMENT SYNTHESIS REPORT, A REPORT OF THE MILLENNIUM ECOSYSTEM ASSESSMENT (Prepublication Final Draft March 23, 2005).

from rivers and lakes doubled between 1960 and 2000, and groundwater use has skyrocketed in many areas as well. In addition to our ethical obligation to preserve and protect other species and their habitats, as recognized in laws such as the Endangered Species Act, many scientists and economists are increasingly taking note of the "ecosystem services" that are lost when species become extinct and other ecosystem resources are lost. *See* NATURE'S SERVICES, SOCIETAL DEPENDENCE ON NATURAL ECOSYSTEMS (GRETCHEN C. DAILY, ed. 1997).

D. IMPLICATIONS FOR ENVIRONMENTAL LAW

In previous sections of the article from which the following is excerpted, Professor Richard Lazarus evaluated the environmental decisions of the U.S. Supreme Court (and of individual Supreme Court justices), and concluded that the Supreme Court has improperly failed to view environmental law as anything more than a subset of general administrative law. In short, it has failed to appreciate the particular characteristics that define and distinguish environmental law. In the following part of the article, Professor Lazarus sets forth his view of what those characteristics are, and their implications.

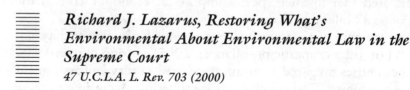

Richard J. Lazarus, Restoring What's Environmental About Environmental Law in the Supreme Court
47 U.C.L.A. L. Rev. 703 (2000)

What Is Environmental About Environmental Law — The Nature of Environmental Injury

What makes environmental law distinctive is largely traceable to the nature of the injury that environmental protection law seeks to reduce, minimize, or sometimes prevent altogether. Environmental law is concerned, in the first instance, with impacts on the natural environment. Hence, although some environmental laws are concerned about human health effects, as are many other types of laws (e.g., food and drug, worker safety, Medicare, and food stamp programs), environmental law is concerned only about human health effects resulting from impacts on the natural environment. And, of course, many environmental laws are concerned only with those impacts and not with possible human health effects at all.

A common denominator, therefore, for environmental law is the ecological injury that serves as the law's threshold and often exclusive focus. That common denominator is also the primary source of the special challenges environmental law presents for lawmaking. Ecological injury has several recurring features that render its redress through law especially difficult. These pertain to both the "cause" and the "effect" of such injury, each of which inevitably becomes a regulatory touchstone in any legal regime for environmental protection. Some of the more obvious features are discussed below.

1. Irreversible, Catastrophic, and Continuing Injury: Environmental law is often concerned about the avoidance of irreversible, catastrophic results. The destruction of an aquifer upon which a community depends for drinking water, the erosion of soil necessary for farming that required centuries to develop, and the destruction of the ozone layer are not possibilities to be lightly taken. Such potential downsides render enormously costly any errors in decision making. Yet, while errors are costly, so too can be delays in decision making. Even the best resolution is worth little if it is developed too late to prevent a chain of events inexorably leading to ecological disaster.

    Finally, a closely related trait of some environmental injury is its continuing nature. Environmental law must address harm that increases over time. The harm is dynamic and not static in character. An oil spill addressed quickly may be confined to manageable dimensions. But conversely, if not quickly addressed, it may rapidly and exponentially increase in scope to overwhelming dimensions. Legal regimes that are inherently cautious and slow to react do not readily lend themselves to the quick action often necessary in the ecological context.

2. Physically Distant Injury: Ecological injury is often not physically confineable. Actions in one location may have substantial adverse effects in very distant locations. This may be because the pollutants actually travel from one place to another. Or it may be as the result of the adverse impacts of activities in one locale on a global commons, upon the viability of which many regions are dependent.

    Long-range transportation of airborne pollutants is an example of the former. The ozone layer in the upper atmosphere exemplifies the transboundary implications of degradation of a commons resource, as the destruction of the ozone layer by activities in one part of the world can have serious environmental and human health effects in other parts of the world. Global warming presents a similar physical dimension.

    For each, the associated challenges for the establishment of any legal regime are great, especially because the costs of control are imposed in one area and the benefits are enjoyed in a very different area. Such a distributional mismatch renders the adoption, implementation, and enforcement of the necessary transboundary legal rules very difficult. This is certainly true in the international arenas, but even far more localized spreadings of causes and effects between states and counties resist ready political resolutions.

3. Temporally Distant Injury: Much of the injury environmental law seeks to address is not imminent. Sometimes actions now may trigger the injury, but the injury itself will be realized only in the distant future. Sometimes the injury will be realized now and will increase, inexorably, over time. To the extent that the latter is occurring, this temporal character to some environmental injury may become, as a practical matter, irreversible and thus collapse into the first feature of ecological injury described above.

    This temporal feature of ecological injuries poses challenges to legal doctrine and lawmaking analogous to those presented by the "physically distant" characteristic discussed above. The same distributional mismatch is presented but even more problematically, because the benefits to be enjoyed will generally inure only to future generations lacking any representation in current lawmaking fora. Such intergenerational effects raise issues regarding the propriety of "discounting" the value of future benefits (including human lives) in selecting environmental controls today. Even more fundamentally, however, the intergenerational dimension to ecological injury raises basic questions regarding the moral responsibilities that current generations have to safeguard the interests of future generations.

4. Uncertainty and Risk: There is much uncertainty associated with environmental injury, which poses even further challenges for lawmaking. The primary source of this uncertainty is the sheer complexity of the natural environment and, accordingly, how much is still unknown about it. This uncertainty expresses itself in our inability to know beforehand the environmental impact of certain actions. It equally undermines our ability to apprehend, after the fact, what precisely caused certain environmental impacts.

    The inevitable upshot is that environmental laws that seek to prevent harm are directed to risk rather than to actual impact. It similarly means that environmental laws that seek to assign responsibility for harm that has already occurred are limited in their ability to do so.

    Because, moreover, environmental law is concerned with risk, there is an inherently psychological dimension to the injury being redressed. The injury is not confined to that which occurs if the risk is itself realized. There is often psychological harm resulting from the risk itself, whether or not ever realized. For this same reason, by failing to address that mental dimension, one can increase the associated injury even if the numerical probability of the risk's physical realization remains the same.

5. Multiple Causes: Ecological injuries are rarely the product of a single action at an isolated moment of time. Putting aside the pervasive

uncertainty issues, environmental harms are more typically the cumulative and synergistic result of multiple actions, often spread over significant time and space. This is primarily traceable to the sharing inherent in any common natural resource base, which is the object of so many simultaneous and sporadic actions over time and space.

6. Noneconomic, Nonhuman Character: Many of the ecological injuries resulting from environmental degradation are not readily susceptible to monetary valuation and have a distinctively nonhuman character. There is simply no readily available market analogue. The nonexclusive nature of the natural resources at stake is often one factor prompting resistance of valuation. Even more generally, the decision to protect the ecological interest in question may have been deliberately made notwithstanding any notion of economic value. It could, of course, be ultimately rooted in notions of uncertainty and concerns about adverse human health affects — e.g., the after-the-fact discovery that the DNA of a subspecies of fly would have cured the common cold. But it may instead be, and often is, based on the deeper notion that there are certain results — such as species extinction or resource destruction — that humankind should strive to avoid because they fall beyond its legitimate authority.

Other kinds of injury that resist ready monetary valuation are the adverse human health effects that can result from environmental degradation, although these valuation issues are shared by all laws designed to safeguard human health. For some economists, all human health effects of this kind must be susceptible to such valuation for the simple reason that tradeoffs are inevitably made in any allocation of limited societal resources. Nothing has infinite value, and each decision has opportunity costs related to opportunities thereby foregone. But some environmental laws reflect a very different philosophy, which posits that there are some adverse human health effects that are presumptively out of bounds for policymakers. For those who share that policy view, economic valuation and tradeoffs are therefore not legitimate topics for policy discussion.

Perhaps, moreover, it is this normative dimension of ecological injury that is ultimately the most telling. The environmental dimension of environmental law teaches that the nonhuman, nonmonetizable dimensions of ecological injury not only exist but are worth protecting. They reflect positive values that are entitled to weight in the balancing in which members of the executive, legislative, and judicial branches are ultimately engaged as part of their respective lawmaking and policymaking responsibilities.

B. Challenges for Law and Lawmaking

Because of these varied features of ecological injuries, the challenges of constructing a legal regime for environmental protection are considerable.

Some of the challenges affect substantive areas of law. Others pertain more to the process of lawmaking and the related institutions than to any distinct area of law. In certain circumstances, a full appreciation of the associated challenges may well justify a modification of current law or the functioning of certain lawmaking institutions, but confined to the environmental context. In other circumstances, however, the lessons to be learned from environmental law may have more far-reaching import. They may suggest that an entire area of law, or the ways in which particular lawmaking institutions operate, should be re-thought. . . .

NOTES AND QUESTIONS ON LAZARUS ARTICLE

1. *Other characteristics?* Would you add anything to Professor Lazarus' list? Would you change or delete anything?

2. *Possible legal solutions?* For each of the six characteristics identified by Professor Lazarus, identify a set of possible legal solutions, perhaps drawing from approaches to similar issues you have learned in other courses. This is a good way to scope out the possible key concepts of environmental law in advance.

E. A CONTINUING CASE STUDY — IS YOUR FRYING PAN HAZARDOUS TO YOUR HEALTH?

Working through problems is a good way to understand how the various concepts we discuss in this book might apply to a real-world situation. We have chosen to use a single, very current, and very difficult real-world situation as the basis for most of the problems throughout this book. We do so for two main reasons. First, we have chosen a problem that we hope will strike a chord in every student who uses this book, because it involves widely-used consumer products. Second, by keeping the fact pattern constant while exploring different ideas about how to regulate environmental hazards, you will better be able to understand the differences among regulatory approaches. (Your analysis of how the approaches differ will not be complicated by application to different sets of facts and circumstances. We use other facts and situations from problems only where our main example does not illustrate a particular problem or issue well.)

The problem we have chosen involves the chemical PFOA (perfluorooctanoic acid) and its various salt forms.[48] PFOA is a synthetic chemical which does not occur naturally in the environment. PFOA is used to manufacture another group of chemicals called fluoropolymers, which are extremely useful in a wide range of products because they are fire resistant, and because they repel water, oil, grease, and stains. As a result, they are used extensively in the aerospace, automotive, construction, chemicals processing, electronics, semiconductor, and textile industries. According to an industry trade organization,[49] these chemicals are vital to public health and safety due to their use in fire-resistant clothing and other materials, and because they help to make safer, less polluting, and more fuel-efficient products, including aircraft and automobiles. In addition, fluoropolymers are key components in several widely used commercial products, such as non-stick cookware (including Teflon and similar products), and, perhaps particularly relevant to many students who choose to study environmental law, waterproof yet breathable and light-weight fabrics such as Gore-Tex.

PFOA is not itself an ingredient in those consumer products. It is used to make them, however, and as explained below, some environmental groups claim that these products break down under certain circumstances into PFOA and similar chemicals, resulting in common human exposure. According to some studies, PFOA is found in the blood of up to 95 percent of the American public. Because these chemicals are *designed* to be extraordinarily stable, they are extremely persistent in the environment, meaning that they break down very slowly, and can remain in our bodies, and the bodies of other animals, for long periods of time. Moreover, some studies suggest that PFOA may cause cancer, birth defects, elevated levels of cholesterol, and other health and environmental problems.

In April, 2003, the Environmental Working Group (EWG), an environmental research and advocacy organization, petitioned EPA to investigate PFOA under the Toxic Substances Control Act (TSCA), 15 U.S.C. §§2610-2692, a federal law that authorizes EPA to regulate the use of toxic chemicals under certain circumstances.[50] EWG alleged that DuPont had violated TSCA's mandatory reporting requirements by hiding information, some of which it allegedly knew for decades, about the risk of birth defects and other adverse health effects of PFOA to exposed workers in some of its factories. EWG also

48. For more basic information on this chemical, its uses, and its potential human health and environmental hazards, see U.S. Environmental Protection Agency, OPPT Fact Sheet, PFOS Q's & A's (August 2004), available at www.epa.gov/oppt/pfoa, from which much of this discussion was taken.

49. The Society of the Plastics Industry, Inc. (SPI). *See* http://www.pfoa-facts.com/.

50. Letter dated April 11, 2003 from Kenneth A. Cook, President, Environmental Working Group, to The Honorable Christine Todd Whitman, Administrator, U.S. Environmental Protection Agency, regarding DuPont's failure to submit key health studies under the requirements of TSCA §8(e), 15 U.S.C. §2607(e). EWG followed up with an additional letter dated August 15, 2003, supplying more information and instances of alleged TSCA violations.

alleges that DuPont secretly tested local water supplies near those plants, and withheld information indicating PFOA contamination of public water supplies.[51] DuPont denies that it withheld information required to be supplied under TSCA, and denies that PFOA is unduly dangerous to human health and the environment. Nevertheless, EPA has taken enforcement action against DuPont under TSCA (discussed in Chapter 15).

Also in April, 2003, EPA released a preliminary assessment of risks associated with PFOA.[52] This preliminary risk assessment was limited to developmental toxicity (possible birth defects in children of mothers exposed to PFOA). It reported evidence of PFOA in U.S. workers at plants where PFOA is used, and of PFOA at much lower levels (parts per billion as opposed to parts per million) in the blood of members of the general public. The preliminary assessment also reported that the available evidence of health risks from PFOA was mixed, with some evidence of an association between PFOA and cancer, elevated levels of some human hormones, and some adverse developmental effects.

EPA is conducting a much broader study to evaluate sources of human exposure to PFOA, and its potential adverse effects, as part of its effort to determine what, if any, regulatory action should be taken under TSCA or other statutes. A more complete risk assessment is being prepared, with the help of a scientific advisory panel. With the cooperation of various companies that use or manufacture PFOA, EPA is collecting more data and conducting more studies. EPA summarized this ongoing effort in the following Federal Register Notice:

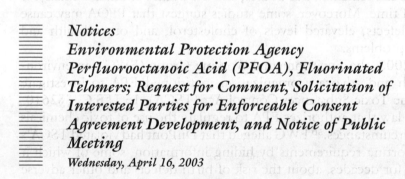

Notices
Environmental Protection Agency
Perfluorooctanoic Acid (PFOA), Fluorinated
Telomers; Request for Comment, Solicitation of
Interested Parties for Enforceable Consent
Agreement Development, and Notice of Public
Meeting
Wednesday, April 16, 2003

Summary: EPA has identified potential human health concerns from exposure to perfluorooctanoic acid (PFOA) and its salts, although there remains considerable scientific uncertainty regarding potential risks. EPA is requesting public comment on pertinent topics of interest, as discussed in this document, and the submission of additional data concerning these chemicals. . . .

    51. For the response by one of the water systems, *see* The Little Hocking Water Association, Inc., News Release # 1, January 15, 2002.
    52. U.S. Environmental Protection Agency, Office of Pollution Prevention and Toxics, Risk Assessment Division, Preliminary Risk Assessment of the Developmental Toxicity Associated with Exposure to Perfluorooctanoic Acid and its Salts (April 10, 2003).

II.   What Action is the Agency Taking?

EPA has prepared a preliminary risk assessment on perfluorooctanoic acid (PFOA) . . . and its salts. . . . This preliminary assessment indicates potential nationwide human exposure to low levels of PFOA. Based on certain animal studies, there could be a potential risk of developmental and other adverse effects associated with these exposures in humans. However, this assessment also reflects substantial uncertainty about the interpretation of the risk. EPA has identified areas where additional information could be very helpful in allowing the Agency to develop a more accurate assessment of the potential risks posed by PFOA and the other compounds addressed in this notice, and to identify what voluntary or regulatory mitigation or other actions, if any, would be appropriate. EPA is making this preliminary assessment public in order to identify the Agency's concerns, to indicate areas where additional information or investigation would be useful, and to request the submission of data addressing these issues. . . .

III.   Background

In 1999, EPA began an investigation after receiving data on perfluorooctyl sulfonate (PFOS) indicating that PFOS was persistent, unexpectedly toxic, and bioaccumulative. These data also showed that PFOS had been found in very low concentrations in the blood of the general population and in wildlife around the world. 3M Company (3M), the sole manufacturer of PFOS in the United States and the principal manufacturer worldwide, announced in May 2000 that it was discontinuing its perfluorooctanyl chemistries, including PFOS. EPA followed the voluntary 3M phaseout with regulatory action under TSCA section 5 to limit any future manufacture or importation of PFOS before EPA has had an opportunity to review activities and risks associated with the proposed manufacture or importation.

In June 2000, EPA indicated that it was expanding its investigation of PFOS to encompass other fluorochemicals, including PFOA, in order to determine whether these other fluorochemicals might present concerns similar to those found with PFOS. EPA was concerned in part because 3M had also found PFOA in human blood during the studies on PFOS. . . . However, as explained in this notice, there remain substantial uncertainties associated with the preliminary risk assessment. EPA believes these uncertainties may be reduced through acquisition of the information described in this notice. EPA is therefore continuing the priority review in order to acquire this information and better inform the Agency's decisionmaking.

A.   PFOA Sources and Uses

PFOA and its salts are fully fluorinated organic compounds that can be produced synthetically and formed through the degradation or metabolism of certain other manmade fluorochemical products. PFOA is a synthetic chemical and is not naturally occurring. Consequently, all PFOA in the environment is attributable to human activity. PFOA is used primarily to produce its salts, which are used as essential processing aids in the production of fluoropolymers and fluoroelastomers. Although they are made using PFOA, finished fluoropolymer and fluoroelastomer products are not expected to contain PFOA. In recent years, less than 600 metric tons per year of PFOA and its salts have been manufactured or imported in the United States. The major fluoropolymers manufactured using PFOA salts are polytetrafluoroethylene (PTFE) and polyvinylidine fluoride (PVDF). PTFE has hundreds of uses in many industrial and consumer products, including soil, stain, grease, and water resistant coatings on textiles and carpet; uses in the automotive, mechanical, aerospace, chemical, electrical, medical, and building/construction industries; personal care products; and non-stick coatings on cookware. PVDF is used primarily in three major industrial sectors: Electrical/electronics, building/construction, and chemical processing. . . .

In addition to releases from the deliberate manufacture of PFOA . . . and from the use of PFOA and its salts in the manufacture and processing of fluoropolymers and fluoroelastomers, PFOA may have entered the environment through other sources. . . .

B. Hazard and Exposure

EPA has conducted a detailed review of all available hazard and exposure information on PFOA. This review is available in the Agency's Revised Draft Hazard Assessment on PFOA and Its Salts. This draft hazard assessment has not been formally peer reviewed, but has been reviewed internally by the EPA Office of Research and Development (ORD).

PFOA is persistent in the environment. It does not hydrolyze, photolyze, or biodegrade under environmental conditions. Based on recent human biomonitoring data provided by industry, which found PFOA in the blood of workers and the general population in all geographic regions of the United States, exposure to PFOA is potentially nationwide, although the routes of exposure for the general population are unknown.

Several epidemiological studies on the effects of PFOA in humans have been conducted on workers. An association with PFOA exposure and prostate cancer was reported in one study; however, this result was not observed in an update to the study in which the exposure categories were modified. A non-statistically significant increase in the levels of the hormone estradiol in workers with high serum PFOA levels (<=30 parts per million (ppm)) was also reported, but none of the other hormone levels analyzed indicated any adverse effects. APFO is the most widely used salt of PFOA, and most animal toxicity studies have been conducted with APFO. An extensive array of animal toxicity studies have been conducted in rodents and monkeys. These studies have shown that APFO exposure can result in a variety of toxic effects in animals including liver toxicity, developmental toxicity, and immunotoxicity. In addition, rodent bioassays have shown that chronic APFO exposure is associated with a variety of tumor types. The mechanisms of APFO tumorigenesis are not clearly understood. At this time, EPA is evaluating the scientific evidence and has not reached any conclusions on the potential significance to humans of the rodent cancer data.

There are marked gender differences in the elimination of PFOA in rats. In addition, there are substantial differences in the half-life of PFOA in rats, monkeys, and humans. The gender and species differences are not completely understood and therefore the extent of potential risks to humans is uncertain. . . .

D. Uncertainties and Data Needs

Although EPA has concerns with respect to the potential nationwide presence of PFOA in blood and with the potential for developmental and other effects suggested by animal studies, there are significant uncertainties in the Agency's quantitative assessment of the risks of PFOA. In addition, the uncertainties discussed in this unit with respect to the identification of the pathway or pathways that result in human exposure to PFOA (air, water, food, etc.), and the uncertainties associated with how PFOA gets into those pathways (including the products or processes that are responsible for the presence of PFOA in the environment) make it difficult to determine what, if any, particular risk mitigation measures would be appropriate. The Agency believes that the additional information identified in this notice would better inform this priority review and Agency decisionmaking with respect to PFOA.

The sources of PFOA in the environment . . . are not fully defined or understood. Historically, direct PFOA releases during the manufacture of PFOA and its use in the manufacture and processing of fluoropolymers and fluoroelastomers have been quantified at some sites. Industry has identified and implemented voluntary control technologies to reduce releases, as well as to improve PFOA recovery for recycling or destruction. The effectiveness of these programs could be assessed . . . by monitoring PFOA levels at the respective facilities and determining if the release reduction and waste management programs are reducing the PFOA levels in the media surrounding the affected facilities. PFOA exposures and releases to the environment may also come from the distribution of PFOA in aqueous dispersions of fluoropolymers used by processors to apply coatings to metals and textiles, a topic which industry is also attempting to resolve.

In addition, the question of the potential contribution to PFOA levels from telomer manufacture and from telomer product degradation remains. The universe of specific telomer chemicals that may ultimately degrade or metabolize to PFOA has not been fully defined. . . . Determining possible telomer product sources of PFOA may be particularly difficult because these fluorochemicals are typically used in products in very low concentrations, indicating that any individual source contribution by specific products could be very small, widely distributed, and difficult to detect. For example, products contaminated with volatile, unreacted telomer alcohol residuals could potentially release those residuals into the environment where they could be subject to biodegradation.

The exposure routes leading to the presence of PFOA in human blood are not known. The nationwide presence of PFOA in human blood, contrasted with the limited geographic locations of fluorochemical plants making or using the chemical, suggests that there must be additional sources of PFOA in the environment, and exposures beyond those attributable to direct releases from industrial facilities. But whether these exposures are due to PFOA in the air, the water, on dusts or sediments, in dietary sources, or through some combination of routes is currently unknown. Data evaluating the environmental presence of PFOA in water are very limited and site-specific. Data on the presence of PFOA in air or soil are not currently available. Data on the presence of PFOA in wildlife suggest that animals are not as likely as humans to have PFOA in their blood, and that PFOA is not found as widely in animals as PFOS. Whether these differences may be due to different exposure pathways or to differences in how the chemicals are processed or retained by animals and humans is unknown. The technical difficulties of detecting and accurately measuring the chemical in all these various media, particularly in the low concentrations that EPA would anticipate, are considerable. . . .

IV. Specific Requests for Comments, Data, and Information

EPA specifically requests comments, data, and information on the following topics.

A. Use and Production Volume Information

What are the specific chemical identities (by Ninth Collective Index name and CAS No., if available) of the telomer chemicals, including polymers derived from these telomers, and of the fluoropolymers and fluoroelastomers made with PFOA or related chemicals, currently in commerce? In what volumes and at what locations are these chemicals manufactured or imported? How and in what volumes are these chemicals used? What are the benefits of these chemicals and products in their specific uses, and what alternatives to these chemicals may be available for specific uses?

B. Exposure Information

How are products containing the chemicals identified in Unit IV.A. used? How are these products disposed of? What environmental releases occur at manufacturing and processing facilities where these chemicals are used? What data are available on worker exposures to these chemicals? What data are available on exposures to the general population? What data are available on measured levels of these chemicals in humans and the environment, in all environmental media? What data are available on the biodegradation of these chemicals, on releases of these chemicals from consumer and industrial products, and on their breakdown during product biodegradation, incineration, and other disposal practices?

C. Monitoring and Related Information

EPA specifically requests that any persons who have in their possession existing human or environmental monitoring data indicating or assessing the presence of PFOA and related fluorochemicals in humans, in wildlife, or in any environmental media, including studies conducted in other countries, provide those data to the Agency in response to the publication of this notice to enhance the understanding of PFOA presence in the environment and of the pathways leading to exposures. EPA includes in this request any existing data not otherwise provided to EPA concerning the toxicity, pharmacokinetics, and half-life of PFOA in organisms. . . .

QUESTIONS AND PROBLEMS ON PFOA

1. *PFOA and scientific uncertainty.* EPA's task is to determine whether the manufacture and use of PFOA warrants additional regulatory action, and if so, what form that action should take. Take note of the degree to which EPA must make those decisions under a cloud of significant uncertainty. Many environmental decisions must be made with incomplete and frequently changing information, but waiting until more or better information is available can pose significant risks in the interim. *See* HENRY POLLACK, UNCERTAIN SCIENCE, UNCERTAIN WORLD (2003). Based on this Federal Register notice, does EPA have enough information to make responsible decisions about whether to regulate PFOA, and how? If not, what additional information is required?

2. *Parties' responses to the notice.* Use this issue to get a preliminary appreciation for what is involved in the *practice* of environmental law.[53] Draw up a brief plan to respond to this notice on behalf of a chemical company that uses or manufactures PFOA, and an environmental group seeking better protection from exposure to PFOA. What information would you try to obtain, and how? What other comments might you submit to EPA? What other actions might you take?

3. *PFOA and the characteristics of environmental law.* Consider the PFOA information in light of the characteristics and challenges of environmental law

---

53. This book is designed mainly for survey courses in the theory and substance of environmental law. It will, however, provide some sense of more practice-oriented issues throughout the book. For a more comprehensive treatment of environmental practice, see JERRY L. ANDERSON and DENNIS D. HIRSCH, ENVIRONMENTAL LAW PRACTICE (2d ed., 2003).

explored in the Lazarus article. Which of these particular challenges are reflected in the PFOA problem, and how? How might each of those problems be addressed by courts, legislatures, administrative agencies, and others?

Ultimately, EPA will address the PFOA problem through a complex set of statutes enacted by Congress and regulations issued by the agency itself. It is possible, however, that some aspects of the PFOA problem might be addressed by common law doctrines that predate the modern regulatory state, and that served as conceptual precursors to modern environmental statutes. In the next chapter, we turn first to common law solutions to environmental problems.

2

Common Law Solutions

Students of environmental law soon learn that complex federal and state statutes currently dominate the field. Even longer sets of implementing regulations and policies dwarf these statutes. These regulatory regimes usually employ a somewhat comprehensive approach, *i.e.*, they might address all sources of a particular type of pollution or regulate entire industries as opposed to individual polluters. For the most part, however, this statutory and regulatory regime only began to develop over the past several decades.[1] Before then, someone who felt sufficiently aggrieved by pollution to seek legal redress would have to resort to common law remedies on a case-by-case basis.

This chapter first explores the major common law doctrines used to redress pollution and other environmental problems. In doing so, we have multiple goals. First, despite the overlay of modern statutes and regulations, the common law is not dead as a tool for addressing environmental problems. Plaintiffs continue to bring common law actions to redress environmental harm for a variety of reasons: there are gaps in the statutory system; the common law may provide superior remedies for particular plaintiffs; and some plaintiffs may believe that a local judge or jury might provide a more receptive audience than a distant bureaucrat. Thus, environmental lawyers should be familiar with the kinds of common law cases that remain available to address environmental issues.

---

1. There are, of course, some exceptions. For example, the Supreme Court construed the Rivers and Harbors Act of 1899, a law originally designed to protect waterways from refuse which would impede navigation for commerce and national defense, in part as an anti-pollution law. *See* United States v. Republic Steel Corp., 362 U.S. 482 (1960); United States v. Standard Oil Co., 384 U.S. 224 (1966). The direct precursor to the modern Clean Water Act was the Water Pollution Control Act of 1948, and the first incarnation of the Clean Air Act was passed in 1955. For the most part, however, common law approaches to most environmental problems were dominant until the 1960s and 1970s.

Second, our environmental statutes were not written on a blank slate. In many cases, Congress (and state legislatures) borrowed concepts from the existing common law, either intact or in modified form, as the basis for statutory regulation. The clearest example is the federal "Superfund" statute,[2] in which Congress adopted certain common law liability rules as the governing substantive law (addressed in Chapter 12), but less explicit use of common law principles is evident in other statutes as well. Thus, a grounding in common law approaches to environmental problems will enhance your understanding of the evolving statutory system.

Third, Congress adopted our modern environmental laws in significant part due to the perceived inadequacy of common law approaches to address the full range and magnitude of environmental problems in an increasingly industrialized world. To understand why those laws were passed, and what they sought to accomplish, it is useful to evaluate both the strengths and the weaknesses of common law approaches.

A. COMMON LAW APPROACHES — FROM STRICT RIGHTS TO BALANCE

Solutions to early environmental problems derived mainly from the law of property and the law of torts. We begin by outlining the most prevalent premises of common law doctrine that are potentially useful for environmental law. Then, we present some of the most noted common law cases in the United States as examples of how those doctrines apply to environmental problems. Finally, we present one of the court opinions in one the most famous "toxic tort" cases (depicted in Jonathan Harr's book, A CIVIL ACTION) as an example of the continuing relevance of common law cases to some plaintiffs. As you read each of these cases, take note of the ways in which common law doctrines provide useful solutions to environmental problems, and the limitations that might have prompted the development of statutory regimes to augment or replace the common law.

As with many aspects of the common law, some doctrines establish strict rights-based approaches in which any impairment of established rights is unlawful *per se*, leaving the nature of the remedy as the only remaining issue. Other doctrines seek to balance the rights and interests of one party against those of others, including the public at large. In some cases, strict rights-based doctrines evolved to reflect more of a balancing approach, as the aesthetic values of once-pastoral societies gave way to the practical needs of the industrial revolution. Pay attention to which aspects of common law doctrine reflect a strict rights-based

---

2. This law is known more formally as the Comprehensive Environmental Response, Compensation, and Liability Act (CERCLA), and is codified at 42 U.S.C. §§9601 *et seq.*

approach, and which reflect more of a balancing method. Both concepts have parallels in various statutory systems you will study later in the book.

1. Trespass

The common law of trespass, an important element of property law, prevents someone from intentionally interfering with your physical possession of land, whether by treading across your prize flower beds or building their new garage on your side of the property line. Likewise, contaminated water or other pollutants flowing onto your fields or into your groundwater can constitute a physical invasion of property. *See, e.g.,* Castles Auto & Truck Service v. Exxon Corp., 16 Fed. Appx. 163 (4th Cir. 2001) (affirming jury verdict of trespass based on migration of petroleum onto plaintiff's property). Should wafts of thick smoke from a nearby factory constitute a physical invasion of property? *See* Stacy v. VEPCO, 7 Envt. Rptr. Cases 1443 (E.D. Va. 1975) (finding "negligence and/or trespass" from power plant emissions that, based on expert testimony, damaged trees 22 miles away). What about invisible but unpleasant odors emanating from a neighboring hog farm? (See discussion of nuisance law below.)

Trespass is a strict liability doctrine for any intentional (and non-consensual) physical invasion of land. Strict liability means that once the elements of the cause of action are established (intentional physical invasion without consent), liability attaches. The only remaining issue is the amount of damages or the nature of other appropriate relief. Moreover, the intent element of trespass requires only that the offending party have the intent to perform the act that results in the physical invasion, rather than an intent to trespass. Thus, trespass reflects a rights-based approach. Property owners are entitled to physical control and enjoyment of their property free from unwanted physical invasions, and the courts strictly protect those rights. Under trespass law, we do not balance the needs and interests of the property owner against those of the intruder.

A somewhat related common law protection against water pollution, also grounded in the law of property, is the doctrine of riparian rights. Law students most commonly study riparian rights in courses in Water Law, with an emphasis on the amount of water flowing past or through one's land. Under the traditional form of this doctrine, developed in England, and then adopted in the eastern United States,[3] riparian landowners are entitled to the "natural flow" of a stream through their property, undiminished in quantity and unimpaired in quality, regardless of hardship to the interests of other users of the waterway. As such, riparian rights resemble trespass in that both doctrines

---

3. The western states adopted the very different prior appropriation doctrine, which in its traditional form protects those who divert water from streams for beneficial uses, regardless of impacts to the environment or to junior (more recent) appropriators.

protect property absolutely against pollution and other forms of impairment. Unlike trespass, however, the law of riparian rights evolved such that courts typically balance the rights, needs, and interests of riparian landowners against those of other water users and the general public. As uses of water grew more common and more intensive, the strict riparian rights doctrine gave way to a "reasonable use" approach in which competing uses of water and waterways — included waste disposal — were weighed, based on factors such as economic utility and the feasibility of abating the harm. *See, e.g.,* Snow v. Parsons, 28 Vt. 459 (1856) (rejecting absolute riparian doctrine in favor of assessment of reasonableness in challenge to discharge of tannery wastes). The Restatement (Second) of Torts (1979), §§850 and 850A also embodies those principles. A similar development occurred in the law of nuisance.

2. Nuisance

As noted by Professor William Rodgers, who penned one of the seminal treatises on modern environmental law, the common law of nuisance has had a formative influence on the entire field of environmental law:

> To a surprising degree, the legal history of the environment has been written by nuisance law. There is no common law doctrine that approaches nuisance in comprehensiveness or detail as a regulator of land use and of technological abuse. Nuisance actions reach pollution of all physical media — air, water, land, groundwater — by a variety of means. Nuisance actions have challenged virtually every major industrial and municipal activity that today is the subject of comprehensive environmental regulation — the operation of land fills, incinerators, sewage treatment plants, activities at chemical plants, aluminum, lead and copper smelters, oil refineries, pulp mills, rendering plants, quarries and mines, textile mills and a host of other manufacturing activities. Nuisance litigation has influenced energy policy at all stages — fuel exploration, transportation, siting of facilities, fuel combustion, waste disposal and reclamation. Nuisance theory is the common law backbone of modern environmental and energy law.

WILLIAM H. RODGERS, JR., ENVIRONMENTAL LAW §2.1, at 112-113 (2d ed. 1994).

One main reason for this pervasive influence of nuisance law is that, whereas trespass law protects against physical invasion of property, nuisance goes farther and protects against any substantial interference with the use and enjoyment of land. *See* Restatement (Second) of Torts §822. To the extent that no physical invasion is required, nuisance law potentially reaches a broader range of actions that may cause environmental harm. *See, e.g.,* O'Neill v. Carolina Freight Carriers Corp., 244 A.2d 372 (Conn. 1968) (awarding damages to homeowner and granting injunctive relief against truck terminal due to excessive noise during nighttime hours); Washington Suburban Sanitary Commission v. CAE-Link Corp., 622 A.2d 745 (Md. 1993) (holding that odors from sewage sludge composting facility constituted a nuisance). An accompanying limitation that actual interference be shown (as opposed to mere physical presence under trespass law) and that the interference be "substantial," however, tempers that breadth.

Nuisance law is divided into two related doctrines, private nuisance and public nuisance, each of which has its own relevance to environmental law. Private nuisance allows private parties to seek redress for injuries to their property rights due to the economic activities of others. As a result, private nuisance claims are available only to those whose property rights are harmed by a particular activity. Public nuisance protects against injuries to the broader public.

Although private nuisance is grounded in property law because of its focus on protecting property rights, it also encompasses various elements of the law of torts. A private nuisance consists of an invasion of property that adversely and substantially affects the use and enjoyment of land, and is either intentional and unreasonable or unintentional but otherwise actionable. As in trespass law, "intentional" means only the intent to perform the act that leads to the invasion and impairment. "Otherwise actionable" can encompass any otherwise valid cause of action, but most commonly means either negligence or strict liability for abnormally dangerous activities, both of which are common law torts.

The concept of "abnormally dangerous activities" has obvious application to environmental cases involving such activities as petrochemical plants or the transportation of toxic or otherwise hazardous materials. Under the principle first established in Fletcher v. Rylands, L.R. 3 H.L. 330 (1868) (finding liability without fault due to dam failure), strict liability may attach to an unduly dangerous thing or activity which a court finds inappropriate to a particular place. *See,* *e.g.,* Crawford v. National Lead Co., 784 F. Supp. 439 (S.D. Ohio 1989) (finding liability for emotional distress and reduced property values due to emissions of uranium and other harmful substances). Under the modern version of the doctrine set forth in the Restatement (Second) of Torts, §520, in deciding whether an activity is abnormally dangerous courts consider the risk of harm, the gravity of harm, whether the risk can be avoided with reasonable care, whether the activity is a "common usage," whether it is inappropriate to a particular place, and the value of the activity to the community. This modern version reflects a balancing of interests rather than a strict protection of property rights.

In its original form, nuisance doctrine imposed strict liability in the same manner as trespass law, on the theory that the right to use and enjoy property should be protected against any unlawful or unreasonable invasion, with the appropriate remedy varying with degree of harm. As industrial activity intensified, however, this strict rights-based approach shifted to a balancing test in which courts weighted the gravity of harm against the utility of the challenged activity. In striking this balance, courts now consider factors such as the extent of harm, the nature of harm, the social value of the competing uses, the suitability of the activity to the place, and the feasibility (or burden) of avoiding the alleged harm. Many modern environmental laws reflect this balancing approach.

Private nuisance cases have only limited utility in redressing widespread environmental harm because those cases require one or more plaintiffs with the requisite degree and kind of harm, as well as sufficient economic means and incentive, to invoke the doctrine. Private nuisance law is less useful where a large number of property owners suffer lesser individual (but cumulatively significant) harm, or where harm occurs to public as opposed to private resources (such as public forests or water bodies). Public nuisance law fills the gap by protecting against an unreasonable interference common to the public. In deciding whether to abate a public nuisance, courts consider the extent to which an activity interferes with public health, safety, peace, and convenience; whether the activity is proscribed by statute or regulation or is otherwise unlawful; and the length and degree of permanence of the harm. *See* Restatement (Second) of Torts, §821C. Traditionally, only public officials could bring public nuisance cases. However, individuals who suffer injuries that are different in kind, not just degree, than those inflicted on the public at large, also may bring public nuisance claims. While monetary damages may be sufficient to redress a private nuisance to a small number of individual property owners, public nuisances are more likely to justify injunctive relief.

B. THE PROMISE AND LIMITS OF COMMON LAW SOLUTIONS

1. The Common Law Tradition

Common law environmental cases are legion. We set forth below some of the most noted cases that have defined common law environmental jurisprudence in the United States. As you read these cases, ask yourself the following questions: (1) In what respects are common law doctrines useful in addressing the range of environmental problems identified in Chapter 1? (2) In what respects are common law approaches potentially inadequate to address those issues and problems? (3) Do these cases suggest anything about whether rights-based or balancing approaches are most appropriate to address environmental issues? (4) What do these cases teach about whether common law doctrines adequately address environmental problems?

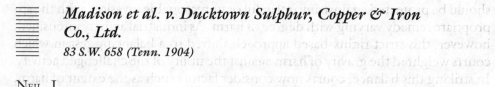

Madison et al. v. Ducktown Sulphur, Copper & Iron Co., Ltd.

83 S.W. 658 (Tenn. 1904)

NEIL, J.

* * * * *

The bills are all based on the ground of nuisance, in that the two companies, in the operation of their plants at and near Ducktown, in Polk county, in the course of reducing copper ore, cause large volumes of smoke to issue from their roast piles, which smoke descends upon the surrounding lands, and injures trees and crops, and renders the homes of complainants less comfortable and their lands less profitable than before. The purpose of all the bills is to enjoin the further operation of these plants. . . .

Ducktown is in a basin of the mountains of Polk county, in this state, not far from the state line of the states of Georgia and North Carolina. This basin is six or eight miles wide. The complainants are the owners of small farms situated in the mountains around Ducktown.

The method used by the defendants in reducing their copper ores is to place the green ore, broken up, on layers of wood, making large open-air piles, called "roast piles," and these roast piles are ignited for the purpose of expelling from the ore certain foreign matters called "sulphurets." In burning, these roast piles emit large volumes of smoke. This smoke, rising in the air, is carried off by air currents around and over adjoining land.

The lands of the complainants [ranged from two to eight miles from the works, with some not specified]. These lands are all thin mountain lands, of little agricultural value. . . .

All of the complainants have owned their several tracts since a time anterior to the resumption of the copper industry at Ducktown in 1891, and have resided on them during this period, with the exception of Avery McGhee, who worked for one of the defendant companies a considerable time, and Margaret Madison, who removed to Snoddy, in Rhea county, two or three years ago.

The general effect produced by the smoke upon the possessions and families of the complainants is as follows, viz.:

Their timber and crop interests have been badly injured, and they have been annoyed and discommoded by the smoke so that the complainants are prevented from using and enjoying their farms and homes as they did prior to the inauguration of these enterprises. The smoke makes it impossible for the owners of farms within the area of the smoke zone to subsist their families thereon with the degree of comfort they enjoyed before. They cannot raise and harvest their customary crops, and their timber is largely destroyed. . . .

The Court of Chancery Appeals finds that the defendants are conducting and have been conducting their business in a lawful way, without any purpose or desire to injure any of the complainants; that they have been and are pursuing the only known method by which these plants can be operated and their business successfully carried on; that the open-air roast heap is the only method known to the business or to science by means of which copper ore of the character mined by the defendants can be reduced; that the defendants have made every effort to get rid of the smoke and noxious vapors, one of the defendants having spent $200,000 in experiments to this end, but without result.

It is to be inferred from the description of the locality that there is no place more remote to which the operations referred to could be transferred.

It is found, in substance, that, if the injunctive relief sought be granted, the defendants will be compelled to stop operations, and their property will become practically worthless, the immense business conducted by them will cease, and they will be compelled to withdraw from the state. It is a necessary deduction from the foregoing that a great and increasing industry in the state will be destroyed, and all of the valuable copper properties of the state become worthless.

The following facts were also found, viz.: [The court itemized tax revenues, employment and production statistics, and other economic benefits provided by the defendants.]

It is quite apparent that the two companies pay out annually vast sums of money, which are necessarily of great benefit to the people of the county, and that they are conducting and maintaining an industry upon which a laboring population of from ten to twelve thousand people are practically dependent; and it is found, in substance, by the Court of Chancery Appeals, that, if these industries be suppressed, these thousands of people will have to wander forth to other localities to find shelter and work. . . .

While there can be no doubt that the facts stated make out a case of nuisance, for which the complainants in actions at law would be entitled to recover damages, yet the remedy in equity is not a matter of course. Not only must the bill state a proper case, but the right must be clear, and the injury must be clearly established, as in doubtful cases the party will be turned over to his legal remedy; and, if there is a reasonable doubt as to the cause of the injury, the benefit of the doubt will be given to the defendant, if his trade is a lawful one, and the injury is not the necessary and natural consequence of the act; and, if the injury can be adequately compensated at law by a judgment for damages, equity will not interfere. . . .

In addition to the principles already announced, the following general propositions seem to be established by the authorities: If the case made out by the pleadings and evidence show with sufficient clearness and certainty grounds for equitable relief it will not be denied because the persons proceeded against are engaged in a lawful business, or because the works complained of are located in a convenient place, if that place be one wherein an actionable injury is done to another; nor will the existence of another nuisance of a similar character at the same place furnish a ground for denying relief if it appear that the defendant has sensibly contributed to the injury complained of. Nor is it a question of care and skill, but purely one of results.

But there is one other principle which is of controlling influence in this department of the law, and in the light of which the foregoing principle must be weighed and applied. This is that the granting of an injunction is not a matter of absolute right, but rests in the sound discretion of the court, to be determined on a consideration of all of the special circumstances of each case, and the situation and surroundings of the parties, with a view to effect the ends of justice.

A judgment for damages in this class of cases is a matter of absolute right, where injury is shown. A decree for an injunction is a matter of sound legal discretion, to be granted or withheld as that discretion shall dictate, after a full and careful consideration of every element appertaining to the injury. . . .

The question now to be considered is, what is the proper exercise of discretion, under the facts appearing in the present case? Shall the complainants be granted, in the way of damages, the full measure of relief to which their injuries entitle them, or shall we go further, and grant their request to blot out two great mining and manufacturing enterprises, destroy half of the taxable values of a county, and drive more than 10,000 people from their homes? We think there can be no doubt as to what the true answer to this question should be.

In order to protect by injunction several small tracts of land, aggregating in value less than $1,000, we are asked to destroy other property worth nearly $2,000,000, and wreck two great mining and manufacturing enterprises, that are engaged in work of very great importance, not only to their owners, but to the state, and to the whole country as well, to depopulate a large town, and deprive thousands of working people of their homes and livelihood, and scatter them broadcast. The result would be practically a confiscation of the property of the defendants for the benefit of the complainants — an appropriation without compensation. The defendants cannot reduce their ores in a manner different from that they are now employing, and there is no more remote place to which they can remove. The decree asked for would deprive them of all of their rights. We appreciate the argument based on the fact that the homes of the complainants who live on the small tracts of land referred to are not so comfortable and useful to their owners as they were before they were affected by the smoke complained of, and we are deeply sensible of the truth of the proposition that no man is entitled to any more rights than another on the ground that he has or owns more property than that other. But in a case of conflicting rights, where neither party can enjoy his own without in some measure restricting the liberty of the other in the use of property, the law must make the best arrangement it can between the contending parties, with a view to preserving to each one the largest measure of liberty possible under the circumstances. We see no escape from the conclusion in the present case that the only proper decree is to allow the complainants a reference for the ascertainment of damages, and that the injunction must be denied to them, except in the qualified manner below indicated.

In the exercise of its discretion to refuse the injunction, the court has power to impose upon the defendants, as a condition annexed to such refusal, that they shall pay such damages as may have accrued to the several complainants up to the filing of the bills below. . . .

Homes and landscape in vicinity of Ducktown Sulphur, Copper & Iron Co., Ltd.

NOTES AND QUESTIONS ON *MADISON v. DUCKTOWN*

1. *Proof and basis for injunctive relief.* Did the plaintiffs in this case prove the elements of a private nuisance claim? If so, why was an injunction denied? What factors might have changed this result?

2. *Propriety of* per se *injunctions.* What problems might arise if a successful private nuisance claim did lead to *per se* injunctive relief?

3. *Measure of damages.* The court indicated that a damage award was appropriate in lieu of injunctive relief. How should the amount of damages be determined? What amount will compensate plaintiffs for their losses? What if the nature or degree of harm changes, or if new information shows that the pollution causes more harm than initially believed?

4. *Assessment of nuisance doctrine.* Based on the case and your answers to the previous questions, what are the major benefits and limitations of private nuisance doctrine in addressing environmental problems?

5. *Public versus private nuisances.* The potential difference between private and public nuisance cases is illustrated by further litigation regarding these same smelters. The same year that the Tennessee Supreme Court denied injunctive relief in *Madison*, the State of Georgia filed an original jurisdiction action in the U.S. Supreme Court to enjoin operation of the smelters because of extensive alleged property damage from emissions that crossed the state border. Georgia v. Tennessee Copper Co., 206 U.S. 230 (1907). Responding to clear proof of a public nuisance, Justice Holmes wrote:

It is a fair and reasonable demand on the part of a sovereign that the air over its territory should not be polluted on a great scale by sulphurous acid gas, that the forests on its mountains, be they better or worse, and whatever domestic destruction they have suffered, should not be further destroyed or threatened by the acts of persons beyond its control, that the crops and orchards on its hills should not be endangered from the same source. If any such demand is to be enforced this must be, notwithstanding the hesitation that we might feel if the suit were between private parties, and the doubt whether for the injuries which they might be suffering to their property they should not be left to an action at law.

[After indicating that the elements of a public nuisance had been shown, Justice Holmes continued:]Whether Georgia by insisting upon this claim is doing more harm than good to her own citizens is for her to determine. The possible disaster to those outside the State must be accepted as a consequence of her standing upon her extreme rights. . . .

If the State of Georgia adheres to its determination, there is no alternative to issuing an injunction, after allowing a reasonable time to the defendants to complete the structures that they now are building, and the effort that they are making, to stop the fumes.

What is the justification for *per se* injunctive relief in a public nuisance case brought by a state (or other political subdivision), relative to a private nuisance case brought by a private party? What prevents one state from shutting down competing industries in other states so long as some nuisance can be shown?

Public nuisance actions do not always succeed, however, as illustrated by the next case.

Missouri v. Illinois
200 U.S. 496 (1906)

JUSTICE HOLMES delivered the opinion of the court.

This is a suit brought by the state of Missouri to restrain the discharge of the sewage of Chicago through an artificial channel into the Desplaines river, in the state of Illinois. That river empties into the Illinois river, and the latter empties into the Mississippi at a point about 43 miles above the city of St. Louis. It was alleged in the bill that the result of the threatened discharge would be to send 1,500 tons of poisonous filth daily into the Mississippi, to deposit great quantities of the same upon the part of the bed of the last-named river belonging to the plaintiff, and so to poison the water of that river, upon which various of the plaintiff's cities, towns, and inhabitants depended, as to make it unfit for drinking, agricultural, or manufacturing purposes. It was alleged that the defendant sanitary district was acting in pursuance of a statute of the state of Illinois, and as an agency of that state. . . . A supplemental bill alleges that since the filing of the original bill the drainage canal has been opened and put into operation, and has produced and is producing all the evils which were apprehended when the injunction first was asked. The answers deny the plaintiff's case, allege that the new plan sends the water of the Illinois river into the Mississippi much purer than it was before, that many towns and cities of the plaintiff along the Missouri and Mississippi discharge their sewage into those rivers, and that if there is any trouble the plaintiff must look nearer home for the cause.

. . . The nuisance set forth in the bill was one which would be of international importance, — a visible change of a great river from a pure stream into a polluted and poisoned ditch. The only question presented was whether, as between the states of the Union, this court was competent to deal with a situation which, if it arose between independent sovereignties, might lead to war. Whatever differences of opinion there might be upon matters of detail, the jurisdiction and authority of this court to deal with such a case as that is not open to doubt. But the evidence now is in, the actual facts have required for their establishment the most ingenious experiments, and for their interpretation the most subtle speculations, of modern science, and therefore it becomes necessary at the present stage to consider somewhat more nicely than heretofore how the evidence in it is to be approached.

[The Court first addressed the threshold question of whether judicial intervention in this interstate water pollution matter was appropriate. After discussing various precedents, the Court wrote:]

. . . The Constitution extends the judicial power of the United States to controversies between two or more states, and between a state and citizens of another state, and gives this court original jurisdiction in cases in which a state shall be a party. Therefore, if one state raises a controversy with another, this court must determine whether there is any principle of law, and, if any, what, on which the plaintiff can recover. But the fact that this court must decide does not mean, of course, that it takes the place of a legislature. Some principles it must have power to declare. . . .

. . . Before this court ought to intervene, the case should be of serious magnitude, clearly and fully proved, and the principle to be applied should be one which the court is prepared deliberately to maintain against all considerations on the other side.

As to the principle to be laid down, the caution necessary is manifest. It is a question of the first magnitude whether the destiny of the great rivers is to be the sewers of the cities along their banks or to be protected against everything which threatens their purity. To decide the whole matter at one blow by an irrevocable fiat would be at least premature. If we are to judge by what the plaintiff itself permits, the discharge of sewage into the Mississippi by cities and towns is to be expected. We believe that the practice of discharging into the river is general along its banks, except where the levees of Louisiana have led to a different course. The argument for the plaintiff asserts it to be proper within certain limits. These are facts to be considered. Even in cases between individuals, some consideration is given to the practical course of events. In the black country of England parties would not be expected to stand upon extreme rights. Where, as here, the plaintiff has sovereign powers, and deliberately permits discharges similar to those of which it complains, it not only offers a standard to which the defendant has the right to appeal, but, as some of those discharges are above the intake of St. Louis, it warrants the defendant in demanding the strictest proof that the plaintiff's own conduct does not produce the result, or at least so conduce to it, that courts should not be curious to apportion the blame.

We have studied the plaintiff's statement of the facts in detail, and have perused the evidence, but it is unnecessary for the purposes of decision to do more than give the general result in a very simple way. At the outset we cannot but be struck by the consideration that if this suit had been brought fifty years ago it almost necessarily would have failed. There is no pretense that there is a nuisance of the simple kind that was known to the older common law. There is nothing which can be detected by the unassisted senses, — no visible increase of filth, no new smell. On the contrary, it is proved that the great volume of pure water from Lake Michigan, which is mixed with the sewage at the start, has improved the Illinois river in these respects to a noticeable extent. Formerly it was sluggish and ill smelling. Now it is a comparatively clear stream to which edible fish have returned. Its water is drunk by the fishermen, it is said without evil results. The plaintiff's case depends upon an inference of the unseen. It draws the inference from two propositions. First, that typhoid fever has increased considerably since the change, and that other explanations have been disproved; and second, that the bacillus of typhoid can and does survive the journey and reach the intake of St. Louis in the Mississippi.

We assume the now-prevailing scientific explanation of typhoid fever to be correct. But when we go beyond that assumption, everything is involved in doubt. The data upon which an increase in the deaths from typhoid fever in St. Louis is alleged are disputed. The elimination of other causes is denied. The experts differ as to the time and distance within which a stream would purify itself. No case of an epidemic caused by infection at so remote a source is brought forward and the cases which are produced are controverted. The plaintiff obviously must be cautious upon this point, for, if this suit should succeed, many others would follow, and it not improbably would find itself a defendant to a bill by one or more of the states lower down upon the Mississippi. The distance which the sewage has to travel (357 miles) is not open to debate, but the time of transit, to be inferred from experiments with floats, is estimated as varying from eight to eighteen and a half days, with forty-eight hours more from intake to distribution, and when corrected by observations of bacteria is greatly prolonged by the defendants. The experiments of the defendant's experts lead them to the opinion that a typhoid bacillus could not survive the journey, while those on the other side maintain that it might live and keep its power for twenty-five days or more, and arrive at St. Louis. Upon the question at issue, whether the new discharge from Chicago hurts St. Louis, there is a categorical contradiction between the experts on the two sides.

The Chicago drainage canal was opened on January 17, 1900. The deaths from typhoid fever in St. Louis, before and after that date, are stated somewhat differently in different places. We give them mainly from the plaintiff's brief: 1890, 140; 1891, 165; 1892, 441; 1893, 215; 1894, 171; 1895, 106; 1896, 106; 1897, 125; 1898, 95; 1899, 131; 1900, 154; 1901, 181; 1902, 216; 1903, 281. It is argued for the defendant that the numbers for the later years have been enlarged by carrying over cases which in earlier years would have been put into a miscellaneous column (intermittent, remittent, typho-malaria, etc., etc.), but we assume that the increase is real. Nevertheless, comparing the last four years with the earlier ones, it is obvious that the ground for a specific inference is very narrow, if we stopped at this point. The plaintiff argues that the increase must be due to Chicago, since there is nothing corresponding to it in the watersheds of the Missouri or Mississippi. On the other hand, the defendant points out that there has been no such enhanced rate of typhoid on the banks of the Illinois as would have been found if the opening of the drainage canal were the true cause.

Both sides agree that the detection of the typhoid bacillus in the water is not to be expected. But the plaintiff relies upon proof that such bacilli are discharged into the Chicago sewage in considerable quantities; that the number of bacilli in the water of the Illinois is much increased, including the *bacillus coli communis*, which is admitted to be an index of contamination, and that the chemical analyses lead to the same inference. To prove that the typhoid bacillus could make the journey an experiment was tried with the *bacillus prodigiosus*, which seems to have been unknown, or nearly unknown, in these waters. After preliminary trials, in which these bacilli emptied into the Mississippi near the mouth of the Illinois were found near the St. Louis intake and in St. Louis in times varying from three days to a month, one hundred and seven barrels of the same, said to contain one thousand million bacilli to the cubic centimeter, were put into the drainage canal near the starting point on November 6, and on December 4 an example was found at the St. Louis intake tower. Four others were found on the three following days, two at the tower and two at the mouth of the Illinois. As this bacillus is asserted to have about the same length of life in sunlight in living waters as the *bacillus typhosus*, although it is a little more hardy, the experiment is thought to prove one element of the plaintiff's case, although the very small number found in many samples of water is thought by the other side to indicate that practically no typhoid germs would get through. It seems to be conceded that the purification of the Illinois by the large dilution from Lake Michigan (nine parts or more in ten) would increase the danger, as it now generally is believed that the bacteria of decay, the saprophytes, which flourish in stagnant pools, destroy the pathogenic germs. Of course, the addition of so much water to the Illinois also increases its speed.

On the other hand, the defendant's evidence shows a reduction in the chemical and bacterial accompaniments of pollution in a given quantity of water, which would be natural in view of the mixture of nine parts to one from Lake Michigan. It affirms that the Illinois is better or no worse at its mouth than it was before, and makes it at least uncertain how much of the present pollution is due to Chicago and how much to sources further down, not complained of in the bill. It contends that if any bacilli should get through, they would be scattered and enfeebled and would do no harm. The defendant also sets against the experiment with the *bacillus prodigiosus* a no less striking experiment with typhoid germs suspended in the Illinois river in permeable sacs. According to this the duration of the life of these germs has been much exaggerated, and in that water would not be more than three or four days. It is suggested, by way of criticism that the germs may not have been of normal strength, that the conditions were less favorable than if they had floated down in a comparatively unchanging body of water, and that the germs may have escaped; but the experiment raises at least a serious doubt. Further, it hardly is denied that there is no parallelism in detail between the increase and decrease of typhoid fever in Chicago and St. Louis. The defendant's experts maintain that the water of the Missouri is worse than that of the Illinois, while it contributes a much larger portion to the intake. The evidence is very strong that it is necessary for St. Louis to take preventive measures, by filtration or otherwise, against the dangers of the plaintiff's own creation or from other sources than Illinois. What will protect against one will protect against another. The presence of causes of infection from the plaintiff's action makes the case weaker in principle as well as harder to prove than one in which all came from a single source.

Some stress was laid on the proposition that Chicago is not on the natural watershed of the Mississippi, because of a rise of a few feet between the Des Plaines and the Chicago rivers. We perceive no reason for distinction on this ground. The natural features relied upon are of the smallest. And if, under any circumstances, they could affect the case, it is enough to say that Illinois brought Chicago into the Mississippi watershed in pursuance, not only of its own statutes, but also of the acts of Congress . . . the validity of which is not disputed. . . . Of course these acts do not grant the right to discharge sewage, but the case stands no differently in point of law from a suit because of the discharge from Peoria into the Illinois, or from any other or all the other cities on the banks of that stream.

We might go more into detail, but we believe that we have said enough to explain our point of view and our opinion of the evidence as it stands. What the future may develop, of course we cannot tell. But our conclusion upon the present evidence is that the case proved falls so far below the allegations of the bill that it is not brought within the principles heretofore established in the cause.

Bill dismissed without prejudice

NOTES AND QUESTIONS ON *MISSOURI v.* *ILLINOIS*

1. *Distinguishing Tennessee Copper.* Why did the plaintiffs succeed in *Georgia v. Tennessee Copper* but not here?

2. *Balancing interests.* In nuisance doctrine, especially in the context of equitable relief (injunctions), courts often balance the needs, interests, and behavior of the various parties. How did that affect the result in *Missouri*? Should it matter that this case was brought by one government against another, as opposed to a government versus private polluter situation such as *Georgia v. Tennessee Copper*?

3. *Nuisance doctrine and new kinds of harm.* Courts developed nuisance doctrine to address obvious sources of annoyance, such as noxious odors, visible wastes, etc. Here, the alleged harm was bacterial, but the water that carried those pathogens looked and smelled better than it did previously. How well suited was nuisance law to handle this new kind of harm?

4. *Causation and injunctive relief.* What degree of causation should be necessary to justify an anti-pollution injunction under common law principles? Is it enough to show an increase in pollution, or does the plaintiff need to prove actual harm to human health?

5. *Burden of proof.* Proving harm can be difficult at the frontiers of science, an issue we will return to in several later chapters. Should the opponent of a polluting activity have to prove an activity is harmful before it can be stopped (the general rule in civil litigation), or should the proponent of the activity bear the burden of proving that the activity is *safe* in the face of uncertainty? As an example, does the following graphic depiction of some of the key evidence indicate that plaintiffs proved that harm was caused by the defendant's conduct?

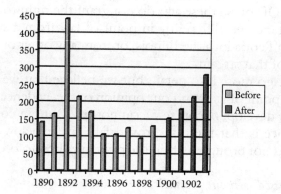

Missouri v. Illinois — Typhoid incidence before and after river re-routed

6. *Prevention versus remediation.* What does this issue say about the ability of the common law to adopt a preventive as opposed to a remedial approach to environmental harm?

2.　Common Law Goals and Coase

We have seen that some common law cases afford plaintiffs a legal right to be free from significant harm from pollution. Others, however, employ some balancing, at least in deciding upon remedies. Which is the proper approach? Consider this seminal law and economics article, which suggests that private bargaining might provide more economically efficient solutions to pollution and other environmental problems:

 ### R. H. Coase, The Problem of Social Cost
3 Journal of Law and Economics 1-44 (1960)

The Problem to Be Examined

This paper is concerned with those actions of business firms which have harmful effects on others. The standard example is that of a factory the smoke from which has harmful effects on those occupying neighboring properties. The economic analysis of such a situation has usually proceeded in terms of a divergence between the private and social product of the factory, in which economists have largely followed the treatment of Pigou in *The Economics of Welfare*. The conclusions to which this kind of analysis seems to have led most economists is that it would be desirable to make the owner of the factory liable for the damage caused to those injured by the smoke, or alternatively, to place a tax on the factory owner varying with the amount of smoke produced and equivalent in money terms to the damage it would cause, or finally, to exclude the factory from residential districts (and presumably from other areas in which the emission of smoke would have harmful effects on others). It is my contention that the suggested courses of action are inappropriate, in that they lead to results which are not necessarily, or even usually, desirable.

The Reciprocal Nature of the Problem

The traditional approach has tended to obscure the nature of the choice that has to be made. The question is commonly thought of as one in which A inflicts harm on B and what has to be decided is: how should we restrain A? But this is wrong. We are dealing with a problem of a reciprocal nature. To avoid the harm to B would inflict harm on A. The real question that has to be decided is: should A be allowed to harm B or should B be allowed to harm A? The problem is to avoid the more serious harm. I instanced in my previous article the case of a confectioner the noise and vibrations from whose machinery disturbed a doctor in his work. To avoid harming the doctor would inflict harm on the confectioner. The problem posed by this case was essentially whether it was worth while, as a result of restricting the methods of production which could be used for the confectioner, to secure more doctoring at the cost of a reduced supply of confectionery products. Another example is afforded by the problem of straying cattle which destroy crops on neighboring land. If it is inevitable that some cattle will stray, an increase in the supply of meat can only be obtained at the expense of a decrease in the supply of crops. The nature of the choice is clear: meat or crops. What answer should be given is, of course, not clear unless we know the value of what is obtained was well as the value of what is sacrificed to obtain it. To give another example, Professor George J. Stigler instances the contamination of a stream. If we assume that the harmful effect of the pollution is that it kills the fish, the question to be decided is: is the value of the fish lost greater or less than the value of the product which the contamination of the stream makes possible. . . .

[Coase proceeds to demonstrate, through a hypothetical arithmetic example which we have spared you, that even absent legal intervention, the parties affected by such choices will bargain to reach the economically optimal result in terms of the values of the resources at issue. Thus, in the case of the cattle straying onto a neighbor's land, if the value of the increased cattle exceeds that of the lost crops, the rancher will pay the farmer the value of the lost crops. If the value of the lost crops exceeds that of the cattle, the farmer will pay the rancher to keep the cattle away. In either instance, he argues, both parties will be better off through this arm's length bargaining process. Moreover, Coase shows that in order to reach such optimal results, it does not matter whether the initial assumption is that the rancher has a right to allow his cattle to roam, or that the farmer has the right to exclude the cattle from her land. Thus, according to Coase, a background rule that automatically places liability on the party causing harm — a presumptive initial delineation of rights — is not necessarily appropriate. In the following section of the article, however, Coase explains a key limitation in this thesis.]

2. The Cost of Market Transactions Taken into Account

The argument has proceeded up to this point on the assumption . . . that there were no costs involved in carrying out market transactions. This is, of course, a very unrealistic assumption. In order to carry out a market transaction it is necessary to discover who it is that one wishes to deal with, to inform people that one wishes to deal and on what terms, to conduct negotiations leading up to a bargain, to draw up the contract, to undertake the inspection needed to make sure that the terms of the contract are being observed, and so on. These operations are often extremely costly, sufficiently costly at any rate to prevent many transactions that would be carried out in a world in which the pricing system worked without cost.

In earlier sections, when dealing with the problem of the rearrangement of legal rights through the market, it was argued that such a rearrangement would be made through the market whenever this would lead to an increase in the value of production. But this assumed costless market transactions. Once the costs of carrying out market transactions are taken into account it is clear that such a rearrangement of rights will only be undertaken when the increase in the value of production consequent upon the rearrangement is greater than the costs which would be involved in bringing it about. When it is less, the granting of an injunction (or the knowledge that it would be granted) or the liability to pay damages may result in an activity being discontinued (or may prevent its being started) which would be undertaken if market transactions were costless. In these conditions the initial delimitation of legal rights does have an effect on the efficiency with which the economic system operates. One arrangement of rights may bring about a greater value of production than any other. But unless this is the arrangement of rights established by the legal system, the costs of reaching the same result by altering and combining rights through the market may be so great that this optimal arrangement of rights, and the greater value of production which it would bring, may never be achieved.

NOTES AND QUESTIONS ON COASE

1. *Pollution as a reciprocal problem.* Do you agree with Coase that pollution is a reciprocal problem? Does a breather of fumes harm the owner of the factory polluting the air? Can one abate pollution without harming the factory or its customers?

2. *Coasian solutions to nuisance cases.* How would you resolve the *Madison* and *Missouri* cases under Coase's approach? Would the approach be different for the private nuisance context of *Madison* as opposed to the public nuisance context of *Missouri v. Illinois*, and if so, why?

3. *Economic efficiency.* Does it make sense to force a cattle rancher to fence in her property, if her neighbor's crops are not as valuable as the extra meat produced when cattle can eat the neighbor's crops? Does it make sense to force a factory owner to abate pollution when doing so will impose a cost on her customers exceeding the value of the fish that the pollution kills? Economists would consider it "inefficient" to impose costs on polluters that exceed the value associated with the resulting environmental benefits. We will return to the efficiency concept when we address the goals of environmental law (Chapter 4) and cost-benefit analysis (Chapter 8).

4. *Private bargaining and public pollution.* Do you read Coase to argue that private bargaining alone provides an adequate solution to pollution problems? Consider that issue as you read the more recent common law cases in the following section, decided at and after the dawn of statutory environmental law.

3.   More recent applications of common law

The court in *Madison* focused on compensation, while the *Missouri* court focused on prevention through injunctive relief. This general issue of prevention versus compensation is revisited in the following case, as well as the willingness of courts to address broader public issues in the context of party-specific litigation:

Boomer et al. v. Atlantic Cement Co., Inc.
257 N.E.2d 870 (N.Y. 1970)

BERGAN, JUDGE.

Defendant operates a large cement plant near Albany. These are actions for injunction and damages by neighboring land owners alleging injury to property from dirt, smoke and vibration emanating from the plant. A nuisance has been found after trial, temporary damages have been allowed; but an injunction has been denied.

The public concern with air pollution arising from many sources in industry and in transportation is currently accorded ever wider recognition accompanied by a growing sense of responsibility in State and Federal Governments to control it. Cement plants are obvious sources of air pollution in the neighborhoods where they operate.

But there is now before the court private litigation in which individual property owners have sought specific relief from a single plant operation. The threshold question raised by the division of view on this appeal is whether the court should resolve the litigation between the parties now before it as equitably as seems possible; or whether, seeking promotion of the general public welfare, it should channel private litigation into broad public objectives.

A court performs its essential function when it decides the rights of parties before it. Its decision of private controversies may sometimes greatly affect public issues. Large questions of law are often resolved by the manner in which private litigation is decided. But this is normally an incident to the court's main function to settle controversy. It is a rare exercise of judicial power to use a decision in private litigation as a purposeful mechanism to achieve direct public objectives greatly beyond the rights and interests before the court.

Effective control of air pollution is a problem presently far from solution even with the full public and financial powers of government. In large measure adequate technical procedures are yet to be developed and some that appear possible may be economically impracticable. It seems apparent that the amelioration of air pollution will depend on technical research in great depth; on a carefully balanced consideration of the economic impact of close regulation; and of the actual effect on public health. It is likely to require massive public expenditure and to demand more than any local community can accomplish and to depend on regional and interstate controls.

A court should not try to do this on its own as a by-product of private litigation and it seems manifest that the judicial establishment is neither equipped in the limited nature of any judgment it can pronounce nor prepared to lay down and implement an effective policy for the elimination of air pollution. This is an area beyond the circumference of one private lawsuit. It is a direct responsibility for government and should not thus be undertaken as an incident to solving a dispute between property owners and a single cement plant — one of many — in the Hudson River valley.

The cement making operations of defendant have been found by the court of Special Term to have damaged the nearby properties of plaintiffs in these two actions. That court, as it has been noted, accordingly found defendant maintained a nuisance and this has been affirmed at the Appellate Division. The total damage to plaintiffs' properties is, however, relatively small in comparison with the value of defendant's operation and with the consequences of the injunction which plaintiffs seek.

The ground for the denial of injunction, notwithstanding the finding both that there is a nuisance and that plaintiffs have been damaged substantially, is the large disparity in economic consequences of the nuisance and of the injunction. This theory cannot, however, be sustained without overruling a doctrine which has been consistently reaffirmed in several leading cases in this court and which has never been disavowed here, namely that where a nuisance has been found and where there has been any substantial damage shown by the party complaining an injunction will be granted.

The rule in New York has been that such a nuisance will be enjoined although marked disparity be shown in economic consequence between the effect of the injunction and the effect of the nuisance . . . but to follow the rule literally in these cases would be to close down the plant at once. This court is fully agreed to avoid that immediately drastic remedy; the difference in view is how best to avoid it.*

One alternative is to grant the injunction but postpone its effect to a specified future date to give opportunity for technical advances to permit defendant to eliminate the nuisance; another is to grant the injunction conditioned on the payment of permanent damages to plaintiffs which would compensate them for the total economic loss to their property present and future caused by defendant's operations. For reasons which will be developed the court chooses the latter alternative.

If the injunction were to be granted unless within a short period — e.g., 18 months — the nuisance be abated by improved methods, there would be no assurance that any significant technical improvement would occur.

The parties could settle this private litigation at any time if defendant paid enough money and the imminent threat of closing the plant would build up the pressure on defendant. If there were no improved techniques found, there

---

*Respondent's investment in the plant is in excess of $45,000.00. There are over 300 people employed there.

would inevitably be applications to the court at Special Term for extensions of time to perform on showing of good faith efforts to find such techniques. Moreover, techniques to eliminate dust and other annoying by-products of cement making are unlikely to be developed by any research the defendant can undertake within any short period, but will depend on the total resources of the cement industry nationwide and throughout the world. The problem is universal wherever cement is made.

For obvious reasons the rate of the research is beyond control of defendant. If at the end of 18 months the whole industry has not found a technical solution a court would be hard put to close down this one cement plant if due regard be given to equitable principles.

On the other hand, to grant the injunction unless defendant pays plaintiffs such permanent damages as may be fixed by the court seems to do justice between the contending parties. All of the attributions of economic loss to the properties on which plaintiffs' complaints are based will have been redressed.

The nuisance complained of by these plaintiffs may have other public or private consequences, but these particular parties are the only ones who have sought remedies and the judgment proposed will fully redress them. The limitation of relief granted is a limitation only within the four corners of these actions and does not foreclose public health or other public agencies from seeking proper relief in a proper court.

It seems reasonable to think that the risk of being required to pay permanent damages to injured property owners by cement plant owners would itself be a reasonable effective spur to research for improved techniques to minimize nuisance.

The power of the court to condition on equitable grounds the continuance of an injunction on the payment of permanent damages seems undoubted. . . .

JASEN, JUDGE (dissenting).

I agree with the majority that a reversal is required here, but I do not subscribe to the newly enunciated doctrine of assessment of permanent damages, in lieu of an injunction, where substantial property rights have been impaired by the creation of a nuisance.

It has long been the rule in this State, as the majority acknowledges, that a nuisance which results in substantial continuing damage to neighbors must be enjoined. To now change the rule to permit the cement company to continue polluting the air indefinitely upon the payment of permanent damages is, in my opinion, compounding the magnitude of a very serious problem in our State and Nation today. . . .

The harmful nature and widespread occurrence of air pollution have been extensively documented. Congressional hearings have revealed that air pollution causes substantial property damage, as well as being a contributing factor to a rising incidence of lung cancer, emphysema, bronchitis and asthma. . . .

I see grave dangers in overruling our long-established rule of granting an injunction where a nuisance results in substantial continuing damage. In permitting the injunction to become inoperative upon the payment of permanent damages, the majority is, in effect, licensing a continuing wrong. It is the same as saying to the cement company, you may continue to do harm to your neighbors so long as you pay a fee for it. Furthermore, once such permanent damages are assessed and paid, the incentive to alleviate the wrong would be eliminated, thereby continuing air pollution of an area without abatement.

It is true that some courts have sanctioned the remedy here proposed by the majority in a number of cases, but none of the authorities relied upon by the majority are analogous to the situation before us. In those cases, the courts, in denying an injunction and awarding money damages, grounded their decision on a showing that the use to which the property was intended to be put was primarily for the public benefit. Here, on the other hand, it is clearly established that the cement company is creating a continuing air pollution nuisance primarily for its own private interest with no public benefit. . . .

I would enjoin the defendant cement company from continuing the discharge of dust particles upon its neighbors' properties unless, within 18 months, the cement company abated this nuisance.

It is not my intention to cause the removal of the cement plant from the Albany area, but to recognize the urgency of the problem stemming from this stationary source of air pollution, and to allow the company a specified period of time to develop a means to alleviate this nuisance.

I am aware that the trial court found that the most modern dust control devices available have been installed in defendant's plant, but, I submit, this does not mean that better and more effective dust control devices could not be developed within the time allowed to abate the pollution.

Moreover, I believe it is incumbent upon the defendant to develop such devices, since the cement company, at the time the plant commenced production (1962), was well aware of the plaintiffs' presence in the area, as well as the probable consequences of its contemplated operation. Yet, it still chose to build and operate the plant at this site.

In a day when there is a growing concern for clean air, highly developed industry should not expect acquiescence by the courts, but should, instead, plan its operations to eliminate contamination of our air and damage to its neighbors.

NOTES AND QUESTIONS ON *BOOMER*

1. Per se *injunctions.* Under prevailing New York State law when this decision was issued, any showing of "substantial damage" required the court to issue an injunction. What is the justification for this *per se* rule, and why did the *Boomer* majority reject this longstanding approach here?

2. *Conditional injunctions.* A somewhat softer form of injunction is a conditional injunction, in which the plant is allowed to operate for a fixed period of time, during which it is expected to develop and implement means to

abate the nuisance. Why does the court reject this approach? Some statutory approaches to environmental law use various means of identifying or forcing development of the "best technology" to control pollution, a concept addressed in Chapter 6.

3. *Judicial solutions to public problems through private litigation.* What do you think concerns the court about whether "seeking promotion of the general public welfare, it should channel private litigation into broad public objectives"? Is the majority most concerned about the nature of the judicial process (resolving site-specific litigation as opposed to broader societal problems), or about its expertise and ability to deal with the complex technical issues of environmental law and management? Does the dissent simply strike a different balance with respect to the appropriate remedy in this case, or does it disagree more fundamentally about the role and capacity of courts to address environmental problems?

Whether or not the courts are competent to resolve environmental issues, or are comfortable doing so, plaintiffs continue to bring common law actions when they believe that they and their families and communities have experienced, and continue to experience, increased risk of environmental harm. The following is one of the many judicial opinions issued in the toxic tort case made famous by Jonathan Harr in *A Civil Action*. This ruling on defendants' motion for summary judgment highlights some of the many issues that arise in the context of modern toxic tort litigation, and sheds additional light on the particular legal problems inherent in judicial resolution of environmental matters.

 ## Anderson v. W.R. Grace & Co.
628 F. Supp. 1219 (D. Mass. 1986)

MEMORANDUM AND ORDER ON
DEFENDANTS' JOINT MOTION FOR PARTIAL
SUMMARY JUDGMENT

SKINNER, DISTRICT JUDGE.

This case arises out of the defendants' alleged contamination of the groundwater in certain areas of Massachusetts, with chemicals, including trichloroethylene and tetrachloroethylene. Plaintiffs allege that two of Woburn's water wells, Wells G and H, drew upon the contaminated water until the wells were closed in 1979 and that exposure to this contaminated water caused them to suffer severe injuries.

Of the 33 plaintiffs in this action, five are the administrators of minors who died of leukemia allegedly caused by exposure to the chemicals. They bring suit for wrongful death and conscious pain and suffering. Sixteen of the 28 living plaintiffs are members of the decedents' immediate families. These plaintiffs seek to recover for the emotional distress caused by witnessing the decedents' deaths. Three of the living plaintiffs also contracted leukemia and currently are either in remission or treatment for the disease. The 25 non-leukemic plaintiffs allege that exposure to the contaminated water caused a variety of illnesses and damaged their bodily systems. All of the living plaintiffs seek to recover for their illnesses and other damage, increased risk of developing future illness, and emotional distress. Six of the plaintiff families still reside in the area above the allegedly contaminated water. These plaintiffs seek injunctive relief under a nuisance theory.

Two of the defendants, W.R. Grace & Co. and Beatrice Foods Co. (collectively defendants), have jointly moved for partial summary judgment on several of plaintiffs' claims. They contend that:

(1)　the wrongful death claims of Michael Zona, James Anderson and Carl Robbins, III are barred by the time limitations of the Massachusetts wrongful death statute;

(2)　the emotional distress claims of the plaintiffs who have not contracted leukemia may not stand because the emotional distress was not caused by any physical injury;

(3)　the plaintiffs' claims for increased risk of developing serious illness in the future are not recognized under Massachusetts law; and

(4)　the plaintiffs lack standing to request injunctive relief under a theory of nuisance.

As these contentions raise discrete issues, I will address each in turn.

A. *Statute of Limitations.*

1. Michael Zona.

Defendants argue that Michael Zona's wrongful death action is barred by the statute of limitations. The Massachusetts wrongful death statute provides in pertinent part: "An action to recover damages under this section shall be commenced within three years from the date of death. . . . " This wrongful death action was filed in May of 1982, more than eight years after Michael Zona died on February 23, 1974. Plaintiffs contend that the action was timely filed because the statute was tolled until May, 1979, when they discovered the alleged cause of Michael Zona's death, by the Massachusetts discovery rule, which tolls the statute of limitations until a plaintiff knows or reasonably should know that he or she has been harmed as a result of the defendant's conduct. The Supreme Judicial Court has not decided whether the discovery rule will toll the statute of limitations contained in the Massachusetts wrongful death statute. . . . [T]he discovery rule is a method of defining when a cause of action accrues. The principle behind the discovery rule is that "a plaintiff should be put on notice before his or her claim is barred by the passage of time." The notice required by the rule includes knowledge of both the injury and its cause — that plaintiff has been harmed as a result of the defendant's conduct.

Arguably, limitation statutes should apply equally to similar facts. Where the circumstances would allow an extension of time under the limitations statute for tort for mere wounding or injury, it may be unjust to permit the fact of death to bar the use of the discovery rule.

The present state of Massachusetts law does not, therefore, foreclose the possibility that a discovery rule might be applied in starting the limitation period notwithstanding the statutory reference to the time of death. . . .

B. *Claims for Emotional Distress.*

Defendants move for summary judgment on plaintiffs' claims of emotional distress on the grounds that the non-leukemic plaintiffs' distress was not caused by any physical injury. They also move for summary judgment on the emotional distress claims of plaintiffs who witnessed a family member die of leukemia, arguing that Massachusetts law does not recognize such a claim. Some plaintiffs are in both of these separate categories.

1. Physical Injury

. . . Defendants attack plaintiffs' claims of emotional distress at three points: they argue that plaintiffs did not suffer physical harm as a result of defendants' allegedly negligent conduct; that, if the plaintiffs did suffer any harm, it was not manifested by objective symptomatology; and that any manifest physical harm did not cause the claimed emotional distress.

The . . . Complaint alleges only that "each plaintiff has suffered a direct adverse physical affect [sic] . . . . " Plaintiffs make a slightly more specific claim to physical injury in their answers to interrogatories. Each plaintiff states that exposure to contaminants in the water drawn from Wells G and H "affected my body's ability to fight disease, [and] caused harm to my body's organ systems, including my respiratory, immunological, blood, central nervous, gastro-intestinal, urinary-renal systems . . . . "

This alleged harm is sufficient to maintain plaintiffs' claims for emotional distress . . . the term "physical harm" denotes harm to the bodies of the plaintiffs. In requiring physical harm rather than mere injury as an element of proof in a claim for emotional distress, the court required that a plaintiff show some actual physical damage as a predicate to suit. Defendants argue that plaintiffs' alleged harm is subcellular and therefore not the type of harm required to support a claim for emotional distress . . . I disagree. The [Massachusetts] Supreme Judicial Court requires that plaintiffs' physical harm be manifested by objective symptomatology and substantiated by expert medical testimony. In setting forth this requirement, the court did not distinguish between gross and subcellular harm. Instead, the court drew a line between harm which can be proven to exist through expert medical testimony based on objective evidence and harm which is merely speculative or based solely on a plaintiff's unsupported assertions. The phrase manifested by objective symptomatology does not indicate that the necessary harm need be immediately apparent but that its existence must be objectively evidenced. Where, as in this case, the harm is not obvious to the layman, its existence may not be demonstrated solely by the complaints of the alleged victim; it must also be substantiated by expert medical testimony. Upon review of the pleadings and the affidavits of plaintiffs' expert, I cannot say as a matter of law that this standard will not be met at trial.

The alleged damage to plaintiffs bodily systems is manifested by the many ailments which plaintiffs claim to have suffered as a result of exposure to the contaminated water.[4] Dr. Levin apparently will testify to the existence of changes in plaintiffs' bodies caused by exposure to the contaminated water. He will base his testimony on objective evidence of these changes, including the maladies listed in footnote four. Although the affidavit does not specifically identify the illnesses suffered by each plaintiff as a result of the changes, nor state that plaintiffs suffered more ailments than the average person would have over the same time span, it is sufficient evidence of harm to support the existence of a factual dispute and bar summary judgment.

[O]f course, injury is not sufficient. The harm allegedly caused by defendants' conduct must either have caused or been caused by the emotional distress. The Complaint does not state that plaintiffs' emotional distress was caused by any physical harm. Plaintiffs only allege that "[a]s a result of the knowledge that they . . . have consumed hazardous chemicals, the plaintiffs have suffered and will continue to suffer great emotional distress."

Plaintiffs provide more specific information about the source of their emotional distress in their answers to defendants' interrogatories. Each plaintiff states that "[a]s a result of the contaminated water . . . I have experienced depression and anxiousness." Plaintiffs also claim that "The defendants' conduct in contributing to the pollution of the groundwater serving Wells G and H and their failure to prevent, monitor, acknowledge, or correct the pollution has affected my mental and emotional state. It has caused me to suffer anxiety, depression, fear, anger, frustration, hopelessness and distress. . . ." None of these claims for emotional distress arise from physical injuries caused by defendants' conduct. Accordingly, they are not compensable. . . .

However, certain elements of plaintiffs' emotional distress stem from the physical harm to their immune systems allegedly caused by defendants' conduct and are compensable. Plaintiffs have stated that the illnesses contributed to by exposure to the contaminated water have caused them anxiety and pain. The excerpts from plaintiffs' depositions appended to defendants' motion indicate that plaintiffs are also worried over the increased susceptibility to

---

4. The list of ailments varies from plaintiff to plaintiff. The ailments include shortness of breath, decreased visual acuity, frequent waking, hoarseness, muscle aching, fatigue, chest pain, sore irritated dry throat, respiratory infections, stress incontinence, tingling, numbness, joint stiffness and aching, dry sensitive skin, rashes, cold sores, red burning eyes, headaches, diarrhea, vomiting, abdominal distress, post nasal discharge, nasal congestion, and nosebleeds.

disease which results from the alleged harm to their immune systems and exposure to carcinogens. As these elements of emotional distress arise out of plaintiffs' injuries, plaintiffs may seek to recover for them.

Defendants contend that plaintiffs' physical harm did not "cause" plaintiffs' distress over their increased susceptibility to disease. . . . They argue that the fear arose out of discussions between plaintiffs and their expert witness, Dr. Levin, in which the expert informed plaintiffs of their suppressed immune systems. Assuming, as I must for purposes of motion, that Dr. Levin is telling the truth, this argument is frivolous.

Plaintiffs can recover "only for that degree of emotional distress which a reasonable person, normally would have experienced under [the] circumstances." The Supreme Judicial Court has explicitly stated that the reasonableness of a claim for emotional distress is to be determined by the trier of fact. Accordingly, defendants' motion for summary judgment on the non-leukemic plaintiffs' claims for emotional distress is DENIED.

2. Witnessing death of a family member.

The second issue raised by defendants' motion is whether Massachusetts recognizes a claim for emotional distress for witnessing a family member die of a disease allegedly caused by defendants' conduct. This differs from the question considered in the preceding section because the concern now is whether the plaintiffs can recover for distress caused by witnessing the injuries of others, not by their own condition. The plaintiffs do not claim any physical harm resulted from this emotional distress. . . .

. . . The basic rule is one of the foreseeability of the emotional harm. Furthermore, in every circumstance but one, the harm for which damages may be recovered is not the emotional distress itself, but physical harm resulting from the emotional distress. In the one additional circumstance, damages may be recovered for emotional distress over injury to a child or spouse when the plaintiff suffers contemporaneous physical injury from the same tortious conduct that caused the injury to the close relative. . . .

. . . For emotional distress to be compensable under Massachusetts law . . . the distress must result from immediate apprehension of the defendant's negligence or its consequences. In each of the cases in which recovery for the emotional distress of a bystander has been allowed, there has been a dramatic traumatic shock causing immediate emotional distress. Such is not the case here. There is no indication in the Massachusetts cases that liability would be extended to a family member's emotional distress which built over time during the prolonged illness of a child. Imposition of liability in that case, while logically indistinguishable from the trauma situation, would violate the Massachusetts court's demonstrated prudential inclination to keep the scope of liability within manageable bounds.

In my opinion, in the present state of the law in Massachusetts, the Supreme Judicial Court would not permit recovery for emotional distress arising from the negligently induced illness of another, and therefore the plaintiffs may not recover for such emotional distress in this case.

C. Claims for increased risk of future illness.

Plaintiffs seek to recover damages for the increased risk of serious illness they claim resulted from consumption of and exposure to contaminated water. Defendants argue that Massachusetts does not recognize a claim for increased risk of future harm, regardless of whether plaintiffs have suffered physical harm. This issue has not been directly addressed by the Massachusetts courts. . . .

Plaintiffs view their claim as merely an element of damages, compensation for the risk of probable future consequences stemming from negligently inflicted present harm. In Massachusetts, [a] plaintiff is entitled to compensation for all damages that reasonably are to be expected to follow, but not to those that possibly may follow, the injury which he has suffered. He is not restricted to compensation for suffering and expense which by a fair preponderance of the evidence he has proved will inevitably follow. He is entitled to compensation for suffering and expense which by a fair preponderance of the evidence he has satisfied the jury reasonably are to be expected to follow, so far as human knowledge can foretell. In addition, when there is a "reasonable probability" that future expenses will be required to remedy the consequences of a defendant's negligence, the jury may consider the expense in awarding damages. Plaintiffs argue that these cases indicate that Massachusetts accepts the general rule of tort law that "[o]ne injured by the tort of another is entitled to recover damages for all harm, past, present and prospective, legally caused by the tort." I agree, subject to two caveats. First, . . . when an injured person seeks to recover for harms that may result in the future, recovery depends on establishing a "reasonable probability" that the harm will occur. Second, recovery for future harm in an action assumes that a cause of action for that harm has accrued at the time recovery is sought.

To view the risk of a future illness as part of damages is to ignore the question of whether a cause of action has accrued. Defendants argue that the cause of action for any future serious illness, including leukemia and other cancers, has not yet accrued because the injury has not yet occurred.[6] This is the rationale of the discovery rule applied to latent disease cases in Massachusetts under which the injury is equated with the manifestation of the disease. The question thus becomes whether, upon the manifestation of one or more diseases, a cause of action accrues for all prospective diseases so that a plaintiff may seek to recover for physically distinct and separate diseases which may develop in the future.

---

6. The weight of authority would deny plaintiffs a cause of action solely for increased risk because no "injury" has occurred. In this case, plaintiffs allege present injuries.

The answer to this question depends on the connection between the illnesses plaintiffs have suffered and fear they will suffer in the future. Unfortunately, the nature of plaintiffs' claim for increased risk of future illness is unclear on two counts. Nothing in the present record indicates the magnitude of the increased risk or the diseases which plaintiffs may suffer. [The] Complaint only alleges the plaintiffs face an "increased risk of serious illness", and the affidavits of plaintiffs' expert only state that exposure to the chemicals "can induce" cancer and result in an "increased susceptibility to disease" including an "increased propensity to serious illnesses as well as cancer." Insofar as plaintiffs seek to recover for their probable future costs and suffering due to ailments of the types they already claim to have endured, they may seek damages in this action. However, plaintiffs also claim an increased risk of leukemia or other cancers. These diseases seem at least qualitatively different from the illnesses plaintiffs have actually suffered. The record is insufficient to determine whether leukemia and other cancers are part of the same disease process as the other illnesses alleged to have resulted from exposure to the contaminated water. If they are part of the same disease process, then plaintiffs may seek recovery for the future illness in this action by showing a "reasonable probability" that they will occur. If, however, they are distinct diseases, then plaintiffs must wait until the disease has manifested itself to sue. . . .

A further reason for denying plaintiffs' damages for the increased risk of future harm in this action is the inevitable inequity which would result if recovery were allowed. "To award damages based on a mere mathematical probability would significantly undercompensate those who actually do develop cancer and would be a windfall to those who do not." In addition, if plaintiffs could show that they were more likely than not to suffer cancer or other future illness, full recovery would be allowed for all plaintiffs, even though only some number more than half would actually develop the illness. In such a case, the defendant would overcompensate the injured class.

Accordingly, action on plaintiffs' claims for the increased risk of serious future illness, including cancer, must be delayed. If the future illnesses stem from the same disease process as the illnesses plaintiffs presently complain of, recovery must be sought in this action. If the disease processes are different, however, the cause of action for the future illness will not accrue until the illness manifests itself.

D. Nuisance claims.

Plaintiffs' final claim is for nuisance. They assert that the alleged contamination of the groundwater from which they formerly drew their water constitutes a nuisance which is "inimical to plaintiffs' health and restricts their access to and use of the groundwater flowing beneath East Woburn and beneath their property". The continued disposal of hazardous substances on the ground and resulting presence of the substances in the soil of defendants' property in East Woburn is also alleged to be a nuisance because it constitutes a "further threat"

to the groundwater. Plaintiffs seek damages and an injunction ordering defendants (1) to halt the disposal of hazardous substances on defendants' property
in Woburn, (2) to remove the substances previously dumped on the property,
and (3) to remove all contamination from the groundwater flowing beneath
East Woburn and plaintiffs' property and "return that groundwater to the
condition it would be in but for the contamination".

The alleged contamination of the groundwater in East Woburn falls into
the category of public nuisances. It is true that pollution of groundwater may
constitute a private nuisance if the polluted water under a property comes into
direct contact with and harms the owner or his property. However, plaintiffs in
this case were only exposed to the water when it was pumped from Wells G and
H by the Town of Woburn. The right to be free of contamination to the
municipal water supply is clearly a "right common to the general public", thus
interference with that right would be a public nuisance.

Defendants argue that plaintiffs, as private persons, have no standing to
bring an action based on the public nuisance of a restriction on use of Woburn's
groundwater. The general rule is that the private injury sustained where a
common right is impaired is "merged in the common nuisance and injury to all
citizens, and the right is to be vindicated [through suit by a public official]."
But when a plaintiff has sustained "special or peculiar damage", he or she may
maintain an individual action. Injuries to a person's health are by their nature
"special and peculiar" and cannot properly be said to be common or public. As
plaintiffs allege that they have suffered a variety of illnesses as a result of
exposure to the contaminated water, they have standing to maintain this
nuisance action.

However, plaintiffs may only seek to obtain damages for their special
injuries. The case upon which plaintiffs rely in their standing argument only
provides that a "person whose property is damaged or whose health is injured
or whose reasonable enjoyment of his estate as a place of residence is impaired
or destroyed . . . may well maintain *an action to recover compensation for the
injury*". If a nuisance is found, plaintiffs are entitled to recover (1) the loss in
rental value of their property, if any, (2) compensation for physical injuries, and
(3) upon a showing of independent personal injury, damages for emotional
distress. Plaintiffs have not claimed any loss of property value.

The injunctive relief requested . . . is sought only on behalf of the six
plaintiff families who still reside in East Woburn. These plaintiffs allege that the
existing groundwater contamination in East Woburn and under their property
is a continuing threat to their health and invasion of their property rights and
constitutes a continuing nuisance. Groundwater pollution may constitute a
nuisance. However, this fact does not permit plaintiffs to raise the claim in a
private action absent some actual detrimental effect on plaintiffs' use or
enjoyment of their land. Plaintiffs' abstract claim of a threat and invasion by the
contaminated groundwater is not the required harm to their use and enjoyment of their property. Plaintiffs have cited no case in which the mere
introduction of foreign material into the ground supported a cause of action.

Nor do plaintiffs' physical injuries support an injunction. Plaintiffs' exposure to the contaminated water ceased in May of 1979, when Wells G and H were closed. The requested relief would not mitigate plaintiffs' special injuries; it would only remedy the public nuisance of groundwater contamination.

This same logic requires that plaintiffs' claim for expenses for abating the nuisance be denied. . . . Plaintiffs in the instant action have alleged no damage to their land other than the contamination of groundwater with which they claim no contact.

Defendants argue that plaintiffs' claims for damages on a theory of nuisance are merely duplicative of their negligence claims. This may well be true in regard to the personal injury claims. However, plaintiffs are entitled to present alternative theories of liability to the jury, so long as appropriate instructions are given to prevent double recovery for any element of damage. . . .

NOTES AND QUESTIONS ON *ANDERSON v. W.R. GRACE*

1. *Alternative Superfund remedy.* Note that the first complaint in this case was filed in 1982, after Congress adopted most of our major environmental statutes. Plaintiffs invoked none of these environmental statutes in the case. However, plaintiffs used information from an ongoing EPA investigation under the recently enacted Superfund statute as part of the basis for their case. After this case was over, EPA brought an action under the Superfund law seeking cleanup of the Woburn site.

2. *Summary judgment.* The court's holdings in this case came in the context of a motion for summary judgment. Did the court find liability for any of the plaintiff's claims? If not, what does the decision hold, and where does it leave the plaintiffs? Is this decision a victory for the plaintiffs or the defendants, and why?

3. *Statutes of limitations in environmental cases.* What is it about claims of environmental damage that can make the statute of limitations inquiry particularly difficult? What implications does this issue have for the adequacy and usefulness of common law environmental claims for the kinds of injury that were at issue in this case?

4. *Unique forms of harm.* This opinion highlights some of the unique kinds of "harm" in environmental cases:

   a. How should the law address the risk of potential future harm (as opposed to demonstrated current harm)? Should any increase in risk be compensable, no matter how small? If not, is there some threshold of increased risk which should be compensable, or must a plaintiff always show actual physical harm?

   b. Should emotional harm be compensable in environmental cases? Why or why not? What about emotional harm from increased *fear* of cancer or other harm?

c. Even where physical harm is manifest, what problems do trial lawyers face in proving causation? Should the rules of causation be any different in environmental cases than in any other tort case?

5. *Sufficiency of bargaining approach.* Does Coase provide an adequate solution to the issues raised in this case, *i.e.,* can a homeowner bargain with a factory to obtain payments to offset an increased risk of cancer to the homeowner and her family?

COMMON LAW REVIEW PROBLEM

As you learned in Chapter 1, EPA is still in the initial stages of deciding whether to regulate PFOA, and if so, how. Meanwhile, there is evidence of PFOA contamination in several public water supply systems near factories that manufacture PFOA or use PFOA in their production processes. Moreover, workers who have been exposed to PFOA exhibit detectable levels of PFOA in their bloodstream, and at least two exposed women workers gave birth to children with birth defects. Finally, much lower levels of PFOA have been detected in members of the general public, but the source of this exposure is currently not known. Because the PFOA issue has only recently been brought to light publicly, there are no public drinking water standards for PFOA under the Safe Drinking Water Act, 42 U.S.C. §§300f *et seq.* (the federal statute that regulates the safety of public drinking water systems), or worker exposure standards under the Occupational Safety and Health Act (OSHA), 29 U.S.C. §§650 *et seq.* (the federal statute governing worker health and safety), including from exposure to toxic chemicals in the workplace.

Assess the viability of bringing common law actions against manufacturers and users of PFOA on behalf of the parties identified below. For each, what kinds of cause of action would you bring? What would you have to do to prove the necessary elements of those claims, and how likely are they to succeed? What major obstacles would you expect if you brought these cases? How would you expect the defendants to respond to these cases?

A. Affected municipal water supply systems.
B. Members of the public who used water from such systems.
C. Women workers who were exposed to PFOA and whose children had birth defects.
D. Other exposed workers (and distinguish between men and women).
E. Members of the general public with measurable levels of PFOA in their blood. (People in the general population may be exposed to PFOA from food packaging and other consumer products.)

4. The Adequacy of the Common Law and a Response to Coase

≣ *Garrett Hardin, The Tragedy of the Commons*
≣   *162 Science 1243-48 (1968)*

The tragedy of the commons develops in this way. Picture a pasture open to all. It is to be expected that each herdsman will try to keep as many cattle as possible on the commons. Such an arrangement may work reasonably satisfactorily for centuries because tribal wars, poaching, and disease keep the numbers of both man and beast well below the carrying capacity of the land. Finally, however, comes the day of reckoning, that is, the day when the long-desired goal of social stability becomes reality. At this point, the inherent logic of the commons remorselessly generates tragedy.

As a rational being, each herdsman seeks to maximize his gain. Explicitly or implicitly, more or less consciously, he asks, "What is the utility *to me* of adding one more animal to my herd?" This utility has one negative and one positive component.

1.   The positive component is a function of the increment of one animal. Since the herdsman receives all the proceeds from the sale of the additional animal, the positive utility is nearly +1.
2.   The negative component is a function of the additional overgrazing created by one more animal. Since, however, the effects of overgrazing are shared by all the herdsmen, the negative utility for any particular decision-making herdsman is only a fraction of −1.

Adding together the component partial utilities, the rational herdsman concludes that the only sensible course for him to pursue is to add another animal to his herd. And another; and another . . . . But this is the conclusion reached by each and every rational herdsman sharing a commons. Therein is the tragedy. Each man is locked into a system that compels him to increase his heard without limit — in a world that is limited. Ruin is the destination toward which all men rush, each pursuing his own best interest in a society that believes in the freedom of the commons. Freedom in a commons brings ruin to all. . . .

The National Parks present another instance of the working out of the tragedy of the commons. At present, they are open to all, without limit. The parks themselves are limited in extent — there is only one Yosemite Valley — whereas population seems to grow without limit. The values that visitors seek in the parks are steadily eroded. Plainly we must soon cease to treat the parks as commons or they will be of no value to anyone.

What shall we do? We have several options. We might sell them off as private property. We might keep them as public property, but allocate the right to enter them. . . .

4. Pollution

In a reverse way, the tragedy of the commons reappears in problems of pollution. Here it is not a question of taking something out of the commons, but of putting something in — sewage, or chemical, radioactive, and heat wastes into water; noxious and dangerous fumes into the air; and distracting and unpleasant advertising signs into the line of sight. The calculations of utility are much the same as before. The rational man finds that his share of the cost of the wastes he discharges into the commons is less than the cost of purifying his wastes before releasing them. Since this is true for everyone, we are locked into a system of "fouling our own nest," so long as we behave only as independent, rational, free-enterprisers.

The tragedy of the commons as a food basket is averted by private property, or something formally like it. But the air and waters surrounding us cannot readily be fenced, and so the tragedy of the commons as a cesspool must be prevented by different means, by coercive laws or taxing devices that make it cheaper for the polluter to treat his pollutants than to discharge them untreated. We have not progressed as far with the solution of this problem as we have with the first. Indeed, our particular concept of private property, which deters us from exhausting the positive resources of the earth, favors pollution. The owner of a factory on the bank of a stream whose property extends to the middle of the stream, often has difficulty seeing why it is not his natural right to muddy the waters flowing past his door. The law, always behind the times, requires elaborate stitching and fitting to adapt it to this newly perceived aspect of the commons.

The pollution problem is a consequence of population. It did not much matter how a lonely American frontiersman disposed of his waste. "Flowing water purifies itself every 10 miles," my grandfather used to say, and the myth was near enough to the truth when he was a boy, for there were not too many people. But as population became denser, the natural chemical and biological recycling processes became overloaded, calling for a redefinition of property rights. . . .

The laws of our society . . . are poorly suited to governing a complex, crowded, changeable world. Our . . . solution is to augment statutory law with administrative law. Since it is practically impossible to spell out all the conditions under which it is safe to burn trash in the back yard or to run an automobile without smog-control, by law we delegate the details to bureaus.

NOTES AND QUESTIONS ON HARDIN

1. *Privatization versus government allocation.* How would Hardin remedy the problem of too many cattle grazing on the commons? Is privatizing the commons a better solution than government allocation of grazing rights? What would Coase have to say about that question?

2. *Role of costs.* Would Hardin favor reducing pollution to levels where all fish survive, regardless of the costs of doing so? Would Coase?

3. *Administrative versus statutory solutions.* Notice that Hardin favors an administrative law solution to the tragedy of the commons over a statutory solution. A statutory solution might involve Congress setting standards for how to burn trash safely or what sort of smog control we should use on automobiles. An administrative approach might have Congress delegating the detailed decisions on these matters to an administrative agency. Why does Hardin favor administrative to statutory law? As you read the next chapter, think about whether a system of statutes granting agencies substantial authority for detailed decisions enjoys important advantages over common law solutions.

3

From Common Law to Administrative Law

In the last chapter, you examined common law solutions to environmental problems. Hopefully, you identified the ways in which common law approaches may be useful in addressing environmental issues, as well as the ways in which those approaches alone may be inadequate in the face of the complexity, uncertainty, and ubiquity of modern environmental problems.

Congress and state legislatures responded to these perceived deficiencies in common law approaches by adopting regulatory statutes designed to address environmental problems in a more comprehensive fashion. Some of these laws are relatively brief. Others, however, are mind-boggling in their length and complexity.[1]

Why are statutory and regulatory approaches useful to solve problems for which the common law was perceived as insufficient? In this chapter, we address this issue in three parts. First, we discuss the basic reasons for statutory approaches to environmental problems, and describe the kinds of mechanisms used to implement those approaches, using the Clean Air Act as an example. Second, we explain the roles of administrative agencies in implementing and enforcing those schemes, and of judicial oversight in ensuring that implementing agencies administer the statutes fairly and reasonably. Third, we revisit the residual role of the common law, which in most respects remains in place, notwithstanding the comprehensive statutory overlay, and explore how the two systems—common law and statutory — relate to each other.

---

1. The National Environmental Policy Act, 42 U.S.C. §§4321-4370, for example, takes just 48 pages in the United States Code. The Clean Air Act, by contrast, now consumes some 800 pages in the United States Code, and, as noted by Justice Rehnquist, the provisions "virtually swim before one's eyes." United States Steel Corp. v. United States EPA, 444 U.S. 1035, 1038 (1980) (Rehnquist, J., dissenting from denial of certiorari). Some commentators believe that the modern regulatory regime has become far too complex and inefficient as a result. *See, e.g.,* Richard Lazarus, *The Tragedy of Distrust in the Implementation of Federal Environmental Law,* 54 L. & Contemp. Probs. 311 (1991).

A. THE IDEA OF STATUTORY SCHEMES

1. *Boomer v. Atlantic Cement*: A Reprise

Recall the reluctance shown by the majority opinion in *Boomer* regarding the appropriate role of common law judges in addressing widespread environmental problems:

> Effective control of air pollution is a problem presently far from solution even with the full public and financial powers of government. In large measure adequate technical procedures are yet to be developed and some that appear possible may be economically impracticable. It seems apparent that the amelioration of air pollution will depend on technical research in great depth; on a carefully balanced consideration of the economic impact of close regulation; and of the actual effect on public health. It is likely to require massive public expenditure and to demand more than any local community can accomplish and to depend on regional and interstate controls.
>
> A court should not try to do this on its own as a by-product of private litigation and it seems manifest that the judicial establishment is neither equipped in the limited nature of any judgment it can pronounce nor prepared to lay down and implement an effective policy for the elimination of air pollution. This is an area beyond the circumference of one private lawsuit. It is a direct responsibility for government and should not thus be undertaken as an incident to solving a dispute between property owners and a single cement plant — one of many — in the Hudson River valley.

The majority in *Boomer* also believed that it was unfair and inappropriate to place on a single company — the defendant in that case — the obligation to research and develop technological solutions to air pollution on behalf of an entire industry:

> Moreover, techniques to eliminate dust and other annoying by-products of cement making are unlikely to be developed by any research the defendant can undertake within any short period, but will depend on the total resources of the cement industry nationwide and throughout the world. The problem is universal wherever cement is made.
>
> For obvious reasons the rate of the research is beyond control of defendant. If at the end of 18 months the whole industry has not found a technical solution a court would be hard put to close down this one cement plant if due regard be given to equitable principles.

The *Boomer* court identified several areas in which it believed that the elected branches of government both bore the responsibility and were better equipped to make the kinds of broad technical and public policy decisions necessary to regulate air pollution at large. In addition to expertise and resources, what other factors might suggest that such decisions are best placed in the hands of the executive and legislative branches of government, rather than the courts?

Consider the problems inherent in determining what pollution controls, or levels of pollution controls, should be imposed not just on one cement plant, but on all cement plants in a region, state, or the country as a whole. Also consider that cement plants might differ in size, materials used, manufacturing methods, energy sources, proximity to homes or other places where the resulting pollution might cause harm, and other factors. In part because of its lack of technological expertise, the *Boomer* court declined to order the defendants to adopt any particular form of pollution controls. Instead, it directed the lower court to assess damages proven by the plaintiffs in this case, leaving it to the defendants to decide whether it would be cheaper to adopt pollution controls in the future to avoid additional monetary damages, and to determine what those controls might be.

Would a statutory system address these issues differently, and if so, how? Among the various pollution control strategies that could be adopted for the entire cement industry, government simply could impose a system of pollution charges similar to the damages assessed in *Boomer*, leaving it to individual plant owners or managers to decide what, if any, controls to adopt. Alternatively, government might choose a single technology for all cement plants, regardless of size, location, and other factors. Or, pollution controls could be set at particular levels, leaving it to each plant to decide how those standards should be met. Are those kinds of choices best made by courts, by legislatures as part of a comprehensive statute, or by government agency officials as part of a broad delegation of authority to regulate air pollution?

Next, consider that cement plants are just one of many sources of air pollution in any community, and in the nation as a whole. Pollution controls that work for cement plants may be inadequate for, or even entirely inapplicable to, coal-fired power plants. Moreover, citizens in any community are likely to breathe a complex mix of pollution from different kinds of factories, power plants, smaller sources, and the ubiquitous motor vehicle. Air pollution might be addressed by focusing on individual pollution sources alone, or by deciding how much *aggregate* pollution is acceptable given the economic and other benefits that might be lost if some sources are shut down or forced to install expensive control systems. Should standards be established to control this aggregate pollution, and if so, for which of the thousands of chemicals that are released into the air routinely from the many different sources of pollution? Which of those sources should be controlled, and to what degree, to assure that the aggregate standards are met?

Congress was also motivated to adopt comprehensive statutory regimes because of public pressure to solve significant environmental problems that simply were not being addressed by common law cases alone. In 1969, the Cuyahoga River in Cleveland, Ohio literally caught fire due to the oil and other industrial wastes floating downstream.[2] Acute air pollution episodes in industrial towns like Donora, Pennsylvania caused large numbers of deaths and serious illnesses. Toxic chemicals buried for decades in the "Love Canal" near Buffalo, New York forced the evacuation of an entire suburban community. A massive oil spill off the coast of Santa Barbara, California highlighted the danger of transporting large quantities of dangerous materials. While these are just some of the more dramatic examples, the problem of pollution was thrust into the public arena at a time when many citizens were demanding more government intervention in a number of areas, from civil rights to social services to environmental protection. *See* Christopher H. Schroeder, *Lost in the Translation: What Environmental Regulation Does That Tort Cannot Duplicate*, 41 Washburn L.J. 583 (2002).

Congress responded to these problems with a series of federal statutes designed to address a range of environmental issues. Below, we summarize the Clean Air Act as one example of how a comprehensive statutory scheme differs from the common law approach.

2. Statutory Responses: The Clean Air Act as an Example

The appellate decision in *Boomer* was issued in 1970, when the perils of air pollution increasingly were becoming known to the American public and its elected officials. On New Year's Eve of the same year, Congress adopted comprehensive amendments to the Clean Air Act (CAA).[3] The House Report on the 1970 Act stated: "A review of achievements to date . . . make abundantly clear that the strategies which we have pursued in the war against air pollution have been inadequate in several important respects, and the methods employed in implementing those strategies often have been slower and less

2. *See* Robert W. Adler, Jessica C. Landman and Diane M. Cameron, The Clean Water Act, Twenty Years Later (1993). For more horror stories about water pollution by the late 1960s, see David Zwick and Marcy Benstock, Water Wasteland (1971).

3. As with some of the other federal environmental laws, in the case of air pollution Congress did not act on a clean slate in 1970. Congress adopted the original "Clean Air Act" in 1955, with amendments in 1963, 1965, 1966 and 1967. The Air Pollution Control Act of 1955, Pub. L. No. 84-159 (July 14, 1955), extended by Pub. L. No. 86-365 (1959); The Clean Air Act of 1963, Pub. L. No. 88-206 (Dec. 17, 1963), as amended by Pub. L. No. 89-272 (Oct. 20, 1965); The Air Quality Act of 1967, Pub. L. 90-148, codified at 42 U.S.C. §§1857 *et seq.* (1967). Earlier legislation, however, was limited largely to authorizing grants and research and development on potential auto emission controls and air quality standards. The 1970 amendments established a comprehensive federal *regulatory* program for air pollution control. The Clean Air Act of 1970, Pub. L. No. 91-604, codified at 42 U.S.C. §§1857 *et seq.* (1970), as amended by Pub. L. No. 95-95, codified at 42 U.S.C. §§7401 *et seq.* (1977), and Pub. L. No. 101-549 (1990). For a complete history, see A. W. Reitze, Jr., Air Pollution Control Law: Compliance and Enforcement (2001), A.W. Reitze, Jr., Overview and Critique: A Century of Air Pollution Control Law: What's Worked; What's Failed; What Might Work, 21 Envtl. L. 1549 (1991).

effective than they might have been." H.R. Rep. 1146, 91st Cong. 2d Sess. 1, reprinted at 1970 U.S. Cong. Code & Admin. News 5356.

As you review the main elements of the Clean Air Act statutory program, ask yourself how Congress sought to address the various problems as compared with the common law approach you identified in the last chapter, and in our reprise of *Boomer* above. In what respects do you think that the statutory approach is superior, and in what ways might it portend problems?

a. Setting Standards for Clean Air

The *Boomer* court was reluctant to decide, for society at large, the proper balance between clean air and economic health. Under this approach, rather than having anyone decide what quality of air is "healthy" or otherwise "appropriate," the quality of the air we actually breathe will depend on the aggregate emissions from all sources, some of which might be lowered due to common law liability, and others of which will remain uncontrolled. In the Clean Air Act, Congress directed the federal government (through the U.S. Environmental Protection Agency (EPA)) to identify those pollutants that may endanger public health or welfare and that derive from numerous or diverse sources (and thus are not likely to be controlled adequately by individual source controls alone). CAA §108, 42 U.S.C. §7408. For those pollutants (at present, EPA has identified six), EPA establishes national air quality standards, which become the mandatory target for clean air programs everywhere in the country. (We discuss these kinds of standards further in Chapter 5.)

b. Setting Standards for Particular Source Controls

The *Boomer* court was also reluctant to decide what level of air pollution control to impose on the defendant cement plant, much less to decide what kinds of controls were available, appropriate, and feasible. Citing technological complexity and other factors, the court used the device of liability to induce pollution control decisions by the plant owners or managers. In the CAA, Congress established a complex system in which EPA and state officials make decisions about the levels of pollution control that can be achieved using various definitions of the "best technology" for particular kinds of pollution sources, from cars to factories to power plants. (We discuss these kinds of standards further in Chapter 6.)

c. Planning for Overall Air Quality

Because the common law approach operates primarily at a site-specific level, discrete decisions by even a large number of individual sources cannot assure that the combination of pollution controls in a region will suffice to "solve" the air pollution problems there. The CAA includes a planning and accounting system in which government officials identify all of the pollution sources, determine how much pollution is emitted from each, and how much total pollution control is necessary in order for the standards to be met, and allocate control requirements among sources so that the air quality standards will be met in each region. (We discuss this kind of process, and how it is divided among different levels of government, in Chapter 13.)

B. THE ROLE OF ADMINISTRATIVE AGENCIES AND JUDICIAL REVIEW

The comprehensive statutory scheme discussed above (and other statutory schemes as well) require an enormous number of decisions regarding very technical issues. Congress cannot possibly make all of these decisions itself, especially when circumstances frequently change (new facilities, changing technology, more research on health and environmental impacts). As a result, Congress delegated significant responsibilities to administrative agencies, which operate under various doctrines of administrative law to ensure that agencies act only within the scope of their delegated powers, and otherwise in accordance with law. Thus, to understand and to practice environmental law, you need to understand both the substantive environmental law, and how it is implemented and reviewed under the rules and procedures of applicable administrative law. For example, you need to understand the rules governing how agencies issue regulations, permits, and other documents; the rights and obligations of other parties with respect to those actions; and how courts review those actions.

The following is a brief survey of the most important rules and principles of *federal* administrative law that are useful in understanding the cases and other materials in this book. These principles are dictated largely by the federal Administrative Procedure Act (APA) and cases applying and interpreting that law, but many environmental statutes and regulations also dictate more specific rules for particular circumstances. Thus, to practice environmental law effectively, lawyers often need to understand (1) the relevant substantive law under applicable federal and state statutes, regulations, and cases; (2) the general principles of administrative law and procedure under the federal APA and potentially its state counterpart; (3) specific procedural requirements in the governing substantive statute and regulations; and (4) how all of those components fit together.

Four main sets of questions dominate federal administrative law as applied to environmental law. First, what kinds of decisions do administrative agencies make, and how much lawmaking authority may be delegated to them? Second, how do federal agencies make those decisions, and how can outside parties influence them (including decisions about what actions to take)? Third, who can challenge agency decisions, and under what circumstances? Fourth, what standards do courts apply in reviewing agency decisions?

1. The Scope of Administrative Agency Authority (Delegation and Nondelegation)

In theory, delegation of legislative authority to agency officials is prohibited by Article I, section 1 of the Constitution, which provides: "All legislative Powers herein granted shall be vested in a Congress of the United States . . . . " As students learn in Constitutional Law classes, on rare occasions dating back to the early New Deal period, the Supreme Court invalidated legislative delegations of authority where there was inadequate definition of the bounds of that power. *See* Panama Refining Co. v. Ryan, 293 U.S. 388 (1935); A.L.A. Schecter Poultry Corp. v. U.S., 295 U.S. 495 (1935). *See also* Carter v. Carter Coal Co., 298 U.S. 238, 310-312 (1936) (holding that delegation of law-making authority to a private board offends due process). Since that time, however, the Supreme Court has regularly upheld delegations of quasi-legislative authority to administrative agencies even when accompanied by very vague statutory instructions. The Court recently reaffirmed that Congress need only set forth some "intelligible principle" to guide agency action in upholding the delegation of authority to EPA to adopt national ambient air quality standards protecting public health. Whitman v. American Trucking Associations, Inc., 531 U.S. 457 (2001).

From a more practical perspective, however, it is important for lawyers to learn how to identify the breadth of delegation conferred in any particular statute or statutory provision. Agency actions can be challenged on the grounds that they exceed (or are outside the bounds of) the delegated authority. In passing environmental laws, Congress has fluctuated between generality and specificity; *i.e.*, between grants of broad and narrow discretion, depending on the program or circumstances, or the politics of the time. In general, Congress has delegated to EPA and other agencies significant amounts of discretion within which to act. In other instances, frustrated with either the pace or manner in which agencies have acted, Congress has adopted far more detailed and specific instructions, choosing to "micro-manage" some agency programs.

Where Congress delegates power broadly, agency lawyers will advise their clients that the agency has more latitude to make different policy choices, and outside parties will have less chance of arguing that an agency has exceeded or otherwise violated its power. Where Congress delegates narrowly, or with very specific rules and conditions, agencies have a smaller ambit within which to act, and outside parties have more ammunition to mount legal challenges to agency action. From a policy perspective, are broad delegations of quasi-legislative authority appropriate? Does it depend on the issues involved? The magnitude and breadth of regulatory impacts? Other factors? Some scholars have argued that excessive delegation, if unchecked by judicial review or legislative oversight, can allow agencies to effectively amend — rather than merely to implement — statutes enacted by Congress. *See* Oliver A. Houck, *The Endangered Species Act and its Implementation by the U.S. Department of Interior and Commerce*, 64 U. Colo. L. Rev. 277 (1993) (arguing that agency regulations effectively amended the Endangered Species Act).

2. Agency Decision Procedures and the Role of Outside Parties

One possible "check" on the ability of administrative agencies to "make law" under legislative delegations of authority involves the procedures that agencies must use to adopt regulations, to issue permits, and to make other decisions. The Administrative Procedure Act (APA) sets forth the general rules governing federal agencies' actions. However, each substantive statute may set forth different or additional procedures that apply for particular actions. Moreover, where neither the APA nor other statutes specify procedures for particular actions, agencies are free to adopt their own practices and procedures, so long as they comport with basic requirements of due process. *See* Vermont Yankee Nuclear Power Corp. v. Natural Resources Defense Council, Inc., 435 U.S. 519 (1978) (rejecting challenge to agency rule-making procedures for nuclear power plant licensing where agency followed minimum statutory procedural requirements); Chemical Waste Management, Inc. v. U.S. Environmental Protection Agency, 873 F.2d 1477 (D.C. Cir. 1989) (upholding informal agency hearing procedures in proceedings regarding corrective actions at contaminated waste sites). Below, we outline the basic procedures by which environmental (and other) agencies operate under the APA.

The APA sets forth two main kinds of actions that agencies may take, rules and orders, with two associated sets of procedures. A "rule" is typically an action that applies prospectively to a class or category of activities, and establishes principles of general applicability. An "order" generally applies to a particular party (or parties) to address particular sites or circumstances. Thus, in the APA, a "rule" is defined as "an agency statement of general or particular applicability and future effect designed to implement, interpret, or prescribe law or policy or describing the organization, procedure, or practice requirements of an agency . . . . " 5 U.S.C. §551(4). An "order," by contrast, constitutes "a final disposition, whether affirmative, negative, injunctive, or declaratory in form, of an agency in a matter other than rule making but including licensing." *Id.* §551(6). For example, EPA might issue a rule requiring all factories of a given type to reduce their emissions by 50 percent. It might issue a site-specific permit dictating exactly how many pounds of pollution must be reduced by a particular factory to comply with that rule, or an adjudication to decide whether the rule has been violated at that site. This distinction can be deceptive, however, because agency applications of law to particular cases can "make law" analogous to the actions of common law judges.

The procedures by which agencies promulgate rules and issue orders and other actions also vary. In general, agencies adopt "rules" most often through informal "notice and comment" procedures, and issue "orders" through more formal adjudicative procedures. In between those two extremes, however, lie a spectrum of procedures (sometimes called "informal adjudications") that may apply to particular actions. The procedures outlined below, along with judicial review discussed in the following section, are important "checks" to ensure that agencies and officials consider a spectrum of views and factors before exercising this authority.[4]

Agency adjudications are trial-type hearings, typically with live witnesses, cross-examination, rules of evidence, and other trial-type procedures. *See* 5 U.S.C. §§556, 557. The basic format resembles civil adjudication and is, therefore, familiar to lawyers and law students and requires no particular elaboration. Informal rule making is a much different process, and is less familiar and perhaps even somewhat strange to many practicing lawyers. Informal rule making consists of three basic steps: (1) notice, (2) opportunity for comment, and (3) evaluation and explanation. 5 U.S.C. §553. Each step is designed to ensure that when agencies exercise their authority, they bear some accountability to diverse interests and values.

First, agencies generally must publish in the Federal Register a "notice of proposed rule making," including:

(1) a statement of the time, place, and nature of public rule making proceedings;
(2) reference to the legal authority under which the rule is proposed; and
(3) either the terms or substance of the proposed rule or a description of the subjects and issues involved.

5 U.S.C. §553(b). This "notice" step ensures that all interested parties — either those who are subject to a regulation or those the regulation should benefit — know about the pending rule and have an opportunity to participate to try to influence the final result.

The second phase of informal rule making provides:

After notice required by this section, the agency shall give interested persons an opportunity to participate in the rule making through submission of written data, views, or arguments with or without opportunity for oral presentation.

---

4. Additional transparency is provided by "open government" statutes such as the Freedom of Information Act, 5 U.S.C. §552, and requirements for open meetings; *see id.* §552b.

After consideration of the relevant matter presented, the agency shall incorporate in the rules adopted a concise general statement of their basis and purpose.

Id. §553(c). The "opportunity to participate" allows parties to submit not only their opinions about whether and how the agency should regulate, but also "data" and "arguments" in support of their positions. This does not typically involve live "witnesses" with cross-examination and formal rules of evidence, although agencies might provide a "public hearing" at which anyone may "testify," *i.e.,* make an oral statement or presentation, as well as the chance to submit written comments, data, studies, etc. This means that there is no formal "gate keeping" process by which the agency may admit or exclude particular "evidence." *Cf.* Daubert v. Merrill Dow Pharmaceuticals, 509 U.S. 579 (1993) (allowing courts to exclude certain kinds of expert testimony from civil trials on grounds of reliability and other factors). Moreover, there is no limit to *who* may submit comments in an informal rule making, *i.e.,* there are no "standing" or other threshold requirements for interested parties.

The open-ended aspect of informal rule making procedure can be significant given the final step mandated by the statute: "After consideration of the relevant matter presented, the agency shall incorporate in the rules adopted a concise general statement of their basis and purpose." In some cases, agencies must reasonably respond to all significant comments, which requires them to sort through massive volumes of comments and carefully address many or all of them.

NOTES AND QUESTIONS ON AGENCY PROCEDURES

1. *Detail in regulatory proposals.* The APA obligates the agency to provide notice of a proposed rule, but in remarkably brief terms: "either the terms or substance of the proposed rule or a description of the subjects and issues involved." In a complex environmental rule making, does this suffice to give interested parties a fair opportunity to comment? The usual agency practice is to publish the full text of the proposed rule, along with a detailed explanation of its purposes, alternatives, and key issues the agency is considering.

2. *Detail in agency explanations of final rules.* The APA calls for a "concise" explanation of the final agency rule or decision. Given that agencies must offer the opportunity for comment to any outside party, and the nature and volume of information that outside parties might present in a complex environmental rule making (a rule regulating PFOA, for instance), just how "concise" would you expect EPA's explanation to be? In practice, EPA and other agencies typically publish very detailed explanations of the final rule, responses to comments, and reasons why they rejected various alternatives proposed by outside parties. The rule making record may include tens of thousands of pages of supporting data and studies. How do you think this affects the agency's ability to promulgate final rules in a timely fashion?

3. *Changes in final regulations.* When an outside party submits comments that are critical of an agency proposal, the agency has several choices. It can stay the course, in which case it must explain why it rejected the comments (for example, why the information submitted is flawed, or why the agency information is superior, or why legal or policy reasons suggest or require the agency approach). It can withdraw the proposal, in which case it must explain why it has done so, especially where other parties supported the proposal. Or, it can modify the proposal to address the information and concerns raised in the comments. In the last option, can the agency simply explain why it changed the proposal, or must it circulate the modified proposal for additional comments? The general rule is that an agency need not seek additional public comment so long as the final rule is a "logical outgrowth" of the original proposal. Does an agency violate the APA when it withdraws a rule making proposal without providing an opportunity for notice and comment? *See* Kennecott Utah Copper Corp. v. U.S. Department of the Interior, 88 F.3d 1191 (D.C. Cir. 1996) (holding that agencies can withdraw proposed regulations submitted for publication even on the eve of actual publication without violating the Federal Register Act). Can an agency simply withdraw a final regulation without an opportunity for notice and comment? *See* Natural Resources Defense Council v. U.S. EPA, 683 F.2d 752 (3d Cir. 1982) (holding that EPA's decision to indefinitely postpone the effective date of amendments to regulations promulgated under the Clean Water Act constituted a "rule" for purposes of the APA).

4. *Failure to comment.* The APA affords parties an opportunity to comment, but what are the ramifications if they fail to do so? The general rule is that parties who fail to raise an issue during the comment period are barred from doing so in subsequent litigation. Sims v. Apfel, 530 U.S. 103 (2000). (One might say that the most fundamental rule of practice in this area is to "comment early and comment often.") There are, however, exceptions for purely legal issues and other circumstances. *See* Chemical Manufacturers Association, et al. v. U.S. Environmental Protection Agency, 870 F.2d 177 (5th Cir. 1989) (finding that EPA's reliance on "undisclosed supplementary data" in a lengthy and complex rule making did not violate the APA where the supplementary data was necessary and a logical and reasonable outgrowth of prior data that had been made available during the rule-making process).

3. The Role of the Courts

Judicial review constitutes the second major "check" on the delegation of significant authority to agencies to formulate national environmental law and policy as they implement statutory schemes. As a practical matter, the availability of judicial review, the ability of parties to compel agencies to act, and the standards under which agency actions are reviewed, all affect the actual breadth of the agency's discretion. The more opportunities parties have to compel and to challenge an agency action, and the stricter the standards for review, the narrower the bounds within which agencies can dictate environmental law and policy. Conversely, where opportunities for judicial review are constrained, and where the standards of review are deferential, agencies enjoy much wider latitude. Where judicial review is constrained, parties usually have better opportunities to influence outcomes by persuading agency officials than they may have of prevailing in court. The combination of various limits on judicial review, relatively narrow, deferential standards for judicial review, and broad delegations of quasi-legislative authority confers substantial authority to "make" environmental law and policy on federal agencies and their state counterparts.

a. The Availability of Judicial Review

The Administrative Procedure Act provides specifically for judicial review of administrative agency actions, under prescribed circumstances. Section 701 first states:

> (a) This chapter applies, according to the provisions hereof, except to the extent that —
>
> (1) statutes preclude judicial review; or
> (2) agency action is committed to agency discretion by law.

5 U.S.C. §701(a). In some statutes, although relatively rarely, Congress expressly prohibits judicial review of certain agency actions and decisions. For example, the Unfunded Mandates Reform Act of 1995, Pub. L. No. 104-4, 109 Stat. 48 (1995), imposes a series of procedural and analytical requirements on various kinds of federal action, most of which are designed to ensure that actions (including laws passed by Congress) are taken with full awareness of the fiscal impacts on state and local governments (and in some cases, the private sector). However, the statute expressly precludes judicial challenges based on alleged violations of those requirements.

The bigger *potential* limitation on judicial review is for "agency action that is committed to agency discretion by law." If interpreted broadly, this language would preclude judicial review of a wide range of agency environmental decisions. The courts, however, have interpreted this provision very narrowly to encompass only those agencies decisions that are so completely subject to agency discretion that there is "no law to apply," an extremely rare situation. *See* Heckler v. Chaney, 470 U.S. 821 (1985) (finding an agency decision not to pursue an enforcement action to be entirely committed to agency discretion and thus not subject to judicial review).[5] This is consistent with the Supreme

---

5. Synthesizing the law of nondelegation with the law of judicial review, however, produces another odd situation. As discussed above, the Supreme Court has found no unlawful

Court's holding in Abbott Laboratories v. Gardner, 387 U.S. 136 (1967), that administrative agency action is subject to a "presumption of reviewability." Section 704 of the APA reinforces this presumption by providing that "Agency action made reviewable by statute and final agency action *for which there is no other adequate remedy in a court* are subject to judicial review." 5 U.S.C. §704 (emphasis added).

Finally, the issue of *who* may challenge a particular agency action is defined in §702 of the APA: "A person suffering legal wrong because of agency action, or adversely affected or aggrieved by agency action within the meaning of a relevant statute, is entitled to judicial review thereof." 5 U.S.C. §702. The issue of who suffers "legal wrong" or is "adversely affected or aggrieved" by agency action is related to principles of standing, which we discuss in Chapter 15. Does it appear that allowing any person aggrieved to challenge agency action offers broader or narrower opportunities to address pollution through litigation than the common law provides? Who could bring suit at common law?

Other principles of justiciability may limit access to court. These principles are based upon statutory, constitutional (Article III "case or controversy") or prudential (gate keeping) factors. For example, under APA §704, as well as the related doctrine of ripeness, only "final agency" action is reviewable, as opposed to "preliminary, procedural, or intermediate agency action." *See, e.g.,* Louisiana Environmental Action Network v. Browner, 87 F.3d 1379 (D.C. Cir. 1996) (EPA rules identifying standards to be used in later final approvals not ripe for review); Clean Air Implementation Project v. EPA, 150 F.3d 1200 (D.C. Cir. 1998) (industry challenge to EPA "any credible evidence" rule not ripe where factual application needed to determine impact of the rule). At the other end of the time spectrum, challenges may be precluded on grounds of mootness where harm no longer exists. *See, e.g.,* Blue Ocean Preservation Society v. Department of Energy, 767 F. Supp. 1518 (D.Haw. 1991) (observing that a lawsuit seeking to compel preparation of an EIS is mooted once the EIS is fully completed). Other potential barriers include exhaustion of administrative remedies,[6] statutes of limitations,[7] abstention and primary jurisdiction,[8]

---

delegation of legislative authority so long as the agency's action is subject to "some intelligible principle" to guide the agency action. One might ask whether there can be "some intelligible principle" if there is "no law to apply" to a particular agency action?

6. *See Chemical Manufacturers Association* case *infra.*

7. *See, e.g.,* Sierra Club v. DOT, 120 F.3d 636 (6th Cir. 1997) (six-year statute of limitations applied to NEPA challenge to highway project); Florida Keys Citizens Coalition v. Army Dept., 996 F. Supp. 1254 (S.D. Fl. 1998) (challenge to regulation barred by statute of limitations).

8. *See* National Solid Waste Management Council v. Ohio, 763 F. Supp. 244 (S.D. Ohio 1991), *rev'd on other grounds,* 959 F.2d 590 (6th Cir. 1992) (abstention not appropriately invoked where challenge was to facial constitutionality of state statute under the Commerce Clause and federal court was not asked to pass on matters of state policy); Culbertson v. Coast American, Inc., 913 F. Supp. 1572 (N.D. Ga. 1995) (abstention raised as defense to citizen suit); Davies v. National Cooperative Refinery Association, 43 ERC 1224 (D. Kan. 1996) (primary jurisdiction and abstention defenses rejected in RCRA case).

and defenses based on sovereign immunity and the Eleventh Amendment.[9] Those issues are best addressed in courses on federal courts and administrative law.

b. Forcing Agency Action

Parties may use the courts to influence the agency agenda by asking judges to order agencies to issue particular rules or to take other actions. When Congress adopts statutory schemes in which it delegates significant implementing authority and responsibility to EPA and other agencies, the force of an agency's power may lie first and foremost in which portions of the statute it elects to implement. Often, Congress establishes an agency agenda by identifying a series of rule-making tasks. Sometimes, Congress prioritizes those tasks by setting statutory deadlines within which agencies must issue rules. If the agency fails to promulgate an essential set of implementing regulations, or to do so within the prescribed deadlines, that part of the statutory scheme might lie dormant. Likewise, if a statute prohibits someone from acting (discharging pollutants into air or water, for instance) without a permit, agency failure to act on a permit application may hinder its operations. An agency might decide not to act because it has too much to do and too few resources; because of lengthy, cumbersome procedural requirements; because it is reluctant to make difficult policy choices; or because it disagrees with a particular program as a matter of policy. (That decision, of course, constitutes a virtual statutory amendment if left unchallenged.) A remarkable amount of environmental law and policy, therefore, has been the product of litigation designed to force an agency to act in particular areas.

Several agency-forcing mechanisms are available to various parties to move matters along. First, most of the major environmental statutes include "citizen suit" provisions that allow "any person" to sue the Administrator of EPA or other agency officials (depending on the statute) for failure to perform any action that is "not discretionary." See, e.g., Clean Water Act §505(a)(2), 33 U.S.C. §1365(a)(2). Obviously, a key determination is whether the official's action is mandatory or discretionary, but agencies clearly have a mandatory duty to comply with a statutory deadline. This kind of citizen suit litigation has driven significant statutory programs. See, e.g., NRDC v. Train, 6 Envt. Law Rptr. (ELI) 20588, 8 Envt. Rptr. Cases (BNA) 2120 (D.C.D.C. 1976)

9. See Maine v. Department of the Navy, 973 F.2d 1007 (1st Cir. 1992) (federal government enjoys sovereign immunity with regard to state-imposed penalties under CERCLA and RCRA); NRDC v. California Department of Transportation, 96 F.3d 420 (9th Cir. 1996); Mancuso v. N.Y. State Thruway Authority, 86 F.3d 289 (2d Cir. 1996) (highway authority not entitled to immunity in Clean Water Act case); New Jersey v. Gloucester Environmental Management Services, 923 F. Supp. 651 (D.N.J. 1995) (state hospital but not state colleges entitled to immunity); California v. Campbell, 138 F.3d 784 (9th Cir. 1998) (court-appointed receiver is not arm of the state for purposes of Eleventh Amendment immunity).

(approving a settlement which dictated EPA's long-term agenda for the regulation of toxic water pollutants and other industrial discharges for decades). What are the policy implications of this kind of citizen suit? On the plus side, clearly it can be used to force a reluctant agency to do the job set out for it by Congress. But where Congress assigns the agency too much to do, with too few resources, who should decide what programs and activities are most important or most pressing: outside groups, the courts, or the agencies themselves? *See, e.g.,* D. Noah Greenwald, Kieran F. Suckling, and Martin Taylor, *The Listing Record*, *in* THE ENDANGERED SPECIES ACT AT THIRTY, REVIEWING THE CONSERVATION PROMISE, VOL. I (GOBLE, SCOTT AND DAVIS eds. 2006), at 51, 63 (discussing and presenting data on the tension between political opposition to new listings of threatened and endangered species and citizen suit pressure to do so).

Second, in some instances Congress takes the initiative in dealing with chronic agency inaction by legislating a default result if the agency fails to act, sometimes known as legislative "hammer provisions." One example is the so-called "land ban" provisions Congress adopted as part of the 1984 amendments to the Resource Conservation and Recovery Act (RCRA). Under this provision, adopted as part of section 3004 of RCRA, 42 U.S.C. §6924, Congress enforced a requirement that EPA write regulations establishing treatment requirements by prohibiting industry from disposing of certain categories of hazardous waste in landfills after certain prescribed dates unless they complied with these new treatment requirements, or met other extremely onerous requirements.

Finally, the APA includes a mandamus-type provision, which may be used where no specific citizen suit authority exists, or where the statute includes no specific deadline for action. The APA requires federal agencies to "give an interested person the right to petition for the issuance, amendment, or repeal of a rule." 5 U.S.C. §553(e). Asking, however, does not mean getting. The statute, therefore, authorizes a reviewing court to "compel agency action unreasonably delayed." 5 U.S.C. §706(1). Suits to remedy unreasonable delay are typically less effective than suits to enforce a firm statutory deadline for several reasons. The issue of what constitutes unreasonable delay is inherently subjective. Further, filing a rule-making petition under section 553(e) is a prerequisite to a mandamus action under section 706(1), meaning that one must first petition the agency for rule making, and then wait a respectable time for the agency to act (or not), before even seeking judicial review of the agency's action or inaction. *See* Oljato Chapter of the Navajo Tribe v. Train, 515 F.2d 654 (D.C. Cir. 1975) (affirming dismissal of challenge to EPA's failure to revise air pollution regulation absent petition for rule making and supporting materials, followed by agency decision on petition). The Supreme Court's decision in Norton v. Southern Utah Wilderness Alliance, 542 U.S. 55 (2004), further limits efforts to force agency action under section 706 of the APA, because the Court held that the term "agency action" does not include discretionary implementation of broad agency programs, such as land use plans, as opposed to discrete actions that laws specifically mandate.

c.   *Challenges on the Merits — Standards of Judicial*
     Review

The APA also provides for judicial review of completed agency action. The standards governing judicial review of agency actions significantly affect the breadth of agency authority to establish environmental law and policy. Along with the authority in section 706(1) to compel agency action unlawfully withheld or unreasonably delayed, section 706 of the APA directs courts to:

> (2) hold unlawful and set aside agency action, findings, and conclusions found to be —
>> (A) arbitrary, capricious, an abuse of discretion, or otherwise not in accordance with law;
>> (B) contrary to constitutional right, power, privilege, or immunity;
>> (C) in excess of statutory jurisdiction, authority, or limitations, or short of statutory right;
>> (D) without observance of procedure required by law;
>> (E) unsupported by substantial evidence in a case subject to sections 556 and 557 of this title or otherwise reviewed on the record of an agency hearing provided by statute; or
>> (F) unwarranted by the facts to the extent that the facts are subject to trial de novo by the reviewing court.

5 U.S.C. §706(2).

First, it is important to understand which of these standards applies to a particular case. Obviously, all agency decisions must be constitutional (subsection B), and comply with the applicable statutes (subsection C) and procedural requirements (subsection D). The standards in subsections E and F, requiring specific degrees of factual support for decisions, apply only to adjudications. The majority of informal agency actions, therefore, such as promulgation of rules and issuance of permits, will be subject to the "arbitrary and capricious" standard set forth in subsection A. The Supreme Court explained the meaning of this key standard in an environmental context in the following seminal case.

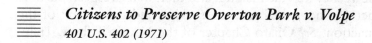

Citizens to Preserve Overton Park v. Volpe
401 U.S. 402 (1971)

Opinion of the Court by JUSTICE MARSHALL, announced by JUSTICE STEWART.

The growing public concern about the quality of our natural environment has prompted Congress in recent years to enact legislation designed to curb the accelerating destruction of our country's natural beauty. We are concerned in this case with §4(f) of the Department of Transportation Act of 1966, as amended, and §18(a) of the Federal-Aid Highway Act of 1968. These statutes prohibit the Secretary of Transportation from authorizing the use of federal funds to finance the construction of highways through public parks if a 'feasible and prudent' alternative route exists. If no such route is available, the statutes allow him to approve construction through parks only if there has been 'all possible planning to minimize harm' to the park.

Petitioners, private citizens as well as local and national conservation organizations, contend that the Secretary has violated these statutes by authorizing the expenditure of federal funds for the construction of a six-lane interstate highway through a public park in Memphis, Tennessee.

Overton Park is 342-acre city park located near the center of Memphis. The park contains a zoo, a nine-hole municipal golf course, an outdoor theater, nature trails, a bridle path, an art academy, picnic areas, and 170 acres of forest. The proposed highway, which is to be a six-lane, high-speed, expressway, will sever the zoo from the rest of the park. Although the roadway will be depressed below ground level except where it crosses a small creek, 26 acres of the park will be destroyed. The highway is to be a segment of Interstate Highway I–40, part of the National System of Interstate and Defense Highways. I–40 will provide Memphis with a major east-west expressway which will allow easier access to downtown Memphis from the residential areas on the eastern edge of the city.

. . . Neither announcement approving the route and design of I–40 was accompanied by a statement of the Secretary's factual findings. He did not indicate why he believed there were no feasible and prudent alternative routes or why design changes could not be made to reduce the harm to the park. Petitioners contend that the Secretary's action is invalid without such formal findings and that the Secretary did not make an independent determination but merely relied on the judgment of the Memphis City Council. They also contend that it would be 'feasible and prudent' to route I–40 around Overton Park either to the north or to the south. And they argue that if these alternative routes are not 'feasible and prudent,' the present plan does not include 'all possible' methods for reducing harm to the park. Petitioners claim that I–40 could be built under the park by using either of two possible tunneling methods, and they claim that, at a minimum, by using advanced drainage techniques the expressway could be depressed below ground level along the entire route through the park including the section that crosses the small creek.

Respondents argue that it was unnecessary for the Secretary to make formal findings, and that he did, in fact, exercise his own independent judgment which was supported by the facts. In the District Court, respondents introduced affidavits, prepared specifically for this litigation, which indicated that the Secretary had made the decision and that the decision was supportable. These affidavits were contradicted by affidavits introduced by petitioners, who also sought to take the deposition of a former Federal Highway Administrator who had participated in the decision to route I–40 through Overton Park.

The District Court and the Court of Appeals found that formal findings by the Secretary were not necessary and refused to order the deposition of the former Federal Highway Administrator because those courts believed that probing of the mental processes of an administrative decisionmaker was prohibited. And, believing that the Secretary's authority was wide and reviewing courts' authority narrow in the approval of highway routes, the lower courts held that the affidavits contained no basis for a determination that the Secretary had exceeded his authority.

We agree that formal findings were not required. But we do not believe that in this case judicial review based solely on litigation affidavits was adequate.

A threshold question — whether petitioners are entitled to any judicial review — is easily answered. Section 701 of the Administrative Procedure Act provides that the action of 'each authority of the Government of the United States,' which includes the Department of Transportation, is subject to judicial review except where there is a statutory prohibition on review or where 'agency action is committed to agency discretion by law.' In this case, there is no indication that Congress sought to prohibit judicial review and there is most certainly no "showing of 'clear and convincing evidence' of a . . . legislative intent" to restrict access to judicial review.

Similarly, the Secretary's decision here does not fall within the exception for action 'committed to agency discretion.' This is a very narrow exception. The legislative history of the Administrative Procedure Act indicates that it is applicable in those rare instances where 'statutes are drawn in such broad terms that in a given case there is no law to apply.'

Section 4(f) of the Department of Transportation Act and §138 of the Federal-Aid Highway Act are clear and specific directives. Both . . . provide that the Secretary 'shall not approve any program or project' that requires the use of any public parkland 'unless (1) there is no feasible and prudent alternative to the use of such land, and (2) such program includes all possible planning to minimize harm to such park. . . .' This language is a plain and explicit bar to the use of federal funds for construction of highways through parks — only the most unusual situations are exempted.

Despite the clarity of the statutory language, respondents argue that the Secretary has wide discretion. They recognize that the requirement that there be no 'feasible' alternative route admits of little administrative discretion. For this exemption to apply the Secretary must find that as a matter of sound engineering it would not be feasible to build the highway along any other route. Respondents argue, however, that the requirement that there be no other 'prudent' route requires the Secretary to engage in a wide-ranging balancing of competing interests. They contend that the Secretary should weigh the detriment resulting from the destruction of parkland against the cost of other routes, safety considerations, and other factors, and determine on the basis of the importance that he attaches to these other factors whether, on balance, alternative feasible routes would be 'prudent.'

But no such wide-ranging endeavor was intended. It is obvious that in most cases considerations of cost, directness of route, and community disruption will indicate that parkland should be used for highway construction whenever possible. Although it may be necessary to transfer funds from one jurisdiction to another, there will always be a smaller outlay required from the public purse when parkland is used since the public already owns the land and there will be no need to pay for right-of-way. And since people do not live or work in parks, if a highway is built on parkland no one will have to leave his home or give up his business. Such factors are common to substantially all highway construction. Thus, if Congress intended these factors to be on an equal footing with preservation of parkland there would have been no need for the statutes.

Congress clearly did not intend that cost and disruption of the community were to be ignored by the Secretary. But the very existence of the statutes indicates that protection of parkland was to be given paramount importance. The few green havens that are public parks were not to be lost unless there were truly unusual factors present in a particular case or the cost or community disruption resulting from alternative routes reached extraordinary magnitudes. If the statutes are to have any meaning, the Secretary cannot approve the destruction of parkland unless he finds that alternative routes present unique problems.

Plainly, there is 'law to apply' and thus the exemption for action 'committed to agency discretion' is inapplicable. But the existence of judicial review is only the start: the standard for review must also be determined. For that we must look to §706 of the Administrative Procedure Act, which provides that a 'reviewing court shall . . . hold unlawful and set aside agency action, findings, and conclusions found' not to meet six separate standards. In all cases agency action must be set aside if the action was 'arbitrary, capricious, an abuse of discretion, or otherwise not in accordance with law' or if the action failed to meet statutory, procedural, or constitutional requirements. In certain narrow, specifically limited situations, the agency action is to be set aside if the action was not supported by 'substantial evidence.' And in other equally narrow circumstances the reviewing court is to engage in a de novo review of the action and set it aside if it was 'unwarranted by the facts.'

Petitioners argue that the Secretary's approval of the construction of I–40 through Overton Park is subject to one or the other of [the last two standards in section 706(2)]. First, they contend that the 'substantial evidence' standard of §706(2)(E) must be applied. In the alternative, they claim that §706(2)(F) applies and that there must be a de novo review to determine if the Secretary's action was 'unwarranted by the facts.' Neither of these standards is, however, applicable. Review under the substantial-evidence test is authorized only when the agency action is taken pursuant to a rulemaking provision of the Administrative Procedure Act itself, or when the agency action is based on a public adjudicatory hearing. The Secretary's decision to allow the expenditure of federal funds to build I–40 through Overton Park was plainly not an exercise of a rulemaking function. And the only hearing that is required by either the Administrative Procedure Act or the statutes regulating the distribution of federal funds for highway construction is a public hearing conducted by local officials for the purpose of informing the community about the proposed project and eliciting community views on the design and route. The hearing is nonadjudicatory, quasi-legislative in nature. It is not designed to produce a record that is to be the basis of agency action — the basic requirement for substantial-evidence review.

Petitioners' alternative argument also fails. De novo review of whether the Secretary's decision was 'unwarranted by the facts' is authorized by §706(2)(F) in only two circumstances. First, such de novo review is authorized when the action is adjudicatory in nature and the agency fact finding procedures are inadequate. And, there may be independent judicial fact finding when issues that were not before the agency are raised in a proceeding to enforce nonadjudicatory agency action. Neither situation exists here.

Even though there is no de novo review in this case and the Secretary's approval of the route of I–40 does not have ultimately to meet the substantial–evidence test, the generally applicable standards of §706 require the reviewing court to engage in a substantial inquiry. Certainly, the Secretary's decision is entitled to a presumption of regularity. But that presumption is not to shield his action from a thorough, probing, in–depth review.

The court is first required to decide whether the Secretary acted within the scope of his authority. This determination naturally begins with a delineation of the scope of the Secretary's authority and discretion. As has been shown, Congress has specified only a small range of choices that the Secretary can make. Also involved in this initial inquiry is a determination of whether on the facts the Secretary's decision can reasonably be said to be within that range. The reviewing court must consider whether the Secretary properly construed his authority to approve the use of parkland as limited to situations where there are no feasible alternative routes or where feasible alternative routes involve uniquely difficult problems. And the reviewing court must be able to find that the Secretary could have reasonably believed that in this case there are no feasible alternatives or that alternatives do involve unique problems.

Scrutiny of the facts does not end, however, with the determination that the Secretary has acted within the scope of his statutory authority. Section 706(2)(A) requires a finding that the actual choice made was not 'arbitrary, capricious, an abuse of discretion, or otherwise not in accordance with law.' To make this finding the court must consider whether the decision was based on a consideration of the relevant factors and whether there has been a clear error of judgment. Although this inquiry into the facts is to be searching and careful, the ultimate standard of review is a narrow one. The court is not empowered to substitute its judgment for that of the agency. The final inquiry is whether the Secretary's action followed the necessary procedural requirements. Here the only procedural error alleged is the failure of the Secretary to make formal findings and state his reason for allowing the highway to be built through the park.

Undoubtedly, review of the Secretary's action is hampered by his failure to make such findings, but the absence of formal findings does not necessarily require that the case be remanded to the Secretary. Neither the Department of Transportation Act nor the Federal-Aid Highway Act requires such formal findings. Moreover, the Administrative Procedure Act requirements that there be formal findings in certain rulemaking and adjudicatory proceedings do not apply to the Secretary's action here. And, although formal findings may be required in some cases in the absence of statutory directives when the nature of the agency action is ambiguous, those situations are rare. Plainly, there is no ambiguity here; the Secretary has approved the construction of I–40 through Overton Park and has approved a specific design for the project. . . .

Moreover, there is an administrative record that allows the full, prompt review of the Secretary's action that is sought without additional delay which would result from having a remand to the Secretary.

That administrative record is not, however, before us. The lower courts based their review on the litigation affidavits that were presented. These affidavits were merely 'post hoc' rationalizations, which have traditionally been found to be an inadequate basis for review. And they clearly do not constitute the 'whole record' compiled by the agency: the basis for review required by s 706 of the Administrative Procedure Act.

Thus it is necessary to remand this case to the District Court for plenary review of the Secretary's decision. That review is to be based on the full administrative record that was before the Secretary at the time he made his decision. But since the bare record may not disclose the factors that were considered or the Secretary's construction of the evidence it may be necessary for the District Court to require some explanation in order to determine if the Secretary acted within the scope of his authority and if the Secretary's action was justifiable under the applicable standard. The court may require the administrative officials who participated in the decision to give testimony explaining their action. Of course, such inquiry into the mental processes of administrative decisionmakers is usually to be avoided. And where there are administrative findings that were made at the same time as the decision, as was the case in Morgan, there must be a strong showing of bad faith or improper behavior before such inquiry may be made. But here there are no such formal findings and it may be that the only way there can be effective judicial review is by examining the decisionmakers themselves.

The District Court is not, however, required to make such an inquiry. It may be that the Secretary can prepare formal findings . . . that will provide an adequate explanation for his action. Such an explanation will, to some extent, be a 'post hoc rationalization' and thus must be viewed critically. If the District Court decides that additional explanation is necessary, that court should consider which method will prove the most expeditious so that full review may be had as soon as possible.

Reversed and remanded.

NOTES AND QUESTIONS ON *OVERTON PARK*

1. *The APA as the basis for judicial review.* The Court found that the agency decision was subject to review under the APA. This ruling exposed to judicial scrutiny under various environmental laws a huge range of decisions by federal agencies whose basic missions have little to do with environmental protection (agencies that build or permit the building of highways, dams, and other projects, or who allow development activities on public lands). It also rendered those decisions subject to review under underlying agency substantive statutes (such as the highway laws at issue in this case), whether or not those laws have independent provisions for judicial review. This holding was particularly significant given the passage of the National Environmental Policy Act (NEPA) just two years earlier, under which all federal agencies, whether or not they have "environmental" responsibilities as part of their primary missions, must evaluate and disclose the environmental impacts of proposed actions and alternatives. Because NEPA itself contains no independent provision for judicial review, the APA provides the only cause of action to challenge an agency NEPA violation. *See* Marsh v. Oregon Natural Resources Council, 490 U.S. 360 (1989).

2. *Deferential standard of review.* At the same time, however, the *Overton Park* decision signaled that the standard of review under the APA arbitrary and capricious language is narrow and, ultimately, deferential to agency policy choices:

> . . . the court must consider whether the decision was based on a consideration of the relevant factors and whether there has been a clear error of judgment. Although this inquiry into the facts is to be searching and careful, the ultimate standard of review is a narrow one. The court is not empowered to substitute its judgment for that of the agency.

3. *Motor vehicles.* In Motor Vehicle Manufacturers Association v. State Farm Mutual Auto Insurance Co., 463 U.S. 29 (1983), the Supreme Court elaborated on the arbitrary and capricious standard of review. While this case involved passive restraint standards for automobile safety, rather than environmental issues, it stands as one of the most revealing articulations of the applicable standard of review under APA §706(2)(A):

> The scope of review under the "arbitrary and capricious" standard is narrow and a court is not to substitute its judgment for that of the agency. Nevertheless, the agency must examine the relevant data and articulate a satisfactory explanation for its action including a "rational connection between the facts found and the choice made." In reviewing that explanation, we must "consider whether the decision was based on a consideration of the relevant factors and whether there has been a clear error of judgment." Normally, an agency rule would be arbitrary

and capricious if the agency has relied on factors which Congress has not intended it to consider, entirely failed to consider an important aspect of the problem, offered an explanation for its decision that runs counter to the evidence before the agency, or is so implausible that it could not be ascribed to a difference in view or the product of agency expertise. The reviewing court should not attempt itself to make up for such deficiencies: "We may not supply a reasoned basis for the agency's action that the agency itself has not given." We will, however, "uphold a decision of less than ideal clarity if the agency's path may reasonably be discerned." For purposes of this case, it is also relevant that Congress required a record of the rulemaking proceedings to be compiled and submitted to a reviewing court, and intended that agency findings would be supported by "substantial evidence on the record considered as a whole."

463 U.S. at 43-44.

This brief excerpt can serve as a template for agency lawyers who want to ensure that agency decisions are likely to withstand judicial review, and for outside parties to guide potential challenges to unfavorable decisions. It can also serve you as a list of the various ways in which agency decisions might be found unlawful, as you read the substantive cases later in the book.

4. *Administrative record.* Last, but not least, the Supreme Court in *Overton Park* clarified the materials a reviewing court may use when evaluating the validity of an agency decision, a process known as "administrative record review." The "administrative record" is comprised of all of the documents and other information that the agency relied upon in reaching its decision, and the agency must compile it contemporaneously throughout the agency's decision-making process. It should include background materials, data, reports and analysis, the agency proposal (or proposals), comments submitted by outside parties, and the agency's responses to those comments, as well as the final decision and any accompanying analysis and rationale for that decision. The concept that review of agency decisions is limited to materials included in the administrative record may have come as a surprise to lawyers used to presenting and cross-examining live witnesses and hand-choosing the documents and other exhibits they want to court to review. It is, however, fundamental to understanding how many environmental decisions are made, and the grounds on which they can be challenged. In addition, it further underscores a point we made earlier in the chapter — the critical importance of submitting comments and relevant data, studies, and other materials on the record during the public comment period. Matters not raised on the record may be precluded from later consideration, although this general rule is subject to several exceptions. *See* Animal Defense Council v. Hodel, 840 F.2d 1432 (9th Cir. 1988) (stating that in deciding a challenge to an agency rule, a district court may look beyond the administrative record and/or pursue any necessary discovery only where (1) the agency relied on materials not included in the administrative record, (2) the court finds review or discovery beyond the administrative record to be "necessary to explain the agency action," or (3) the court finds that the agency has acted in bad faith).

5. *Deference to agencies.* Is the level of deference to agency policy decisions afforded in cases like *Overton Park* and *Motor Vehicle Manufacturers* appropriate? Why or why not?

Arguably, the "arbitrary and capricious" portion of the APA standard applies to agency policy decisions that are within the bounds of discretion delegated by Congress, while more of a purely legal determination is involved when a party challenges agency actions as "not in accordance with law" (subsection A) or "in excess of statutory jurisdiction, authority, or limitations, or short of statutory right" (subsection C). The opening sentence of section 706 provides: "To the extent necessary to decision and when presented, the reviewing court shall decide all relevant questions of law, interpret constitutional and statutory provisions, and determine the meaning or applicability of the terms of an agency action." Does this language suggest more of a *de novo* judicial review of purely legal issues? Is this not the primary role of the judiciary? Before making a final call on this issue, read the following case.

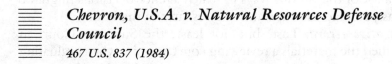

Chevron, U.S.A. v. Natural Resources Defense Council
467 U.S. 837 (1984)

JUSTICE STEVENS delivered the opinion of the Court.

In the Clean Air Act Amendments of 1977, Congress enacted certain requirements applicable to States that had not achieved the national air quality standards established by the Environmental Protection Agency (EPA) pursuant to earlier legislation. The amended Clean Air Act required these "nonattainment" States to establish a permit program regulating "new or modified major stationary sources" of air pollution. Generally, a permit may not be issued for a new or modified major stationary source unless several stringent conditions are met.[1] The EPA regulation promulgated to implement this permit requirement allows a State to adopt a plantwide definition of the term "stationary source."[2] Under this definition, an existing plant that contains several pollution-emitting devices may install or modify one piece of equipment without meeting the permit conditions if the alteration will not increase

1. Section 172(b)(6), 42 U.S.C. §7502(b)(6), provides: "The plan provisions required by subsection (a) shall —

"(6) require permits for the construction and operation of new or modified major stationary sources in accordance with section 173 (relating to permit requirements)." 91 Stat. 747.

2. "(i) 'Stationary source' means any building, structure, facility, or installation which emits or may emit any air pollutant subject to regulation under the Act.

"(ii) 'Building, structure, facility, or installation' means all of the pollutant-emitting activities which belong to the same industrial grouping, are located on one or more contiguous or adjacent properties, and are under the control of the same person (or persons under common control) except the activities of any vessel." 40 CFR §§51.18(j)(1)(i) and (ii) (1983).

the total emissions from the plant. The question presented by these cases is whether EPA's decision to allow States to treat all of the pollution-emitting devices within the same industrial grouping as though they were encased within a single "bubble" is based on a reasonable construction of the statutory term "stationary source." . . .

The Court of Appeals set aside the regulations. . . .

The court observed that the relevant part of the amended Clean Air Act "does not explicitly define what Congress envisioned as a 'stationary source,' to which the permit program . . . should apply," and further stated that the precise issue was not "squarely addressed in the legislative history." In light of its conclusion that the legislative history bearing on the question was "at best contradictory," it reasoned that "the purposes of the nonattainment program should guide our decision here." Based on two of its precedents concerning the applicability of the bubble concept to certain Clean Air Act programs, the court stated that the bubble concept was "mandatory" in programs designed merely to maintain existing air quality, but held that it was "inappropriate" in programs enacted to improve air quality. Since the purpose of the permit program — its "raison d'être," in the court's view — was to improve air quality, the court held that the bubble concept was inapplicable in these cases under its prior precedents. It therefore set aside the regulations embodying the bubble concept as contrary to law. We granted certiorari to review that judgment, and we now reverse. The basic legal error of the Court of Appeals was to adopt a static judicial definition of the term "stationary source" when it had decided that Congress itself had not commanded that definition. . . .

II

When a court reviews an agency's construction of the statute which it administers, it is confronted with two questions. First, always, is the question whether Congress has directly spoken to the precise question at issue. If the intent of Congress is clear, that is the end of the matter; for the court, as well as the agency, must give effect to the unambiguously expressed intent of Congress.[9] If, however, the court determines Congress has not directly addressed the precise question at issue, the court does not simply impose its own construction on the statute, as would be necessary in the absence of an administrative interpretation. Rather, if the statute is silent or ambiguous with

9. The judiciary is the final authority on issues of statutory construction and must reject administrative constructions which are contrary to clear congressional intent. If a court, employing traditional tools of statutory construction, ascertains that Congress had an intention on the precise question at issue, that intention is the law and must be given effect.

respect to the specific issue, the question for the court is whether the agency's answer is based on a permissible construction of the statute.[11]

"The power of an administrative agency to administer a congressionally created . . . program necessarily requires the formulation of policy and the making of rules to fill any gap left, implicitly or explicitly, by Congress." If Congress has explicitly left a gap for the agency to fill, there is an express delegation of authority to the agency to elucidate a specific provision of the statute by regulation. Such legislative regulations are given controlling weight unless they are arbitrary, capricious, or manifestly contrary to the statute. Sometimes the legislative delegation to an agency on a particular question is implicit rather than explicit. In such a case, a court may not substitute its own construction of a statutory provision for a reasonable interpretation made by the administrator of an agency.

We have long recognized that considerable weight should be accorded to an executive department's construction of a statutory scheme it is entrusted to administer, and the principle of deference to administrative interpretations.

In light of these well-settled principles it is clear that the Court of Appeals misconceived the nature of its role in reviewing the regulations at issue. Once it determined, after its own examination of the legislation, that Congress did not actually have an intent regarding the applicability of the bubble concept to the permit program, the question before it was not whether in its view the concept is "inappropriate" in the general context of a program designed to improve air quality, but whether the Administrator's view that it is appropriate in the context of this particular program is a reasonable one. Based on the examination of the legislation and its history . . . we agree with the Court of Appeals that Congress did not have a specific intention on the applicability of the bubble concept in these cases, and conclude that the EPA's use of that concept here is a reasonable policy choice for the agency to make. . . .

Policy

The arguments over policy that are advanced in the parties' briefs create the impression that respondents are now waging in a judicial forum a specific policy battle which they ultimately lost in the agency and in the 32 jurisdictions opting for the "bubble concept," but one which was never waged in the Congress. Such policy arguments are more properly addressed to legislators or administrators, not to judges. In these cases, the Administrator's interpretation represents a reasonable accommodation of manifestly competing interests and is entitled to deference: the regulatory scheme is technical and complex, the agency considered the matter in a detailed and reasoned fashion, and the decision involves reconciling conflicting policies. Congress intended to accommodate both interests, but did not do so itself on the level of specificity

11. The court need not conclude that the agency construction was the only one it permissibly could have adopted to uphold the construction, or even the reading the court would have reached if the question initially had arisen in a judicial proceeding.

presented by these cases. Perhaps that body consciously desired the Administrator to strike the balance at this level, thinking that those with great expertise and charged with responsibility for administering the provision would be in a better position to do so; perhaps it simply did not consider the question at this level; and perhaps Congress was unable to forge a coalition on either side of the question, and those on each side decided to take their chances with the scheme devised by the agency. For judicial purposes, it matters not which of these things occurred. Judges are not experts in the field, and are not part of either political branch of the Government. Courts must, in some cases, reconcile competing political interests, but not on the basis of the judges' personal policy preferences. In contrast, an agency to which Congress has delegated policy-making responsibilities may, within the limits of that delegation, properly rely upon the incumbent administration's views of wise policy to inform its judgments. While agencies are not directly accountable to the people, the Chief Executive is, and it is entirely appropriate for this political branch of the Government to make such policy choices — resolving the competing interests which Congress itself either inadvertently did not resolve, or intentionally left to be resolved by the agency charged with the administration of the statute in light of everyday realities. When a challenge to an agency construction of a statutory provision, fairly conceptualized, really centers on the wisdom of the agency's policy, rather than whether it is a reasonable choice within a gap left open by Congress, the challenge must fail. In such a case, federal judges — who have no constituency — have a duty to respect legitimate policy choices made by those who do. The responsibilities for assessing the wisdom of such policy choices and resolving the struggle between competing views of the public interest are not judicial ones: "Our Constitution vests such responsibilities in the political branches."

We hold that the EPA's definition of the term "source" is a permissible construction of the statute which seeks to accommodate progress in reducing air pollution with economic growth. "The Regulations which the Administrator has adopted provide what the agency could allowably view as . . . [an] effective reconciliation of these twofold ends. . . . "

The judgment of the Court of Appeals is reversed.

NOTES AND QUESTIONS ON *CHEVRON*

1. *Holding.* Articulate the two-part test identified in this decision for when a court reviews an agency decision involving statutory interpretation. Does this standard of review comport with the role of courts articulated in the first sentence of APA §706, set forth above? What are the implications of this standard for the breadth of agency authority to "make" environmental law and policy?

2. *Strategy.* What prong of the two-part test is preferred by parties who challenge agency decisions? What prong is preferred by agency lawyers who defend those decisions?

3. *Plain language versus legislative history.* Among other factors, the *Chevron* doctrine re-affirms the traditional role of legislative history in construing statutes. Courts use various canons of construction, as well as relevant statements in congressional reports and debates, to ascertain what Congress intended in the face of otherwise ambiguous statutory text. However, the Court has also tended in recent years to decline *Chevron* deference by construing statutes based on the plain statutory text where possible. *See, e.g.,* City of Chicago v. Environmental Defense Fund, 511 U.S. 328, 337 (1994) ("it is the statute, not the Committee Report, which is the authoritative expression of the law") (Scalia, J.); Solid Waste Agency of Northern Cook County v. U.S. Army Corps of Engineers, 531 U.S. 159, 172 (2001) (declining *Chevron* deference where statutory text is clear). *See generally* ANTONIN SCALIA, A MATTER OF INTERPRETATION: FEDERAL COURTS AND THE LAW 23 (1997) (arguing that the plain meaning of statutes should be construed "reasonably, to contain all that it fairly means"); Thomas Merrill, *Textualism and the Future of the Chevron Doctrine,* 72 Wash. U. L.J. 351 (1994).

4. *Evolution of* Chevron *doctrine.* Lest you begin to think that it is virtually impossible to challenge administrative agency decisions, in addition to the trend toward textualism discussed above, the *Chevron* doctrine has experienced some significant erosion since it was adopted. Perhaps most notably, in U.S. v. Mead, 533 U.S. 718 (2001), the Supreme Court clarified that *Chevron* deference is appropriate only where an agency's statutory interpretation forms part of an action promulgated formally through notice and comment rule making or some other formal proceedings. *See, e.g.,* Catskill Mountains Chapter of Trout Unlimited, Inc. v. The City of New York, 273 F.3d 487 (2d Cir. 2001) (declining to defer to EPA interpretation of Clean Water Act that was not embodied in a formal rule-making action). In *Solid Waste Agency of Northern Cook County,* the Court also declined to afford *Chevron* deference where the administrative interpretation would raise "serious constitutional problems," unless the result would plainly contradict Congress' intent. 531 U.S. at 160.

Review — Key APA Provisions Governing Administrative Process

Section of APA	Provision
5 U.S.C. §551(4)	Defines "rule" as "an agency statement of general or particular applicability and future effect designed to implement, interpret or prescribe law or policy."
5 U.S.C. §551(6)	Defines "order" as "a final disposition, whether affirmative, negative, injunctive, or declaratory in form, of an agency in a matter other than rule making but including licensing."

Section of APA	Provision
5 U.S.C. §553(a)-(c)	Establishes "notice and comment" rule making process in which agencies must (1) publish notices of proposed rule making (including a description of the substance of the proposal or its subjects and issues); (2) allow interested persons an opportunity to comment on the proposal or otherwise to participate in the rule making; and (3) consider and respond to comments before issuing a final rule.
5 U.S.C. §553(e)	Requires agencies to provide any interested person the right to petition for the issuance, amendment, or repeal of rules.
5 U.S.C. §§554, 556	Establishes procedures for administrative adjudications.
5 U.S.C. §702	Allows judicial review by any person who suffers legal wrong or is adversely affected or aggrieved by agency action.
5 U.S.C. §704	Provides for judicial review of agency actions made reviewable by statute, or other final agency actions for which there is no other adequate remedy in court.
5 U.S.C. §706(1)	Allows parties to ask a reviewing court to "compel agency action unlawfully withheld or unreasonably delayed."
5 U.S.C. §706(2)	Establishes standards of judicial review of agency actions, providing relief for actions which are (A) "arbitrary, capricious, an abuse of discretion, or otherwise not in accordance with law," (B) unconstitutional, (C) beyond the scope of agency authority, (D) adopted contrary to applicable procedures, or (E) and (F) insufficiently supported by evidence or facts.

C. RECAPITULATION: THE RESIDUAL ROLE OF THE COMMON LAW IN A STATUTORY WORLD

While Congress and state legislatures augmented the common law with comprehensive statutory schemes, in most cases they did not replace common law solutions. Rather, common law remedies remain to fulfill their original purposes, and to fill in gaps in the modern regulatory regime. Modern statutes may regulate activities prospectively, require cleanup of environmental hazards caused by past activities, and provide for restoration of public resources, but they do not provide for compensation to injured private parties. The Superfund statute, for example, allows public trustees to collect natural resource damages from past releases of hazardous substances, but does not allow pollution victims to obtain compensation. *See* 42 U.S.C. §9607(a). Pollution victims may, however, bring private damage actions as in the Woburn, Massachusetts toxic tort case studied in Chapter 2.

Whether a particular statute allows pre-existing common law claims to continue is governed by the law of preemption. Under the Supremacy Clause in Article VI of the U.S. Constitution, the preemption doctrine governs whether a provision of federal law supersedes or overrides state or local law. In this section, we use the Clean Water Act (CWA) as an example of the relationship between the new statutory regime and the common law. The CWA is a good case study of the statutory-common law intersection because the Supreme Court has decided several major cases that define this relationship. Because the result in this and similar cases depends on the specific language and legislative history of each statute, however, be careful not to assume that the results of this inquiry will be the same under other statutes. In Chapter 12, for example, you will learn that in Superfund, Congress deliberately embraced existing principles of common law liability within the statutory system in a way that leaves particular applications subject to the common law of individual states. Recently, the U.S. Supreme Court ruled that the Federal Insecticide, Fungicide, and Rodenticide Act (FIFRA) does not preempt common law and state statutory claims by farmers against herbicide manufacturers. Bates v. Dow Agrosciences LLC, 125 S. Ct. 1788 (2005). *See generally* Robert L. Glicksman, *Federal Preemption and Private Legal Remedies for Pollution*, 134 U. Pa. L. Rev. 121 (1985) (surveying cases and evaluating the legal and policy arguments for and against preserving common law remedies).

You will recall from your reading of *Missouri v. Illinois* that water systems respect no geopolitical boundaries. There are often upstream polluters and downstream recipient communities, raising the question of who should make water pollution policy. It is no surprise, then, that a major context for disputes over the continuing utility and role of the common law has been in water bodies that cross those borders (including interstate waters and coastal waters). An open question, however, is the degree to which the comprehensive statutory scheme in the CWA supplants or supplements common law remedies. Moreover, if common law claims survive in the statutory era, what body of common law controls in cases of interstate pollution, federal common law, the law of the discharging state, or the law of the receiving state?

The first major word in the CWA-common law saga was a decision by Justice Douglas in a case involving sewage pollution in Lake Michigan, decided a half year *before* Congress adopted its comprehensive amendments to the Federal Water Pollution Control Act (commonly known as the Clean Water Act), which established the current regulatory approach to water pollution. Against the backdrop of the existing federal statute, which left most authority to the states, the Court announced the following about the law of interstate water pollution control:

≣ *Illinois v. City of Milwaukee*
≡ *406 U.S. 91 (1972)*

JUSTICE DOUGLAS delivered the opinion of the Court.

This is a motion by Illinois to file a bill of complaint under our original jurisdiction against four cities of Wisconsin, the Sewerage Commission of the City of Milwaukee, and the Metropolitan Sewerage Commission of the County of Milwaukee. The cause of action alleged is pollution by the defendants of Lake Michigan, a body of interstate water. According to plaintiff, some 200 million gallons of raw or inadequately treated sewage and other waste materials are discharged daily into the lake in the Milwaukee area alone. Plaintiff alleges that it and its subdivisions prohibit and prevent such discharges, but that the defendants do not take such actions. Plaintiff asks that we abate this public nuisance. . . .

III

Congress has enacted numerous laws touching interstate waters. In 1899 it established some surveillance by the Army Corps of Engineers over industrial pollution, not including sewage. . . .

The 1899 Act has been reinforced and broadened by a complex of laws recently enacted. The Federal Water Pollution Control Act tightens control over discharges into navigable waters so as not to lower applicable water quality standards. . . . Congress has evinced increasing concern with the quality of the aquatic environment as it affects the conservation and safeguarding of fish and wildlife resources. . . .

The Federal Water Pollution Control Act . . . declares that it is federal policy 'to recognize, preserve, and protect the primary responsibilities and rights of the States in preventing and controlling water pollution.' But the Act makes clear that it is federal, not state, law that in the end controls the pollution of interstate or navigable waters. While the States are given time to establish water quality standards, if a State fails to do so the federal administrator promulgates one. Section 10(a) makes pollution of interstate or navigable waters subject 'to abatement' when it 'endangers the health or welfare of any persons.' The abatement that is authorized follows a long-drawn out procedure unnecessary to relate here. It uses the conference procedure, hoping for amicable settlements. But if none is reached, the federal administrator may request the Attorney General to bring suit on behalf of the United States for abatement of the pollution.

The remedy sought by Illinois is not within the precise scope of remedies prescribed by Congress. Yet the remedies which Congress provides are not necessarily the only federal remedies available. 'It is not uncommon for federal courts to fashion federal law where federal rights are concerned.' When we deal with air and water in their ambient or interstate aspects, there is a federal common law. . . . [5]

The application of federal common law to abate a public nuisance in interstate or navigable waters is not inconsistent with the Water Pollution Control Act. Congress provided in §10(b) of that Act that, save as a court may decree otherwise in an enforcement action, '(s)tate and interstate action to abate pollution of interstate or navigable waters shall be encouraged and shall not . . . be displaced by Federal enforcement action. . . . '

When it comes to water pollution this Court has spoken in terms of 'a public nuisance,'. . . . It may happen that new federal laws and new federal regulations may in time pre-empt the field of federal common law of nuisance. But until that comes to pass, federal courts will be empowered to appraise the equities of the suits alleging creation of a public nuisance by water pollution. While federal law governs, consideration of state standards may be relevant. Thus, a State with high water-quality standards may well ask that its strict standards be honored and that it not be compelled to lower itself to the more degrading standards of a neighbor. There are no fixed rules that govern; these will be equity suits in which the informed judgment of the chancellor will largely govern. . . .

NOTES AND QUESTIONS ON *ILLINOIS v. CITY OF MILWAUKEE*

1. *Purpose of retaining common law.* At the time this case was decided, Congress had adopted legislation governing water pollution for at least 73 years. Why, then, did the Court find a residual role for the common law, and what purpose was it supposed to serve?

2. *Why federal common law?* Given that common law under our system of federalism typically is formulated by individual states, what was the Supreme Court's justification for declaring that a *federal* common law of nuisance should govern this case? Is this sound as a matter of environmental policy?

3. *Aftermath.* A half year after this case was decided, Congress adopted its extensive amendments to the Federal Water Pollution Control Act. Then, another several years (including three years of discovery) passed before this case went to trial, which was six months long. The trial court granted relief imposing additional pollution control requirements on the defendants, along with a mandatory construction and compliance schedule. The court of appeals modified this relief, holding that, notwithstanding the Supreme Court's decision in *Milwaukee I*, any federal common law claim must be judged in light of the new statute. The Supreme Court reviewed this decision in *Milwaukee II*:

---

5. While the various federal environmental protection statutes will not necessarily mark the outer bounds of the federal common law, they may provide useful guidelines in fashioning such rules of decision.

≣ *City of Milwaukee v. Illinois*
≣ *451 U.S. 304 (1981)*

JUSTICE REHNQUIST delivered the opinion of the Court.

When this litigation was first before us we recognized the existence of a federal "common law" which could give rise to a claim for abatement of a nuisance caused by interstate water pollution. Subsequent to our decision, Congress enacted the Federal Water Pollution Control Act Amendments of 1972. We granted certiorari to consider the effect of this legislation on the previously recognized cause of action. . . .

I

[The Court reiterated, in somewhat more detail, the sewage pollution problems for which the plaintiffs sought redress, along with the Supreme Court's prior decision and the relief granted by the district court.]

Five months [after the new complaint was filed in district court] Congress, recognizing that "the Federal water pollution control program . . . has been inadequate in every vital aspect," passed the Federal Water Pollution Control Act Amendments of 1972. The Amendments established a new system of regulation under which it is illegal for anyone to discharge pollutants into the Nation's waters except pursuant to a permit. To the extent that the Environmental Protection Agency, charged with administering the Act, has promulgated regulations establishing specific effluent limitations, those limitations are incorporated as conditions of the permit. Permits are issued either by the EPA or a qualifying state agency. Petitioners operated their sewer systems and discharged effluent under permits issued by the Wisconsin Department of Natural Resources (DNR) . . . . Petitioners did not fully comply with the requirements of the permits and, as contemplated by the Act, the state agency brought an enforcement action in state court. On May 25, 1977, the state court entered a judgment requiring discharges from the treatment plants to meet the effluent limitations set forth in the permits and establishing a detailed timetable for the completion of planning and additional construction to control sewage overflows.

Trial on Illinois' claim commenced on January 11, 1977. On July 29 the District Court rendered a decision finding that respondents had proved the existence of a nuisance under federal common law, both in the discharge of inadequately treated sewage from petitioners' plants and in the discharge of untreated sewage from sewer overflows. The court ordered petitioners to eliminate all overflows and to achieve specified effluent limitations on treated sewage. A judgment order entered on November 15 specified a construction timetable for the completion of detention facilities to eliminate overflows. Separated sewer overflows are to be completely eliminated by 1986; combined sewer overflows by 1989. The detention facilities to be constructed must be large enough to permit full treatment of water from any storm up to the largest storm on record for the Milwaukee area. Both the aspects of the decision concerning overflows and concerning effluent limitations . . . went considerably beyond the terms of petitioners' previously issued permits and the enforcement order of the state court.

On appeal, the Court of Appeals for the Seventh Circuit affirmed in part and reversed in part. The court ruled that the 1972 Amendments had not pre-empted the federal common law of nuisance, but that "[i]n applying the federal common law of nuisance in a water pollution case, a court should not ignore the Act but should look to its policies and principles for guidance." The court reversed the District Court insofar as the effluent limitations it imposed on treated sewage were more stringent than those in the permits and applicable EPA regulations. The order to eliminate all overflows, however, and the construction schedule designed to achieve this goal, were upheld.

II

Federal courts, unlike state courts, are not general common-law courts and do not possess a general power to develop and apply their own rules of decision. Erie R. Co. v. Tompkins . . . The enactment of a federal rule in an area of national concern, and the decision whether to displace state law in doing so, is generally made not by the federal judiciary, purposefully insulated from democratic pressures, but by the people through their elected representatives in Congress. *Erie* recognized as much in ruling that a federal court could not generally apply a federal rule of decision, despite the existence of jurisdiction, in the absence of an applicable Act of Congress. When Congress has not spoken to a particular issue, however, and when there exists a "significant conflict between some federal policy or interest and the use of state law," the Court has found it necessary, in a "few and restricted" instances, to develop federal common law. Nothing in this process suggests that courts are better suited to develop national policy in areas governed by federal common law than they are in other areas, or that the usual and important concerns of an appropriate division of functions between the Congress and the federal judiciary are inapplicable. We have always recognized that federal common law is "subject to the paramount authority of Congress." It is resorted to "[i]n absence of an applicable Act of Congress" . . . Federal common law is a "necessary expedient," and when Congress addresses a question previously governed by a decision rested on federal common law the need for such an unusual exercise of lawmaking by federal courts disappears. . . .

III

We conclude that, at least so far as concerns the claims of respondents, Congress has not left the formulation of appropriate federal standards to the

courts through application of often vague and indeterminate nuisance concepts and maxims of equity jurisprudence, but rather has occupied the field
through the establishment of a comprehensive regulatory program supervised
by an expert administrative agency. The 1972 Amendments to the Federal
Water Pollution Control Act were not merely another law "touching interstate
waters" . . . . Rather, the Amendments were viewed by Congress as a "total
restructuring" and "complete rewriting" of the existing water pollution legislation considered in that case. Congress' intent in enacting the Amendments
was clearly to establish an all-encompassing program of water pollution
regulation. Every point source discharge is prohibited unless covered by a
permit, which directly subjects the discharger to the administrative apparatus
established by Congress to achieve its goals. The "major purpose" of the
Amendments was "to establish a comprehensive long-range policy for the
elimination of water pollution." No Congressman's remarks on the legislation
were complete without reference to the "comprehensive" nature of the
Amendments. . . . The establishment of such a self-consciously comprehensive program by Congress, which certainly did not exist when Illinois v.
Milwaukee was decided, strongly suggests that there is no room for courts to
attempt to improve on that program with federal common law.[14]

Turning to the particular claims involved in this case, the action of
Congress in supplanting the federal common law is perhaps clearest when the
question of effluent limitations for discharges from the two treatment plants is
considered. The duly issued permits under which the city Commission discharges treated sewage . . . incorporate, as required by the Act, the specific
effluent limitations established by EPA regulations. . . . There is thus no
question that the problem of effluent limitations has been thoroughly addressed through the administrative scheme established by Congress, as contemplated by Congress. This being so there is no basis for a federal court to
impose more stringent limitations than those imposed under the regulatory
regime by reference to federal common law, as the District Court did in this
case. . . . Federal courts lack authority to impose more stringent effluent
limitations under federal common law than those imposed by the agency
charged by Congress with administering this comprehensive scheme. . . .

The invocation of federal common law by the District Court and the
Court of Appeals in the face of congressional legislation supplanting it is

14. This conclusion is not undermined by Congress' decision to permit States to establish
more stringent standards. While Congress recognized a role for the States, the comprehensive
nature of its action suggests that it was the exclusive source of federal law. Cases recognizing that
the comprehensive character of a federal program is an insufficient basis to find pre-emption of
state law are not in point, since we are considering which branch of the Federal Government is
the source of federal law, not whether that law pre-empts state law. Since federal courts create
federal common law only as a necessary expedient when problems requiring federal answers are
not addressed by federal statutory law, see supra, at 1790-1791, the comprehensive character of
a federal statute is quite relevant to the present question, while it would not be were the question
whether state law, which of course does not depend upon the absence of an applicable Act of
Congress, still applied.

peculiarly inappropriate in areas as complex as water pollution control. . . . Not only are the technical problems difficult — doubtless the reason Congress vested authority to administer the Act in administrative agencies possessing the necessary expertise — but the general area is particularly unsuited to the approach inevitable under a regime of federal common law. Congress criticized past approaches to water pollution control as being "sporadic" and "ad hoc," characterizations of any judicial approach applying federal common law.

It is also significant that Congress addressed in the 1972 Amendments one of the major concerns underlying the recognition of federal common law in Illinois v. Milwaukee. We were concerned in that case that Illinois did not have any forum in which to protect its interests unless federal common law were created. In the 1972 Amendments Congress provided ample opportunity for a State affected by decisions of a neighboring State's permit-granting agency to seek redress. [The Court described the statutory mechanism by which a downstream state may ask EPA to reject or modify a permit issued by an upstream state, noting that the plaintiffs did not avail themselves of these statutory mechanisms.] The statutory scheme established by Congress provides a forum for the pursuit of such claims before expert agencies by means of the permit-granting process. It would be quite inconsistent with this scheme if federal courts were in effect to "write their own ticket" under the guise of federal common law after permits have already been issued and permittees have been planning and operating in reliance on them.

Respondents argue that congressional intent to preserve the federal common-law remedy recognized in Illinois v. Milwaukee is evident in §§510 and 505(e) of the statute. Section 510 provides that nothing in the Act shall preclude States from adopting and enforcing limitations on the discharge of pollutants more stringent than those adopted under the Act.[20] It is one thing, however, to say that States may adopt more stringent limitations through state administrative processes, or even that States may establish such limitations through state nuisance law, and apply them to in-state discharges. It is quite another to say that the States may call upon federal courts to employ federal common law to establish more stringent standards applicable to out-of-state

---

20. In full, §510 provides:

"Except as expressly provided in this chapter, nothing in this chapter shall (1) preclude or deny the right of any State or political subdivision thereof or interstate agency to adopt or enforce (A) any standard or limitation respecting discharges of pollutants, or (B) any requirement respecting control or abatement of pollution; except that if any effluent limitation, or other limitation, effluent standard, prohibition, pretreatment standard, or standard of performance is in effect under this chapter, such State or political subdivision or interstate agency may not adopt or enforce any effluent limitation, or other limitation, effluent standard, prohibition, pretreatment standard, or standard of performance which is less stringent than the effluent limitation, or other limitation, effluent standard, prohibition, pretreatment standard, or standard of performance under this chapter; or (2) be construed as impairing or in any manner affecting any right or jurisdiction of the States with respect to the waters (including boundary waters) of such States."

dischargers. Any standards established under federal common law are federal standards, and so the authority of States to impose more stringent standards under §510 would not seem relevant. Section 510 clearly contemplates state authority to establish more stringent pollution limitations; nothing in it, however, suggests that this was to be done by federal-court actions premised on federal common law.

Subsection 505(e) provides:

> "Nothing *in this section* shall restrict any right which any person (or class of persons) may have under any statute or common law to seek enforcement of any effluent standard or limitation or to seek any other relief (including relief against the Administrator or a State agency)" (emphasis supplied).

Respondents argue that this evinces an intent to preserve the federal common law of nuisance. We, however, are inclined to view the quoted provision as meaning what it says: that nothing in §505, the citizen-suit provision, should be read as limiting any other remedies which might exist. Subsection 505(e) is virtually identical to subsections in the citizen-suit provisions of several environmental statutes. The subsection is common language accompanying citizen-suit provisions and we think that it means only that the provision of such suit does not revoke other remedies. It most assuredly cannot be read to mean that the Act as a whole does not supplant formerly available federal common-law actions but only that the particular section authorizing citizen suits does not do so. No one, however, maintains that the citizen-suit provision pre-empts federal common law. We are thus not persuaded that §505(e) aids respondents in this case, even indulging the unlikely assumption that the reference to "common law" in §505(e) includes the limited federal common law as opposed to the more routine state common law. . . . [22]

We therefore conclude that no federal common-law remedy was available to respondents in this case. The judgment of the Court of Appeals is therefore vacated, and the case is remanded for proceedings consistent with this opinion.

It is so ordered.

JUSTICE BLACKMUN, with whom JUSTICE MARSHALL and JUSTICE STEVENS join, dissenting. . . .

---

22. The dissent's criticism of our reading of §505(e), post, at 1805, is misplaced. There is nothing unusual about Congress enacting a particular provision, and taking care that this enactment by itself not disturb other remedies, without considering whether the rest of the Act does so or what other remedies may be available. The fact that the language of §505(e) is repeated *in haec verba* in the citizen-suit provisions of a vast array of environmental legislation, indicates that it does not reflect any considered judgment about what other remedies were previously available or continue to be available under any particular statute. The dissent refers to our reading as "extremely strained," but the dissent, in relying on §505(e) as evidence of Congress' intent to preserve the federal common-law nuisance remedy, must read "nothing in this section" to mean "nothing in this Act." We prefer to read the statute as written. Congress knows how to say "nothing in this Act" when it means to.

It is well settled that a body of federal common law has survived the decision in Erie R. Co. v. Tompkins. Erie made clear that federal courts, as courts of limited jurisdiction, lack general power to formulate and impose their own rules of decision. The Court, however, did not there upset, nor has it since disturbed, a deeply rooted, more specialized federal common law that has arisen to effectuate federal interests embodied either in the Constitution or an Act of Congress. Chief among the federal interests served by this common law are the resolution of interstate disputes and the implementation of national statutory or regulatory policies.

Both before and after Erie, the Court has fashioned federal law where the interstate nature of a controversy renders inappropriate the law of either State. When such disputes arise, it is clear under our federal system that laws of one State cannot impose upon the sovereign rights and interests of another. . . .

II

In my view, the language and structure of the Clean Water Act leaves no doubt that Congress intended to preserve the federal common law of nuisance. Section 505(e) of the Act reads: "Nothing in this section shall restrict any right which any person (or class of persons) may have under any statute or common law to seek enforcement of any effluent standard or limitation or to seek any other relief (including relief against the Administrator or a State agency)."

The Act specifically defines "person" to include States, and thus embraces respondents Illinois and Michigan. It preserves their right to bring an action against the governmental entities who are charged with enforcing the statute. Most important, as succinctly stated by the Court of Appeals in this case: "There is nothing in the phrase 'any statute or common law' that suggests that this provision is limited to state common law." To the best of my knowledge, every federal court that has considered the issue has concluded that, in enacting §505(e), Congress meant to preserve federal as well as state common law.

Other sections of the Clean Water Act also support the conclusion that Congress in 1972 had no intention of extinguishing the federal common law of nuisance. Although the Act established a detailed and comprehensive regulatory system aimed at eliminating the discharge of pollutants into all navigable waters, it did not purport to impose a unitary enforcement structure for abating water pollution. In particular, Congress expressly provided that the effluent limitations promulgated under the Act do not preclude any State from establishing more stringent limitations. It also made clear that federal officers or agencies are not foreclosed from adopting or enforcing stricter pollution controls and standards than those required by the Act.

Thus, under the statutory scheme, any permit issued by the EPA or a qualifying state agency does not insulate a discharger from liability under other federal or state law. To the contrary, the permit granted pursuant to §402(k) confers assurances with respect to certain specified sections of the Act, but the requirements under other provisions as well as separate legal obligations remain unaffected. Congress plainly anticipated that dischargers might be required to meet standards more stringent than the minimum effluent levels approved by the EPA. Those more stringent standards would necessarily be established by other statutes or by common law. Because the Act contemplates a shared authority between the Federal Government and the individual States, it is entirely understandable that Congress thought it neither imperative nor desirable to insist upon an exclusive approach to the improvement of water quality. . . .

NOTES AND QUESTIONS ON *MILWAUKEE II*

1. *Holding and aftermath.* Does the court hold that the CWA preempts all state law? Does the court hold that the CWA preempts *all* common law claims, or simply those based on *federal* common law? On remand in *Milwaukee III*, 519 F. Supp. 292 (D.C. Ill. 1981), the district court interpreted *Milwaukee II* to permit state common law claims for liability resulting from interstate water pollution and allowed Illinois to proceed against the city of Milwaukee under the Illinois law of nuisance. The Seventh Circuit reversed, 731 F.2d 403 (7th Cir. 1984), *cert. denied*, 469 U.S. 1196 (1985), holding that the CWA precluded a state claiming injury from asserting its own laws, whether statutory or common law, as a basis for imposing liability on a discharging sister state. The Seventh Circuit reasoned that the CWA:

> may well preserve a right under statutes or the common law of the state within which a discharge occurs (State I) to obtain enforcement of prescribed standards or limitations, and we see no reason why such a right could not be asserted by an out-of-state plaintiff injured as a result of the violation. However, it seems implausible that Congress meant to preserve or confer any right of the state claiming injury (State II) or its citizens to seek enforcement of limitations on discharges in State I by applying the statutes or common law of State II.

731 F.2d at 414. The Supreme Court agreed with this result six years later, holding that the law of the discharging state controls in order to preserve the comprehensive regulatory regime envisioned by the CWA, thus precluding suits based on the common law of the receiving state, but not those based on the common law of the source state. International Paper v. Ouellette, 479 U.S. 481 (1987).

2. *Role of comprehensive scheme.* If this decision merely bars federal common law claims, how relevant to the holding is the fact that Congress adopted a comprehensive statutory scheme? Should that not also bar state common law claims as well? And if so, what did Congress intend to accomplish in the section 505(e) savings clause?

3. *Institutional factors.* In some ways, the majority opinion echoes the reluctance of the *Boomer* court to address complex environmental issues, in favor of an approach that relies on legislative action and the expertise of

administrative agencies rather than judicial discretion. If the major purpose of statutory schemes was to replace the unpredictable, uncertain nature of case-by-case decisions as a means of environmental protection, isn't the Court correct here to reject that approach once a comprehensive administrative regime is in place? Should the residual role of the common law be limited to damages, as opposed to corrective action?

4. *Sea Clammers.* In the same term, the Supreme Court decided in Middlesex County Sewerage Authority v. National Sea Clammers Association, 453 U.S. 1 (1981), that the Clean Water Act similarly preempted any federal common law claims regarding ocean pollution. The *Sea Clammers* decision also held that neither the CWA nor the Marine Protection, Research, and Sanctuaries Act (MPRSA, or Ocean Dumping Act) included an implied right of action other than the specific citizen suit and other remedies expressly provided in those laws.

5. *State of the law.* Reading all of the opinions together (*Milwaukee I and II*, along with *International Paper* and *Sea Clammers*), the result is that the Supreme Court has held that Congress intended to preempt the federal common law of nuisance and the common law of states that may receive pollution from other states, but not the common law of the discharging state. How does this view of the residual role of the common law fit with the regulatory programs in the statute, and how might a broader common law role interfere with those programs?

4

The Goals and Objectives of Environmental Statutes

In Chapter 3, we described why Congress augmented the common law approach with a set of statutory schemes designed to address a wide range of environmental problems. We also addressed the basic principles of administrative law that govern how those laws are implemented, and the relationship between the common law and statutory approaches. Before exploring the major concepts in those laws in more detail, it is useful to ask what Congress is trying to accomplish in those statutory schemes.

In describing the common law in Chapter 2, we introduced the tension between an absolutist approach to health and environmental protection and an approach that balances those goals with economic considerations. Congress faced similar choices in writing our environmental statutes. Did it want to *eliminate* all health and environmental risks regardless of the costs of doing so? Did it want implementing agencies to calculate levels of environmental risk, and reduce that risk to a degree deemed "acceptable"? Should the benefits of particular environmental standards be balanced against the costs to society of meeting them (economic efficiency)? Or, should we worry more about achieving a fair distribution of environmental risks and benefits, and the costs of achieving them (equity)?

In the opening provision (or provisions) of many environmental statutes, Congress identified a series of goals and objectives. This chapter explores the goals of some of the Nation's major environmental statutes, and asks what those provisions suggest about the basic approaches to environmental protection and regulation adopted by Congress. We begin in Section A by asking you to consider what goals *might* be or *should* be included in environmental statutes, based on a series of excerpts from significant environmental writings. In Section B, we set forth the goals provisions of some of the major environmental statutes, and ask you to consider which kinds of goals Congress chose, and what those goals might mean. At the same time, this exercise will give you a basic introduction to what problems each of those laws were designed to address.

113

A. WHAT SHOULD THE GOALS OF ENVIRONMENTAL LAW BE?

What principles should inform the goals of environmental law more broadly, including the goals for statutory schemes? There is a rich literature in environmental writing from a wide range of disciplines, including ecology, ethics, and economics (as well as literature itself). *See, e.g.,* THE NORTON BOOK OF NATURE WRITING (ROBERT FINCH AND JOHN ELDER eds., 2002). We can draw upon much of this writing and thinking to help inform and explain the history (and the future) of environmental policy. Consider the following readings, each of which adopts a different approach to environmental issues and problems. To some extent, each of these ideas are reflected in the statutory goals presented later in this chapter, and in the more detailed strategies of environmental protection explored throughout the rest of the book.

1. Ecology, Rights and Ethics

Conservation is a state of harmony between men and land. By land is meant all of the things on, over, or in the earth. Harmony with land is like harmony with a friend; you cannot cherish his right hand and chop off his left. That is to say, you cannot love game and hate predators; you cannot conserve the waters and waste the ranges; you cannot build the forest and mine the farm. The land is one organism. Its parts, like our own parts, compete with each other and co-operate with each other. The competitions are as much a part of the inner workings as the co-operations. You can regulate them — cautiously — but not abolish them.

The outstanding scientific discovery of the twentieth century is not television, or radio, but rather the complexity of the land organism. Only those who know the most about it can appreciate how little is known about it. The last word in ignorance is the man who says of an animal or plant: 'What good is it?' If the land mechanism as a whole is good, then every part is good, whether we understand it or not. If the biota, in the course of eons, has built something we like but do not understand, then who but a fool would discard seemingly useless parts? To keep every cog and wheel is the first precaution of intelligent tinkering. . . .

It is inconceivable to me that an ethical relation to land can exist without love, respect, and admiration for land, and a high regard for its value. By value, I of course mean something far broader than mere economic value; I mean value in the philosophical sense.

Perhaps the most serious obstacle impeding the evolution of a land ethic is the fact that our educational and economic system is headed away from, rather than toward, an intense consciousness of land. . . . The 'key-log' which must be moved to release the evolutionary process for an ethic is simply this: quit thinking about decent land-use as solely an economic problem. Examine each question in terms of what is ethically and esthetically right, as well as what is economically expedient. A thing is right as it tends to preserve the integrity, stability, and beauty of the biotic community. It is wrong when it tends otherwise.

ALDO LEOPOLD, SAND COUNTY ALMANAC 189-190, 261-262 (Oxford Univ. Press ed., 1966) (first published 1949).

Leopold is considered one of the parents of the modern conservation movement, especially for his concept of the "land ethic." *See* Eric T. Freyfogle, *The Land Ethic and Pilgrim Leopold*, 61 U. Colo. L. Rev. 217 (1990). Leopold's concepts anticipated the huge advances in the ecological sciences since then, which have increased our understanding of the extent to which human welfare depends on ecological integrity. *See* NATURE'S SERVICES, SOCIETAL DEPENDENCE ON NATURAL ECOSYSTEMS (GRETCHEN C. DAILY ed., 1997). Based on the writings of Leopold and others, however, some have argued for legal rights on behalf of nature independent of human welfare. *See* CHRISTOPHER D. STONE, SHOULD TREES HAVE STANDING, AND OTHER ESSAYS ON LAW, MORALS AND THE ENVIRONMENT (1996). Deep Ecologists take this concept one step farther, rejecting an anthropocentric approach emphasizing enhancement of the quality of human life, in favor of the belief that the interests of nonhuman life deserve paramount protection, regardless of that life's impact on humans. *See generally*, BILL DEVALL AND GEORGE SESSIONS, DEEP ECOLOGY: LIVING AS IF NATURE MATTERED (1985). Alternatively, Professor Amy Sinden defends a rights-based approach to environmental law on the basis of pragmatic considerations rooted in a view of how administrative law functions. *See* Amy Sinden, *In Defense of Absolutes: Combating the Politics of Power in Environmental Law*, 90 Iowa L. Rev. 1405 (2005). She argues that concentrated corporate economic interests have much more power than the relatively diffuse, albeit numerous, proponents of environmental protection. As a result, special interests skew the administrative process to compromise efforts to achieve environmental goals. She argues that absolutism in the goals of environmental law helps provide a counterweight to this power imbalance.

2. Human Health and Prevention

The battle of living things against cancer began so long ago that its origin is lost in time. But it must have begin in a natural environment, in which whatever life inhabited the earth was subjected, for good or ill, to influences that had their origin in sun and storm and the ancient nature of the earth. Some of the elements of this environment created hazards to which life had to adjust or perish. The ultraviolet radiation in sunlight could cause malignancy. So could radiation from certain rocks, or arsenic washed out of soil or rocks to contaminate food or water supplies.

The environment contained these hostile elements even before there was life; yet life arose, and over millions of years it came to exist in infinite numbers and endless variety. Over the eons of unhurried time that is nature's, life reached an adjustment with destructive forces as selection weeded out the less adaptable and only the most resistant survived. These natural cancer-causing agents are still a factor in causing malignancy; however, they are few in number and they belong to that ancient array of forces to which life has become accustomed from the beginning.

With the advent of man the situation began to change, for man, alone of all forms of life, can *create* cancer-producing substances, which in medical terminology are called carcinogens. A few man-made carcinogens have been part of the environment for centuries. An example is soot, containing aromatic hydrocarbons. With the dawn of the industrial era the world became a place of continuous, ever-accelerating change. Instead of the natural environment there was rapidly substituted an artificial one composed entirely of new chemical and physical agents, many of them possessing powerful capacities for inducing biologic change. Against these carcinogens which his own activities had created man had no protection, for even as his biological heritage has evolved slowly, so it adapts slowly to new conditions. As a result these powerful substances could easily penetrate the inadequate defenses of the body. . . .

The task is by no means a hopeless one. In one important respect the outlook is more encouraging than the situation regarding infectious disease at the turn of the [twentieth] century. The world was then full of disease germs, as today it is full of carcinogens. But man did not put the germs into the environment and his role *has* put the vast majority of carcinogens into the environment, and he can, if he wishes, eliminate many of them. The chemical agents of cancer have become entrenched in our world in two ways: first, and ironically, through man's search for a better and easier way of life; second, because the manufacture and sale of such chemicals has become an accepted part of our economy and our way of life.

It would be unrealistic to suppose that all chemical carcinogens can or will be eliminated from the modern world. But a very large proportion are by no means necessities of life. By their elimination the total load of carcinogens would be enormously lightened, and the threat that [so many people] will develop cancer would at least be greatly mitigated. The most determined effort should be made to eliminate those carcinogens that now contaminate our food, our water supplies, and our atmosphere, because these provide the most dangerous type of contact — minute exposures, repeated over and over throughout the years.

Among the most eminent . . . in cancer research are many who share [the] belief that malignant diseases can be reduced significantly by determined efforts to identify the environmental causes and to eliminate them or reduce their impact. For those in whom cancer is already a hidden or visible presence, efforts to find cures must of course continue. But for those not yet touched by the disease and certainly for the generations yet unborn, prevention is the imperative need.

RACHEL CARSON, SILENT SPRING 215-216 (1962).

Like Aldo Leopold, Carson is given credit for stimulating the modern environmental movement, and in particular, the nation's first major anti-pollution statutes. *See* Peter M. Manus, *Natural Resource Damages from Rachel Carson's Perspective: A Rite of Spring in American Environmentalism*, 37 Wm. & Mary L. Rev. 381 (1996). While the above excerpt focuses on cancer, Carson's charges against synthetic chemicals in general and pesticides in particular extended to a wider range of adverse human health and environmental harms, and are credited with, among other reforms, the ban on the use of DDT and other highly toxic pesticides in the United States. *See* JOHN WARGO, OUR CHILDREN'S TOXIC LEGACY, HOW SCIENCE AND LAW FAIL TO PROTECT US FROM PESTICIDES 80-85

(1996). We will discuss environmental standards based on strict protection of human health and the environment in Chapter 5, and the concept of bans in Chapter 8. Ironically, Carson died of cancer just two years after publication of *Silent Spring. Id.* at 84.

3. Economic Efficiency

The first and most fundamental step toward solution of our environmental problems is a clear recognition that our objective is not pure air or water but rather some optimal state of pollution. That step immediately suggests the question: How do we define and attain the level of pollution that will yield the maximum possible amount of human satisfaction?

Low levels of pollution contribute to human satisfaction but so do food and shelter and education and music. To attain ever lower levels of pollution, we must pay the cost of having these other things. . . .

People enjoy watching penguins. They enjoy relatively clean air and smog-free vistas. Their health is improved by relatively clean water or air. Each of these benefits is a type of good or service. As a society we would be well advised to give up one washing machine if the resources that would have gone into that washing machine can yield greater human satisfaction when diverted into pollution control. We should give up one more hospital if the resources thereby freed would yield more human satisfaction when devoted to elimination of noise in our cities. And so on, trade-off by trade-off, we should divert our productive capacities from the production of existing goods and services to the production of a cleaner, quieter, more pastoral nation up to — and no further than — the point at which we value more highly the next washing machine or hospital that we would have to do without than we value the next unit of environmental improvement that the diverted resources would create.

WILLIAM F. BAXTER, PEOPLE OR PENGUINS, THE CASE FOR OPTIMAL POLLUTION 8-9, 12 (1974).

Baxter was among a group of economists who, consistent with Coase's theories presented in Chapter 2, believed that an absolute rights-based approach to environmental protection does not necessarily maximize human welfare. These ideas gave birth to a number of market-based approaches in lieu of, or in addition to, government regulation. *See generally* TERRY L. ANDERSON AND DONALD R. LEAL, FREE MARKET ENVIRONMENTALISM (revised ed. 2001). We will explore these ideas further in Chapters 7 and 9.

4. Equity and Environmental Justice

The EPA defines environmental justice as "the fair treatment and meaningful involvement of all people regardless of race, color, national origin, or income with respect to the development, implementation, and enforcement of environmental laws, regulations, and policies. Fair treatment means that no group of

people, including racial, ethnic, or socio-economic groups, should bear a disproportionate share of the negative environmental consequences resulting from
industrial, municipal, and commercial operations or the execution of federal,
state, local, and tribal programs and policies." Poverty and pollution are intri-
cately linked.

Numerous studies have documented the fact that, in the United States,
people of color are disproportionately affected by environmental hazards in their
homes, neighborhoods, and workplaces. In 1999, the Institute of Medicine of
the National Academies, a nongovernmental organization that provides guidance on matters of science and medicine, issued *Toward Environmental Justice:
Research, Education and Health Policy Needs.* This report concluded that communities populated by low-income groups and people of color are exposed to
higher levels of pollution than the rest of the nation, and that these same
populations experience certain diseases in greater numbers than more affluent
white communities. . . .

Despite significant improvements in environmental protection over the past
thirty-five years, however, millions of Americans continue to live, work, play, and
go to school in unsafe and unhealthy physical environments. Over the past three
decades, the EPA has not always recognized that many government and industry
practices (whether intended or unintended) have had an adverse impact on poor
people and people of color. Grassroots community resistence emerged in response to practices, policies, and conditions that residents judged to be unjust,
unfair, and illegal. Discrimination is a fact of life in America. Racial discrimination
is also illegal.

The EPA is mandated to enforce the nation's environmental laws and regulations equally across the board. It is also required to protect all Americans — not
just individuals or groups who can afford lawyers, lobbyists, and experts. Environmental protection is a right, not a privilege reserved for a few who can fend off environmental stressors that address environmental inequities.

Equity may mean different things to different people. Equity can be distilled
into three broad categories: procedural, geographic, and social equity. *Procedural
equity* refers to the "fairness" question: the extent to which governing rules, regulations, evaluation criteria, and enforcement are applied uniformly across the
board. Unequal protection might result from nonscientific and undemocratic
decisions, exclusionary practices, public hearings held in remote locations and at
inconvenient times, and the use of English alone in communicating information
about, and conducting hearings for, the non-English-speaking public. *Geographic
equity* refers to location and spatial configuration of communities and their proximity to environmental hazards and locally unwanted land uses such as landfills,
incinerators, sewer treatment plants, lead smelters, refineries, and other noxious
facilities. For example, unequal protection may result from land use decisions that
determine the location of residential amenities and dis-amenities. Communities
that are unincorporated, poor, and populated by people of color often suffer triple
vulnerability to the siting of noxious facilities simply because of these characteristics. *Social equity* assesses the role of sociological factors, such as race, ethnicity,
class, culture, lifestyles, political power, and so on, in environmental decision
making. Poor people and people of color often work in the most dangerous jobs
and live in the most polluted neighborhoods, and their children are exposed to a
host of environmental toxins on the playgrounds and in their homes.

Robert D. Bullard, The Quest for Environmental Justice, Human Rights and the Politics of Pollution 4, 30-31(2005).

Bullard and his colleagues helped give birth to the environmental justice movement in the late 1980s and early 1990s. *See* Robert D. Bullard, Dumping in Dixie, Race, Class and Environmental Quality (1990); Unequal Protection, Environmental Justice and Communities of Color (Robert D. Bullard, ed., 1994). This has led to a considerable amount of grassroots activism, as well as an academic debate about whether disproportionate environmental impacts stem from racial, economic, or other factors. *Compare* Eileen Gauna, *An Essay on Environmental Justice: The Past, the Present, and Back to the Future*, 42 Nat. Resources J. 701 (2002) *with* Vicki Been, *Locally Undesirable Land Uses in Minority Neighborhoods: Disproportionate Siting or Market Dynamics*, 103 Yale L.J. 1383 (1994).

5. Sustainable Development

[I]t is impossible for the world economy to grow its way out of poverty and environmental degradation. In other words, sustainable growth is impossible. In its physical dimensions the economy is an open subsystem of the earth ecosystem, which is finite, nongrowing, and materially closed. As the economic subsystem grows it incorporates an ever greater proportion of the total ecosystem into itself and must reach a limit at 100 percent, if not before. Therefore its growth is not sustainable. The term "sustainable growth" when applied to the economy is a bad oxymoron. . . .

The term "sustainable development" therefore makes sense for the economy, but only if it is understood as "development without growth" — i.e., qualitative improvement of a physical economic base that is maintained in a steady state by a throughput of matter-energy that is within the regenerative and assimilative capacities of the ecosystem. Currently the term "sustainable development" is used as a synonym for the oxymoronic "sustainable growth." It must be saved from this perdition.

Politically it is very difficult to admit that growth, with its almost religious connotations of ultimate goodness, must be limited. But . . . [t]here is a limit to the population of trees the earth can support, just as there is a limit to the populations of humans and of automobiles.

Every day we read about stress-induced feedbacks from the ecosystem to the economy, such as greenhouse buildup, ozone layer depletion, acid rain, etc., which constitute evidence that even the present scale is unsustainable.

An economy in sustainable development adapts and improves in knowledge, organization, technical efficiency, and wisdom; and it does this without assimilating or accreting, beyond some point, an ever greater percentage of the matter-energy of the ecosystem into itself, but rather stops at a scale at which the remaining ecosystem (the environment) can continue to function and renew itself year after year. The non-growing economy is not static — it is being continually maintained and renewed as environment.

What policies are implied by the goal of sustainable development, as here defined? . . . Strive to hold throughput constant at present levels (or reduced truly sustainable levels) by taxing resource extraction, especially energy, very heavily. . . .

At the project level there are some additional policy guidelines for sustainable development. Renewable resources should be exploited in a manner such that:

(1) harvesting rates do not exceed regeneration rates; and
(2) waste emissions do not exceed the renewable assimilative capacity of the local environment . . .

Nonrenewable resources should be depleted at a rate equal to the rate of creation of renewable substitutes.

Herman E. Daly, *Sustainable Growth: An Impossibility Theorem, in* VALUING THE EARTH 267-271 (HERMAN E. DALY AND KENNETH N. TOWNSEND eds., 1992).

A number of international environmental legal instruments embrace the goal of sustainable development. *See, e.g.,* WORLD COMMISSION ON ENVIRONMENT AND DEVELOPMENT, OUR COMMON FUTURE 43 (1987); Rio Declaration of Environment and Development, U.N. Conference on Environment and Development (UNCED), U.N. Doc. A/Conf.151/5/Rev. 1, 31 I.L.M. 874 (1992). Not everybody, however, agrees with Daly's definition of sustainable development. Some practitioners argue that the concept implies an integrated participatory process for environmental decision-making. *See* John C. Dernbach, *Sustainable Development: Now More than Ever, in* STUMBLING TOWARD SUSTAINABILITY 51-53, 56 (JOHN C. DERNBACH ed., 2002). Others emphasize equity between developed and less developed countries, with a need to reduce consumption in northern countries that have an adequate material basis for life, while increasing economic development in impoverished countries. *Id.* at 55-57.

NOTES AND QUESTIONS ON GOALS

1. *What goals?* What goals for environmental law do each of these writings suggest? To what extent are they compatible or mutually exclusive?

2. *Theory and reality.* Which of these writings (and the goals they suggest) do you most agree with philosophically? Which are most likely to result in a desirable degree of environmental protection, and why? Did you choose the same approaches for both questions?

3. *The role of environmental law.* Should environmental law address all of these goals? For example, should economic efficiency and racial discrimination be addressed by environmental law, or by other sets of laws and policies, leaving environmental law to focus exclusively on protecting the environment?

4. *PFOA.* What responses to the PFOA problem are suggested by each of these approaches?

B. THE GOALS OF SOME OF THE MAJOR FEDERAL ENVIRONMENTAL STATUTES

Now that you have thought some about what the goals of environmental law should be, we can begin to study the actual goals of environmental law. Think about the extent to which the goals of environmental law match your views of appropriate goals.

1. The Clean Water Act

In the 1972 amendments to the Federal Water Pollution Control Act (now known commonly as the Clean Water Act), Congress articulated as its overarching objective one of the broadest ecosystem restoration and protection aspirations in all of environmental law: "The objective of this chapter is to restore and maintain the chemical, physical, and biological integrity of the Nation's waters." 33 U.S.C. §1251(a). Congress followed up on its sweeping declaration of a goal of ecosystem integrity with a series of more specific goals and objectives, the relevant provisions of which are set forth below:

> In order to achieve this objective it is hereby declared that, consistent with the provisions of this chapter —
> (1) it is the national goal that the discharge of pollutants into the navigable waters be eliminated by 1985;
> (2) it is the national goal that wherever attainable, an interim goal of water quality which provides for the protection and propagation of fish, shellfish, and wildlife and provides for recreation in and on the water be achieved by July 1, 1983;
> (3) it is the national policy that the discharge of toxic pollutants in toxic amounts be prohibited; . . . .

NOTES AND QUESTIONS ON CLEAN WATER ACT GOALS

1. *What goals?* Which of the possible statutory goals you identified in Section A did Congress include in the Clean Water Act? Which of the goals are most important?

2. *Balance?* The opening objective ("to restore and maintain the chemical, physical, and biological integrity of the Nation's waters") seems to establish environmental protection as the primary goal of the statute. Is the primary statutory objective absolute, *i.e.*, do you think Congress intended that it be achieved at any and all costs, or does other language in section 101(a)

suggest some tempering of the apparently absolutist goals? Lest you get the wrong impression at this preliminary phase of your study, economic factors are included in many of the substantive provisions of the statute. *See, e.g.,* 33 U.S.C. §§1311(c) (economic variances from control requirements), 1314(b) (consideration of economic factors in establishing certain control requirements).

3. *Implications for scope.* Is the objective of the Clean Water Act simply to address water pollution in the lay sense, *i.e.,* to reduce or eliminate releases of chemicals from factory pipes? Or does it require actions to redress the many other ways in which human activities impair the integrity of aquatic ecosystems? Consider the following examples:

a.   Dams transform free-flowing rivers and streams into placid lakes, with very different water chemistry and biological communities. Physical integrity is altered significantly by armoring river banks, channelization, and construction of levees to prevent flooding. Must these structures be removed to meet the statutory goals?

b.   Does stocking streams with non-native rainbow trout alter the biological integrity of those waters?

c.   We have significantly de-watered western waterways for irrigation and other water uses. Are those actions inconsistent with the Clean Water Act's goals?

4. *Endangered Species Act.* A similar problem occurs in interpreting the breadth of the Endangered Species Act (ESA), 16 U.S.C. §§1531 *et seq.,* which authorizes the federal government to identify threatened and endangered species, and to protect those species and their habitats. The purposes of the ESA are "to provide a means whereby the ecosystems upon which endangered species and threatened species depend may be conserved, [and] to provide a program for the conservation of such endangered species and threatened species . . . ." *Id.* §1531(b). Is the main purpose of the ESA to protect individual threatened and endangered species, as the name of the statute suggests, or to protect whole ecosystems? The two key operative provisions of the law seem to focus on individual species. *See id.* §1536 (prohibiting federal agencies from taking any action that jeopardizes the continued existence of listed species, without first consulting with the U.S. Fish and Wildlife Service (or National Marine Fisheries Service for marine species)); and *id.* §1538 (prohibiting private parties from "taking" endangered species). In Babbitt v. Sweet Home Chapter of Communities for a Great Oregon, 515 U.S. 687 (1995), however, the Supreme Court upheld a Fish and Wildlife Service regulation that defines unlawful "taking" as including "significant habitat modification or degradation where it actually kills or injures wildlife by significantly impairing essential behavioral patterns, including breeding, feeding, or sheltering." 50 C.F.R. §17.3.

5. *Ambitious goals: symbolic or real?* Is the goal that waters be clean enough by 1983 to protect fish and wildlife as well as public recreation (the so-called "fishable and swimmable waters" goal) reasonable? What about the "zero discharge" goal articulated in section 101(a)(1)? In some cases, broad statutory goals and objectives have direct parallels within the law's operative provisions, and thereby carry significant substantive force. In others, they remain as hortatory guideposts that, at best, will influence the way in which the rest of the statute operates. One court noted in the context of the Clean Water Act: "[A]s any student of the legislative process soon learns, it is one thing for Congress to announce a grand goal, and another for it to mandate full implementation of that goal." National Wildlife Federation v. Gorsuch, 693 F.2d 156, 178 (D.C. Cir. 1982). A charitable explanation is that Congress believes that it is important to establish long-term environmental aspirations, but realizes that economic, technological, and other factors must be considered in providing for short-term progress toward those goals. A somewhat less flattering view is that members of Congress like to claim that they are solving broad environmental problems comprehensively, but are not willing to adopt specific statutory solutions strong enough to do the job for fear of alienating powerful constituents and other interest groups. Congress instead leaves that harder task to the agencies and the courts. Professor John Dwyer referred to this as the "pathology of symbolic legislation":

> Most regulatory statutes instruct agencies to balance competing concerns in setting standards. Some regulatory statutes, however, impose short deadlines and stringent standard-setting criteria that are designed to address a single, overriding concern to the exclusion of other factors. Typically addressed to exotic and particularly dreaded health threats, this type of legislation reflects the public's urgent desire to avoid such risks. . . . The programs mandated by such legislation are more symbolic than functional. Frequently, the legislature has failed to address the administrative and political constraints that will block implementation of the statute. By enacting this type of statute, legislators reap the political benefits of voting for "health and the environment" and against "trading lives for dollars," and successfully sidestep the difficult policy choices that must be made in regulating public health and the environment. Thus, while the statute, literally read, promises a risk-free environment, the hard issues involved in defining acceptable risk are passed on to the regulatory agency or to the courts. The actual regulatory program takes shape only after additional legislative, administrative, or judicial developments that transform symbolic guarantees into enforceable standards.
>
> The enactment of symbolic legislation reflects a breakdown of the legislative policymaking machinery, a system that all too frequently addresses real social problems in an unrealistic fashion. It also creates a dilemma for regulators and judges. While they generally are reluctant to usurp the legislature's policymaking prerogatives by substituting their own version of appropriate public policy, they also are loath to implement and enforce a statute whose costs are grossly disproportionate to its benefits. The critical issue, then, is whether and how the agency or court should take the initiative to transform symbolic legislation into a functional regulatory program.

Believing that it would be irresponsible and politically mad to interpret and implement symbolic statutory provisions literally, the agency's usual response is to resist implementation. Although an agency may experiment with interpretations that moderate the stringent statutory standard-setting criteria, it will implement its reformulation slowly in order to delay judicial review. As a result, the agency adopts very few standards.

The most significant problem with symbolic legislation, however, is not delay; it is the resulting distortions in the regulatory process. Symbolic legislation hobbles the regulatory process by polarizing public discussion in agency proceedings and legislative hearings. Environmental groups take the legislation's promise of a risk-free environment at face value and tend to refuse to compromise the "rights" inherent in such promises. Industry fears that regulators will implement the statute literally and, consequently, vigorously opposes the regulatory process at every stage. By making promises that cannot be kept, and by leaving no middle ground for accommodation, the legislature makes it more difficult to reach a political compromise (either in the agency or the legislature) that would produce a functional regulatory program.

John P. Dwyer, *The Pathology of Symbolic Legislation*, 17 Ecol. L.Q. 233 (1990). *See also* David Schoenbrod, *Goals Statutes or Rules Statutes: The Case of the Clean Air Act*, 30 U.C.L.A. L. Rev. 740 (1983).

2. The Clean Air Act

Compare the lofty aspirations Congress articulated in the Clean Water Act (restoring chemical, physical, and biological integrity; zero discharge of pollutants; no toxics in toxic amounts) with the one major substantive goal stated in the Clean Air Act:

The purposes of this subchapter are —
(1) to protect and enhance the quality of the Nation's air resources so as to promote the public health and welfare and the productive capacity of its population;. . . .

42 U.S.C. §7401(b).

NOTES AND QUESTIONS ON CLEAN AIR ACT GOALS

1. *Compare with Clean Water Act.* Is this goal as specific and ambitious as the goals stated in the Clean Water Act? Is the language more or less protective of human health and the environment? Why are the goals different?

2. *Balance?* What is Congress' principal focus here? Does this provision suggest that Congress meant to balance costs and benefits, or does it instead omit economics from the statutory purposes?

3. *Missing goals.* In some of the nation's most important environmental statutes, Congress included no statement of statutory objectives, goals or policies. Key examples include the Superfund statute (formally known as the Comprehensive Environmental Response, Compensation, and Liability Act (CERCLA)), 42 U.S.C. §§9601 *et seq.*, which governs the cleanup of hazardous waste sites and seeks to prevent future such sites; the Safe Drinking Water Act, 42 U.S.C. §§300f to 300j-26, which governs the safety of water supplies; and FIFRA, governing the manufacture, sale, and use of pesticides. For these laws, how should agencies and courts determine Congress' intent?

3. The Toxic Substances Control Act

The Toxic Substances Control Act (TSCA) requires EPA to evaluate, and to regulate as appropriate, the manufacture of new chemicals that may pose risks to human health and the environment. Read TSCA's statement of "Findings, Policy, and Intent of Congress":

(a) Findings
The Congress finds that —
(1) human beings and the environment are being exposed each year to a large number of chemical substances and mixtures;
(2) among the many chemical substances and mixtures which are constantly being developed and produced, there are some whose manufacture, processing, distribution in commerce, use, or disposal may present an unreasonable risk of injury to health or the environment; . . . .
(b) Policy
It is the policy of the United States that —
(1) adequate data should be developed with respect to the effect of chemical substances and mixtures on health and the environment and that the development of such data should be the responsibility of those who manufacture and those who process such chemical substances and mixtures;
(2) adequate authority should exist to regulate chemical substances and mixtures which present an unreasonable risk of injury to health or the environment, and to take action with respect to chemical substances and mixtures which are imminent hazards; and
(3) authority over chemical substances and mixtures should be exercised in such a manner as not to impede unduly or create unnecessary

economic barriers to technological innovation while fulfilling the primary purpose of this chapter to assure that such innovation and commerce in such chemical substances and mixtures do not present an unreasonable risk of injury to health or the environment.

(c) Intent of Congress

It is the intent of Congress that the Administrator shall carry out this chapter in a reasonable and prudent manner, and that the Administrator shall consider the environmental, economic, and social impact of any action the Administrator takes or proposes to take under this chapter.

15 U.S.C. §2601.

NOTES AND QUESTIONS ON TOXIC SUBSTANCES CONTROL ACT

1. *Information.* Clearly, one problem Congress sought to address in enacting TSCA was that large numbers of new, potentially toxic chemicals (such as PFOA) were being invented, manufactured, and used without adequate information on their potential impacts to human health and the environment. (Rachel Carson identified this problem in *Silent Spring.*) Does this make better information *per se* a statutory "goal"?

2. *Unreasonable risk.* Congress uses the phrase "unreasonable risk of injury to health or the environment" in subsections (a)(2) and (b)(2). Is some form of balancing of risk against product benefits necessary to determine what level of risk is "unreasonable," or can that decision be made purely as a matter of public health and environmental policy?

3. *Product innovation.* In subsection (b)(3), Congress expressed concern about preserving "technological innovation" while still protecting human health and the environment. How does Congress appear to strike that "balance" between industrial and commercial innovation and environmental protection?

4. *Why different goals here?* Assuming that Congress adopted a balancing approach in TSCA, as opposed to a more absolutist approach in the Clean Air Act and the Clean Water Act, what might explain that difference? Note that the Clean Air Act and Clean Water Act regulate waste byproducts generated while producing or using goods and services, while TSCA authorizes EPA to ban or otherwise limit the manufacturing or use of chemical substances. (The same is true for the Federal Insecticide, Fungicide and Rodenticide Act (FIFRA), 7 U.S.C. §§136 *et seq.*, which governs potentially dangerous chemicals used to kill insects, weeds, and rodents.)

4. The Resource Conservation and Recovery Act

The Solid Waste Disposal Act (more commonly known as the Resource Conservation and Recovery Act (RCRA), after the name of the 1976 amendments to that statute), establishes a comprehensive program for the regulation of solid and hazardous wastes. In section 1003 of the Act, Congress articulated two statutory objectives, a list of ways to achieve those objectives, and a statement of national policy. The relevant provisions follow:

(a) Objectives
The objectives of this chapter are to promote the protection of health and the environment and to conserve valuable material and energy resources by . . . .

(3) prohibiting future open dumping on the land and requiring the conversion of existing open dumps to facilities which do not pose a danger to the environment or to health;

(4) assuring that hazardous waste management practices are conducted in a manner which protects human health and the environment;

(5) requiring that hazardous waste be properly managed in the first instance thereby reducing the need for corrective action at a future date;

(6) minimizing the generation of hazardous waste and the land disposal of hazardous waste by encouraging process substitution, materials recovery, properly conducted recycling and reuse, and treatment; . . . .

(b) National policy
The Congress hereby declares it to be the national policy of the United States that, wherever feasible, the generation of hazardous waste is to be reduced or eliminated as expeditiously as possible. Waste that is nevertheless generated should be treated, stored, or disposed of so as to minimize the present and future threat to human health and the environment.

42 U.S.C. §6902.

NOTES AND QUESTIONS ON RESOURCE CONSERVATION AND RECOVERY ACT

1. *Health and environmental protection.* Like the Clean Air Act and the Clean Water Act, RCRA begins by proclaiming the objective "to promote the

protection of health and the environment . . . . " Based on the specific methods listed in the balance of section 1003(a), and the "national policy" articulated in section 1003(b), is this statute more or less protective of health and the environment than the Clean Water Act? The Clean Air Act? TSCA?

2. *Prevention.* The word "prevention" is included twice in the statement of goals in the Clean Air Act, but is that concept addressed more rigorously in the RCRA objectives and policy? Is "prevention" a statutory "goal," or a mechanism to attain the statutory goals?

3. *Conflicting objectives?* In the opening sentence of RCRA, Congress asserts an objective "to conserve valuable material and energy resources . . . . " Read together with the remaining language of section 1003, is the primary goal of this statute to protect human health and the environment, to reduce or eliminate the generation of solid and hazardous waste, or to promote the recycling of waste and the accompanying recovery of usable materials from that waste? Is there an apparent conflict between those three goals, or are they entirely consistent?

5. The National Environmental Policy Act

The National Environmental Policy Act (NEPA), enacted by Congress in 1969 and signed into law by President Nixon on the first day of the new decade, was the first of the "modern" environmental statutes. The best-known provision of this law, indeed one of the few aspects of modern environmental law that can be said to approach the common knowledge of the lay public, requires "environmental impact statements" in advance of major federal actions that may affect the quality of the environment (an information-generating process addressed in more detail in Chapter 10). Perhaps because it focused on environmental quality generally rather than on a particular problem (such as air or water pollution), the goals set forth in NEPA's opening sections are possibly the broadest of any of the nation's environmental laws. Section 2, entitled "Congressional declaration of purpose," provides:

> The purposes of this chapter are: To declare a national policy which will encourage productive and enjoyable harmony between man and his environment; to promote efforts which will prevent or eliminate damage to the environment and biosphere and stimulate the health and welfare of man; to enrich the understanding of the ecological systems and natural resources important to the Nation; and to establish a Council on Environmental Quality.

43 U.S.C. §4321. Now consider the far more detailed "declaration of national environmental policy" included in section 101 of NEPA:

> (a) The Congress, recognizing the profound impact of man's activity on the interrelations of all components of the natural environment,

particularly the profound influences of population growth, high-density urbanization, industrial expansion, resource exploitation, and new and expanding technological advances and recognizing further the critical importance of restoring and maintaining environmental quality to the overall welfare and development of man, declares that it is the continuing policy of the Federal Government, in cooperation with State and local governments, and other concerned public and private organizations, to use all practicable means and measures, including financial and technical assistance, in a manner calculated to foster and promote the general welfare, to create and maintain conditions under which man and nature can exist in productive harmony, and fulfill the social, economic, and other requirements of present and future generations of Americans.

(b) In order to carry out the policy set forth in this chapter, it is the continuing responsibility of the Federal Government to use all practicable means, consistent with other essential considerations of national policy, to improve and coordinate Federal plans, functions, programs, and resources to the end that the Nation may —

(1) fulfill the responsibilities of each generation as trustee of the environment for succeeding generations;

(2) assure for all Americans safe, healthful, productive, and esthetically and culturally pleasing surroundings;

(3) attain the widest range of beneficial uses of the environment without degradation, risk to health or safety, or other undesirable and unintended consequences;

(4) preserve important historic, cultural, and natural aspects of our national heritage, and maintain, wherever possible, an environment which supports diversity and variety of individual choice;

(5) achieve a balance between population and resource use which will permit high standards of living and a wide sharing of life's amenities; and

(6) enhance the quality of renewable resources and approach the maximum attainable recycling of depletable resources.

(c) The Congress recognizes that each person should enjoy a healthful environment and that each person has a responsibility to contribute to the preservation and enhancement of the environment.

43 U.S.C. §4331.

NOTES AND QUESTIONS ON NATIONAL ENVIRONMENTAL POLICY ACT

1. *Section 2.* What environmental and other values did Congress seek to promote in section 2 of NEPA? In seeking "harmony between man and his environment," does Congress mean that people should achieve harmony by

minimizing their impact on the nonhuman physical and biological environment, or does the term "harmony" suggest a balance between human needs and environmental quality?

2. *Section 101.* What additional environmental values are added in section 101 of NEPA? Does the "assurance" in subsection (b)(2), along with the "recognition" in subsection(c), create any legal "right" to a clean environment?

3. *Information versus policy; substance versus procedure.* Compare the "purpose" in section 2 and the "policy" articulated in section 101(a) with the opening language in section 102:

> The Congress authorizes and directs that, to the fullest extent possible: (1) the policies, regulations, and public laws of the United States shall be interpreted and administered in accordance with the policies set forth in this chapter, and (2) all agencies of the Federal Government shall —

43 U.S.C. §4332. (The specific requirements of this pivotal section of NEPA will be addressed in Chapter 10.) What words distinguish this section from the previous two? In the first decade of NEPA implementation, courts debated whether Congress intended the law to have substantive force, or merely to establish procedures for better-informed environmental decision making. In Calvert Cliffs Coordinating Committee v. Atomic Energy Commission, 449 F.2d 1109 (D.C. Cir. 1971), Judge Skelly Wright held that NEPA establishes an environmental balancing process:

> We conclude, then, that Section 102 of NEPA mandates a particular sort of careful and informed decisionmaking process and creates judicially enforceable duties. The reviewing courts probably cannot reverse a substantive decision on its merits, under Section 101, unless it be shown that the actual balance of costs and benefits that was struck was arbitrary or clearly gave insufficient weight to environmental values. But if the decision was reached procedurally without individualized consideration and balancing of environmental factors — conducted fully and in good faith — it is the responsibility of the courts to reverse. As one District Court has said of Section 102 requirements: "It is hard to imagine a clearer or stronger mandate to the Courts."

The Supreme Court eventually ruled that NEPA imposes procedural but not substantive duties on federal agencies. Early in the history of NEPA, at least some Supreme Court Justices leaned in the direction of affording NEPA's substantive goals and policies enforceable legal effect: "NEPA is more than a technical statute of administrative procedure. It is a commitment to the preservation of our natural environment." Aberdeen & Rockfish R.R. Co. v. Students Challenging Regulatory Agency Procedures (SCRAP II), 422 U.S. 289, 331 (1975) (Douglas, J., dissenting). *See also,* United States v. Students Challenging Regulatory Agency Procedures (SCRAP I), 412 U.S. 669, 699–700 (1975) (Douglas, J., dissenting); *id.* at 731–732 (Marshall, J., dissenting). In Vermont Yankee Nuclear Power Corporation v. Natural Resources Defense Council, however, the Court suggested: "NEPA does set forth significant substantive goals for the Nation, but its mandate to the agencies is essentially procedural." 435 U.S. 519, 558 (1978). Two years later, the Court reversed a decision by the Second Circuit invalidating an agency's substantive decision on NEPA grounds: "[I]n the present case there is no doubt that [the agency] considered the environmental consequences of its decision to designate the proposed site for low-income housing. NEPA requires no more." Strycker's Bay Neighborhood Council, Inc. v. Karlen, 444 U.S. 223 (1980). Nearly another decade passed, however, before the Court hammered the nail in the coffin of substantive NEPA review, acknowledging that while Congress did announce substantive policy goals in NEPA, they are implemented through purely procedural devices. Robertson v. Methow Valley Citizens Council, 490 U.S. 332, 350 (1989) (excerpted in Chapter 10). If NEPA requires only better informed decisions, rather than particular environmental results, is the "goal" of NEPA better information, as opposed to the environmental values articulated in section 101?

4. *Lynton Caldwell.* At least one knowledgeable commentator, who was personally involved in the creation of NEPA, disagrees strongly with the Supreme Court's conclusion that Congress intended NEPA to impose only procedural obligations. Professor Lynton Caldwell, who worked closely with Senator Henry Jackson in drafting the legislation, believes that Congress did intend NEPA to have substantive as well as procedural import:

> Few statutes of the United States are intrinsically more important and less understood that is the National Environmental Policy Act of 1969. This comprehensive legislation, the first of its kind to be adopted by any national government, and now widely emulated throughout the world, has achieved notable results, yet its basic intent has not been fully achieved. Its purpose and declared principles have not been thoroughly internalized in the assumptions and practices of American government. Nevertheless, there appears to be a growing consensus among the American people that environmental quality is a public value, and that development of the economy does not require a trade-off between environmental quality and economic well-being. Voluntary compliance with NEPA principles may one day become standard policy and procedure for government and business; meanwhile, it is in the national interest to understand the historical developments that led to NEPA and the subsequent course of its implementation. There have been numerous and often contradictory evaluations of its intent and effectiveness.
>
> The legislative history of NEPA and the policy concepts it declared are more extensive and accessible than some of its critics recognize. Treating NEPA as if it were a special application of the Administrative Procedures Act of 1946 misreads its principal purpose and misdirects criticism. NEPA declares public values and directs policy, but it is not "regulatory" in the ordinary sense. A decade of thought, advocacy, and negotiation in and out of Congress preceded the legislation of 1969. Dissatisfaction with NEPA and its implementing institution — the Council on Environmental Quality — should not be directed

against this innovative and well-considered statute, but rather toward those authorities who have not seriously attempted to understand its purpose, to reinforce its administration, or to support its intent. This does not imply that a more explicit and extended revision of NEPA could never be enacted. But it cannot be successfully undertaken until a critical mass of the voting public acquiesces.

Through the judicially enforceable process of impact analysis, NEPA has significantly modified the environmental behavior of Federal agencies and, indirectly, of State and local governments and private undertakings. Relative to many other statutory policies, NEPA must be accounted an important success. But implementation of the substantive principles of national policy declared in NEPA requires a degree of political will not yet evident in the Congress or the White House. The public-at-large, which has received little help in understanding the purpose of the Act or the requirements for its implementation, has not audibly demanded that NEPA be put into effect.

A quarter-century, however, is a very short time for a new aspect of public policy — the environment — to attain the importance and priority accorded such century-old concerns as taxation, defense, education, civil liberties, and the economy. The goals declared in NEPA are as valid today as they were in 1969. Indeed, perhaps more so, as the Earth and its biosphere are stressed by human demands to a degree that has no precedent. But "environment" in its full dimensions is not easily comprehended. Human perceptions are culturally and physically limited, but science has been extending environmental horizons from the cosmic to the microcosmic. Even so, the word "environment" does not yet carry to most people the scope, complexity, or dynamic of its true dimensions.

If NEPA continues to be interpreted narrowly and exclusively by the courts, more compelling legislation may be required. A statutory amendment may be necessary to give its substantive provisions operative legal status. . . .

LYNTON KEITH CALDWELL, THE NATIONAL ENVIRONMENTAL POLICY ACT: AN AGENDA FOR THE FUTURE 23-24 (1998). Professor Caldwell obviously is disappointed that the substantive aspects of NEPA have not been implemented properly. Who does he seem to blame for this failure? Administrative agencies? The courts? The public at large?

II

GOALS FOR PARTICULAR REGULATIONS

You have seen that statutes have general goals (Chapter 4). To meet these goals, Congress has created complex statutory schemes that require numerous particular regulatory decisions. Congress often delegates many of these decisions to administrative agencies (recall Chapter 3). In detailed statutory provisions, Congress establishes the criteria that govern these decisions. One can think of these criteria as establishing goals governing particular regulations, for they give agencies guidance as to how strict a regulation should be, in other words, guidance about how much pollution reduction to demand. These policies may contribute to meeting statutory goals, even when they do not precisely track statutory goals.

These statutory provisions list a wide variety of considerations for agencies to take into account in setting standards. But a fairly limited set of concepts underlies these provisions. This part begins with a chapter on "effects-based" standards. These standards seek to protect public or the environment adequately, and stringency decisions taken under these provisions depend upon estimates of the effects of pollution on the environment and health and agency views about how much protection meets particular statutory criteria defining health and environmental goals. The next chapter, Chapter 6, addresses technology-based standards, standards set by assessing the capabilities of technology. Chapter 7 addresses cost-benefit approaches, which involves comparing the costs of various levels of regulation to the benefits various potential regulations might bring to help determine levels of stringency. As you read these materials, ask yourself which approach is best. And try to get a sense for the particular problems and dilemmas the various approaches create for regulatory agencies.

5

Effects-Based Standards

One potential answer to the question of what the goal of environmental law should be is that the basic goal of environmental statutes should be to control or prevent the adverse *effects* of pollution and other sources of environmental harm. This, you might think, seems incredibly obvious. What other purpose is there to environmental law if not to control or prevent adverse environmental effects? Establishing environmental standards on the basis of adverse effects, however, implies far more than is immediately apparent.

All environmental standards seek to reduce adverse effects in some way. Effects-based environmental standards, often referred to as "health-based" or "environment-based" standards, do so by expressly determining the level of environmental quality deemed acceptable as a goal. (This could be viewed from the opposite perspective as the residual level of environmental harm permitted.) In establishing effects-based standards, we ask what level of environmental quality is adequate, or necessary, to protect health or environmental resources. The difficult part is deciding what is "adequate." That question is answered in part by the language of particular statutes, and in part by the manner in which the statutes are interpreted and administered by agencies and courts.

In Section A, we introduce the basic idea of effects-based standards, the threshold for deciding when such standards are needed, and the degree to which a precautionary as opposed to a reactive approach is used in writing those standards. One kind of effects-based standard, known as an "ambient standard," dictates acceptable levels of environmental quality in the ambient environment, such as the air we breathe or the water we use in rivers for swimming or drinking. Key examples are the National Ambient Air Quality Standards promulgated by EPA under the Clean Air Act, and water quality standards generally developed by states under the Clean Water Act. Rather than focusing upon individual pollution sources, or even categories of sources, ambient standards govern aggregate impacts from all of the sources that contribute to a particular kind of pollution in a defined geographic region (an airshed or a stretch of river, for example). We explore those kinds of standards in Section B of this chapter. Alternatively, effects-based standards can control the health or environmental impacts of particular pollution sources or categories of sources (automobiles, for example). "Output standards" or "release standards" define how much pollution a particular type of source may release into the environment, rather than how dirty the environmental medium may become. While output or release standards from individual sources can also be based on other concepts, such as the best available control technology approach discussed in Chapter 6, in Section C of this chapter we describe output or release standards, the stringency of which is determined by reference to health and environmental effects.

A. DEFINING "EFFECTS" — CONCEPTS OF RISK AND PRECAUTION

The following case addresses EPA's authority under section 211(c) of the Clean Air Act either to control, or to prohibit altogether, motor vehicle fuels or fuel additives. Section 211 is a very long, complex provision, which Congress amended several times after this case was decided. To understand this case, you only need to read the portions of the statute included in the case excerpt. To put the case in context, you should understand that: (1) automobiles and other motor vehicles are one of the major sources of air pollution nationally; (2) the manner in which gasoline and other fuels are manufactured can contribute significantly to that pollution; and (3) the use of lead as a fuel additive was the principle gasoline component of concern when Congress first adopted this section of the law. Therefore, in addition to regulating tailpipe emissions from cars and trucks directly, Congress authorized EPA to regulate motor vehicle fuels that contribute to those emissions. In section 211, Congress authorized EPA to regulate fuel additives in two separate circumstances. In the provision not at issue in this case, EPA could prohibit or regulate fuels or fuel additives that would interfere with the new technologies designed to control tailpipe emissions (especially catalytic converters). Under the subsection at issue here, EPA could regulate fuels or fuel components which, at the time this case was decided, the Administrator of EPA found "will endanger the public health or welfare. . . . " In reading this case, focus on the threshold of harm, i.e., what "effects" were necessary to justify EPA regulation under this provision, and with what degree of certainty.

Ethyl Corporation v. Environmental Protection Agency

541 F.2d 1 (D.C. Cir. 1976) (en banc)

J. SKELLY WRIGHT, CIRCUIT JUDGE.

[Environmental agencies] must deal with predictions and uncertainty, with developing evidence, with conflicting evidence, and, sometimes, with little or no evidence at all. Today we address the scope of the power delegated one such watchdog, the Environmental Protection Agency (EPA). We must determine the certainty required by the Clean Air Act before EPA may act to protect the health of our populace from the lead particulate emissions of automobiles.

Section 211(c)(1)(A) of the Clean Air Act authorizes the Administrator of EPA to regulate gasoline additives whose emission products "will endanger the public health or welfare. . . . " Acting pursuant to that power, the Administrator, after notice and comment, determined that the automotive emissions caused by leaded gasoline present "a significant risk of harm" to the public health. Accordingly, he promulgated regulations that reduce, in step-wise fashion, the lead content of leaded gasoline. We must decide whether the Administrator properly interpreted the meaning of Section 211(c)(1)(A) and the scope of his power thereunder, and, if so, whether the evidence adduced at the rule-making proceeding supports his final determination. Finding in favor of the Administrator on both grounds, and on all other grounds raised by petitioners, we affirm his determination.

I. The Facts, The Statute, The Proceedings, And The Regulations

Hard on the introduction of the first gasoline-powered automobiles came the discovery that lead "antiknock" compounds, when added to gasoline, dramatically increase the fuel's octane rating. Increased octane allows for higher compression engines, which operate with greater efficiency. Since 1923 antiknocks have been regularly added to gasoline, and a large industry has developed to supply those compounds. Today, approximately 90 percent of motor gasoline manufactured in the United States contains lead additives, even though most 1975 and 1976 model automobiles are equipped with catalytic converters, which require lead-free gasoline. From the beginning, however, scientists have questioned whether the addition of lead to gasoline, and its consequent diffusion into the atmosphere from the automobile emission, poses a danger to the public health. As use of automobiles, and emission of lead particulates, has accelerated in the last quarter century, this concern has mounted. The reasons for concern are obvious (and essentially undisputed by petitioners): (1) lead in high concentrations in the body is toxic; (2) lead can be absorbed into the body from the ambient air; and (3) lead particulate emissions from gasoline engines account for approximately 90 percent of the lead in our air. Despite these apparent reasons for concern, hard proof of any danger caused by lead automotive emissions has been hard to come by. Part of the reason for this lies in the multiple sources of human exposure to lead.

Lead is an ubiquitous element. It is found in the land, in the sea, in plants, in animals, and, ultimately, in humans. Traces of lead ranging from 10 to 40 micrograms per 100 grams of blood (10-40 μg/100g) are found in everyone, including those living in environments with almost no atmospheric lead. Despite its universal presence, however, lead serves no known purpose in the human body, and at higher concentrations is toxic, causing anemia, severe intestinal cramps, paralysis of nerves, fatigue, and even death. Clinical symptoms of lead poisoning appear at blood lead levels of 80-100 μg or higher, and symptomatic lead poisoning may appear at levels of 50-60 μg, particularly in the presence of anemia.

Human body lead comes from three major sources. In most people, the largest source is the diet. . . . This daily intake, which may be highly variable depending on individual diets, is generally regarded as, for all practical purposes, uncontrollable.

A second major source of the body's lead burden, at least among urban children, is regarded as controllable, although effective control may be both difficult and expensive to achieve. Ingestion of lead paint by children with pica (the abnormal ingestion of non-food substances, a relatively common trait in pre-school children, particular ages 1-3) is generally regarded as "the principal environmental source in cases of severe acute lead poisoning in young children." . . .

The last remaining major source of lead exposure for humans is the ambient air. This source is easily the most controllable, since approximately 90 percent of lead in the air comes from automobile emissions, and can be simply eliminated by removing lead from gasoline. While the extent to which such lead actually enters the body is vigorously contested by petitioners and lies at the heart of this appeal, all parties agree that, to some extent at least, airborne lead can be absorbed through the lungs as a person breathes lead-contaminated air and that it can be eaten by children with pica after larger lead particles fall to the ground and mix with dust. Once the lead is in the body, however, its source becomes irrelevant; all lead in the bloodstream, from whatever source, is essentially fungible. Thus so long as there are multiple sources of lead exposure it is virtually impossible to isolate one source and determine its particular effect on the body. The effect of any one source is meaningful only in cumulative terms.

The multiple sources of human exposure to lead explain in part why it has been difficult to pinpoint automobile lead emissions as a danger to public health. Obviously, any danger is caused only by the additive effect of lead emissions on the other, largely uncontrollable, sources of lead. For years the lead antiknock industry has refused to accept the developing evidence that lead emissions contribute significantly to the total human lead body burden. In the

Clean Air Act Amendments of 1970, however, Congress finally set up a legal mechanism by which that evidence could be weighed in a more objective tribunal. It gave the newly-created EPA authority to control or prohibit the sale or manufacture of any fuel additive whose emission products "will endanger the public health or welfare. . . . " 42 U.S.C. §1857f–6c(c)(1)(A) (1970). It is beyond question that the fuel additive Congress had in mind was lead. . . .

On October 28, 1973 . . . this court ordered EPA to reach within 30 days a final decision on whether lead additives should be regulated for health reasons. . . . Under the final regulations, lead in all gasoline would be reduced over a five-year period to an average of 0.5 grams per gallon.

Petitioners, various manufacturers of lead additives and refiners of gasoline, appealed the promulgation of low-lead regulations to this court under Section 307 of the Clean Air Act. . . .

The regulations are challenged by petitioners on a variety of grounds, all of which will be addressed below. Their primary claims, and the ones on which the division majority based its reversal, are that the Administrator misinterpreted the statutory standard of "will endanger" and that his application of that standard is without support in the evidence and arbitrary and capricious.

II. The Statutory Requirements

Under Section 211(c)(1)(A) the Administrator may, on the basis of all the information available to him, promulgate regulations that control or prohibit the manufacture, introduction into commerce, offering for sale, or sale of any fuel or fuel additive for use in a motor vehicle or motor vehicle engine (A) if any emission products of such fuel or fuel additive will endanger the public health or welfare. . . . The Administrator cannot act under Section 211(c)(1)(A), however, until after "consideration of all relevant medical and scientific evidence available to him, including consideration of other technologically or economically feasible means of achieving emission standards under (Section 202)." Section 211(c)(2)(A). Section 202 of the Act allows the Administrator to set standards for emission of pollutants from automobiles (as opposed to standards for the composition of the gasoline that produces the emissions), and is thus the preferred although not the mandatory alternative under the statutory scheme, presumably because it minimizes Agency interference with manufacturer prerogatives.[14]

The Administrator is also required, before prohibiting a fuel or fuel additive under Section 211(c)(1)(A), to find, and publish the finding, that in

----

14. When EPA acts under §211(c)(1)(A) it is essentially telling manufacturers how to make their fuels, a task Congress felt the Agency should enter upon only with trepidation. See e.g., 116 Cong.Rec. 32920 (1970) (remarks of Sen. Baker); id. at 19229 (remarks of Reps. Rogers & Waggoner). On the other hand, when the Agency acts under §202, it is only mandating an end product regulated emissions. The method for achieving the required result is entirely in the hands of the manufacturers.

his judgment any fuel or fuel additive likely to replace the prohibited one will not "endanger the public health or welfare to the same or greater degree. . . . " Section 211(c)(2)(C). It is significant that this is the only conclusion the Administrator is expressly required to "find" before regulating a fuel or fuel additive for health reasons.

A. *The Threshold Determination*

In making his threshold determination that lead particulate emissions from motor vehicles "will endanger the public health or welfare," the Administrator provided his interpretation of the statutory language by couching his conclusion in these words: such emissions "present a significant risk of harm to the health of urban populations, particularly to the health of city children." By way of further interpretation, he added that it was his view that the statutory language . . . does not require a determination that automobile emissions alone create the endangerment on which controls may be based. Rather, the Administrator believes that in providing this authority, the Congress was aware that the public's exposure to harmful substances results from a number of sources which may have varying degrees of susceptibility to control. It is petitioners' first claim of error that the Administrator has erroneously interpreted Section 211(c)(1)(A) by not sufficiently appreciating the rigor demanded by Congress in establishing the "will endanger" standard. Therefore, petitioners argue, the Administrator's action is "short of statutory right," in violation of Section 10(e)(2)(C) of the Administrative Procedure Act (APA).

Petitioners argue that the "will endanger" standard requires a high quantum of factual proof, proof of actual harm rather than of a "significant risk of harm." Since, according to petitioners, regulation under Section 211(c)(1)(A) must be premised upon factual proof of actual harm, the Administrator has, in their view, no power to assess risks or make policy judgments in deciding to regulate lead additives. Moreover, petitioners argue, regulation must be based on the danger presented by lead additives "in and of themselves," so it is improper to consider, as the Administrator did, the cumulative impact of lead additives on all other sources of human exposure to lead. We have considered these arguments with care and find them to be without merit. It is our view that the Administrator's interpretation of the standard is the correct one.

1. The Precautionary Nature of "Will Endanger."

Simply as a matter of plain meaning, we have difficulty crediting petitioners' reading of the "will endanger" standard. The meaning of "endanger" is not disputed. Case law and dictionary definition agree that endanger means something less than actual harm.[17] When one is endangered, harm is

---

17. It is linguistically clear, of course, that one can be "endangered" without actually being harmed. Nonetheless, some risk of harm is necessary. State v. Fine, 324 Mo. 194, 23

threatened; no actual injury need ever occur. Thus, for example, a town may be "endangered" by a threatening plague or hurricane and yet emerge from the danger completely unscathed. A statute allowing for regulation in the face of danger is, necessarily, a precautionary statute. Regulatory action may be taken before the threatened harm occurs; indeed, the very existence of such precautionary legislation would seem to demand that regulatory action precede, and, optimally, prevent, the perceived threat. As should be apparent, the "will endanger" language of Section 211(c)(1)(A) makes it such a precautionary statute.

The Administrator read it as such, interpreting "will endanger" to mean "presents a significant risk of harm." We agree with the Administrator's interpretation. . . .

Perhaps because it realized that the above interpretation was the only possible reading of the statutory language, petitioner Ethyl addresses this interpretation and argues that even if actual harm is not required for action under Section 211(c)(1)(A), the occurrence of the threatened harm must be "probable" before regulation is justified. While the dictionary admittedly settles on "probable" as its measure of danger, we believe a more sophisticated case-by-case analysis is appropriate. Danger, the Administrator recognized, is not set by a fixed probability of harm, but rather is composed of reciprocal elements of risk and harm, or probability and severity. Cf. Carolina Environmental Study Group v. United States, 166 U.S.App.D.C. 416, 419, 510 F.2d 796, 799 (1975); Reserve Mining Co. v. EPA, supra, 514 F.2d at 519-520. That is to say, the public health may properly be found endangered both by a lesser risk of a greater harm and by a greater risk of a lesser harm.[32] Danger depends upon the relation between the risk and harm presented by each case, and cannot legitimately be pegged to "probable" harm, regardless of whether that harm be great or small. As the Eighth Circuit found in Reserve Mining, these concepts "necessarily must apply in a determination of whether any relief should be given in cases of this kind in which proof with certainty is impossible." 514 F.2d at 520. . . .

S.W.2d 7, 9 (1929). Webster defines "endanger" as "to bring into danger or peril of *probable* harm or loss." Webster's Third New International Dictionary 748 (1961) (emphasis added).

32. This proposition must be confined to reasonable limits, however. In Carolina Environmental Study Group v. United States, 166 U.S.App.D.C. 416, 510 F.2d 796 (1975), a division of this court found the possibility of a Class 9 nuclear reactor disaster, a disaster of ultimate severity and horrible consequences, to be so low that the Atomic Energy Commission's minimal consideration of the effects of such a disaster in an environmental impact statement prepared for a new reactor was sufficient. Likewise, even the absolute certainty of de minimis harm might not justify government action. Under §211 the threatened harm must be sufficiently significant to justify health-based regulation of national impact. Ultimately, of course, whether a particular combination of slight risk and great harm, or great risk and slight harm, constitutes a danger must depend on the facts of each case.

NOTES AND QUESTIONS ON *ETHYL CORPORATION*

1. *Uncertainty.* Identify all of the components of uncertainty that complicated EPA's decision and ultimately caused the industry to challenge EPA's finding of "endangerment." Then, explain how EPA and the court's interpretation of the statutory language justified the regulation of lead in motor vehicle fuels notwithstanding this uncertainty.

2. *Precautionary principle.* The Court refers to the "precautionary nature" of the statutory language. A similarly phrased "precautionary principle" has been adopted as one of the bedrock principles of international environmental law. *See* Rio Declaration on Environment and Development, U.N. Conference on Environment and Development, U.N. Doc. A/CONF.151/5/Rev.1, 31 I.L.M. 874 (1992). How does the CAA statutory approach compare with the common law standards studied in Chapter 3 under which this issue would be addressed?

3. *Reserve Mining and the Clean Water Act.* EPA's and the Court's precautionary interpretation of the "will endanger" standard was also supported in part by the Eighth Circuit's holding in Reserve Mining Co. v. EPA, 514 F.2d 492 (8th Cir. 1975) (en banc). *Reserve Mining* involved EPA's request, under the statutory predecessor to the current Clean Water Act, for an injunction against the continued discharge of mine tailings that contained asbestos fibers into waters of Lake Superior used as public water supply for the City of Duluth, Minnesota. As in *Ethyl Corp.*, considerable scientific uncertainty surrounded the issue of whether the fibers caused demonstrable harm to public health. While the Eighth Circuit held that the degree of scientific uncertainty should be considered in determining the nature and terms of the injunction, it ruled that uncertainty does not preclude such relief under the language of the statute in effect at the time: "In the context of this environmental legislation, we believe that Congress used the term 'endangering' in a precautionary or preventive sense, and, therefore, evidence of potential harm as well as actual harm comes within the purview of that term." *Id.* at 528. The D.C. Circuit noted in *Ethyl Corp.* that similar provisions of the Clean Air Act and the Clean Water Act, adopted contemporaneously, often are interpreted similarly. 541 F.2d at 17. This is one of many examples. *See also Natural Resources Defense Council, Inc. v. Train,* 510 F.2d 692, 701-702 (D.C. Cir. 1975).

4. *Statutory amendment.* The panel decision preceding the *en banc* opinion presented above struck down the lead rule as contrary to the "will endanger" standard. Ethyl Corp. v. EPA, 7 ERC 1353, 5 Envtl. L. Rep. 20,096 (D.C. Cir. 1975). Congress later amended the relevant statutory language to: "(A) if in the judgment of the Administrator any emission product of such fuel or fuel additive causes, or contributes to, air pollution which may reasonably be anticipated to endanger the public health or welfare." 42 U.S.C. §7545(c)(1)(A). In what

ways does this amendment affect EPA's ability to regulate fuels or fuel additives under this provision?

5. *Health-based trigger.* The Court referred to the standards reviewed in *Ethyl Corp.* as "health-based regulations," apparently to distinguish them from standards adopted under the "sister provision" in section 211(b)(1)(B), which are established to protect the operation of emissions control devices in motor vehicles. This terminology, however, is potentially misleading. It is very important conceptually to distinguish these "health-based regulations," in which the need for regulation is triggered by adverse health effects, from the "health-and-environment-based" ambient standards that will be addressed in the next section of this chapter. EPA evaluated and made findings regarding the potential health effects of leaded gasoline in making the threshold determination that it had authority to adopt the lead phase-out regulation. It did not, however, explicitly tie the "pooled average" levels of lead allowed under the regulation to particular health effects, and did not seek to justify the regulatory level on those grounds. As you read the provisions addressed in the following section, and in the cases interpreting them, make sure you understand the conceptual differences between an effects-based trigger for regulation and an effects-based regulatory level. Also consider the practical implications of that difference in terms of what issues the agency can and cannot consider in writing the rules, and in what information interested parties should include in comments on proposed rules.

B. AMBIENT EFFECTS-BASED STANDARDS

Some effects-based standards define environmental quality goals in the ambient environment. "Ambient" means "surrounding on all sides." In this context, it means setting effects-based standards in the environment at large — such as the air we breathe and the water in rivers and lakes. The most notable examples of ambient environmental standards are the National Ambient Air Quality Standards (NAAQS) promulgated by EPA under the Clean Air Act, and water quality standards (WQS) generally issued by individual states under the Clean Water Act. These two main examples are similar in many respects, but different in others. Read the following two cases, one regarding NAAQS and the other WQS, for two main purposes. First, try to ascertain the major characteristics of ambient effects-based standards. What factors and information can the issuing agencies consider, and what is out of bounds? What is the scope of the standards, and what kinds of environmental harm can they address? Second, in what ways are ambient standards similar or different under the two statutes, and what are the practical implications of those differences?

1.   National Ambient Air Quality Standards

Lead Industries Association, Inc. v. Environmental Protection Agency
647 F.2d 1130 (D.C. Cir. 1980)

J. SKELLY WRIGHT, CHIEF JUDGE.

. . . In the present consolidated cases we are asked to review EPA regulations establishing national ambient air quality standards for lead. These air quality standards prescribe the maximum concentrations of lead that will be permitted in the air of our country. We must decide whether EPA's Administrator acted within the scope of his statutory authority in promulgating these regulations and, if so, whether the evidence adduced at the rulemaking proceeding supports his final determinations. . . .

II.   The Statutory Scheme

The first step toward establishing national ambient air quality standards for a particular pollutant is its addition to a list, compiled by EPA's Administrator, of pollutants that cause or contribute to air pollution "which may reasonably be anticipated to endanger public health or welfare(.)" Section 108(a)(1), 42 U.S.C. §7408(a)(1). Within twelve months of the listing of a pollutant under Section 108(a) the Administrator must issue "air quality criteria" for the pollutant. Section 108 makes it clear that the term "air quality criteria" means something different from the conventional meaning of "criterion"; such "criteria" do not constitute "standards" or "guidelines," but rather refer to a document to be prepared by EPA which is to provide the scientific basis for promulgation of air quality standards for the pollutant. This criteria document must "accurately reflect the latest scientific knowledge useful in indicating the kind and extent of all identifiable effects on public health or welfare which may be expected from the presence of such pollutant in the ambient air, in varying quantities." Section 108(a)(2), 42 U.S.C. §7408(a)(2).

At the same time as he issues air quality criteria for a pollutant, the Administrator must also publish proposed national primary and secondary air quality standards for the pollutant. Section 109(a)(2), 42 U.S.C. §§7409(a)(2). National primary ambient air quality standards are standards "the attainment and maintenance of which in the judgment of the Administrator, based on such criteria and allowing an adequate margin of safety, are requisite to protect the public health." Section 109(b)(1), 42 U.S.C. §7409(b)(1). Secondary air quality standards "specify a level of air quality the attainment and maintenance of which in the judgment of the Administrator, based on such criteria, is requisite to protect the public welfare from any known or anticipated adverse effects associated with the presence of such air pollutant in the ambient air." Section 109(b)(2), 42 U.S.C. §7409(b)(2). Effects on "the public welfare" include "effects on soils, water, crops, vegetation, manmade materials, animals, wildlife, weather, visibility, and climate, damage to and deterioration of property, and hazards to transportation, as well as effects on economic values and on personal comfort and well-being." Section 302(h), 42 U.S.C. §7602(h). The Administrator is required to submit the proposed air quality standards for public comment in a rulemaking proceeding, the procedure for which is prescribed by Section 307(d) of the Act, 42 U.S.C. §7607(d).

Within six months of publication of the proposed standards the Administrator must promulgate final primary and secondary ambient air quality standards for the pollutant. Section 307(d)(10), 42 U.S.C. §7607(d)(10). Once EPA has promulgated national ambient air quality standards, responsibility under the Act shifts from the federal government to the states. Within nine months of promulgation of the standards each state must prepare and submit to EPA for approval a state implementation plan. Section 110(a)(1), 42 U.S.C. §7410(a)(1). These state implementation plans must contain emission limitations and all other measures necessary to attain the primary standards "as expeditiously as practicable," but no later than three years after EPA approval of the plan, and to attain the secondary standards within a reasonable period of time. Section 110(a)(2)(A) & (B), 42 U.S.C. §7410(a)(2)(A) & (B). . . .

III. The Lead Standards Rulemaking Proceedings

As required by statute, EPA's first step toward promulgating air quality standards for lead was to prepare a criteria document. The Lead Criteria Document was the culmination of a process of rigorous scientific and public review, and thus is a comprehensive and thoughtful analysis of the most current scientific information on the subject. . . .

[The opinion summarized the adverse health effects of lead identified in EPA's Criteria Document. Lead levels in blood are measured as micrograms of lead per deciliter of blood (µg Pb/dl). The ambient air quality standards are expressed as micrograms of lead per cubic meter of air (µg Pb/m³). EPA found that people with elevated blood lead (about 40 µg Pb/dl in children and about 50 µg Pb/dl in adults) experienced anemia due to destruction of red blood cells, and due to impaired synthesis of hemoglobin, the protein that carries oxygen in the blood. EPA also identified "subclinical effects" at lower blood levels. Subclinical effects include impairment of various physiological functions, but at levels that do not produce the kinds of symptoms discovered in routine medical examinations. EPA found one such effect, lead-related elevation of erythrocyte protoporphyrin (EP elevation), in children and women is at blood lead levels of 15-20 µg Pb/dl, and 25-30 µg Pb/dl in adult males.]

In addition to examining the health effects of lead exposure, the Criteria Document also discussed other issues critical to the task of setting air quality standards for lead. One of these issues is the relationship between air lead exposure and blood lead levels, a relationship commonly referred to as the air lead/blood lead ratio. . . . [A]ir lead/blood lead ratios fall within a range of 1:1 to 1:2 (μg Pb/m 3 air):(μg Pb/dl blood) at the levels of lead exposure generally encountered by the population, i.e., blood lead levels increase by between 1 and 2 μg Pb/dl of blood for every 1 μg Pb/m 3 of air. (Air lead content is measured in micrograms of lead per cubic meter of air μg Pb/m 3.) The Criteria Document reported that the studies indicate that the ratio for children is at the upper end of this range or even slightly above it.

Finally, the Criteria Document also examined the distribution of blood lead levels throughout the population, concluding that there is a significant variability in individual blood lead responses to any particular level of air lead exposure. . . . [P]reschool-age children and pregnant women are particularly sensitive to lead exposure, the latter mainly because of the risk to the unborn child. . . .

D. The Final Air Quality Standards for Lead

The Administrator promulgated the final air quality standards on October 5, 1978, prescribing national primary and secondary ambient air quality standards for lead of 1.5 μg Pb/m^3, averaged over a calendar quarter. . . . The Administrator . . . focused on two key questions: (1) What is the maximum safe individual blood lead level for children? and (2) what proportion of the target population should be kept below this blood lead level? Addressing the first issue required a review of the health effects of lead exposure discussed in the Criteria Document. The Administrator concluded that, although EP elevation beginning at blood lead levels of 15-20 μg Pb/dl is potentially adverse to the health of children, only when blood lead concentration reaches a level of 30 μg Pb/dl is this effect significant enough to be considered adverse to health. Accordingly, he selected 30 μg Pb/dl as the maximum safe individual blood lead level for children. The Administrator based this choice on three mutually supporting grounds. First, it is at this blood lead level that the first adverse health effect of lead exposure impairment of heme synthesis begins to occur in children. Second, a maximum safe individual blood lead level of 30 μg Pb/dl would allow an adequate margin of safety in protecting children against more serious effects of lead exposure anemia, symptoms of which begin to appear in children at blood lead levels of 40 μg Pb/dl, and central nervous system deficits which start to occur in children at blood lead levels of 50 μg Pb/dl. Third, the Administrator reasoned that the maximum safe individual blood lead level should be no higher than the blood lead level used by the Center for Disease Control in screening children for lead poisoning 30 μg Pb/dl.

Having determined the maximum safe individual blood lead level for the target population, the Administrator next focused on the question of what percentage of children between the ages of 1 and 5 years the standard should attempt to keep below this blood lead level. According to the 1970 census, there are approximately 20 million children under the age of 5 years in the United States, 12 million of them in urban areas and 5 million in inner cities where lead exposure may be especially high. The Administrator concluded that in order to provide an adequate margin of safety, and to protect special high risk sub-groups, the standards should aim at keeping 99.5% of the target population below the maximum safe individual blood lead level of 30 µg Pb/dl. . . . The result was an ambient air quality standard of 1.5 µg Pb/m3. . . .

V. Statutory Authority

The petitioners' first claim is that the Administrator exceeded his authority under the statute by promulgating a primary air quality standard for lead which is more stringent than is necessary to protect the public health because it is designed to protect the public against "sub-clinical" effects which are not harmful to health. According to petitioners, Congress only authorized the Administrator to set primary air quality standards that are aimed at protecting the public against health effects which are known to be clearly harmful. They argue that Congress so limited the Administrator's authority because it was concerned that excessively stringent air quality standards could cause massive economic dislocation.

In developing this argument St. Joe contends that EPA erred by refusing to consider the issues of economic and technological feasibility in setting the air quality standards for lead. St. Joe's claim that the Administrator should have considered these issues is based on the statutory provision directing him to allow an "adequate margin of safety" in setting primary air quality standards. In St. Joe's view, the Administrator must consider the economic impact of the proposed standard on industry and the technological feasibility of compliance by emission sources in determining the appropriate allowance for a margin of safety. St. Joe argues that the Administrator abused his discretion by refusing to consider these factors in determining the appropriate margin of safety for the lead standards, and maintains that the lead air quality standards will have a disastrous economic impact on industrial sources of lead emissions.

This argument is totally without merit. St. Joe is unable to point to anything in either the language of the Act or its legislative history that offers any support for its claim that Congress, by specifying that the Administrator is to allow an "adequate margin of safety" in setting primary air quality standards, thereby required the Administrator to consider economic or technological feasibility. To the contrary, the statute and its legislative history make clear that economic considerations play no part in the promulgation of ambient air quality standards under Section 109.

Where Congress intended the Administrator to be concerned about economic and technological feasibility, it expressly so provided. For example, Section 111 of the Act directs the Administrator to consider economic and technological feasibility in establishing standards of performance for new stationary sources of air pollution based on the best available control technology. In contrast, Section 109(b) speaks only of protecting the public health and welfare. Nothing in its language suggests that the Administrator is to consider economic or technological feasibility in setting ambient air quality standards.

The legislative history of the Act also shows the Administrator may not consider economic and technological feasibility in setting air quality standards; the absence of any provision requiring consideration of these factors was no accident; it was the result of a deliberate decision by Congress to subordinate such concerns to the achievement of health goals. . . .

For its part, LIA maintains that its claim that the Administrator exceeded the bounds of his statutory authority does not depend on the supposition that he is required, or even permitted, to consider economic and technological feasibility in setting air quality standards. LIA contends that, instead, its argument is based on the fact that Congress itself was concerned about the question of the economic feasibility of compliance with air quality standards, a concern which was reflected in the statute it enacted. According to LIA, Congress was mindful of the possibility that air quality standards which are too stringent could cause severe economic dislocation. For this reason it only granted the Administrator authority to adopt air quality standards which are "designed to protect the public from adverse health effects that are clearly harmful (.)" LIA finds support for its interpretation of congressional intent in various portions of the legislative history of the Act. . . . LIA then argues that the Administrator based the lead air quality standards on protecting children from "subclinical" effects of lead exposure which have not been shown to be harmful to health, that in so doing the Administrator ignored the clear limitation that Congress imposed on his standard-setting powers, and that the Administrator's action will in fact cause the very result that Congress was so concerned about avoiding. . . .

Section 109(b) does not specify precisely what Congress had in mind when it directed the Administrator to prescribe air quality standards that are "requisite to protect the public health." The legislative history of the Act does, however, provide some guidance. The Senate Report explains that the goal of the air quality standards must be to ensure that the public is protected from "adverse health effects." And the report is particularly careful to note that especially sensitive persons such as asthmatics and emphysematics are included within the group that must be protected. It is on the interpretation of the phrase "adverse health effects" that the disagreement between LIA and EPA about the limits of the Administrator's statutory authority appears to be based. LIA argues that the legislative history of the Act indicates that Congress only intended to protect the public against effects which are known to be clearly harmful to health, maintaining that this limitation on the Administrator's statutory authority is necessary to ensure that the standards are not set at a level which is more stringent than Congress contemplated. The Administrator, on the other hand, agrees that primary air quality standards must be based on protecting the public from "adverse health effects," but argues that the meaning LIA assigns to that phrase is too limited. In particular, the Administrator contends that LIA's interpretation is inconsistent with the precautionary nature of the statute, and will frustrate Congress' intent in requiring promulgation of air quality standards.

The Administrator begins by pointing out that the Act's stated goal is "to protect and enhance the quality of the Nation's air resources so as to promote the public health and welfare and the productive capacity of its population (.)" Section 101(b)(1). This goal was reaffirmed in the 1977 Amendments. For example, the House Report accompanying the Amendments states that one of its purposes is "(t)o emphasize the preventive or precautionary nature of the act, i.e., to assure that regulatory action can effectively prevent harm before it occurs; to emphasize the predominant value of protection of public health(.)" The Administrator notes that protecting the public from harmful effects requires decisions about exactly what these harms are, a task Congress left to his judgment. He notes that the task of making these decisions is complicated by the absence of any clear thresholds above which there are adverse effects and below which there are none. Rather, as scientific knowledge expands and analytical techniques are improved, new information is uncovered which indicates that pollution levels that were once considered harmless are not in fact harmless. Congress, the Administrator argues, was conscious of this problem, and left these decisions to his judgment partly for this reason. In such situations the perspective that is brought to bear on the problem plays a crucial role in determining what decisions are made. Because it realized this, Congress, the Administrator maintains, directed him to err on the side of caution in making these judgments. First, Congress made it abundantly clear that considerations of economic or technological feasibility are to be subordinated to the goal of protecting the public health by prohibiting any consideration of such factors. Second, it specified that the air quality standards must also protect individuals who are particularly sensitive to the effects of pollution. Third, it required that the standards be set at a level at which there is "an absence of adverse effect" on these sensitive individuals. Finally, it specifically directed the Administrator to allow an adequate margin of safety in setting primary air quality standards in order to provide some protection against effects that research has not yet uncovered. The Administrator contends that these indicia of congressional intent, the precautionary nature of the statutory mandate to protect the public health, the broad discretion Congress gave him to decide what effects to protect against, and the uncertainty that must be part of any attempt to determine the health effects of air pollution, are all extremely difficult to reconcile with LIA's suggestion that he can only set standards which are designed to protect against effects which are known to be clearly harmful to health.

We agree that LIA's interpretation of the statute is at odds with Congress' directives to the Administrator. . . .

NOTES AND QUESTIONS ON *LEAD INDUSTRIES*

1. *Holding.* What is the textual basis for the court's holding that EPA may not consider economic factors in setting ambient air quality standards? What is the relationship between section 108 and section 109 of the statute, *i.e.*, how does section 108 govern the appropriate interpretation of section 109? Is this the only plausible way to interpret this statutory language?

2. *Rule making practice and administrative record.* What kinds of issues and information may EPA consider in establishing (or revising) an ambient air quality standard? What other issues and information, in addition to purely economic factors, is EPA prohibited from considering? Is it realistic to assume that EPA can ignore those issues entirely?

3. *Policy.* What are the policy implications of developing ambient air quality standards solely on the basis of health and environmental factors, and with no consideration of economic impacts or attainability? The NAAQS drive much of the rest of the statute, but taken alone impose no requirements on sources of air pollution. In the opening section of the opinion describing the overall legal scheme, the court identifies the State Implementation Plans (SIPs), which must include emissions limitations and other requirements on particular pollution sources, as necessary to implement the NAAQS. In later chapters, you will learn the extent to which costs and other factors may be taken into account in adopting those source control requirements.

4. *Later cases.* The D.C. Circuit repeatedly reaffirmed in later decisions that EPA may not consider cost in setting the NAAQS. American Petroleum Institute v. Costle, 665 F.2d 1176 (D.C. Cir. 1981), *cert. denied*, 455 U.S. 1034 (1982); Natural Resources Defense Council v. Administrator, U.S. EPA, 902 F.2d 962 (D.C. Cir. 1990) (per curiam), *opinion dismissed in part and vacated in part*, 921 F.2d 326 (D.C. Cir. 1991); American Lung Association v. EPA, 134 F.3d 388 (D.C. Cir. 1998). The cost issue later reached the U.S. Supreme Court in the context of allegations that EPA surreptitiously (that is, not on the record) considered economic factors in amending some of the NAAQS. Justice Scalia rejected the argument that EPA may consider cost in establishing the NAAQS:

> The text of §109(b), interpreted in its statutory and historical context and with appreciation for its importance to the CAA as a whole, unambiguously bars cost considerations from the NAAQS-setting process, and thus ends the matter for us as well as the EPA.

Whitman v. American Trucking Associations, Inc., 531 U.S. 457, 471 (2001). With respect to the argument that EPA secretly did consider economic factors, the Court said:

Respondents' speculation that the EPA is secretly considering the costs of attainment without telling anyone is irrelevant to our interpretive inquiry. If such an allegation could be proved, it would be grounds for vacating the NAAQS, because the Administrator had not followed the law.

Id. n. 4.

5. *Complexity.* This case provides a sense of some of the scientific, policy, ethical, and other issues involved in identifying a numeric criterion that defines, for the ambient air in the entire nation, what level of air quality is "requisite to protect the public health" with an "adequate margin of safety." Here is a summary of the lead health effects considered in this rule making:

Threshold lead impacts (μg Pb/dl)

*	15-20	EP elevation children (subclinical)
*	5-20	EP elevation in adults
*	30	CDC screening level
*	40	Anemia in children
*	50	Anemia in adults
*	80-100	Neurological effects in children
*	100-200	Neurological effects in adults

While a full understanding of those complex issues requires a much more detailed inquiry, consider the following issues raised by the lead rule making:

a. Why can EPA consider "subclinical" health effects in establishing NAAQS? What kinds of "effects" count as "public health impairment?" Irritation to eyes and lungs, at levels that are annoying but present no long-term risk of illness or diminution of life span? What if you are a runner and shortness of breath from air pollution adds a minute to your time in your next recreational 5K race?

b. What portion of the population should be the focal point of health-effects-based regulations? Certain sub-populations may be more susceptible to adverse health effects than the general population, including children, the elderly, and individuals who already suffer respiratory, cardiovascular, or other illnesses. Are those sub-populations the appropriate focus for rules designed to protect the "public health" nationally?

c. Should the most susceptible individuals be protected in the standards, or a population average? For an interesting analysis of the degree to which genetic predisposition to illness should be considered in effects-based rules, *see* Jamie A. Grodsky, *Genetics and Environmental Law: Redefining Public Health*, 93 Cal. L. Rev. 171 (2005).

d. What if certain racial or ethnic groups face disproportionate impacts from a particular air pollutant, either because of where they live or other risk factors? Should EPA modify a national air quality standard to protect such sub-populations?

6. *Primary and secondary standards.* What is the difference between "primary" and "secondary" ambient air quality standards? From a practical perspective, EPA has almost invariably determined that human health impacts occur at lower levels than other adverse air pollution effects to "human welfare." As a result, the primary and secondary standards are identical in most cases. *See* 40 C.F.R. §§50.6-50.12 (NAAQS for particulate matter, carbon monoxide, ozone, nitrogen dioxide, and lead). For sulfur oxides, EPA has established somewhat different primary and secondary standards. *Id.* §§50.4, 50.5.

2. Critiques of Ambient Standards

From the outset, the concept of uniform national ambient air quality standards has been controversial. Consider the following critique, published just a few years after the 1970 Clean Air Act was passed:

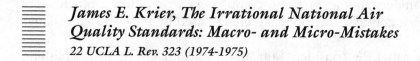

James E. Krier, The Irrational National Air Quality Standards: Macro- and Micro-Mistakes
22 UCLA L. Rev. 323 (1974-1975)

. . . I begin with the assertion that uniform national ambient standards represent a fundamental error in our approach to air pollution control. . . .

A. A Test for Resource Allocation

It is well worth keeping in mind that the air is a resource used by all of us (although in many different ways) and valued by all of us (although to varying degrees, depending upon our own individual frame of preferences and upon the uses to which we put the air environment). Government long ago concluded, quite justifiably, that a laissez-faire market could not adequately allocate this resource among all the differently valued divergent uses, and that government intervention was necessary. The task of government is then to allocate the resource *wisely*.

At a minimum, wise resource allocation entails recognition of two propositions: *First*, that while use of a resource in certain ways may result in costs, avoidance of those uses (or the costs of those uses) also results in costs; *second*, that society is using a resource most efficiently (though not necessarily most fairly, an important point to which we shall return) when the total of these costs is as low as possible. Applying these propositions to the air resource, we should first recognize that using the air as a pollutant receptacle entails costs such as discomfort, ill health, crop damage, materials damage, and scenic blight. But we should also realize that avoiding these pollution costs requires expenditures of time, effort, and money. At least from the standpoint of efficiency, therefore, our goal for air quality — for allocating the air to polluting and nonpolluting uses — appears to be quite clear: The air should be cleaned (or polluted, depending upon one's perspective) to the level that minimizes the sum of (a) the costs of pollution, plus (b) the costs of avoiding the costs of pollution.

B. Applying the Test to Uniform Air Quality Standards

Let us turn to applying the resource allocation test to the federal requirement of uniform national air quality standards. Do such standards represent an efficient allocation of the air resource?

I think it clear that at one level of analysis the answer to this question must be no. To justify uniform standards as efficient in cost-minimization terms one would have to assume that the costs of a given level of pollution and a given level of control are the same across the nation. This assumption, however, is manifestly not valid. For example, aesthetic costs and materials losses will be functions of the varying resource endowments, degrees of development, and human attitudes that exist in different regions. Even health costs — which were of the greatest concern to Congress in passing the 1970 legislation — vary from place to place. Since such costs represent the aggregate of individual health effects, and since population varies significantly by region, so too will health costs. If one believes that per capita and not aggregate health costs should be the relevant factor, efficiency considerations would still suggest some variation in air quality levels. This is because the costs of pollution control will also vary, depending upon population, density and nature of development, and meteorological and topographical conditions in any particular region. In short, since the costs of pollution and the costs of control vary across the country, it is difficult to see how a uniform standard can begin to take the varying costs into account. The standard that minimizes total costs for a region in Iowa is hardly likely to do so for all the regions of California or New York or Colorado as well. To require adherence to the same stringent standard everywhere will in many areas result in the imposition of control costs which are much larger than the pollution costs avoided. . . .

NOTES AND QUESTIONS ON KRIER CRITIQUE

1. *Allocating clean air.* Do you agree with Professor Krier that air pollution control is a matter of "resource allocation," *i.e.*, that air is a resource to be allocated among "polluting and nonpolluting uses"? If not, what other perspective on the issue would you suggest, and how does that affect the issue of what approach we take to air quality control?

2. *Uniformity.* Professor Krier criticizes the national uniformity inherent in the NAAQS. Professor Krier prefers an approach in which decisions about ambient air quality standards are based on more localized assessments of the impacts of air pollution in different areas, and the costs of controlling it. Later in this chapter, you will see that Congress adopted such an approach in the Clean Water Act, in which states adopt their own water quality criteria, subject to EPA review and approval. Do not, however, confuse the issue of uniformity with the level of government at which more localized decisions might be made. In theory, EPA, rather than the states could adopt air quality standards that vary in stringency around the country. Indeed, Professor Krier states that he prefers federally promulgated non-uniform standards. *See* James E. Krier, *On the Topology of Uniform Environmental Standards in a Federal System — and Why it Matters*, 54 Md. L. Rev. 1226 (1995). What are the advantages and disadvantages of adopting non-uniform ambient standards at the national as opposed to the state (or local) levels?

3. *Costs versus benefits.* Krier's critique of the effects-based standards approach, however, also runs much deeper. He suggests that ambient air quality standards should reflect the health and other costs of air pollution relative to the costs of controlling that pollution, in order to reach an "optimal" level of pollution (or air quality) from an overall societal perspective (as suggested by Baxter in *People or Penguins*, excerpted in Chapter 4). In essence, Krier argues that ambient air quality standards should be set based on a cost-benefit analysis, rather than the assumption that all adverse air pollution effects should be eliminated or at least minimized. Environmental standards based on cost-benefit principles are addressed in Chapter 7.

3. Water Quality Standards

In some major respects, ambient air and water quality standards share common characteristics. In some ways they are quite different. While EPA establishes uniform ambient air quality standards for the entire nation, Congress directed each state to adopt its own water quality standards specific to individual bodies of water or categories of waters, subject to EPA review and approval. (The federalism aspects of this system are addressed in Chapter 13.) Therefore, developing water quality standards involves a two-step process. States first designate the particular uses for which each kind of water body is to be protected (such as drinking water, cold water fish, or swimming). Second, they adopt standards deemed adequate to protect those uses. While air quality standards have focused primarily on human health impacts, water quality standards address a wide range of factors that impair the "physical, chemical, and biological integrity of the nation's waters," the overriding objective of the CWA you read about in Chapter 4. Therefore, while water quality standards may focus on human health issues related to fishing, swimming, or drinking water, they also address toxicity and other adverse impacts to fish and aquatic life. Protecting so many different kinds of uses requires states to adopt different kinds of water quality standards. These variations make the water quality standard process more complex than the NAAQS process in several ways, as illustrated in the following case:

 PUD No. 1 of Jefferson County v. Washington Department of Ecology
511 U.S. 700 (1994)

Justice O'Connor delivered the opinion of the Court.

Petitioners, a city and a local utility district, want to build a hydroelectric project on the Dosewallips River in Washington State. We must decide whether respondent state environmental agency (hereinafter respondent) properly conditioned a permit for the project on the maintenance of specific minimum stream flows to protect salmon and steelhead runs.

I

This case involves the complex statutory and regulatory scheme that governs our Nation's waters, a scheme that implicates both federal and state administrative responsibilities. The Federal Water Pollution Control Act, commonly known as the Clean Water Act, 86 Stat. 816, as amended, 33 U.S.C. §1251 et seq., is a comprehensive water quality statute designed to "restore and maintain the chemical, physical, and biological integrity of the Nation's waters." §1251(a). The Act also seeks to attain "water quality which provides for the protection and propagation of fish, shellfish, and wildlife." §1251(a)(2).

To achieve these ambitious goals, the Clean Water Act establishes distinct roles for the Federal and State Governments. Under the Act, the Administrator of the Environmental Protection Agency (EPA) is required, among other things, to establish and enforce technology-based limitations on individual discharges into the country's navigable waters from point sources. See §§1311, 1314. Section 303 of the Act also requires each State, subject to federal approval, to institute comprehensive water quality standards establishing water quality goals for all intrastate waters. §§1311(b)(1)(C), 1313. These state water quality standards provide "a supplementary basis . . . so that numerous point sources, despite individual compliance with effluent limitations, may be further regulated to prevent water quality from falling below acceptable levels."

A state water quality standard "shall consist of the designated uses of the navigable waters involved and the water quality criteria for such waters based upon such uses." 33 U.S.C. §1313(c)(2)(A). In setting standards, the State must comply with the following broad requirements:

"Such standards shall be such as to protect the public health or welfare, enhance the quality of water and serve the purposes of this chapter. Such standards shall be established taking into consideration their use and value for public water supplies, propagation of fish and wildlife, recreational [and other purposes.]"

Ibid. See also §1251(a)(2).

A 1987 amendment to the Clean Water Act makes clear that §303 also contains an "antidegradation policy" — that is, a policy requiring that state standards be sufficient to maintain existing beneficial uses of navigable waters, preventing their further degradation. Specifically, the Act permits the revision of certain effluent limitations or water quality standards "only if such revision is subject to and consistent with the antidegradation policy established under this section." §1313(d)(4)(B). Accordingly, EPA's regulations implementing the Act require that state water quality standards include "a statewide antidegradation policy" to ensure that "[e]xisting instream water uses and the level of water quality necessary to protect the existing uses shall be maintained and protected." 40 CFR §131.12 (1993). At a minimum, state water quality standards must satisfy these conditions. The Act also allows States to impose more stringent water quality controls. See 33 U.S.C. §§1311(b)(1)(C), 1370. See also 40 CFR §131.4(a) (1993) ("As recognized by section 510 of the Clean Water Act [33 U.S.C. §1370], States may develop water quality standards more stringent than required by this regulation").

The State of Washington has adopted comprehensive water quality standards intended to regulate all of the State's navigable waters. The State created an inventory of all the State's waters, and divided the waters into five classes. Each individual fresh surface water of the State is placed into one of these classes. The Dosewallips River is classified AA, extraordinary. The water quality standard for Class AA waters . . . identifies the designated uses of Class AA waters as well as the criteria applicable to such waters.

In addition to these specific standards applicable to Class AA waters, the State has adopted a statewide antidegradation policy. That policy provides:

"(a) Existing beneficial uses shall be maintained and protected and no further degradation which would interfere with or become injurious to existing beneficial uses will be allowed.
"(b) No degradation will be allowed of waters lying in national parks, national recreation areas, national wildlife refuges, national scenic rivers, and other areas of national ecological importance. . . .
"(f) In no case, will any degradation of water quality be allowed if this degradation interferes with or becomes injurious to existing water uses and causes long-term and irreparable harm to the environment."

As required by the Act, EPA reviewed and approved the State's water quality standards. Upon approval by EPA, the state standard became "the water quality standard for the applicable waters of that State." 33 U.S.C. §1313(c)(3). . . .

III

The principal dispute in this case concerns whether the minimum stream flow requirement that the State imposed on the Elkhorn Project is a permissible condition . . . under the Clean Water Act. [The Court first determined the breadth of the State's authority to condition federal licenses and permits under section 401 of the CWA, one of the provisions that authorizes states to implement and enforce WQS. In the following section of the opinion, the Court decided whether states can establish minimum stream flows as part of their WQS:]

B

Having concluded that, pursuant to §401, States may condition certification upon any limitations necessary to ensure compliance with state water quality standards or any other "appropriate requirement of State law," we consider whether the minimum flow condition is such a limitation. Under §303, state water quality standards must "consist of the designated uses of the navigable waters involved and the water quality criteria for such waters based upon such uses." In imposing the minimum stream flow requirement, the State determined that construction and operation of the project as planned would be inconsistent with one of the designated uses of Class AA water, namely "[s]almonid [and other fish] migration, rearing, spawning, and harvesting." The designated use of the river as a fish habitat directly reflects the Clean Water Act's goal of maintaining the "chemical, physical, and biological integrity of the Nation's waters." 33 U.S.C. §1251(a). Indeed, the Act defines pollution as "the man-made or man induced alteration of the chemical, physical, biological, and radiological integrity of water." §1362(19). Moreover, the Act expressly requires that, in adopting water quality standards, the State must take into consideration the use of waters for "propagation of fish and wildlife." §1313(c)(2)(A).

Petitioners assert, however, that §303 requires the State to protect designated uses solely through implementation of specific "criteria." According to petitioners, the State may not require them to operate their dam in a manner consistent with a designated "use"; instead, say petitioners, under §303 the State may only require that the project comply with specific numerical "criteria."

We disagree with petitioners' interpretation of the language of §303(c)(2)(A). Under the statute, a water quality standard must "consist of the designated uses of the navigable waters involved *and* the water quality criteria for such waters based upon such uses." 33 U.S.C. §1313(c)(2)(A) (emphasis added). The text makes it plain that water quality standards contain two components. We think the language of §303 is most naturally read to require that a project be consistent with both components, namely, the designated use and the water quality criteria. Accordingly, under the literal terms of the statute, a project that does not comply with a designated use of the water does not comply with the applicable water quality standards. . . .

EPA has not interpreted §303 to require the States to protect designated uses exclusively through enforcement of numerical criteria. In its regulations governing state water quality standards, EPA defines criteria as "*elements* of State water quality standards, expressed as constituent concentrations, levels, or narrative statements, representing a quality of water that supports a particular use." 40 CFR §131.3(b) (1993) (emphasis added). The regulations further provide that "[w]hen criteria are met, water quality will *generally* protect the designated use." Ibid. (emphasis added). Thus, the EPA regulations implicitly recognize that in some circumstances, criteria alone are insufficient to protect a designated use.

Petitioners also appear to argue that use requirements are too open ended, and that the Act only contemplates enforcement of the more specific and objective "criteria." But this argument is belied by the open-ended nature of the criteria themselves. As the Solicitor General points out, even "criteria" are often expressed in broad, narrative terms, such as " 'there shall be no discharge of toxic pollutants in toxic amounts.' " See American Paper Institute, Inc. v. EPA, 996 F.2d 346, 349 (CADC 1993). In fact, under the Clean Water Act, only one class of criteria, those governing "toxic pollutants listed pursuant to section 1317(a)(1)," need be rendered in numerical form. See 33 U.S.C. §1313(c)(2)(B); 40 CFR §131.11(b)(2) (1993).

Washington's Class AA water quality standards are typical in that they contain several open-ended criteria which, like the use designation of the river as a fishery, must be translated into specific limitations for individual projects. For example, the standards state that "[t]oxic, radioactive, or deleterious material concentrations shall be less than those which may affect public health, the natural aquatic environment, or the desirability of the water for any use." Similarly, the state standards specify that "[a]esthetic values shall not be impaired by the presence of materials or their effects, excluding those of natural origin, which offend the senses of sight, smell, touch, or taste." We think petitioners' attempt to distinguish between uses and criteria loses much of its force in light of the fact that the Act permits enforcement of broad, narrative criteria based on, for example, "aesthetics."

Petitioners further argue that enforcement of water quality standards through use designations renders the water quality criteria component of the standards irrelevant. We see no anomaly, however, in the State's reliance on both use designations and criteria to protect water quality. The specific numerical limitations embodied in the criteria are a convenient enforcement mechanism for identifying minimum water conditions which will generally achieve the requisite water quality. And, in most circumstances, satisfying the criteria will, as EPA recognizes, be sufficient to maintain the designated use. Water quality standards, however, apply to an entire class of water, a class which contains numerous individual water bodies. For example, in the State of Washington, the Class AA water quality standard applies to 81 specified fresh surface waters, as well as to all "surface waters lying within the mountainous regions of the state assigned to national parks, national forests, and/or wilderness areas," all "lakes and their feeder streams within the state," and all "unclassified surface waters that are tributaries to Class AA waters." While enforcement of criteria will in general protect the uses of these diverse waters, a complementary requirement that activities also comport with designated uses enables the States to ensure that each activity — even if not foreseen by the criteria–will be consistent with the specific uses and attributes of a particular body of water.

Under petitioners' interpretation of the statute, however, if a particular criterion, such as turbidity, were missing from the list contained in an individual state water quality standard, or even if an existing turbidity criterion were insufficient to protect a particular species of fish in a particular river, the State would nonetheless be forced to allow activities inconsistent with the existing or designated uses. We think petitioners' reading leads to an unreasonable interpretation of the Act. The criteria components of state water quality standards attempt to identify, for all the water bodies in a given class, water quality requirements generally sufficient to protect designated uses. These criteria, however, cannot reasonably be expected to anticipate all the water quality issues arising from every activity that can affect the State's hundreds of individual water bodies. Requiring the States to enforce only the criteria component of their water quality standards would in essence require the States to study to a level of great specificity each individual surface water to ensure that the criteria applicable to that water are sufficiently detailed and individualized to fully protect the water's designated uses. Given that there is no textual support for imposing this requirement, we are loath to attribute to Congress an intent to impose this heavy regulatory burden on the States.

The State also justified its minimum stream flow as necessary to implement the "antidegradation policy" of §303. When the Clean Water Act was enacted in 1972, the water quality standards of all 50 States had antidegradation provisions. These provisions were required by federal law. By providing in 1972 that existing state water quality standards would remain in force until revised, the Clean Water Act ensured that the States would continue their antidegradation programs. EPA has consistently required that revised state standards incorporate an antidegradation policy. And, in 1987, Congress explicitly recognized the existence of an "antidegradation policy established under [§303]."

EPA has promulgated regulations implementing §303's antidegradation policy, a phrase that is not defined elsewhere in the Act. These regulations require States to "develop and adopt a statewide antidegradation policy and identify the methods for implementing such policy." 40 CFR §131.12 (1993). These "implementation methods shall, at a minimum, be consistent with the . . . [e]xisting instream water uses and the level of water quality necessary to protect the existing uses shall be maintained and protected." Ibid. EPA has

explained that under its antidegradation regulation, "no activity is allowable
. . . which could partially or completely eliminate any existing use." Thus,
States must implement their antidegradation policy in a manner "consistent"
with existing uses of the stream. The State of Washington's antidegradation
policy in turn provides that "[e]xisting beneficial uses shall be maintained and
protected and no further degradation which would interfere with or become
injurious to existing beneficial uses will be allowed." The State concluded that
the reduced stream flows would have just the effect prohibited by this policy.
The Solicitor General, representing EPA, asserts, and we agree, that the State's
minimum stream flow condition is a proper application of the state and federal
antidegradation regulations, as it ensures that an "existing instream water
us[e]" will be "maintained and protected."

Petitioners also assert more generally that the Clean Water Act is only
concerned with water "quality," and does not allow the regulation of water
"quantity." This is an artificial distinction. In many cases, water quantity is
closely related to water quality; a sufficient lowering of the water quantity in a
body of water could destroy all of its designated uses, be it for drinking water,
recreation, navigation or, as here, as a fishery. In any event, there is recognition
in the Clean Water Act itself that reduced stream flow, i.e., diminishment of
water quantity, can constitute water pollution. First, the Act's definition of
pollution as "the man-made or man induced alteration of the chemical,
physical, biological, and radiological integrity of water" encompasses the
effects of reduced water quantity. 33 U.S.C. §1362(19). This broad concep-
tion of pollution — one which expressly evinces Congress' concern with the
physical and biological integrity of water — refutes petitioners' assertion that
the Act draws a sharp distinction between the regulation of water "quantity"
and water "quality." . . .

NOTES AND QUESTIONS ON *JEFFERSON COUNTY*

1. *Designated uses and water quality criteria.* Ambient air quality standards consist of one component, the standards themselves. Water quality
standards consist of two major components: designated uses and water quality
criteria to protect those uses. What explains this difference? What happens if
different criteria are necessary to protect different designated uses?

2. *Enforceability.* What did the Supreme Court say in *Jefferson County*
about the enforceable nature of both components of the standards (designated
uses and criteria), and why is that important? How does it further distinguish
ambient water quality standards from ambient air quality standards?

3. *Scope.* EPA has adopted ambient air quality standards for only six
pollutants. By contrast, it has issued water quality criteria guidance under
section 304 of the CWA for over a hundred toxic and other water pollutants.
Under pressure from Congress, most states have adopted water quality standards for most of those pollutants, as well as others. What explains this

difference? *Compare* CAA section 108(a), 42 U.S.C. §7408(a), *with* CWA section 303(c)(2)-(4), 33 U.S.C. §1313(c)(2)(-(4).

4. *Format.* Ambient air quality criteria are universally expressed in numeric terms, in concentrations of a particular pollutant over a specified unit of time. For example, the primary NAAQS for sulfur dioxide is 80 micrograms per cubic meter as an annual arithmetic mean, and 365 micrograms per cubic meter over a 24-hour period. Setting different standards for different time periods can protect against different kinds of adverse health and other impacts. For example, some kinds of illness (shortness of breath or other acute respiratory impacts) can occur during brief periods of very high exposure. Other effects can occur due to long-term exposure at somewhat lower concentrations.

Water quality standards, by contrast, come in more flavors that have evolved over time, and that continue to evolve in order to address a suite of factors that determine whether various uses of water bodies will be protected:

a. *Narrative criteria.* As discussed in *Jefferson County*, the most general forms of water quality standards are narrative standards, which articulate in plain English the acceptable condition of a water body. Examples of narrative criteria include statements that water bodies must be "free from floatable wastes" or contain "no toxics in toxic amounts." *See* Environmental Defense Fund v. Costle, 657 F.2d 275, 288 (D.C. Cir. 1981) (approving the use of narrative rather than numeric criteria for salinity). From the perspective of an environmental agency, what is useful about such broad narrative criteria? What might make them difficult to implement in practice?

b. *Numeric criteria.* States also adopt specific numeric water quality criteria similar in nature to the numeric air quality standards. The Supreme Court highlighted the utility of numeric standards in EPA v. California Water Resources Control Board, 426 U.S. 200 (1976), noting that one of the key purposes of the 1972 amendments was to translate general water quality requirements into specific obligations of individual dischargers. *See also* Natural Resources Defense Council, Inc. v. EPA, 915 F.2d 1314 (9th Cir. 1990) (describing water quality criteria as the "maximum concentration of pollutants that could occur without jeopardizing the use").

c. *Whole effluent toxicity criteria.* Why might numeric criteria for a long list of pollutants not suffice to protect water body uses? To address the additive and synergistic effects of multiple pollutants on aquatic life, states also may issue "whole effluent toxicity" (WET) criteria, which measure the combined effects of toxic pollutants on test organisms that may be in the polluted water body. The legality of these criteria was upheld in American Paper Institute, Inc. v. EPA, 996 F.2d 346 (D.C. Cir. 1993), and in Natural Resources Defense Council, Inc. v. EPA, 859 F.2d 156 (D.C. Cir. 1988).

d. *Biocriteria.* All of the above forms of water quality criteria address the "chemical" aspect of the Clean Water Act's overriding objective to restore the chemical, physical, and biological integrity of the nation's waters. Physical and biological impairments to water bodies are notably absent from the criteria described above, but are far more difficult to articulate as criteria. A more recent innovation to fill this gap is the establishment of biological water quality criteria (biocriteria) which define the health of aquatic ecosystems by comparing the biota in a given water body with those in the least-altered natural system of the same or similar type, using a rigorous set of statistical measurements. *See* Robert W. Adler, *The Two Lost Books in the Water Quality Trilogy: The Elusive Objectives of Physical and Biological Integrity,* 33 Envtl. L. 29, 70-75 (2003).

e. *Antidegradation criteria.* Yet another form of "ambient water quality standard" is reflected in the "antidegradation" provisions of EPA's regulations, 40 C.F.R. §131.12, as discussed in the *Jefferson County* decision. Antidegradation standards require the protection of all designated uses and water quality at levels necessary to protect those uses, and further require that water quality above that level be maintained and protected except under prescribed conditions. Similar requirements are included in the Prevention of Significant Deterioration (PSD) provisions of the Clean Air Act. Briefly, the PSD provisions in the CAA require states to limit air quality degradation even where air quality is better than required by the NAAQS. These provisions are designed to prevent future violations due to additional growth or other factors, and to protect visibility afforded by particularly clean air, especially in National Parks and other scenic places.

5. *The Endangered Species Act.* In Chapter 8, we describe the Endangered Species Act (ESA) as a statute that acts by imposing a ban on certain activities, such as the "taking" of endangered species. In other respects, however, the ESA can be viewed as an example of an effects-based statute. The purpose of the statute is to provide "means whereby the ecosystems upon which endangered species depend may be conserved. . . . " 16 U.S.C. §1531(b). Preventing impairment of healthy ecosystems on which species depend, therefore, is the primary statutory goal, and areas of "critical habitat" are identified to serve that goal. *Id.* §1533(b)(6)(C). Congress defined "conserve" to mean "all methods and procedures which are necessary to bring any endangered species or threatened species to the point at which" additional corrective actions are not necessary. *Id.* §1532(3). Species recovery, therefore, is the measuring stick by which statutory implementation is gauged, and species-specific recovery plans are adopted to define the actions necessary to achieve recovery, and the criteria by which recovery will be ascertained. *Id.* §1533(f).

C. EFFECTS-BASED OUTPUT STANDARDS (RELEASE LIMITS)

A key characteristic of both the ambient air quality standards and the ambient water quality standards is that they define how clean the air and water, respectively, must be in the environment as a whole. As such, to provide for attainment of the ambient standards, we must consider the combined effects of all sources of that pollutant within a given area. We address this implementation problem in Chapter 13. Effects-based standards, however, also can be written at the level of individual pollution sources. Effects-based output standards (or release limits) dictate the amount of pollution that can be released from a particular smokestack or pipe or similar facility, and are known as "emission limits" in the CAA and "effluent standards" in the CWA. Like effects-based ambient standards, regulators dictate effects-based output standards based on adverse health and environmental effects. The scientific and regulatory problems inherent in establishing effects-based output standards, therefore, closely resemble those confronted in setting ambient effects-based standards. These issues are described in the following case, which pondered the establishment of effects-based source standards for toxic air pollutants under the pre-1990 version of the Clean Air Act.

 Natural Resources Defense Council, Inc., v. U.S. Environmental Protection Agency
824 F.2d 1146 (D.C. Cir. 1987)

BORK, CIRCUIT JUDGE [en banc].

Current scientific knowledge does not permit a finding that there is a completely safe level of human exposure to carcinogenic agents. The Administrator of the Environmental Protection Agency, however, is charged with regulating hazardous pollutants, including carcinogens, under section 112 of the Clean Air Act by setting emission standards "at the level which in his judgment provides an ample margin of safety to protect the public health." 42 U.S.C. §7412(b)(1)(B) (1982). We address here the question of the extent of the Administrator's authority under this delegation in setting emission standards for carcinogenic pollutants.

Petitioner Natural Resources Defense Council ("NRDC") contends that the Administrator must base a decision under section 112 exclusively on health-related factors and, therefore, that the uncertainty about the effects of carcinogenic agents requires the Administrator to prohibit all emissions. The Administrator argues that in the face of this uncertainty he is authorized to set standards that require emission reduction to the lowest level attainable by best available control technology whenever that level is below that at which harm to humans has been demonstrated. We find no support for either position in the language or legislative history of the Clean Air Act. We therefore grant the petition for review and remand to the Administrator for reconsideration in light of this opinion.

I

Section 112 of the Clean Air Act provides for regulation of hazardous air pollutants, which the statute defines as "air pollutant[s] to which no ambient air quality standard is applicable and which in the judgment of the Administrator cause[ ], or contribute[ ] to, air pollution which may reasonably be anticipated to result in an increase in mortality or an increase in serious irreversible, or incapacitating reversible, illness." 42 U.S.C. §7412(a)(1) (1982). . . . The statute directs the Administrator to set an emission standard promulgated under section 112 "at the level which in his judgment provides an ample margin of safety to protect the public health." *Id.*

This case concerns vinyl chloride regulations. Vinyl chloride is a gaseous synthetic chemical used in the manufacture of plastics and is a strong carcinogen. In late 1975, the Administrator issued a notice of proposed rulemaking to establish an emission standard for vinyl chloride. In the notice, the EPA asserted that available data linked vinyl chloride to carcinogenic, as well as some noncarcinogenic, disorders and that "[r]easonable extrapolations" from this data suggested "that present ambient levels of vinyl chloride may cause or contribute to . . . [such] disorders." The EPA also noted that vinyl chloride is "an apparent non-threshold pollutant," which means that it appears to create a risk to health at all non-zero levels of emission. Scientific uncertainty, due to the unavailability of dose-response data and the twenty-year latency period between initial exposure to vinyl chloride and the occurrence of disease, makes it impossible to establish any definite threshold level below which there are no adverse effects to human health. The notice also stated the "EPA's position that for a carcinogen it should be assumed, in the absence of strong evidence to the contrary, that there is no atmospheric concentration that poses absolutely no public health risk."

Because of this assumption, the EPA concluded that it was faced with two alternative interpretations of its duty under section 112. First, the EPA determined that section 112 might require a complete prohibition of emissions of non-threshold pollutants because a "zero emission limitation would be the only emission standard which would offer absolute safety from ambient exposure." The EPA found this alternative "neither desirable nor necessary" because "[c]omplete prohibition of all emissions could require closure of an entire industry," a cost the EPA found "extremely high for elimination of a risk to health that is of unknown dimensions."

The EPA stated the second alternative as follows:

An alternative interpretation of section 112 is that it authorizes setting emission standards that require emission reduction to the lowest level achievable by use of the best available control technology in cases involving apparent non-threshold pollutants, where complete emission prohibition would result in widespread industry closure and EPA has determined that the cost of such closure would be grossly disproportionate to the benefits of removing the risk that would remain after imposition of the best available control technology.

The EPA adopted this alternative on the belief that it would "produce the most stringent regulation of hazardous air pollutants short of requiring a complete prohibition in all cases."

[The Environmental Defense Fund challenged these regulations. After settlement of this litigation and another decade of rule making proceedings, EPA adopted only minor changes to the rule, which was then challenged by the Natural Resources Defense Council (NRDC).] . . .

III

The NRDC's challenge . . . is simple: because the statute adopts an exclusive focus on considerations of health, the Administrator must set a zero level of emissions when he cannot determine that there is a level below which no harm will occur.

. . . We find no support in the text or legislative history for the proposition that Congress intended to require a complete prohibition of emissions whenever the EPA cannot determine a threshold level for a hazardous pollutant. Instead, there is strong evidence that Congress considered such a requirement and rejected it.

Section 112 commands the Administrator to set an "emission standard" for a particular "hazardous air pollutant" which in his "judgment" will provide an "ample margin of safety." Congress' use of the term "ample margin of safety" is inconsistent with the NRDC's position that the Administrator has no discretion in the face of uncertainty. The statute nowhere defines "ample margin of safety." The Senate Report, however, in discussing a similar requirement in the context of setting ambient air standards under section 109 of the Act, explained the purpose of the "margin of safety" standard as one of affording "a reasonable degree of protection . . . against hazards which research has not yet identified." This view comports with the historical use of the term in engineering as "a safety factor . . . meant to compensate for uncertainties and variabilities." Furthermore, in a discussion of the use of identical language in the Federal Water Pollution Control Act, this court has recognized that, in discharging the responsibility to assure "an ample margin of safety," the Administrator faces "a difficult task, indeed, a veritable paradox — calling as it does for knowledge of that which is unknown — [but] . . . the term 'margin of safety' is Congress's directive that means be found to carry out the task and to reconcile the paradox." Environmental Defense Fund v. EPA, 598 F.2d 62, 81 (D.C.Cir.1978). And while Congress used the modifier "ample" to exhort the Administrator not to allow "the public [or] the environment . . . to be exposed to anything resembling the maximum risk" and, therefore, to set a margin "greater than 'normal' or 'adequate,'" Congress still left the EPA "great latitude in meeting its responsibility."

Congress' use of the word "safety," moreover, is significant evidence that it did not intend to require the Administrator to prohibit all emissions of non-threshold pollutants. As the Supreme Court has recently held, "safe" does not mean "risk-free." Industrial Union Dep't, AFL-CIO v. American Petroleum Inst., 448 U.S. 607, 642, 100 S.Ct. 2844, 2864, 65 L.Ed.2d 1010 (1980). Instead, something is "unsafe" only when it threatens humans with "a significant risk of harm." *Id.*

Thus, the terms of section 112 provide little support for the NRDC's position. The uncertainty about the effects of a particular carcinogenic pollutant invokes the Administrator's discretion under section 112. In contrast, the NRDC's position would eliminate any discretion and would render the standard "ample margin of safety" meaningless as applied to carcinogenic pollutants.[1] Whenever any scientific uncertainty existed about the ill effects of a nonzero level of hazardous air pollutants — and we think it unlikely that science will ever yield absolute certainty of safety in an area so complicated and rife with problems of measurement, modeling, long latency, and the like — the Administrator would have no discretion but would be required to prohibit all emissions. Had Congress intended that result, it could very easily have said so by writing a statute that states that no level of emissions shall be allowed as to which there is any uncertainty. But Congress chose instead to deal with the pervasive nature of scientific uncertainty and the inherent limitations of scientific knowledge by vesting in the Administrator the discretion to deal with uncertainty in each case. . . .

IV

We turn now to the question whether the Administrator's chosen method for setting emission levels above zero is consistent with congressional intent. The Administrator's position is that he may set an emission level for non-threshold pollutants at the lowest level achievable by best available control technology when that level is anywhere below the level of demonstrated harm and the cost of setting a lower level is grossly disproportionate to the benefits of removing the remaining risk. The NRDC argues that this standard is arbitrary and capricious because the EPA is never permitted to consider cost and technological feasibility under section 112 but instead is limited to consideration of health-based factors. Thus, before addressing the Administrator's method of using cost and technological feasibility in this case, we must determine whether he may consider cost and technological feasibility at all.

1. With the exception of mercury, every pollutant the Administrator has listed or intends to list under §112 is a non-threshold carcinogen. . . .

A.

On its face, section 112 does not indicate that Congress intended to preclude consideration of any factor. Though the phrase "to protect the public health" evinces an intent to make health the primary consideration, there is no indication of the factors the Administrator may or may not consider in determining, in his "judgment," what level of emissions will provide "an ample margin of safety." Instead, the language used, and the absence of any specific limitation, gives the clear impression that the Administrator has some discretion in determining what, if any, additional factors he will consider in setting an emission standard. . . .

The legislative history is simply ambiguous with respect to the question of whether the Administrator may permissibly consider cost and technological feasibility under section 112. In the course of the compromise, the House lost a provision which would have permitted consideration of non-health based factors and the Senate lost a provision which would have limited the Administrator to consideration of health-based factors. The resulting standard neither permits nor prohibits consideration of any factor. Thus, we cannot find a clear congressional intent in the language, structure, or legislative history of the Act to preclude consideration of cost and technological feasibility under section 112.

C.

The petitioner argues next that a finding that section 112 does not preclude consideration of cost and technological feasibility would render the Clean Air Act structurally incoherent and would be inconsistent with the Supreme Court's interpretation of section 110 of the Act . . . , and this court's interpretation of section 109 of the Act, see Lead Indus. Ass'n v. EPA, as precluding consideration of these factors. We do not believe that our decision here is inconsistent with either the holding or the statutory interpretation. . . .

First, as discussed below, the court in [*Lead Industries* and *Union Electric,* infra] rejected an argument that the EPA must consider cost and technological feasibility as factors equal in importance to health. We reject the same argument here. In this case, however, we must also address the question of whether the Administrator may consider these factors if necessary to further protect the public health. This issue was not addressed in . . . *Lead Industries.* . . .

In *Lead Industries,* we held that the Administrator is not required to consider cost and technology under the mandate in section 109 of the Clean Air Act to promulgate primary air quality standards which "allow [ ] an adequate margin of safety . . . to protect the public health." 42 U.S.C. §7409(b)(1) (1982). The NRDC argues that the decision in *Lead Industries,* which involved the more permissive language "adequate," rather than "ample," "margin of safety," compels the conclusion that section 112 precludes consideration of economic and technological feasibility. We think not.

The *Lead Industries* court did note that the statute on its face does not allow consideration of technological or economic feasibility, but the court based its decision that section 109 does not allow consideration of these factors in part on structural aspects of the ambient air pollution provisions that are not present here. First, besides "allowing an adequate margin of safety," ambient air standards set under section 109(b) must be based on "air quality criteria," which section 108 defines as comprising several elements, all related to health. The court reasoned that the exclusion of economic and technological feasibility considerations from air quality criteria also foreclosed reliance on such factors in setting the ambient air quality standards based on those criteria. The court also relied on the fact that state implementation plans, the means of enforcement of ambient air standards, could not take into account economic and technological feasibility if such consideration interfered with the timely attainment of ambient air standards, and that the Administrator could not consider such feasibility factors in deciding whether to approve the state plans. This provided further grounds for the court to believe that Congress simply did not intend the economics of pollution control to be considered in the scheme of ambient air regulations.

In *Lead Industries,* moreover, the relevant Senate Report stated flatly that "existing sources of pollutants either should meet the standard of the law or be closed down." This is a far clearer statement than anything in the present case that Congress considered the alternatives and chose to close down sources or even industries rather than to allow risks to health.

The substantive standard imposed under the hazardous air pollutants provisions of section 112, by contrast with sections 109 and 110, is not based on criteria that enumerate specific factors to consider and pointedly exclude feasibility. Section 112(b)(1)'s command "to provide an ample margin of safety to protect the public health" is self-contained, and the absence of enumerated criteria may well evince a congressional intent for the Administrator to supply reasonable ones. . . .

Thus, in *Lead Industries,* the court found clear evidence that Congress intended to limit the factors the Administrator is permitted to consider in setting a "margin of safety" under section 109. The "margin of safety" standard in section 112 is not so adorned. For that reason, *Lead Industries* does not control this case. . . .

V

Since we cannot discern clear congressional intent to preclude consideration of cost and technological feasibility in setting emission standards under section 112, we necessarily find that the Administrator may consider these factors. We must next determine whether the Administrator's use of these factors in this case is "based on a permissible construction of the statute. . . . "

Given the foregoing analysis of the language and legislative history of section 112, it seems to us beyond dispute that Congress was primarily concerned with health in promulgating section 112. Every action by the Administrator in setting an emission standard is to be taken "to protect the public health." In setting an emission standard for vinyl chloride, however, the Administrator has made no finding with respect to the effect of the chosen level of emissions on health. Nor has the Administrator stated that a certain level of emissions is "safe" or that the chosen level will provide an "ample margin of safety." Instead, the Administrator has substituted "best available technology" for a finding of the risk to health. . . .

Thus, in setting emission standards for carcinogenic pollutants, the Administrator has decided to determine first the level of emissions attainable by best available control technology. He will then determine the costs of setting the standard below that level and balance those costs against the risk to health below the level of feasibility. If the costs are greater than the reduction in risk, then he will set the standard at the level of feasibility. This exercise, in the Administrator's view, will always produce an "ample margin of safety." . . .

We find that the congressional mandate to provide "an ample margin of safety" "to protect the public health" requires the Administrator to make an initial determination of what is "safe." This determination must be based exclusively upon the Administrator's determination of the risk to health at a particular emission level. Because the Administrator in this case did not make any finding of the risk to health, the question of how that determination is to be made is not before us. We do wish to note, however, that the Administrator's decision does not require a finding that "safe" means "risk-free," or a finding that the determination is free from uncertainty. Instead, we find only that the Administrator's decision must be based upon an expert judgment with regard to the level of emission that will result in an "acceptable" risk to health. In this regard, the Administrator must determine what inferences should be drawn from available scientific data and decide what risks are acceptable in the world in which we live. This determination must be based solely upon the risk to health. The Administrator cannot under any circumstances consider cost and technological feasibility at this stage of the analysis. The latter factors have no relevance to the preliminary determination of what is safe. Of course, if the Administrator cannot find that there is an acceptable risk at any level, then the Administrator must set the level at zero.

Congress, however, recognized in section 112 that the determination of what is "safe" will always be marked by scientific uncertainty and thus exhorted the Administrator to set emission standards that will provide an "ample margin" of safety. This language permits the Administrator to take into account scientific uncertainty and to use expert discretion to determine what action should be taken in light of that uncertainty. In determining what is an "ample margin" the Administrator may, and perhaps must, take into account the inherent limitations of risk assessment and the limited scientific knowledge of the effects of exposure to carcinogens at various levels, and may therefore decide to set the level below that previously determined to be "safe." This is especially true when a straight line extrapolation from known risks is used to estimate risks to health at levels of exposure for which no data is available. This method, which is based upon the results of exposure at fairly high levels of the hazardous pollutants, will show some risk at every level because of the rules of arithmetic rather than because of any knowledge. In fact the risk at a certain point on the extrapolated line may have no relationship to reality; there is no particular reason to think that the actual line of the incidence of harm is represented by a straight line. Thus, by its nature the finding of risk is uncertain and the Administrator must use his discretion to meet the statutory mandate. It is only at this point of the regulatory process that the Administrator may set the emission standard at the lowest level that is technologically feasible. In fact, this is, we believe, precisely the type of policy choice that Congress envisioned when it directed the Administrator to provide an "ample margin of safety." Once "safety" is assured, the Administrator should be free to diminish as much of the statistically determined risk as possible by setting the standard at the lowest feasible level. Because consideration of these factors at this stage is clearly intended "to protect the public health," it is fully consistent with the Administrator's mandate under section 112. . . .

NOTES AND QUESTIONS ON
VINYL CHLORIDE CASE

1. *Zero risk.* If EPA must adopt effects-based standards at levels necessary to "protect public health," and if some cancer may occur at any level of vinyl chloride emissions, why is EPA *not* required to establish a zero emissions level? Does the decision prohibit EPA from adopting a zero emission standard?

2. *Lead Industries.* Does the Court convincingly distinguish section 109 of the CAA, as interpreted in *Lead Industries*? In choosing an effects level at which some risk to public health remains, are we not at least implicitly allowing EPA to balance economic impacts (closing factories, losing jobs) against the remaining risk of cancer?

3. *Technology-based approach.* Why did the Court reject EPA's approach of reducing releases to the maximum extent possible given available technology? Why was it not within EPA's discretion to find that reducing emissions by the maximum amount possible provides the largest margin of safety possible?

4. *Two-step approach.* What guidance did the court give as to how EPA *should* develop toxic air pollutant emissions standards? Under the Court's two-step procedure, when and how may EPA consider economic and similar factors, and when is it prohibited from doing so?

5. *Statutory amendments.* Three years after this decision was issued, as part of the comprehensive 1990 amendments to the Clean Air Act, Congress adopted wholesale revisions to section 112. Congress replaced the effects-based emissions standards for hazardous air pollutants with a system of technology-based requirements augmented by an effects-based backup. For a very long list of hazardous air pollutants identified by Congress in the statute

itself (a highly unusual move),[1] EPA must promulgate a comprehensive set of technology-based emissions standards by industrial category. These kinds of standards are discussed in Chapter 6. However, the revised provision also includes the following, in section 112(d)(4):

> With respect to pollutants for which a health threshold has been established, the Administrator may consider such threshold level, with an ample margin of safety, when establishing emission standards under this subsection.

Moreover, under section 112(f), Congress required EPA to report on remaining health risks following implementation of the technology-based standards, and provide recommendations for additional legislation to address such risks. If Congress fails to act on such recommendations, within eight years after promulgation of the categorical technology-based standards for each category of sources, EPA must issue supplemental effects based standards "in order to provide an ample margin of safety to protect public health in accordance with this section (as in effect before November 15, 1990) or to prevent, taking into consideration costs, energy, safety, and other relevant factors, an adverse environmental effect." *Id.* §112(f)(2)(A). In another unusual step, Congress dictated that EPA must issue such standards whenever the technology-based standards fail to reduce the lifetime cancer risk to the "individual most exposed to emissions from a source in the category or subcategory to less than one in a million. . . ." *Id.* What continued relevance does the *Vinyl Chloride* decision have to any effects-based emissions standards issued by EPA under this backup provision?

6. *Clean Water Act.* A similar regulatory/legislative saga unfolded under the CWA, but with somewhat different results. Under the version of section 307(a) of the CWA enacted in 1972, Congress directed EPA to identify and issue effects-based source standards (known in the water context as "effluent standards" rather than "emissions standards") for toxic water pollutants. The CWA standards, however, required a lengthy quasi-adjudicative hearing process, which made the issuance of those standards even more difficult administratively. The long saga of one of EPA's rule making proceedings under this provision is described in Environmental Defense Fund v. EPA, 598 F.2d 62 (D.C. Cir. 1978). Due to EPA's glacial pace of issuing effects-based effluent standards for toxic water pollutants, Congress amended the CWA in both 1977 and 1987, in ways designed to promote more efficient attention to the problem of toxic water pollution. Section 307(a) now requires EPA to develop technology-based requirements, by categories and subcategories of sources, for all toxic pollutants identified on a list compiled in the legislative history. 33 U.S.C. §1317(a). EPA retains the discretion to adopt effects-based standards on a pollutant-specific basis, but has not done so since the 1977 amendments were adopted. (Unlike the amended section 112 of the CAA, EPA's residual

---

1. In section 112(b)(2), Congress provided EPA with the authority to modify this list.

authority to adopt effects-based effluent standards under the CWA is entirely discretionary.) In 1987, Congress also required individual states, or EPA if they fail to do so, to promulgate ambient water quality criteria for toxic pollutants. 33 U.S.C. §1313(c)(2)(B). The history of EPA's implementation of the original provision, and Congress' response, is detailed in Oliver A. Houck, *The Regulation of Toxic Pollutants Under the Clean Water Act*, 21 Envtl. L. Rptr. 10,528 (1991).

ISSUES IN RISK ASSESSMENT AND DECISION MAKING

General Background on Risk Assessment and Management

> "The risks are all acceptable; acceptable to who?"
> Folksinger/songwriter Charlie King

While environmental lawyers do not need to become experts in risk assessment and related disciplines, in part because they will work with experts in those fields, they do need to understand the basics of how risk assessment methodology is used in the regulatory process. As you saw in the above cases, changes in methods, assumptions, and data can have a dramatic influence on the final regulatory standards. We will begin with some basic terminology:

- **Risk assessment** is a process by which we try to characterize the risk of harm from exposure to a particular environmental cause. Risk assessment can consist solely of a qualitative assessment, as in the *Ethyl* case. Quantitative risk assessment involves an effort to evaluate the magnitude of particular harm from a particular cause. Quantitative risk assessment might involve estimating the lifetime incremental risk of getting cancer due to exposure to a particular chemical, with "incremental risk," meaning the added probability of cancer from that exposure above the background cancer rate in the population. Or, it might predict that a certain number of people will experience difficulty breathing due to a certain level of an air pollutant, or that there is an X percent chance that the population of an endangered species might decline by another Y percent if a particular highway is built. Risk assessment relies upon scientific data, but usually requires extrapolation from limited scientific evidence and interpretation of relevant science.
- **Risk management** is a policy inquiry in which we make regulatory and other decisions based on the risk assessment process and results. Using risk management, we might decide to choose regulatory standard A over standard B based on the degree of risk we are willing to tolerate. Or, we might choose to site a new hazardous waste landfill at site C

rather than D based on the relative risks between the sites, or issue the landfill permit or not, based on how severe we predict the risks will be.

Risk assessment requires an understanding of several factors. First, how much of a pollutant is emitted into the environment? Second, what is the pathway by which the pollutant reaches an individual who might be harmed? This inquiry, in turn, involves questions about the fate and persistence of the pollutant. (Does it break down into another substance? Does it dissipate over time or through dilution? Does it evaporate into the air? Does it concentrate in various places in the environment, for example, through bioconcentration or biomagnification?) Third, what is the effect or potential effect on the recipient? This last inquiry might involve what parts of the individual are exposed, what kinds of effects might occur, and the probability that those effects will occur, all of which involve complex and difficult data collection and analysis.

Based on this information, to what degree is risk assessment a purely "objective" scientific inquiry? Where might more subjective, policy factors enter the risk assessment process? What additional factors are considered in risk management? To what degree are those decisions guided by science, law, policy, economics, ethics, or other factors? Revisit these issues after you evaluate the PFOA example below.

Figure 5-1 – The Risk Assessment Process

Risk Assessment

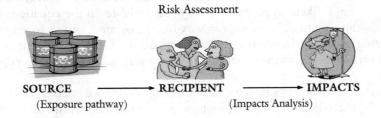

| SOURCE | → | RECIPIENT | → | IMPACTS |
| (Exposure pathway) | | | (Impacts Analysis) | |

PFOA — AN EXAMPLE FOR DISCUSSION

You are the chief of the water quality bureau for a state with a factory that releases PFOA into a river, and determine that it is appropriate to promulgate an ambient water quality criterion for PFOA. Because the PFOA problem is so new, EPA has not issued a recommended water quality criterion under section 304(a) of the CWA. Moreover, the applicable EPA regulation provides rather sparse guidance on how states are to adopt criteria for toxic pollutants:

(a) *Inclusion of pollutants.*
(1) States must adopt those water quality criteria that protect the designated use. Such criteria must be based on sound scientific rationale and must contain sufficient parameters orconstituents to protect the designated use. For waters with multiple use designations, the criteria shall support the most sensitive use.

(2) *Toxic pollutants.* States must . . . identify specific water bodies where toxic pollutants may be adversely affecting water quality or the attainment of the designated water use or where the levels of toxic pollutants are at a level to warrant concern and must adopt criteria for such toxic pollutants applicable to the water body sufficient to protect the designated use. . . .

(B) Form of criteria: In establishing criteria, States should:

(1) Establish numerical values based on:

(i) 304(a) Guidance; or

(ii) 304(a) Guidance modified to reflect site-specific conditions; or

(iii) Other scientifically defensible methods; . . . .

40 C.F.R. §131.12.

Under EPA's standard risk assessment procedure, water quality criteria for nonthreshold carcinogens are based on a mathematical formula (or "model"). While we will spare you the details, application of the formula involves choices between a number of "assumptions" or "inputs" into the equation. For some of these factors, relatively standard values are typically used (such as the assumption that people drink about two liters of water a day). Others may be more controversial, but are likely to have only a very small impact on the final result. For example, one might argue that using the weight of the average adult male (70 kilograms (kg)) produces a criterion weaker than necessary to protect women, who on average have lower body weights. But the difference between using 70 or, say, 60 kg, is likely to be dwarfed by other variables in the equation. Other factors in the equation, however, can vary by one or more orders of magnitude depending on policy decisions and what science is used. Using different assumptions for those factors in the equation can have a very dramatic effect on the final result:

1. The risk level is a policy determination of the "acceptable" level of risk chosen by the regulatory agency, such as an incremental lifetime cancer risk of one in a million (10^{-6}) above the background cancer risk to the population absent PFOA exposure. EPA uses a suggested one in a million cancer risk level (10^{-6}). However, EPA guidance indicates that it will generally approve state water quality criteria that use human health risk levels of between one in a hundred thousand and one in ten million (1×10^{-5} to 1×10^{-7}). Thus, choosing different risk levels within this range can change the resulting water quality criterion by 100-fold. In adopting a water quality criterion for PFOA, how would you decide which level of cancer risk to choose? Assume that using a one in a hundred thousand risk level will require no additional controls by the factory; one in a million will require use of expensive but available controls; and one in ten million will require the factory to close. Can you take those factors into account?

2. The cancer potency factor is a scientifically derived estimate of the relationship between exposure at a given level and the increased likelihood of getting cancer (the dose-response curve), *i.e.*, a measure of the "strength" of the carcinogen. Large variations between the agency estimates occur because of difficulties in extrapolating from actual evidence of cancer (tumors) caused when test animals are exposed to relatively high doses of a toxin, to the much smaller doses at which environmental exposure usually occurs. Uncertainty and debate

arises about such issues as: (1) the validity of comparing cancer in test animals to effects in humans, due to genetic and other differences between species; (2) the proper way to translate animal data to humans based on differences in size and weight; (3) the validity of extrapolating from high-dose, short-term exposures to low-dose, long-term exposure, and the resulting "shape" of the dose-response curve at very low exposure levels, for which no real data exist. The following graph illustrates the typical nature and uncertainties in dose-response curves. Note that at the lower end of the curve (very small doses), where regulatory standards typically are set, the shape of the curve is based on extrapolations from higher doses rather than real data. The shape of the curve at such low levels can have a large impact on the standard chosen, but is the subject of intense scientific disagreement.

Assume that you have a choice between one PFOA cancer potency factor derived by scientists at the state university, whose research is sponsored by the chemical industry, and a factor ten times higher calculated by EPA scientists (predicting that PFOA is a more potent carcinogen). The water quality criterion for PFOA thus would vary by another ten-fold based on which potency factor is used. On what basis would you choose between these estimates? Under the EPA regulation quoted above (40 C.F.R. §131.12), would the criterion be legally vulnerable if you choose the weaker estimate?

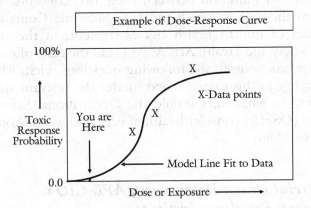

3. The nearest large city that uses water from the river for public drinking water is 20 miles downstream, by which time the PFOA is diluted because of inflows from several tributaries in between. Do you think you can you take that fact into account in issuing the water quality criterion? What if a Native American Tribe takes drinking water from the river much closer to the source, but its population is very small, so only several hundred people are affected?

4. If evidence surfaces that PFOA causes reproductive failure in a small specie of minnow at lower levels than you deem necessary to protect human health against cancer risks, should that require a change in the water quality criterion for PFOA?

The PFOA problem above assumes that drinking water is the only source of human exposure to PFOA from the river. For other pollutants, particularly those that tend to concentrate in fat or other parts of fish, much higher exposures can

occur due to fish consumption. This adds additional complications, such as
estimating the degree to which pollutants bioconcentrate in fish (occur in fish
tissue at levels higher than in the water column). Many of these issues were
addressed in Natural Resources Defense Council, Inc. v. U.S. Environmental
Protection Agency, 16 F.3d 1395 (4th Cir. 1993) (upholding EPA's approval of
dioxin water quality criteria issued by Virginia and Maryland that were 100-fold
weaker than those recommended by EPA).

D. POSTSCRIPT: A SEGUE FROM EFFECTS-BASED TO TECHNOLOGY-BASED REGULATION

This chapter explored effects-based regulations. The following chapter
will discuss technology-based regulation. In some statutory provisions, however, Congress did not choose so clearly among those options. Some statutes
reflect what my be called a "hybrid" of the two approaches, and provide a
useful way for us to transition between these two concepts. The following
excerpt is from the case in which the U.S. Supreme Court most squarely
addressed issues of human health risk assessment, in the context of the
Occupational Safety and Health Act. As you read the case, often known as the
"Benzene" case, ask yourself the following questions. First, what role is risk
assessment playing in this case? Second, under the relevant statutory provisions, when and in what ways should the Occupational Safety and Health
Administration (OSHA) consider health effects, and when should it consider
technological feasibility?

*Industrial Union Department, AFL-CIO v.
American Petroleum Institute*
448 U.S. 607 (1980)

JUSTICE STEVENS announced the judgment of the Court and delivered an
opinion, in which THE CHIEF JUSTICE and MR. JUSTICE STEWART joined and in
Parts I, II, III-A, III-B, III-C and III-E of which MR. JUSTICE POWELL joined.

The Occupational Safety and Health Act of 1970 (Act) was enacted for
the purpose of ensuring safe and healthful working conditions for every
working man and woman in the Nation. This litigation concerns a standard
promulgated by the Secretary of Labor to regulate occupational exposure to
benzene, a substance which has been shown to cause cancer at high exposure
levels. The principal question is whether such a showing is a sufficient basis for
a standard that places the most stringent limitation on exposure to benzene
that is technologically and economically possible.

The Act delegates broad authority to the Secretary to promulgate different kinds of standards. The basic definition of an "occupational safety and health standard" is found in §3(8), which provides:

The term 'occupational safety and health standard' means a standard which requires conditions, or the adoption or use of one or more practices, means, methods, operations, or processes, reasonably necessary or appropriate to provide safe or healthful employment and places of employment.

Where toxic materials or harmful physical agents are concerned, a standard must also comply with §6(b)(5), which provides:

The Secretary, in promulgating standards dealing with toxic materials or harmful physical agents under this subsection, shall set the standard which most adequately assures, to the extent feasible, on the basis of the best available evidence, that no employee will suffer material impairment of health or functional capacity even if such employee has regular exposure to the hazard dealt with by such standard for the period of his working life. . . .

Wherever the toxic material to be regulated is a carcinogen, the Secretary has taken the position that no safe exposure level can be determined and that §6(b)(5) requires him to set an exposure limit at the lowest technologically feasible level that will not impair the viability of the industries regulated. In this case, after having determined that there is a causal connection between benzene and leukemia (a cancer of the white blood cells), the Secretary set an exposure limit on airborne concentrations of benzene of one part benzene per million parts of air (1 ppm), regulated dermal and eye contact with solutions containing benzene, and imposed complex monitoring and medical testing requirements on employers whose workplaces contain 0.5 ppm or more of benzene.

On pre-enforcement review, the United States Court of Appeals for the Fifth Circuit held the regulation invalid. The court concluded that the Occupational Safety and Health Administration (OSHA) had exceeded its standard-setting authority because it had not shown that the new benzene exposure limit was "reasonably necessary or appropriate to provide safe or healthful employment" as required by §3(8), and because §6(b)(5) does "not give OSHA the unbridled discretion to adopt standards designed to create absolutely risk-free workplaces regardless of costs." Reaching the two provisions together, the Fifth Circuit held that the Secretary was under a duty to determine whether the benefits expected from the new standard bore a reasonable relationship to the costs that it imposed. The court noted that OSHA had made an estimate of the costs of compliance, but that the record lacked substantial evidence of any discernible benefits.

We agree with the Fifth Circuit's holding that §3(8) requires the Secretary to find, as a threshold matter, that the toxic substance in question poses a significant health risk in the workplace and that a new, lower standard is therefore "reasonably necessary or appropriate to provide safe or healthful employment and places of employment." Unless and until such a finding is made, it is not necessary to address the further question whether the Court of Appeals correctly held that there must be a reasonable correlation between costs and benefits, or whether, as the federal parties argue, the Secretary is then required by §6(b)(5) to promulgate a standard that goes as far as technologically and economically possible to eliminate the risk....

I

The entire population of the United States is exposed to small quantities of benzene, ranging from a few parts per billion to 0.5 ppm, in the ambient air. Over one million workers are subject to additional low-level exposures as a consequence of their employment....

As early as 1928, some health experts theorized that there might also be a connection between benzene in the workplace and leukemia....

Between 1974 and 1976 additional studies were published which tended to confirm the view that benzene can cause leukemia, at least when exposure levels are high. In ... August 1976 ... NIOSH [OSHA's research arm] stated that these studies provided "conclusive" proof of a causal connection between benzene and leukemia. Although it acknowledged that none of the intervening studies had provided the dose-response data it had found lacking two years earlier, NIOSH nevertheless recommended that the exposure limit be set low as possible. As a result of this recommendation, OSHA contracted with a consulting firm to do a study on the costs to industry of complying with the 10 ppm standard then in effect or, alternatively, with whatever standard would be the lowest feasible.

In October 1976, NIOSH sent another memorandum to OSHA, seeking acceleration of the rulemaking process and "strongly" recommending the issuance of an emergency temporary standard pursuant to §6(c) of the Act for benzene and two other chemicals believed to be carcinogens. NIOSH recommended that a 1 ppm exposure limit be imposed for benzene.

In [response to new evidence], OSHA issue[d] an emergency standard effective May 21, 1977, reducing the benzene exposure limit from 10 ppm to 1 ppm, the ceiling for exposures of up to 10 minutes from 25 ppm to 5 ppm, and eliminating the authority for peak concentrations of 50 ppm. 42 Fed.Reg. 22516 (1977). In its explanation accompanying the emergency standard, OSHA stated that benzene had been shown to cause leukemia at exposures below 25 ppm and that, in light of its consultant's report, it was feasible to reduce the exposure limit to 1 ppm....

On May 19, 1977, the Court of Appeals for the Fifth Circuit entered a temporary restraining order preventing the emergency standard from taking effect. Thereafter, OSHA abandoned its efforts to make the emergency standard effective and instead issued a proposal for a permanent standard patterned almost entirely after the aborted emergency standard.

In its published statement giving notice of the proposed permanent standard, OSHA did not ask for comments as to whether or not benzene presented a significant health risk at exposures of 10 ppm or less. Rather, it asked for comments as to whether 1 ppm was the minimum feasible exposure limit. As OSHA's Deputy Director of Health Standards, Grover Wrenn, testified at the hearing, this formulation of the issue to be considered by the Agency was consistent with OSHA's general policy with respect to carcinogens. Whenever a carcinogen is involved, OSHA will presume that no safe level of exposure exists in the absence of clear proof establishing such a level and will accordingly set the exposure limit at the lowest level feasible. The proposed 1 ppm exposure limit in this case thus was established not on the basis of a proven hazard at 10 ppm, but rather on the basis of "OSHA's best judgement at the time of the proposal of the feasibility of compliance with the proposed standard by the [a]ffected industries." Given OSHA's cancer policy, it was in fact irrelevant whether there was any evidence at all of a leukemia risk at 10 ppm. The important point was that there was no evidence that there was *not* some risk, however small, at that level. The fact that OSHA did not ask for comments on whether there was a safe level of exposure for benzene was indicative of its further view that a demonstration of such absolute safety simply could not be made. The final standard was issued on February 10, 1978. In its final form, the benzene standard is designed to protect workers from whatever hazards are associated with low-level benzene exposures by requiring employers to monitor workplaces to determine the level of exposure, to provide medical examinations when the level rises above 0.5 ppm, and to institute whatever engineering or other controls are necessary to keep exposures at or below 1 ppm.

As presently formulated, the benzene standard is an expensive way of providing some additional protection for a relatively small number of employees. According to OSHA's figures, the standard will require capital investments in engineering controls of approximately $266 million, first-year operating costs (for monitoring, medical testing, employee training, and respirators) of $187 million to $205 million and recurring annual costs of approximately $34 million. The figures outlined in OSHA's explanation of the costs of compliance to various industries indicate that only 35,000 employees would gain any benefit from the regulation in terms of a reduction in their exposure to benzene. . . .

Although OSHA did not quantify the benefits to each category of worker in terms of decreased exposure to benzene, it appears from the economic impact study done at OSHA's direction that those benefits may be relatively small. Thus, although the current exposure limit is 10 ppm, the actual exposures outlined in that study are often considerably lower. For example, for the period 1970-1975 the petrochemical industry reported that, out of a total of 496 employees exposed to benzene, only 53 were exposed to levels between

1 and 5 ppm and only 7 (all at the same plant) were exposed to between 5 and 10 ppm.

II

The critical issue at this point in the litigation is whether the Court of Appeals was correct in refusing to enforce the 1 ppm exposure limit on the ground that it was not supported by appropriate findings.

Any discussion of the 1 ppm exposure limit must, of course, begin with the Agency's rationale for imposing that limit. The written explanation of the standard fills 184 pages of the printed appendix. Much of it is devoted to a discussion of the voluminous evidence of the adverse effects of exposure to benzene at levels of concentration well above 10 ppm. This discussion demonstrates that there is ample justification for regulating occupational exposure to benzene and that the prior limit of 10 ppm, with a ceiling of 25 ppm (or a peak of 50 ppm) was reasonable. It does not, however, provide direct support for the Agency's conclusion that the limit should be reduced from 10 ppm to 1 ppm. . . .

The Agency made no finding that . . . any . . . empirical evidence, or any opinion testimony demonstrated that exposure to benzene at or below the 10 ppm level had ever in fact caused leukemia.

In the end OSHA's rationale for lowering the permissible exposure limit to 1 ppm was based, not on any finding that leukemia has ever been caused by exposure to 10 ppm of benzene and that it will *not* be caused by exposure to 1 ppm, but rather on a series of assumptions indicating that some leukemias might result from exposure to 10 ppm and that the number of cases might be reduced by reducing the exposure level to 1 ppm. In reaching that result, the Agency first unequivocally concluded that benzene is a human carcinogen. Second, it concluded that industry had failed to prove that there is a safe threshold level of exposure to benzene below which no excess leukemia cases would occur. . . .

Third, the Agency applied its standard policy with respect to carcinogens, concluding that, in the absence of definitive proof of a safe level, it must be assumed that *any* level above zero presents *some* increased risk of cancer. . . .

Fourth, the Agency reiterated its view of the Act, stating that it was required by §6(b)(5) to set the standard either at the level that has been demonstrated to be safe or at the lowest level feasible, whichever is higher. If no safe level is established, as in this case, the Secretary's interpretation of the statute automatically leads to the selection of an exposure limit that is the lowest feasible. Because of benzene's importance to the economy, no one has ever suggested that it would be feasible to eliminate its use entirely, or to try to limit exposures to the small amounts that are omnipresent. Rather, the Agency selected 1 ppm as a workable exposure level, and then determined that compliance with that level was technologically feasible and that "the economic impact of . . . [compliance] will not be such as to threaten the financial welfare of the affected firms or the general economy." It therefore held that 1 ppm was the minimum feasible exposure level within the meaning of §6(b)(5) of the Act.

Finally, although the Agency did not refer in its discussion of the pertinent legal authority to any duty to identify the anticipated benefits of the new standard, it did conclude that some benefits were likely to result from reducing the exposure limit from 10 ppm to 1 ppm. This conclusion was based, again, not on evidence, but rather on the assumption that the risk of leukemia will decrease as exposure levels decrease. . . .

III

Our resolution of the issues in these cases turns, to a large extent, on the meaning of and the relationship between §3(8), which defines a health and safety standard as a standard that is "reasonably necessary and appropriate to provide safe or healthful employment," and §6(b)(5), which directs the Secretary in promulgating a health and safety standard for toxic materials to "set the standard which most adequately assures, to the extent feasible, on the basis of the best available evidence, that no employee will suffer material impairment of health or functional capacity. . . . "

In the Government's view, §3(8)'s definition of the term "standard" has no legal significance or at best merely requires that a standard not be totally irrational. It takes the position that §6(b)(5) is controlling and that it requires OSHA to promulgate a standard that either gives an absolute assurance of safety for each and every worker or reduces exposures to the lowest level feasible. The Government interprets "feasible" as meaning technologically achievable at a cost that would not impair the viability of the industries subject to the regulation. The respondent industry representatives, on the other hand, argue that the Court of Appeals was correct in holding that the "reasonably necessary and appropriate" language of §3(8), along with the feasibility requirement of §6(b)(5), requires the Agency to quantify both the costs and the benefits of a proposed rule and to conclude that they are roughly commensurate.

In our view, it is not necessary to decide whether either the Government or industry is entirely correct. For we think it is clear that §3(8) does apply to all permanent standards promulgated under the Act and that it requires the Secretary, before issuing any standard, to determine that it is reasonably necessary and appropriate to remedy a significant risk of material health impairment. Only after the Secretary has made the threshold determination that such a risk exists with respect to a toxic substance, would it be necessary to decide whether §6(b)(5) requires him to select the most protective standard he can consistent with economic and technological feasibility, or whether, as respondents argue, the benefits of the regulation must be commensurate with the costs of its implementation. Because the Secretary did not make the required threshold finding in these cases, we have no occasion to determine whether costs must be weighed against benefits in an appropriate case.

A

Under the Government's view, §3(8), if it has any substantive content at all, merely requires OSHA to issue standards that are reasonably calculated to produce a safer or more healthy work environment. Apart from this minimal requirement of rationality, the Government argues that §3(8) imposes no limits on the Agency's power, and thus would not prevent it from requiring employers to do whatever would be "reasonably necessary" to eliminate all risks of any harm from their workplaces. With respect to toxic substances and harmful physical agents, the Government takes an even more extreme position. Relying on §6(b)(5)'s direction to set a standard "which most adequately assures . . . that no employee will suffer material impairment of health or functional capacity," the Government contends that the Secretary is required to impose standards that either guarantee workplaces that are free from any risk of material health impairment, however small, or that come as close as possible to doing so without ruining entire industries.

If the purpose of the statute were to eliminate completely and with absolute certainty any risk of serious harm, we would agree that it would be proper for the Secretary to interpret §§3(8) and 6(b)(5) in this fashion. But we think it is clear that the statute was not designed to require employers to provide absolutely risk-free workplaces whenever it is technologically feasible to do so, so long as the cost is not great enough to destroy an entire industry. Rather, both the language and structure of the Act, as well as its legislative history, indicate that it was intended to require the elimination, as far as feasible, of significant risks of harm.

B

By empowering the Secretary to promulgate standards that are "reasonably necessary or appropriate to provide safe or healthful employment and places of employment," the Act implies that, before promulgating any standard, the Secretary must make a finding that the workplaces in question are not safe. But "safe" is not the equivalent of "risk-free." There are many activities that we engage in every day — such as driving a car or even breathing city air — that entail some risk of accident or material health impairment; nevertheless, few people would consider these activities "unsafe." Similarly, a workplace can hardly be considered "unsafe" unless it threatens the workers with a significant risk of harm.

Therefore, before he can promulgate *any* permanent health or safety standard, the Secretary is required to make a threshold finding that a place of employment is unsafe — in the sense that significant risks are present and can be eliminated or lessened by a change in practices. This requirement applies to permanent standards promulgated pursuant to §6(b)(5), as well as to other types of permanent standards. For there is no reason why §3(8)'s definition of a standard should not be deemed incorporated by reference into §6(b)(5). The standards promulgated pursuant to §6(b)(5) are just one species of the genus of standards governed by the basic requirement. That section repeatedly uses the term "standard" without suggesting any exception from, or qualification of, the general definition; on the contrary, its directs the Secretary to select "*the* standard" — that is to say, one of various possible alternatives that satisfy the basic definition in §3(8) — that is most protective. Moreover, requiring the Secretary to make a threshold finding of significant risk is consistent with the scope of the regulatory power granted to him by §6(b)(5), which empowers the Secretary to promulgate standards, not for chemicals and physical agents generally, but for "*toxic* materials" and "*harmful* physical agents."

Thus, in this case, the Secretary was required to find that exposures at the current permissible exposure level of 10 ppm present a significant risk of harm in the workplace.

In the absence of a clear mandate in the Act, it is unreasonable to assume that Congress intended to give the Secretary the unprecedented power over American industry that would result from the Government's view of §§3(8) and 6(b)(5), coupled with OSHA's cancer policy. Expert testimony that a substance is probably a human carcinogen — either because it has caused cancer in animals or because individuals have contracted cancer following extremely high exposures — would justify the conclusion that the substance poses some risk of serious harm no matter how minute the exposure and no matter how many experts testified that they regarded the risk as insignificant. That conclusion would in turn justify pervasive regulation limited only by the constraint of feasibility. In light of the fact that there are literally thousands of substances used in the workplace that have been identified as carcinogens or suspect carcinogens, the Government's theory would give OSHA power to impose enormous costs that might produce little, if any, discernible benefit. . . .

If the Government was correct in arguing that neither §3(8) nor §6(b)(5) requires that the risk from a toxic substance be quantified sufficiently to enable the Secretary to characterize it as significant in an understandable way, the statute would make such a "sweeping delegation of legislative power" that it might be unconstitutional under the Court's reasoning in *A.L.A. Schechter Poultry Corp. v. United States*, 295 U.S. 495 and *Panama Refining Co. v. Ryan*, 293 U.S. 388. A construction of the statute that avoids this kind of open-ended grant should certainly be favored. . . .

D

Given the conclusion that the Act empowers the Secretary to promulgate health and safety standards only where a significant risk of harm exists, the critical issue becomes how to define and allocate the burden of proving the significance of the risk in a case such as this, where scientific knowledge is imperfect and the precise quantification of risks is therefore impossible. The Agency's position is that there is substantial evidence in the record to support its conclusion that there is no absolutely safe level for a carcinogen and that, therefore, the burden is properly on industry to prove, apparently beyond a shadow of a doubt, that there *is* a safe level for benzene exposure. The Agency argues that, because of the uncertainties in this area, any other approach would render it helpless, forcing it to wait for the leukemia deaths that it believes are likely to occur before taking any regulatory action.

We disagree. As we read the statute, the burden was on the Agency to show, on the basis of substantial evidence, that it is at least more likely than not that long-term exposure to 10 ppm of benzene presents a significant risk of material health impairment. Ordinarily, it is the proponent of a rule or order who has the burden of proof in administrative proceedings.

In this case OSHA did not even attempt to carry its burden of proof. The closest it came to making a finding that benzene presented a significant risk of harm in the workplace was its statement that the benefits to be derived from lowering the permissible exposure level from 10 to 1 ppm were "likely" to be "appreciable." The Court of Appeals held that this finding was not supported by substantial evidence. Of greater importance, even if it were supported by substantial evidence, such a finding would not be sufficient to satisfy the Agency's obligations under the Act. . . .

OSHA is not required to support its finding that a significant risk exists with anything approaching scientific certainty. Although the Agency's findings must be supported by substantial evidence, 29 U.S.C. §655(f), §6(b)(5) specifically allows the Secretary to regulate on the basis of the "best available evidence." As several Courts of Appeals have held, this provision requires a reviewing court to give OSHA some leeway where its findings must be made on the frontiers of scientific knowledge. Thus, so long as they are supported by a body of reputable scientific thought, the Agency is free to use conservative assumptions in interpreting the data with respect to carcinogens, risking error on the side of overprotection rather than underprotection. . . .

The judgment of the Court of Appeals remanding the petition for review to the Secretary for further proceedings is affirmed.

JUSTICE POWELL, concurring in part and concurring in the judgment.

I agree that §§6(b)(5) and 3(8) of the Occupational Safety and Health Act of 1970, 29 U.S.C. §§655(b)(5) and 652(8), must be read together. They require OSHA to make a threshold finding that proposed occupational health standards are reasonably necessary to provide safe workplaces. When OSHA acts to reduce existing national consensus standards, therefore, it must find that (i) currently permissible exposure levels create a significant risk of material health impairment; and (ii) a reduction of those levels would significantly reduce the hazard.

[Justice Powell argues that OSHA did find significant risk, but that substantial evidence does not support this finding.]

II

I conclude that the statute also requires the agency to determine that the economic effects of its standard bear a reasonable relationship to the expected benefits. An occupational health standard is neither "reasonably necessary" nor "feasible," as required by statute, if it calls for expenditures wholly disproportionate to the expected health and safety benefits. . . .

Although one might wish that Congress had spoken with greater clarity, the legislative history and purposes of the statute do not support OSHA's interpretation of the Act. It is simply unreasonable to believe that Congress intended OSHA to pursue the desirable goal of risk-free workplaces to the extent that the economic viability of particular industries — or significant segments thereof — is threatened. . . .

I therefore would not lightly assume that Congress intended OSHA to require reduction of health risks found to be significant *whenever* it also finds that the affected industry can bear the costs. Perhaps more significantly, however, OSHA's interpretation of §6(b)(5) would force it to regulate in a manner inconsistent with the important health and safety purposes of the legislation we construe today. Thousands of toxic substances present risks that fairly could be characterized as "significant." Even if OSHA succeeded in selecting the gravest risks for earliest regulation, a standard-setting process that ignored economic considerations would result in a serious misallocation of resources and a lower effective level of safety than could be achieved under standards set with reference to the comparative benefits available at a lower cost. I would not attribute such an irrational intention to Congress.

I join the Court's judgment affirming the judgment of the Court of Appeals.

Justice Marshall, with whom Justice Brennan, Justice White, and Justice Blackmun join, dissenting.

The plurality ignores the plain meaning of the Occupational Safety and Health Act of 1970 in order to bring the authority of the Secretary of Labor in line with the plurality's own views of proper regulatory policy. The unfortunate consequence is that the Federal Government's efforts to protect American workers from cancer and other crippling diseases may be substantially impaired . . . .

In this case the Secretary of Labor found, on the basis of substantial evidence, that (1) exposure to benzene creates a risk of cancer, chromosomal damage, and a variety of nonmalignant but potentially fatal blood disorders, even at the level of 1 ppm; (2) no safe level of exposure has been shown; (3) benefits in the form of saved lives would be derived from the permanent standard; (4) the number of lives that would be saved could turn out to be either substantial or relatively small; (5) under the present state of scientific knowledge, it is impossible to calculate even in a rough way the number of lives that would be saved, at least without making assumptions that would appear absurd to much of the medical community; and (6) the standard would not materially harm the financial condition of the covered industries. The Court does not set aside any of these findings. Thus, it could not be plainer that the Secretary's decision was fully in accord with his statutory mandate "most adequately [to] assur[e] . . . that no employee will suffer material impairment of health or functional capacity. . . ."

The plurality's conclusion to the contrary is based on its interpretation of 29 U.S.C. §652(8), which defines an occupational safety and health standard as one "which requires conditions . . . reasonably necessary or appropriate to provide safe or healthful employment. . . ." According to the plurality, a standard is not "reasonably necessary or appropriate" unless the Secretary is able to show that it is "at least more likely than not" that the risk he seeks to regulate is a "significant" one. Nothing in the statute's language or legislative history, however, indicates that the "reasonably necessary or appropriate" language should be given this meaning. Indeed, both demonstrate that the plurality's standard bears no connection with the acts or intentions of Congress and is based only on the plurality's solicitude for the welfare of regulated industries. And the plurality uses this standard to evaluate not the agency's decision in this case, but a strawman of its own creation.

Unlike the plurality, I do not purport to know whether the actions taken by Congress and its delegates to ensure occupational safety represent sound or unsound regulatory policy. The critical problem in cases like the ones at bar is scientific uncertainty. While science has determined that exposure to benzene at levels above 1 ppm creates a definite risk of health impairment, the magnitude of the risk cannot be quantified at the present time. The risk at issue has hardly been shown to be insignificant; indeed, future research may reveal that the risk is in fact considerable. But the existing evidence may frequently be inadequate to enable the Secretary to make the threshold finding of "significance" that the Court requires today. If so, the consequence of the plurality's approach would be to subject American workers to a continuing risk of cancer and other fatal diseases, and to render the Federal Government powerless to take protective action on their behalf. Such an approach would place the burden of medical uncertainty squarely on the shoulders of the American worker, the intended beneficiary of the Occupational Safety and Health Act. It is fortunate indeed that at least a majority of the Justices reject the view that the Secretary is prevented from taking regulatory action when the magnitude of a health risk cannot be quantified on the basis of current techniques. . . .

I

Congress enacted the Occupational Safety and Health Act as a response to what was characterized as "the grim history of our failure to heed the occupational health needs of our workers." . . .

The Act is enforced primarily through two provisions. First, a "general duty" is imposed upon employers to furnish employment and places of employment "free from recognized hazards that are causing or are likely to cause death or serious physical harm. . . . " Second, the Secretary of Labor is authorized to set "occupational safety and health standards," defined as standards requiring "conditions, or the adoption or use of one or more practices, means, methods, operations, or processes, reasonably necessary or appropriate to provide safe or healthful employment and places of employment."

The legislative history of the Act reveals Congress' particular concern for health hazards of "unprecedented complexity" that had resulted from chemicals whose toxic effects "are only now being discovered." Members of Congress made repeated references to the dangers posed by carcinogens and to the defects in our knowledge of their operation and effect. One of the primary purposes of the Act was to ensure regulation of these "insidious 'silent' killers."

This special concern led to the enactment of the first sentence of 29 U.S.C. §655(b)(5), which, as noted above, provides:

> The Secretary, in promulgating standards dealing with toxic materials or harmful physical agents under this subsection, shall set the standard which most adequately assures, to the extent feasible, on the basis of the best available evidence, that no employee will suffer material impairment of health or functional capacity even if such employee has regular exposure to the hazard dealt with by such standard for the period of his working life."

This directive is designed to implement three legislative purposes. First, Congress recognized that there may be substances that become dangerous only upon repeated or frequent exposure. The Secretary was therefore required to provide protection even from substances that would cause material impairment only upon exposure occurring throughout an employee's working life. Second, the requirement that the Secretary act on the basis of "the best available evidence" was intended to ensure that the standard-setting process would not be destroyed by the uncertainty of scientific views. Recognizing that existing knowledge may be inadequate, Congress did not require the Secretary to wait until definitive information could be obtained. Thus "it is not intended that the Secretary be paralyzed by debate surrounding diverse medical opinions." Third, Congress' special concern for the "silent killers" was felt to justify an especially strong directive to the Secretary in the standard-setting process.

The authority conferred by §655(b)(5), however, is not absolute. The subsection itself contains two primary limitations. The requirement of "material" impairment was designed to prohibit the Secretary from regulating substances that create a trivial hazard to affected employees. Moreover, all standards promulgated under the subsection must be "feasible." During the floor debates Congress expressed concern that a prior version of the bill, not clearly embodying the feasibility requirement, would require the Secretary to close down whole industries in order to eliminate risks of impairment. This standard was criticized as unrealistic. The feasibility requirement was imposed as an affirmative limit on the standard-setting power.

The remainder of §655(b)(5), applicable to all safety and health standards, requires the Secretary to base his standards "upon research, demonstrations, experiments, and such other information as may be appropriate." In setting standards, the Secretary is directed to consider "the attainment of the highest degree of health and safety protection for the employee" and also "the latest available scientific data in the field, the feasibility of the standards, and experience gained under this and other health and safety laws." . . .

II

The plurality's discussion of the record in this case is both extraordinarily arrogant and extraordinarily unfair. It is arrogant because the plurality presumes to make its own factual findings with respect to a variety of disputed issues relating to carcinogen regulation. It should not be necessary to remind the Members of this Court that they were not appointed to undertake independent review of adequately supported scientific findings made by a technically expert agency. And the plurality's discussion is unfair because its characterization of the Secretary's report bears practically no resemblance to what the Secretary actually did in this case. Contrary to the plurality's suggestion, the Secretary did not rely blindly on some Draconian carcinogen "policy." If he had, it would have been sufficient for him to have observed that benzene is a carcinogen, a proposition that respondents do not dispute. Instead, the Secretary gathered over 50 volumes of exhibits and testimony and offered a detailed and evenhanded discussion of the relationship between exposure to benzene at all recorded exposure levels and chromosomal damage, aplastic anemia, and leukemia. In that discussion he evaluated, and took seriously, respondents' evidence of a safe exposure level. . . .

The Secretary discussed the contention that a safe level of exposure to benzene had been demonstrated. From the testimony of numerous scientists, he concluded that it had not. He also found that although no dose-response curve could be plotted, the extent of the risk would decline with the exposure level. Exposure at a level of 1 ppm would therefore be less dangerous than exposure at one of 10 ppm. The Secretary found that the existing evidence justified the conclusion that he should not "wait for answers" while employees continued to be exposed to benzene at hazardous levels.

Finally, the Secretary responded to the argument that the permissible exposure level should be zero or lower than 1 ppm. Even though many industries had already achieved the 1 ppm level, he found that a lower level would not be feasible.

Costs and benefits. The Secretary offered a detailed discussion of the role that economic considerations should play in his determination. He observed that standards must be "feasible," both economically and technologically. In his view the permanent standard for benzene was feasible under both tests. The economic impact would fall primarily on the more stable industries, such as petroleum refining and petrochemical production. These industries would be able readily to absorb the costs or to pass them on to consumers. None of the 20 affected industries, involving 157,000 facilities and 629,000 exposed employees would be unable to bear the required expenditures. He concluded that the compliance costs were "well within the financial capability of the covered industries.". . .

III

A

This is not a case in which the Secretary found, or respondents established, that no benefits would be derived from a permanent standard, or that the likelihood of benefits was insignificant. Nor was it shown that a quantitative estimate of benefits could be made on the basis of "the best available evidence." Instead, the Secretary concluded that benefits will result, that those benefits "may" be appreciable, but that the dose-response relationship of low levels of benzene exposure and leukemia, nonmalignant blood disorders, and chromo-somal damage was impossible to determine. The question presented is whether, in these circumstances, the Act permits the Secretary to take regula-tory action, or whether he must allow continued exposure until more definitive information becomes available.

As noted above, the Secretary's determinations must be upheld if sup-ported by "substantial evidence in the record considered as a whole." This standard represents a legislative judgment that regulatory action should be subject to review more stringent than the traditional "arbitrary and capricious" standard for informal rulemaking. We have observed that the arbitrary and capricious standard itself contemplates a searching "inquiry into the facts" in order to determine "whether the decision was based on a consideration of the relevant factors and whether there has been a clear error of judgment. Careful performance of this task is especially important when Congress has imposed the comparatively more rigorous "substantial evidence" requirement. As we have emphasized, however, judicial review under the substantial evidence test is ultimately deferential. The agency's decision is entitled to the traditional presumption of validity, and the court is not authorized to substitute its judgment for that of the Secretary. If the Secretary has considered the decisional factors and acted in conformance with the statute, his ultimate decision must be given a large measure of respect.

The plurality is insensitive to three factors which, in my view, make judicial review of occupational safety and health standards under the substantial evidence test particularly difficult. First, the issues often reach a high level of technical complexity. In such circumstances the courts are required to immerse themselves in matters to which they are unaccustomed by training or experience. Second, the factual issues with which the Secretary must deal are frequently not subject to any definitive resolution. Often "the factual finger points, it does not conclude." Causal connections and theoretical extrapolations may be uncertain. Third, when the question involves determination of the acceptable level of risk, the ultimate decision must necessarily be based on considerations of policy as well as empirically verifiable facts. Factual determinations can at most define the risk in some statistical way; the judgment whether that risk is tolerable cannot be based solely on a resolution of the facts.

The decision to take action in conditions of uncertainty bears little resemblance to the sort of empirically verifiable factual conclusions to which the substantial evidence test is normally applied. Such decisions were not intended to be unreviewable; they too must be scrutinized to ensure that the Secretary has acted reasonably and within the boundaries set by Congress. But a reviewing court must be mindful of the limited nature of its role. It must recognize that the ultimate decision cannot be based solely on determinations of fact, and that those factual conclusions that have been reached are ones which the courts are ill-equipped to resolve on their own.

Under this standard of review, the decision to reduce the permissible exposure level to 1 ppm was well within the Secretary's authority. The Court of Appeals upheld the Secretary's conclusions that benzene causes leukemia, blood disorders, and chromosomal damage even at low levels, that an exposure level of 10 ppm is more dangerous than one of 1 ppm, and that benefits will result from the proposed standard. It did not set aside his finding that the number of lives that would be saved was not subject to quantification. Nor did it question his conclusion that the reduction was "feasible."

In these circumstances, the Secretary's decision was reasonable and in full conformance with the statutory language requiring that he "set the standard which most adequately assures, to the extent feasible, on the basis of the best available evidence, that no employee will suffer material impairment of health or functional capacity even if such employee has regular exposure to the hazard dealt with by such standard for the period of his working life." 29 U.S.C. §655(b)(5). On this record, the Secretary could conclude that regular exposure above the 1 ppm level would pose a definite risk resulting in material impairment to some indeterminate but possibly substantial number of employees. Studies revealed hundreds of deaths attributable to benzene exposure. Expert after expert testified that no safe level of exposure had been shown and that the extent of the risk declined with the exposure level. There was some direct evidence of incidence of leukemia, nonmalignant blood disorders, and chromosomal damage at exposure levels of 10 ppm and below. Moreover, numerous experts testified that existing evidence required an inference that an exposure level above 1 ppm was hazardous. We have stated that "well-reasoned expert testimony — based on what is known and uncontradicted by empirical evidence — may in and of itself be 'substantial evidence' when first-hand evidence on the question is unavailable." Nothing in the Act purports to prevent the Secretary from acting when definitive information as to the quantity of a standard's benefits is unavailable. Where, as here, the deficiency in knowledge relates to the extent of the benefits rather than their existence, I see no reason to hold that the Secretary has exceeded his statutory authority. . . .

In passing the Occupational Safety and Health Act of 1970, Congress was aware that it was authorizing the Secretary to regulate in areas of scientific uncertainty. But it intended to require stringent regulation even when definitive information was unavailable. In reducing the permissible level of exposure to benzene, the Secretary applied proper legal standards. His determinations are supported by substantial evidence The Secretary's decision was one, then, which the governing legislation authorized him to make.

IV

In recent years there has been increasing recognition that the products of technological development may have harmful effects whose incidence and severity cannot be predicted with certainty. The responsibility to regulate such products has fallen to administrative agencies. Their task is not an enviable one. Frequently no clear causal link can be established between the regulated substance and the harm to be averted. Risks of harm are often uncertain, but inaction has considerable costs of its own. The agency must decide whether to take regulatory action against possibly substantial risks or to wait until more definitive information becomes available — a judgment which by its very nature cannot be based solely on determinations of fact.

Those delegations, in turn, have been made on the understanding that judicial review would be available to ensure that the agency's determinations are supported by substantial evidence and that its actions do not exceed the limits set by Congress. In the Occupational Safety and Health Act, Congress expressed confidence that the courts would carry out this important responsibility. But in these cases the plurality has far exceeded its authority. The plurality's "threshold finding" requirement is nowhere to be found in the Act and is antithetical to its basic purposes. "The fundamental policy questions appropriately resolved in Congress . . . are *not* subject to re-examination in the federal courts under the guise of judicial review of agency action." Surely this is no less true of the decision to ensure safety for the American worker than the decision to proceed with nuclear power.

Because the approach taken by the plurality is so plainly irreconcilable with the Court's proper institutional role, I am certain that it will not stand the test of time. In all likelihood, today's decision will come to be regarded as an extreme reaction to a regulatory scheme that, as the Members of the plurality perceived it, imposed an unduly harsh burden on regulated industries. But as the Constitution "does not enact Mr. Herbert Spencer's Social Statics," *Lochner v. New York*, 198 U.S. 45, 75 (1905) (Holmes, J., dissenting), so the responsibility to scrutinize federal administrative action does not authorize this

Court to strike its own balance between the costs and benefits of occupational safety standards. I am confident that the approach taken by the plurality today, like that in *Lochner* itself, will eventually be abandoned, and that the representative branches of government will once again be allowed to determine the level of safety and health protection to be accorded to the American worker.

NOTES AND QUESTIONS ON *BENZENE*

1. *Holding.* Does the case resolve the question decided in the Court of Appeals, whether OSHA must find a reasonable relationship between costs and benefits? Is there a majority opinion? Does Justice Steven's opinion require effects-based standards?

2. *Basis for ruling.* What section of the statute does the plurality opinion rely upon? What parts of the statute do the dissenters rely upon? Does the section relied upon by the plurality justify the requirement to find a significant risk before regulating?

3. *Safety and risk.* Does safe mean "risk free?" If not, what does it mean?

4. *Quantification.* Must the agency quantify the risk in order to meet the burden of proof imposed by the plurality opinion?

OSHA justified setting the benzene standard at the lowest feasible level by stating that "there is no safe level of exposure . . . and that it is impossible to precisely quantify the anticipated benefits." This approach reflected a generic cancer policy being advocated in the federal government as a method of avoiding revisiting similar cancer scientific policy issues in each chemical-specific rule making.

The Court claimed that a requirement to demonstrate significant risk will not stymie regulation of carcinogens for the following reasons:

> First, the requirement that a "significant" risk be identified is not a mathematical straitjacket. It is the Agency's responsibility to determine, in the first instance, what it considers to be a "significant" risk. Some risks are plainly acceptable and others are plainly unacceptable. If, for example, the odds are one in a billion that a person will die from cancer by taking a drink of chlorinated water, the risk clearly could not be considered significant. On the other hand, if the odds are one in a thousand that regular inhalation of gasoline vapors that are 2% benzene will be fatal, a reasonable person might well consider the risk significant and take appropriate steps to decrease or eliminate it. Although the Agency has no duty to calculate the exact probability of harm, it does have an obligation to find that a significant risk is present before it can characterize a place of employment as "unsafe."

If the agency is not able to quantify the risks, are these suggestions helpful? Can OSHA justify a finding of significant risk without quantification? If not, can it adequately protect workers' health?

5. *Agency response.* Suppose that you are counsel for OSHA. The head of OSHA and her staff remain convinced that the existing 10 ppm standard does not adequately protect workers and would like to promulgate a stricter standard. How would you recommend that the agency justify this standard?

6. *Aftermath.* Although the *Benzene* case produced no majority opinion, it had a profound impact upon agency practice. It led federal regulatory agencies to abandon formal generic cancer policy articulating general presumptions to apply in cases of uncertainty in favor of case-by-case quantitative risk assessment. Thomas O. McGarity, *The Story of the Benzene Case: Judicially Imposed Regulatory Reform through Risk Assessment, in* ENVIRONMENTAL LAW STORIES 165-68 (RICHARD J. LAZARUS AND OLIVER A. HOUCK eds., 2005).

Nevertheless, as a science policy matter, the federal agencies, with support from the Scientific Advisory Board, have continued to assume, as OSHA had in the "Benzene" case, that absent contrary evidence for a particular carcinogen, no safe threshold exists for carcinogens. Industry and the conservative think tanks it funds have attacked this presumption for many years.

6

Technology-Based Standard Setting

Many statutory provisions require agencies to set standards that available (or potentially available) technologies are capable of achieving. Typically, agencies establish these standards by asking some variation of the following question: What level of emission reductions can the best technology for this kind of pollution from this kind of facility allow a polluter to achieve? Answering this sort of question can prove deceptively difficult.

The Clean Water Act relies heavily upon this approach in its National Pollutant Discharge Elimination Standards (NPDES) program for point sources (pollutants discharged through some sort of discrete conveyance). *See, e.g.,* 33 U.S.C. §§1311, 1362(11), (14). The Clean Air Act relies heavily upon technology-based standards as well. *See, e.g.,* 42 U.S.C. §§7411, 7412(d). Many technology-based provisions require the maximum feasible reductions of pollution. *See, e.g.,* 42 U.S.C. §7412(d); 33 U.S.C. §1316(a)(1). But others are less demanding. *See, e.g.,* 42 U.S.C. §7502(c)(1).

This chapter will explore the major concepts and problems associated with technology-based standards, using a few examples. These concepts will help you understand any technology-based standard setting provision and will enable you to address any problem under such a provision, even one you have not encountered before.

A. FEASIBILITY

The *Benzene* case (see Chapter 5) might lead one to expect that the technology-based approach to standard setting plays no role in setting toxics standards under the OSH Act. The *Cotton Dust* case, decided one year after *Benzene*, addresses the question of how OSHA should determine the stringency of toxics standards under that statute.

 ### *American Textile Manufacturers Institute, Inc. v. Donovan [Cotton Dust Case]*
452 U.S. 490 (1981)

BRENNAN, J.

Congress enacted the Occupational Safety and Health Act of 1970 (Act) "to assure so far as possible every working man and woman in the Nation safe and healthful working conditions" 29 U.S.C. §651(b). The Act authorizes the Secretary of Labor to establish, after notice and opportunity to comment, mandatory nationwide standards governing health and safety in the workplace. 29 U.S.C. §§655(a),(b). In 1978, the Secretary, acting through the Occupational Safety and Health Administration (OSHA), promulgated a standard limiting occupational exposure to cotton dust, an airborne particle byproduct of the preparation and manufacture of cotton products, exposure to which induces a "constellation of respiratory effects" known as "byssinosis." This disease was one of the expressly recognized health hazards that led to passage of the Act. . . .

Byssinosis, known in its more severe manifestations as "brown lung" disease, is a serious and potentially disabling respiratory disease primarily caused by the inhalation of cotton dust. . . .

The Cotton Dust Standard promulgated by OSHA establishes mandatory [permissible exposure limits] PELs over an 8-hour period of 200 [micrograms per cubic meter of air] $\mu g/m^3$ for yarn manufacturing, 750 $\mu g/m^3$ for slashing and weaving operations, and 500 $\mu g/m^3$ for all other processes in the cotton industry. These levels represent a relaxation of the proposed PEL of 200 $\mu g/m^3$ for all segments of the cotton industry. . . .

In promulgating the Cotton Dust Standard, OSHA interpreted the Act to require adoption of the most stringent standard to protect against material health impairment, bounded only by technological and economic feasibility. . . .

The Court of Appeals upheld the Standard in all major respects. The court held that "Congress itself struck the balance between costs and benefits in the mandate to the agency" under §6(b)(5) of the Act, 29 U.S.C. §655 (b)(5), and that OSHA is powerless to circumvent that judgment by adopting less than the most protective feasible standard. Finally, the court held that the agency's determination of technological and economic feasibility was supported by substantial evidence in the record as a whole.

We affirm. . . .

II

The principal question presented in these cases is whether the Occupational Safety and Health Act requires the Secretary, in promulgating a standard pursuant to §6(b)(5) of the Act, 29 U.S.C. §655(b)(5), to determine that the costs of the standard bear a reasonable relationship to its benefits. Relying on §§6(b)(5) and 3(8) of the Act, 29 U.S.C. §§655(b)(5) and 652(8), petitioners urge not only that OSHA must show that a standard addresses a significant risk of material health impairment, see Industrial Union Dept. v. American Petroleum Institute, 448 U.S., at 639 (plurality opinion), but also that OSHA must demonstrate that the reduction in risk of material health impairment is significant in light of the costs of attaining that reduction. Respondents on the other hand contend that the Act requires OSHA to promulgate standards that eliminate or reduce such risks "to the extent such protection is technologically and economically feasible." To resolve this debate, we must turn to the language, structure, and legislative history of the Act.

A

The starting point of our analysis is the language of the statute itself. Section 6(b)(5) of the Act, 29 U.S.C. §655(b)(5) (emphasis added), provides:

> The Secretary, in promulgating standards dealing with toxic materials or harmful physical agents under this subsection, shall set the standard which most adequately assures, *to the extent feasible*, on the basis of the best available evidence, that no employee will suffer material impairment of health or functional capacity even if such employee has regular exposure to the hazard dealt with by such standard for the period of his working life.

Although their interpretations differ, all parties agree that the phrase "to the extent feasible" contains the critical language in §6(b)(5) for purposes of these cases. The plain meaning of the word "feasible" supports respondents' interpretation of the statute. According to Webster's Third New International Dictionary of the English Language 831 (1976), "feasible" means "capable of being done, executed, or effected." Thus, §6(b)(5) directs the Secretary to issue the standard that "most adequately assures . . . that no employee will suffer material impairment of health," limited only by the extent to which this is "capable of being done." In effect then, as the Court of Appeals held, Congress itself defined the basic relationship between costs and benefits, by placing the "benefit" of worker health above all other considerations save those making attainment of this "benefit" unachievable. Any standard based on a balancing of costs and benefits by the Secretary that strikes a different balance than that struck by Congress would be inconsistent with the command set forth in §6(b)(5). Thus, cost-benefit analysis by OSHA is not required by the statute because feasibility analysis is. See Industrial Union Dept. v. American

Petroleum Institute, 448 U.S., at 718-719 (MARSHALL, J., dissenting). When Congress has intended that an agency engage in cost-benefit analysis, it has clearly indicated such intent on the face of the statute. One early example is the Flood Control Act of 1936: "[T]he Federal Government should improve or participate in the improvement of navigable waters or their tributaries, including watersheds thereof, for flood-control purposes *if the benefits to whomsoever they may accrue are in excess of the estimated costs. . . .* "

B

Even though the plain language of §6(b)(5) supports this construction, we must still decide whether §3(8), the general definition of an occupational safety and health standard, either alone or in tandem with §6(b)(5), incorporates a cost-benefit requirement for standards dealing with toxic materials or harmful physical agents. Section 3(8) of the Act, 29 U.S.C. §652(8) (emphasis added), provides:

> The term 'occupational safety and health standard' means a standard which requires conditions, or the adoption or use of one or more practices, means, methods, operations, or processes, *reasonably necessary or appropriate* to provide safe or healthful employment and places of employment.

Taken alone, the phrase "reasonably necessary or appropriate" might be construed to contemplate some balancing of the costs and benefits of a standard. Petitioners urge that, so construed, §3(8) engrafts a cost-benefit analysis requirement on the issuance of §6(b)(5) standards, even if §6(b)(5) itself does not authorize such analysis. We need not decide whether §3(8), standing alone, would contemplate some form of cost-benefit analysis. For even if it does, Congress specifically chose in §6(b)(5) to impose separate and additional requirements for issuance of a subcategory of occupational safety and health standards dealing with toxic materials and harmful physical agents: it required that those standards be issued to prevent material impairment of health *to the extent feasible*. Congress could reasonably have concluded that health standards should be subject to different criteria than *safety* standards because of the special problems presented in regulating them. See Industrial Union Dept. v. American Petroleum Institute, 448 U.S., at 649, n.54 (plurality opinion).

Agreement with petitioners' argument that §3(8) imposes an additional and overriding requirement of cost-benefit analysis on the issuance of §6(b)(5) standards would eviscerate the "to the extent feasible" requirement. Standards would inevitably be set at the level indicated by cost-benefit analysis, and not at the level specified by §6(b)(5). For example, if cost-benefit analysis indicated a protective standard of 1,000 μg/m³ PEL, while feasibility analysis indicated a 500 μg/m³ PEL, the agency would be forced by the cost-benefit requirement to choose the less stringent point. We cannot believe that Congress intended the general terms of §3(8) to countermand the specific feasibility requirement of §6(b)(5).

Adoption of petitioners' interpretation would effectively write §6(b)(5) out of the Act. We decline to render Congress' decision to include a feasibility requirement nugatory, thereby offending the well-settled rule that all parts of a statute, if possible, are to be given effect. Congress did not contemplate any further balancing by the agency for toxic material and harmful physical agents standards, and we should not " 'impute to Congress a purpose to paralyze with one hand what it sought to promote with the other.' "

C

The legislative history of the Act, while concededly not crystal clear, provides general support for respondents' interpretation of the Act. The congressional Reports and debates certainly confirm that Congress meant "feasible" and nothing else in using that term. Congress was concerned that the Act might be thought to require achievement of absolute safety, an impossible standard, and therefore insisted that health and safety goals be capable of economic and technological accomplishment. Perhaps most telling is the absence of any indication whatsoever that Congress intended OSHA to conduct its own cost-benefit analysis before promulgating a toxic material or harmful physical agent standard. The legislative history demonstrates conclusively that Congress was fully aware that the Act would impose real and substantial costs of compliance on industry, and believed that such costs were part of the cost of doing business. . . .

Not only does the legislative history confirm that Congress meant "feasible" rather than "cost-benefit" when it used the former term, but it also shows that Congress understood that the Act would create substantial costs for employers, yet intended to impose such costs when necessary to create a safe and healthful working environment. Congress viewed the costs of health and safety as a cost of doing business. . . .

Accordingly, the judgment of the Court of Appeals is affirmed. It is so ordered.

NOTES AND QUESTIONS ON THE
COTTON DUST CASE

1. *Consistency with Benzene.* Is the *Cotton Dust* case (as the *Donovan* case above is called) consistent with *Benzene*? How does the *Cotton Dust* Court seek to reconcile these cases?

2. *Criterion.* What criterion determines the stringency of standards under *Cotton Dust*? Does the *Cotton Dust* Court embrace or reject cost-benefit analysis as the method for determining the stringency of standards under the OSH Act? Does it reject consideration of cost altogether?

3. *Congressional balance.* The Court explains that Congress itself determined the balance to be struck between costs and benefits. What does it mean by that? Should Congress perform that role, or should administrative agencies?

Notice that Congress has apparently agreed not to fully protect the health of workers, if doing so is not feasible. This points up a general point about technology-based standards. If one uses technological capability to determine the amount of clean-up to demand, that level might inadequately protect health or the environment. Conversely, it is possible that the level of clean-up demanded may be more than is needed to fully protect health and the environment. While technology-based standards by themselves have no clear relationship to health or environmentally protective goals, they often serve as mechanisms to advance those goals. For example, the Clean Air Act requires states with unhealthy air quality to impose "reasonably available control" technology on major sources of pollution as a means toward the end of meeting the health-based NAAQS. *See* 42 U.S.C. §7502(c)(1).

The *Cotton Dust* case leads to some questions not only about the OSH Act, but about technology-based standard setting in general. How should an administrative agency determine what is feasible, *i.e.*, what a regulated industry is "capable of doing"? The courts, in interpreting relevant statutory provisions, have generally answered this question (both before and after the *Cotton Dust* decision) by requiring that agency standards meet tests of both technical and economic feasibility.

1. Technical Feasibility

a. Demonstrated Technology

The case below is fairly typical of cases raising concerns about technical feasibility. EPA set a new source performance standard (NSPS) for lime kilns. NSPS is a type of technology-based standard that EPA writes for major new stationary sources under the Clean Air Act, based on its assessment of technological capability. The owners of these facilities challenged the standards in court, arguing that the technology on which EPA based its standards is not capable of meeting the performance standard EPA promulgated. Therefore, they argue, compliance with the standard is not feasible. Owners of regulated facilities have made similar arguments with varying degrees of success in dozens of reported cases. *See, e.g.,* National Petrochemical & Refiners Ass'n v. EPA, 287 F.3d 1130, 1151 (D.C. Cir. 2002) (upholding limits on diesel engine exhaust emissions); Husqvarna AB v. EPA, 254 F.3d 195, 203 (D.C. Cir. 2001) (upholding air pollution standards for new handheld nonroad engines); AFL-CIO v. OSHA, 965 F.2d 962, 981 (11th Cir. 1992) (rejecting agency conclusion that "existing engineering controls are available" to meet its standards for air contaminants, because of lack of information about how specific industries will meet the standards); FMC Corp. v. Train, 539 F.2d 973,

982 (4th Cir. 1976) (rejecting reliance upon single plant's achievement and prediction that the regulated parties could apply their expertise to meet limits, when record does not identify plant or provide details); Tanners' Council of America v. Train, 540 F.2d 1188, 1193 (4th Cir. 1976) (rejecting regulation of tannery effluent).

National Lime Association v. Environmental Protection Agency
627 F.2d 416 (D.C. Cir. 1980)

WALD, CIRCUIT JUDGE.

The National Lime Association (NLA), representing ninety percent of this country's commercial producers of lime and lime hydrate (the industry), challenges the new source performance standards (NSPS) for lime manufacturing plants issued by the Environmental Protection Agency (EPA, Administrator or Agency) under §111 of the Clean Air Act (the Act), The standards limit the mass of particulate that may be emitted in the exhaust gas from all lime-hydrating and from certain lime-manufacturing facilities and limit the permitted visibility of exhaust gas emissions from some facilities manufacturing lime. We find inadequate support in the administrative record for the standards promulgated and therefore remand to the Administrator.

II. PROCEDURAL HISTORY

Section 111 of the Clean Air Act . . . authorizes the Administrator to limit the air pollutants that can lawfully be emitted from newly constructed[22] or modified[23] plants. This the Administrator can do by promulgating new source performance standards requiring new or modified plants to meet standards which can be met through application of the best system of emission reduction (considering costs) which has been "adequately demonstrated." The purpose is to assure that new or modified plants will not create significant new air pollution problems. . . .

---

22. A "new source" is defined by the Act to mean: any stationary source, the construction or modification of which is commenced after the publication of regulations (or, if earlier, proposed regulations) prescribing a standard of performance under this section which will be applicable to such source.

23. "Modification" of a source is defined to mean: any physical change in, or change in the method of operation of, a stationary source which increases the amount of any air pollutant emitted by such source or which results in the emission of any air pollutant not previously emitted. Conversion of a kiln from natural gas or fuel oil to coal firing may constitute a "modification," triggering application of the NSPS here promulgated.

III.   PREVIOUS REVIEW UNDER SECTION 111

As amended in 1977, section 111 of the Clean Air Act requires the Administrator to prescribe standards of performance for new statutory sources that reflect the degree of emission limitation and the percentage reduction achievable through the application of the best technological system of continuous emission reduction which (taking into consideration the cost of achieving such emission reduction, any nonair quality health and environmental impact and energy requirements), the Administrator determines has been adequately demonstrated . . . 42 U.S.C. §7411(a).

[Our] decisions have established a rigorous standard of review under section 111 . . . . [W]hile we remain diffident in approaching problems of this technical complexity, . . . the necessity to review agency decisions, if it is to be more than a meaningless exercise, requires enough steeping in technical matters to determine whether the agency "has exercised a reasoned discretion." . . . We cannot substitute our judgment for that of the agency, but it is our duty to consider whether "the decision was based on a consideration of the relevant factors and whether there has been a clear error of judgment." Ultimately, we believe, that the cause of a clean environment is best served by reasoned decision-making.

Section 111 requires that the emissions control system considered able to meet the standard be "adequately demonstrated" and the standard itself "achievable." 42 U.S.C. §7411(a).

The issue presented here is primarily one of the adequacy of EPA's test data on which the industry standards are based. NLA disagrees with EPA's conclusion that the standards are achievable under the "best technological system of continuous emission reduction which . . . the Administrator determines has been adequately demonstrated." Specifically, NLA claims that the test data underlying the development of the standards do not support the Administrator's conclusion that the promulgated emission levels are in fact "achievable" on a continuous basis. Promulgation of standards based upon inadequate proof of achievability would defy the Administrative Procedure Act's mandate against action that is "arbitrary, capricious, an abuse of discretion, or otherwise not in accordance with law."

IV.   ASSESSMENT OF THE OBJECTIONS RAISED
BY THE INDUSTRY

Our review has led us to conclude that the record does not support the "achievability" of the promulgated standards for the industry as a whole. This conclusion is a cumulative one, resulting from our assessment of the many points raised by the industry at the administrative level and in this court; no one point made is so cogent that remand would necessarily have followed on that basis alone. In the analysis that follows, common threads will be discerned in our discussions of individual points. Chief among these common threads is a concern that the Agency consider the representativeness for the industry as a whole of the tested plants on which it relies, at least where its central argument is that the standard is achievable because it has been achieved (at the tested plants). The Agency's failure to consider the representativeness along various relevant parameters of the data relied upon is the primary reason for our remand. The locus of administrative burdens of going forward or of persuasion may shift in the course of a rulemaking proceeding, but we think an initial burden of promulgating and explaining a non-arbitrary, non-capricious rule rests with the Agency and we think that by failing to explain how the standard proposed is achievable under the range of relevant conditions which may affect the emissions to be regulated, the Agency has not satisfied this initial burden.

Bearing this initial burden will involve first, identifying and verifying as relevant or irrelevant specific variable conditions that may contribute substantially to the amount of emissions, or otherwise affect the efficiency of the emissions control systems considered. And second, where test results are relied upon, it should involve the selection or use of test results in a manner which provides some assurance of the achievability of the standard for the industry as a whole, given the range of variable factors found relevant to the standards' achievability.

EPA itself acknowledged in this case that "standards of performance . . . must . . . meet these conditions for all variations of operating conditions being considered anywhere in the country." As set forth in the standards support statement, EPA's guidelines require data to be assessed with consideration of the "representativeness" of the source tested, including the "feedstock, operation, size and age" of the source. Furthermore, the record strongly suggests other factors that may affect the particulate emissions from lime plants. Yet at no point does EPA evaluate the relevance or irrelevance of such factors to regulable emissions; nor does the Agency explain how such factors might have been taken into account in choosing test plant sites or in analyzing the data from the sites it chose.

The critical question presented here is whether the regulated industry, through its trade association, should have borne the entire burden of demonstrating the unreliability for the industry as a whole of the conclusions drawn by the EPA. In this connection we are candidly troubled by the industry's failure to respond, at a crucial juncture in the standards development process, to the Agency's invitation to submit data supporting a fundamental industry objection to the achievability of the standard. We would have expected the industry to have been eager to supply supporting data for its position, assuming the "cost" of obtaining such data were less than the "cost" of compliance with a standard that was argued to be unachievable on any reliably repetitive basis for the industry as a whole. We cannot help but wonder if the industry's failure to supply such data means that the data available or obtained would not be favorable to the industry's position. Nevertheless we remand because we think, on balance, EPA must affirmatively show that its standard reflects consideration of the range of relevant variables that may affect emissions in different plants.

The showing we require does not mean that EPA must perform repeated tests on every plant operating within its regulatory jurisdiction. It does, however, mean that due consideration must be given to the possible impact on emissions of recognized variations in operations and some rationale offered for the achievability of the promulgated standard given the tests conducted and the relevant variables identified. To facilitate public comment, we think this rationale should have appeared in the Agency's initial standards support statement.

We must remand to the Agency for a more adequate explanation or, if necessary, for supplementary data to justify the standard in terms of the "representativeness" of the sources tested. The specific doubts generated by our review of the record in light of the lime industry's attack on the standard are more fully explained below.

A. The Particulate Emission Standards

1. Rotary Kilns

EPA tested emissions at six plants before it proposed its mass emission standard for rotary lime kilns. These six plants were selected for testing on the basis of visits to thirty-nine plants, during which the visibility of emissions was observed and information obtained on the emissions control systems employed. The thirty-nine plants were themselves selected because they had been identified as effectively controlled after a review of the literature and contact with industry representatives. The results of the tests of one plant (Plant A) which could not meet the proposed standard were excluded from consideration because the plant was thought not to represent best technology. From what we can gather from the record, three plants were able to meet the standard consistently.

Our doubts about the representativeness of the data relied upon are grouped under [these] subheadings. Variations in Quantity of Particulate Generated in the Kiln [and] Variations in Controllability of Particulate Generated . . . Under the subheading Variations in Quantity of Particulate Generated in the Kiln, we discuss the possible impact on the standard's achievability of composite dust levels generated by the tested plants and two factors (feedstock variations and gas velocity) that may contribute to composite dust levels. Under the subheading Variations in Controllability of Particulate Generated, we discuss two factors apart from sheer quantity of dust that may affect emissions control: coal usage and particulate size. . . .

a. Variations in Quantity of Particulate Generated
    in the Kiln

That the quantity of dust produced in the kilns would affect the control-lability of emissions and the achievability of the standards does not seem an unreasonable expectation. The Agency, however, appears to have taken con-flicting positions on the reasonableness of this expectation and perhaps as a consequence has devoted inadequate attention to several variables which EPA's own documents and the industry suggest may affect the volume of dust produced in different kilns.

(1) Feedstock Variations

For example, the record suggests that the size and chemical composition of the limestone feedstock used will affect the amount of dust produced.

This suggests to us that some analysis should have been performed or tests conducted which took into account significant variations in limestone feed, or other variables relevant to dust generation.

For all we know, the six plants tested could be using kinds and sizes of feed which are representative of only a small segment of the industry spectrum. If that were true the plants may not be "representative" and the regulation might not be "achievable" by the industry as a whole. . . .

(2) Gas Velocity and Operation Levels

According to the [consultant's] [r]eport [found in the record], dust generation is in part a function of gas velocity in the kiln. Gas velocity appears in turn to depend on several factors, including the percentage of capacity at which the kiln is operating. Thus the level of capacity at which the plant was operating at the time of sampling and the gas velocity would appear relevant to the representativeness of the test data.

Data on the production level and air flow rate (velocity) at the tested plants were included in the support document filed in this case. . . .

Having stated that much, however, the Agency did not explain how the range of test results fully takes account of any significant differences in operating conditions in the industry. The support document is totally devoid of analysis of the relevance or irrelevance of operating level or gas velocity to the achievability of the standard, notwithstanding assertions in the EPA's own contracted-for report that gas velocity bears upon dust generation rates.

(3) Dust Levels at the Tested Plants . . .

As laypersons it seems entirely logical to us to suppose that dust genera-tion levels would directly affect emissions controllability, viz., the higher the dust generation, the more difficult the achievability of the standard by the technological control device. But the exact relationship between volume of dust generated and the efficiency of the emissions control systems is never clearly stated or explained by the Agency. Instead, the Agency sends us several mixed signals. . . .

Our examination of the record thus yields a conflict: while in one breath EPA appears to acknowledge the relevance of dust generation levels to the proposed standard, in another breath the relevance is denied. In our view, the conflict is not adequately explained, nor is the industry-wide achievability of the standard adequately justified, in light of the acknowledged possibility that heavy dusting creates a more difficult control problem. From what appears in the record, both variations in dust volume produced and its contributing factors received inadequate attention from the Agency in the development and explanation of this standard.

b. Variations in Controllability of Particulate Generated

The record points to other variables which were also given short shrift in the stated rationale: the use of coal to fuel the kiln (as it relates to controllability of emissions); and variations in size of emitted particles. The record strongly supports the relevance of coal usage to the efficiency of at least the [electrostatic precipitator] (ESP) . . . control method and it also suggests a relationship between particle size and the efficiency of both the ESP and the baghouse control method. Nothing indicates how if at all variations in these factors were considered in proposing an "achievable" standard. . . .

(2) Particle Size

Although there is (a) considerable evidence in the record that the efficiency of available control technology varies with emitted particle size and (b) that lime dust particle size varies regionally (probably due to feedstock variation), the EPA (c) undertook no analysis of the impact of particle size distribution on the achievability of its standard. Each of these points is discussed under separate subheadings below.

(a) The relationship of particle size to efficiency of control methods.

That particle size affects the efficiency of at least two of the three "best" technological control systems seems clear. . . .

(b) Regional variations in particle size

Two early studies on which EPA relies in support of its standard strongly suggest regional or temporal variations in lime particle size . . . . When particle size was identified as a potentially important variable, both the Agency and the industry failed to pick up the ball.

(c)   EPA's lack of analysis

As far as we can tell the Agency gathered no data on particle size distribution at the tested plants or in the industry generally, either before or after the industry meeting which focused on this factor. Whether the EPA took particle size into account in developing and promulgating its proposed standard cannot be determined from this record.

Understandably, the Agency's main defense in court centers on the industry's total failure to respond positively to EPA's suggestion that the industry either suggest additional test sites or submit data on the basis of which EPA might reconsider or subcategorize the standard to conform to local variations. EPA's point is a sympathetic one, but not, we think, dispositive. EPA has a statutory duty to promulgate achievable standards. This requires that they approach that task in a systematic manner that identifies relevant variables and ensures that they are taken account of in analyzing test data. EPA's own support document recognizes particle size as a variable but enigmatically does not discuss it at any length or explain its importance in emissions control. That the industry did not assist the Agency in any meaningful way by data or even by suggestions for additional testing is certainly discouraging. But we do not think that inaction lamentable though it may be lifted the burden from the Agency of pursuing what appears to be a relevant variable or at the least discussing in its document why it was not considered important.

In this respect, we believe that the industry's comments, concerning particle size distribution, when viewed in light of the material contained in EPA's own support statement and in light of the background documents on which it relied, met a "threshold requirement of materiality," mandating an Agency response which was not forthcoming here.

B.   The Opacity Standard . . .

Both in this court and at the administrative level EPA emphasizes the overwhelming extent to which the plants tested were able to meet the ten percent opacity standard. But without knowing the representativeness of the plants tested or of test conditions, we cannot say that the standard is neither arbitrary nor capricious. Certainly the fact that virtually all plants tested were able to meet the standard is an important consideration, but our doubts are sufficient, when coupled with our doubts concerning the mass emissions standard (discussed above), to remand to the Agency for amplification of the record.

V.   THE STANDARD OF REVIEW AS APPLIED

Our requirement that the EPA consider the representativeness of the test data relied upon in the development and justification of its standard does not presage any new or more stringent standard of judicial review. The rigorous-ness of the review in which this court has engaged in previous NSPS decisions known to some as the "hard look" standard has already been described. . . .

Both decisions reviewing the NSPS and those reviewing other adminis-trative determinations under the Clean Air Act evince a concern that variables be accounted for, that the representativeness of test conditions be ascertained, that the validity of tests be assured and the statistical significance of results determined. Collectively, these concerns have sometimes been expressed as a need for "reasoned decision-making" and sometimes as a need for adequate "methodology." However expressed, these more substantive concerns have been coupled with a requirement that assumptions be stated, that process be revealed, that the rejection of alternate theories or abandonment of alternate courses of action be explained and that the rationale for the ultimate decision be set forth in a manner which permits the public to exercise its statutory prerogative of comment and the courts to exercise their statutory responsibility upon review. . . .

Our opinion should not suggest the necessity of "ninety-five percent certainty" in all the "facts" which enter into the Agency's decision. We would require only that the Agency provide sufficient data to demonstrate a system-atic approach to problems, not that it adduce vast quantities of factual data. However, where the facts pertinent to the standard's feasibility are available and easily discoverable by conventional technical means, there is somewhat less reason for so limited a data base. Nothing in the record suggests the relevant facts are not readily accessible to the Agency; the number of plants is large, use of the control methods found by the Agency to represent the "best systems" is widespread, and stack emission measurement techniques have been known and applied for many years.

With respect to the standard's achievability we are thus not presented with the question how much deference is owed a judgment predicated on limited evidence when additional evidence cannot be adduced or adduced in the near future. We do not depart from some of the most carefully considered and closely reasoned decisions of this court which permit an agency latitude to exercise its discretion in accordance with the remedial purposes of the control-ling statute where relevant facts cannot be ascertained or are on the frontiers of scientific inquiry.

A systematic approach may not necessarily require a conclusion grounded in actual test results. We do not intend to bridle the Agency's discretion to make well-founded assumptions even where the assumption could be replaced by valid test results, but we think first, the assumption should be stated and second, where test data could have verified the assumption, a reason for not testing or relying on such data should be given.

We recognize, for example, that the finding of facts, especially through elaborate testing, is costly and the costs of additional testing may be added by the Agency to the costs of delay in issuing the proposed rule and the sum of these costs weighed against the benefit of proposing a rule without additional data.

We leave to the Agency on remand the decision whether additional Agency-conducted testing is appropriate in this case. Data may already be available to the Administrator which would support the achievability of these standards for the industry as a whole. If so, satisfaction of the concerns we have expressed in this opinion may be a fairly simple matter.

To ensure that the Agency has engaged in reasoned decision-making, we remand. We have outlined our substantive misgivings; the Agency may choose the appropriate method of response.

Remanded.

NOTES ON *NATIONAL LIME*

1. *Burden of production.* One could imagine a court holding that EPA had met its initial burden by showing that some facilities could meet EPA's standards. Once this initial burden is met, the regulated industry must bring forth test data to show that variability in operating conditions makes achievement of the standards impossible. But the court did not do this. Should the court have put the burden upon EPA of showing in the administrative record that EPA's standards are achievable by the whole industry?

2. *Information asymmetry.* Judge Wald expresses dismay at the industry's failure to come forward with test results. A significant problem afflicting technology-based standards involves what economists call an information asymmetry. Often the regulated industry has better information about its own operations, and thus the potential for (or problems with) pollution control, than the agency. Does the *National Lime* case provide the proper incentives to overcome problems of information asymmetry?

3. *Remand.* What should EPA do on remand, assuming it does not have a sufficient budget to test all of the plants in the industry? EPA has authority under the Clean Air Act (as it has under other statutes) to order industry to monitor and report its emissions and to inspect facilities in order to facilitate standard setting. *See* 42 U.S.C. §7414(a). Would this authority suffice to develop the information needed to address the court's concern on remand?

One might think that this authority to require emissions reports would overcome some information asymmetries. The Paperwork Reduction Act, which authorizes the Office of Management and Budget (OMB) to review the burdens involved in government paperwork requirements, may provide a disincentive to liberal exercise of this authority. *See* General Accounting Office, Environmental Regulation: Differences Remain Between EPA and OMB over Paperwork Requirements (RCED-94-254) (1994) (describing the difficulties EPA has experienced in seeking and obtaining approval of reporting requests). Also, polluters may require significant amounts of time to provide useful information, which can delay standard setting unless begun well in advance of a rule making effort. Information procured early in the rule making process, on the other hand, can become outdated before a rule is promulgated. Also, in using this information, EPA may not disclose trade secrets. *See* 42 U.S.C. §7414(c). This can limit opportunities for the public to use facility-provided information to influence the outcome of rules and of the agencies to rely upon the information to justify a rule publicly.

In *National Lime,* EPA itself took the position that it must show that the industry could meet its standard under the operating conditions prevailing in the industry. Suppose that EPA instead took the position that the owners of the plants could control all of the operational variables that might make meeting promulgated emission standards problematic. This position might be tenable with respect to some of the variables at issue in *National Lime.* For example, owners might have a choice of feedstock materials, a variable that industry and EPA agreed might affect emissions. And the agency could take the position that pollution control considerations should influence industry feedstock selection. Should a position that companies can adjust their operating conditions cause a court to uphold EPA's rule, even if the test data does not adequately account for the variables that might influence emissions?

A Note on the Follow-the-Leader Principle, the Problem of Categorization, and Variances

In the 1990 Amendments to the Clean Air Act, Congress responded to the dampening effect the *National Lime* case had on stringent standard setting when it created, for the first time, technology-based requirements for sources of hazardous air pollutants (recall that Congress used a health-based approach to these pollutants prior to 1990, as in the *Vinyl Chloride* case in Chapter 5). *See* 42 U.S.C. §7412(d). Practitioners refer to these standards as "MACT" standards because they generally require standards reflecting the "maximum achievable control technology."

In order to relieve the agency of the burden of proving that all sources could meet a standard, Congress required EPA to set standards for existing sources that were at least as strict as the "average emission limit achieved by the best performing 12 percent of the existing sources . . . " in an industrial category or subcategory. 42 U.S.C. §7412(d)(3). With respect to new sources of hazardous air pollutants, Congress required EPA to set standards at least as stringent as that achieved by the "best controlled similar source." Practitioners refer to these requirements as the "MACT floor" provisions, because the statute authorizes EPA to set standards even stricter than those achieved by the best performing sources, but does not allow standards less strict than the best source (for new sources) or the average of the best 12 percent (for existing sources). Yet, Congress did not enact similar amendments to section 111, the section at issue in *National Lime,* which governs standard setting applying to new sources for non-hazardous pollutants. In spite of this congressional fix to the *National Lime* problem in section 112, EPA has been reluctant to impose standards for hazardous air pollutants without a high degree of confidence that all regulated plants are capable of achieving the standards with a technology the agency knows about. *See, e.g.,* Sierra Club v. EPA, 167 F.3d 658 (D.C. Cir. 1999) (remanding rule because EPA did not adequately explain its determination of the "MACT floor"); National Lime Ass'n v. EPA, 233 F.3d 625, 632 (D.C. Cir. 2000) (same, with EPA trying to defend its method as justified by the need to show that all sources can achieve the standards set under the most adverse conditions). Why do you suppose that EPA feels compelled to show that all facilities can meet its emission limits, even when there is some indication that Congress is trying to give it some latitude?

The MACT floor provides a recent example of congressional adoption of a "follow-the-leader" principle for determining feasibility. This principle requires that EPA set standards at least as stringent as those achieved in practice by the best controlled similar plants. The Supreme Court recognized that Congress has intended this principle to govern best practicable control technology (BPT) standards under the Clean Water Act. *See* E.I. du Pont de Nemours v. Train, 430 U.S. 112, 131 n.21 (1977) (BPT limitations should be based upon the average of the best performers). BPT standards form part of the Clean Water Act's suite of technology-based standards, serving as a prelude to more stringent Best Available Technology standards. Is the follow-the-leader principle consistent with the EPA's position that it must show that all plants can meet the standard it imposed? If this principle is not followed, will the agency be forced to adopt extremely lax standards in order to make sure that the most antiquated poorly equipped plants can meet them?

Notice that the follow-the-leader principle may have some harsh consequences. It could require an implementing agency to set a standard that some facilities cannot comply with, because of the kinds of variations in operating conditions that *National Lime* discusses, which may cause some plants to close. The legislative history of several technology-based provisions, however, shows that Congress did intend to require standards sufficiently stringent to allow marginal or laggard facilities to go out of business. *See, e.g.,* Industrial Union Dep't, AFL-CIO v. Hodgson, 499 F.2d 467, 477 (D.C. Cir. 1974) (Occupational Safety & Health Act allows a laggard in protecting the health and safety of workers to go out of business). Does the desire for a level playing field justify this approach? *See* Wendy A. Wagner, *Innovations in Environmental Policies: The Triumph of Technology-Based Standards,* 2000 U. Ill. L. Rev. 83, 103-04 (technology-based standards create a level playing field by treating all companies in the same class the same). Should all companies that compete with each other have to meet the same standards regardless of variations in circumstances?

The statutes contain several mechanisms to ameliorate the potential harshness of strict uniform standards for a broad category of facilities. First, they sometimes authorize agencies to set different standards for different subcategories of facilities. *See, e.g.,* American Iron & Steel Inst. v. EPA, 568 F.2d 284, 297-300 (3d Cir. 1977) (adjudicating dispute about subcategorization). Does subcategorization undercut the follow-the-leader principle?

What policy goals should guide EPA in its use of authority to subcategorize? Should it only consider physical differences among plants, or also take differences in economic capabilities into account? There is some evidence that Congress intended that this authority be used to avoid widespread shutdowns, but not to avoid the shutdown of a few laggard facilities:

> [T]he [Clean Water] Act's supporters in both Houses acknowledged and accepted the possibility that its 1977 requirements might cause individual plants to go out of business. They self-consciously made the legislative determination that the health and safety gains that achievement of the Act's aspirations would bring to future generations will in some cases outweigh the economic dislocation it causes to the present generation.

Weyerhaeuser Co. v. Costle, 590 F.2d 1011, 1036-37 (D.C. Cir. 1978). Is that the right policy?

Another technique for ameliorating the potential harshness of imposing strict standards on a broad category of plants involves offering variances for individual plants that have difficulty in complying. If an adjustment mechanism is desired, which mechanism is better, subcategorization or variances? In EPA v. National Crushed Stone Ass'n, 449 U.S. 64, 76-77 (1980), the Supreme Court disallowed a general variance from BPT standards under the Clean Water Act based on the individual polluter's economic capabilities as inconsistent with the follow-the-leader approach. On the other hand, the Court stated that a variance might be appropriate if the polluter can show that "its situation, including its costs of compliance, is outside the range or circumstances" EPA considered when establishing the standards. Id. at 77.

By contrast, consider the variance criterion that section 301(c) of the FWPCA applies to polluters subject to Best Available Technology (BAT) standards, stricter standards imposed to limit water pollution after laxer BPT standards have been met. That section allows a variance if the applicant shows that the modified requirements represent "the maximum use of technology within" the owner's "economic capability" and produces "reasonable further progress" toward the "elimination" of pollution discharges. Notice that this does allow a limited variance based on the polluter's economic capability. See Crushed Stone, 449 U.S. at 73. Why would Congress allow EPA to take economic capability into account in granting BAT variances, but not in granting BPT variances? Does allowing a variance for lack of economic capability undermine the level playing field ideal?

A Note on The Value of Uniformity

Congress in many instances required EPA to set uniform standards for polluters in a source category. Why not adopt individually tailored standards instead, since different facilities have different physical characteristics and different owners have different economic capabilities?

Congress clearly hoped to achieve economies of scale through uniform standard setting. Setting individual standards for each facility can prove enormously resource intensive. Setting a uniform standard for an entire industrial subcategory allows simultaneous regulation of a large number of facilities. The level playing field idea also helps explain why Congress (and sometimes industry) supports uniform standards. Of course, the provisions for subcategorization and variances raise questions about whether the standards are as uniform in practice as they appear to be in theory. We will consider some criticisms of uniformity at the end of this chapter.

b. Technology-Forcing

In *National Lime*, EPA claimed that existing technology that it had identified and already tested could enable lime kilns to meet the adopted standard. Section 111 requires standards reflecting the capabilities of the best emission reduction system that EPA "determines has been adequately demonstrated." 42 U.S.C. §7411(a). While an early decision interpreted this language to allow EPA to base standards on technology that has not been used but might be created in response to its standard setting, *see* Portland Cement Ass'n v. Ruckelshaus, 486 F.2d 375, 391 (D.C. Cir. 1973) (analogizing NSPS provisions to technology-forcing standards for mobile sources), EPA has generally based its NSPS standards on existing technology, *cf.* Lignite Energy Council v. EPA, 198 F.3d 930, 933 (D.C. Cir. 1999) (New Source Performance Standards are not technology-forcing).

By contrast, the subsection of the Clean Air Act requiring EPA to regulate non-road engines (such as those found in power mowers and weed trimmers) requires EPA to set standards to "achieve the greatest degree of emission reduction achievable through the application of technology which the Administrator determines *will be* available. . . . " 42 U.S.C. §7547(a)(3). The United States Court of Appeals for the District of Columbia Circuit has held that this provision authorizes or requires technology-forcing regulation, *i.e.*, regulation that might force companies to come up with technology not yet developed or successfully employed. *See* Husqvarna AB v. EPA, 254 F.3d 195, 201 (D.C. Cir. 2001).

In general, the Supreme Court has explained that the Clean Air Act is a "technology forcing" statute. *See* Union Electric v. EPA, 427 U.S. 246, 257 (1976). The idea of technology-forcing comes from the legislative history of the Clean Air Act Amendments of 1970, which established the modern statute's basic contours. Congress feared that industry would resist standards by claiming that clean-up was impossible. Such claims might defeat efforts to establish the standards needed to produce clean air.

Senator Muskie responded to concerns that achievement of clean air might be impossible in a very interesting way. He did not simply deny the validity of the concern, by claiming that achievement of the 1970 Amendment's standards was possible. Rather, he argued that Congress' proper role is to protect public health, leaving industry to figure out how to clean up. 116 Cong. Rec. 32901-32902 (1970) (statement of Senator Muskie). If after a good faith effort to comply with the 1970 Amendments, industry could not do so, it should then come back to Congress for relief. Industry has done this many times over the years, and received exemptions and extensions of deadlines. The legislative history specifically reflects an intention to force the development of technology that would make it possible to achieve levels of cleanup that might "appear" impossible. *Id. See Union Electric*, 427 U.S. at 259.

Two features of the 1970 Amendments are most closely associated with the technology-forcing philosophy. The rejection of administrative consideration of cost in setting the health-based National Ambient Air Quality Standards (recall *Lead Industries*) implies that states must ultimately come up with sufficiently stringent emission standards to protect public health. *Union Electric*, 427 U.S. at 258-59. Congress deemed this cost-blindness appropriate in part because it believed that industry would develop the technologies needed to protect health if required to do so. Thus, health-based standards (or other effects-based standards) can force technology, because EPA sets them without considering cost or technological feasibility in establishing a standard's stringency.

Second, statutory provisions governing emissions from automobiles also reflected the technology-forcing philosophy. These provisions required industry to meet strict numerical limits that Congress wrote into the 1970 Amendments, notwithstanding auto industry claims that the standards were impossible to meet. But Congress provided an escape valve, authorizing EPA to delay compliance with these standards, which it did.

In 1970, Congress also authorized EPA to set "feasible" technology-forcing limits on its own to supplement the specific limits Congress created. These provisions are technology-based standards that require the consideration of cost and technology. But they permit the agency to rely upon technologies not yet adequately developed in justifying a standard. Similar provisions in the subsequent 1977 Amendments gave rise to the following case:

Natural Resources Defense Council, Inc. v. U.S. Environmental Protection Agency
655 F.2d 318 (D.C. Cir. 1981)

Mikva, Circuit Judge.

These consolidated cases present a variety of challenges to actions of the EPA in setting standards to govern emissions of particulate matter and oxides of nitrogen from diesel vehicles . . . . General Motors Corporation (GM) and Intervenors Mercedes-Benz of North America, Inc., and Volkswagen of America, Inc., assert that . . . the standards are too strict. Finding that the agency has stated adequate reasons for its decisions . . . we uphold the challenged regulations in their entirety. . . .

B.   Technological Feasibility

The EPA's choice of the 0.20 [grams per mile] gpm standard for light-duty diesels in 1985 was the result of adjusting current diesel particulate emission data by the percentage of reduction expected from certain technological improvements, most notably the trap-oxidizer. The manufacturers' attack on the standard focuses on the EPA's prediction concerning the probable pace of development of trap-oxidizer technology. Before examining the details of the agency's reasoning and the industry challenges, however, we find it useful to discuss the legal standard that governs our inquiry.

1.   The Standard of Review

The standard of review in this case is the traditional one for judicial scrutiny of agency rulemaking: we are to set aside any action found to be "arbitrary, capricious, an abuse of discretion, or otherwise not in accordance with law." Act §307(d)(9)(A). As nonscientists, we must recall that "(o)ur 'expertise' is not in setting standards for emission control but in determining if the standards as set are the result of reasoned decisionmaking." Despite this limited role, our examination of the record must be searching, for the necessity to review agency decisions, if it is to be more than a meaningless exercise, requires enough steeping in technical matters to determine whether the agency "has exercised a reasoned discretion." . . . We cannot substitute our own judgment for that of the agency, but it is our duty to consider whether "the decision was based on a consideration of the relevant factors and whether there has been a clear error of judgment."

In the present case, GM attacks the EPA's estimation of the period of time "necessary to permit the development and application of the requisite technology" to achieve compliance with the 1985 particulate standards. The agency has determined that the technology will be available in time, and now seeks to defend its conclusion as a product of reasoned decisionmaking. Such predictions inherently involve a greater degree of uncertainty than estimations of the effectiveness of current technology. If we judge the EPA's action by the standard of certainty appropriate to current technology, the agency will be unable to set pollutant levels until the necessary technology is already available.

The legislative history of both the 1970 and the 1977 amendments demonstrates that Congress intended the agency to project future advances in pollution control capability. . . .

This court has upheld the agency's power to make such projections, while recognizing that it is "subject to the restraints of reasonableness, and does not open the door to ' "crystal ball" inquiry.' "[sic] The Clean Air Act requires the EPA to look to the future in setting standards, but the agency must also provide a reasoned explanation of its basis for believing that its projection is reliable. This includes a defense of its methodology for arriving at numerical estimates.

The EPA has generally been granted "considerable latitude in extrapolating from today's technology" when it predicts future technological developments for the purposes of the Clean Water Act. The courts have had numerous occasions to review EPA determinations that a given control technique constitutes the "best available technology economically achievable" in the 1980s. Most of the opinions . . . steer close by the shores of their factual contexts and yield little in the way of explicit doctrine. But their essential requirement is that the agency provide "a reasonable basis for belief that a new technology will be available and economically achievable." When a technology is already in use in other industries, the court often expects more solid evidence that the technology can be transferred to the industry in question, or at least that relevant dissimilarities have been considered.

The EPA's decision must be judged in terms of record evidence available in early 1980, allowing a "time frame of 2–2½ years for completion of the design development phase (and) 2–2½ years of production lead time."

Given this time frame, we feel that there is substantial room for deference to the EPA's expertise in projecting the likely course of development. The essential question in this case is the pace of that development, and absent a revolution in the study of industry, defense of such a projection can never possess the inescapable logic of a mathematical deduction. We think that the EPA will have demonstrated the reasonableness of its basis for prediction if it answers any theoretical objections to the trap-oxidizer method, identifies the major steps necessary in refinement of the device, and offers plausible reasons for believing that each of those steps can be completed in the time available. If the agency can make this showing, then we cannot say that its determination was the result of crystal ball inquiry, or that it neglected its duty of reasoned decisionmaking.

2. *The Time "Necessary to Permit the Development and Application of the Requisite Technology"* . . .

The EPA has predicted that trap-oxidizers will be available for use in model year 1985 vehicles. As the agency has repeatedly observed, the trap-oxidizer is familiar and unobjectionable as a concept. It is not only theoretically sound — experimental data demonstrate that periodic incineration can maintain efficiency for over 10,000 miles. But to date, no filter material has been found that can withstand periodic incineration of the accumulated particulates throughout the 50,000-mile useful life of the vehicle while maintaining a high level of trapping efficiency. . . .

The EPA is not obliged to provide detailed solutions to every engineering problem posed in the perfection of the trap-oxidizer. In the absence of theoretical objections to the technology, the agency need only identify the major steps necessary for development of the device, and give plausible reasons for its belief that the industry will be able to solve those problems in the time remaining. The EPA is not required to rebut all speculation that unspecified factors may hinder "real world" emission control.

The EPA has identified as the necessary remaining steps in development of trap-oxidizer technology — the choice of a durable, efficient filter material, the selection of an incineration method, and the refinement of a control mechanism to bring about automatic initiation of the regeneration process. GM agrees with the agency's specification of these aspects of the trap-oxidizer as the ones requiring further research.

a.   Development of a Durable Filter

The most vigorously controverted issue in this case concerns durability, which the EPA has recognized as the key remaining problem. "Collection efficiencies and regeneration techniques have progressed to the point where the most critical issue is whether the efficiency and regeneration mechanism can be maintained over the useful life of the vehicle." Both parties focus on the GM Opel test, in which a metal mesh trap survived over 12,000 miles; the EPA views this test as a stirring demonstration of how far research had progressed in the brief springtime of trap-oxidizer research, while GM sees the 12,000-mile mark as insubstantial compared to the 50,000- to 100,000-mile goal.

The EPA has predicted that the necessary work can be accomplished in time for 1985 model year production. The agency points to the wide variety of materials that have demonstrated appropriate initial efficiencies; several of these are hybrids, suggesting that new combinations of present candidates, rather than hitherto untested substances, may provide the answer. The EPA noted the rapid pace of achievement since attention turned to trap-oxidizers . . . :

Considerable progress has occurred in the last 1½ years. . . .

We conclude that these are plausible reasons for a determination that the industry is capable of solving the durability problem in the allotted time. The EPA could reasonably refuse to be discouraged by the limited initial success, as the project is relatively young. The rapidity of recent progress is a factor that the agency may consider in making a prediction of future capabilities. And the industry's own predictions, while not determinative, support the view that success in this kind of research can realistically be expected within the proposed time frame. We conclude that the EPA's durability prediction, though uncertain, is no more uncertain than such estimates inherently must be, and that the EPA has met the requirement of "reasoned decisionmaking."

d. Conclusion

In summary, we find sufficient support for the EPA's necessarily predictive judgment and therefore uphold the EPA's particulate standard. The agency has given the manufacturers substantial lead time, and there is room for interim adjustments to the standard without significant hardship. Under those circumstances, the applicable standard of review allows the EPA considerable latitude to exercise its expertise through reasoned projections. We find that the agency has given an adequate explanation of its reasons for believing that the necessary steps in improving trap-oxidizer technology can be completed in the time remaining. . . .

V. Conclusion

In the Clean Air Act, Congress encouraged the EPA to set standards for the future without specifying the methodology the agency must follow to determine the probable course of future technological growth. In these circumstances, a reviewing court's role is to make sure that the agency has acted responsibly in formulating a reasoned prediction. It is not our task to decide whether the agency is correct, or to require proof to a mathematical certainty. We must be satisfied if the agency has undertaken its analysis with the degree of precision and clarity that the subject inherently permits. The EPA has done so in this case . . . .

The regulations reviewed in this proceeding, in their entirety, are Affirmed.

NOTES AND QUESTIONS ON *NRDC v. EPA* AND TECHNOLOGY–FORCING

1. *1970 Amendments.* Both EPA and Congress delayed implementation of the numerical standards for automobile emissions many times. But ultimately, the game of chicken worked, and the automobile industry did comply with the standards enacted. Some scholars, however, have claimed that these standards did not truly force development of new technology, but instead simply forced adoption of already existing technology that industry was resisting as impracticable. D. Bruce La Pierre, *Technology-Forcing and Federal Environmental Protection Statutes*, 62 Iowa L. Rev. 771, 796 (1977) (concluding that the automobile standards have not sparked efforts "to develop a variety of innovative controls"); Richard B. Stewart, *Regulation, Innovation, and Administrative Law: A Conceptual Framework*, 69 Cal. L. Rev. 1256, 1304 (1981) (automobile standards forced "the rapid commercialization and diffusion of add-on catalysts," but failed to produce "basic changes in engine technologies").

2. *California LEV standards.* The state of California has always played a leading role in developing automobile standards and forcing technology. In the 1990s, California introduced Low Emissions Vehicle (LEV) standards to force

further technological development and cleanup from the automobile industry. As originally enacted, these standards demanded improvements in emission levels that would require increasingly radical technological change over a long period of time, culminating in a zero emission standard that probably would require some sort of electric vehicle not using gasoline at all. Industry has successfully pressured California to relax and delay these standards in various ways, largely out of concern about the zero emission mandate. Still these standards, which a number of states have copied, have led to the introduction of cars with substantially lower emissions, some of which use new "hybrid technology." Hybrid technology uses a combination of gasoline and electric power to reduce fuel consumption and emissions, and sales of hybrid vehicles have been rising. While some zero emission vehicles exist, they have not penetrated the market widely as of this writing.

   3. *What must government know about technology?* Should Congress or administrative agencies impose standards (such as LEV) without knowing how companies can meet them? Do the standards the D.C. Circuit has developed provide a sufficient framework for judicial review of such standards?

2. Economic Feasibility

   The technology-based standard setting provisions generally require agencies to consider the costs of compliance, not just the technical feasibility of installing and operating particular pollution control technologies. But how should they analyze costs and take them into account?

   The law could require agencies to consider costs to determine whether facility owners can afford the cost of compliance, *i.e.*, to analyze whether a standard is economically feasible. Agencies might instead compare the costs to the societal benefits of regulation (in reduced health and environmental impacts), *i.e.*, engage in cost-benefit analysis. Or agencies might analyze the dollars that must be expended for each marginal increment in pollution reduction, a marginal cost effectiveness analysis.

   One of us has described the restraints the feasibility principle imposes in the following manner:

> The feasibility principle . . . generally requires stringent regulation, but presumptively subjects this demand for stringency to two constraints. First, the principle authorizes government agencies to forego physically impossible environmental improvements. Second, the principle authorizes government agencies to forego constraints so costly that they cause widespread plant shutdowns. . . .
> The cost constraint requires assessment of cost and the technological constraint requires assessment of engineering possibilities, i.e. a technological assessment. But cost assessment presupposes technological assessment. The cost of making any environmental improvement equals the cost incurred in making the physical changes necessary to accomplish it. Nobody can begin to estimate the cost of an environmental improvement until an engineer describes the technologies regulated parties will use to make that improvement. . . .

The cost constraint, however, implies that the regulator must analyze whether the cost of implementing the technologically possible reductions would lead to plant shutdowns. This implies that regulators must compare cost, not to benefits, but to net earnings prior to regulation and the value of corporate assets. Costs significant enough to render plants *unprofitable* could lead their owners to shut them down. For that reason, feasibility analysis also includes an assessment of the cost's impact on shutdowns. . . .

The feasibility principle does not, however, consist wholly of constraints. This principle requires maximum reductions at least up to the point where plant closures begin to occur.

David M. Driesen, *Distributing the Costs of Environmental, Health and Safety Protection: The Feasibility Principle, Cost-Benefit Analysis, and Regulatory Reform*, 32 B.C. Envtl. Aff. L. Rev. 1, 9-16 (2005).

Does the idea that regulators should "avoid widespread plant shutdowns" offer a good interpretation of what it means for a regulation to be feasible? What else might the idea of economic feasibility mean?

Agencies and courts have not been clear and consistent in how they interpret the economic constraint on feasibility. Furthermore, Professor Driesen only argues that the requirement to maximize reductions that do not shut down plants offers a good presumptive interpretation of statutory provisions employing maximizing language, such as requirements for the "maximum" achievable emissions reduction, *see* 42 U.S.C. §7412(d), and the "best" available technology, *see* 33 U.S.C. §1311(b)(2). He does not argue, for example, that the provision of the Clean Air Act requiring states to impose limits reflecting "reasonably available control technology" on major existing sources, for example, requires regulators to maximize reductions up to the point of widespread plant closures. For that provision does not have any language indicating an intent to "maximize" reductions or employ the "best" technology.

In the case below, EPA established effluent limitations (a form of technology-based regulation) under two separate statutory provisions. One requires it to set standards based on the "best practicable control technology" (BPT); another required standards based on the "best available technology" (BAT). Consider whether the statutory language of either of these standards embodies something like the feasibility principle. Does it demand consideration of economic feasibility, cost-benefit analysis, or marginal cost effectiveness analysis?

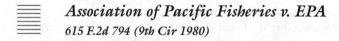

Association of Pacific Fisheries v. EPA
615 F.2d 794 (9th Cir 1980)

KENNEDY, CIRCUIT JUDGE.

In 1972 Congress, intending "to restore and maintain the chemical, physical, and biological integrity of the Nation's waters," amended the Federal

Water Pollution Control Act (Act). Congress established national pollution goals to be achieved by specific dates. By July 1, 1977, industries discharging pollutants into the nation's waters were to have achieved "the best practicable control technology currently available (BPT)." Section 301(b)(1)(A), 33 U.S.C. §1311(b)(1)(A). By 1983, industry is to achieve "the best available technology economically achievable [BAT]." Section 301(b)(2)(A), 33 U.S.C. §1311(b)(2)(A). The Environmental Protection Agency (EPA or Agency) was entrusted with the responsibility of defining and policing the efficient and prompt achievement of these goals.

This case involves a challenge to regulations promulgated by the Agency establishing effluent guidelines for the Canned and Preserved Seafood Processing Point Source Category. . . . The effluent which is the subject of the regulations consists of unused fish residuals. This discharge includes heads, tails, and internal residuals of the processed fish. Substantial quantities of water are used at various stages of the plant operations. This water comes into contact with the fish residuals and contains pollutants when discharged. The regulations prescribe limitations on discharge, and utilize three measures of pollution: five-day biochemical oxygen demand (BOD 5); total suspended solids (TSS); and oil and grease (O & G). The regulations establish daily maximum levels and monthly average levels for each subcategory, and are measured in terms of the amount of pollutant per thousand pounds of fish processed.

The prescribed 1977 BPT for processors not located in Alaska, and Alaska processors located in "population or processing centers," is the installation of screens to trap the larger fish particles before the effluent is discharged from the plant. . . .

By 1983 the fisheries must comply with more rigorous technology requirements and effluent limitations. For nonremote facilities, the Agency directed that a dissolved air flotation unit be installed at each location and that the end-of-pipe effluent be channeled through this system before it is discharged into the receiving water. These regulations apply to all nonremote subcategories except Subpart V, Conventional Bottomfish. There, the Administrator has prescribed aerated lagoons as the BAT. Remote Alaska fish processors will be required by the 1983 regulations to screen the effluent before discharging it into the receiving waters.

Scope of Review

The scope of our review in cases like this is well-settled and need not be restated at length. Our task is to insure that the Agency has accumulated sufficient material upon which to make a reasoned decision, reviewed that material, and promulgated regulations that are the result of reasoned decision-making. . . .

1977 Regulations

The petitioners contend that the cost of operating the required technology is wholly disproportionate to the resulting pollution control benefits, and that both costs and benefits were erroneously calculated by the Agency. . . .

B. Cost-Benefit Comparisons and the Question of Screening

The parties dispute whether or not the requirement of screening plus barging or land-based disposal was reached after a proper evaluation of costs and benefits. The disagreement extends both to questions of interpreting the statute and to whether the Agency followed the Act even assuming its own interpretation is correct.

Section 304(b)(1)(B) of the Act provides in part:

Factors relating to the assessment of best practicable control technology currently available to comply with subsection (b)(1) of section 301 of this Act shall include consideration of the total cost of application of technology in relation to the effluent reduction benefits to be achieved from such application. . . .

We think it plain that, as a general rule, the EPA is required to consider the costs and benefits of a proposed technology in its inquiry to determine the BPT. The Agency has broad discretion in weighing these competing factors, however. When considering different levels of technology, it must be shown that increased costs are wholly disproportionate to potential effluent reduction before the Agency is permitted to rely on a cost-benefit comparison to select a lower level of technology as the BPT. This conclusion is consistent with the interpretation of section 304(b)(1)(B) given in the Conference Report on the bill which ultimately became the Act. The Report states:

The balancing test between total cost and effluent reduction benefits is intended to limit the application of technology only where the additional degree of effluent reduction is wholly out of proportion to the costs of achieving such marginal level of reduction for any class or category of sources.

It is relevant in this case, moreover, to consider the definition of the benefits the Agency is directed to weigh. We agree with the Agency's contention that Congress intended BPT standards to be based primarily on employment of available technology for reducing effluent discharge, and not primarily on demonstrated changes in water quality. Congress was aware that prior enforcement efforts based on water quality standards had not been successful. It determined, accordingly, that the Agency should have the authority to require effluent reduction benefits as defined by the amount or degree of reduction achieved by a level of technology applied to discharge, without the necessity of demonstrating the incremental effect of that technology on the quality of the receiving water . . . . [T]he "effluent reduction benefits" referred to in the Act are not primarily water quality benefits; rather, "(e)ffluent reduction occurs whenever less effluent is discharged, i. e., whenever a plant treats its wastes before discharge. . . . "

The costs of screening were also considered by the Agency. . . . After estimating the costs for affected subcategories, the Agency concluded the total internal costs of the 1977 effluent limitations would be $6.2 million for investment and $1.3 million of annual expenditures. External costs included a minor effect on prices and the expected closure of some processing plants because of inability to comply economically with the regulations. The effect of these closures on the domestic industry capacity was anticipated to be small.

Petitioners argue that the number of plants estimated to close as a result of the regulations demonstrates that the costs of implementing the technology are wholly out of proportion to the effluent reduction benefits, and thus that the regulations do not prescribe a practicable technology. We do not find the Agency's action can be set aside on this issue.

Precisely how many plants in nonremote locations the EPA estimated would close as a result of the 1977 BPT is not completely clear from the record. In the Preamble to the Regulations, 40 Fed. Reg. 55777, the Agency states only that "a number of small plants are projected to be adversely affected by the effluent limitations." The record shows that in affected subcategories 28 out of 172 plants were projected to close as a result of the 1977 BPT. In its brief, the Agency argues that for several reasons, stated in the record, its original estimate of the number of plant closings was too high. It does not, however, point to any revised estimate. Thus, the most concrete estimate available is that contained in EPA's Economic Analysis. These data also disclose that in Alaska nonremote subcategories the Alaska subcategories where screening is the BPT seven out of sixteen plants were predicted to close as a result of inability to meet BPT.

Petitioners agree Congress contemplated that implementing BPT might result in plant closures in some industries. The proportion of plants estimated to close in the nonremote Alaska subcategories (57% for nonremote Alaskan fresh and frozen salmon and 33% for nonremote Alaskan salmon canning) is substantially higher than that approved in some other cases. See, e.g., Weyerhaeuser, 590 F.2d at 1047 (summarizing facts in American Paper Inst. v. Train, 543 F.2d 328, 338-39 (D.C. Cir.) (out of 270 mills and 120,000 people, 8 mills estimated to close and 1800 people laid off; in three subcategories, of 30 mills, 3 estimated to close). The Agency determined, however, that the effect on prices of implementing the BPT would be small: "price increases generally in the range of 0.3 to 0.5 percent are projected," 40 Fed.Reg. at 55777. It also found that "domestic industry capacity is not expected to be affected by the potential closure of these particular small plants." *Id.* The percentage of estimated plant closures in the seafood processing category generally is low. Given these findings, the estimated number of plant closings in the nonremote Alaska subcategories, standing by itself, does not invalidate its cost/benefit analysis or require us to set aside the Agency's determination that the required technology was practicable.

The Agency need not balance the costs of compliance against effluent reduction benefits with pinpoint precision, in part because many of the benefits resulting from the effluent reduction are incapable of precise quantification. Cf. American Petroleum Inst. v. EPA, 540 F.2d 1023, 1038 (10th Cir. 1976) ("The value of the resulting benefits is not capable of present-day determination."). See also Appalachian Power Co. v. Train, 545 F.2d 1351, 1361 (4th Cir. 1976) ("(W)e (reject) Industry's contention that benefits derived from a particular level of effluent reduction must be quantified in monetary terms. This reflects the simple fact that such benefits often cannot be reduced to dollars and cents.").

The Agency, upon consideration of the effluent reduction benefits thought to be achieved by screening, both the water quality benefits and the amount of pollutants discharged into the receiving waters, determined that the costs of screening were justified. We conclude the Agency complied with the Act's mandate to consider the costs of technology in relation to effluent reduction benefits.

1983 Regulations

The regulations promulgated by the Administrator for 1983 are to reflect the "best available technology economically achievable." Section 301(b)(2)(A), 33 U.S.C. §1311(b)(2)(A). For the regulations to be affirmed, the Agency must demonstrate that the technology required is "available" and the effluent limitations are "economically achievable."

. . . [The Court upheld the EPA's conclusion that its BAT limits were technically achievable.]

The next question is whether the Agency properly evaluated the costs of meeting the 1983 guidelines. In describing the role of costs in promulgating [BAT], the Conference Report stated:

> While cost should be a factor in the Administrator's judgment, no balancing test will be required. The Administrator will be bound by a test of reasonableness. In this case, the reasonableness of what is 'economically achievable' should reflect an evaluation of what needs to be done to move toward the elimination of the discharge of pollutants and what is achievable through the application of available technology without regard to cost.

Although the wording of the statute clearly states that the 1983 limitations must be "economically achievable," there is some disagreement among the circuits as to whether the costs of compliance should be considered in a review of the 1983 limitations. We hold . . . that the EPA must consider the economic consequences of the 1983 regulations, along with the other factors mentioned in section 304(b)(2)(B), 33 U.S.C. §1314(b)(2)(B).

Petitioners maintain that the Agency must balance the ecological benefits against the associated costs in determining whether the technology is economically achievable. They cite in support of this proposition Appalachian Power Co. v. Train, supra. In remanding the 1983 regulations affecting electrical power companies, the court there stated:

(I)n choosing among alternative strategies, EPA must not only set forth the cost of achieving a particular level of heat reduction but must also state the expected environmental benefits, that is to say the effect on the environment, which will take place as a result of reduction, for it is only after EPA has fully explicated its course of conduct in this manner that a reviewing court can determine whether the agency has, in light of the goal to be achieved, acted arbitrarily or capriciously in adopting a particular effluent reduction level.

According to petitioners, the Agency did not consider the incremental benefit to the environment to be achieved by the dissolved air flotation units, and the regulations must be set aside. We cannot agree. As noted by the court in Weyerhaeuser, the language of the statute indicates that the EPA's consideration of costs in determining BPT and [BAT] was to be different. In prescribing the appropriate 1977 technology, the Agency was to "include consideration of the total cost of application of technology *in relation to the effluent reduction benefits to be achieved from such application.*" Section 304(b)(1)(B) (emphasis added). In determining the 1983 control technology, however, the EPA must "take into account . . . the cost of achieving such effluent reduction," along with various other factors. Section 304(b)(2)(B). The conspicuous absence of the comparative language contained in section 304(b)(1)(B) leads us to the conclusion that Congress did not intend the Agency or this court to engage in marginal cost-benefit comparisons.

The intent of Congress is stated in 33 U.S.C. §1251(a)(1): "(I)t is the national goal that the discharge of pollutants into the navigable waters be eliminated by 1985." The regulations that will be applied in 1983 are intended to result "in reasonable further progress toward the national goal of eliminating the discharge of all pollutants. . . . " 33 U.S.C. §1311(b)(2)(A). These express declarations of congressional intent cannot be ignored in determining the reasonableness of the 1983 regulations. So long as the required technology reduces the discharge of pollutants, our inquiry will be limited to whether the Agency considered the cost of technology, along with the other statutory factors, and whether its conclusion is reasonable. Of course, at some point extremely costly more refined treatment will have a de minimis effect on the receiving waters. But that point has not been reached in these [BAT] regulations.

The record discloses that the Agency studied the cost of complying with the 1983 regulations. It set forth the cost of compliance for plants that produced various amounts of effluent per minute, both in terms of capital costs and operation and maintenance costs. The projections include estimates of the costs of construction, labor, power, chemicals and fuel. Although land acquisition costs were not considered, the amount of land necessary for the air flotation unit is minimal. In contrast to our conclusion regarding aerated lagoons, the Agency was not arbitrary in concluding that the DAF unit could be installed on existing plant locations without necessitating additional land acquisitions. . . .

Finally, it does not appear that the cost of complying with the 1983 regulations is unreasonable. The cost of compliance for the Northwest Canned

Salmon subcategory, for example, is estimated to be $157,000 for initial investment and $32,000 of annual expenditures for the average size plants. According to the EPA's economic analysis, the total annual costs of pollution abatement averaged between one and two percent of the total sales figures of each subcategory. Depreciation is available for the capital outlays and tax deductions are available for business expenses. The Agency concluded that the benefits justified the costs, and petitioners have not shown that conclusion to be arbitrary or capricious.

Although the number of plants estimated to close as a result of the 1983 regulations was not stated clearly to us, it appears to be a lesser proportion of affected plants than that which we approved for the 1977 regulations. Since Congress contemplated the closure of some marginal plants, we do not consider the regulations to be arbitrary and capricious.

For these reasons, we conclude that the 1983 regulations requiring dissolved air flotation units for West Coast fish processors should be upheld.

[The Court remanded part of the regulation, because EPA had not adequately demonstrated the technical feasibility of plants achieving the limits EPA said that aerated lagoons can enable them to achieve or the costs of land acquisition associated with this technology.]

AFFIRMED in part and REMANDED in part.

NOTES ON *PACIFIC FISHERIES* AND ECONOMIC FEASIBILITY

1. *Considering Cost.* The Clean Water Act requires EPA to consider the cost of its technology-based effluent regulations. According to this case, how precisely must the agency do so, and in what respects?

2. *CBA?* In the next chapter, we will consider cost-benefit analysis (CBA) and its role in regulation. Some commentators regard any regulatory process that involves consideration and analysis of cost as an instance of CBA. Does the Clean Water Act require CBA in this sense? This book and most commentators who write about this subject frequently employ a narrower definition of CBA. Under this definition, CBA requires a comparison between the costs of regulation and its benefits, and the benefits must be monetized, *i.e.*, expressed in dollar terms. Do the statutory provision governing BPT and BAT require CBA in this sense? Do these provisions differ in how they treat cost, and if so, how?

3. *Facility closure.* EPA predicted that its regulations would close some facilities. Did that make the standards unachievable in the court's view? What degree of plant closures would make a regulation "unachievable"? The court noted that this regulation would close a larger number of facilities than is typical. For many regulations, EPA projects no plant closures at all. *See* Driesen, *Feasibility Principle, supra,* at 43. When it does project plant closures, it usually expects 3% or less of regulated plants to close. *See id.*

4. *Feasibility and cost.* Notice that if the economic feasibility test is understood as a prohibition against widespread plant closures, decisions about feasibility do not depend upon the relationship between costs and benefits. Rather, they depend upon the relationship between costs and the economic capabilities of regulated industry. *See, e.g.,* National Wildlife Federation v. EPA, 286 F.3d 554, 564 (D.C. Cir. 2002) (plant closures predicted when net earnings fall below the salvage value of a regulated mill).

5. *Definition of benefits for BPT.* With respect to BPT, the court defined the benefit of the regulation in terms of the amount of effluent reduction, rather than in terms of "water quality benefits." In Weyerhauser v. Costle, 590 F.2d 1011 (D.C. Cir. 1978), the court explained the reasons to avoid considering water quality benefits in rejecting paper mill owners' argument that EPA must consider the capacity of ocean waters to dilute effluent in setting BPT limits:

[For 24 years], Congress attempted to use receiving water quality as a basis for setting effluent standards. At the end of that period, Congress realized not only that its water pollution efforts . . . had failed, but also that reliance on receiving water capacity as a crucial test for permissible pollution levels had contributed greatly to that failure.

Based on this experience, Congress adopted a new approach in 1972. Under the Act, 'a discharger's performance is . . . measured against strict technology-based effluent limitations — specified levels of treatment — to which it must conform, rather than against limitations derived from water quality standards to which it and other polluters must collectively conform.'

The new approach reflected developing views on practicality and rights. Congress concluded that water pollution seriously harmed the environment, and that although the cost of control would be heavy, the nation would benefit from controlling that pollution. Yet scientific uncertainties made it difficult to assess the benefits to particular bodies of receiving water. Even if the federal government eventually could succeed at the task at which [sic] had failed for 24 years and thus could determine benefits and devise water quality standards, Congress concluded that the requisite further delay was too long for the nation to wait.

Moreover, by eliminating the issue of the capacity of particular bodies of receiving water, Congress made nationwide uniformity in effluent limitations possible. . . .

More fundamentally, the new approach implemented changing views as to the relative rights of the public and of industrial polluters. Hitherto, the right of the polluter was pre-eminent, unless the damage caused by pollution could be proven. Henceforth, the right of the public to a clean environment would be pre-eminent, unless pollution treatment was impractical or unachievable. . . . This view of relative rights was based in part on hard-nosed assessment of our scientific ignorance. . . .

Weyerhauser, 590 F.2d at 1042-43.

One cannot monetize the benefits of regulation without taking into account the impact of specific dischargers on specific water bodies. To monetize benefits, EPA would have to assess not just the tons of pollution reduced and the cost of pollution control, but also the degree of benefit these reductions would bring to fish, wildlife, aesthetics, water-based recreation, and other discrete benefits associated with improved water quality. Such an analysis would prove difficult or impossible in the context of national standard setting, because the water quality benefit of a particular quantity of reduction would vary with the quality of particular receiving waters, and the state of controls on sources other than the ones being regulated. The benefit would not be uniform nationally. Because the legislative history on the BPT cost-benefit provision recognizes this problem, courts have rejected the claim that the requirement to consider the costs and benefits of effluent reductions for purposes of establishing BPT requires consideration of water quality.

6. *Costs disproportionate to benefits.* The *Pacific Fisheries* court interpreted the statutory language governing BPT standards to allow EPA to set less stringent regulations than a feasibility test might indicate if costs are wholly disproportionate to benefits. If a regulation required removal of 100 million pounds of total suspended solids, how would EPA determine the point at which costs would be "wholly disproportionate" to those benefits? ($100 million? $200 million? $500 million?) Is it possible to make that determination without translating the amount of effluent reduction into water quality benefits? Would translation of the benefit into estimates of water quality benefits make it possible to determine proportionality?

7. *Marginal cost effectiveness analysis.* EPA has relied primarily upon marginal cost effectiveness analysis in comparing costs to effluent reduction benefits for purposes of setting BPT standards. Thus, in a subsequent case, EPA successfully defended BPT standards for the chemical industry by asserting that $76.6 million of annualized compliance cost after an initial capital investment of $215.8 million was reasonable, since its regulations would remove 108 million pounds of conventional pollutants annually. *See* Chemical Mfrs. Ass'n v. EPA, 870 F.2d 177, 204 (5th Cir. 1989). In *Chemical Mfrs. Ass'n,* the chemical industry invoked marginal cost effectiveness analysis to challenge EPA's BPT requirements. It argued that in going from 96 to 99 percent removal, costs increased from 38 cents per pound to 71 cents per pound. *Id.* at 205.

The court upheld the regulations anyway, refusing to require a "knee of the curve test" that would prohibit regulations that made a curve drawn showing the marginal cost per marginal pound of abatement sloping sharply upward. *Id.* at 204.

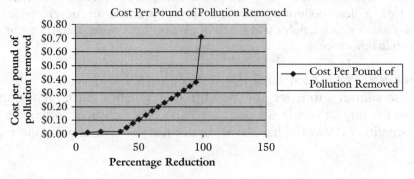

Cost Per Pound of Pollution Removed

Did the court properly interpret the BPT requirements, and if so, are they appropriate? Suppose that the average costs were reasonable, but the curve did rise sharply in going from 96 to 99 percent. Should the agency avoid the sharp rise in marginal abatement cost?

8. *Rationale for the feasibility principle.* Consider the following defense of the feasibility principle:

> If one believes, as many CBA proponents do, that environmental regulators should consider the distribution of costs and benefits of environmental regulation, the feasibility principle has much to recommend it. This approach focuses regulators' attention on significant costs and avoids wasting resources considering finely calibrated responses to costs having minor impacts on society.
>
> This approach relies primarily upon information about the distribution of costs to separate significant from insignificant costs. When economic losses become concentrated in ways that devastate individuals, they can have drastic effects, even if the total amount of cost is low. Conversely, widely distributed costs can have minor effects, even if total aggregate costs are high. This "concentration" principle suggests that the distribution of costs can tell us a lot about their significance. . . .
>
> As a general rule, environmental regulations may lead owners of regulated facilities to increase employment. Regulations often force companies to hire more workers or pay contractors to install and operate pollution controls or to redesign processes to prevent pollution. Indeed, more stringent and costly regulation may force more pollution-control related hiring than less stringent and costly regulation, as long as the regulation does not make plants unprofitable and lead to shutdowns.
>
> Often costs imposed on companies become distributed so widely that they have little real impact on human lives. . . . Furthermore, firms can creatively compensate for or avoid costs. Indeed, when environmental regulation has been demanding, firms have often engaged in innovative changes to avoid the costs of regulation. . . .
>
> By contrast, regulations that force a plant owner to shutdown decrease employment, at least in the short run. This can concentrate severe economic losses on small numbers of workers who can ill afford them. This sort of loss can have a devastating impact on workers' lives, leading to depression, a terrible feeling of loss, and an inability to cope economically, especially if unemployment or very severe underemployment proves permanent. . . .
>
> While firms often can systematically distribute regulatory costs widely or avoid them altogether, harms from pollution often devastate randomly selected individuals. Cancer, for example, can lead to a long slow painful death for some unfortunates. Birth defects can ruin the lives of children born with them and afflict their parents with enormous burdens. Asthma can make its victims gasp for air, send asthmatics to hospital emergency rooms in summer, and force children from

the playground on hot days. As these examples demonstrate, we should think of most pollution control programs as efforts to ameliorate concentrated harms.

Furthermore, while imposition of regulatory costs tends to spawn cost avoidance behavior, some of which can be very socially productive, pollution can impose burdens that one cannot easily escape. Since people must breathe, they cannot escape air pollution. Of course, relatively wealthy individuals can choose among the cleanest areas and escape some of the worst effects of pollution. But others have fewer options. . . .

The feasibility constraint focuses analytical attention on costs likely to be significant, in the sense of having a distribution likely to have a serious impact on people's lives. It avoids lavishing administrative resources on calibrating responses to what one might call de minimis costs.

The feasibility principle offers an appropriate response to problems characterized by de minimis cost and concentrated harms. It calls for stringent regulation. On the other hand, it constrains regulation when the costs concentrate in ways likely to produce greater than de minimis impacts.

Driesen, *Feasibility Principle, supra*, at 34-41.

If you were a member of Congress, would you vote to eliminate or to expand EPA's authority to reject feasible requirements where costs are wholly disproportionate to benefits? Or would you substitute a cost-benefit test for the feasibility tests found in many existing statutory provisions?

9. *Overestimating cost.* In practice, EPA usually overestimates the cost of its regulations. It often relies upon regulated industry for estimates of the cost of the technologies involved, and regulated industry has an incentive to exaggerate costs in order to persuade EPA to set lax standards. *See* Thomas O. McGarity & Ruth Ruttenberg, *Counting the Cost of Health Safety and Environmental Regulation,* 80 Tex. L. Rev. 1997, 1998 (2002) (*ex ante* cost estimates have been higher than actual costs incurred, sometimes by orders of magnitude); Winston Harrington, Richard D. Morgenstern, and Peter Nelson, *On the Accuracy of Regulatory Cost Estimates*, 19 J. Pol'y Analysis and Management 297 (2000). Also, once a regulation is promulgated, industry acquires an incentive to lower the cost of compliance as much as possible, either through competitive bidding processes or through innovation in applying new approaches or technologies. David M. Driesen, *The Societal Cost of Environmental Protection: Beyond Administrative Cost-Benefit Analysis,* 24 Ecology L.Q. 545, 600-01 (1997). Should this influence how the agencies or courts evaluate technological achievability? If so, how?

B. THE VARIETY OF TECHNOLOGY-BASED STANDARDS

While it is impossible to learn all of the statutory details for each of the technology-based provisions Congress has drafted in an introductory environmental law course, you should be aware of some of the patterns found in technology-based provisions.

First, the statutes often apply stricter standards to new sources than to existing sources. This reflects Congress' view that costs of retrofitting old sources might be very high, but that the installation of new equipment provides an opportunity for cost effective emissions control. Thus, for example, the Clean Air Act requires that new and modified sources conform to federal new source performance standards (NSPS), which we have seen, envision limits reflecting the best adequately demonstrated emission control technology, considering cost and some other factors. *See* 42 U.S.C. §7411(a). *See also* 33 U.S.C. §1316 (requiring strict new source performance standards under the Clean Water Act). Yet, states need only require emission levels reflecting "reasonably available control technology" (RACT) of major existing sources. 42 U.S.C. §7502(c)(1).

Second, the Clean Air Act tends to apply more comprehensive and strict standards to areas that have not attained the NAAQS than to areas that have met them. Thus, states must require new and modified major sources to attain the "lowest achievable emission" rate (LAER) in nonattainment areas (where the NAAQS have not been attained) and the emission level reflecting the best available control technology (BACT) in attainment areas (where the NAAQS has been attained). *See* 42 U.S.C. §§7501(3), 7503(a)(2), 7479. LAER is generally considered stricter. Can you see why?

Overall, this scheme looks like this:

Selected Clean Air Act Technology-Based Standards

	Attainment Area	Non-Attainment Area
Existing Sources		RACT
New Sources	NSPS, BACT	NSPS, LAER

Notice the blank in the upper left hand corner (standards for existing sources in attainment areas). Why do you suppose Congress did not generally require technology-based regulation of existing sources in attainment areas?

The NSPS standards are federal standards promulgated for selected categories of sources. The BACT and LAER standards are source-specific standards applicable to any major source. Why do we have both? Given the limitations that *National Lime* places on national standard setting, can you see why BACT and LAER requirements might usefully supplement NSPS standards?

Third, a common pattern involves progressing from relatively undemanding standards for "reasonably available" control technology to stricter standards governed by the feasibility principle. This is most obvious in the Federal Water Pollution Control Act, which, as we have seen, required Best Practicable Control Technology (BPCT) by July 1, 1977 and Best Available Technology (BAT) by July 1, 1983. *See* 33 U.S.C. §1311(b)(1), (2). *Cf.* 33 U.S.C. §1317(a) (requiring BAT for toxic pollutants). Since the Clean Air Act applies strict new source standards to modified sources, and most facility owners eventually modify their facilities, one can likewise view the Clean Air Act as contemplating a progression toward stricter standards.

Fourth, Congress has tended to treat toxic pollutants, those associated with acute hazards like cancer, differently. Thus, while Congress only requires states to apply RACT under the Clean Air Act to existing sources of conventional pollutants in nonattainment areas, it has required the emission limits based on the Maximum Achievable Control Technology (MACT) nationwide for the first phase of regulation of toxic (or hazardous) air pollutants. *See* 42 U.S.C. §7412(d).

Do these patterns reflect sound policy? Why or why not?

TECHNOLOGY-BASED STANDARD SETTING SAMPLE PROBLEM

Electric utility steam-generating units emit mercury, which is a potent bioaccumulative neurotoxin that threatens fetal development, when they burn coal to produce electricity. Mercury emissions depose in water and go up the food chain. Almost all of the states have issued advisories against catching fish, because of high levels of mercury in the fish. EPA has advised pregnant women to avoid eating fish, because of concerns about danger mercury poses to the development of unborn children.

Section 112(n)(1) of the Clean Air Act requires EPA to study the hazards electric utility mercury emissions pose to public health and to regulate the emissions "under this section if EPA finds such regulation is appropriate and necessary" after considering the results of the study. The subsection also requires EPA to "develop and describe" in its "report to Congress alternative control strategies." EPA conducted the study and found that electric utility mercury emissions are of great concern from a public health perspective, because mercury is highly toxic, persistent, and bioaccumulates in food chains. *See* 65 Fed. Reg. 79830 (2000). Electric utilities, according to EPA, are the largest source of man-made mercury emissions. EPA therefore made a formal finding that regulation under section 112 was appropriate and subsequently issued a notice of proposed rule making under section 112(d)(2), (3) of the Clean Air Act, which provides:

> (2) Standards and Methods
>
>   Emissions standards promulgated under this subsection . . . shall require the maximum degree of reduction in emissions of the hazardous air pollutants subject to this section . . . that [EPA], taking into consideration the cost of achieving such emission reduction, and any non-air quality health and environmental impacts . . . , determines is achievable for- . . . sources in the category or subcategory to which such emission standard applies. . . .
>
> (3) New and Existing Sources

> The maximum degree of reductions that is deemed achievable for new sources in a category or subcategory . . . shall not be less stringent than the emission control that is achieved in practice by the best controlled similar source. . . . Emission standards promulgated under this subsection for existing sources . . . shall not be less stringent than
>
> > (A) the average emission limitation achieved by the best performing 12 percent of the existing sources (for which the Administrator has emissions information . . .) . . . in the category or subcategory. . . .

42 U.S.C. §7412(d)(2),(3).

EPA studied the technologies available to limit mercury emission from electric power plants. It concluded that conventional technologies currently being used to limit emissions of other pollutants are capable of producing a 33 percent reduction of mercury emissions. *See* Supplemental Notice for the Proposed National Emission Standards for Hazardous Air Pollutants; and, in the Alternative, Proposed Standards for Performance for New and Existing Stationary Sources: Electric Utility Steam Generating Units, 69 Fed. Reg. 12398, 12402 (March 16, 2004). The technologies include scrubbers, selective catalytic reduction, and fabric filters. Sorbent injection technologies have achieved emission reductions as high as 90 percent of inlet mercury levels when plants burn **bituminous** coal. These technologies have been widely used to reduce mercury emissions from municipal waste combustors and medical waste incinerators, but have been used sparingly by electric utilities. Power plants burning **subbituminous** coals on the other hand, have experienced reductions of up to 65 percent reduction in mercury using sorbent injection technologies. All of the results regarding Sorbent Injection Technologies came from short-term tests, lasting four to nine days. *See* U.S. EPA, Office of Research and Development, Memorandum: Control of Mercury Emissions from Coal-fired Electric Utility Boilers 4-5 (February 2004).

EPA proposed to create two separate sub-categories for power plants, one for plants burning bituminous and another for plants burning subbituminous coal. EPA had test results for 32 bituminous coal-fired units. The four best units reported emission rates ranging from .1062 pounds per Trillion British Thermal Units of energy (lb/TBtu) to .1316 lb/TBtu, with an average of .118 lb/TBtu. Proposed National Emission Standards for Hazardous Air Pollutants; and in the Alternative, Proposed Standards of Performance for New and Existing Stationary Sources, 69 Fed. Reg. 4652, 4673 (January 30, 2004) [hereinafter Proposed NESHAP]. EPA proposed that the MACT floor for this subcategory be 2 lb/TBtu.

For subbituminous coal-fired units, EPA also had test results from 32 units. The best four plants had emission rates ranging from .4606 lb/TBtu to 1.207 lb/TBtu. EPA proposed that the MACT floor be 5.8 lb/TBtu.

In explaining its proposed MACT floors, EPA expressed concern about the fact that emissions can vary depending on the type of coal and even the particular seam, as well as other factors. EPA decided to develop a variability factor to "assure that" the emission limit "was representative of what was actually being achieved by the best-performing units under all conditions expected to be encountered by those units." *Id.* at 4670. In order to do this, EPA sought to determine how the best performing sources "will perform over the full range of operating conditions they will reasonably expect to encounter." *Id.* Based on a technical analysis, its proposal concluded that it needed to apply a variability factor to the actual test results in order to predict real world performance over a long period of time. This led to the adjusted MACT floors described above. This floor represents approximately a 33 percent cut in emissions. *See* Memorandum from EPA, Clean Air Markets Division to Docket, January 28, 2004.

EPA's proposal then considered going well beyond this MACT floor to reach the 90 percent or better controls potentially available from activated carbon injection and other sorbent technologies. Proposed NESHAP, 69 Fed. Reg. at 4676. The proposal rejected that option, because it was not currently "commercially available" (even though other types of facilities use it), and it had never been installed on any electric utility unit in the United States, except in the short-term trials discussed above.

You are EPA's lawyer and the agency asks your advice about what decisions to make in the final rule. What limits do you propose that EPA set?

1. *MACT floor.* Do you think that the proposed limits at the MACT floor as adjusted to account for variability conform to section 112(d)(3)?

2. *MACT level.* Do you think that the agency should demand the 90 percent reduction that the limited data indicate might be achievable? If so, should it demand this level for all plants or just bituminous plants? Do you think either 90 percent limit is legally permissible? Is the agency's proposed basis for rejecting the 90 percent limit adequate? Would it be wise policy?

3. *MACT v. NSPS.* Suppose that the political leadership of the agency and/or the Office of Management and Budget thinks that the MACT limits are too stringent and wants to proceed under section 111. Assuming that section 111 authorizes regulation of mercury emissions from existing and new electric utilities, would this allow the agency to forego regulation under section 112? If the agency could substitute regulations under section 111, could it more easily justify weaker standards than it would have to promulgate under section 112? What should the new source standards require as emission limits under section 112? What about under section 111? Recall that section 111 requires a standard that:

> reflects the degree of emission limitation achievable through the best system of emission reduction which (taking into account the cost of achieving such reduction and any nonair quality health and environmental impact and energy requirements) the Administrator determines has been adequately demonstrated.

42 U.S.C. §7411(a). If section 111(d) authorizes regulation of mercury, it would do so by allowing EPA to demand that states impose section 111(a) standards upon existing sources. *See* 42 U.S.C. §7411(d)(1). Would these standards be less stringent than the MACT standards for existing sources?

4. *Categorization.* Should EPA put bituminous and non-bituminous coal burning plants in separate subcategories? Notice that the bituminous plants generally perform better on emission tests. If the agency combines the subcategories into a single category, will this raise or lower the MACT floor relative to the floor

for bituminous plants? What about relative to subbituminous plants? Should the agency base the standards for all plants on what the best plants burning bituminous coal can achieve? If plant operators could switch fuels would that affect your answer? What if they could switch, but only with some modification of the physical plant?

5. *Cost.* So far, the questions have focused upon technical feasibility. Suppose that EPA's proposed MACT floor would generate $1.6 billion in annual cost, which would increase electricity production costs by 1.9 percent, raising electricity prices by .6 percent. EPA, Clean Air Markets Division to Docket, January 28, 2004, at 2, 8. Suppose that going to 90 percent control would raise the costs to $3.2 billion in annual cost, raising electricity prices by 1.2 percent. Would this influence your decision? What if this price increase implied that no plants would shut down under either scenario? Suppose that no plant closures were predicted at the MACT floor, but that EPA projected that some of the older coal-fired power plants would shut down if 90 percent reduction obligations were imposed, representing 5 percent of the plants. Would these shutdown projections influence your choice? What if the 90 percent reduction would close down 30 percent of the plants?

C. TECHNOLOGY-BASED STANDARD SETTING'S RECORD

Congress introduced technology-based output standards into the Clean Water Act in response to failed efforts to base reduction requirements on ambient water quality standards. As the *Weyerhauser* Court suggested, the process of back calculating emission or effluent limitations from ambient air quality or water quality standards has always been extraordinarily complex and difficult. The Supreme Court explained:

> Before it was amended in 1972, the Federal Water Pollution Control Act employed ambient water quality standards specifying acceptable levels of pollution in a State's interstate navigable waters as the primary mechanism for the control of water pollution. This program based on water quality standards, which were to serve both to guide performance by polluters and to trigger legal action to abate pollution, proved ineffective. The problems stemmed from the character of the standards themselves, which focused on the tolerable effects rather than the preventable causes of water pollution, from the awkwardly shared federal and state responsibility for promulgating such standards, and from the cumbersome enforcement procedures. These combined to make it very difficult to develop and enforce standards to govern the conduct of individual polluters.

EPA v. California ex rel. State Water Resources Control Bd., 426 U.S. 200, 202-03 (1976).

Oliver Houck, a leading water pollution expert, has written that "Ambient-based management has not worked well in any media-air, water, or waste." *See, e.g.*, OLIVER A. HOUCK, THE CLEAN WATER ACT TMDL PROGRAM: LAW, POLICY, AND IMPLEMENTATION 165 (2d ed. 2002). By contrast, a consensus exists that technology-based regulations have produced significant reductions in pollution. *See, e.g., id.* at 3; Wendy A. Wagner, *Innovations in Environmental Policies: The Triumph of Technology-Based Standards,* 2000 U. Ill. L. Rev. 83, 94-107; Sidney A. Shapiro and Thomas O. McGarity, *Not So Paradoxical: The Rationale for Technology-Based Regulation,* 1991 Duke L. J. 729, 739-42. While the standard setting process has been somewhat treacherous, understanding technological possibilities is not as difficult as risk-based standard setting. And technology-based standards, once promulgated, can produce large amounts of reduction in a variety of pollutants across a wide geographic area. We shall see, however, that scholars have harshly criticized "command and control" regulation as inefficient and otherwise defective.

The history of pollution control efforts in the United States contains many instances of Congress converting risk-based programs into technology-based programs, because the risk-based programs did not work. For example, the 1970 Clean Air Act Amendments required EPA to regulate hazardous air pollutants to achieve an ample margin of safety. (Recall the *Vinyl Chloride* case, *supra.*) EPA only regulated seven pollutants in 20 years under this risk-based approach. *See* David M. Driesen, *Getting Our Priorities Straight: One Strand of the Regulatory Reform Debate,* 31 Envt'l L. Rep. 10003, 10007 (2001). Some observers attribute this to EPA's fear of having to put industry out of business in order to implement a mandate to protect public health. Others attribute it to the difficulty of analyzing the health effects data. But Congress clearly concluded in 1990 that this program had failed and substituted a technology-based standard setting program for 189 pollutants that Congress listed in the statute. This program has succeeded in producing a large number of standards, but we have inadequate information about the amount of reductions these standards have achieved in practice. The statute still contemplates a second phase of regulation to eliminate residual risk. See 42 U.S.C. §7412(f).

A similar history comes from the Clean Water Act. The Natural Resources Defense Council (NRDC), an environmental group, sued EPA for failing to implement that statute's mandate for protective regulation of toxic water pollutants. NRDC, industry, and EPA agreed to regulate a list of "priority" pollutants negotiated between the parties. They agreed that rather than strictly following the risk-based approach in the statute, EPA would base these limits on technological capability. Congress subsequently ratified this approach when it amended the Clean Water Act. This approach has produced significant reductions in toxic effluent.

On the other hand, industry lobbyists frequently criticize technology-based standard setting as "control for control's" sake. They have a point, don't they? After all, we regulate to achieve environmental benefits. Technology-based standard setting becomes simple at the cost of not considering the precise environmental benefit involved. It focuses primarily on what can be done, rather than the value of reductions to the environment.

Scholars have frequently criticized technology-based standards as inefficient. They rely on the sort of variability in plant conditions that *National Lime* discusses. These variations imply that the cost of achieving a given level of pollution reduction is relatively high at some plants and low at others, something nobody doubts. Uniform standards can prove inefficient because they do not take this variability into account. Does this criticism apply only to technology-based uniform standards? Would it apply to health-based uniform standards? Cost-benefit-based uniform standards?

Scholars have also attacked technology-based standard setting as providing insufficient incentives for innovation. For example, Bruce Ackerman and Richard Stewart write:

> BAT controls can ensure the diffusion of established control technologies. But they do not provide strong incentives for the development of new environmentally superior strategies and may actually discourage their development. Such innovations are essential if we are to maintain economic growth in the long run without simultaneously increasing pollution and other forms of environmental degradation.

Reforming Environmental Law: The Democratic Case for Market Incentives, 13 Colum. J. Envtl. L. 171, 174 (1988).

Because of a dearth of post-compliance studies, we do not know how often technology-based regulations encourage innovation. Nevertheless, a number of scholars share Ackerman's and Stewart's views. On the other hand, we know that in some instances technology-based regulation has encouraged innovation. *See* David M. Driesen, The Economic Dynamics of Environmental Law 53 (2003); David Popp, *Pollution Control Innovations and the 1990 Clean Air Act Amendments,* 22 J. Pol'y Analysis and Management 641 (2003); UNITED STATES CONGRESS, OFFICE OF TECHNOLOGY ASSESSMENT, GAUGING CONTROL TECHNOLOGY AND REGULATORY IMPACTS IN OCCUPATIONAL SAFETY AND HEALTH-AN APPRAISAL OF OSHA'S ANALYTICAL APPROACH 64 (1995); Nicholas A. Ashford, Christine Ayers and Robert F. Stone, *Using Regulation to Change the Market for Innovation,* 9 Harv. Envt'l L. Rev. 419, 440-41 (1985); Nicholas A. Ashford and George R. Heaton Jr., *Regulation and Technological Innovation in the Chemical Industry,* 46 Law & Contemporary Probs. 109, 139-40 (1983).

What variables do you suppose might influence innovation rates? Do you think that more stringent and costly regulation would increase or decrease incentives for innovation? Would health-based standards encourage innovation better than technology-based regulation? What about standards based on cost-benefit analysis?

Many scholars have argued that the law's tendency to impose stricter standards on new sources than on existing sources also tends to discourage innovation. Is this really a criticism of technology-based standard setting?

Suppose that the federal government amended the environmental statutes to impose equally strict requirements on new and existing sources, but based both on technological capability. Would this solve the problem of discouraging cleaner new sources? Recall (from *National Lime, supra*) that new source controls under the Clean Air Act apply to modified sources as well as existing sources. The Clean Air Act defines modification as a physical or operational change at an existing pollution source that increases emissions. Can one argue, given the applicability of new source controls to modified existing sources, that existing law discourages emission decreasing modernization by imposing stricter requirements on new sources than on existing ones? Would strict application of new source controls to modified sources remove the disincentives for new sources? Are pollution control costs significant enough to influence firms' technological choices in a significant way? What data would you like to have to answer this question?

Scholars who criticize technology-based regulation for imposing too much cost while discouraging innovation usually recommend emissions trading programs as a remedy. We will consider the value of emissions trading and the theoretical arguments about innovation in a section addressing the means of environmental protection. In the next chapter, we consider the alternative to technology-based standard setting advocated by industry in the *Benzene* and *Pacific Fisheries* cases, standards based on cost-benefit analysis.

7
Cost-Benefit Approaches

Recently, government has placed a great deal of emphasis on using cost-benefit analysis (CBA) to guide environmental decision-making, which has had a relatively confined role in the past. CBA involves comparing the costs of a proposed action to its benefits. If the action consists of an economic development project, such as the building of a dam, the project will typically generate economic benefits (*e.g.*, electricity) and environmental costs (*e.g.*, damage to fisheries). By contrast, a regulation requiring pollution reduction typically generates environmental benefits (*e.g.*, more fish, less illness) and economic costs. This chapter focuses primarily upon the use of CBA to guide pollution control decisions.

When the action consists of a government regulation requiring reduction or elimination of pollution, the direct costs typically consist of the monies regulated firms or individuals must spend to comply with regulatory requirements. CBA may also include estimates of indirect impacts upon employment and the economy. Calculating the direct costs of environmental regulation for purposes of cost-benefit analysis is basically the same as calculating direct costs to set a technology-based standard. (Recall that the technology-based standard provisions typically required consideration of cost, but did not require CBA.)

The benefits consist of the environmental improvements the pollution reduction will bring about. Estimating the value of these benefits proves more difficult than the estimation of the cost of compliance. Estimation of benefits involves two steps. First, the analyst must engage in quantitative risk assessment, which you learned about in Chapter 5. Then, she must monetize the benefits, *i.e.*, assign a dollar value to the health and environmental consequences of the regulation. Conversion of environmental benefits into dollars allows the regulator to compare the value of environmental benefits to the costs.

The quantitative risk assessment step requires government officials to estimate the number of deaths, illnesses, and other consequences a proposed regulation would prevent. Usually, the agency is unable to quantify many significant environmental and health effects, because of lack of sufficient data. An example of a case where quantification was impossible involves the rule considered in *Lead Industries*. Even though abundant data existed showing that lead was harmful, EPA lacked sufficient information about the contribution of *leaded gasoline* to even prove that leaded gasoline posed a problem, let alone to quantify the problem's extent. The rule upheld in *Lead Industries*, however, ultimately generated data showing that the rule had an enormous positive impact on health. Those data then made it possible to at least estimate some of the health consequences of later reductions of lead.

Quantifying the amount of ecological damage a regulation might avoid usually proves especially difficult. How much is it worth to have bald eagles, to see a beautiful view unmarred by haze, or to be able to exercise outdoors without harm to one's health? While economists have tried to estimate the dollar value of some environmental amenities, *see, e.g.,* Ohio v. Dep't of Interior, 880 F.2d 432, 475 (D.C. Cir. 1989) (discussing various ways of assessing natural resource damages), critics question whether these techniques adequately capture the true value.

Almost always, quantification involves substantial uncertainties. For example, carcinogens usually command regulatory attention because data from experiments on animals indicate that the animals contract cancer when consuming too much of a substance. *See* Wendy E. Wagner, *The Science Charade in Toxic Risk Regulation*, 95 Colum. L. Rev. 1613, 1625 (1995) (discussing the problem of extrapolating human health effects from high dose animal experiments). If we have human exposure data, those data usually come from rare accidental occupational exposures to unusually high doses of the chemical, much higher and of shorter duration than typical environmental exposures. Estimation of the effects of continuous low dose exposure upon humans requires extrapolation from the animal data and (if it exists) data about human response to temporary high doses. Unfortunately, we do not understand cancer well enough to know how to make this extrapolation. For that reason, the National Academy of Sciences has recommended providing a range of estimates, rather than a point estimate. Frequently, the range of plausible estimates is so large as to provide relatively little guidance. Cass R. Sunstein, *The Arithmetic of Arsenic*, 90 Geo. L. J. 2255, 2257 (2002). *See also* Donald T. Hornstein, *Reclaiming Environmental Law: A Normative Critique of Comparative Risk Analysis*, 92 Colum. L. Rev. 562, 572 (1992) (the National Academy of Sciences has identified 50 "inference options," where a policy decision must be made to extrapolate a risk assessment from limited data). You learned about the uncertainty inherent in extrapolation from limited data in the PFOA problem presented in Chapter 5.

The agency must then attempt to monetize the benefits. EPA, for example, usually assumes that a human life is worth $6.1 million. This monetization is extremely controversial. Critics claim that we ought not treat life like a commodity and that assigning it a dollar value is arbitrary. Furthermore, they claim that data limitations make a lot of this monetization ludicrous and they question the value choices imbedded in the assumptions underlying the choice of dollar values. *See* FRANK ACKERMAN AND LISA HEINZERLING, PRICELESS: ON KNOWING THE PRICE OF EVERY-THING AND THE VALUE OF NOTHING (2004). Others, however, believe this process appropriate, even if imprecise, because of the need to improve priority setting, advance overall well-being (including economic well-being), and improve the rationality of regulation. *See, e.g.*, CASS R. SUNSTEIN, THE COST-BENEFIT STATE: THE FUTURE OF REGULATORY PROTECTION (2002); CASS R. SUNSTEIN, RISK AND REASON: SAFETY, LAW, AND THE ENVIRONMENT (2002); Matthew D. Adler and Eric A. Posner, *Rethinking Cost-Benefit Analysis*, 109 Yale L. J. 165 (1999). After monetizing benefits, the agency must then compare costs and benefits in some fashion.

A. CBA IN THE TOXIC SUBSTANCES CONTROL ACT AND THE FEDERAL INSECTICIDE, FUNGICIDE, AND RODENTICIDE ACT

The following case history involves an EPA proposal to ban most uses of asbestos under the Toxic Substances Control Act (TSCA). This proposal followed a series of actions seeking to limit asbestos exposure in various settings. For example, the *Reserve Mining* case discussed in a note in Chapter 5 (on effects-based regulation) sought to limit asbestos as a water pollutant. Asbestos is a fire-proofing material often used in construction and brake linings. Asbestos causes two diseases not significantly associated with other causes, asbestosis and mesothelioma. It also causes a number of cancers, such as lung and gastrointestinal cancers, that other toxic substances can also trigger. By the time EPA promulgated its asbestos ban, successful toxic tort suits were well on their way to driving the asbestos industry into bankruptcy. Apparently, juries were satisfied that asbestos was causing serious injuries to those who had worked with the substance.

Consider first the following questions. Does section 6 of the Toxic Substances Control Act require CBA? How should EPA go about deciding whether a ban is appropriate? Section 6 provides:

§2605. Regulation of hazardous chemical substances and mixtures

(a) Scope of regulation. If the Administrator finds that there is a reasonable basis to conclude that the manufacture, processing, distribution in commerce, use, or disposal of a chemical substance or mixture, or that any combination of such activities, presents or will present an unreasonable risk of injury to health or the environment, the Administrator shall by rule apply one or more of the following requirements to such substance or mixture to the extent necessary to protect adequately against such risk using the least burdensome requirements:

(1) A requirement (A) prohibiting the manufacturing, processing, or distribution in commerce of such substance or mixture, or (B) limiting the amount of such substance or mixture which may be manufactured, processed, or distributed in commerce.

(2) A requirement —

(A) prohibiting the manufacture, processing, or distribution in commerce of such substance or mixture for (i) a particular use or (ii) a particular use in a concentration in excess of a level specified by the Administrator in the rule imposing the requirement, or

(B) limiting the amount of such substance or mixture which may be manufactured, processed, or distributed in commerce for (i) a particular use or (ii) a particular use in a concentration in excess of a level specified by the Administrator in the rule imposing the requirement.

(3) A requirement that such substance or mixture or any article containing such substance or mixture be marked with or accompanied by clear and adequate warnings and instructions with respect to its use, distribution in commerce, or disposal or with respect to any combination of such activities. The form and content of such warnings and instructions shall be prescribed by the Administrator.

(4) A requirement that manufacturers and processors of such substance or mixture make and retain records of the processes used to manufacture or process such substance or mixture and monitor or conduct tests which are reasonable and necessary to assure compliance with the requirements of any rule applicable under this subsection.

(5) A requirement prohibiting or otherwise regulating any manner or method of commercial use of such substance or mixture.

(6) (A) A requirement prohibiting or otherwise regulating any manner or method of disposal of such substance or mixture, or of any article containing such substance or mixture, by its manufacturer or processor or by any other person who uses, or disposes of, it for commercial purposes.

(B) A requirement under subparagraph (A) may not require any person to take any action which would be in violation of any law or requirement of, or in effect for, a State or political subdivision, and shall require each person subject to it to notify each State and political subdivision in which a required disposal may occur of such disposal.

(7) A requirement directing manufacturers or processors of such substance or mixture (A) to give notice of such unreasonable risk of injury to distributors in commerce of such substance or mixture and, to the extent reasonably ascertainable, to other persons in possession of such substance or mixture or exposed to such substance or mixture, (B) to give public notice of such risk of injury, and (C) to replace or repurchase such

substance or mixture as elected by the person to which the requirement is directed.

Does this language require that the benefits of an asbestos ban outweigh the costs? Suppose that EPA concludes that all of the options except a ban would not adequately prevent a risk of contracting cancer? May it still choose one of the less drastic options? Would your answer change if the cost of a ban outweighed the benefits? *See* Thomas O. McGarity, *The Courts and the Ossification of Rulemaking: A Response to Professor Seidenfeld*, 75 Tex. L. Rev. 525, 541-49 (1997).

EPA decided to ban most uses of asbestos. But it provided that it would exempt particular asbestos uses from the ban if an applicant could demonstrate that she "has made demonstrable good faith efforts to develop substitutes for its product and that granting the exemption will not result in an unreasonable risk of injury to human health." EPA's decision and interpretation of section 6 are explained in the Federal Register notice announcing the asbestos ban:

Asbestos; Manufacture, Importation, Processing, and Distribution in Commerce Prohibitions
54 Fed. Reg. 29460 (July 12, 1989)

* * *

V. Regulatory Assessment

Section 6 of TSCA authorizes EPA to promulgate a rule prohibiting or limiting the amount of a chemical substance that may be manufactured, processed, or distributed in commerce in the U.S. if EPA finds that there is a reasonable basis to conclude that the manufacturer, processing, distribution in commerce, use, or disposal of the chemical substance, or any combination of these activities, presents or will present an unreasonable risk of injury to human health or the environment.

Section 6(c)(1) of TSCA requires EPA to consider the following factors when determining whether a chemical substance presents an unreasonable risk:

1.   The effects of such substance on human health and the magnitude of the exposure of human beings to such substance.
2.   The effects of such substance on the environment and the magnitude of the exposure of the environment to such substance or mixture.
3.   The benefits of such substance for various uses and the availability of substitutes for such uses.
4.   The reasonably ascertainable economic consequences of the rule, after consideration of the effect on the national economy, small

businesses, technological innovation, the environment, and public health.

To determine whether a risk from activities involving asbestos-containing products presents an unreasonable risk, EPA must balance the probability that harm will occur from the activities against the effects of the proposed regulatory action on the availability to society of the benefits of asbestos. EPA has considered these factors in conjunction with the extensive record gathered in the development of this rule. EPA has concluded that the continued manufacture, importation, processing, and distribution in commerce of most asbestos-containing products poses an unreasonable risk to human health. This conclusion is based on information summarized in the following paragraphs and discussed in the units that follow.

EPA has concluded that exposure to asbestos during the life cycles of many asbestos-containing products poses an unreasonable risk of injury to human health. EPA has also concluded that section 6 of TSCA is the ideal statutory authority to regulate the risks posed by asbestos exposure. This rule's pollution prevention actions under TSCA are both the preferable and the least burdensome means of controlling the exposure risks posed throughout the life cycle of asbestos-containing products. Findings supporting this conclusion include the following:

1. Exposure to asbestos causes many painful, premature deaths due to mesothelioma and lung, gastrointestinal, and other cancers, as well as asbestosis and other diseases. Risks attributable to asbestos exposure and addressed by this rule are serious and are calculated for this rule using direct evidence from numerous human epidemiological studies. Studies show that asbestos is a highly potent carcinogen and that severe health effects occur after even short-term, high-level or longer-term, low-level exposures to asbestos. Asbestos exposure is compatible with a linear, nonthreshold dose-response model for lung cancer. In addition, there is no undisputed evidence of quantitative differences in potency based on fiber size or type.

For the quantitative risk assessment performed as part of this rulemaking, EPA used dose-response constants for lung cancer and mesothelioma that were the geometric means of the "best estimates" from a number of epidemiological studies. If EPA had instead used an upper bound estimate, as is normally done by the scientific community and in EPA regulatory risk assessment when only data from animal studies is available to extrapolate human health risk, predicted lung cancer deaths could increase by a factor of 10 and mesothelioma deaths could increase by a factor of 20.

2. People are frequently unknowingly exposed to asbestos and are rarely in a position to protect themselves. Asbestos is generally invisible,

odorless, very durable, and highly aerodynamic. It can travel long distances and exist in the environment for extended periods. Therefore, exposure can take place long after the release of asbestos and at a distant location from the source of release.

3. Additions to the current stock of asbestos-containing products would contribute to the environmental loading of asbestos. This poses the potential for an increased risk to the general population of asbestos-related disease and an increased risk to future generations because of asbestos' longevity.

4. Asbestos fibers are released to the air at many stages of the commercial life of the products that are subject to this rule. Activities that might lead to the release of asbestos include mining of the substance, processing asbestos fibers into products, and transport, installation, use, maintenance, repair, removal, and disposal of asbestos-containing products. EPA has found that the occupational and non-occupational exposure existing over the entire life cycles of each of the banned asbestos-containing products poses a high level of individual risk. EPA has determined that thousands of persons involved in the manufacture, processing, transport, installation, use, repair, removal, and disposal of the asbestos-containing products affected by this rule are exposed to a serious lifetime asbestos exposure risk, despite OSHA's relatively low workplace PEL. In addition, according to the EPA Asbestos Modeling Study, millions of members of the general U.S. population are exposed to elevated levels of lifetime risk due to asbestos released throughout the life cycle of asbestos-containing products. EPA believes that the exposure quantified for the analyses supporting this rule represent an understatement of actual exposure.

5. Release of asbestos fibers from many products during life cycle activities can be substantial. OSHA stated in setting its PEL of 0.2 f/cc that remaining exposures pose a serious risk because of limitations on available exposure control technologies. Even with OSHA's controls, thousands of workers involved in the manufacture and processing of asbestos-containing products are exposed to a lifetime risk of 1 in 1,000 of developing cancer. Many other exposures addressed by this rule are not affected by engineering controls required by OSHA's PEL or by other government regulation. Because asbestos is a highly potent carcinogen, the uncontrolled high peak episodic exposures that are faced by large populations pose a significant risk.

6. Because of the life cycle or "cradle-to-grave" nature of the risk posed by asbestos, attempts by OSHA, the Consumer Product Safety Commission (CPSC), and other EPA offices to regulate the continued commercial use of asbestos still leave many persons unprotected from the hazards of asbestos exposure. Technological limitations inhibit the effectiveness of existing or possible exposure control actions under non-TSCA authorities. Many routes of asbestos exposure posed by the

products subject to this rule are outside the jurisdictions of regulatory authorities other than TSCA. EPA has determined that the residual exposure to asbestos that exists despite the actions taken under other authorities poses a serious health risk throughout the life cycle of many asbestos-containing products. This residual exposure can only be adequately controlled by the exposure prevention actions taken in this rule.

7. Despite the proven risks of asbestos exposure and the current or imminent existence of suitable substitutes for most uses of asbestos, asbestos continues to be used in large quantities in the U.S. in the manufacture or processing of a wide variety of commercial products. Total annual U.S. consumption of asbestos dropped from a 1984 total of about 240,000 metric tons to less than 85,000 metric tons in 1987, according to the U.S. Department of Interior, Bureau of Mines data. This change suggests that the use of substitutes has increased markedly since the proposal. However, the 1987 consumption total indicates that significant exposure due to the commercial use of asbestos and the resultant risks would continue for the foreseeable future absent the actions taken in this rule.

Evidence supports the conclusion that substitutes already exist or will soon exist for each of the products that are subject to the rule's bans. In scheduling products for the different stages of the bans, EPA has analyzed the probable availability of non-asbestos substitutes. In the rule, the various asbestos products are scheduled to be banned at times when it is likely that suitable non-asbestos substitutes will be available. However, the rule also includes an exemption provision to account for instances in which technology might not have advanced sufficiently by the time of a ban to produce substitutes for certain specialized or limited uses of asbestos.

8. EPA has calculated that the product bans in this rule will result in the avoidance of 202 quantifiable cancer cases, if benefits are not discounted, and 148 cases, if benefits are discounted at 3 percent. The figures decrease to 164 cases, if benefits are not discounted, and 120 cases, if benefits are discounted at 3 percent, if analogous exposures are not included in the analysis. In all likelihood, the rule will result in the avoidance of a large number of other cancer cases that cannot be quantified, as well as many cases of asbestos related diseases. Estimates of benefits resulting from the action taken in this rule are limited to mesothelioma and lung and gastrointestinal cancer-cases-avoided, and do not include cases of asbestosis and other diseases avoided and avoided costs from treating asbestos diseases, lost productivity, or other factors. EPA has estimated that the cost of this rule, for the 13-year period of the analyses performed, will be approximately $458.89 million, or $806.51 million if a 1 percent

annual decline in the price of substitutes is not assumed. This cost will be spread over time and a large population so that the cost to any person is likely to be negligible. In addition, the rule's exemption provision is a qualitative factor that supports the actions taken in this rule. EPA has concluded that the quantifiable and unquantifiable benefits of the rule's staged-ban of the identified asbestos-containing products will outweigh the resultant economic consequences to consumers, producers, and users of the products.

9. EPA has determined that, within the findings required by section 6 of TSCA, only the staged-ban approach employed in this final rule will adequately control the asbestos exposure risk posed by the product categories affected by this rule. Other options either fail to address significant portions of the life cycle risk posed by products subject to the rule or are unreasonably burdensome. EPA has, therefore, concluded that the actions taken in this rule represent the least burdensome means of reducing the risk posed by exposure to asbestos during the life cycles of the products that are subject to the bans.

10. Based on the reasons summarized in this preamble, this rule bans most asbestos-containing products in the U.S. because they pose an unreasonable risk to human health. These banned products account for approximately 94 percent of U.S. asbestos consumption, based on 1985 consumption figures. The actions taken will result in a substantial reduction in the unreasonable risk caused by asbestos exposure in the U.S.

A few minor uses of asbestos and asbestos products are not included in the ban. These uses, which account for less than 6 percent of U.S. asbestos consumption based on 1985 data, do not pose an unreasonable risk, based on current knowledge. . . .

The United States Court of Appeals for the Fifth Circuit reversed EPA's ban. Focus on whether the court's statutory interpretation differed from that of EPA, and if so, how.

Corrosion Proof Fittings v. EPA
947 F.2d 1201 (5th Cir. 1991)

SMITH, CIRCUIT JUDGE.

The Environmental Protection Agency (EPA) issued a final rule under section 6 of the Toxic Substances Control Act (TSCA) to prohibit the future manufacture, importation, processing, and distribution of asbestos in almost all products. Petitioners claim that the EPA's . . . rule was not promulgated on the basis of substantial evidence . . . . Because the EPA failed to muster substantial evidence to support its rule, we remand this matter to the EPA for further consideration in light of this opinion.

I. Facts and Procedural History

Asbestos is a naturally occurring fibrous material that resists fire and most solvents. Its major uses include heat-resistant insulators, cements, building materials, fireproof gloves and clothing, and motor vehicle brake linings. Asbestos is a toxic material, and occupational exposure to asbestos dust can result in mesothelioma, asbestosis, and lung cancer.

The EPA began these proceedings in 1979, when it issued an Advanced Notice of Proposed Rulemaking announcing its intent to explore the use of TSCA "to reduce the risk to human health posed by exposure to asbestos." *See* 54 Fed. Reg. 29,460 (1989). While these proceedings were pending, other agencies continued their regulation of asbestos uses, in particular the Occupational Safety and Health Administration (OSHA), which in 1983 and 1984 involved itself with lowering standards for workplace asbestos exposure.

An EPA-appointed panel reviewed over one hundred studies of asbestos and conducted several public meetings. Based upon its studies and the public comments, the EPA concluded that asbestos is a potential carcinogen at all levels of exposure, regardless of the type of asbestos or the size of the fiber. The EPA concluded in 1986 that exposure to asbestos "poses an unreasonable risk to human health" and thus proposed at least four regulatory options for prohibiting or restricting the use of asbestos, including a mixed ban and phase-out of asbestos over ten years; a two-stage ban of asbestos, depending upon product usage; a three-stage ban on all asbestos products leading to a total ban in ten years; and labeling of all products containing asbestos.

Over the next two years, the EPA updated its data, received further comments, and allowed cross-examination on the updated documents. In 1989, the EPA issued a final rule prohibiting the manufacture, importation, processing, and distribution in commerce of most asbestos-containing products. Finding that asbestos constituted an unreasonable risk to health and the environment, the EPA promulgated a staged ban of most commercial uses of asbestos. The EPA estimates that this rule will save either 202 or 148 lives, depending upon whether the benefits are discounted, at a cost of approximately $ 450-800 million, depending upon the price of substitutes.

The rule is to take effect in three stages, depending upon the EPA's assessment of how toxic each substance is and how soon adequate substitutes will be available. The rule allows affected persons one more year at each stage to sell existing stocks of prohibited products. The rule also imposes labeling requirements on stage 2 or stage 3 products and allows for exemptions from the rule in certain cases.

[P]etitioners challenge the EPA's final rule, claiming that the EPA's rulemaking procedure was flawed and that the rule was not promulgated based upon substantial evidence . . . .

IV. The Language of TSCA

A. *Standard of Review*

Our inquiry into the legitimacy of the EPA rulemaking begins with a discussion of the standard of review governing this case. EPA's phase-out ban of most commercial uses of asbestos is a TSCA §6(a) rulemaking. TSCA provides that a reviewing court "shall hold unlawful and set aside" a final rule promulgated under §6(a) "if the court finds that the rule is not supported by substantial evidence in the rulemaking record . . . taken as a whole."

Substantial evidence requires "something less than the weight of the evidence, and the possibility of drawing two inconsistent conclusions from the evidence does not prevent an administrative agency's finding from being supported by substantial evidence." This standard requires (1) that the agency's decision be based upon the entire record, taking into account whatever in the record detracts from the weight of the agency's decision; and (2) that the agency's decision be what "a reasonable mind might accept as adequate to support [its] conclusion." Thus, even if there is enough evidence in the record to support the petitioners' assertions, we will not reverse if there is substantial evidence to support the agency's decision. . . .

In evaluating whether the EPA has presented substantial evidence, we examine (1) whether the quantities of the regulated chemical entering into the environment are "substantial" and (2) whether human exposure to the chemical is "substantial" or "significant." An agency may exercise its judgment without strictly relying upon quantifiable risks, costs, and benefits, but it must "cogently explain why it has exercised its discretion in a given manner" and "must offer a 'rational connection between the facts found and the choice made.'"

We note that in undertaking our review, we give all agency rules a presumption of validity, and it is up to the challenger to any rule to show that the agency action is invalid. The burden remains on the EPA, however, to justify that the products it bans present an unreasonable risk, no matter how regulated. Finally, as we discuss in detail *infra*, because TSCA instructs the EPA to undertake the least burdensome regulation sufficient to regulate the substance at issue, the agency bears a heavier burden when it seeks a partial or total ban of a substance than when it merely seeks to regulate that product.

B. *The EPA's Burden Under TSCA*

TSCA provides, in pertinent part, as follows:

(a) Scope of regulation. — If the Administrator finds that there is a *reasonable basis* to conclude that the manufacture, processing, distribution in commerce, use, or disposal of a chemical substance or mixture, or that any combination of such activities, presents or will present an *unreasonable risk of injury* to health or the environment, the Administrator shall by rule apply one or more of the following requirements to such substance or mixture to the extent necessary *to protect adequately* against such risk using the *least burdensome* requirements.

As the highlighted language shows, Congress did not enact TSCA as a zero-risk statute. The EPA, rather, was required to consider both alternatives to a ban and the costs of any proposed actions and to "carry out this chapter in a reasonable and prudent manner [after considering] the environmental, economic, and social impact of any action." 15 U.S.C. §2601(c).

We conclude that the EPA has presented insufficient evidence to justify its asbestos ban. We base this conclusion upon two grounds: the failure of the EPA to consider all necessary evidence and its failure to give adequate weight to statutory language requiring it to promulgate the least burdensome, reasonable regulation required to protect the environment adequately. Because the EPA failed to address these concerns, and because the EPA is required to articulate a "reasoned basis" for its rules, we are compelled to return the regulation to the agency for reconsideration.

1. Least Burdensome and Reasonable

TSCA requires that the EPA use the least burdensome regulation to achieve its goal of minimum reasonable risk. This statutory requirement can create problems in evaluating just what is a "reasonable risk." Congress's rejection of a no-risk policy, however, also means that in certain cases, the least burdensome yet still adequate solution may entail somewhat more risk than would other, known regulations that are far more burdensome on the industry and the economy. The very language of TSCA requires that the EPA, once it has determined what an acceptable level of non-zero risk is, choose the least burdensome method of reaching that level.

In this case, the EPA banned, for all practical purposes, all present and future uses of asbestos — a position the petitioners characterize as the "death penalty alternative," as this is the *most* burdensome of all possible alternatives listed as open to the EPA under TSCA. TSCA not only provides the EPA with a list of alternative actions, but also provides those alternatives in order of how burdensome they are. The regulations thus provide for EPA regulation ranging from labeling the least toxic chemicals to limiting the total amount of chemicals an industry may use. Total bans head the list as the most burdensome regulatory option.

By choosing the harshest remedy given to it under TSCA, the EPA assigned to itself the toughest burden in satisfying TSCA's requirement that its alternative be the least burdensome of all those offered to it. Since, both by definition and by the terms of TSCA, the complete ban of manufacturing is the most burdensome alternative — for even stringent regulation at least allows a manufacturer the chance to invest and meet the new, higher standard — the EPA's regulation cannot stand if there is any other regulation that would achieve an acceptable level of risk as mandated by TSCA.

We reserve until a later part of the opinion a product-by-product review of the regulation. Before reaching this analysis, however, we lay down the inquiry that the EPA should undertake whenever it seeks total ban of a product.

The EPA considered, and rejected, such options as labeling asbestos products, thereby warning users and workers involved in the manufacture of asbestos-containing products of the chemical's dangers, and stricter workplace rules. EPA also rejected controlled use of asbestos in the workplace and deferral to other government agencies charged with worker and consumer exposure to industrial and product hazards, such as OSHA, the CPSC, and the MSHA. The EPA determined that deferral to these other agencies was inappropriate because no one other authority could address all the risks posed "throughout the life cycle" by asbestos, and any action by one or more of the other agencies still would leave an unacceptable residual risk.

Much of the EPA's analysis is correct, and the EPA's basic decision to use TSCA as a comprehensive statute designed to fight a multi-industry problem was a proper one that we uphold today on review. What concerns us, however, is the manner in which the EPA conducted some of its analysis. TSCA requires the EPA to consider, along with the effects of toxic substances on human health and the environment, "the benefits of such substance[s] or mixture[s] for various uses and the availability of substitutes for such uses," as well as "the reasonably ascertainable economic consequences of the rule, after consideration for the effect on the national economy, small business, technological innovation, the environment, and public health." *Id.* §2605(c)(1)(C-D).

The EPA presented two comparisons in the record: a world with no further regulation under TSCA, and a world in which no manufacture of asbestos takes place. The EPA rejected calculating how many lives a less burdensome regulation would save, and at what cost. Furthermore the EPA, when calculating the benefits of its ban, explicitly refused to compare it to an improved workplace in which currently available control technology is utilized. This decision artificially inflated the purported benefits of the rule by using a baseline comparison substantially lower than what currently available technology could yield.

Under TSCA, the EPA was required to evaluate, rather than ignore, less burdensome regulatory alternatives. TSCA imposes a least-to-most-burdensome hierarchy. In order to impose a regulation at the top of the hierarchy — a total ban of asbestos — the EPA must show not only that its proposed action reduces the risk of the product to an adequate level, but also that the actions Congress identified as less burdensome also would not do the job. The failure of the EPA to do this constitutes a failure to meet its burden of showing that its actions not only reduce the risk but do so in the Congressionally-mandated *least burdensome* fashion.

Thus it was not enough for the EPA to show, as it did in this case, that banning some asbestos products might reduce the harm that could occur from the use of these products. If that were the standard, it would be no standard at all, for few indeed are the products that are so safe that a complete ban of them would not make the world still safer.

This comparison of two static worlds is insufficient to satisfy the dictates of TSCA. While the EPA may have shown that a world with a complete ban of asbestos might be preferable to one in which there is only the current amount of regulation, the EPA has failed to show that there is not some intermediate state of regulation that would be superior to both the currently-regulated and the completely-banned world. Without showing that asbestos regulation would be ineffective, the EPA cannot discharge its TSCA burden of showing that its regulation is the least burdensome available to it.

Upon an initial showing of product danger, the proper course for the EPA to follow is to consider each regulatory option, beginning with the least burdensome, and the costs and benefits of regulation under each option. The EPA cannot simply skip several rungs, as it did in this case, for in doing so, it may skip a less-burdensome alternative mandated by TSCA. Here, although the EPA mentions the problems posed by intermediate levels of regulation, it takes no steps to calculate the costs and benefits of these intermediate levels. Without doing this it is impossible, both for the EPA and for this court on review, to know that none of these alternatives was less burdensome than the ban in fact chosen by the agency.

The EPA's offhand rejection of these intermediate regulatory steps is "not the stuff of which substantial evidence is made." While it is true that the EPA considered five different ban options, these differed solely with respect to their effective dates. The EPA did not calculate the risk levels for intermediate levels of regulation, as it believed that there was no asbestos exposure level for which the risk of injury or death was zero. Reducing risk to zero, however, was not the task that Congress set for the EPA in enacting TSCA. The EPA thus has failed "cogently [to] explain why it has exercised its discretion in a given manner," by failing to explore in more than a cursory way the less burdensome alternatives to a total ban.

2. The EPA's Calculations

Furthermore, we are concerned about some of the methodology employed by the EPA in making various of the calculations that it did perform. In order to aid the EPA's reconsideration of this and other cases, we present our concerns here.

First, we note that there was some dispute in the record regarding the appropriateness of discounting the perceived benefits of the EPA's rule. In choosing between the calculated costs and benefits, the EPA presented variations in which it discounted only the costs, and counter-variations in which it discounted both the costs and the benefits, measured in both monetary and human injury terms. As between these two variations, we choose to evaluate the EPA's work using its discounted benefits calculations.

Although various commentators dispute whether it ever is appropriate to discount benefits when they are measured in human lives, we note that it would skew the results to discount only costs without according similar treatment to the benefits side of the equation. Adopting the position of the commentators who advocate not discounting benefits would force the EPA similarly not to calculate costs in present discounted real terms, making comparisons difficult. Furthermore, in evaluating situations in which different options incur costs at varying time intervals, the EPA would not be able to take into account that soon-to-be-incurred costs are more harmful than postponable costs. Because the EPA must discount costs to perform its evaluations properly, the EPA also should discount benefits to preserve an apples-to-apples comparison, even if this entails discounting benefits of a non-monetary nature. *See What Price Posterity?*, The Economist, March 23, 1991, at 73 (explaining use of discount rates for non-monetary goods). . . .

Of more concern to us is the failure of the EPA to compute the costs and benefits of its proposed rule past the year 2000, and its double-counting of the costs of asbestos use. In performing its calculus, the EPA only included the number of lives saved over the next thirteen years, and counted any additional lives saved as simply "unquantified benefits." 54 Fed. Reg. at 29,486. The EPA and intervenors now seek to use these unquantified lives saved to justify calculations as to which the benefits seem far outweighed by the astronomical costs. For example, the EPA plans to save about three lives with its ban of asbestos pipe, at a cost of $128-227 million (*i.e.*, approximately $43-76 million per life saved). Although the EPA admits that the price tag is high, it claims that the lives saved past the year 2000 justify the price.

Such calculations not only lessen the value of the EPA's cost analysis, but also make any meaningful judicial review impossible. While TSCA contemplates a useful place for unquantified benefits beyond the EPA's calculation, unquantified benefits never were intended as a trump card allowing the EPA to justify any cost calculus, no matter how high.

The concept of unquantified benefits, rather, is intended to allow the EPA to provide a rightful place for any remaining benefits that are impossible to quantify after the EPA's best attempt, but which still are of some concern. But the allowance for unquantified costs is not intended to allow the EPA to perform its calculations over an arbitrarily short period so as to preserve a large unquantified portion.

Unquantified benefits can, at times, permissibly tip the balance in close cases. They cannot, however, be used to effect a wholesale shift on the balance beam. Such a use makes a mockery of the requirements of TSCA that the EPA weigh the costs of its actions before it chooses the least burdensome alternative.

We do not today determine what an appropriate period for the EPA's calculations would be, as this is a matter better left for agency discretion. We do note, however, that the choice of a thirteen-year period is so short as to make the unquantified period so unreasonably large that any EPA reliance upon it must be displaced. . . .

3. Reasonable Basis

In addition to showing that its regulation is the least burdensome one necessary to protect the environment adequately, the EPA also must show that it has a reasonable basis for the regulation. 15 U.S.C. §2605(a). To some extent, our inquiry in this area mirrors that used above, for many of the methodological problems we have noted also indicate that the EPA did not have a reasonable basis. We here take the opportunity to highlight some areas of additional concern.

Most problematical to us is the EPA's ban of products for which no substitutes presently are available. In these cases, the EPA bears a tough burden indeed to show that under TSCA a ban is the least burdensome alternative, as TSCA explicitly instructs the EPA to consider "the benefits of such substance or mixture for various uses and the availability of substitutes for such uses." *Id.* §2605(c)(1)(C). These words are particularly appropriate where the EPA actually has decided to ban a product, rather than simply restrict its use, for it is in these cases that the lack of an adequate substitute is most troubling under TSCA.

As the EPA itself states, "when no information is available for a product indicating that cost-effective substitutes exist, the estimated cost of a product ban is very high." Because of this, the EPA did not ban certain uses of asbestos, such as its use in rocket engines and battery separators. The EPA, however, in several other instances, ignores its own arguments and attempts to justify its ban by stating that the ban itself will cause the development of low-cost, adequate substitute products.

As a general matter, we agree with the EPA that a product ban can lead to great innovation, and it is true that an agency under TSCA, as under other regulatory statutes, "is empowered to issue safety standards which require improvements in existing technology or which require the development of new technology." As even the EPA acknowledges, however, when no adequate substitutes currently exist, the EPA cannot fail to consider this lack when formulating its own guidelines. Under TSCA, therefore, the EPA must present a stronger case to justify the ban, as opposed to regulation, of products with no substitutes.

We note that the EPA does provide a waiver provision for industries where the hoped-for substitutes fail to materialize in time. Under this provision, if no adequate substitutes develop, the EPA temporarily may extend the planned phase-out.

The EPA uses this provision to argue that it can ban any product, regardless of whether it has an adequate substitute, because inventive companies soon will develop good substitutes. The EPA contends that if they do not, the waiver provision will allow the continued use of asbestos in these areas, just as if the ban had not occurred at all.

The EPA errs, however, in asserting that the waiver provision will allow a continuation of the status quo in those cases in which no substitutes materialize. By its own terms, the exemption shifts the burden onto the waiver proponent to convince the EPA that the waiver is justified. As even the EPA acknowledges, the waiver only "may be granted by [the] EPA in very limited circumstances."

The EPA thus cannot use the waiver provision to lessen its burden when justifying banning products without existing substitutes. While TSCA gives the EPA the power to ban such products, the EPA must bear its heavier burden of justifying its total ban in the face of inadequate substitutes. Thus, the agency cannot use its waiver provision to argue that the ban of products with no substitutes should be treated the same as the ban of those for which adequate substitutes are available now.

We also are concerned with the EPA's evaluation of substitutes even in those instances in which the record shows that they are available. The EPA explicitly rejects considering the harm that may flow from the increased use of products designed to substitute for asbestos, even where the probable substitutes themselves are known carcinogens. The EPA justifies this by stating that it has "more concern about the continued use and exposure to asbestos than it has for the future replacement of asbestos in the products subject to this rule with other fibrous substitutes." The agency thus concludes that any "regulatory decisions about asbestos which poses well-recognized, serious risks should not be delayed until the risk of all replacement materials are fully quantified . . . "

EPA cannot say with any assurance that its regulation will increase workplace safety when it refuses to evaluate the harm that will result from the increased use of substitute products. While the EPA may be correct in its conclusion that the alternate materials pose less risk than asbestos, we cannot say with any more assurance than that flowing from an educated guess that this conclusion is true. Eager to douse the dangers of asbestos, the agency inadvertently actually may increase the risk of injury Americans face. The EPA's explicit failure to consider the toxicity of likely substitutes thus deprives its order of a reasonable basis.

Our opinion should not be construed to state that the EPA has an affirmative duty to seek out and test every workplace substitute for any product it seeks to regulate. TSCA does not place such a burden upon the agency. We do not think it unreasonable, however, once interested parties introduce credible studies and evidence showing the toxicity of workplace substitutes, or the decreased effectiveness of safety alternatives such as non-asbestos brakes, that the EPA then consider whether its regulations are even increasing workplace safety, and whether the increased risk occasioned by dangerous substitutes makes the proposed regulation no longer reasonable. In the words of the EPA's own release that initiated the asbestos rulemaking, we direct that the agency consider the adverse health effects of asbestos substitute "for comparison with the known hazards of asbestos," so that it can conduct, as it promised in 1979, a "balanced consideration of the environmental, economic, and social impact of any action taken by the agency."

In short, a death is a death, whether occasioned by asbestos or by a toxic substitute product, and the EPA's decision not to evaluate the toxicity of known carcinogenic substitutes is not a reasonable action under TSCA. Once an interested party brings forth credible evidence suggesting the toxicity of the probable or only alternatives to a substance, the EPA must consider the comparative toxic costs of each. Its failure to do so in this case thus deprived its regulation of a reasonable basis, at least in regard to those products as to which petitioners introduced credible evidence of the dangers of the likely substitutes.

4. Unreasonable Risk of Injury

The final requirement the EPA must satisfy before engaging in any TSCA rulemaking is that it only take steps designed to prevent "unreasonable" risks. In evaluating what is "unreasonable," the EPA is required to consider the costs of any proposed actions and to "carry out this chapter in a reasonable and prudent manner [after considering] the environmental, economic, and social impact of any action." 15 U.S.C. §2601(c).

As the District of Columbia Circuit stated when evaluating similar language governing the Federal Hazardous Substances Act, "the requirement that the risk be 'unreasonable' necessarily involves a balancing test like that familiar in tort law: The regulation may issue if the severity of the injury that may result from the product, factored by the likelihood of the injury, offsets the harm the regulation itself imposes upon manufacturers and consumers. . . . "

That the EPA must balance the costs of its regulations against their benefits further is reinforced by the requirement that it seek the least burdensome regulation. While Congress did not dictate that the EPA engage in an exhaustive, full-scale cost-benefit analysis, it did require the EPA to consider both sides of the regulatory equation, and it rejected the notion that the EPA should pursue the reduction of workplace risk at any cost. Thus, "Congress also plainly intended the EPA to consider the economic impact of *any* actions taken by it under . . . TSCA."

Even taking all of the EPA's figures as true, and evaluating them in the light most favorable to the agency's decision (non-discounted benefits, discounted costs, analogous exposure estimates included), the agency's analysis results in figures as high as $74 million per life saved. For example, the EPA states that its ban of asbestos pipe will save three lives over the next thirteen years, at a cost of $128-227 million ($43-76 million per life saved), depending upon the price of substitutes; that its ban of asbestos shingles will cost $23-34 million to save 0.32 statistical lives ($72-106 million per life saved); that its ban of asbestos coatings will cost $46-181 million to save 3.33 lives ($14-54 million per life saved); and that its ban of asbestos paper products will save 0.60 lives at a cost of $4-5 million ($7-8 million per life saved). Were the analogous exposure estimates not included, the cancer risks from substitutes such as ductile iron pipe factored in, and the benefits of the ban appropriately discounted from the time of the manifestation of an injury rather than the time of exposure, the costs would shift even more sharply against the EPA's position.

While we do not sit as a regulatory agency that must make the difficult decision as to what an appropriate expenditure is to prevent someone from incurring the risk of an asbestos-related death, we do note that the EPA, in its zeal to ban any and all asbestos products, basically ignored the cost side of the TSCA equation. The EPA would have this court believe that Congress, when it enacted its requirement that the EPA consider the economic impacts of its regulations, thought that spending $200-300 million to save approximately seven lives (approximately $30-40 million per life) over thirteen years is reasonable.

As we stated in the OSHA context, until an agency "can provide substantial evidence that the benefits to be achieved by [a regulation] bear a reasonable relationship to the costs imposed by the reduction, it cannot show that the standard is reasonably necessary to provide safe or healthful workplaces." Although the OSHA statute differs in major respects from TSCA, the statute does require substantial evidence to support the EPA's contentions that its regulations both have a reasonable basis and are the least burdensome means to a reasonably safe workplace.

The EPA's willingness to argue that spending $23.7 million to save less than one-third of a life reveals that its economic review of its regulations, as required by TSCA, was meaningless. As the petitioners' brief and our review of EPA case law reveals, such high costs are rarely, if ever, used to support a safety regulation. If we were to allow such cavalier treatment of the EPA's duty to consider the economic effects of its decisions, we would have to excise entire sections and phrases from the language of TSCA. Because we are judges, not surgeons, we decline to do so. . . .

VI. Conclusion

In summary, of most concern to us is that the EPA has failed to implement the dictates of TSCA and the prior decisions of this and other courts that, before it impose a ban on a product, it first evaluate and then reject the less burdensome alternatives laid out for it by Congress. While the EPA spent much time and care crafting its asbestos regulation, its explicit failure to consider the alternatives required of it by Congress deprived its final rule of the reasonable basis it needed to survive judicial scrutiny.

[T]he EPA failed to provide a reasonable basis for the purported benefits of its proposed rule by refusing to evaluate the toxicity of likely substitute products that will be used to replace asbestos goods. While the EPA does not have the duty under TSCA of affirmatively seeking out and testing all possible substitutes, when an interested party comes forward with credible evidence that the planned substitutes present a significant, or even greater, toxic risk than the substance in question, the agency must make a formal finding on the record that its proposed action still is both reasonable and warranted under TSCA.

We regret that this matter must continue to take up the valuable time of the agency, parties and, undoubtedly, future courts. The requirements of TSCA, however, are plain, and the EPA cannot deviate from them to reach its desired result. We therefore GRANT the petition for review, VACATE the EPA's proposed regulation, and REMAND to the EPA for further proceedings in light of this opinion.

NOTES AND QUESTIONS ON *CORROSION PROOF FITTINGS*, TSCA, AND FIFRA

1. *Remand.* Can the agency expect to meet the Fifth Circuit's demands on remand? What should it do if it wants to try?

2. *Aftermath.* The court was wrong to think that this matter would continue to take up valuable judicial time. After this decision, EPA never again regulated any new substance under section 6 of the Toxic Substances Control Act and it never again sought to apply section 6 authority to asbestos. Why do you think paralysis followed this decision? EPA spent ten years preparing the rule reversed in *Corrosion Proof Fittings* and it spent between $5 and $10 million on consultants as part of its cost-benefit analysis. *See* Economic Analysis at EPA: Assessing Regulatory Impact 173 (Richard Morgenstern ed., 1997) [hereinafter *Economic Analysis*].

3. *Statutory interpretation.* How did the court's statutory interpretation differ from that of EPA in the Federal Register notice, and why? The court demanded more than an EPA finding that the benefits of banning asbestos outweigh the costs, and a finding that the alternatives to a ban failed to protect public health. It required EPA to weigh the costs and benefits of each alternative to the a ban.

4. *The most burdensome option.* The court says that the ban chosen by EPA is the "most burdensome" option. If a substitute for asbestos proves no more costly than asbestos itself, will the substitution impose any net burden on consumers? On the manufacturer? *Cf.* Honeywell Intern., Inc. v. EPA, 374 F.3d 1363 (D.C. Cir. 2004) (discussing the potential economic benefits of bans for manufacturers of substitutes and issues posed by the variations in costs among the substitutes). Which burden should matter the most in deciding whether to ban the substance? For more information on how EPA quantified the costs of switching products, *see Economic Analysis, supra,* at 182-89.

5. *Non-quantified benefits.* The court said that EPA could consider non-quantified benefits, but could not assign them great weight. Does the fact that a benefit cannot be quantified mean that it is trivial? Should it matter that EPA considered its monetization of benefits an understatement? Consider the following:

> There were . . . many instances where there was good reason to believe that exposure occurred, but there were no data as to the level of exposure. . . .

Although benefits were estimated assuming zero exposure where no data was available, unless the exposures to asbestos from those products was in fact zero, this procedure would clearly bias the benefit-cost information in the direction of not supporting a regulation when regulation is warranted.

Economic Analysis, supra., at 191-92. What should EPA do in this circumstance?

6. *Discounting.* The court requires discounting future benefits, *i.e.*, assigning a future benefit a lower value than the same benefit would receive if realized immediately. The notion that agencies should discount future compliance *costs* in assessing regulations is not controversial. The reason is fairly simple. Suppose that the prevailing interest rates today is 5 percent. If a manufacturer needs to spend $1 million to comply with a regulation, it needs $1 million. Suppose, however, that the manufacturer must spend $1 million five years from now to comply. The manufacturer need not put aside $1 million today to fund that obligation. Because the money put aside will earn 5 percent interest, the manufacturer can put aside significantly less than $1 million, because the money saved will earn interest at a 5 percent rate. To take this into account, regulators must discount future compliance expenditures, applying a discount rate corresponding to estimates of prevailing interest rates.

Most economists believe that regulatory agencies monetizing benefits should discount future benefits in a similar fashion. But is a life saved tomorrow worth less than a life saved today? Why does the court insist on discounting benefits? Do you agree with its reasoning? Should it defer to the agency's judgment on this?

The decision to use a discount rate and the choice of which discount rate to apply can have an enormous impact on the calculations of costs and benefits.[1] For example, a regulation saving 100 lives 30 years from now at a discount rate of 3 percent has a present value of 41.2 lives. If one increases the discount rate to 6 percent, the regulation saves the equivalent of 17.41 lives today, less than half the number of present lives saved with a 3 percent assumption.   *See*   http://www.progressiveregulation.org/perspectives/costbenefit.cfm (online calculator). If the regulator values each life saved at

---

1. *See* Douglas A. Kysar, *Climate Change, Cultural Transformation, and Comprehensive Rationality*, 31 B.C. Envt'l Aff. L. Rev. 555, 578-585 (2004) (discussing discounting's moral issues in the climate change context); Lisa Heinzerling, *The Rights of Statistical People*, 24 Harv. Envtl. L. Rev. 189 (2000); Armatya Sen, *The Discipline of Cost-Benefit Analysis*, 29 J. Legal Stud. 931 (2000); Henry Richardson, *The Stupidity of Cost-Benefit Analysis*, 29 J. Legal Stud. 971 (2000); Richard L. Revesz, *Environmental Regulation, Cost-Benefit Analysis, and the Discounting of Human Lives*, 99 Colum. L. Rev. 941 (1999); Lisa Heinzerling, *Discounting Life*, 108 Yale L. J. 1911 (1999); John J. Donohue, III, *Why We Should Discount the Views of Those Who Discount Discounting*, 108 Yale L. J. 1901 (1999); Daniel A. Farber and Paul A. Hemmersbaugh, *The Shadow of the Future: Discount Rates, Later Generations, and the Environment*, 46 Vand. L. Rev. 267 (1993). *See also* Edith Brown Weiss, *The Planetary Trust: Conservation and Intergenerational Equity*, 11 Ecology L.Q. 495 (1984).

$6.3 million, then selecting the higher discount rate (6 percent) can reduce the estimate of the regulatory benefit by $150 million.

7. *Risk/risk analysis.* A number of commentators have emphasized the value of risk/risk analysis. It is possible that companies might respond to an asbestos ban by introducing a more hazardous substance to perform the functions asbestos used to perform. It is also possible that banning asbestos, which is used as fireproofing, would increase the number of fires. What did the court hold respecting risk/risk analysis? If EPA must evaluate all possible substitutes, how would it go about doing so?

Some commentators cite the value of risk/risk analysis as a reason to favor cost-benefit based standard setting. Is it possible to consider the problem of environmental solutions causing worse risks without using CBA? Consider section 112(d)(2) of the Clean Air Act (the section addressing technology-based MACT standards), which states:

> Emission standards promulgated under this subsection . . . shall require the maximum degree of reduction in emissions of the hazardous air pollutants subject to this section . . . that the Administrator, taking into consideration the cost of achieving such emission reductions, and *any non-air quality health and environmental impacts* . . . determines is achievable. . . .

42 U.S.C. §7412(d)(2) (emphasis added). Under this section, what should EPA do if it discovers that a potential air pollution reduction technique has a negative impact on water quality? Is this a cost-benefit provision or a technology-based provision? Similar language exists in other technology-based standard setting provisions. *See, e.g.,* 33 U.S.C. §1314(b)(2)(B); BP Exploration & Oil Co., Inc. v. U.S. E.P.A., 66 F.3d 784, 796-97 (6th Cir. 1995) (upholding EPA's decision not to require zero discharge limits for offshore oil and gas production in light of air quality and solid waste impacts associated with the technology needed to meet a zero limit for water pollution).

8. *FIFRA.* The courts have also interpreted the Federal, Insecticide, Fungicide, and Rodenticide Act to apply a cost-benefit test to decisions about whether to register a pesticide. EPA has authority to ban or drastically limit the use of pesticides, but it rarely uses that authority. Experts on this statute agree that the requirement to quantify the risks of pesticides has paralyzed EPA:

> The informational demands of risk analysis doom the regulatory process to a perpetual state of slow motion . . . "[A]fter 20 years collecting data to reevaluate the health and environmental effects of 19,000 older pesticides, EPA . . . had reregistered only 2 products."

Donald Hornstein, *Lessons from Federal Pesticide Regulation on the Paradigm and Politics of Environmental Law Reform,* 10 YALE J. ON REG. 369, 437-38 (1993).

B. REVIEW UNDER THE EXECUTIVE ORDERS

President Reagan heavily promoted cost-benefit analysis in order to "reduce the burdens" on regulated industry. *See* Executive Order (E.O.) 12291, 46 Fed. Reg. 13193 (February 17, 1981). He issued an Executive Order requiring the Office of Management and Budget (OMB) to apply a cost-benefit test to major regulations to the extent consistent with applicable law. Specifically, the Executive Order required "to the extent permitted by law" that "regulation shall not be undertaken unless the potential benefits to society . . . outweigh the potential costs. . . . " *Id.* §2(b).

Does the law permit this cost-benefit test to apply to decisions to set national ambient air quality standards under section 109? *See* Whitman v. American Trucking Ass'ns, 531 U.S. 457, 464-71 (2001). Recall that this section requires health protective standards and does not authorize the consideration of cost. Does the law permit a cost-benefit test to apply to a cost-sensitive technology-based decision, like those undertaken in setting Best Available Technology and Best Practicable Control Technology decisions under the Clean Water Act? Recall *Pacific Fisheries'* discussion of the consideration of cost.

Reagan's order led to charges that OMB was forcing EPA to violate the law. *See* Erik Olson, *The Quiet Shift of Power: Office of Management and Budget Supervision of Environmental Protection Agency Rulemaking Under Executive Order 12,291*, 4 Va. J. Nat. Res. L. 1, 51 (1984). Would a requirement that benefits must outweigh costs ever require the agency to make a regulation more stringent? Or is it a one-way ratchet making regulations less stringent? *See* David M. Driesen, *Is Cost-Benefit Analysis Neutral?* 72 U. Colo. L. Rev. 335, 387-89 (2006). *Cf.* E.O. 12291 §2 (requiring that regulatory objectives be chosen to maximize net benefits to society). Critics also accused OMB of functioning as a secretive back channel helping industry undermine environmental, health, and safety protection. *See* Olson, *supra*, at 55-57.

Support for CBA, however, clearly became wider during the 1980s. When President Clinton came into office, he continued the practice of OMB review ostensibly based on CBA. *See* E.O. 12866, 58 Fed. Reg. 51,735 (September 30, 1993). This order stated that regulation should only be adopted if "the benefits of the . . . regulation justify the costs." *Id.* §1(b)(6). Does this criterion differ materially from that imposed by President Reagan? Is it a one-way ratchet or not? *Cf. id.* §1(a) (agencies should select "approaches" that "maximize net benefits"); Driesen, *supra*, at 341, 387-87 (discussing the "indeterminate position" that regulators should consider CBA). The Clinton order aimed to increase the transparency of the process and focus it on economically significant rules. *Cf.* UNITED STATES GENERAL ACCOUNTING OFFICE, RULEMAKING: OMB's ROLE IN REVIEWS OF AGENCIES' DRAFT RULES AND THE TRANSPARENCY OF THOSE REVIEWS (2003) (discussing the extent to which transparency had taken hold during the Bush Administration). Congress, which had initially been very skeptical of CBA, lent its support in 1995 when it passed the Unfunded Mandates Reform Act (UMRA), Pub. L. No. 104-4, §202, codified at 2 U.S.C. §1532. UMRA required CBA of rules generating over $100 million in annual compliance expenditures "unless otherwise prohibited by law."

The executive orders mention another criterion, maximizing net benefits. As a technical economic matter, this should mean that marginal costs are set equal to marginal benefits. HORST SIEBERT, ECONOMICS OF THE ENVIRONMENT: THEORY AND POLICY 65 (5th rev. ed. 1998). Economists define "optimal pollution levels" as those reflecting equalization of costs and benefits at the margin. This means that the cost of the last increment of pollution control should provide a benefit equal to the cost. Since marginal pollution control cost (*i.e.*, the cost associated with each increment of stringency) typically rises as a standards become more stringent, one can graph this concept as follows:

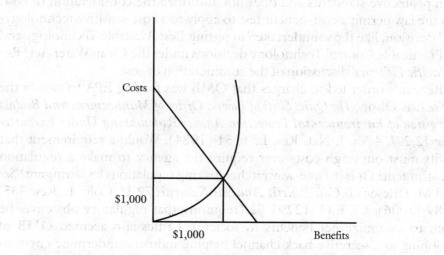

Does this criterion act as a one-way ratchet?

Assume that controlling air emissions at a plant producing teflon coatings using mediocre pollution control equipment costs $50 per pound for the last unit of control. And assume that this last unit of control produces $75 worth of benefit at the margin (*i.e.*, for last unit of control only). A more stringent approach would cost $80 per pound at the margin, and would produce $80 worth of benefits.

Which option does the maximize net benefits criterion suggest the regulator should choose? Does this criterion make sense as a policy matter?

C. THE POLICY DEBATE

1. The Supermandate Idea

About the time that Congress passed the Unfunded Mandates Reform Act, it considered superseding almost all environmental statutory provisions with a "supermandate" applying a cost-benefit test to all environmental statutes. Do you think such a supermandate is a good idea? *See* William W. Buzbee, *Regulatory Reform or Statutory Muddle: The "Legislative Mirage" of Single Statute Regulatory Reform*, 5 N.Y.U. Envt'l L.J. 298 (1996). Many legislators, even some who favored a supermandate, would have limited the use of judicial review in enforcing it. Does the *Corrosion Proof Fittings* case counsel against judicially reviewable CBA?

2. Priority Setting and Dollars per Life Saved Tables

Supporters of CBA claim that environmental law has been very bad at priority setting. They cite tables developed by an OMB economist showing that the dollars per lives saved for various regulatory interventions have varied wildly and argue that CBA is needed as a rationalizing reform. *See, e.g.* Cass Sunstein, Risk and Reason: Safety, Law, and the Environment 19-27 (2002). Opponents of CBA claim that these tables include regulations that were never promulgated and that the table's authors used their own questionable assumptions to doctor government estimates of costs and benefits. *See* Richard W. Parker, *Grading Government*, 70 U. Chi. L. Rev. 1345 (2003); Lisa Heinzerling, *Regulatory Costs of Mythic Proportions*, 107 Yale L. J. 1981 (1998). *Cf.* John F. Morrall, *Saving Lives: A Review of the Record*, 27 J. Risk & Uncertainty (2003) (defending his tables). If regulation does have discrepancies in dollars per life saved, does that make regulation irrational *per se*? Suppose that regulation is technology-based. Will that approach produce even cost-benefit ratios? Is it irrational to base regulation on what the regulated are capable of doing? What if a regulation with very high dollars per life saved brings an enormous ecological benefit. Does that matter? Is it correct to think of decisions about regulatory stringency as priority setting decisions? *See* David M. Driesen, *Getting Our Priorities Straight: One Strand of the Regulatory Reform Debate*, 31 Envt'l L. Rep. (Envt'l L. Inst.) 10003 (2001); Stephen Breyer, Breaking the Vicious Circle: Toward Effective Risk Regulation (1993).

3. Tradeoffs

Proponents of CBA argue that environmental law must take tradeoffs into account and that CBA helps it do that. *See, e.g.,* Sunstein, *supra,* at 5. Resources used for environmental protection will not be available for other uses. *See* WILLIAM BAXTER, PEOPLE OR PENGUINS: THE CASE FOR OPTIMAL POLLUTION (1974) (excerpted in Chapter 4). Regulatory reformers argue that regulations costing more than they are worth waste money that could be used to save even more lives. Does relaxing a regulation limiting emissions of hazardous air pollutants from a factory using PFOA to produce teflon help fund childhood vaccinations, which might deserve higher priority from a public health standpoint?

The degree of stringency, CBA proponents argue, should reflect the magnitude of the harm and the amount of costs. Otherwise, in the words politicians use to advocate CBA, we might impose regulations that do more harm than good. Should environmental regulation countenance tradeoffs or should it involve an uncompromising search for full protection of the environment and public health? *See* JOSEPH SAX, MOUNTAINS WITHOUT HANDRAILS: REFLECTIONS ON THE NATIONAL PARKS (1980). If tradeoffs must be taken into account, does it follow that we must use CBA to do so? *See BP Exploration, supra.* Do health-based standards take tradeoffs into account? What about technology-based standards? Does the feasibility principle take tradeoffs into account? What about a system that forbids agencies from taking tradeoffs into account? Would such a system forbid Congress from countermanding overly aggressive agency action from time to time? Is such an approach, combining absolutist administrative law with occasional political intervention to correct abuses, an adequate way to take tradeoffs into account?

4. Quantifying Risk and Ecological Harm

The argument that environmental law should consider the magnitude of the harm leads directly to efforts to quantify the risks. But even proponents of CBA recognize that many harms cannot be quantified, because of data gaps. Quantifying ecological harms can be especially difficult. *See generally* Amy Sinden, *The Economics of Endangered Species: Why Less is More in the Economic Analysis of Critical Habitat Designations,* 28 Harv. Envtl. L. Rev. 129, 146-151 (2004) (explaining the difficulties of quantifying benefits in the Endangered Species context). CBA proponents usually argue that regulators should consider the non-quantified harms as well as the quantified ones. Suppose that the monetized costs exceed the monetized benefits, but the EPA Administrator believed that the non-monetized benefits justify the regulation. How could she rationally explain why these unquantified benefits outweigh a particular cost? Could she make an explanation that would survive judicial review?

How helpful is CBA when not all of the benefits can be monetized? Consider this statement by an EPA senior scientist:

Typically, only a few potential health or other benefits can be quantified, and even fewer can be valued monetarily. Consequently, when the sum of the limited subset of benefits that can be quantified and monetized is shown to be less than the estimated costs, it is often impossible to conclude anything about the relative magnitude of the full benefits.

Ronnie Levin, *Lead in Drinking Water*, in *Economic Analysis, supra*, at 230. Is the opposite true? If the monetizable benefits are shown to be more than the estimated costs, it is possible to tell whether the benefits outweigh the costs?

When risks can be quantified, the benefits range can be quite large, depending upon the underlying assumptions chosen in the risk assessment and monetization process. Professors Shapiro and McGarity state that the range of risk estimates for a carcinogen approximates the difference between the size of the national debt (circa 1990) and the price of a cup of coffee (regular coffee, not lattes). *See* Sidney A. Shapiro & Thomas O. McGarity, *Not So Paradoxical: The Rationale for Technology-Based Regulation*, 1991 Duke L.J. 729, 731. If that's true, how useful can CBA be in decision-making? See Amy Sinden, *Cass Sunstein's Cost-Benefit Lite: Economics for Liberals*, 29 Colum. J. Envtl. L. 191, 210-11 (2004) (arguing that CBA expands agency discretion and exacerbates problems of special interest influence).

5. Preferences and Statistical Life

The CBA controversy reflects wider debates about the role of economics in legal policy. The cost-benefit approach basically treats environmental protection like the purchase of a consumer good, rather than as harm prevention. *See* David M. Driesen, *The Societal Cost of Environmental Regulation: Beyond Administrative Cost-Benefit Analysis*, 24 Ecology L.Q. 545, 560-63 (1997). The theory posits that the amount of money spent on this good should not exceed what a rational consumer of the health and environmental benefits would pay for them. What consumers are willing to pay reflects consumer preferences.

The $6.1 million figure for the value of human life comes from surveys that economists have interpreted as showing that labor markets charge "risk premiums." In other words, jobs with greater danger from occupational hazards command higher wages. The hypothesis underlying the number assumes that these differentials reflect how much the worker is willing to accept to put up with greater risk. Some, however, have questioned whether that is so. *See* Ackerman and Heinzerling, *supra*, at 77 (pointing out that workers may have limited choices in jobs and may not understand the risks that they supposedly have accepted).

More generally, some writers have raised questions about whether consumer "preferences" should dictate policy choices. The philosopher Mark Sagoff has argued that using preferences to decide policy involves a "category mistake." Marg Sagoff, The Economy of the Earth: Philosophy, Law and the

ENVIRONMENT (1988). *Cf.* Carol M. Rose, *Environmental Faust Succumbs to Temptations of Economic Mephistopheles, or, Value by Any Other Name is Preference*, 87 Mich. L. Rev. 1631 (1987) (critiquing Sagoff's work). Professor Sagoff argues that public policy should flow from a debate about what sort of society we want to have. He makes a distinction between what people want as consumers and what they, as citizens, wish society to achieve. So, for example, a consumer may prefer to have a deduction for mortgage interest on a second home as a consumer, but disfavor such a deduction as a matter of public policy, because she thinks that tax breaks for the well-off are not good policy. And policy positions of a society can adjust themselves as members of the polity learn from each other and clarify values in public debates.

On the other hand, Matthew Adler and Eric Posner, who reject the notion that public policy should involve the mere summation of preferences, generally tilt toward CBA. Matthew D. Adler and Eric A. Posner, *Rethinking Cost-Benefit Analysis*, 109 Yale L.J. 165 (1999). They argue that CBA, as adjusted in ways necessary to overcome the problems with preferences, reasonably approximates overall well-being. *Cf.* David M. Driesen, *Distributing the Cost of Environmental, Health, and Safety Protection: The Feasibility Principle, Cost-Benefit Analysis, and Regulatory Reform*, 32 B.C. Envt'l Aff. L. Rev. 1, 69-75 (2005) (critiquing this view).

6. Transparency

Several writers have argued that CBA enhances the transparency of the decision-making process. Suppose that an agency concludes that eliminating teflon would produce $1 million worth of annual benefits at a cost of $500,000 a year. Does this information improve the transparency of the reasons for eliminating teflon? Would it be any less transparent if the agency simply stated that information exists suggesting that teflon causes cancer? Aren't both of these decisions less than fully transparent? Why did the agency choose the $1 million figure? Why did it think that the information suggesting that teflon causes cancer was sufficiently compelling to justify the decision? Would a technology-based decision, which reflects some judgment about the capabilities of technology, be more or less transparent than a cost-benefit based or health-based judgment? What sorts of information and explanations would aid transparency?

7. Comprehensive Rationality

One can think of the debate about CBA as a discussion of the merits of "comprehensive rationality." *See* THOMAS O. MCGARITY, REINVENTING RATIONALITY: THE ROLE OF REGULATORY ANALYSIS IN THE FEDERAL BUREAUCRACY 5-16 (1991). CBA proponents seem to view CBA as a means to allow agencies to consider everything. They then should make the most sensible decision based on all of the information before them. This vision suggests that there might be some ultimately optimal decision that can be made independent of categorical value choices about what is important. By contrast, a vision of instrumental rationality requires some political value choice about goals. Under this view, administrative agencies are (or should be) engaged in figuring out how to achieve these goals. The instrumental rationality approach lends itself to specific statutory mandates and limiting the inquiry of agencies into the matters most important to figuring out how to meet statutory goals. Which of these two visions leads to more agency discretion? Which relies more heavily upon congressional decision-making?

PFOA PROBLEM

Analyze what, if any standards, would be appropriate to regulate PFOA under a health-based, technology-based, or CBA-based approach. For each approach, list the information you need to establish the regulation and think about what analysis you need to conduct. Consider the following information.

Recall that PFOA has appeared in the bloodstream of many Americans and that EPA's preliminary risk assessment found some evidence of cancer, increased levels of some hormones, and some adverse developmental effects. EPA has information indicating that the general U.S. population may be exposed to PFOA at very low levels. But it has little information about the exposure routes and its information about health risks comes from animal studies and very limited studies of occupational exposure (which are typically much higher than environmental exposures). Furthermore, these compounds are extremely stable, so that they may persist in the environment for a long time.

Fluoropolymer manufacturers have indicated that there are no known alternatives to PFOA. But some manufacturing processes currently employing PFOA can use technologies that do not use PFOA.

DuPont has announced that it is employing technology that can reduce air emissions by as much as 99 percent and is sharing it with other manufacturers. *DuPont Responds to EPA Complaint on Alleged PFOA Reporting Violations: Company reaffirms it complied with all laws, continues to support EPA review process* (August 12, 2004), available at http://www1.dupont.com/NASApp/ dupontglobal/corp/index.jsp?page=/content/US/en_US/news/releases/ 2004/nr08_12_04a.html. PFOA has also been detected in drinking water, which has led to class action law suits. PFOA has also been detected in some consumer products.

If EPA thinks that it should reduce exposure, should EPA give priority to TSCA regulations, Clean Air Act regulations, or Clean Water Act regulations? What sorts of considerations would govern standard setting under these statutes? Which sort of standard would be easiest to establish, given this information? What additional information should EPA seek in order to set standards?

III

The Means of Environmental Protection

The previous part focused on how agencies make decisions about the stringency of environmental standards (both ambient and output standards). We discovered that environmental law uses effects-based, technological, or cost-benefit criteria to guide agency stringency determinations.

These stringency determinations set enforceable objectives for improving the environment. This part discusses the means of realizing these environmental improvements. Once the agency has chosen a level of protection, it must decide whether to command use of a particular technology or technique, require a particular level of performance from regulated parties, employ an "economic incentive" to encourage reduced environmental damage, use information to motivate change, or try to encourage or require pollution prevention. The legislature faces the same choices if it decides to make detailed decisions itself, rather than delegate them to an administrative agency.

We explore the choice of means through chapters on traditional regulation, economic incentive approaches, including informational approaches, and pollution prevention. The choice about the means of meeting environmental goals can influence cost, enforceability, and fairness, so it raises extremely important practical issues that influence policy-making.

8

Traditional Regulation

This book uses the term "traditional regulation" to refer to performance standards, work practice standards, and bans. For convenience, this chapter uses the term "work practice standards" in a generic sense to refer to any standard dictating a particular method of obtaining emission reductions, a definition that includes design, equipment, or operational standards. *Cf.* 42 U.S.C. §7412(h)(1). We contrast traditional regulation with approaches, such as emissions trading, that most experts think of as economic incentive programs.

Most writing about the means of environmental regulation contrasts "command and control regulation" with economic incentives. Some writers use the term "command and control regulation" to refer to work practice standards. Others use the term to refer to both work practice standards and standards requiring a particular level of performance. This book's use of the term "traditional regulation" generally tracks this broader definition of command and control regulation.

A. PERFORMANCE STANDARDS

A performance standard quantitatively limits the amount of pollution or natural resource destruction. For example, EPA has traditionally limited air emissions from electric utilities with standards limiting the pounds per million British Thermal Units (BTUs are a measure of heat energy) that the utility can emit. It has often regulated vehicle emissions by limiting the grams of a pollutant emitted per mile. Here's one court's description of a traditional utility performance standard:

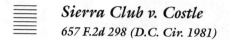

Sierra Club v. Costle
657 F.2d 298 (D.C. Cir. 1981)

I. INTRODUCTION

WALD, CIRCUIT JUDGE.

A. The Challenged Standards

The Clean Air Act provides for direct federal regulation of emissions from new stationary sources of air pollution by authorizing EPA to set performance standards for significant sources of air pollution which may be reasonably anticipated to endanger public health or welfare. In June 1979 EPA promulgated the [New Source Performance Standards] NSPS involved in this case. The new standards increase pollution controls for new coal-fired electric power plants by tightening restrictions on emissions of sulfur dioxide and particulate matter. Sulfur dioxide emissions are limited to a maximum of 1.2 lbs./MBtu[1] . . . and a 90 percent reduction of potential uncontrolled sulfur dioxide emissions is required except when emissions to the atmosphere are less than 0.60 lbs./MBtu. When sulfur dioxide emissions are less than 0.60 lbs./MBtu potential emissions must be reduced by no less than 70 percent. In addition, emissions of particulate matter are limited to 0.03 lbs./MBtu.

II. The Variable Percentage Reduction Option

[T]he final NSPS adopted by EPA include an optional variable percentage reduction standard. Under this optional standard a utility plant can permissibly reduce its sulfur dioxide emissions by less than 90 percent of potential uncontrolled emissions if the amount of sulfur dioxide emitted following the use of pollution control technology is less than 0.60 lbs./MBtu. In no instance, however, can a plant reduce emissions by less than 70 percent of potential uncontrolled emissions. As a result of this option, the NSPS requirements for percentage reduction of sulfur dioxide removal vary on a sliding scale ranging from a minimum of 70 percent to a maximum of 90 percent. There is no dispute that the 70 percent floor in the standard necessarily means that, given the present state of pollution control technology, utilities will have to employ some form of flue gas desulfurization (. . . . "scrubbing") technology.

---

1. MBtu refers to Million British thermal units which is a measure of heat energy. A single Btu is the amount of energy required to raise the temperature of one pound of water one degree Fahrenheit. This measure is appropriate here because utility plants combust coal to heat water which produces steam used for generating electricity.

NOTES ON THE PERFORMANCE STANDARD IN
SIERRA CLUB v. COSTLE

1. *Flexibility of performance standards.* The court states, "*[G]iven the present state of pollution control technology,* utilities will have to employ some form of flue gas desulfurization ("FGD" or "scrubbing") technology." [emphasis added]. *Sierra Club,* 657 F.2d at 316. Suppose that a utility invents a new form of technology capable of meeting the numerical standards in the regulation. May the utility use this alternative technology under this standard as written?

2. *Coal washing.* On the other hand, coal washing technology, which would usually cost much less than scrubbing, reduces emissions by 20-40 percent. *See* BRUCE A. ACKERMAN & WILLIAM T. HASSLER, CLEAN COAL/DIRTY AIR: OR HOW THE CLEAN AIR ACT BECAME A MULTIBILLION-DOLLAR BAIL-OUT FOR HIGH SULFUR COAL PRODUCERS AND WHAT SHOULD BE DONE ABOUT IT 15, 66-68 (1981). Does the standard described in this case preclude complete reliance upon coal washing for compliance? Why did EPA rule out a nice cheap control option?

3. *CWA statutory language.* Many statutes contain language calling for performance standards. For example, section 304(b)(2)(A) of the Clean Water Act requires technology-based standards identifying "the degree of effluent reduction attainable through the application of the best control measures and practices achievable including treatment techniques, process and procedure innovations, operating methods, and other alternatives ... " 33 U.S.C. §1314(b)(2)(A). Do you see why this language requires a performance standard, rather than a specification of technique? If that is so, why does the provision mention techniques?

4. *Ends and means.* In *Costle,* the Clean Air Act required EPA to use a technology-based approach to choosing its performance standard. *See* 42 U.S.C. §7411(a)(1). Can an agency use a health-based approach or a cost-benefit approach to setting a performance standard? Would these sorts of standards look any different in the Code of Federal Regulations, which codifies the standards themselves, but not the explanation for standards found in the Federal Register?

Technological Innovation

1. *Views of scholars.* While performance standards seem to allow technological innovations that make equal or better environmental performance possible at lower cost, some writers have claimed that in practice performance standards discourage innovation. Consider the views of Professor Stewart:

Richard Stewart, Regulation, Innovation, and Administrative Law: A Conceptual Framework
69 Cal. L. Rev. 1256, 1268-69 (1981)

3. Performance, Specification, and Engineering Standards

The conduct required by standards may be expressed in terms of a performance characteristic (*e.g.*, m.p.g. fuel economy, quantity of emissions, toxicity of ingredients). Alternately, a standard may specify a particular input, such as low-sulphur fuel oil, or a particular engineering design or piece of equipment, such as a flue gas desulphurization "scrubber." Performance standards allow regulated firms flexibility to select the least costly or least burdensome means of achieving compliance. For instance, cost considerations might cause a firm to change its internal processes rather than to incorporate an "end-of-pipe" control to meet standards. Specification standards, on the other hand, offer administrative simplicity and ease of enforcement. Technology to monitor emissions, particularly from industrial sources, in many cases has been expensive, cumbersome, and not very accurate. These drawbacks have allowed regulated firms to resist enforcement through legal challenges related to evidentiary and technical issues. Also, agency monitoring and enforcement resources are often quite limited. With specification standards, enforcement personnel need only check fuel supply invoices or determine whether control equipment is operating.

Engineering standards are a hybrid of performance standards and specifications. In form, they are expressed as pure performance standards. In practice, they are based upon the level of performance that can be achieved by a specific input or technology. Administrators rely on these specific control measures to determine the required level of performance in order to simplify standard setting, to meet legal challenges to standards' feasibility, and to facilitate enforcement. While regulated firms are in theory free to meet the required level of performance any way they choose, they have strong incentives to adopt the particular technology underlying the standard because its use will readily persuade regulators of compliance.

Professor Stewart's statement suggesting that in practice technology-based performance standards discourage even compliant innovations seems to assume that the work of evaluating a technology's feasibility in setting a limit influences firm's decisions about what technology to adopt. Does this argument that performance standards discourage innovation apply to a performance standard adopted using a health-based approach to standard setting? In that situation, the regulator might not have relied upon the performance of any particular technology to arrive at the decision about what level of reductions to require. Would his argument apply to a standard set using CBA? Professor Stewart's argument, while very influential, has been contested:

> Professor Richard Stewart of New York University, however, has stated that polluters have "strong incentives to adopt the particular technology underlying" a technology-based performance standard because "its use will readily persuade regulators of compliance." He does not explain why this countervailing persuasion incentive would overcome the economic incentive to realize savings through an effective and cheaper innovation, even if the persuasiveness incentive were powerful. Polluters, after all, have a number of means of persuading regulators that their innovations perform adequately if they in fact do so. First, polluters may monitor their pollution directly to demonstrate compliance. Second, in some cases polluters may eliminate regulated chemicals, which certainly demonstrates compliance.

DAVID M. DRIESEN, THE ECONOMIC DYNAMICS OF ENVIRONMENTAL LAW 52 (MIT Press 2003).

2. *Client counseling.* Imagine that you represent a company required to comply with a performance standard. Suppose that your client's engineers have figured out how to eliminate the pollution the performance standard regulates. What factors would you consider in deciding whether to counsel your client to adopt this pollution prevention method? What if your client has a control technology that it thinks superior, but the regulator has never seen it?

If your client thinks there is some risk of not meeting the standard both with the technology the agency evaluated in setting the standard and an alternative being offered by a vendor, which would you select? In the event of a failure to meet the performance standard, would (or should) the choice of technology influence the court's decision about the size of the penalty?

3. *Empirical information.* The question of whether performance standards discourage innovation should be empirically testable. The literature does show some cases where polluters have innovated in response to performance standards. *See* Kurt Strasser, *Clean Technology, Pollution Prevention, and Environmental Regulation*, 9 Fordham Envt'l L. J. 1, 32 (1997); U.S. CONGRESS, OFFICE OF TECHNOLOGY ASSESSMENT, GAUGING CONTROL TECHNOLOGY AND REGULATORY IMPACTS IN OCCUPATIONAL SAFETY AND HEALTH — AN APPRAISAL OF OSHA'S ANALYTICAL APPROACH 64 (1995); Nicholas A. Ashford, Christine Ayers, and Robert F. Stone, *Using Regulations to Change the Market for Innovation*, 9 Harv. Envtl. L. Rev. 419, 440-41 (1985); Nicholas Ashford and George R. Heaton Jr., *Regulation and Technological Innovation in the Chemical Industry*, 46 Law & Contemp. Probs. 109, 139-40 (1983). Yet, we simply have no good information about precisely how polluters have responded to most standards. And many experts believe that traditional regulation has not proven very successful at promoting innovation.

B. WORK PRACTICE STANDARDS

In contrast to performance standards, work practice standards specifically require use of a particular technique. Why would a regulatory agency ever mandate a technique, rather than at least provide some potential for flexibility through a performance standard? Consider a typical provision governing the use of work practice standards from section 112 of the Clean Air Act:

42 U.S.C. §7412. Hazardous air pollutants

(h) Work practice standards and other requirements
(1) In general
For purposes of this section, if it is not feasible in the judgment of the Administrator to prescribe or enforce an emission standard for control of a hazardous air pollutant or pollutants, the Administrator may, in lieu thereof, promulgate a design, equipment, work practice, or operational standard, or combination there of. . . .
(2) Definition
For the purpose of this subsection, the phrase "not feasible to prescribe or enforce an emission standard" means any situation in which the Administrator determines that —
(A) a hazardous air pollutant or pollutants cannot be emitted through a conveyance designed and constructed to emit or capture such pollutant . . . or
(B) the application of measurement methodology to a particular class of sources is not practicable due to technological and economic limitations. . . .
(4) Numerical standard required
Any standard promulgated under paragraph (1) shall be promulgated in terms of an emission standard whenever it is feasible to promulgate and enforce a standard in such terms.

Section 112(h) distinguishes work practice standards from design, equipment, or operational standards. Recall, however, that this textbook uses the term "work practice" standard to include these similar prescriptive requirements. If it is impossible to measure pollution, can a performance standard be enforced? Does the statute favor or disfavor work practice standards? The following case offers an example of a work practice standard.

≣ *Adamo Wrecking Co. v. United States*
    434 U.S. 275 (1978)

JUSTICE REHNQUIST delivered the opinion of the Court.

The Clean Air Act authorizes the Administrator of the Environmental Protection Agency to promulgate "emission standards" for hazardous air pollutants "at the level which in his judgment provides an ample margin of safety to protect the public health." The emission of an air pollutant in violation of an applicable emission standard is prohibited by section 112(c)(1)(B) of the Act. The knowing violation of the latter section, in turn, subjects the violator to fine and imprisonment under the provisions of §113(c)(1)(C) of the Act. The final piece in this statutory puzzle is §307(b) of the Act, which provides in pertinent part:

(1) A petition for review of action of the Administrator in promulgating . . . any emission standard under section 112 . . . may be filed only in the United States Court of Appeals for the District of Columbia. . . . Any such petition shall be filed within 30 days from the date of such promulgation or approval, or after such date if such petition is based solely on grounds arising after such 30th day.

(2) Action of the Administrator with respect to which review could have been obtained under paragraph (1) shall not be subject to judicial review in civil or criminal proceedings for enforcement.

I

It is within this legislative matrix that the present criminal prosecution arose. Petitioner was indicted in the United States District Court for the Eastern District of Michigan for violation of §112(c)(1)(B). The indictment alleged that petitioner, while engaged in the demolition of a building in Detroit, failed to comply with 40 CFR §61.22(d)(2)(I) (1975). That regulation, described in its caption as a "National Emission Standard for Asbestos," specifies procedures to be followed in connection with building demolitions, but does not by its terms limit emissions of asbestos which occur during the course of a demolition. The District Court granted petitioner's motion to dismiss the indictment on the ground that no violation of §112(c)(1)(B), necessary to establish criminal liability under §113(c)(1)(C), had been alleged, because the cited regulation was not an "emission standard" within the meaning of §112(c). The United States Court of Appeals for the Sixth Circuit reversed holding that Congress had in §307(b) precluded petitioner from questioning in a criminal proceeding whether a regulation ostensibly promulgated under §112(b)(1)(B) was in fact an emission standard. We granted certiorari, and we now reverse.

We do not intend to make light of a difficult question of statutory interpretation when we say that the basic question in this case may be phrased:

"When is an emission standard not an emission standard?" Petitioner contends, and the District Court agreed, that while the preclusion and exclusivity provisions of §307(b) of the Act prevented his obtaining "judicial review" of an emission standard in this criminal proceeding, he was nonetheless entitled to claim that the administrative regulation cited in the indictment was actually not an emission standard at all. The Court of Appeals took the contrary view. It held that a regulation designated by the Administrator as an "emission standard," however different in content it might be from what Congress had contemplated when it authorized the promulgation of emission standards, was sufficient to support a criminal charge based upon §112(c), unless it had been set aside in an appropriate proceeding commenced in the United States Court of Appeals for the District of Columbia Circuit pursuant to §307(b). . . .

. . . A federal court in which a criminal prosecution under §113(c)(1)(C) of the Clean Air Act is brought may determine whether or not the regulation which the defendant is alleged to have violated is an "emission standard" within the meaning of the Act. We are aware of the possible dangers that flow from this interpretation; district courts will be importuned, under the guise of making a determination as to whether a regulation is an "emission standard," to engage in judicial review in a manner that is precluded by §307(b)(2) of the Act. This they may not do. The narrow inquiry to be addressed by the court in a criminal prosecution is not whether the Administrator has complied with appropriate procedures in promulgating the regulation in question, or whether the particular regulation is arbitrary, capricious, or supported by the administrative record. Nor is the court to pursue any of the other familiar inquiries which arise in the course of an administrative review proceeding. The question is only whether the regulation which the defendant is alleged to have violated is on its face an "emission standard" within the broad limits of the congressional meaning of that term.

IV

It remains to be seen whether the District Court reached the correct conclusion with regard to the regulation here in question. In the Act, Congress has given a substantial indication of the intended meaning of the term "emission standard." Section 112 on its face distinguishes between emission standards and the techniques to be utilized in achieving those standards. Under §112(c)(1)(B)(ii), the Administrator is empowered temporarily to exempt certain facilities from the burden of compliance with an emission standard, "if he finds that such period is necessary for the installation of controls." In specified circumstances, the President, under §112(c)(2), has the same power, "if he finds that the technology to implement such standards is not available." Section 112(b)(2) authorizes the Administrator to issue information on "pollution control techniques."

Most clearly supportive of petitioner's position that a standard was intended to be a quantitative limit on emissions is this provision of §112(b)(1)(B): "The Administrator shall establish any such standard *at the level* which in his judgment provides an ample margin of safety to protect the public health from such hazardous air pollutant." (Emphasis added.) All these provisions lend force to the conclusion that a standard is a quantitative "level" to be attained by use of "techniques," "controls," and "technology." This conclusion is fortified by recent amendments to the Act, by which Congress authorized the Administrator to promulgate a "design, equipment, work practice, or operational standard" when "it is not feasible to prescribe or enforce an emission standard." Clean Air Act Amendments of 1977, Pub. L. 95-95, §110, 91 Stat. 703.

This distinction, now endorsed by Congress, between "work practice standards" and "emission standards" first appears in the Administrator's own account of the development of this regulation. Although the Administrator has contended that a "work practice standard" is just another type of emission standard, the history of this regulation demonstrates that he chose to regulate work practices only when it became clear he could not regulate emissions. The regulation as originally proposed would have prohibited all visible emissions of asbestos during the course of demolitions. In adopting the final form of the regulation, the Administrator concluded "that the no visible emission requirement would prohibit repair or demolition in many situations, since it would be impracticable, if not impossible, to do such work without creating visible emissions." Therefore the Administrator chose to "specif[y] certain work practices" instead.

The Government concedes that, prior to the 1977 Amendments, the statute was ambiguous with regard to whether a work-practice standard was properly classified as an emission standard, but agues that this Court should defer to the Administrator's construction of the Act. While such deference is entirely appropriate under ordinary circumstances, in this case the 1977 Amendments to the Clean Air Act tend to undercut the administrative construction. The Senate Report reiterated its "strong preference for numerical emission limitations," but endorsed the addition of §112(e) to the Act to allow the use of work-practice standards "in a very few limited cases." Although the Committee agreed that the Amendments would authorize the regulation involved here, it refrained from endorsing the Administrator's view that the regulation had previously been authorized as an emission standard under §112(c). The clear distinction drawn in §112(e) between work-practice standards and emission standards practically forecloses any such inference.

For all of the foregoing reasons, we conclude that the work-practice standard involved here was not an emission standard. The District Court's order dismissing the indictment was therefore proper, and the judgment of the Court of Appeals is Reversed.

JUSTICE STEVENS, dissenting.

The reason Congress attached "the most stringent criminal liability" to the violation of an emission standard for a "hazardous air pollutant" is that substances within that narrow category pose an especially grave threat to human health. That is also a reason why the Court should avoid a construction of the statute that would deny the Administrator the authority to regulate these poisonous substances effectively.

The reason the Administrator did not frame the emission standard for asbestos in numerical terms is that asbestos emissions cannot be measured numerically. For that reason, if Congress simultaneously commanded him (a) to regulate asbestos emissions by establishing and enforcing emission standards and (b) never to use any kind of standard except one framed in numerical terms, it commanded an impossible task.

Nothing in the language of the 1970 statute, or in its history, compels so crippling an interpretation of the Administrator's authority. On the contrary, I am persuaded (1) that the Administrator's regulation of asbestos emissions was entirely legitimate; (2) that if this conclusion were doubtful, we would nevertheless be required to respect his reasonable interpretation of the governing statute; (3) that the 1977 Amendments, fairly read, merely clarified his pre-existing authority; and (4) that the Court's reading of the statute in its current form leads to the anomalous conclusion that work-practice rules, even though properly promulgated, are entirely unenforceable. Accordingly, . . . I cannot accept Part IV's disposition of the most important issue in this case.

The regulation which petitioner is accused of violating requires that asbestos insulation and fireproofing in large buildings be watered down before the building is demolished. The effect of the regulation is to curtail the quantity of asbestos which is emitted into the open air during demolition. Because neither the rule nor its limiting effect is expressed in numerical terms, the Court holds that the asbestos regulation cannot be a "standard" within the meaning of §112(b)(1) of the Clean Air Act. This conclusion is not compelled by the use of the word "standard" or by Congress' expectation that standards would normally be expressed in numerical terms; for the statute contains no express requirements that standards always be framed in such language. There is no semantic reason why the word "standard" may not be used to describe the watered down asbestos standard involved in this case.

The promulgated standard is entirely consistent with congressional intent. Congress had indicated a preference for numerical emission standards.[13] Congress had also expressed a willingness to accept the serious economic hardships that a total prohibition of asbestos emissions would have caused. But there is no evidence that Congress intended to require the Administrator to

---

13. Congress apparently believed that too frequent resort to work-practice rules or equipment specifications would discourage the private market's pursuit of "the most economic, acceptable technique to apply." S. Rep. No. 91-1196, at 17.

make a choice between the extremes of closing down an entire industry and imposing no regulation on the emission of a hazardous pollutant; Congress expressed no overriding interest in using a numerical standard when industry is able to demonstrate that a less drastic control technique is available,[14] and that it provides an ample margin of safety to the public health. . . .

IV

A reading of the entire statute, as amended in 1977, confirms my opinion that the asbestos regulation is, and since its promulgation has been, an emission standard. If this is not true, as the Court holds today, it is unenforceable, and will continue to be unenforceable even if promulgated anew pursuant to the authority expressly set forth in the 1977 Amendments.

The Clean Air Act treats the Administrator's power to promulgate emission standards separately from his power to enforce them. While it is §112(b) that gives the Administrator authority to promulgate an "emission standard," it is §112(c) that prohibits the violation of an "emission standard." Presumably the Court's holding that a work-practice rule is not an "emission standard" applies to both of these sections. Under that holding a work-practice rule may neither be enforced nor promulgated as an emission standard. This holding will not affect the Administrator's power to promulgate work-practice rules, because the 1977 Amendments explicitly recognize that power. But Congress has not amended §112(c), which continues to permit enforcement only of "emission standards." Accordingly, the Court's holding today has effectively made the asbestos regulation, and any other work-practice rule as well, unenforceable.

Ironically, therefore, the 1977 Amendments, which were intended to lift the cloud over the Administrator's authority, have actually made his exercise of that authority ineffectual. This is the kind of consequence a court risks when it substitutes its reading of a complex statute for that of the Administrator charged with the responsibility of enforcing it. Moreover, it is a consequence which would be entirely avoided by recognizing that the Administrator acted well within his statutory authority when he promulgated the asbestos regulation as an "emission standard" for hazardous air pollutants. I would affirm the judgment of the Court of Appeals for the Sixth Circuit.

---

14. A summary of the conference agreement states that §112 "could mean, effectively, that a plant would be required to close because of the absence of control techniques." This statement implies that the Administrator should avoid setting emission standards that will require plant closings if alternative control techniques — including work-practice rules — can provide an ample margin of safety. It is unlikely that Congress intended, by expressing a modest preference for numerical standards, to mandate plant closings under a numerical standard when a work-practice rule would achieve the same level of protection with less economic disruption.

NOTES ON *ADAMO WRECKING* AND WORK PRACTICE STANDARDS

1. *Subsequent history.* Congress promptly superseded this decision with a statutory amendment making sure that EPA could criminally enforce work practice standards promulgated under section 112. *See* United States v. Ethyl Corp., 576 F. Supp. 80, 82 (M.D. La. 1983), *rev'd on other grounds*, 761 F.2d 1153 (5th Cir. 1985), *cert. denied*, 474 U.S. 1070 (1986). No authority, however, has called the Court's description of the difference between work practice and emission standards into question. Even though that distinction has ceased to matter for purposes of the applicability of criminal sanctions, the choice between those forms of standards remains an issue that arises regularly in agency rule making. Agencies must implement the congressional policies respecting which type of standard to promulgate.

2. *Why?* Why did EPA write a work practice standard instead of an emissions standard?

3. *Reasons to prefer performance standards.* Note that in explaining the congressional preference for emission standards rather than work practice standards, the Court explains:

> Congress apparently believed that too frequent resort to work-practice rules or equipment specifications would discourage the private market's pursuit of "the most economic, acceptable technique to apply."

Adamo Wrecking, 434 U.S. at 299, n.13.

4. *Other statutory provisions.* The strong congressional preference for emissions standards is not unique to section 112 of the Clean Air Act. *See* 42 U.S.C. §7411(h); PPG Industries v. Harrison, 660 F.2d 628, 636 (5th Cir. 1981) (authority to set performance standards does not include authority to specify fuels); American Petroleum Institute v. EPA, 52 F.3d 1113 (1995) (EPA may not limit use of ethanol in reformulated gasoline, because Clean Air Act mandates performance standards).

5. *Counseling EPA.* You are an EPA attorney advising EPA's Office of Solid Waste. That office has drafted regulations addressing the treatment of hazardous waste exempted from RCRA's ban on land disposal of certain waste. This ban proceeds in phases, but allows EPA to exempt waste from the ban if the ban "is not required in order to protect human health and the environment." 42 U.S.C. §6924(d)-(g). While that office believes that it is possible to measure the levels of waste being released into the environment, it would prefer to simply mandate its preferred treatment technology in order to reduce enforcement and monitoring costs. Would you recommend that it do so? The relevant statutory language follows:

> the Administrator shall promulgate regulations specifying those levels or methods of treatment, if any, which substantially diminish the toxicity of waste or

substantially reduce the likelihood of migration of hazardous constituents from the waste so that short-term and long-term threats to human health and the environment are minimized.

42 U.S.C. §6924(m)(1).

Suppose that you transfer to the Office of Air and Radiation and confront the same question, *i.e.*, the Office of Air would prefer to mandate its preferred technology even though measurement of pollution levels is possible. Would you give the same advice in a rule making governed by CAA section 112(h), the provision involved in *Adamo Wrecking*?

C. BANS

Governments may choose to simply ban environmentally destructive substances and practices. The pollution control statutes tend to employ more modest approaches that limit rather than ban pollution. *But see* 33 U.S.C. §1311(b)(2)(A) (requiring elimination of discharges when achievable); Environmental Defense Fund v. EPA, 489 F.2d 1247 (D.C. Cir. 1973) (affirming ban of DDT); 42 U.S.C. §§7671c-7671e (phasing out ozone depleting substances); 42 U.S.C. §7545(n) (ban of lead in gasoline). The Endangered Species Act, 16 U.S.C. §§1531-44, however, relies on a ban upon harming an endangered species as its principal approach (albeit with numerous exceptions). The following materials discuss the occasional bans found in pollution control law and then provide an introduction to the Endangered Species Act.

1. Bans as a Method of Pollution Control

Congress and EPA have occasionally elected to simply ban hazardous substances of various kinds. Congress, for example, generally banned manufacture of polychlorinated biphenyls when it passed TSCA. *See* 15 U.S.C. §2605(e)(3)(A). EPA banned DDT under the Federal Insecticide, Fungicide, and Rodenticide Act.

Congress also required EPA to phase out ozone-depleting substances under the 1990 Amendments to the Clean Air Act. Scientists had found that a host of substances used as refrigerants, solvents, and pesticides were depleting the stratospheric ozone layer, which shields us from ultraviolet rays. This depletion posed serious risks of producing skin cancer, cataracts, and immune deficiencies. Accordingly, the United States spearheaded an international agreement to phase out the most serious ozone-depleting substances, called the Montreal Protocol to the Vienna Convention on Ozone Depleting Substances. Title VI of the Clean Air Act Amendments of 1990 implements these agreements, and indeed, requires more rapid phase-out than the agreements require in some respects. *See* 42 U.S.C. §§7671-7671q.

Prior to the signing of the Montreal Protocol, ozone-depleting substances were widely used and well entrenched. It was not clear whether adequate substitutes could be found and it was considered possible that any substitutes would prove costly. *See* EDWARD A. PARSON, PROTECTING THE OZONE LAYER: SCIENCE AND STRATEGY 9 (Oxford U. Press 2003). Nevertheless, all of the principal manufacturing countries agreed to phase out production of ozone depleting chemicals. The phase-out proved relatively inexpensive and produced a raft of innovative substitutes in a variety of applications.

At first glance, it might appear that a ban is simply an extremely stringent performance standard, a zero emissions standard. Alternatively, one might think of it as a very specific work practice standard.

While both of these views are plausible, a ban has special characteristics that require some discussion. First of all, as both EPA and the *Corrosion Proof Fittings* court recognized when EPA attempted to phase out asbestos, a ban does more than reduce releases to zero in a given medium. It eliminates a particular substance as a future threat to all media — air, water, and land. *See, e.g.,* Richard B. Alexander and Richard A. Smith, *Trends in Lead Concentrations in Major U.S. Rivers and Their Relation to Historical Changes in Gasoline-Lead Consumption,* 24 Water Res. Bull. 557, 568 (1988) (ban on lead in gasoline, while motivated by concerns about air emissions, reduced water pollution).

On the other hand, a ban does not address continuing use of substances already manufactured. Thus, for example, even as EPA banned future production of freon, an ozone-depleting substance that auto manufacturers used as a coolant for vehicle air conditioners, EPA found it necessary to write work practice standards to govern the disposal of freon already in use. Still, over the long term, bans can be extremely effective. On the other hand, they can, as the *Corrosion Proof Fittings* court recognized, raise risk/risk tradeoffs. For example, some of the substitutes for ozone-depleting chemicals in solvents were as benign as soap and water, but others were toxic chemicals that posed cancer risks.

A work practice standard like that in *Adamo* may appear to share a lot in common with a ban. Both involve very specific government orders. But there's a significant difference. The work practice standard told asbestos contractors what to do, *i.e.,* to wet down buildings undergoing demolition. A ban tells manufacturers what not to do, *i.e.,* do not continue to use or manufacture the dangerous substance.

While orders telling people precisely what to do by their nature greatly limit flexibility, orders prohibiting a dangerous substance allow manufacturers to do anything but that which is prohibited. Thus, phase-outs can serve as catalysts for innovation. *Accord* Kurt Strasser, *Cleaner Technology, Pollution Prevention, and Environmental Regulation,* 9 Fordham Envtl. L.J. 1, 38-40 (1997). They prohibit manufacture of substances with an established market niche and thus open up space for competitors to do something new. Indeed, if the old way of doing something is forbidden, manufacturers have to attempt something new if they want to profit from meeting the need that created the demand for a product in the first place.

Bans can obviously disrupt existing industry. The degree of the disruption, however, may vary. For example, manufacturers of ozone-depleting chemicals ultimately supported the phase-out of ozone-depleting chemicals, because they believed that they could manufacture profitable substitutes. Would you expect the same reaction if EPA announced that it was banning all chemical pesticides, because organic agriculture or genetically modified organisms make them unnecessary? What if EPA decided to phase out the use of coal in power plants? What about eliminating PFOA as an aid to manufacturing Teflon coatings? What about a general ban on PFOA? When government wishes to ban a material, it frequently phases it out over time to give industry time to adjust and to minimize disruption.

2. The Endangered Species Act

A number of statutes seek to protect natural resources from a broad array of threats, rather than only prevent pollution. Natural resources, as we learned in Chapter 1, suffer threats from economic development of land, extraction of timber, oil, minerals, and other resources, and many other human activities. A number of federal and state statutes address these issues, with most of the federal statutes addressing the use of federal lands, such as National Parks and Forests.

Most statutes addressing natural resources destruction stop short of banning all activities harming a resource. For example, under the Multiple Use Sustained Yield Act (MUSY), which governs National Forests, the Forest Service must balance competing uses of the national forests in some fashion. Thus, the statute clearly contemplates some use of forests as sources of timber, notwithstanding logging operations' potential to harm the environment. Many other public land statutes likewise envision some sort of balancing.

But Congress employed a much firmer approach to address the extinction of species, as the following case illustrates:

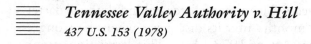

Tennessee Valley Authority v. Hill
437 U.S. 153 (1978)

Chief Justice Burger delivered the opinion of the Court.

The questions presented in this case are (a) whether the Endangered Species Act of 1973 requires a court to enjoin the operation of a virtually completed federal dam — which had been authorized prior to 1973 — when, pursuant to authority vested in him by Congress, the Secretary of the Interior has determined that operation of the dam would eradicate an endangered species; and (b) whether continued congressional appropriations for the dam after 1973 constituted an implied repeal of the Endangered Species Act, at least as to the particular dam.

The Little Tennessee River originates in the mountains of northern Georgia and flows through the national forest lands of North Carolina into Tennessee, where it converges with the Big Tennessee River near Knoxville.

[T]he Tennessee Valley Authority, a wholly owned public corporation of the United States, began constructing the Tellico Dam and Reservoir Project in 1967, shortly after Congress appropriated initial funds for its development. Tellico is a multipurpose regional development project designed principally to stimulate shoreline development, generate sufficient electric current to heat 20,000 homes, and provide flatwater recreation and flood control, as well as improve economic conditions in "an area characterized by underutilization of human resources and outmigration of young people." Of particular relevance to this case is one aspect of the project, a dam which TVA determined to place on the Little Tennessee, a short distance from where the river's waters meet with the Big Tennessee. When fully operational, the dam would impound water covering some 16,500 acres — much of which represents valuable and productive farmland — thereby converting the river's shallow, fast-flowing waters into a deep reservoir over 30 miles in length.

The Tellico Dam has never opened, however, despite the fact that construction has been virtually completed and the dam is essentially ready for operation. Although Congress has appropriated monies for Tellico every year since 1967, progress was delayed, and ultimately stopped, by a tangle of lawsuits and administrative proceedings.

Exploring the area around Coytee Springs, which is about seven miles from the mouth of the river, a University of Tennessee ichthyologist, Dr. David A. Etnier, found a previously unknown species of perch, the snail darter, or *Percina (Imostoma) tanasi*. This three-inch, tannish-colored fish, whose numbers are estimated to be in the range of 10,000 to 15,000, would soon engage the attention of environmentalists, the TVA, the Department of the Interior, the Congress of the United States, and ultimately the federal courts, as a basis to halt construction of the dam.

Until recently the finding of a new species of animal life would hardly generate a cause célèbre. This is particularly so in the case of darters, of which there are approximately 130 known species, 8 to 10 of these having been identified only in the last five years. The moving force behind the snail darter's sudden fame came some four months after its discovery, when the Congress passed the Endangered Species Act of 1973 (Act). This legislation, among other things, authorizes the Secretary of the Interior to declare species of animal life "endangered"[8] and to identify the "critical habitat"[9] of these

8. An "endangered species" is defined by the Act to mean "any species which is in danger of extinction throughout all or a significant portion of its range other than a species of the Class Insecta determined by the Secretary to constitute a pest whose protection under the provisions of this chapter would present an overwhelming and overriding risk to man." 16 U.S.C. §1532 (4) (1976 ed.).

creatures. When a species or its habitat is so listed, the following portion of the Act — relevant here — becomes effective:

"The Secretary [of the Interior] shall review other programs administered by him and utilize such programs in furtherance of the purposes of this chapter. All other Federal departments and agencies shall, in consultation with and with the assistance of the Secretary, utilize their authorities in furtherance of the purposes of this chapter by carrying out programs for the conservation of endangered species and threatened species listed pursuant to section 1533 of this title and *by taking such action necessary to insure that actions authorized, funded, or carried out by them do not jeopardize the continued existence of such endangered species and threatened species or result in the destruction or modification of habitat of such species* which is determined by the Secretary, after consultation as appropriate with the affected States, to be critical."

16 U.S.C. §1536 (1976 ed.) (emphasis added).

In January 1975, the respondents in this case . . . petitioned the Secretary of the Interior to list the snail darter as an endangered species. [T]he Secretary formally listed the snail darter as an endangered species on October 8, 1975. In so acting, . . . the Secretary determined that the snail darter apparently lives only in that portion of the Little Tennessee River which would be completely inundated by the reservoir created as a consequence of the Tellico Dam's completion.[12] The Secretary went on to explain the significance of the dam to the habitat of the snail darter:

"The act covers every animal and plant species, subspecies, and population in the world needing protection. There are approximately 1.4 million full species of animals and 600,000 full species of plants in the world. Various authorities calculate as many as 10% of them — some 200,000 — may need to be listed as Endangered or Threatened. When one counts in subspecies, not to mention individual populations, the total could increase to three to five times that number."

9. The Act does not define "critical habitat," but the Secretary of the Interior has administratively construed the term:

"'Critical habitat' means any air, land, or water area (exclusive of those existing man-made structures or settlements which are not necessary to the survival and recovery of a listed species) and constituent elements thereof, the loss of which would appreciably decrease the likelihood of the survival and recovery of a listed species or a distinct segment of its population. The constituent elements of critical habitat include, but are not limited to: physical structures and topography, biota, climate, human activity, and the quality and chemical content of land, water, and air. Critical habitat may represent any portion of the present habitat of a listed species and may include additional areas for reasonable population expansion." 43 Fed. Reg. 874 (1978) (to be codified as 50 CFR §402.02).

12. Searches by TVA in more than 60 watercourses have failed to find other populations of snail darters. The Secretary has noted that "more than 1,000 collections in recent years and additional earlier collections from central and east Tennessee have not revealed the presence of the snail darter outside the Little Tennessee River." It is estimated, however, that the snail darter's range once extended throughout the upper main Tennessee River and the lower

"[The] snail darter occurs only in the swifter portions of shoals over clean gravel substrate in cool, low-turbidity water. Food of the snail darter is almost exclusively snails which require a clean gravel substrate for their survival. *The proposed impoundment of water behind the proposed Tellico Dam would result in total destruction of the snail darter's habitat.*" *Ibid.* (emphasis added).

Subsequent to this determination, the Secretary declared the area of the Little Tennessee which would be affected by the Tellico Dam to be the "critical habitat" of the snail darter. Using these determinations as a predicate, and notwithstanding the near completion of the dam, the Secretary declared that pursuant to §7 of the Act, "all Federal agencies must take such action as is necessary to insure that actions authorized, funded, or carried out by them do not result in the destruction or modification of this critical habitat area." This notice, of course, was pointedly directed at TVA and clearly aimed at halting completion or operation of the dam. . . .

Meanwhile, Congress had also become involved in the fate of the snail darter. Appearing before a Subcommittee of the House Committee on Appropriations in April 1975 — some seven months before the snail darter was listed as endangered — TVA representatives described the discovery of the fish and the relevance of the Endangered Species Act to the Tellico Project. . . . Thereafter, the House Committee on Appropriations, in its June 20, 1975, Report, stated the following in the course of recommending that an additional $29 million be appropriated for Tellico:

"The *Committee* directs that the project, for which an environmental impact statement has been completed and provided the Committee, should be completed as promptly as possible" H. R. Rep. No. 94-319, p. 76 (1975). (Emphasis added.)

Congress then approved the TVA general budget, which contained funds for continued construction of the Tellico Project. In December 1975, one month after the snail darter was declared an endangered species, the President signed the bill into law. . . .

The District Court found that closure of the dam and the consequent impoundment of the reservoir would "result in the adverse modification, if not complete destruction, of the snail darter's critical habitat," making it "highly probable" that "the continued existence of the snail darter" would be "jeopardize[d]." Despite these findings, the District Court declined to embrace the plaintiffs' position on the merits: that once a federal project was shown to jeopardize an endangered species, a court of equity is compelled to issue an injunction restraining violation of the Endangered Species Act.

In reaching this result, the District Court stressed that the entire project was then about 80% complete and, based on available evidence, "there [were]

---

portions of its major tributaries above Chattanooga — all of which are now the sites of dam impoundments.

no alternatives to impoundment of the reservoir, short of scrapping the entire project." The District Court also found that if the Tellico Project was permanently enjoined, "[s]ome $53 million would be lost in nonrecoverable obligations," meaning that a large portion of the $78 million already expended would be wasted. The court also noted that the Endangered Species Act of 1973 was passed some seven years after construction on the dam commenced and that Congress had continued appropriations for Tellico, with full awareness of the snail darter problem. Assessing these various factors, the District Court concluded:

> "At some point in time a federal project becomes so near completion and so incapable of modification that a court of equity should not apply a statute enacted long after inception of the project to produce an unreasonable result. . . . Where there has been an irreversible and irretrievable commitment of resources by Congress to a project over a span of almost a decade, the Court should proceed with a great deal of circumspection."

To accept the plaintiffs' position, the District Court argued, would inexorably lead to what it characterized as the absurd result of requiring "a court to halt impoundment of water behind a fully completed dam if an endangered species were discovered in the river on the day before such impoundment was scheduled to take place. We cannot conceive that Congress intended such a result."

Thereafter, in the Court of Appeals, respondents argued that the District Court had abused its discretion by not issuing an injunction in the face of "a blatant statutory violation." The Court of Appeals agreed, and on January 31, 1977, it reversed, remanding "with instructions that a permanent injunction issue halting all activities incident to the Tellico Project which may destroy or modify the critical habitat of the snail darter.". . . .

We granted certiorari to review the judgment of the Court of Appeals.

II

We begin with the premise that operation of the Tellico Dam will either eradicate the known population of snail darters or destroy their critical habitat. Petitioner does not now seriously dispute this fact. In any event, under §4(a)(1) of the Act the Secretary of the Interior is vested with exclusive authority to determine whether a species such as the snail darter is "endangered" or "threatened" and to ascertain the factors which have led to such a precarious existence. By §4(d) Congress has authorized — indeed commanded — the Secretary to "issue such regulations as he deems necessary and advisable to provide for the conservation of such species." 16 U.S.C. §1533(d) (1976 ed.). As we have seen, the Secretary promulgated regulations which declared the snail darter an endangered species whose critical habitat would be destroyed by creation of the Tellico Dam. . . .

Starting from the above premise, two questions are presented: (a) would TVA be in violation of the Act if it completed and operated the Tellico Dam as planned? (b) if TVA's actions would offend the Act, is an injunction the appropriate remedy for the violation? For the reasons stated hereinafter, we hold that both questions must be answered in the affirmative.

(A)

It may seem curious to some that the survival of a relatively small number of three-inch fish among all the countless millions of species extant would require the permanent halting of a virtually completed dam for which Congress has expended more than $ 100 million. The paradox is not minimized by the fact that Congress continued to appropriate large sums of public money for the project, even after congressional Appropriations Committees were apprised of its apparent impact upon the survival of the snail darter. We conclude, however, that the explicit provisions of the Endangered Species Act require precisely that result.

One would be hard pressed to find a statutory provision whose terms were any plainer than those in §7 of the Endangered Species Act. Its very words affirmatively command all federal agencies "to *insure* that actions *authorized, funded,* or *carried out* by them do not *jeopardize* the continued existence" of an endangered species or "*result* in the destruction or modification of habitat of such species." 16 U.S.C. §1536 (1976 ed.). (Emphasis added.) This language admits of no exception. Nonetheless, petitioner urges, as do the dissenters, that the Act cannot reasonably be interpreted as applying to a federal project which was well under way when Congress passed the Endangered Species Act of 1973. To sustain that position, however, we would be forced to ignore the ordinary meaning of plain language. It has not been shown, for example, how TVA can close the gates of the Tellico Dam without "carrying out" an action that has been "authorized" and "funded" by a federal agency. Nor can we understand how such action will *"insure"* that the snail darter's habitat is not disrupted.[18] Accepting the Secretary's determinations, as

---

18. In dissent, JUSTICE POWELL argues that the meaning of "actions" in §7 is "far from 'plain,' " and that "it seems evident that the 'actions' referred to are not all actions that an agency can ever take, but rather actions that the agency is *deciding whether* to authorize, to fund, or to carry out." Aside from this bare assertion, however, no explanation is given to support the proffered interpretation. This recalls Lewis Carroll's classic advice on the construction of language:

" 'When *I* use a word,' Humpty Dumpty said, in rather a scornful tone, 'it means just what *I* choose it to mean — neither more nor less.' " Through the Looking Glass, in The Complete Works of Lewis Carroll 196 (1939).

Aside from being unexplicated, the dissent's reading of §7 is flawed on several counts. First, under its view, the words "or carry out" in §7 would be superfluous since all prospective actions of an agency remain to be "authorized" or "funded." Second, the dissent's position logically means that an agency would be obligated to comply with §7 only when a project is in the planning stage. But if Congress had meant to so limit the Act, it surely would have used

we must, it is clear that TVA's proposed operation of the dam will have precisely the opposite effect, namely the *eradication* of an endangered species.

Concededly, this view of the Act will produce results requiring the sacrifice of the anticipated benefits of the project and of many millions of dollars in public funds. But examination of the language, history, and structure of the legislation under review here indicates beyond doubt that Congress intended endangered species to be afforded the highest of priorities.

By 1973, when Congress held hearings on what would later become the Endangered Species Act of 1973, it was informed that species were . . . being lost at the rate of about one per year, 1973 House Hearings 306 (statement of Stephen R. Seater, for Defenders of Wildlife), and "the pace of disappearance of species" appeared to be "accelerating." H. R. Rep. No. 93-412, p. 4 (1973). Moreover, Congress was also told that the primary cause of this trend was something other than the normal process of natural selection:

"[Man] and his technology has *[sic]* continued at an ever-increasing rate to disrupt the natural ecosystem. This has resulted in a dramatic rise in the number and severity of the threats faced by the world's wildlife. The truth in this is apparent when one realizes that half of the recorded extinctions of mammals over the past 2,000 years have occurred in the most recent 50-year period." 1973 House Hearings 202 (statement of Assistant Secretary of the Interior).

That Congress did not view these developments lightly was stressed by one commentator:

"The dominant theme pervading all Congressional discussion of the proposed [Endangered Species Act of 1973] was the overriding need *to devote whatever effort and resources were necessary* to avoid further diminution of national and worldwide wildlife resources. Much of the testimony at the hearings and much debate was devoted to the biological problem of extinction. Senators and Congressmen uniformly deplored the irreplaceable loss to aesthetics, science, ecology, and the national heritage should more species disappear."

The legislative proceedings in 1973 are, in fact, replete with expressions of concern over the risk that might lie in the loss of *any* endangered species. Typifying these sentiments is the Report of the House Committee on Merchant Marine and Fisheries on H. R. 37, a bill which contained the essential features of the subsequently enacted Act of 1973; in explaining the need for the legislation, the Report stated:

"As we homogenize the habitats in which these plants and animals evolved, and as we increase the pressure for products that they are in a position to supply (usually unwillingly) we threaten their — and our own — genetic heritage. *"The value of this genetic heritage is, quite literally, incalculable.*

words to that effect, as it did in the National Environmental Policy Act, 42 U.S.C. §§4332(2)(A), (C).

"From the most narrow possible point of view, *it is in the best interests of mankind to minimize the losses of genetic variations.* The reason is simple: they are potential resources. They are keys to puzzles which we cannot solve, and may provide answers to questions which we have not yet learned to ask.

"To take a homely, but apt, example: one of the critical chemicals in the regulation of ovulations in humans was found in a common plant. Once discovered, and analyzed, humans could duplicate it synthetically, but had it never existed — or had it been driven out of existence before we knew its potentialities — we would never have tried to synthesize it in the first place.

"Who knows, or can say, what potential cures for cancer or other scourges, present or future, may lie locked up in the structures of plants which may yet be undiscovered, much less analyzed? Sheer self-interest impels us to be cautious.

"*The institutionalization of that caution* lies at the heart of H. R. 37 . . ." H. R. Rep. No. 93-412, pp. 4-5 (1973). (Emphasis added.)

As the examples cited here demonstrate, Congress was concerned about the *unknown* uses that endangered species might have and about the *unforeseeable* place such creatures may have in the chain of life on this planet.

In shaping legislation to deal with the problem thus presented, Congress started from the finding that "[t]he two major causes of extinction are hunting and destruction of natural habitat." Of these twin threats, Congress was informed that the greatest was destruction of natural habitats. Witnesses recommended, among other things, that Congress require all land-managing agencies "to avoid damaging critical habitat for endangered species and to take positive steps to improve such habitat." . . .

As it was finally passed, the Endangered Species Act of 1973 represented the most comprehensive legislation for the preservation of endangered species ever enacted by any nation. Its stated purposes were "to provide a means whereby the ecosystems upon which endangered species and threatened species depend may be conserved," and "to provide a program for the conservation of such species" 16 U.S.C. §1531(b) (1976 ed.). In furtherance of these goals, Congress expressly stated in §2(c) that "all Federal departments and agencies *shall* seek *to conserve endangered species* and threatened species." 16 U.S.C. §1531(c) (1976 ed.). (Emphasis added.) Lest there be any ambiguity as to the meaning of this statutory directive, the Act specifically defined "conserve" as meaning "to use and the use of *all methods and procedures which are necessary* to bring *any endangered species* or threatened species to the point at which the measures provided pursuant to this chapter are no longer necessary." §1532(2). (Emphasis added.) Aside from §7, other provisions indicated the seriousness with which Congress viewed this issue: Virtually all dealings with endangered species, including taking, possession, transportation, and sale, were prohibited, 16 U.S.C. §1538 (1976 ed.), except in extremely narrow circumstances, see §1539(b). The Secretary was also given extensive power to develop regulations and programs for the preservation of endangered and threatened species. Citizen involvement was encouraged by the Act, with provisions allowing interested persons to petition the Secretary to list a species as endangered or threatened and bring civil suits in United States district courts to force compliance with any provision of the Act. . . .

The plain intent of Congress in enacting this statute was to halt and reverse the trend toward species extinction, whatever the cost. This is reflected not only in the stated policies of the Act, but in literally every section of the statute. All persons, including federal agencies, are specifically instructed not to "take" endangered species, meaning that no one is "to harass, harm, pursue, hunt, shoot, wound, kill, trap, capture, or collect" such life forms. 16 U.S.C. §§1532(14), 1538(a)(1)(B) (1976 ed.). Agencies in particular are directed by §§2(c) and 3(2) of the Act to "use . . . *all methods* and procedures which are necessary" to preserve endangered species. 16 U.S.C. §§1531(c), 1532(2) (1976 ed.) (emphasis added). In addition, the legislative history undergirding §7 reveals an explicit congressional decision to require agencies to afford first priority to the declared national policy of saving endangered species. The pointed omission of the type of qualifying language previously included in endangered species legislation reveals a conscious decision by Congress to give endangered species priority over the "primary missions" of federal agencies.

Congress foresaw that §7 would, on occasion, require agencies to alter ongoing projects in order to fulfill the Act's goal. . . .[32]

One might dispute the applicability of these examples to the Tellico Dam by saying that in this case the burden on the public through the loss of millions of unrecoverable dollars would greatly outweigh the loss of the snail darter. But neither the Endangered Species Act nor Art. III of the Constitution provides federal courts with authority to make such fine utilitarian calculations. On the contrary, the plain language of the Act, buttressed by its legislative history, shows clearly that Congress viewed the value of endangered species as "incalculable." Quite obviously, it would be difficult for a court to balance the loss of a sum certain — even $100 million — against a congressionally declared "incalculable" value, even assuming we had the power to engage in such a weighing process, which we emphatically do not.

In passing the Endangered Species Act of 1973, Congress was also aware of certain instances in which exceptions to the statute's broad sweep would be necessary. Thus, §10, 16 U.S.C. §1539 (1976 ed.), creates a number of limited "hardship exemptions," none of which would even remotely apply to the Tellico Project. In fact, there are no exemptions in the Endangered Species

---

32. JUSTICE POWELL characterizes the result reached here as giving "retroactive" effect to the Endangered Species Act of 1973. We cannot accept that contention. Our holding merely gives effect to the plain words of the statute, namely, that §7 affects all projects which remain to be authorized, funded, or carried out. Indeed, under the Act there could be no "retroactive" application since, by definition, any *prior* action of a federal agency which *would* have come under the scope of the Act must have already *resulted* in the destruction of an endangered species or its critical habitat. In that circumstance the species would have already been extirpated or its habitat destroyed; the Act would then have no subject matter to which it might apply.

Act for federal agencies, meaning that under the maxim *expressio unius est exclusio alterius*, we must presume that these were the only "hardship cases" Congress intended to exempt.

Notwithstanding Congress' expression of intent in 1973, we are urged to find that the continuing appropriations for Tellico Dam constitute an implied repeal of the 1973 Act, at least insofar as it applies to the Tellico Project. In support of this view, TVA points to the statements found in various House and Senate Appropriations Committees' Reports; as described in Part I, *supra*, those Reports generally reflected the attitude of the *Committees* either that the Act did not apply to Tellico or that the dam should be completed regardless of the provisions of the Act. Since we are unwilling to assume that these latter Committee statements constituted advice to ignore the provisions of a duly enacted law, we assume that these Committees believed that the Act simply was not applicable in this situation. But even under this interpretation of the Committees' actions, we are unable to conclude that the Act has been in any respect amended or repealed.

There is nothing in the appropriations measures, as passed, which states that the Tellico Project was to be completed irrespective of the requirements of the Endangered Species Act. These appropriations, in fact, represented relatively minor components of the lump-sum amounts for the *entire* TVA budget. To find a repeal of the Endangered Species Act under these circumstances would surely do violence to the "'cardinal rule that repeals by implication are not favored . . . .'"

(B)

Having determined that there is an irreconcilable conflict between operation of the Tellico Dam and the explicit provisions of §7 of the Endangered Species Act, we must now consider what remedy, if any, is appropriate. It is correct, of course, that a federal judge sitting as a chancellor is not mechanically obligated to grant an injunction for every violation of law. . . .

But these principles take a court only so far. Our system of government is, after all, a tripartite one, with each branch having certain defined functions delegated to it by the Constitution. While "[i]t is emphatically the province and duty of the judicial department to say what the law is," Marbury v. Madison, 1 Cranch 137, 177 (1803), it is equally — and emphatically — the exclusive province of the Congress not only to formulate legislative policies and mandate programs and projects, but also to establish their relative priority for the Nation. Once Congress, exercising its delegated powers, has decided the order of priorities in a given area, it is for the Executive to administer the laws and for the courts to enforce them when enforcement is sought.

Here we are urged to view the Endangered Species Act "reasonably," and hence shape a remedy "that accords with some modicum of common sense and the public weal." But is that our function? We have no expert knowledge on the subject of endangered species, much less do we have a mandate from the people to strike a balance of equities on the side of the Tellico Dam. Congress has spoken in the plainest of words, making it abundantly clear that the balance has been struck in favor of affording endangered species the highest of priorities, thereby adopting a policy which it described as "institutionalized caution."

Our individual appraisal of the wisdom or unwisdom of a particular course consciously selected by the Congress is to be put aside in the process of interpreting a statute. Once the meaning of an enactment is discerned and its constitutionality determined, the judicial process comes to an end. . . .

JUSTICE POWELL, with whom JUSTICE BLACKMUN joins, dissenting.

The Court today holds that §7 of the Endangered Species Act requires a federal court, for the purpose of protecting an endangered species or its habitat, to enjoin permanently the operation of any federal project, whether completed or substantially completed. This decision casts a long shadow over the operation of even the most important projects, serving vital needs of society and national defense, whenever it is determined that continued operation would threaten extinction of an endangered species or its habitat. This result is said to be required by the "plain intent of Congress" as well as by the language of the statute.

In my view §7 cannot reasonably be interpreted as applying to a project that is completed or substantially completed when its threat to an endangered species is discovered. Nor can I believe that Congress could have intended this Act to produce the "absurd result" — in the words of the District Court — of this case. If it were clear from the language of the Act and its legislative history that Congress intended to authorize this result, this Court would be compelled to enforce it. It is not our province to rectify policy or political judgments by the Legislative Branch, however egregiously they may disserve the public interest. But where the statutory language and legislative history, as in this case, need not be construed to reach such a result, I view it as the duty of this Court to adopt a permissible construction that accords with some modicum of common sense and the public weal.

I

. . . In 1975, 1976, and 1977, Congress, with full knowledge of the Tellico Project's effect on the snail darter and the alleged violation of the Endangered Species Act, continued to appropriate money for the completion of the Project. In doing so, the Appropriations Committees expressly stated that the Act did not prohibit the Project's completion, a view that Congress presumably accepted in approving the appropriations each year. . . .

II

Today the Court, like the Court of Appeals below, adopts a reading of §7 of the Act that gives it a retroactive effect and disregards 12 years of consistently expressed congressional intent to complete the Tellico Project. With all due respect, I view this result as an extreme example of a literalist construction, not required by the language of the Act and adopted without regard to its manifest purpose. Moreover, it ignores established canons of statutory construction.

A

The starting point in statutory construction is, of course, the language of §7 itself. I agree that it can be viewed as a textbook example of fuzzy language, which can be read according to the "eye of the beholder." The critical words direct all federal agencies to take "such action [as may be] necessary to insure that actions authorized, funded, or carried out by them do not jeopardize the continued existence of . . . endangered species . . . or result in the destruction or modification of [a critical] habitat of such species. . . . " Respondents — as did the Sixth Circuit — read these words as sweepingly as possible to include all "actions" that any federal agency ever may take with respect to any federal project, whether completed or not.

The Court today embraces this sweeping construction. Under the Court's reasoning, the Act covers every existing federal installation, including great hydroelectric projects and reservoirs, every river and harbor project, and every national defense installation — however essential to the Nation's economic health and safety. The "actions" that an agency would be prohibited from "carrying out" would include the continued operation of such projects or any change necessary to preserve their continued usefulness. The only precondition, according to respondents, to thus destroying the usefulness of even the most important federal project in our country would be a finding by the Secretary of the Interior that a continuation of the project would threaten the survival or critical habitat of a newly discovered species of water spider or amoeba.

"[F]requently words of general meaning are used in a statute, words broad enough to include an act in question, and yet a consideration of the whole legislation, or of the circumstances surrounding its enactment, or of the absurd results which follow from giving such broad meaning to the words, makes it unreasonable to believe that the legislator intended to include the particular act." Church of the Holy Trinity v. United States, 143 U.S. 457, 459 (1892). The result that will follow in this case by virtue of the Court's reading of §7 makes it unreasonable to believe that Congress intended that reading. Moreover, §7 may be construed in a way that avoids an "absurd result" without doing violence to its language.

The critical word in §7 is "actions" and its meaning is far from "plain." It is part of the phrase: "actions authorized, funded or carried out." In terms of planning and executing various activities, it seems evident that the "actions" referred to are not all actions that an agency can ever take, but rather actions that the agency is *deciding whether* to authorize, to fund, or to carry out. In short, these words reasonably may be read as applying only to *prospective actions, i.e.*, actions with respect to which the agency has reasonable decision-making alternatives still available, actions *not yet* carried out.

. . . This is a reasonable construction of the language and also is supported by the presumption against construing statutes to give them a retroactive effect. . . .

B

[The Court] finds that the "totality of congressional action makes it abundantly clear that the result we reach today [j]ustifying the termination or abandonment of any federal project] is wholly in accord with both the words of the statute and the intent of Congress." Yet, in the same paragraph, the Court acknowledges that "there is no discussion in the legislative history of precisely this problem." The opinion nowhere makes clear how the result it reaches can be "abundantly" self-evident from the legislative history when the result was never discussed. . . . [16]

If the relevant Committees that considered the Act, and the Members of Congress who voted on it, had been aware that the Act could be used to terminate major federal projects authorized years earlier and nearly completed, or to require the abandonment of essential and long-completed federal installations and edifices, we can be certain that there would have been hearings, testimony, and debate concerning consequences so wasteful, so inimical to purposes previously deemed important, and so likely to arouse public outrage. The absence of any such consideration by the Committees or in the floor debates indicates quite clearly that no one participating in the legislative process considered these consequences as within the intendment of the Act.

As indicated above, this view of legislative intent at the time of enactment is abundantly confirmed by the subsequent congressional actions and expressions. . . .

JUSTICE REHNQUIST, dissenting.

In the light of my Brother POWELL's dissenting opinion, I am far less convinced than is the Court that the Endangered Species Act of 1973 was intended to prohibit the completion of the Tellico Dam. But the very difficulty and doubtfulness of the correct answer to this legal question convinces me that the Act did *not* prohibit the District Court from refusing, in the exercise of its traditional equitable powers, to enjoin petitioner from completing the Dam. . . .

---

16. I cannot believe that Congress would have gone this far to imperil every federal project, however important, on behalf of any living species however unimportant, without a clear declaration of that intention. The more rational interpretation is consistent with Representative Dingell's obvious thinking: The Act is addressed to prospective action where reasonable options exist; no thought was given to abandonment of completed projects.

. . . [T]he District Court's refusal to issue an injunction was not an abuse of its discretion. I therefore dissent from the Court's opinion holding otherwise.

NOTES ON THE ENDANGERED
SPECIES ACT AS A BAN

1. *The case.* Do you agree with the majority opinion or the dissent, and why?

2. *Section 9.* This case primarily addresses section 7 of the Act, which imposes obligations upon the federal government to protect threatened and endangered species. Section 9 of the Act limits private actions that can harm an endangered species. It generally (*i.e.*, with significant exceptions) forbids any action harming an endangered species. *See* Babbitt v. Sweet Home Chapter of Communities for a Greater Oregon, 515 U.S. 687 (1995). This prohibition may preclude private development activities that destroy habitat that a species needs for its survival. For that reason, the Act has been the focal point of significant controversy.

3. *What sort of ban?* While the Endangered Species Act (ESA) does ban some activities as a regulatory technique, note that the ban operates very differently from bans enacted in pollution control statutes. For one thing, the ESA's prohibitions generally have a geographically restricted reach. Section 7's prohibition became operative in the *TVA* case only after two steps took place. First, the Secretary of the Interior listed the snail darter as endangered. Second, it designated the relevant portion of the Tennessee River as "critical habitat." The prohibition on building the dam arose from the obligation section 7 imposes on federal agencies to avoid damaging critical habitat. Thus, the ESA did not prohibit dam building as a general approach to generating electricity, but only the construction of this particular dam in this particular place.

Section 7 does not, however, only prohibit "destruction or adverse modification of habitat." *See* 16 U.S.C. §1536. It also requires all federal agencies to "insure that any action authorized, funded, or carried out by such agency is not likely to jeopardize the continued existence of any endangered or threatened species." *Id.* Because most endangered species have limited geographic ranges, this clause also tends to have a geographically limited impact.

Section 9 enacts a nationwide ban on some activities, such as importing or exporting an endangered species. *See* 16 U.S.C. §1538(a)(1)(A). Section 9's limitations on private land uses harming endangered species have been even more controversial. Since most species have a limited range, section 9 generally has a geographically limited reach. Do the geographic limits implicit in sections 7 and 9 significantly limit the potential harshness of the ESA?

4. *Is a ban justified?* Is it appropriate to protect species regardless of cost? *See* John Copeland Nagle, *Playing Noah,* 82 Minn. L. Rev. 1171 (1998) (discussing biblical lessons about endangered species). Should the obligation to

protect endangered species trump Indian treaty rights to hunt and fish? *See* Mary Gray Holt, *Choosing Harmony: Indian Rights and the Endangered Species Act, in* ENDANGERED SPECIES ACT: LAW, POLICY, AND PERSPECTIVES 155-178 (DONALD C. BAUR AND WM. ROBERT IRVIN eds., 2001). What if the obligation to avoid harming a species effectively eliminated the economy of a ranching community that has persisted for generations? Should all pollutants that can kill a human being be banned? What about all pollutants that can kill thousands of human beings?

5. *The debate about absolutism.* Sections 7 and 9 potentially impose broad prohibitions on activities harming endangered species. Commentators have sometimes claimed that such an absolutist approach creates perverse incentives. Think about how the possibility of stringent prohibitions might influence the Department of Interior, which administers the Act. None of these prohibitions attach until the agency lists a species as endangered. The determination of whether a species is endangered or not involves an element of judgment in the face of substantial scientific uncertainty. *See generally* Holly Doremus, *Listing Decisions Under the Endangered Species Act: Why Better Science isn't Always Better Policy,* 75 Wash. U. L.Q. 1029 (1997). Substantial scientific evidence exists that some salmon species and sub-species are becoming extinct. But listing all endangered species and sub-species of salmon might conceivably put pressure on federal agencies not just to keep the floodgates closed on a completed dam, but to take down dams that have been providing electricity for decades. Such listing decisions would almost certainly influence water allocation decisions that greatly impact farmers, fishermen, and ranchers. Is it possible that the Department of Interior might prove reluctant to list some salmon species or sub-species because of the potentially difficult consequences?

This same concern about counterproductive stringency arose under section 112 of the Clean Air Act prior to 1990, when it required protection of public health with an ample margin of safety from hazardous air pollutants. Since many listed pollutants had no threshold where they were known to be safe, section 112 could be read to require zero emission levels (although the court of appeals rejected this interpretation more than a decade after section 112 became law). Some commentators attributed EPA's failure to list substantial numbers of pollutants under section 112 for regulation to this potential consequence. But others attributed this failure to the general scientific difficulties of determining health-based levels.

Some commentators have also claimed that the ESA creates perverse incentives for private landholders. Since a listing may limit property development, does it create incentives to kill off species that might subsequently be listed, or will it instead encourage landlords to care for the species, so that it will breed and escape actual endangerment? *See* J.B. Ruhl, *The Endangered Species Act and Private Property: A Matter of Timing and Location,* 8 Cornell J. L. & Pub. Pol'y 37, 42-43 (1998).

Even if absolutist approaches do create some perverse incentives, does that make them bad? If one believes (as apparently the enacting Congress did) that protecting endangered species should be of paramount importance, is there an alternative likely to do a better job of protecting species than a ban of activities harming them? If the statute was less draconian, would there be less slippage (failures to list endangered species, etc.) or would the slippage just retreat from a weaker baseline to a still weaker form of protection? *See* Amy Sinden, *In Defense of Absolutes: Combating the Politics of Power in Environmental Law*, 90 Iowa L. Rev. 1405 (2005) (arguing that absolutism provides a useful counterweight to powerful interests seeking to undermine environmental protection). *See generally* Daniel A. Farber, *Taking Slippage Seriously: Noncompliance and Creative Compliance in Environmental Law*, 23 Harv. Envtl. L. Rev. 297 (1999) (discussing the problem of "slippage" where implementation seriously deviates from statutory design). We will take up some of the alternatives issues later in this chapter and lay some groundwork for that here.

6. *Escape valves.* The ESA is not as absolute as it might seem at first glance.

a. Section 7 Flexibility.

Congress enacted the Act's most well-known escape hatch, the so-called "God Squad" provision, in response to the *Snail Darter* case. That provision allows a committee made up of cabinet members to exempt a particular federal action from the section 7(a)(2) prohibition on harming species or their habitat. *See* 16 U.S.C. §1536(a)(2), (e)-(h).

While most readers of *TVA v. Hill* might assume that the snail darter saga involved an extreme example of economic folly, the halting of a nearly completed dam to save a minor species, the subsequent history, which includes the first use of the God Squad, demonstrates that the converse was true. The decision to halt the dam made good economic sense, but did not prove essential to the snail darter's survival. The God Squad unanimously decided not to exempt the Tellico dam from operation of the ESA on economic, not environmental grounds. The chair of Council of Economic Advisors prompted this decision by arguing that the costs of finishing off the mostly completed dam exceeded the benefits. Partrick A. Parenteau, *The Exemption Process and the God Squad, in Endangered Species, supra*, at 144. Congress, however, passed an appropriations rider ordering the dam to begin operation, in spite of information indicating that it made no economic or environmental sense. But the snail darter had the last laugh. Other populations of the snail darter appeared in tributaries of the Little Tennessee River. *Id.* at 145.

In twenty years, the God Squad has only met twice. *Id.* at 143. The second meeting (after the meeting on the Tellico and Grey Rocks dam projects) approved 13 timber sales, but denied exemptions for 31 additional sales, in land designated as habitat for the listed spotted owl. *Id.* at 150. Nor is the God Squad the leading check on absolutism. A leading natural resources scholar explains:

> While the God Squad provision only rarely applies, still the ESA rarely stops projects: In the Act's implementation, 'mitigation' is the watchword." Mitigation essentially means a new form of accommodative flexibility.

George Cameron Coggins, *A Premature Evaluation of American Endangered Species Law, in Endangered Species Act, supra*, at 7. *TVA v. Hill* explains that agencies have a duty not to jeopardize an endangered species. To carry out this obligation, they must consult with the Fish and Wildlife Service or the National Marine Fisheries Service, which advises agencies about the effects of their actions on listed species. The following statutory provisions govern these "jeopardy findings."

16 U.S.C. §1536(b) . . .

(3) (A) . . . If jeopardy or adverse modification is found, the Secretary shall suggest those reasonable and prudent alternatives which he believes would not violate subsection (a)(2) of this section and can be taken by the Federal agency or applicant in implementing the agency action. . . .

(4) If after consultation under subsection (a)(2) of this section, the Secretary concludes that —

(A) the agency action will not violate such subsection, or offers reasonable and prudent alternatives which the Secretary believes would not violate such subsection;

(B) the taking of an endangered species or a threatened species incidental to the agency action will not violate such subsection; and

(C) if an endangered species or threatened species of a marine mammal is involved, the taking is authorized pursuant to section 1371 (a)(5) of this title;

the Secretary shall provide the Federal agency and the applicant concerned, if any, with a written statement that —

(i) specifies the impact of such incidental taking on the species,

(ii) specifies those reasonable and prudent measures that the Secretary considers necessary or appropriate to minimize such impact,

(iii) in the case of marine mammals, specifies those measures that are necessary to comply with section 1371(a)(5) of this title with regard to such taking, and

(iv) sets forth the terms and conditions (including, but not limited to, reporting requirements) that must be complied with by the Federal agency or applicant (if any), or both, to implement the measures specified under clauses (ii) and (iii).

You can see that these provisions emphasize mitigation of impacts and alternatives to the precise projects proposed, rather than necessarily stopping projects altogether. In the 1980s, less than 1 percent of the jeopardy consultations called for in these provisions produced an opinion that a project would jeopardize a listed species. Of this 1 percent, the government cancelled only one in eight projects. *Id.* Mitigation of potential impacts upon endangered species through adjustments as to how and when projects are carried out occur far more commonly than project cancellations.

b. Exception to Section 9 Prohibition on Taking Species.

Even though section 9's prohibition on private parties taking endangered species has been defined broadly to prohibit actions harming a species, section 10 of the Act sets out a variety of exceptions that mitigate the absolutism of section 9. *See* 16 U.S.C. §1539. For example, the implementing agencies can grant "incidental take" permits. Such permits can authorize federal, state, or private actions that "take" a species under some circumstances. *See* 16 U.S.C. §1539(a)(2). Would the breadth of the otherwise applicable prohibitions provide an incentive to construe these exemptions broadly? We will consider these exemptions in materials in Chapter 10 on "information" as a regulatory technique, for the issuance of these permits depends heavily upon gathering information about alternatives and mitigation measures. The important point here though, is that in practice, the ESA has had much less drastic impact than a mere reading of *TVA v. Hill* might lead one to believe.

7. *Success or failure?* The Department has listed 990 species as endangered. The Department has removed fourteen species from the list because they recovered and seven because they became extinct. Ruhl, *supra*, at 23. Does this mean the Act is a success or failure? What else would you like to know to evaluate this issue? Consider Professor Doremus' view:

> Because the ESA is currently the most effective source of protection against the single most important threat to listed species, habitat destruction, the vast majority of listed species will not be delisted in the near future. . . . That does not mean that the ESA is a failure. Rather it points up the critical importance of the ESA for conservation. While the ESA can and should bring most species to the point where they are biologically functional elements of their ecosystems, only substantial regulatory or cultural changes will make the protections of the ESA superfluous.

Holly Doremus, *Delisting Endangered Species: An Aspirational Goal, Not a Realistic Expectation*, 30 Envt'l L. Rep. (Envt'l L. Inst.) 10434, 10435 (2000). Do you agree?

9

Economic Incentives

This chapter will address the use of economic incentives as techniques for realizing environmental goals. While traditional regulatory approaches use monetary penalties to induce compliance, thus relying on economic incentives, this chapter focuses on alternatives to traditional regulatory approaches.

Some academics have criticized environmental law because it relies, at least ostensibly, upon uniform output standards for industrial categories. Because plants have uneven compliance costs, uniform standards can produce very high costs for some plants and relatively low costs for others.

In theory, it is possible to achieve the same reduction of total pollution for less cost by requiring more reductions from facilities with low compliance costs and less reductions from facilities with high compliance costs. In practice, the difficulty of obtaining marginal plant-specific control cost information makes it difficult for agencies to fine-tune standards in this way. *See generally* Howard Latin, *Ideal Versus Real Regulatory Efficiency: Implementation of Uniform Standards and "Fine-Tuning" Regulatory Reforms*, 37 Stan. L. Rev. 1267 (1985). Consider the Supreme Court's response to the argument that Clean Water Act variances should be available for facilities facing greater than average control costs:

> The approach of giving variances to pollution controls based on economic grounds has long ago shown itself to be a risky course: All too often the variances become a tool used by powerful interests to obtain so many exemptions for pollution control standards and timetables on the flimsiest of pretenses that they become meaningless. In short, with variances, exceptions to pollution cleanup can become the rule, meaning further tragic delay in stopping the destruction of our environment.

EPA v. National Crushed Stone Ass'n, 449 U.S. 64, 81 (1980). *Cf.* Chemical Mfrs. Ass'n v. Natural Resources Defense Council, 470 U.S. 116, 129-31

(1985) (stating that "fundamentally different factor" variances do not undermine statutory goals).

Economists have suggested two reforms that might seize the opportunity to realize environmental goals at lower cost: pollution taxes and pollution trading. They tend to favor pollution taxes. We will begin with pollution taxes, even though pollution trading has proven a much more popular reform in the United States.

A. ECO-TAXES

A tax on pollution requires the polluter to pay the government a set sum for every pound of pollution released into the environment. Pollution taxes should prove more cost-effective than a uniform standard because, at least in theory, polluters will respond to the tax differently depending on their pollution control cost. Imagine a pollution tax of $1.00 per pound of nitrogen oxide emitted into the air. How would a polluter who faces control costs of $1.50 per pound of nitrogen oxide respond to the tax? Economists predict that such a polluter would pay the tax, rather than reduce pollution, since this would cost less. Now suppose that a different polluter can reduce nitrogen oxides at a cost of 50 cents per pound. How would that polluter respond? Economists predict that this polluter would prefer to reduce her pollution in order to avoid paying the tax. Notice that a tax should produce cost-effective abatement. Polluters facing relatively high control costs will pay the tax, but polluters with low control costs will prefer pollution abatement.

In fact, facilities' pollution control costs can vary with the degree of reduction. While the first pounds of reduction might prove cheap, the marginal costs of additional reduction can prove relatively expensive. Consider the following hypothetical example:

Marginal Control Costs

Pounds of Reduction	Cost Per Pound of Reduction
1000-2000	$.50
2001-4000	$.75
4001-6000	$1.25
6001-10000	$2.00

Notice that the marginal cost rises steeply as more reductions are produced. This is a fairly typical pattern. How many pounds of reduction would a rational polluter facing a $1.00 per pound tax make?

While the United States used a pollution tax in conjunction with the phase-out of ozone-depleting substances, it has not relied heavily upon pollution taxes as a principal method for reducing pollution. President Clinton proposed an energy tax to address climate change, but this proposal did not pass. Some taxes, such as gasoline taxes, do not tax pollution directly, but, in theory, might encourage reductions of consumption that would reduce pollution impacts. Subsidies and tax breaks, however, may offset the potentially positive environmental impacts of some taxes. The environmental statutes contain some provisions requiring permit fees. But these fee provisions seek only to recover government administrative costs. They are probably not high enough to motivate much pollution reduction. Pollution taxes only motivate pollution reduction if they exceed the cost of pollution control.

The European Union has made greater use of pollution taxes than the United States. Several European countries have established effluent taxes, which some use to fund waste treatment, and carbon taxes. Most developed countries also impose higher gasoline taxes than the United States does.

Suppose that you had authority to establish a pollution tax. How would you go about establishing the tax rate? Notice that this decision, like the decision about how stringent a performance standard should be, will strongly influence the amount of pollution reduction that will be realized. A higher tax rate will induce more pollution reduction than a lower rate.

In principle, it might be possible for an administrator with taxation authority to use any of the standard setting criteria mentioned previously to establish the tax rate. Economists tend to favor establishing a tax rate equal to the dollar value of the harms the taxed pollutant causes. Notice that implementing this approach requires monetization of environmental harms, a direct analogue to the monetization of environmental benefits of regulation sought through the executive orders on cost-benefit analysis. Thus, this approach involves the same quantification and monetization difficulties that beset cost-benefit analysis. This approach would therefore prove difficult to implement.

Governments, however, can establish tax rates without cost-benefit analysis. Indeed, one of the first pollution tax proposals considered in Congress would have employed a technology-based approach to taxation.

Eco-taxes can, in theory, raise production costs and therefore deter consumption. Lessening consumption can help conserve natural resources and reduce pollution. Should the United States charge fees for water used by farmers, industry, and city dwellers that flows from federal irrigation projects? Overuse of water can leave streams and rivers depleted, thereby destroying fisheries and disrupting ecosystems. Should we at least eliminate subsidies for resource use, such as those that encourage grazing and use of scarce water in the west?

State regulators have historically regulated electricity rates. Consumption of electricity leads to the use of power plants to generate electricity. Power plants produce enormous amounts of serious air pollution. Should regulators raise electricity rates to reduce consumption? In general, pricing and taxation policy can have an impact on pollution and the use of natural resources.

B. POLLUTION TRADING

Pollution trading provides another method for improving the cost effectiveness of environmental regulation. In a pollution trading system, the government determines the amount of reductions, just as it would in establishing a performance standard. But it authorizes those subject to its limits to pay other parties to make reductions in their stead.

Consider the following simplified example. An agency wishes to secure 10 tons of cumulative reduction from two pollution sources, each of which currently emit 10 tons. It could require 5 tons of reduction from each polluter, a uniform standard:

Uniform Standards Example

Plant Name	Reductions Required	Cost per Ton of Reduction
Expensive	5 tons	$5,000
Cheap	5 tons	$1,000

If the costs are as set out in the chart above, this requirement would produce 10 tons of reductions (5 + 5) at a total cost of $30,000 ((5 × $5,000) + (5 × $1,000)). Now suppose that the regulator set the same limits, but allowed trades. Plant Expensive could pay Plant Cheap to make reductions in its stead. If this occurred, we'd have this situation:

Trading Example

Plant Name	Reductions Made	Cost Per Ton of Reduction
Expensive	0 tons	$5,000
Cheap	10 tons	$1,000

Now the total cost of making the 10 tons of reductions has dropped from $30,000 in the uniform standards example to $10,000 (10 × $1,000) in the trading example. Notice that Plant Expensive makes less than the required reductions, but that Plant Cheap makes more than the minimum requirement to make up the shortfall.

Many supporters of trading claim that trading not only encourages cost-effective reductions, but also provides superior incentives for innovation. Innovation in pollution control techniques can increase our future capacity to reduce pollution without economic disruption.

1. Early History: The Bubble

The trading concept involves allowing pollution reductions in one place to substitute for reductions in another. The trading concept made its way into environmental law gradually, first as a means of ameliorating the Clean Air

Act's impact on new pollution sources. While the trading concept envisions trades among different facilities, the early history often involved authority to make trades among polluting units at a single facility.

The statute generally requires major new pollution sources to conform to pollution control requirements reflecting the capabilities of state-of-the-art technology. *See, e.g.*, 42 U.S.C. §7411. It provided, however, that existing sources would only have to conform to requirements states developed in order to meet air quality goals. *See, e.g.*, 42 U.S.C. §7502(c)(1) (requiring "reasonably available control methods" in state implementation plans). The differential reflected congressional concern that retrofitting existing facilities would prove costly. Nevertheless, Congress limited the grandfathering of existing sources. It required existing sources to conform to new source requirements when their owners "modified" their facilities. *See* 42 U.S.C. §7411(a)(2). And the statute defined modification broadly as any operational or physical change increasing emissions. 42 U.S.C. §7411(a)(4). Clean Air Act experts sometimes refer to the set of requirements applicable to new and modified sources as the new source review program.

The Act, however, imposed a ban on new construction in areas that failed to meet ambient air quality standards by the Act's deadlines. When states missed the attainment deadlines, this construction ban became very controversial. In response, EPA developed the concept of an "offset." It would allow construction of new sources in areas that had missed the deadline, but only if the owners of new sources offset their emissions by procuring greater emission reductions from some other source. Notice that this approach uses the trading concept to produce reductions of emissions, when a ban on new construction would only keep emissions from increasing.

Subsequent amendments incorporated this offset requirement into new source review more generally, even before states had missed revised attainment deadlines incorporated in later versions of the Act. *See, e.g.*, 42 U.S.C. §7511a(a)(4), (b)(5), (c)(10), (d)(2), (e)(1). Thus, both new and modified sources in areas that violated air quality standards would not only install state-of-the-art controls, but also deliver offsetting reductions more than compensating for the remaining emissions. This offset requirement leads, in principle, to improvements in air quality.

Owners of existing facilities found the new source review requirements onerous and clamored for relief. EPA responded by redefining the modification trigger for new source review of projects at existing sources. EPA at first defined a modification as a change increasing emissions at a particular smokestack or other emitting unit. Under pressure from polluters eager to avoid new source review, EPA eventually redefined an emission increase as an increase in the emissions from the entire plant. *See* Alabama Power v. Costle, 636 F.2d 323, 400-01 (D.C. Cir. 1979) (applying this approach to areas that comply with air quality standards). Under this approach, an emission increase at one unit would not trigger new source requirements at that unit, if the plant owner could show a reduction at some other unit. This allowed plants to "net out" of new source review. This involves trading within a plant.

For example, consider the following illustration:

Netting-Out Illustration

Unit Number	Pre-Change Emissions	Post-Change Emissions
1	200 tons	300 tons
2	100 tons	100 tons
3	500 tons	400 tons
Totals	800 tons	800 tons

If EPA defines modification as an increase in emissions at a unit, then an increase triggering new source requirement occurred at unit 1. If, however, EPA defines a modification as requiring a plant-wide increase, no new source requirement apply to this facility, for the net plant-wide emissions did not increase.

When EPA chose to allow netting out in non-attainment areas, the D.C. Circuit reversed, because it found netting out inconsistent with the air quality improvement purposes of the Act. *See* Natural Resources Defense Council v. Gorsuch, 685 F.2d 718, 726-27 (D.C. Cir. 1982), *reversed sub nom.* Chevron v. Natural Resources Defense Council, 467 U.S. 837 (1984). By contrast, the court upheld netting out in areas that had met air quality standards, since the Act sought only to maintain, rather than improve, air quality in attainment areas. *See id.* at 720. The Supreme Court reviewed this decision in *Chevron v. Natural Resources Defense Council,* which we encountered earlier as a leading case on statutory interpretation:

> In the Clean Air Act Amendments of 1977 . . . Congress enacted certain requirements applicable to States that had not achieved the national air quality standards established by the Environmental Protection Agency (EPA) pursuant to earlier legislation. The amended Clean Air Act required these "nonattainment" States to establish a permit program regulating "new or modified major stationary sources" of air pollution. Generally, a permit may not be issued for a new or modified major stationary source unless several stringent conditions are met. The EPA regulation promulgated to implement this permit requirement allows a State to adopt a plantwide definition of the term "stationary source." Under this definition, an existing plant that contains several pollution-emitting devices may install or modify one piece of equipment without meeting the permit conditions if the alteration will not increase the total emissions from the plant. The question presented by these cases is whether EPA's decision to allow States to treat all of the pollution-emitting devices within the same industrial grouping as though they were encased within a single "bubble" is based on a reasonable construction of the statutory term "stationary source."

Chevron v. Natural Resources Defense Council, 467 U.S. 837, 839-40 (1984). The Court, as you may recall, went on to uphold the EPA's decision to allow netting out, even in nonattainment areas. *Id.* at 866.

Thinking about the relationship between netting out and offsets can help you to understand the impact of the *Chevron* decision on air quality. Suppose that a plant owner modifies an existing unit in a way that increases emissions at a single unit by 100 tons. Netting out is not allowed; EPA imposes a 2:1 offset requirement; and the state-of-the-art pollution control required by new source review reduces emissions by 90 percent. Reducing emissions by 90 percent leaves 10 tons of residual emissions. The offset requirement would require the plant operator to make or purchase an additional 20 tons of pollution reductions. New source review in this situation produces a 10 ton net reduction in pollution (10 tons minus 20 tons).

Now consider the same situation when netting out is allowed and emissions have declined at a non-modified unit within the facility. Suppose that plant owner modifies a unit in a way that raises pollution by 100 tons (as before), but reduced the same pollutant by 100 tons at another unit. Because there is no net emissions increase, new source review does not apply, and the plant operator need not obtain offsets or install state-of-the-art control. Net emissions neither increase nor decrease. Is netting out environmentally better than prohibiting netting out in the context of an environmentally favorable offset requirement?

EPA has also encouraged plant-wide emission limits for existing sources, sometimes called "bubbles." These requirements treat the plant as if it were encased within a bubble and measure reductions by adding together the emissions estimated at various units. Sometimes pollution control experts use the term "bubble" as the *Chevron* Court used it, as a generic term to describe "netting-out," offsets, and plant-wide existing source control standards. Sometimes, however, the term "bubble" is used more narrowly to describe a plant-wide approach to existing sources, which may be contrasted with offsets and netting-out. The link to the trading concept is that "bubble" approaches essentially allow trades, at least within a plant.

The following chart illustrates the types of "bubble"-like arrangements used by EPA prior to 1990:

Term	*Meaning*
Offset	Requirement to offset pollution added by new source
Netting-out	Allowing sources modifying a unit to avoid new source review if net emissions at the facility did not increase
Bubble	Plant-wide requirements for existing sources

The bubble programs produced enormous cost savings. But they often did so by providing cover for various forms of evasion of requirements to provide fresh emission reductions. *See* RICHARD A. LIROFF, REFORMING AIR POLLUTION REGULATION: THE TOIL AND TROUBLE OF EPA'S BUBBLE 22, 28-29 (1986); CALIFORNIA AIR RESOURCES BOARD AND UNITED STATES ENVIRONMENTAL PROTECTION AGENCY, PHASE III RULE EFFECTIVENESS STUDY OF THE AEROSPACE COATING INDUSTRY (1990). Consider the following case:

Citizens Against the Refinery's Effects v. EPA
643 F.2d 183 (4th Cir. 1981)

HALL, CIRCUIT JUDGE.

Citizens Against the Refinery's Effects (CARE) appeals from a final ruling by the Administrator of the Environmental Protection Agency (EPA) approving the Virginia State Implementation Plan (SIP) for reducing hydrocarbon pollutants. The plan requires the Virginia Highway Department to decrease usage of a certain type of asphalt, thereby reducing hydrocarbon pollution by more than enough to offset expected pollution from the Hampton Roads Energy Company's (HREC) proposed refinery. We affirm the action of the administrator in approving the state plan.

The Act

The Clean Air Act establishes National Ambient Air Quality Standards (NAAQS) for five major air pollutants. . . . Where the standard has not been attained for a certain pollutant, the state must develop a State Implementation Plan designed to bring the area into attainment within a certain period. In addition, no new source of that pollutant may be constructed until the standard is attained.

The Clean Air Act created a no-growth environment in areas where the clean air requirements had not been attained. EPA recognized the need to develop a program that encouraged attainment of clean air standards without discouraging economic growth. Thus the agency proposed an Interpretive Ruling in 1976 which allowed the states to develop an "offset program" within the State Implementation Plans. 41 Fed. Reg. 55524 (1976). The offset program, later codified by Congress in the 1977 Amendments to the Clean Air Act, permits the states to develop plans which allow construction of new pollution sources where accompanied by a corresponding reduction in an existing pollution source. In effect, a new emitting facility can be built if an existing pollution source decreases its emissions or ceases operations as long as a positive net air quality benefit occurs. . . .

The Refinery

HREC proposes to build a petroleum refinery and offloading facility in Portsmouth, Virginia. Portsmouth has been unable to reduce air pollution enough to attain the national standard for one pollutant, photochemical oxidants, which is created when hydrocarbons are released into the atmosphere and react with other substances. Since a refinery is a major source of hydrocarbons, the Clean Air Act prevents construction of the HREC plant until the area attains the national standard. . . .

The Virginia Board proposed to offset the new HREC hydrocarbon pollution by reducing the amount of cutback asphalt used for road paving operations in three highway districts by the Virginia Department of Highways. By switching from "cutback" to "emulsified" asphalt, the state can reduce hydrocarbon pollutants by the amount necessary to offset the pollutants from the proposed refinery.

CARE insists that the offset plan should have been disapproved since the state is voluntarily reducing usage of cutback asphalt anyway. . . .

[T]he standard of review here is whether the agency action was arbitrary, capricious, an abuse of discretion, or otherwise not in accordance with law. . . .

The Legally Binding Plan

For several years, Virginia has pursued a policy of shifting from cutback asphalt to the less expensive emulsified asphalt in road-paving operations. The policy was initiated in an effort to save money, and was totally unrelated to a State Implementation Plan. Because of this policy, CARE argues that hydrocarbon emissions were decreasing independent of this SIP and therefore are not a proper offset against the refinery. They argue that there is not, in effect, an actual reduction in pollution.

The Virginia voluntary plan is not enforceable and therefore is not in compliance with the 1976 Interpretive Ruling which requires that the offset program be enforceable. 41 Fed. Reg. 55526 (1976). The EPA, in approving the state plan, obtained a letter from the Deputy Attorney General of Virginia in which he stated that the requisites had been satisfied for establishing and enforcing the plan with the Department of Highways. Without such authority, no decrease in asphalt-produced pollution is guaranteed. In contrast to the voluntary plan, the offset plan guarantees a reduction in pollution resulting from road-paving operations.

Conclusion

In approving the state plan, EPA thoroughly examined the data, requested changes in the plan, and approved the plan only after the changes were made. There is no indication that the agency acted in an arbitrary or capricious manner or that it stepped beyond the bounds of the Clean Air Act. We affirm the decision of the administrator in approving the state plan.

NOTES ON *CITIZENS AGAINST*
THE REFINERY'S EFFECTS

1. *Surplus.* Citizens argued that the changes in highway asphalt producing the offset would have been undertaken anyway. The court apparently agrees that this is true. But what is the legal and policy significance of that fact?

2. *Actual reduction.* Citizens argued that the asphalt offset does not produce an actual emission reduction. Is that correct?

3. *Enforceability.* Does the court address Citizens' argument? Is Citizens' argument really directed at the enforceability of the offset?

4. *Baselines and net pollution.* Suppose that the switch in asphalt usage would produce a 100 ton reduction in hydrocarbon emissions. Assume that the new petroleum refinery produces 90 tons of pollution. Is net pollution increasing or decreasing? By how much?

Now assume that construction of the refinery is prohibited because of the construction ban. Are there reductions from asphalt usage? Is net pollution (from the refinery and asphalt usage) rising or decreasing? By how much?

Suppose that the refinery is built, but the regulator denies permission to use the asphalt reductions as an offset. Because of this the refinery must find other fresh offsets. Is net pollution increased or reduced? By how much?

5. *Fraud.* Is this transaction fraudulent? Most scholarly supporters of trading recognize that trading can only work when reliable monitoring is feasible. Volatile organic compounds, the predominant target of the bubble programs, are notoriously difficult to monitor. EPA has historically been reluctant to make stringent monitoring a prerequisite for trading, but, in 1990, Congress enacted a program that required strict monitoring.

2. The Acid Rain Trading Program

In the 1990 Clean Air Act Amendments, Congress created a model trading program limiting sulfur dioxide emissions from power plants, the chief precursors of acid rain. Electric utilities emit sulfur dioxide and nitrogen oxides into the air. Some of this pollution deposes in water, *i.e.*, acts as "acid rain" when wet deposition occurs (some of the deposition, however, is dry). Because these compounds are highly acidic, they tend to acidify lakes, streams, and ecosystems. This acidification has damaged ecosystems, producing a loss of fish, acidification of soils, and extensive damage to trees. Congress designed the acid rain trading program to address this problem.

Unlike the bubble programs, the acid rain program featured continuous emissions monitoring, a cap on the mass of emissions, and largely game-proof rules. It has produced cost savings while delivering the planned emission reductions:

Byron Swift, Command Without Control: Why Cap-and-Trade Should Replace Rate Standards for Regional Pollutants
31 Envtl. L. Rep. (Envtl. L. Inst.) 10330 (2001)

* * *

II.   An Overview of SO$_2$ [sulfur dioxide] and NOx [nitrogen oxide] Regulation in the Power Generation Sector

A.   *Regulation of Existing Sources: Title IV and Ozone Transport Commission (OTC) Standards*

Emissions of NOx and SO$_2$ from most existing power generation sources are regulated under Title IV of the CAA established in the CAA Amendments of 1990. Title IV creates two very different systems to achieve major reductions in SO$_2$ and NOx emission from utility sources: a national emissions cap and allowance trading approach for SO$_2$, and rate-based standards for NOx. . . .

1.   Emissions Cap and Allowance Trading Program for SO$_2$

Electric utilities are responsible for 60% of national SO$_2$ emissions, and Title IV imposes a permanent cap on utility SO$_2$ emissions at 8.95 million tons, roughly one-half the 1980 baseline. Title IV, unlike traditional regulation that imposes source-specific rate limits, implements an industrywide mass standard known as an emissions cap. The emissions cap and allowance trading program for the SO$_2$ program is divided in two phases. Phase I began in 1995 and required the 263 dirtiest coal-fired electric-generating units (referred to as Table A units) to reduce their emissions to a base level of 5.7 million tons of SO$_2$. Phase II implements a stricter standard in the year 2000, and requires all generating units larger than 25 megawatts to reduce their emissions to the final cap amount.

To implement the cap, allowances equivalent to a ton of SO$_2$ are assigned to each affected generating unit based on their generation rates from the historic base period of 1985-1987, scaled down so that the aggregate emissions equaled the target emissions cap. Although the annual and the bonus allowances are allocated without charge to existing sources, a limited number of allowances also are available for purchase through an annual U.S. Environmental Protection Agency (EPA) auction. Title IV, therefore, implements a zero new source standard, as any new generating source must purchase all its needed allowances. In another departure from traditional regulation, Title IV allows individual sources to trade their unused allowances to other sources or bank them for future use.

Finally, Title IV incorporates an extremely strict monitoring and compliance system. Monitoring is required by continuous emissions monitoring devices (CEMS) that collect data every 15 minutes, with consolidated data reported hourly. The monitors must also regularly transmit data that indicates that the monitor is functioning properly. CEMS are expensive, costing almost $1 million per stack. Compliance procedures are also strict and include an automatic $2,000 fine per ton and forfeiture of an additional ton of reductions.

Utilities responded to the Title IV program by reducing SO_2 emissions by eight million tons, almost 50% below their 1990 emissions level and 30% below the cap in Phase I. The most significant use of the flexibility mechanisms of Title IV was banking, or emitting below the standards and saving the allowances for later use. About 75% of total allowances created were banked, as a more stringent cap on all units would be imposed in 2000. Another major use of a flexibility provision was trading, which was used by 30 of the 51 firms for intra-firm averaging. Although trading volume increased throughout the program as firms became more comfortable with trading and some began to trade for arbitrage purposes, only 3 of the 51 firms used inter-firm trading to emit over their allowance allocation.

Figure 1: 1990-1999 SO$_2$ Allocated Allowances and Emissions

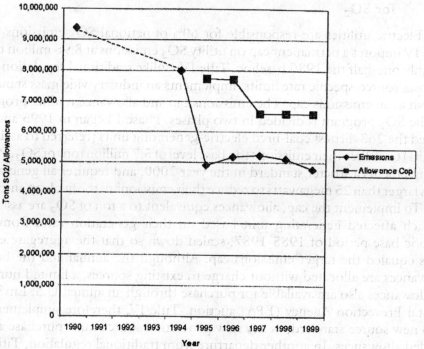

A major story of Phase I compliance under the SO_2 program was the low cost of compliance. This was due to the flexibility of Title IV, derived primarily from the cap approach, which allows greater flexibility than the rate-based standards, and also the ability to trade allowances. Initial expectations by industry in 1991 were for allowance prices of $300 to $1,000 during Phase I. In 1992 and 1993, the earliest signals began to show that prices would be substantially lower, and EPA's first auction of allowances in March 1993, revealed prices at $131. Allowance prices then continued in the $100 range until they began to climb toward $200 as Phase II approached.

The lower cost of compliance was driven by cost reductions and innovation in both of the principal means of compliance — the use of low-sulfur coal and scrubbing. The widespread use of low-sulfur coal has been a major component of compliance strategy for Phase I, resulting in over seven million tons of net reductions (over one-half of net reductions). This use was catalyzed by the flexibility afforded by Title IV, which allowed low-sulfur coal to compete with scrubbing as a compliance method. This led to experimentation and innovation in fuel blending techniques that allowed greater than expected use of low-sulfur western coals, and greater incentives to use eastern low- and medium-sulfur coals. These innovations, together with reduction in rail costs due to competition among railroads, lowered the cost premium for low-sulfur coal and dramatically increased their use, which has been a major driving force in lowering the cost of compliance in Phase I of Title IV.

Scrubbing was the second principal strategy to reduce SO_2 in Phase I, and accounts for 3.5 million tons of emissions reductions (rising to 5.5 million tons if bonus allowances allocated to scrubbed units are counted). Scrubbers were installed for 27 Table A units, promoted in part by the bonus allowances, although several firms canceled scrubber contracts when the low prices for low-sulfur coal became apparent in the early 1990s. The cost of scrubbing also fell significantly during the compliance period, due to innovation in design and materials as well as the significantly lower need for redundancy to comply with Title IV's annual standard, in comparison to previous scrubbers that had been built to meet the new source standard.

Although the Phase I cap required only a moderate SO_2 reduction of around 30%, the cap-and-trade approach exerted continuous pressure to innovate and create lower cost reductions. The cap has prompted continuing innovation in fuel blending techniques and rail infrastructure relating to low-sulfur coal, and also in scrubbing, the cost of which has declined steadily since competition was created with low-sulfur coal. The ability to trade allowances has led to a fully integrated cost of sulfur in the coal market, integrating an environmental parameter into the price of coal. Finally, the monetization of environmental costs and benefits under the cap-and-trade approach has allowed the fuller integration of environmental considerations into the regular financially based decisionmaking throughout a company.

Overall, the shift in Title IV away from scrubber use and toward low-sulfur coal had economic, environmental, and political consequences. The investment in rail infrastructure, innovation in fuel blending and rail transport, and competition among railroads led to low compliance costs that benefitted both the industry and ratepayers. The principal environmental benefit is the reduction and permanent cap on SO_2 emissions, together with the greater political possibility of further reductions given the low cost of compliance. Other environmental benefits of the move to cleaner fuels include the benefits of pollution prevention, in avoiding the direct 1.5% energy loss and significant resource use and waste disposal consequences of scrubbing. Political consequences were also significant, and include the move from unionized coal-mining jobs in midwestern states with high-sulfur coal to western and Appalachian states with low-sulfur coal. Notwithstanding these shifts, the success of the Title IV SO_2 cap-and-trade program in overachieving a strict standard at low cost has led some to include it among the most successful programs under the CAA.

NOTES ON THE ACID RAIN PROGRAM

1. *Cost savings.* Should one attribute the cost savings observed to trading? After all, only 3 of 51 firms engaged in inter-firm trading. In addition, post-compliance studies (where they exist) tend to show that compliance costs for traditional regulation falls below the amounts predicted. *See* Thomas O. McGarity and Ruth Ruttenberg, *Counting the Cost of Health Safety and Environmental Regulation*, 80 Tex. L. Rev. 1997 (2002). Subsequently, by the way, trading increased. While one may question attribution of all of the observed cost savings to trading, surely the theoretical reasons to expect trades (even intra-facility trades) to save money justify confidence that significant cost savings are associated with trading. Why would a facility operator engage in any trades if she did not save money by doing so?

2. *Innovation in the acid rain program.* This article, like many others, claims that the acid rain program stimulated innovation. Some commentators have cited the use of low-sulfur coal and scrubbing as innovations. Consider the following Federal Register notice from 1981:

> Environmental laws have caused massive shifts in coal consumption patterns. The Clean Air Act Amendments of 1970 caused many Midwestern utilities to purchase low-sulfur "compliance coal" from Western coal producers. The subsequent geographic expansion of the market to comprise both the Midwestern and Western regions effectively lowered seller concentration levels, which were higher in the Midwest than in any other region. . . .
>
> With the implementation of the 1970 amendments, utilities could choose medium- or high-sulfur coal (usually located in the East or Midwest) with a scrubber, or use more distant low-sulfur coal (usually located in the West). . . .

Coal Competition Prospects for the 1980s: Request for Written Comments on Draft Report, 46 Fed. Reg. 10686, 10692, 10698 (1981). Is it appropriate to describe techniques available since the 1970s as innovations when employed in the 1990s?

3. *Emissions trading and innovation in general.* The standard economic theory states that emissions trading provides superior incentives to innovate, because it makes going beyond compliance profitable. While it is true that low cost sources acquire an incentive to go beyond compliance, high cost sources make fewer local reductions under a trading program than under a comparable traditional regulation. They purchase credits in lieu of making local reductions. Thus, they have less of an incentive to innovate under a trading program than they would under a traditional regulation. Do you think that trading would provide a greater net incentive to innovate than a traditional performance standard? *See* David M. Driesen, *Does Emissions Trading Encourage Innovation?*, 33 Envtl L. Rep. (Envtl. L. Inst.) 10094 (2003).

A thorough empirical review of sulfur dioxide control technology's evolution over time concluded that the "majority of the performance and capitol cost improvements in the dominant technology to achieve SO_2 control occurred before the 1990 Amendments," which contain the acid rain trading program. Margaret A. Taylor, Edward S, Rubin and David A. Hounshell, *Regulation as the Mother of Innovation: The Case for SO_2 Control*, 27 Law & Pol'y 348, 369 (2005). Similarly, Professor Popp, an environmental economist, compared the level of patent activity associated with the New Source Performance Standards (including the standard upheld in *Sierra Club*) and the electric utility industry with that associated with the subsequent acid rain trading program. *See* David Popp, *Pollution Control Innovations and the Clean Air Act of 1990*, 22 J. Pol'y Analysis & Mgmt. 641 (2003). He concludes that more patenting of new technology occurred under the old performance standard than under the trading program. But he claims that the trading program induced more patents of environmentally better technology. The traditional regulation tended to encourage patenting of cheaper methods for achieving the same amount of reductions. In both cases, companies filed patents focusing on better scrubber designs, rather than radical innovations.

4. *Radical innovation.* There seems to be no evidence that the acid rain program encouraged radical innovation, such as wider deployment of solar energy. Why not?

5. *Design.* Design of trading programs is critical. Few, if any, programs have been as well designed as the acid rain program. Yet, trading is being used extensively in a wide variety of areas. *See, e.g.,* Ann Powers, *Reducing Nitrogen Loading on Long Island Sound: Is there a Place for Pollutant Trading?* 23 Colum J. Envtl. L. 137 (1998); David M. Driesen, *Free Lunch or a Cheap Fix?: The Emissions Trading Idea and the Climate Change Convention*, 26 B. C. Envtl. Aff. L. Rev. 1 (1998); Suitum v. Tahoe Reg'l Planning Agency, 520 U.S. 725, 728-31 (1997) (discussing use of "Transferable Development Rights" under interstate compact); Robert W. Adler, *Economic Incentives for Wetlands*

and Water Quality Protection: A Public Perspective, 110 Env't Counselor 2 (1997); Royal C. Gardner, *Banking on Entrepreneurs: Wetlands, Mitigation Banking, and Takings*, 81 Iowa L. Rev. 527 (1996).

3. Policy Issues

a. Environmental Justice, Hot Spots and Currency

A significant concern about trading involves the potential for creation of "hot spots," areas where emissions remain high or even increase, even while emissions elsewhere go down. This concern arises from the ability of pollution sources under trading to forego reductions to the extent they purchase compensating reductions from elsewhere. If many of the polluters in a particular area fail to make reductions, then people (or environmental resources) in that area may have a disproportionate pollution burden.

For this reason, trading is generally thought appropriate only when the effects of pollution do not vary significantly with location. Where pollutants have strong local effects, trading can raise serious equitable and pragmatic issues.

The equitable concerns that trading raises become especially acute in the case of toxic pollution. Does a reduction of cancer risk in one community justify allowing a cancer risk in another community to remain high or even increase? EPA's traditional answer to this question has been no. It has generally disallowed trading of air toxics under programs aiming to reduce the risks of toxic exposures. Recently, however, EPA has proposed to apply a trading approach to reductions of mercury emissions, which depose in water and contaminate fish. This application of trading has raised concerns about leaving groups that consume a lot of fish, such as some Indian tribes, exposed to high levels of mercury even as overall levels decline. *See* Catherine A. O'Neill, *Mercury, Risk and Justice*, 34 Envtl. L. Rep. (Envtl. L. Inst.) 11070 (2004).

Some environmentalists have also criticized California's RECLAIM program for volatile organic compounds as unjust to a community of color living near a petroleum refinery. The program allowed a petroleum refinery to avoid reducing its own emissions if it purchased credits for reductions from cars (obtained partly by junking older vehicles that might otherwise emit high volumes of pollutants). Both the car emissions and the refinery emissions contributed to high regional ozone pollution, which exacerbates asthma, especially in the elderly and in children. The petroleum refinery's volatile organic compounds were also highly toxic and posed risks of cancer for the community of color living near the refinery's gates. The trading program allowed these toxic emissions to continue without abatement, but the resulting reductions in vehicle emissions would not necessarily reduce the cancer risks of the community living near the refinery.

Will trading systematically disadvantage communities of color? *See* Stephen M. Johnson, *Economics versus Equity: Do Market-Based Reforms Exacerbate Environmental Injustice?*, 56 Wash. & Lee L. Rev. 111 (1999).

On the other hand, Congress, EPA, and most of the environmental community embraced trading under the acid rain program, because the ecological problems were a product of atmospheric loadings across a wide area. In such situations, the location of particular pollution sources (credit buyers and sellers) becomes much less important. Nevertheless, Congress authorized EPA to set a "deposition" standard if need be. The idea is that if an ecologically sensitive area (such as New York's Adirondack park) became a hot spot, then EPA would impose additional geographically targeted reductions to address the problem. Would such a problem arise if all of the polluters downwind of the park were credit sellers? What if they were all buyers? This problem did not arise and EPA did not establish a deposition standard.

A related concern about trading involves the issue of currency:

 James Salzman and J.B. Ruhl, *Currencies and the Commodification of Environmental Law*
53 Stan. L. Rev. 607, 609-613 (2000)

[E]nvironmental trading markets (ETMs) now operate in a range of regulatory settings where parties exchange credits to emit air pollutants, extract natural resources, and develop habitat. In fact, every major environmental policy review in the last five years has called for even greater use of ETMs. Markets for environmental commodities represent the new wave of environmental protection and, despite critiques both subtle and shrill, they are still building.

[Yet] a basic aspect of trading has largely escaped attention. Perhaps because it is so obvious, there has been scant consideration of the simple question — what is actually being traded?

If one compares trading programs, they all seem to share a basic feature. The CFC, fisheries, and proposed greenhouse gas ETMs, for example, all exchange commodities that appear to be fungible. One molecule of CFC, kilo of halibut, or ton of carbon dioxide seems much the same as another, both in terms of identity and impact. It is trading apples for apples (or pork bellies for pork bellies). Thus ETMs are considered a type of commodity market, where environmental credits go to the highest bidder. And for good reason, since the Chicago Board of Trade now sells rights to emit sulfur dioxide alongside pork bellies, orange juice, and grain futures.

Indeed ETMs must assume fungibility — that the things exchanged are sufficiently similar in ways important to the goals of environmental protection — otherwise there would be no assurance that trading ensured environmental protection. While the precondition of fungibility may seem self-evident, this core assumption turns out to be more problematic than it first appears.

As an example of why fungibility matters, consider wetlands mitigation banking. This policy permits developers, once they have taken steps to avoid and minimize wetland loss, to compensate for wetlands that will be destroyed through development by ensuring the restoration of wetlands in another location. The regulations mandate trades that ensure equivalent value and function between destroyed and restored wetlands. In practice, however, most trades are valued in units of acreage. Within very loose guidelines, trades between productive (though soon to be destroyed) wetlands and restored wetlands are approved on an acre-for-acre basis. More sophisticated banks require ratios, trading development on one acre of productive wetlands for, say, restoring four or five acres of wetlands somewhere else. Counting acres may make for easy accounting, but it is poor policy.

Why? The social value of the habitat is absent from the transaction. The ecosystem services provided by the wetlands — positive externalities such as water purification, groundwater recharge, and flood control — are largely ignored. Opinions may differ over the value of a wetland's scenic vista, but they are in universal accord over the contributions of clean water and flood control to social welfare. Trading acres for acres provides an inadequate measure to capture what is really being traded of significance. To be sure, such a simple metric allows trades, but other important, unaccounted trade-offs are occurring. The program can suffer from a lack of accountability (or, more accurately, a lack of countability).

In fact, upon close inspection, it turns out that most ETMs involve commodities and trades that exhibit a range of fungibilities. Legal trades can range from relatively straightforward kilos of surf clams to trades involving the exchange of different types of habitat (that may provide very different social benefits). To achieve the optimal outcome from ETMs, we need to understand and account much better for the qualities being traded. To do so requires careful consideration of the measure of exchange — the currency — since in the final analysis the currency forms the very basis of the transaction. The trading currency superficially makes the commodities fungible, determining what is being traded and, therefore, protected.

Many of the currencies employed by ETMs present trades of an acre of wetland here for an acre of wetland there, or a ton of emissions here for a ton there, as a basic exchange of apples for apples. In reality, though, this is a misleading description. More times than one might think, we are trading Macintoshes for Granny Smiths, apples for oranges, and, in some cases, apples for Buicks. Put simply, we can end up trading the wrong things.

NOTES ON HOT SPOTS AND CURRENCY

1. *Responses to currency problems.* Should regulators forego trading where simple currencies do not work? Or are the cost savings from trading so important that regulators should continue to use simple currencies even when

they do not capture important environmental values? Should regulators instead use a more complex currency, and if so, what currency should they use?

2. *Wetlands example.* To make the possibility of a complex currency concrete, consider the following. Suppose that developers who choose to use wetland protection credits to justify filling in a wetland must obtain credits from projects of equivalent ecological value. Imagine that the wetland being developed and creating the debit offers very good flood control potential, habitat for some common migratory birds, and little scenic value. The wetland being protected for credit does not provide any flood control value, provides habitat for several endangered species, but no migratory birds, and appeared beautiful to one third of the surrounding community. How should a regulator decide whether protecting the creditable wetland in exchange for developing the other one constitutes a good deal? Is there a scientific basis for declaring flood control more important than protecting an endangered species, or is public input necessary to make such choices? Won't public hearings for each trade create transaction costs impeding trading? The federal government has, in fact, developed an approach that tries to distinguish between different wetland types, values, and functions for purposes of mitigation and potentially, mitigation banking — a form of trading. *See The National Action Plan to Implement the Hydrogeomorphic Approach to Assessing Wetland Functions,* 62 Fed. Reg. 33607 (June 20, 1997).

3. *Comparing contexts.* Perhaps the problem of currency is more acute in the case of wetlands protection than in the case of acid rain. Do tons of sulfur dioxide mean the same thing regardless of location? Sulfur dioxide can travel hundreds of miles. In the midwest and east, prevailing winds tend to blow the sulfur dioxide toward the east. In terms of impacts, is a ton of sulfur dioxide from a plant on Long Island (in eastern New York) the same as a ton of sulfur dioxide from a plant in West Virginia?

4. *Geographical restrictions.* One approach to trying to address the problem of equivalent masses of pollution having different effects depending upon geography has been to place geographical restrictions in trades. For example, Clean Water Act effluent trading has been confined to trades within a watershed. Would that help solve the problem of treating tons of pollution as a currency, even when the effects of that pollution vary with geography?

b. Emissions Trading Versus Best Available Technology

Now that you have some understanding of emissions trading, you can start to evaluate its desirability. The article that appears below predates the acid rain program. It argues that emissions trading is superior to a "Best Available Technology" system. Consider these arguments in light of the information you have about technology-based standard setting. *See infra*, Chapter 6, at 235-238. How prescient have these arguments been in light of the subsequent experience with emissions trading discussed above?

Bruce A. Ackerman and Richard B. Stewart,
Comment: Reforming Environmental Law
37 Stan. L. Rev. 1333 (1985)

The existing system of pollution regulation . . . is primarily based on a Best Available Technology (BAT) strategy. If an industrial process or product generates some nontrivial risk, the responsible plant or industry must install whatever technology is available to reduce or eliminate this risk, so long as the costs of doing so will not cause a shutdown of the plant or industry. BAT requirements are largely determined through uniform federal regulations. Under the Clean Water Act's BAT strategy, the EPA adapts nationally uniform effluent limitations for some 500 different industries. A similar BAT strategy is deployed under the Clean Air Act for new industrial sources of air pollution, new automobiles, and industrial sources of toxic air pollutants. BAT strategies are also widely used in many fields of environmental regulation other than air and water pollution.

BAT was embraced by Congress and administrators in the early 1970s in order to impose immediate, readily enforceable federal controls on a relatively few widespread pollutants, while avoiding widespread industrial shutdowns. Subsequent experience and analysis has demonstrated:

1. Uniform BAT requirements waste many billions of dollars annually by ignoring variations among plants and industries in the cost of reducing pollution and by ignoring geographic variations in pollution effects. A more cost-effective strategy of risk reduction could free enormous resources for additional pollution reduction or other purposes.

2. BAT controls, and the litigation they provoke, impose disproportionate penalties on new products and processes. A BAT strategy typically imposes far more stringent controls on new sources because there is no risk of shutdown. Also, new plants and products must run the gauntlet of lengthy regulatory and legal proceedings to win approval; the resulting uncertainty and delay discourage new investment. By contrast, existing sources can use the delays and costs of the legal process to burden regulators and postpone or "water-down" compliance. BAT strategies also impose disproportionate burdens on more productive and profitable industries because these industries can "afford" more stringent controls. This "soak the rich" approach penalizes growth and international competitiveness.

3. BAT controls can ensure that established control technologies are installed. They do not, however, provide strong incentives for the development of new, environmentally superior strategies, and may actually discourage their development. Such innovations are essential for maintaining long-term economic growth without simultaneously increasing pollution and other forms of environmental degradation.

4. BAT involves the centralized determination of complex scientific, engineering, and economic issues regarding the feasibility of controls on hundreds of thousands of pollution sources. Such determinations impose massive information-gathering burdens on administrators, and provide a fertile ground for complex litigation in the form of massive adversary rulemaking proceedings and protracted judicial review. Given the high costs of regulatory compliance and the potential gains from litigation brought to defeat or delay regulatory requirements, it is often more cost-effective for industry to "invest" in such litigation rather than to comply.

5. A BAT strategy is inconsistent with intelligent priority setting. Simply regulating to the hilt whatever pollutants happen to get on the regulatory agenda may preclude an agency from dealing adequately with more serious problems that come to scientific attention later. BAT also tends to reinforce regulatory inertia. Foreseeing that "all or nothing" regulation of a given substance under BAT will involve large administrative and compliance costs, and recognizing that resources are limited, agencies often seek to limit sharply the number of substances on the agenda for regulatory action.

When a polluter receives an air or water permit under existing law . . . the permit tries to be as quantitatively precise as possible, telling each discharger how much of the regulated pollutants he may discharge.

. . . [O]ur reforms build upon, rather than abandon, this basic permit system. Indeed, we have only two, albeit far-reaching, objections to the existing permit mechanism. First, existing permits are free. This is bad because it gives the polluter no incentive to reduce his wastes below the permitted amount. Second, they are non-transferable. This is bad because polluter A is obliged to cut back his own wastes even if it is cheaper for him to pay his neighbor B to undertake the extra cleanup instead.

Our basic reform would respond to these deficiencies by allowing polluters to buy and sell each other's permits — thereby creating a powerful financial incentive for those who can clean up most cheaply to sell their permits to those whose treatment costs are highest. This reform will, at one stroke, cure many of the basic flaws of the existing command-and-control regulatory systems discussed earlier.

A system of tradeable rights will tend to bring about a least cost allocation of control burdens, saving many billions of dollars annually. It will eliminate the disproportionate burdens that BAT imposes on new and more productive industries by treating all sources of the same pollutant on the same basis. It will provide positive economic rewards for polluters who develop environmentally superior products and processes. It will, as we show below, reduce the incentives for litigation, simplify the issues in controversy, and facilitate more intelligent setting of priorities.

Would allowing the sale of permits lead to a bureaucratic nightmare? Before proceeding to the new administrative burdens marketablity with generate, it is wise to pause . . . to consider marketability's great administrative advantages.

First, marketability would immediately eliminate most of the information-processing tasks that are presently overwhelming the federal and state bureaucracies. No longer would the EPA be required to conduct endless adversary proceedings to determine the best available control technologies in each major industry of the United States, and to defend its determinations before the courts; nor would federal and state officials be required to spend vast amounts of time and energy in adapting these changing national guidelines to the particular conditions of every important pollution source in the United States. Instead of giving the job of economic and technological assessment to bureaucrats, the marketable rights mechanism would put the information-processing burden precisely where it belongs: upon business managers and engineers who are in the best position to figure out how to cut back on their plants' pollution costs. If the managers operating plant A think they can clean up a pollutant more cheaply than those in charge of plant B, they should be expected to sell some of their pollution rights to B at a mutually advantageous price; cleanup will occur at the least cost without the need for constant bureaucratic decisions about the best available technology. . . . [T]he existing system of command-and-control regulation . . . envisions inevitably ill-informed bureaucrats continually "fine-tuning" technological and economic decisions best made by the people operating the plants.

Second, marketable permits would open up enormous financial resources for effective and informed regulation. While polluters would have the right to trade their permits among themselves during the n years they are valid, they would be obliged to buy new ones when their permits expired at an auction held by the EPA in each watershed and air quality control region. These auctions would raise substantial sums of money for the government on a continuing basis. . . .

Third, the auction system would help correct one of the worst weaknesses of the present system: the egregious failure of the EPA and associated state agencies to enforce the laws on the books in a timely and effective way. Part of the problem stems from the ability of existing polluters to delay regulatory implementation by using legal proceedings to challenge the economic and engineering bases of BAT regulations and permit conditions. But agencies also invest so little in monitoring that they must rely on polluters for the bulk of their data on discharges. Since polluters are predictably reluctant to report their own violations, the current system perpetuates a Panglossian view of regulatory reality. For example, a General Accounting Office investigation of 921 major air polluters officially considered to be in compliance revealed 200, or 22%, to be violating their permits; in one region, the number not complying was 52%. Even when illegal polluters are identified, they are not effectively sanctioned: The EPA's Inspector General in 1984 found that it was a common practice for water pollution officials to respond to violations by issuing administrative orders that effectively legitimized excess discharges. Thus, while the system may, after protracted litigation, eventually "work" to force the slow installation of expensive control machinery, there is no reason to think this machinery will run well when eventually installed. Although there are many reasons for this appalling weakness in enforcement, one stands out above all others: The present system does not put pressure on agency policymakers to make the large investments in monitoring and personnel that are required to make the tedious and unending work of credible enforcement a bureaucratic reality.

The auction system would change existing compliance incentives dramatically. It would reduce the opportunity and incentive of polluters to use the legal system for delay and obstruction by finessing the complex BAT issues, and it would limit dispute to the question of whether a source's discharges exceeded its permits. It would also eliminate the possibility of using the legal system to postpone implementation of regulatory requirements by requiring the polluter that lost its legal challenge to pay for the permits it would have been obliged to buy during the entire intervening period of noncompliance (plus interest).

The marketable permit system would also provide much stronger incentives for effective monitoring and enforcement. If polluters did not expect rigorous enforcement during the term of their permits, this fact would show up at the auction in dramatically lower bids: Why pay a lot for the right to pollute legally when one can pollute illegally without serious risk of detection? Under a marketable permit approach, this problem would be at the center of bureaucratic attention. For if, as we envisage, the size of the budget available to the EPA and state agencies would depend on total auction revenues, the bureaucracy's failure to invest adequately in enforcement would soon show up in a potentially dramatic drop in auction income available for the next budgetary period. This is not a prospect that top EPA administrators will take lightly. Monitoring and enforcement will become agency priorities of the first importance. Moreover, permit holders may themselves support strong enforcement in order to ensure that cheating by others does not depreciate the value of the permit holders' investments.

A system of marketable permits, then, not only promises to save Americans many billions of dollars a year, to reward innovative improvements in existing clean-up techniques, and to eliminate the BAT system's penalty on new, productive investment. It also offers formidable administrative advantages. It relieves agencies of the enormous information-processing burdens that overwhelm them under the BAT system; it greatly reduces litigation and delay; it offers a rich source of budgetary revenue in a period of general budgetary stringency; and it forces agencies to give new importance to the critical business of enforcing the law in a way that America's polluters will take seriously. . . .

The reformed system we have described involves the execution of four bureaucratic tasks. First, the agency must estimate how much pollution presently is permitted by law in each watershed and air quality region. Second, it must run a system of fair and efficient auctions in which polluters can regularly buy rights for limited terms. Third, it must run an efficient title registry in each region that will allow buyers and sellers to transfer rights in a legally effective way. Fourth, it must consistently penalize polluters who discharge more than their permitted amounts.

And that's that. . . .

NOTES ON THE ACKERMAN AND STEWART CRITIQUE

1. *Waste*. Ackerman and Stewart claim that BAT controls are wasteful. What precisely do they mean by that?

2. *Regulating to the hilt*. Ackerman and Stewart criticize BAT for "regulating to the hilt whatever pollutants happen to get on the regulatory agenda," which they characterize as inconsistent with good priority setting. Would these problems be avoided by trading programs?

3. *New sources*. Ackerman and Stewart criticize BAT for requiring more stringent controls of new sources.[1] But is this an inherent characteristic of technology-based performance standards? Is it possible to use traditional regulatory approaches that treat new and existing sources equally? Congress introduced differential treatment because it considered retrofitting costly and awkward. It required owners of existing sources to employ stricter new source controls when they modified their facilities. Should Congress require all facilities to meet strict new source standards? Should it instead relax new source standards to comport with less stringent regulation for existing sources?

Should Congress retain a differential favoring existing sources? Or should it reverse it, applying stricter standards to existing sources than it applies to new sources in hopes of pressuring plants into modernizing or shutting down? If Swift, *supra*, is correct that all new pollution sources in the acid rain program must purchase allowances, even though existing sources get them for free, then does trading solve the problem of discrimination against new sources?

4. *Information burdens*. Ackerman and Stewart criticize BAT because of the information burdens involved in determining feasibility. Would the information burdens prove lighter for health-based or cost-benefit-based standards? Recall that trading does not obviate the need to set limits. Wouldn't an agency establishing a trading program need to use some version of the standard setting rubrics used for traditional regulation to establish the limits? Are Ackerman and Stewart assuming that Congress, rather than an administrative agency, sets

---

1. While Ackerman and Stewart are correct that the Clean Water Act contemplates stricter standards for new sources, in practice EPA often sets NSPS limits for new water pollution sources equal to BAT limits for existing sources.

the trading program's limits? Could Congress set the limits for a non-trading program?

5. *Auctions.* Ackerman and Stewart call for an auction of pollution permits. While Congress adopted their recommendation to use trading in the acid rain program, Congress gave away most of the permits instead of auctioning them off. To what extent does this giveaway weaken the argument for trading?

6. *Enforcement.* Will trading improve enforcement of the law? To what extent does Ackerman's and Stewart's argument on this point disappear when the government gives away rather than sells allowances? The acid rain program suggests that their argument that trading would provide incentives to improve monitoring and enforcement has proven prescient. Congress required continuous emission monitors in order to make the program credible and obviated the need for large investments in enforcement. On the other hand, some subsequent programs have not featured good monitoring. Consider the following:

> Spatial specificity . . . helps make standards enforceable. A regulatory agency, citizen group, or corporation seeking to evaluate compliance must generally look at each place where regulated pollution escapes into the environment in order to determine whether emission reductions have occurred. Hence, it seems logical to specify obligations for specific places where emission reductions can be verified. Where a company cannot reliably measure emissions, a regulator or citizen may determine whether a reduction has occurred at these places by determining whether the polluter has properly applied a technique known to reduce emissions at that particular place. An understanding of the reasons for spatial specificity need not lead to the conclusion that only traditional regulation makes sense. However, programs that lessen spatial specificity only produce real verifiable emission reductions when they adequately address the enforcement problems they create. Lack of spatial specificity complicates enforcement by increasing the number and variety of claims, transactions, and activities that a regulator must evaluate to detect noncompliance. . . .
>
> Furthermore, most scholars recognize that emissions trading requires good monitoring in order to succeed. Because pollution sources have an economic incentive to try to exaggerate the value of reduction credits and to understate the value of debits in an emissions trading scheme, good monitoring is essential. For some pollution sources, however, good monitoring simply is not technically feasible.
>
> For this reason, emissions trading cannot supplant true command and control regulation. Normally, command and control regulation exists precisely because an agency has determined that it cannot measure emission reductions. Emissions trading may sometimes provide a good alternative to performance standards, but it will function poorly if used to supplant true command and control regulation. Hence, the command and control/economic incentive dichotomy not only unfairly disparages traditional regulation, it suggests application of emissions trading precisely in areas where it cannot work.

David M. Driesen, *Is Emissions Trading an Economic Incentive Program?:
Replacing the Command and Control/Economic Incentive Dichotomy,* 55 Wash.
& Lee L. Rev. 289, 303-04, 310-311 (1998).

Do you think trading will improve compliance incentives for the reasons
Ackerman and Stewart suggest? Would it instead make enforcement more
difficult? Or does the choice between trading and traditional regulation make
no difference? Will the answer vary with context? If so, what variables will
influence compliance?

10

Information-Based Approaches

Generation of information about the environmental consequences of actions can provide a means of encouraging better environmental performance. The materials in this section address two basic functions that information plays.

First, information helps inform government decisions about how and whether to protect the environment. *See generally* Daniel C. Esty, *Environmental Protection in the Information Age*, 79 N.Y.U. L. Rev. 115, 121-140 (2004) (delineating information's role in some detail). The National Environmental Policy Act (NEPA) and the testing requirements of the Toxic Substances Control Act (TSCA) provide prominent examples of laws seeking information to inform the government and the public before the government makes key decisions. NEPA generates information about the environmental impact of significant proposed federal actions and alternatives to those actions. TSCA generates information on hazardous chemicals to inform regulatory decisions about toxic substances.

Second, information sometimes motivates private cleanup and/or avoidance of environmental problems. Prominent examples of laws that have motivated cleanup include federal "Right-to-Know" provisions requiring reporting of information about releases of toxic pollution into the environment and California's Proposition 65, which requires labels warning consumers about carcinogens in consumer products.

A. INFORMATION IN GOVERNMENT ENVIRONMENTAL DECISION-MAKING

1. NEPA and Its Analogues

Government needs information to make good environmental decisions. Congress recognized this in one of the first modern environmental statutes it enacted, the National Environmental Policy Act of 1969 (NEPA), 42 U.S.C. §4321 *et seq.* This statute plays an especially important role in the management of natural resources, for it requires analysis of the environmental impacts of major proposals for federal actions significantly affecting the environment (known as environmental impact statements (EIS)). Many of these actions involve decisions the federal government makes about how to manage federal lands.

A federal obligation to prepare an EIS only applies to proposed "federal" actions, but state law sometimes requires an EIS for state actions. Federal actions, however, encompass much more than purely federal projects. They include many decisions by the federal government to grant permits and licenses to others, *see, e.g.,* Davis v. Morton, 469 F.2d 593, 598 (10th Cir. 1972) (the Bureau of Indian Affairs must comply with NEPA before approving a lease for development purposes on tribal lands), and to fund projects that the federal government does not carry out, *see, e.g.,* Blue Ocean Preservation Society v. Watkins, 754 F. Supp. 1450, 1461 (D. Haw. 1991) (EIS required for state proposal to develop geothermal resources when federal funds support the project); Don't Ruin Our Park v. Stone, 749 F. Supp. 1386 (M.D. Pa. 1990), *aff'd mem.,* 931 F.2d 49 (3d Cir. 1991) (EIS required for relocation of a Pennsylvania National Guard unit to a location adjacent to a state park because of federal funding); *cf.* National Organization for the Reform of Marijuana Laws v. Drug Enforcement Administration, 545 F. Supp. 981, 985 (D.D.C. 1982) (federal technical assistance not a sufficient basis to make marijuana spraying a federal action); Sierra Club v. Stamm, 507 F.2d 788 (10th Cir. 1974) (federal subsidies used for pesticide and herbicide spraying does not make a federal action when the federal agency did not control the subsidies' use).

NEPA only requires an EIS when a proposed federal action "significantly" affects the environment. *See* Minnesota Public Interest Research Group v. Butz (I), 498 F.2d 1314 (8th Cir. 1974); 40 C.F.R. §1508.18. Most courts assess significance by examining both the magnitude of harm emanating from a project and the extent to which it will cause adverse effects "in excess of those created by additional uses." *See* Hanly v. Kleindienst, 471 F.2d 823 (2d Cir. 1972), *cert. denied,* 412 U.S. 908 (1973); 40 C.F.R. §1508.27. Some courts require impact statements whenever the actions are "arguably" significant and demand a convincing agency case for insignificance before excusing agency preparation of an EIS. *See, e.g.,* Maryland-National Capital Park and Planning Commission v. United States Postal Service, 487 F.2d 1029 (D.C. Cir. 1973).

By only requiring an EIS for actions that may have significant effects, the statute recognizes that generating analysis and information is costly and ought be undertaken only where the impacts of an action might be serious. Implementing this requirement to prepare an EIS for significant actions poses a problem. How can the agency know if a contemplated action is significant enough to warrant an EIS without preparing an EIS? Generally, agencies that believe that a contemplated action might be too minor to warrant preparation of an EIS conduct a much less intensive "Environmental Assessment" to determine if an EIS is needed. *See* DANIEL R. MANDELKER, NEPA LAW AND LITIGATION §7.11(2006). If the agency concludes that its contemplated action will not have significant effects triggering the obligation to prepare an EIS, it publishes a "Finding of No Significant Impact" (FONSI). These findings sometimes prove controversial and lead to litigated cases about whether the agency's reasons for its FONSI were arbitrary and capricious. *Cf.* Marsh v. Oregon Natural Resources Council, 490 U.S. 360, 379 (1989) (upholding decision not to file a supplemental environmental impact statement as reasonable in spite of pertinent new information).

The following cases address this question: Once an agency or court determines that an action has a sufficiently significant effect to trigger an EIS, how should the agency evaluate the impact? Notice that an EIS typically must involve substantial uncertainty and judgment, because it provides an estimate of the future impacts of a decision that has not yet been made. The case that follows addresses the question of how the agency should handle that problem.

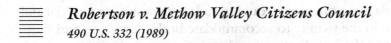

Robertson v. Methow Valley Citizens Council
490 U.S. 332 (1989)

JUSTICE STEVENS delivered the opinion of the Court.

We granted certiorari to decide two questions of law. As framed by petitioners, they are:

"1. Whether the National Environmental Policy Act requires federal agencies to include in each environmental impact statement: (a) a fully developed plan to mitigate environmental harm; and (b) a 'worst case' analysis of potential environmental harm if relevant information concerning significant environmental effects is unavailable or too costly to obtain.

"2. "Whether the Forest Service may issue a special use permit for recreational use of national forest land in the absence of a fully developed plan to mitigate environmental harm."

. . .

I

The Forest Service is authorized by statute to manage the national forests for "outdoor recreation, range, timber, watershed, and wildlife and fish purposes." Pursuant to that authorization, the Forest Service has issued "special use" permits for the operation of approximately 170 Alpine and Nordic ski areas on federal lands.

The Forest Service permit process involves three separate stages. The Forest Service first examines the general environmental and financial feasibility of a proposed project and decides whether to issue a special use permit. Because that decision is a "major Federal action" within the meaning of NEPA, it must be preceded by the preparation of an Environmental Impact Statement (EIS). If the Service decides to issue a permit, it then proceeds to select a developer, formulate the basic terms of the arrangement with the selected party, and issue the permit. The special use permit does not, however, give the developer the right to begin construction. In a final stage of review, the Service evaluates the permittee's "master plan" for development, construction, and operation of the project. Construction may begin only after an additional environmental analysis (although it is not clear that a second EIS need always be prepared) and final approval of the developer's master plan. This case arises out of the Forest Service's decision to issue a special use permit authorizing the development of a major destination Alpine ski resort at Sandy Butte in the North Cascade Mountains.
. . .

In 1978, Methow Recreation, Inc. (MRI), applied for a special use permit to develop and operate its proposed "Early Winters Ski Resort" on Sandy Butte and an 1,165-acre parcel of land it had acquired adjacent to the National Forest. The proposed development would make use of approximately 3,900 acres of Sandy Butte; would entice visitors to travel long distances to stay at the resort for several days at a time; and would stimulate extensive commercial and residential growth in the vicinity to accommodate both vacationers and staff.

In response to MRI's application, the Forest Service, in cooperation with state and county officials, prepared an EIS known as the Early Winters Alpine Winter Sports Study (Early Winters Study or Study). The stated purpose of the EIS was "to provide the information required to evaluate the potential for skiing at Early Winters" and "to assist in making a decision whether to issue a Special Use Permit for downhill skiing on all or a portion of approximately 3,900 acres of National Forest System land." . . .

The Early Winters Study is a printed document containing almost 150 pages of text and 12 appendices. It evaluated five alternative levels of development of Sandy Butte that might be authorized, the lowest being a "no action" alternative and the highest being development of a 16-lift ski area able to accommodate 10,500 skiers at one time. The Study considered the effect of each level of development on water resources, soil, wildlife, air quality, vegetation, and visual quality, as well as land use and transportation in the Methow

Valley, probable demographic shifts, the economic market for skiing and other summer and winter recreational activities in the Valley, and the energy require- ments for the ski area and related developments. The Study's discussion of possible impacts was not limited to on-site effects, but also, as required by Council on Environmental Quality (CEQ) regulations, see 40 CFR §1502.16(b) (1987), addressed "off-site impacts that each alternative might have on community facilities, socio-economic and other environmental con- ditions in the Upper Methow Valley." As to off-site effects, the Study explained that "due to the uncertainty of where other public and private lands may become developed," it is difficult to evaluate off-site impacts, and thus the document's analysis is necessarily "not site-specific". Finally, the Study out- lined certain steps that might be taken to mitigate adverse effects, both on Sandy Butte and in the neighboring Methow Valley, but indicated that these proposed steps are merely conceptual and "will be made more specific as part of the design and implementation stages of the planning process."

The effects of the proposed development on air quality and wildlife received particular attention in the Study. In the chapter on "Environmental Consequences," the first subject discussed is air quality. As is true of other subjects, the discussion included an analysis of cumulative impacts over several years resulting from actions on other lands as well as from the development of Sandy Butte itself. The Study concluded that although the construction, maintenance, and operation of the proposed ski area "will not have a measur- able effect on existing or future air quality," the off-site development of private land under all five alternatives — including the "no action" alternative — "will have a significant effect on air quality during severe meteorological inversion periods." The burning of wood for space heat, the Study explained, would constitute the primary cause of diminished air quality, and the damage would increase incrementally with each of the successive levels of proposed develop- ment. The Study cautioned that without efforts to mitigate these effects, even under the "no action" alternative, the increase in automobile, fireplace, and wood stove use would reduce air quality below state standards, but added that "[t]he numerous mitigation measures discussed" in the Study "will greatly reduce the impacts presented by the model."

In its discussion of air-quality mitigation measures, the EIS identified actions that could be taken by the county government to mitigate the adverse effects of development, as well as those that the Forest Service itself could implement at the construction stage of the project. The Study suggested that Okanogan County develop an air quality management plan, requiring weath- erization of new buildings, limiting the number of wood stoves and fireplaces, and adopting monitoring and enforcement measures. In addition, the Study suggested that the Forest Service require that the master plan include proce- dures to control dust and to comply with smoke management practices.

In its discussion of adverse effects on area wildlife, the EIS concluded that no endangered or threatened species would be affected by the proposed development and that the only impact on sensitive species was the probable loss of a pair of spotted owls and their progeny. With regard to other wildlife, the Study considered the impact on 75 different indigenous species and predicted that within a decade after development vegetational change and increased human activity would lead to a decrease in population for 31 species, while causing an increase in population for another 24 species on Sandy Butte. Two species, the pine marten and nesting goshawk, would be eliminated altogether from the area of development.

In a comment in response to the draft EIS, the Washington Department of Game voiced a special concern about potential losses to the State's largest migratory deer herd, which uses the Methow Valley as a critical winter range and as its migration route. The state agency estimated that the total population of mule deer in the area most likely to be affected was "better than 30,000 animals" and that "the ultimate impact on the Methow deer herd could exceed a 50 percent reduction in numbers." The agency asserted that "Okanogan County residents place a great deal of importance on the area's deer herd." In addition, it explained that hunters had "harvested" 3,247 deer in the Methow Valley area in 1981, and that, since in 1980 hunters on average spent $1,980 for each deer killed in Washington, they had contributed over $6 million to the State's economy in 1981. Because the deer harvest is apparently proportional to the size of the herd, the state agency predicted that "Washington business can expect to lose over $3 million annually from reduced recreational opportunity." The Forest Service's own analysis of the impact on the deer herd was more modest. It first concluded that the actual operation of the ski hill would have only a "minor" direct impact on the herd, but then recognized that the off-site effect of the development "would noticeably reduce numbers of deer in the Methow [Valley] with any alternative." Although its estimate indicated a possible 15 percent decrease in the size of the herd, it summarized the State's contrary view in the text of the EIS, and stressed that off-site effects are difficult to estimate due to uncertainty concerning private development.

As was true of its discussion of air quality, the EIS also described both on-site and off-site mitigation measures. Among possible on-site mitigation possibilities, the Study recommended locating runs, ski lifts, and roads so as to minimize interference with wildlife, restricting access to selected roads during fawning season, and further examination of the effect of the development on mule deer migration routes. Off-site options discussed in the Study included the use of zoning and tax incentives to limit development on deer winter range and migration routes, encouragement of conservation easements, and acquisition and management by local government of critical tracts of land. As with the measures suggested for mitigating the off-site effects on air quality, the proposed options were primarily directed to steps that might be taken by state and local government.

Ultimately, the Early Winters Study recommended the issuance of a permit for development at the second highest level considered — a 16-lift ski area able to accommodate 8,200 skiers at one time. On July 5, 1984, the Regional Forester decided to issue a special use permit as recommended by the

Study. In his decision, the Regional Forester found that no major adverse effects would result directly from the federal action, but that secondary effects could include a degradation of existing air quality and a reduction of mule deer winter range. He therefore directed the supervisor of the Okanogan National Forest, both independently and in cooperation with local officials, to identify and implement certain mitigating measures.

Four organizations (respondents) . . . brought this action under the Administrative Procedure Act, 5 U.S.C. §§701-706, to obtain judicial review of the Forest Service's decision. Their principal claim was that the Early Winters Study did not satisfy the requirements of NEPA, 42 U.S.C. §4332. With the consent of the parties, the case was assigned to a United States Magistrate. After a trial, the Magistrate filed a comprehensive written opinion and concluded that the EIS was adequate. Specifically, he found that the EIS had adequately disclosed the adverse impacts on the mule deer herd and on air quality and that there was no duty to prepare a "worst case analysis" because the relevant information essential to a reasoned decision was available. In concluding that the discussion of off-site, or secondary, impacts was adequate, the Magistrate stressed that courts apply a "rule of reason" in evaluating the adequacy of an EIS and "take the uncertainty and speculation involved with secondary impacts into account in passing on the adequacy of the discussion of secondary impacts." On the subject of mitigation, he explained that "[m]ere listing . . . is generally inadequate to satisfy the CEQ regulations," but found that "in this EIS there is more — not much more — but more than a mere listing of mitigation measures." Moreover, emphasizing the tiered nature of the Forest Service's decisional process, the Magistrate noted that additional mitigation strategies would be included in the master plan, that the Forest Service continues to develop mitigation plans as further information becomes available, and that the Regional Forester's decision conditioned issuance of the special use permit on execution of an agreement between the Forest Service, the State of Washington, and Okanogan County concerning mitigation.

Concluding that the Early Winters Study was inadequate as a matter of law, the Court of Appeals reversed. The court held that the Forest Service could not rely on "the implementation of mitigation measures" to support its conclusion that the impact on the mule deer would be minor, "since not only has the effectiveness of these mitigation measures not yet been assessed, but the mitigation measures themselves have yet to be developed." It then added that if the agency had difficulty obtaining adequate information to make a reasoned assessment of the environmental impact on the herd, it had a duty to make a so called "worst case analysis." Such an analysis is "formulated on the basis of available information, using reasonable projections of the worst possible consequences of a proposed action."

The court found a similar defect in the EIS' treatment of air quality. Since the EIS made it clear that commercial development in the Methow Valley will result in violations of state air-quality standards unless effective mitigation measures are put in place by the local governments and the private developer,

the Court of Appeals concluded that the Forest Service had an affirmative duty to "develop the necessary mitigation measures *before* the permit is granted." The court . . . read the statute as imposing a substantive requirement that "action be taken to mitigate the adverse effects of major federal actions." For this reason, it concluded that "an EIS must include a thorough discussion of measures to mitigate the adverse environmental impacts of a proposed action."
. . .

II

Section 101 of NEPA declares a broad national commitment to protecting and promoting environmental quality. To ensure that this commitment is "infused into the ongoing programs and actions of the Federal Government, the act also establishes some important 'action-forcing' procedures." Section 102 thus, among other measures

> "directs that, to the fullest extent possible . . . all agencies of the Federal Government shall —
> . . .
>
> "(C) include in every recommendation or report on proposals for legislation and other major Federal actions significantly affecting the quality of the human environment, a detailed statement by the responsible official on —
> "(i) the environmental impact of the proposed action,
> "(ii) any adverse environmental effects which cannot be avoided should the proposal be implemented,
> "(iii) alternatives to the proposed action,
> "(iv) the relationship between local short-term uses of man's environment and the maintenance and enhancement of long-term productivity, and
> "(v) any irreversible and irretrievable commitments of resources which would be involved in the proposed action should it be implemented."

42 U.S.C. §4332.

The statutory requirement that a federal agency contemplating a major action prepare such an environmental impact statement serves NEPA's "action-forcing" purpose in two important respects. It ensures that the agency, in reaching its decision, will have available, and will carefully consider, detailed information concerning significant environmental impacts; it also guarantees that the relevant information will be made available to the larger audience that may also play a role in both the decisionmaking process and the implementation of that decision.

Simply by focusing the agency's attention on the environmental consequences of a proposed project, NEPA ensures that important effects will not be overlooked or underestimated only to be discovered after resources have been committed or the die otherwise cast. Moreover, the strong precatory language of §101 of the Act and the requirement that agencies prepare detailed impact statements inevitably bring pressure to bear on agencies "to respond to the needs of environmental quality."

Publication of an EIS, both in draft and final form, also serves a larger informational role. It gives the public the assurance that the agency "has indeed considered environmental concerns in its decisionmaking process," and, perhaps more significantly, provides a springboard for public comment. Thus, in this case the final draft of the Early Winters Study reflects not only the work of the Forest Service itself, but also the critical views of the Washington State Department of Game, the Methow Valley Citizens Council, and Friends of the Earth, as well as many others, to whom copies of the draft Study were circulated. Moreover, with respect to a development such as Sandy Butte, where the adverse effects on air quality and the mule deer herd are primarily attributable to predicted off-site development that will be subject to regulation by other governmental bodies, the EIS serves the function of offering those bodies adequate notice of the expected consequences and the opportunity to plan and implement corrective measures in a timely manner.

The sweeping policy goals announced in §101 of NEPA are thus realized through a set of "action-forcing" procedures that require that agencies take a "'hard look' at environmental consequences," and that provide for broad dissemination of relevant environmental information. Although these procedures are almost certain to affect the agency's substantive decision, it is now well settled that NEPA itself does not mandate particular results, but simply prescribes the necessary process. If the adverse environmental effects of the proposed action are adequately identified and evaluated, the agency is not constrained by NEPA from deciding that other values outweigh the environmental costs. In this case, for example, it would not have violated NEPA if the Forest Service, after complying with the Act's procedural prerequisites, had decided that the benefits to be derived from downhill skiing at Sandy Butte justified the issuance of a special use permit, notwithstanding the loss of 15 percent, 50 percent, or even 100 percent of the mule deer herd. Other statutes may impose substantive environmental obligations on federal agencies, but NEPA merely prohibits uninformed — rather than unwise — agency action.

To be sure, one important ingredient of an EIS is the discussion of steps that can be taken to mitigate adverse environmental consequences. The requirement that an EIS contain a detailed discussion of possible mitigation measures flows both from the language of the Act and, more expressly, from CEQ's implementing regulations. Implicit in NEPA's demand that an agency prepare a detailed statement on "any adverse environmental effects which cannot be avoided should the proposal be implemented," is an understanding that the EIS will discuss the extent to which adverse effects can be avoided. More generally, omission of a reasonably complete discussion of possible mitigation measures would undermine the "action forcing" function of NEPA. Without such a discussion, neither the agency nor other interested groups and individuals can properly evaluate the severity of the adverse effects. An adverse effect that can be fully remedied by, for example, an inconsequential public expenditure is certainly not as serious as a similar effect that can only be modestly ameliorated through the commitment of vast public and private resources. Recognizing the importance of such a discussion in guaranteeing that the agency has taken a "hard look" at the environmental consequences of proposed federal action, CEQ regulations require that the agency discuss possible mitigation measures in defining the scope of the EIS in discussing alternatives to the proposed action, and consequences of that action, and in explaining its ultimate decision.

There is a fundamental distinction, however, between a requirement that mitigation be discussed in sufficient detail to ensure that environmental consequences have been fairly evaluated, on the one hand, and a substantive requirement that a complete mitigation plan be actually formulated and adopted, on the other. In this case, the off-site effects on air quality and on the mule deer herd cannot be mitigated unless nonfederal government agencies take appropriate action. Since it is those state and local governmental bodies that have jurisdiction over the area in which the adverse effects need be addressed and since they have the authority to mitigate them, it would be incongruous to conclude that the Forest Service has no power to act until the local agencies have reached a final conclusion on what mitigating measures they consider necessary. Even more significantly, it would be inconsistent with NEPA's reliance on procedural mechanisms — as opposed to substantive, result-based standards — to demand the presence of a fully developed plan that will mitigate environmental harm before an agency can act.

We thus conclude that the Court of Appeals erred, first, in assuming that "NEPA requires that 'action be taken to mitigate the adverse effects of major federal actions,'" and, second, in finding that this substantive requirement entails the further duty to include in every EIS "a detailed explanation of specific measures which *will* be employed to mitigate the adverse impacts of a proposed action."

III

The Court of Appeals also concluded that the Forest Service had an obligation to make a "worst case analysis" if it could not make a reasoned assessment of the impact of the Early Winters project on the mule deer herd. Such a "worst case analysis" was required at one time by CEQ regulations, but those regulations have since been amended. Moreover, although the prior regulations may well have expressed a permissible application of NEPA, the Act itself does not mandate that uncertainty in predicting environmental harms be addressed exclusively in this manner. Accordingly, we conclude that the Court of Appeals also erred in requiring the "worst case" study.

In 1977, President Carter directed that CEQ promulgate binding regulations implementing the procedural provisions of NEPA. Exec. Order No. 11991, 3 CFR §123 (1977 Comp.). Pursuant to this Presidential order, CEQ promulgated implementing regulations. Under §1502.22 of these regulations — a provision which became known as the "worst case requirement" — CEQ provided that if certain information relevant to the agency's evaluation of the proposed action is either unavailable or too costly to obtain, the agency must include in the EIS a "worst case analysis and an indication of the probability or improbability of its occurrence." 40 CFR §1502.22 (1985). In 1986, however, CEQ replaced the "worst case" requirement with a requirement that federal agencies, in the face of unavailable information concerning a reasonably foreseeable significant environmental consequence, prepare "a summary of existing credible scientific evidence which is relevant to evaluating the adverse impacts" and prepare an "evaluation of such impacts based upon theoretical approaches or research methods generally accepted in the scientific community." 40 CFR §1502.22(b) (1987). The amended regulation thus "retains the duty to describe the consequences of a remote, but potentially severe impact, but grounds the duty in evaluation of scientific opinion rather than in the framework of a conjectural 'worst case analysis.'" 50 Fed. Reg. 32237 (1985).

The Court of Appeals recognized that the "worst case analysis" regulation has been superseded, yet held that "[t]his rescission . . . does not nullify the requirement . . . since the regulation was merely a codification of prior NEPA case law." This conclusion, however, is erroneous in a number of respects. Most notably, review of NEPA case law reveals that the regulation, in fact, was not a codification of prior judicial decisions. The cases cited by the Court of Appeals ultimately rely on the Fifth Circuit's decision in *Sierra Club* v. *Sigler*, 695 F. 2d 957 (1983). *Sigler*, however, simply recognized that the "worst case analysis" regulation codified the "judicially created principl[e]" that an EIS must "consider the probabilities of the occurrence of any environmental effects it discusses." As CEQ recognized at the time it superseded the regulation, case law prior to the adoption of the "worst case analysis" provision did require agencies to describe environmental impacts even in the face of substantial uncertainty, but did not require that this obligation necessarily be met through the mechanism of a "worst case analysis." CEQ's abandonment of the "worst case analysis" provision, therefore, is not inconsistent with any previously established judicial interpretation of the statute.

Nor are we convinced that the new CEQ regulation is not controlling simply because it was preceded by a rule that was in some respects more demanding. In *Andrus v. Sierra Club*, 442 U.S., at 358, we held that CEQ regulations are entitled to substantial deference. In that case we recognized that although less deference may be in order in some cases in which the "administrative guidelines" conflict "with earlier pronouncements of the agency," substantial deference is nonetheless appropriate if there appears to have been good reason for the change. Here, the amendment only came after the prior regulation had been subjected to considerable criticism. Moreover, the amendment was designed to better serve the twin functions of an EIS — requiring agencies to take a "hard look" at the consequences of the proposed action and providing important information to other groups and individuals. CEQ explained that by requiring that an EIS focus on reasonably foreseeable impacts, the new regulation "will generate information and discussion on those consequences of greatest concern to the public and of greatest relevance to the agency's decision," rather than distorting the decisionmaking process by overemphasizing highly speculative harms. In light of this well-considered basis for the change, the new regulation is entitled to substantial deference. Accordingly, the Court of Appeals erred in concluding that the Early Winters Study is inadequate because it failed to include a "worst case analysis."

* * *

V

In sum, we conclude that NEPA does not require a fully developed plan detailing what steps *will* be taken to mitigate adverse environmental impacts and does not require a "worst case analysis." . . . The judgment of the Court of Appeals is accordingly reversed, and the case is remanded for further proceedings consistent with this opinion.

It is so ordered.

NOTES ON *ROBERTSON v. METHOW VALLEY CITIZENS COUNCIL*

1. *Information motivating action.* Note that even as the Court refuses to hold that NEPA requires any particular decision respecting the ski resort, it affirms that the NEPA process is "almost certain to affect the agency's substantive decision." *Robertson*, 490 U.S. at 350. If the Court is right, why is it right? One possibility is that the professionals in the agency will prove responsive to significant information once they assemble it, because their sense of professionalism will make them responsive. Another possibility is that the disclosure of adverse environmental impacts to the public will create sufficient political pressure to force the agency to mitigate or avoid significant environmental impacts. A third possibility is that the agency decisions will remain subject to judicial review. The agency will have to explain why it made its decision to a court. Perhaps information about negative environmental impacts makes it harder to provide non-arbitrary rationales for carrying out decisions likely to seriously harm the environment. A fourth possibility is that information that the EIS generates will identify potential violations of other laws and regulations.

In spite of the Forest Service's victory in the *Methow Valley* case, the ski resort was not built. The Ninth Circuit found the EIS inadequate not only with respect to the issues raised in the Supreme Court, but on other grounds as well. As a result, the Forest Service had to revise its impact statement even after prevailing in the Supreme Court. Environmentalists continued to press their case. Eventually, the developer abandoned the plan to build the resort. Does this suggest that NEPA is working well or badly?

2. *What sort of analysis?* Does NEPA mandate formal cost-benefit analysis, in which agencies must explicitly compare, in monetary terms, the economic costs of implementing a particular action with the economic benefits to be derived, and to approve the action only where the ratio of benefits to costs is positive? *See* 42 U.S.C. §4332; Calvert Cliffs Coordinating Committee v. Atomic Energy Commission, 449 F.2d 1109, 1115 (D.C. Cir. 1971) (suggesting that a court may reverse an agency action under NEPA if the agency strikes an arbitrary "balance of costs and benefits"). Some courts have imposed an obligation to consider environmental costs, while others have overseen the content of the analysis. *See, e.g.,* Sierra Club v. Sigler, 695 F.2d 957, 974 (5th Cir. 1983) (requiring worst case analysis and analysis of the environmental costs of digging a deeper channel); Johnston v. Davis, 698 F.2d 1088 (9th Cir. 1983) (approving fairly cursory analysis of some environmental costs, but requiring the Soil Conservation Service to take the artificially low discount rate it used in evaluating its proposed project into account).

3. *Public participation.* Public participation in creating the information also plays a role in shaping decisions. NEPA typically creates several opportunities for the public and non-federal government entities to participate in shaping the analysis. Once an agency decides to prepare an EIS, it usually engages in a "scoping" process to determine which issues the EIS will focus upon. *See* Mandelker, *supra*, §7:12. Agencies typically solicit the views of other government agencies and the public in this process. *See* 40 C.F.R. §1501.7. *But see* Northwest Coalition for Alternatives to Pesticides v. Lyng, 844 F.2d 588 (9th Cir. 1988) (finding no prejudicial error when agency failed to notify environmental groups). Agencies also solicit public comment once they have prepared a draft environmental impact statement. 40 C.F.R. §1503.1(4). Do you see any evidence that local and state agencies took advantage of these opportunities in the *Methow Valley* case?

The agency then responds to the public comments in writing the final environmental impact statement. 40 C.F.R. §1503.4. The process culminates in a "record of decision" that explains the decision, the alternatives considered under NEPA, and whether the agency has used all practicable means to minimize environmental harm. 40 C.F.R. §1505.2. CEQ regulations also require the agency to explain why any measure capable of mitigating harm has not been adopted. 40 C.F.R. §1505.2(c). Given this last requirement, do you think agencies are likely to seriously engage in mitigation even after *Methow Valley?*

4. *Mitigation.* Suppose that the environmental impact statement had fully discussed the environmental impacts, but failed to discuss how government officials might mitigate those impacts. Would such a statement pass muster? In this case, most of the mitigation measures discussed required action of local government. Suppose that an EIS identified a number of mitigation measures that the federal government could take. Would NEPA require the federal government to take such measures if they would avoid otherwise serious environmental impacts?

May the agency assume that environmental impacts are trivial, because it can envision mitigation measures that would make it trivial, without their actual adoption?

5. *Worst case analysis.* Do you read the statutory language set out in the opinion as requiring worse case analysis? *See Robertson,* 490 U.S. at 348. The Court traced the requirement for worst case analysis back to *Sierra Club v. Sigler,* which it characterizes as "simply" recognizing that the "worst case analysis" regulation codified the "judicially created principle" that an EIS "must consider the probabilities of the occurrences of any environmental effects." *Id.* at 355. The *Sigler* court, however, characterized its conclusion in the following way: "Because [the worst case requirement] is in accord with the language and legislative history of NEPA and closely tracks NEPA case law, we conclude that it is not beyond the statutory minima of NEPA." Sierra Club v. Sigler, 695 F.2d 957, 971 (5th Cir. 1983). The *Sigler* court also states that NEPA's "literal language does not require a worst case analysis." *Id.* at 969. Should the Supreme Court have considered whether NEPA's legislative history and purposes require worst case analysis? Which court was correct? Regardless of the results of this case, many environmental impact statements lead to the adoption of measures reducing a project's environmental impacts.

6. *The mitigation concept.* While the Court rejected a requirement to actually undertake mitigation measures under NEPA, such requirements do exist under other statutes. NEPA spawned a number of state environmental policy acts. *See generally* Mandelker, *supra,* §12. Some of these may force mitigation:

> Mitigation plays a heightened role under the California Environmental Quality Act; once an environmental impact has been declared to be "significant" . . . the agency is required to find that sufficient mitigation measures have been taken to lessen the project's impact. If the agency finds that alternatives or mitigation measures are not feasible, the agency must adopt a statement of overriding considerations which states the specific reasons why "the project's benefit outweighs the unmitigated effects. . . . "

City of Carmel-by-the-Sea v. United States DOT, 123 F.3d 1142, 1164 (9th Cir. 1997).

Moreover, many federal actions that are subject to NEPA are subject to mitigation under other environmental statutes, such as section 404 of the CWA and various provisions of the Endangered Species Act, discussed in a note below. By forcing consideration of mitigation options, NEPA may make mitigation opportunities required by those laws more apparent.

7. *Worst case policy and uncertainty.* In almost all cases, the future environmental impacts of significant federal actions are uncertain. Also, scientific information that might help us make reasonable predictions usually has serious gaps. Given the pervasiveness of uncertainty, should worst case analysis be mandatory?

Would your answer change if the possible impacts of decisions were very serious and the worst case scenario helped inform the emergency planning of the police, fire fighters, medical personnel, and other disaster relief agencies? This is not an academic question. Chemical accidents killed or injured more than 2,000 people between 1994 and 2004. As a result, the Clean Air Act requires chemical companies to create risk management plans to "detect and prevent or minimize" accidents. *See* 42 U.S.C. §7412(r)(7)(B)(ii). The planning requirements for larger plants include:

A hazard assessment to assess the potential effects of an accidental release of any regulated substance. This assessment shall include an estimate of potential release quantities and a determination of downwind effects, including potential exposures to affected populations. Such assessments shall include a previous release history for the past 5 years, including the size concentration, and duration of release; and shall include an evaluation of *worst case accidental releases,* . . . .

42 U.S.C. §7412(r)(7)(B)(ii)(I) [emphasis added]. The Clean Air Act further requires that chemical plant operators make these plans public and share them with local officials. 42 U.S.C. §7412(r)(7)(H). The Emergency Planning and Community Right-to-Know-Act requires chemical plants to report accidental releases of extremely hazardous substances to local authorities and sets up a planning procedure for local governments to prepare to address chemical accidents. *See* 42 U.S.C. §§11001-11005.

After the World Trade Center Bombing on September 11, 2001, the Bush Administration pulled this emergency planning information from the Internet, apparently from fear that terrorists would use it to select facilities to target. *See* 42 U.S.C. §7412(r)(7)(H)(ii)(I)(aa). Is this an appropriate response? Will public access increase the accountability of local officials for appropriate emergency planning? What sort of information do you think would prove most useful for terrorists? Should the problem of potential terrorism lead government to abandon worst case analysis? Should it be available at public libraries, but not the Internet?

a. *Alternatives Analysis*

NEPA requires agencies to consider the environmental impacts of alternatives to its proposed action in the EIS. Notice that the Early Winters Study considered five different alternative levels of development. In this context, the agency considered whether a smaller number of lifts serving fewer skiers (and therefore generating less traffic and surrounding development) might work.

Council of Environmental Quality regulations require discussion of the no-action alternative — doing nothing. 40 C.F.R. §1502.14(d). But what other alternatives should the agency discuss? Suppose that the Forest Services proposes to authorize the cutting of 500 trees in a forest. What alternatives should it study? Suppose that the Bureau of Land Management proposes to authorize oil drilling in a beautiful canyon. What alternatives should it study?

At first blush, one might think that the agency should consider all conceivable alternatives. The United States Court of Appeals for the Fourth Circuit explains why this cannot be the answer in a case rejecting a citizen demand that the Department of Transportation consider a route in between two routes considered for a highway:

> [The] cases construe the provisions for consideration and discussion of alternatives as subject to a construction of reasonableness. The gist of all of the opinions is that an infinite variety of alternatives is permissible in almost every administrative decision of this nature, which should be especially true here when it is considered that the administrative authorities have considered a "do nothing" alternative. This being so, there must be an end to the process somewhere or no federal-aid highway would ever be built. So long as there are unexplored and undiscussed alternatives that inventive minds can suggest, without a rule of reason, it will be technically impossible to prepare a correct environmental impact statement. . . . We think that what NEPA, 42 USC §4332(C)(iii), demands is the "study, development, and description of reasonable alternatives," that is to say, "realistic alternatives that will be reasonably available within the time the decision making official intends to act." . . . [I]f this requirement is not rubber, neither is it iron. The statute must be construed in the light of reason if it is not to demand what is, fairly speaking, not meaningfully possible, given the obvious, that the resources of energy and research — and time — available to meet the Nation's needs are not infinite.

Fayetteville Area Chamber of Commerce v. Volpe, 515 F.2d 1021, 1027 (4th Cir. 1975). *But see* Utahns for Better Transportation v. U.S. Dep't of Transp., 305 F.3d 1152 (10th Cir. 2002), *modified on other grounds,* 319 F.3d 1207 (10th Cir. 2003) (remanding for, *inter alia*, evaluation of alternative highway routes).

The courts regularly apply a "rule of reason" to their evaluation of agency selection of alternatives to study in the EIS. While such a rule suggests deference to agencies, courts sometimes find NEPA violations when the agency discusses an inadequate range of alternatives.

The following two cases involve selection of alternatives for study in deciding upon what federal lands to protect from development. Ask yourself whether these cases are consistent and what principles should govern selection of alternatives.

≣ *California v. Block*
≣ *690 F.2d 753 (9th Cir. 1982)*

TANG, CIRCUIT JUDGE.

This appeal is from a summary judgment and injunction entered against the Forest Service for failing to comply with the National Environmental Policy Act in preparing an environmental impact statement ("EIS") on a Forest Service decision to allocate National Forest System land among three management categories. . . . Did the district court err in holding that . . . the Final EIS did not consider an adequate range of alternatives?

We affirm.

FACTS

This litigation concerns how the Forest Service intends to manage 62 million acres of the National Forest System. . . . Under the mandate of the enabling legislation, the Secretary of Agriculture is directed to recommend to Congress "primitive" areas that should be added to the Wilderness System. [Land not designated as wilderness receives much less protection, as this land can be used to supply timber and for other uses incompatible with wilderness designation.]

In 1972, the Forest Service made an abortive attempt to devise a national planning document for the management of "roadless areas" within the National Forest System. Dubbed "Roadless Area Review and Evaluation (RARE I)," this effort ended when a federal court enjoined development pursuant to the plan until the Forest Service completed an EIS.

In 1977, the Forest Service made a second attempt to evaluate programmatically the roadless areas in the National Forest System. This project, named RARE II, inventoried all roadless areas within the National Forest System and allocated each area to one of three planning categories: Wilderness, Further Planning and Nonwilderness. Areas designated as Wilderness were to be recommended to Congress for inclusion in the [National Wilderness Preservation System] NWPS. A Further Planning designation meant that an area would be protected pending completion of unit management plans which would consider whether to recommend the area for inclusion in the NWPS. No controversy surrounds the Wilderness or Further Planning designations. The parties here dispute what a Nonwilderness designation means.

A draft EIS on the RARE II project was released to the public on June 15, 1978. The document . . . identified ten alternative allocation methods which resulted in different allocations between the three planning categories, but did not tentatively endorse any of the alternatives as a Proposed Action. Each alternative reflected a different combination of decisional criteria. The criteria included Forest Service resource planning goals, wilderness attributes, public accessibility to wilderness areas, public comment and the economic effects of Wilderness classification.

Public comment was solicited concerning the decisional criteria, the allocations that resulted from the alternatives, and possible alternative approaches not considered in the draft. The draft EIS prompted over 264,000 comments.

The Final EIS was filed on January 4, 1979. It identified for the first time the Forest Service's Proposed Action and called for allocating 15 million acres of RARE II lands to Wilderness, 10.8 million acres to Further Planning, and 36 million acres to Nonwilderness. The Proposed Action was not one of the alternatives considered in the draft EIS, but represented an amalgam of all the decisional criteria considered in the draft EIS alternatives. The percentage allocation produced by the Proposed Action was within the range of percentage allocations produced by the draft EIS alternatives, but was not roughly identical to any one set of allocation percentages considered in the earlier alternatives. *See* Table # 1, *infra*.

. . .

On July 25, 1979, the State of California brought action in federal district court against the Secretary of Agriculture and the Forest Service, alleging violations of the National Environmental Policy Act ("NEPA"). . . .

California specifically challenged the Forest Service decision to designate forty-seven RARE II areas in California as Nonwilderness. On January 8, 1980, the district court granted California's motion for summary judgment. . . . [T]he court held that the RARE II Final EIS was inadequate to support the Nonwilderness designations of the disputed areas and therefore violated NEPA. It ruled that the Final EIS was deficient [because] . . . the EIS did not consider an adequate range of alternatives.

Pursuant to [this holding], the district court enjoined the Forest Service from taking any action that might change the wilderness character of the disputed areas in California until it filed an EIS that satisfied NEPA's requirements and considered the impact of the decision upon the wilderness characteristics of these areas. . . .

The Forest Service appeals from the summary judgment and injunction. . . .

DISCUSSION

* * *

II. Did the RARE II Final EIS consider a reasonable range of alternatives?

The Final EIS lists eleven alternatives, of which three — "all Wilderness", "no Wilderness" and "no action" — were included as points of reference rather than as seriously considered alternatives. . . .

The area allocations resulting from these various alternatives are summarized in Table # 1. None of the eight alternatives seriously considered by the Forest Service designates more than thirty-three percent of the roadless acreage to Wilderness, and none designates less than thirty-seven percent of that acreage to Nonwilderness. More than one-half of the roadless acreage is allocated to Nonwilderness in six of the eight alternatives.

TABLE # 1
Percent of Acreage of RARE II Areas in Each RARE II Planning Category.*

Alternative	Non-Wilderness	Further Planing	Wilderness
C	68	18	14
D	48	38	19
E	94	1	6
F	55	36	9
G	79	1	21
H	73	11	16
I	37	30	33
Proposed Action	59	18	23

*Alternatives A, B, and J were included in the EIS as points of reference and were not seriously considered. See RARE II Final EIS at 26. Alternatives C-I were included in the draft EIS. The Proposed Action, the alternative ultimately selected by the Forest Service, first appeared in the Final EIS.

The district court held that the RARE II Final EIS failed to consider an adequate range of alternatives. The court ruled that the EIS should have considered. . . . :

— Allocating to Wilderness a share of the RARE II acreage at an intermediate percentage between 34% and 100%.

California v. Bergland, 483 F. Supp. at 492-93.
. . .

Our standard of review is well-established. NEPA requires a "detailed statement . . . on . . . alternatives to the proposed action. . . . " 42 U.S.C. §4332(2)(C)(1976). Agencies are also under a mandate to "study, develop, and describe appropriate alternatives to recommend courses of action in any proposal which involves unresolved conflicts concerning alternative uses of available resources." *Id.* at §4332(2)(E). Judicial review of the range of alternatives considered by an agency is governed by a "rule of reason" that requires an agency to set forth only those alternatives necessary to permit a "reasoned choice." An EIS, however, need not consider an alternative "whose effect cannot be reasonably ascertained, and whose implementation is deemed remote and speculative." As with the standard employed to evaluate the detail that NEPA requires in discussing a decision's environmental consequences, the touchstone for our inquiry is whether an EIS's selection and discussion of alternatives fosters informed decision-making and informed public participation.

. . .

. . . [W]e . . . affirm the district court's ruling that NEPA requires the Forest Service to consider an alternative that allocates more than a third of the RARE II acreage to Wilderness. Whether the RARE II decision is viewed as a decision to develop or merely as the first step in a protracted planning process, it is puzzling why the Forest Service did not seriously consider an alternative that allocated more than a third of the RARE II acreage to Wilderness. All of the RARE II acreage, by definition, met the minimum criteria for inclusion in the NWPS. Nonetheless, without any explanation the Final EIS seriously considered only those alternatives that allocate more acreage to Nonwilderness than to Wilderness. Moreover, with the sole exception of Alternative I, Nonwilderness acreage allocations exceed Wilderness allocations by a substantial margin, ranging from five-to-two for Alternative D, to nineteen-to-one for Alternative E. While nothing in NEPA prohibits the Forest Service from ultimately implementing a proposal that allocates more acreage to Nonwilderness than to Wilderness, it is troubling that the Forest Service saw fit to consider from the outset only those alternatives leading to that end result.

. . .

THE ROADLESS SAGA CONTINUES

The task the Forest Service confronted in inventorying and making decisions about huge expanses of roadless areas proved overwhelming. No doubt the requirement to provide detailed environmental analysis added to its woes.

After roadless area review had gone on for almost three inconclusive decades, the Clinton Administration decided to seriously limit development in roadless areas. The following case ensued.

 ### *Kootenai Tribe of Idaho v. Veneman*
313 F.3d 1094 (9th Cir. 2002)

GOULD, CIRCUIT JUDGE.

I

This case involves procedural challenges to a United States Forest Service rule, known commonly as the "Roadless Rule," with a potential environmental impact restricting development in national forest lands representing about two percent of the United States land mass. These challenges in essence urge that the Roadless Rule was promulgated without proper process and that it is invalid. . . .

. . .

. . . The district court granted plaintiffs' motions for preliminary injunction against the implementation of the Roadless Rule. . . .

We hold . . . that the district court abused its discretion in granting preliminary injunction against implementation of the Roadless Rule.

II

In the 1970s, the United States Forest Service ("Forest Service") began to study and evaluate roadless areas in national forests. The Forest Service developed an "inventory" of roadless areas, each larger than five thousand acres. There are now 58.5 million acres of inventoried roadless areas in the National Forest System.

Since 1982, the Forest Service has permitted road construction, industrial logging and other development in the inventoried roadless areas on a local, site-specific basis. *See California v. Block*, 690 F.2d 753 (9th Cir. 1982). In the past two decades, 2.8 million acres of roadless areas have been developed by the Forest Service.

On October 13, 1999, President William Jefferson Clinton ordered the United States Forest Service to initiate a nationwide plan to protect inventoried and uninventoried roadless areas within our treasured national forests. . . .

. . . On January 5, 2001, the Forest Service issued the Final [Roadless] Rule, applicable to the 58.5 million acres identified in the [Final Environmental Impact Statement] FEIS. It was to be implemented on March 13, 2001. It generally banned road building. . . . Henceforth, this vast national forest acreage, for better or worse, was more committed to pristine wilderness, and less amenable to road development for purposes permitted by the Forest Service.

B. Procedural History

On January 8, 2001, three days after the Final Rule was issued, the Kootenai Tribe, and the private and county plaintiffs joined with it, filed suit alleging that the Roadless Rule was illegal. On January 9, 2001, the Idaho plaintiffs filed suit with similar claims. Both sets of plaintiffs alleged violations of the NEPA and the APA.

On January 20, 2001, newly-inaugurated President George Walker Bush issued an order postponing by sixty days the effective date of all the prior administration's regulations and rules not yet implemented. The effective date of the Roadless Rule was thus postponed until May 12, 2001. Before then, on February 20, 2001, the Kootenai Tribe and its co-plaintiffs moved for a preliminary injunction against implementation of the Roadless Rule. The Idaho plaintiffs did the same on March 7, 2001. Both sets of plaintiffs argued that the Roadless Rule would cause them irreparable harm by preventing their access to the national forests for proper purposes. Plaintiffs argued that such access was necessary to counter wildfires and threats from insects and disease. The plaintiffs based their motion for preliminary injunction upon alleged violations of NEPA . . .

Thereafter, on March 14, 2001, the district court granted the motion of the Idaho Conservation League, joined by other environmental organizations (collectively, "ICL") to intervene as defendants in both cases. The district court also granted the motion of the Forest Service Employees for Environmental Ethics ("FSEEE") to intervene as a defendant in the complaint brought by Kootenai Tribe and its co-plaintiffs.

. . . [T]he district court found that the plaintiffs had shown that there was "a strong likelihood of success on the merits"; that there existed, absent amendments to the Roadless Rule proposed by the federal government under President Bush's administration, a "substantial possibility that the Roadless Rule will result in irreparable harm to the National Forests"; that there was no date certain for amendments nor guarantee that amendments would "cure the defects identified by the Court and acknowledged to exist by the Federal Government"; and finally and accordingly, that "the Court finds that Plaintiffs have made the minimal showing of irreparable harm and will order that the injunction issue."

ICL and FSEEE filed their Notices of Appeal on May 11 and May 15, 2001, respectively. The federal defendants did not appeal.

III

This appeal presents an unusual procedural setting: The federal defendants, enjoined from "implementing all aspects of the Roadless Area Conservation Rule," have not appealed the injunctions. The interlocutory appeals before us were brought by the environmental groups granted status as defendant-intervenors by the district court. [The court upheld the right of the environmental intervenors to appeal the judgment, notwithstanding the Bush Administration's acquiescence.] . . .

VI

. . .

A. *Success on the Merits*

. . .

2. Consideration of a Reasonable Range of Alternatives

Plaintiffs allege that the alternatives to the Roadless Rule proposed by the Forest Service in the [Draft Environmental Impacts Statement] DEIS and

FEIS were impermissibly narrow under NEPA. The district court held that the Forest Service failed to consider the full range of reasonable alternatives consonant with its policy objectives, stressing that the Forest Service considered only three viable alternatives, all of which included a total ban on road construction within roadless areas. We disagree with the district court's conclusion in this regard. We conclude that the DEIS and FEIS analyzed an adequate range of alternatives. The NEPA alternatives requirement must be interpreted less stringently when the proposed agency action has a primary and central purpose to conserve and protect the natural environment, rather than to harm it. Certainly, it was not the original purpose of Congress in NEPA that government agencies in advancing conservation of the environment must consider alternatives less restrictive of developmental interests. The reason for a proper concern with alternatives here is that plaintiffs have urged that an excess of conservation will be harmful to the environment by precluding appropriate actions in developing roads useful for fighting fires, or insects, or other hazards.

Under NEPA, the Forest Service was under a mandate to "study, develop, and describe appropriate alternatives to recommended courses of action." 42 U.S.C. §4332(E). The Forest Service was also required to include in its EIS a "detailed statement . . . on . . . alternatives to the proposed action." 42 U.S.C. §4332(C)(iii). NEPA regulations describe this alternatives requirement as the "heart" of the EIS and require the agency to produce an EIS that "rigorously explores and objectively evaluates all reasonable alternatives" so that the agency can "sharply define the issues and provide a clear basis for choice among options by the decisionmaker and the public." 40 C.F.R. §1502.14. In this case, the DEIS and FEIS considered three action alternatives for the inventoried roadless areas: (1) prohibit road construction and reconstruction and allow timber harvest; (2) prohibit road construction, reconstruction, and timber harvest except for stewardship purposes (e.g., disease, insect and fire prevention); and (3) prohibit road construction, reconstruction, and all timber harvest within inventoried roadless areas. The district court concluded that each of these three alternatives essentially "banned road construction and reconstruction in inventoried roadless areas and only differed as to the level of restriction imposed on timber harvesting." The district court was concerned that notably absent from the DEIS and FEIS was a consideration of alternatives that did not include a near-total, nationwide prohibition on road construction in inventoried roadless areas.

We disagree. We think that defendant-intervenors are correct in arguing that any inclusion of alternatives that allowed road construction outside of the few exceptions allowed in the Roadless Rule would be inconsistent with the Forest Service's policy objective in promulgating the Rule. That objective, as described by the Forest Service itself in the FEIS was to "prohibit[ ] activities that have the greatest likelihood of degrading desirable characteristics of inventoried roadless areas and [to] ensure that ecological and social characteristics of inventoried roadless areas are identified and evaluated through local land management planning efforts." The Forest Service defined these values as, among other things, undisturbed landscapes, sources of water, biological diversity, protection against invasive species, and educational opportunities.

The district court also paid no heed to other interests asserted by intervenors such as FSEEE which, through its declarants, pointed out that there were inadequate funds available to maintain with safety existing Forest Service roads. The Roadless Rule ban would help ensure that adequate resources were available to keep existing roads in roaded areas safe. Stated another way, budget and safety considerations were offered by Forest Service to justify the Roadless Rule, in addition to the compelling environmental, conservation and wilderness values asserted by declarants and by Forest Service.

The district court's opinion, in our view, gives inadequate weight to analysis of the conservation and environmental values supporting the Rule and of the budgetary and safety considerations pertinent to it. All these values are worthy and they deserve consideration. As explained in the Final Rule, roadless areas contribute to the health of the public because they help preserve the forest system's watersheds, the rivers, streams, lakes, and wetlands that "are the circulatory system of ecosystems, and water is the vital fluid for inhabitants of these ecosystems, including people." The roadless areas also provide "important habitat for a variety of terrestrial and aquatic wildlife and plants, including hundreds of threatened, endangered, and sensitive species." Roadless areas in our national forests also help conserve some of the last unspoiled wilderness in our country. The unspoiled forest provides not only sheltering shade for the visitor and sustenance for its diverse wildlife but also pure water and fresh oxygen for humankind. In contrast, road construction and reconstruction facilitates forest management by timber harvest and possibly aiding fire prevention, but it is to a degree inimical to conservation. Given the importance of roadless lands as a resource and the ease with which they may be irretrievably damaged, and the amount of forest land already crossed by roads that facilitate active management of vast acreages, a near total ban on further road construction in the remaining and precious roadless areas within our national forests is not the drastic measure that the plaintiffs make it out to be. In contrast to the development of roads sought by plaintiffs, which may inevitably and finally alter the character of developed forest land, the Roadless Rule is benign in that it can be undone so that any development that has been forestalled under the rule may be resumed, or limited development may proceed under the exceptions it contemplates.

The Forest Service was not required under NEPA to consider alternatives in the DEIS and FEIS that were inconsistent with its basic policy objectives. Although plaintiffs are correct that the Forest Service could not "define its objectives in unreasonably narrow terms," there is no indication that it did so here. Protecting the roadless areas of our national forests from further degradation can hardly be termed unreasonably narrow. Moreover, given that the conservation and preventative goals of the Forest Service in promulgating the

Roadless Rule are entirely consistent with the policy objectives of NEPA,[26] as well as with the Forest Service's own mission, it would turn NEPA on its head to interpret the statute to require that the Forest Service conduct in-depth analyses of environmentally damaging alternatives that are inconsistent with the Forest Service's conservation policy objectives. While NEPA's procedural safeguards may be used to benefit those who assert development interests, just as the safeguards may be used to benefit those who assert conservation interests, NEPA's policy objectives must not be thwarted in the process.

As the case law and the statute itself reflect, the policy of NEPA is first and foremost to protect the natural environment. NEPA may not be used to preclude lawful conservation measures by the Forest Service and to force federal agencies, in contravention of their own policy objectives, to develop and degrade scarce environmental resources. The Forest Service, as steward of our priceless national forests, is in the best position, after hearing from the

---

26. NEPA's policy objectives are set forth in 42 U.S.C. §4331, which provides in pertinent part:

(a) Creation and maintenance of conditions under which man and nature can exist in productive harmony. The Congress, recognizing the profound impact of man's activity on the interrelations of all components of the natural environment, particularly the profound influences of population growth, high-density urbanization, industrial expansion, resource exploitation, and new and expanding technological advances and recognizing further the critical importance of restoring and maintaining environmental quality to the overall welfare and development of man, declares that it is the continuing policy of the Federal Government, in cooperation with State and local governments, and other concerned public and private organizations, to use all practicable means and measures, including financial and technical assistance, in a manner calculated to foster and promote the general welfare, to create and maintain conditions under which man and nature can exist in productive harmony, and fulfill the social, economic, and other requirements of present and future generations of Americans.

(b) Continuing responsibility of Federal Government to use all practicable means to improve and coordinate Federal plans, functions, programs, and resources. In order to carry out the policy set forth in this chapter, it is the continuing responsibility of the Federal Government to use all practicable means, consistent with other essential considerations of national policy, to improve and coordinate Federal plans, functions, programs, and resources to the end that the Nation may —

(1) fulfill the responsibilities of each generation as trustee of the environment for succeeding generations;

(2) assure for all Americans safe, healthful, productive, and esthetically and culturally pleasing surroundings;

(3) attain the widest range of beneficial uses of the environment without degradation, risk to health or safety, or other undesirable and unintended consequences;

(4) preserve important historic, cultural, and natural aspects of our national heritage, and maintain, wherever possible, an environment which supports diversity and variety of individual choice;

(5) achieve a balance between population and resource use which will permit high standards of living and a wide sharing of life's amenities; and

(6) enhance the quality of renewable resources and approach the maximum attainable recycling of depletable resources.

public, to assess whether current roads adequately aid forest management practices and whether a general ban on new roads in roadless areas of national forest serves appropriate conservation and budgetary interests.

The district court held that the Forest Service did not consider in the DEIS and FEIS less prohibitive restrictions that could have both protected roadless area values *and* permitted road construction that allowed for more active forest management. We conclude that this finding is clearly erroneous. The Forest Service's consideration of the three alternatives was adequate, and the selection of the preferred alternative does not appear to have been predetermined. Moreover, having considered additional alternatives in a preliminary manner, the Forest Service could reasonably conclude that only a near total ban on road construction in roadless areas could satisfy its policy objectives.

. . .

VII

. . .

. . . Because of its incorrect legal conclusion on prospects of success, the district court proceeded on an incorrect legal premise, applied the wrong standard for injunction, and abused its discretion in issuing a preliminary injunction.

REVERSED AND REMANDED for proceedings consistent with this opinion.

KLEINFELD, Circuit Judge, concurring in part and dissenting in part.

. . .

B. *The Preliminary Injunction*

. . .

The majority correctly notes that the Forest Service must consider alternatives to the proposed rule under NEPA, and appropriately recognizes that the regulations demand the Service produce a statement that "rigorously explores and objectively evaluates all reasonable alternatives." The majority notes the stated objective of the Service was to "prohibit[ ] activities that have the greatest likelihood of degrading desirable characteristics of inventoried roadless areas." The so-called action "alternatives" offered by the Forest Service were: 1) ban road construction and repair but allow timber harvesting, 2) ban road construction and repair but allow timber harvesting only for stewardship purposes, and 3) ban road construction and repair and all timber harvesting. These "alternatives" differ only in how they handle timber harvesting; all of them ban road construction. They omit the obvious alternative of *not* banning road construction and repair. Thus the agency failed, as the district court found and the agency concedes, to give a "hard look" at all the alternatives.

The majority defends the "alternatives" offered by the Service on the ground that to offer other alternatives would have been "inconsistent" with the policy objectives of the Service. That contention is belied by the majority's own characterization of the Service's objective as preventing degradation of roadless areas. There are innumerable alternatives that would have met this objective. To name a few: allowing road construction with limits on density, allowing construction of roads made of certain materials only, or limiting use of the roads to low-emission vehicles. We have held previously, "The existence of a viable but unexamined alternative renders an environmental impact statement inadequate. An agency's consideration of alternatives is adequate if it considers an appropriate range of alternatives, even if it does not consider every available alternative." The alternatives in this case do not meet that standard, and the alternatives requirement is "the heart of the environmental impact statement." The majority writes as if the stated objective were banning roads in roadless areas. Such was not the case, and could not be the case under circuit precedent. Roads may be necessary to protect the forests and those who have property affected by them from avoidable destruction by fire, insects, and disease.

The majority claims "The NEPA alternatives requirement must be interpreted less stringently when the proposed agency action has a primary and central purpose to conserve and protect the natural environment, rather than to harm it." No citation of authority for this proposition is provided. It makes no sense. The national forests were established to provide a source of timber and to protect the flow of water. "National forests [at their creation] were not to be reserved for aesthetic, environmental, recreational, or wildlife-preservation purposes." They are not the same as wilderness areas, and the national forests are not "natural environments." They've been a managed rather than a natural environment for a hundred years. For most of that time they were managed to serve as a federal tree farm, supplying timber as a renewable resource. It also makes no sense to assume, as the majority opinion does, that roadlessness will "conserve and protect" the forests. The plaintiffs submitted evidence that roadlessness may promote forest fires, insect infestation, and disease.

. . .

The Roadless Rule does not preserve the status quo. It changes it, massively, for two percent of the entire land area of the United States. And by increasing the risk of forest fires, it threatens additional land and people, such as the Kootenai Tribe and the people of Idaho who brought this suit.

What we have here is a case where the agency attempted a massive management change for two percent of the nation's land on the eve of an election, and shoved it through without the "hard look" NEPA required, as the district court so found and the agency itself now acknowledges. The majority says, "No, it was a good enough look," but the agency prefers to take a harder look at all the alternatives. To the extent that policy preferences, for pristine wilderness, or fire suppression, or logging, or recreation, or anything else, bear on the issue, the elected organs of government ought to balance those interests. There is no justification for abandoning our precedents on intervention in NEPA actions in order to prevent the government from taking a harder look at a massive policy change.

NOTES ON THE ROADLESS AREA CASES

1. *Consistency.* Is the range of alternatives narrower in *Block* than in *Kootenai*? How does the *Kootenai* court justify accepting such a narrow range of alternatives? A federal district court subsequently issued an opinion at odds with the Ninth Circuit's view that the range of alternatives in the Clinton rule was adequate. *See* Wyoming v. United States Dep't Agric., 277 F. Supp. 2d 1197, 1222-26 (D. Wyo. 2003), *vacated as moot*, 414 F.3d 1207 (10th Cir. 2005).

2. *Range of alternatives.* Since studying every alternative is not possible, how should government agencies select the range of alternatives to focus on? Should a federal agency consider an alternative that only a state agency could implement? *See* 40 C.F.R. §1502.14(c) (requiring consideration of alternatives not within the jurisdiction of the lead agency). Should the agency only study alternatives that meet agency objectives? *See* Robert L. Glicksman, *Traveling in Opposite Directions: Roadless Area Management Under the Clinton and Bush Administrations,* 34 Envtl. L. 1143, 1188 (2004). Should it consider alternatives that would be illegal to implement? *Cf.* Southwest Center for Biological Diversity v. Bureau of Reclamation, 143 F.3d 515 (9th Cir. 1998) (upholding Bureau of Reclamation decision under the Endangered Species Act not to consider alternatives prohibited by applicable law governing management of the Colorado River). When an agency is considering constructing a dam as a source of hydropower, should it limit its choices to alternative sites for the dam, or should it also consider alternative designs at the same site? Other sources of energy?

3. *Agency discretion as to purpose.* The *Kootenai* majority justifies allowing the Clinton administration to consider a narrow group of alternatives, in part, on the grounds that the Forest Service need not consider alternatives "inconsistent with its basic policy objectives." *Kootenai*, 313 F.3d at 1121. On the other hand, the majority concedes that the Forest Service "could not 'define its objective in unreasonably narrow terms.'" *Id.* Why doesn't this characterization of the law on how agency purposes can limit the range of alternatives lead the dissent to agree with the majority?

In *Kootenai*, the Forest Service, according to the majority, defined its objective as "protecting roadless areas . . . from further degradation." *Id.* at 1122. Does this selection of purpose stack the deck against alternatives that involve leaving some roadless areas outside of wilderness areas? Is this appropriate? In Citizens Against Burlington, Inc. v. Busey, 938 F.2d 190 (D.C. Cir. 1991), then Judge (now Supreme Court Justice) Thomas rejected a citizen group's argument that the Federal Aviation Administration needed to consider alternative locations for an airport expansion, even though the proposed expansion was near a public park. He relied heavily on the FAA's narrow definition of its purposes:

> The FAA's reasoning fully supports its decision to evaluate only the preferred and do-nothing alternatives. The agency first examined Congress's views on how this country is to build its civilian airports. As the agency explained, Congress has told the FAA to nurture aspiring cargo hubs. At the same time, however, Congress has also said that the free market, not an ersatz Gosplan for aviation, should determine the siting of the nation's airports. Congress has expressed its intent by statute, and the FAA took both of Congress's messages seriously.
>
> The FAA also took into account the Port Authority's reasons for wanting a cargo hub in Toledo. In recent years, more than fifty major companies have left the Toledo metropolitan area, and with them, over seven thousand jobs. The Port Authority expects the cargo hub at Toledo Express to create immediately more than two hundred permanent and six hundred part-time jobs with a total payroll value of more than $10 million. After three years, according to the Port Authority, the hub should create directly more than one thousand permanent jobs at the airport and one hundred and fifty other, airport-related jobs. The University of Toledo estimates that the new Toledo Express will contribute at least $42 million to the local economy after one full year of operation and nearly $68 million per year after three. In addition, the Port Authority expects the expanded airport, and Burlington's presence there, to attract other companies to Toledo. All of those factors, the Port Authority hopes, will lead to a renaissance in the Toledo metropolitan region.
>
> Having thought hard about these appropriate factors, the FAA defined the goal for its action as helping to launch a new cargo hub in Toledo and thereby helping to fuel the Toledo economy. The agency then eliminated from detailed discussion the alternatives that would not accomplish this goal. Each of the different geometric configurations would mean technological problems and extravagant costs. So would plans to route traffic differently at Toledo Express, or to build a hub at one of the other airports in the city of Toledo. None of the airports outside of the Toledo area would serve the purpose of the agency's action. The FAA thus evaluated the environmental impacts of the only proposal that might reasonably accomplish that goal — approving the construction and operation of a cargo hub at Toledo Express. It did so with the thoroughness required by law.
>
> We conclude that the FAA acted reasonably in defining the purpose of its action, in eliminating alternatives that would not achieve it, and in discussing (with the required do-nothing option) the proposal that would. The agency has therefore complied with NEPA.

Busey, 938 F.2d at 197-98. Suppose that the FAA had defined its purpose as supporting airport expansion, rather than as supporting airport expansion at the Toledo site. Would consideration of alternative sites have been consistent with this broader objective? Was it appropriate for the agency to define its objective so narrowly? Judge Buckley, writing in dissent, opined that the

Federal Aviation Administration had impermissibly allowed the primary beneficiary of the airport expansion, a company which had sought to relocate to the Toledo airport from nearby Fort Wayne, to define the limits of its NEPA review. *Id.* at 207.

A Note On Alternatives and Mitigation in the Wetlands and Endangered Species Context

NEPA uses information to stimulate what one might call voluntary standard setting. The agency undertaking NEPA analysis may modify its conduct in order to lessen its action's environmental impact, or choose a less damaging alternative, but NEPA does not require that the agency choose environmentally preferred alternatives or mitigate the impacts of an environmentally destructive federal action. Section 404 of the Clean Water Act, however, does require the federal agencies implementing the dredge and fill program to employ an approach, called sequencing, that mandates use of alternatives and mitigation. Thus, information about the availability of alternatives to a proposal to dredge or fill wetlands or other United States waters and mitigation measures to reduce the impacts of authorized dredging and filling shapes requirements in section 404 permits.

Wetlands, a major focus of the section 404 program, recharge aquifers, filter pollution, help control floods, and provide critical habitat for many plants and animals. In order to preserve wetlands without completely stopping all development where wetlands exist, EPA has historically applied a structured "sequencing" approach to use of mitigation and alternatives:

> In the context of existing wetlands regulation, mitigation generally refers to avoidance, minimization, and compensation. These steps are frequently applied in a sequential manner. First, a party seeking a permit for a project that affects wetlands must demonstrate that the least environmentally damaging alternative will be used. Second, the permit applicant must develop a plan to minimize the environmental harm from any unavoidable impacts. For example, the applicant might minimize the impact of a project by scheduling construction in a manner that would reduce interference with spawning or nesting seasons. Finally, the applicant must compensate for or offset any harm done to wetland functions and values which is not avoided or minimized.

Royal C. Gardner, *Banking on Entrepreneurs: Wetlands, Mitigation Banking, and Takings*, 81 Iowa L. Rev. 527, 535 (1995-96). *See* 40 C.F.R. §230.10. Why does the agency give priority to avoidance of harm, rather than mitigation? Is the requirement that permit applicants employ the least damaging alternative sufficient to meet the statutory goal of avoiding harms to aquatic ecosystems? Is avoidance more likely to achieve this goal than minimization of harm and compensation?

In the 1990s, the federal government adopted a policy of "no-net loss of wetlands." *See* WHITE HOUSE OFFICE ON ENVIRONMENTAL POLICY, PROTECTING AMERICA'S WETLANDS: A FAIR, FLEXIBLE AND EFFECTIVE APPROACH 4 (August 24, 1993); *Memorandum of Agreement Between the Environmental Protection Agency and the Department of the Army Concerning the Determination of Mitigation under the Clean Water Act Section 404(b)(1) Guidelines*, 55 Fed. Reg. 9210, 9211 (March 12, 1990). Does the sequencing approach to mitigation and alternatives adequately serve this no-net-loss goal? Does a shift from a no-loss to a no-net-loss goal have any implications for the appropriateness of sequencing?

Should this mandatory approach to mitigation measures and implementation of alternatives apply more generally to environmentally destructive actions? Should it apply to particular types of activities outside the wetlands context? Or should the federal government avoid mandatory sequencing for wetlands in favor of a system of informed discretion like that used in NEPA? In thinking about this last question, consider that scientists have been alarmed by wetlands loss and consider it a serious ecological problem. On the other hand, the wetlands protection program has been extraordinarily controversial because it can limit all sorts of development projects. For that reason, the administrative agencies have tended to exempt smaller projects from mandatory sequencing. *See* Gardner, *supra*, at 537-39. Indeed, the Army Corps of Engineers, which implements the wetlands program along with EPA, has issued "general permits" that authorize whole classes of activities without requiring any individualized mitigation or consideration of alternatives. When an obligation to employ available alternatives applies, its effect can be malleable:

> By "alternatives" we may mean other locations for the proposed activity, other activities for the proposed location, other activities elsewhere, or even other actors. At the outer edge, an applicant for a waterfront condominium might, alternatively, go open a store in Des Moines. Somewhat closer on the spectrum of reasonableness, most electric utilities could meet demand at less cost by selling insulation rather than nuclear power. Each of these possibilities begs the question: Alternative to what? What is the project for? . . . Every section 404 decision, from the smallest bulkhead to the largest commercial development, turns on these same vexing questions of perspectives.

Oliver A. Houck, *Hard Choices: The Analysis of Alternatives Under Section 404 of the Clean Water Act and Similar Environmental Laws*, 60 U. Colo. L. Rev. 773, 774 (1989).

The Endangered Species Act also employs a concept of mandatory mitigation. Recall that the law as originally enacted prohibited private parties from "taking" an endangered species. But Congress amended the statute in 1982 to authorize the taking of species incidental to "otherwise lawful activity." 16 U.S.C. §1539(a)(1)(B). The United States Fish and Wildlife Service and the National Marine Fisheries Service can only grant an incidental take permit, as the permits authorizing takings are called, if "the applicant will, to the maximum extent practicable, minimize and mitigate the impact of such takings," 16 U.S.C. §1539(a)(2)(B)(ii), and "the taking will not appreciably reduce" the species' "likelihood of survival," 16 U.S.C. §1539(a)(2)(B)(iv).

This provision authorizes habitat conservation plans, such as that used to preserve and enhance the habitat of endangered butterflies near the San Bruno Mountain area south of San Francisco, while authorizing limited development that might otherwise have violated section 9 of the Act. *See* Karen Donovan, *HCPs — Important Tools for Conserving Habitat and Species, in* ENDANGERED SPECIES ACT: LAW, POLICY, AND PERSPECTIVES 321 (DONALD C. BAUR & WM. ROBERT IRVIN eds., 2002). In spite of the introduction of statutory authority to sanction such habitat conservation plans (HCPs) through incidental take permits, the federal government only approved 38 such plans between 1982 and 1994. *Id.* at 326.

The Clinton Administration greatly increased the use of HCPs by introducing a "no surprises" rule that forbids the agency issuing an incidental take permit based on an HCP from adding developmental restrictions later on. *Id.* at 326. Is such a "no surprises rule" good policy? *See* John Kostyack, *Tipping the Balance, in Endangered Species Act, supra,* at 339-358 (arguing that it is not). Is such a policy consistent with section 10(a)(2)(C) of the Act which requires revocation of a permit if the "permittee is not complying with" permit terms? 16 U.S.C. §1539(2)(C). *See* Spirit of the Sage Council v. Norton, 411 F.3d 225 (D.C. Cir. 2005) (dismissing challenge to a district court order suspending the no surprises rule while agency corrects procedural irregularities in its rulemaking).

b. Tiering, Timing and Scope

One of the difficulties that plagued the Forest Service in carrying out Roadless Area Review involved the problem of evaluating such a broad decision. The negative environmental impacts from Roadless Area Review would come from development activities in lands not designated for wilderness. But the Roadless Area Review program has a relatively narrow, albeit important, purpose — to designate some land as wilderness and to leave other lands subject to multiple uses (with some being studied further). Uncertain decisions about how much development to permit in the areas not designated as wilderness would ultimately determine the extent of environmental destruction associated with not preserving particular areas.

This complex process of land use decisions over time raises a question about the appropriate timing and scope of an EIS. Perhaps the agency should wait until it is about to make the concrete permitting decisions that would make the contours of development clear before carrying out an EIS. Perhaps it should carry out project-specific assessment for each timber cut, mining lease, ski development, etc., like the EIS reviewed in the *Methow Valley* case. While this narrows the scope of the action being evaluated and makes the assessment more concrete, it has its own problems. First, while one timber sale (or ski resort, or mining project) might have a limited effect, perhaps all of the timber sales would cumulatively have a serious impact on water resources, wildlife, and the land itself. Project-specific environmental analysis might miss this bigger picture. Another problem involves the practical problem of agency inertia and commitment. Once the Forest Service commits a parcel of land to multiple uses, it probably will not protect it as it would a wilderness. Should the environmental impact of wilderness designations (or, more to the point, multiple use designations) be studied before the agency has made the commitment to fully protect some lands and not others? The programmatic evaluations at issue in *Block* and *Kootanai* respond to this problem by evaluating a broad program-wide decision about the general contours of land use. CEQ regulations counsel the use of tiering to try and carry out environmental analysis prior to "irretrievable commitment of resources," assess cumulative impacts, and properly account for project-specific impacts. Tiering involves using a sequence of program-wide and site-specific studies to properly assess impacts in a timely and informed manner. The following case reviews an agency decision to address the tiering problem.

Kleppe v. Sierra Club
427 U.S. 390 (1976)

Justice Powell delivered the opinion of the Court.

. . .

I

Respondents, several organizations concerned with the environment, brought this suit in July 1973 in the United States District Court for the District of Columbia. The defendants in the suit, petitioners here, were the officials of the Department [of Interior] and other federal agencies responsible for issuing coal leases, approving mining plans, granting rights-of-way, and taking the other actions necessary to enable private companies and public utilities to develop coal reserves on land owned or controlled by the Federal Government. Citing widespread interest in the reserves of a region identified as the "Northern Great Plains region," and an alleged threat from coal-related operations to their members' enjoyment of the region's environment, respondents claimed that the federal officials could not allow further development without preparing a "comprehensive environmental impact statement" under §102(2)(C) on the entire region. They sought declaratory and injunctive relief.

[The District Court granted the government's motion for summary judgment. The court of appeals reversed and enjoined four mining plans in the Powder River Coal Basin.]

II

[An inter-agency task force carried out an "interim" study called the Northern Great Plains Resources Program (NGPRP), which assessed "'the potential social, economic and environmental impacts' from resource development in . . . Montana, Wyoming, South Dakota, North Dakota, and Nebraska."]

In addition, since 1973 the Department has engaged in a complete review of its coal-leasing program for the entire Nation. On February 17 of that year the Secretary announced the review and announced also that during study a "short-term leasing policy" would prevail, under which new leasing would be restricted to narrowly defined circumstances and even then allowed only when an environmental impact statement had been prepared if required under NEPA. The purpose of the program review was to study the environmental impact of the Department's entire range of coal-related activities and to develop a planning system to guide the national leasing program. The impact statement, known as the "Coal Programmatic EIS," went through several drafts before issuing in final form on September 19, 1975 — shortly before the petitions for certiorari were filed in this case. The Coal Programmatic EIS proposed a new leasing program . . . and assessed the prospective environmental impact of the new program as well as the alternatives to it. We have been informed by the parties to this litigation that the Secretary is in the process of implementing the new program.

. . .

III

. . . [NEPA] §102(2)(C) requires an impact statement "in every recommendation or report on proposals for legislation and other major Federal actions significantly affecting the quality of the human environment." Since no one has suggested that petitioners have proposed legislation on respondents' region, the controlling phrase in this section of the Act, for this case, is "major Federal actions." Respondents can prevail only if there has been a report or recommendation on a proposal for major federal action with respect to the Northern Great Plains region. Our statement of the relevant facts shows there has been none; instead, all proposals are for actions of either local or national scope.

The local actions are the decisions by the various petitioners to issue a lease, approve a mining plan, issue a right-of-way permit, or take other action to allow private activity at some point within the region identified by respondents. Several Courts of Appeals have held that an impact statement must be included in the report or recommendation on a proposal for such action if the private activity to be permitted is one "significantly affecting the quality of the human environment" within the meaning of §102(2)(C). The petitioners do not dispute this requirement in this case, and indeed have prepared impact statements on several proposed actions of this type in the Northern Great Plains during the course of this litigation.[10] Similarly, the federal petitioners agreed at oral argument that §102(2)(C) required the Coal Programmatic EIS that was prepared in tandem with the new national coal-leasing program and included as part of the final report on the proposal for adoption of that program. Their admission is well made, for the new leasing program is a coherent plan of national scope, and its adoption surely has significant environmental consequences.

But there is no evidence in the record of an action or a proposal for an action of regional scope. The District Court, in fact, expressly found that there was no existing or proposed plan or program on the part of the Federal Government for the regional development of the area described in respondents' complaint. It found also that . . . the NGPRP — [was] not [part] of any plan or program to develop or encourage development of the Northern Great Plains. That court found no evidence that the individual coal development projects undertaken or proposed by private industry and public utilities in that part of the country are integrated into a plan or otherwise interrelated. These findings were not disturbed by the Court of Appeals, and they remain fully supported by the record in this Court.

Quite apart from the fact that the statutory language requires an impact statement only in the event of a proposed action, respondents' desire for a regional environmental impact statement cannot be met for practical reasons. In the absence of a proposal for a regional plan of development, there is nothing that could be the subject of the analysis envisioned by the statute for an impact statement. Section 102(2)(C) requires that an impact statement contain, in essence a detailed statement of the expected adverse environmental consequences of an action, the resource commitments involved in it, and the alternatives to it.[13] Absent an overall plan for regional development, it is

---

10. In an affidavit submitted in support of the application for a stay of the Court of Appeals' injunction, the Secretary described four impact statements completed by the petitioners on coal-related activity in Montana and Wyoming. One was the multiproject statement on the Powder River Coal Basin that was the subject of that injunction. Another was on the single mining plan subsequently brought under the injunction as modified by the District Court. A third covered one leased tract, and apparently was occasioned by an application for approval of a new mining plan on the tract. The fourth, on another single mining plan, has been the subject of litigation, on the merits of which we intimate no view.

13. Section 102(2)(C) states that the statement must be a detailed statement on —

"(i) the environmental impact of the proposed action,

"(ii) any adverse environmental effects which cannot be avoided should the proposal be implemented,

"(iii) alternatives to the proposed action,

"(iv) the relationship between local short-term uses of man's environment and the maintenance and enhancement of long-term productivity, and

"(v) any irreversible and irretrievable commitments of resources which would be involved in the proposed action should it be implemented."

impossible to predict the level of coal-related activity that will occur in the region identified by respondents, and thus impossible to analyze the environmental consequences and the resource commitments involved in, and the alternatives to, such activity. A regional plan would define fairly precisely the scope and limits of the proposed development of the region. Where no such plan exists, any attempt to produce an impact statement would be little more than a study along the lines of the NGPRP, containing estimates of potential development and attendant environmental consequences. There would be no factual predicate for the production of an environmental impact statement of the type envisioned by NEPA.[14]

IV

A

The Court of Appeals, in reversing the District Court, did not find that there was a regional plan or program for development of the Northern Great Plains region. It accepted all of the District Court's findings of fact, but concluded nevertheless that the petitioners "contemplated" a regional plan or program. . . . It . . . concluded that the interim report of the NGPRP, then expected to be released at any time, would provide the petitioners with the information needed to formulate the regional plan they had been "contemplating." The Court therefore remanded with instructions to the petitioners to inform the District Court of their role in the further development of the region within 30 days after the NGPRP interim report issued; if they decided to control that development, an impact statement would be required.
. . .

Even had the record justified a finding that a regional program was contemplated by the petitioners, the legal conclusion drawn by the Court of Appeals cannot be squared with the Act. The court recognized that the mere "contemplation" of certain action is not sufficient to require an impact statement. But it believed the statute nevertheless empowers a court to require the preparation of an impact statement to begin at some point prior to the formal recommendation or report on a proposal. The Court of Appeals accordingly devised its own four-part "balancing" test for determining when, during the contemplation of a plan or other type of federal action, an agency

14. In contrast, with both an individual coal-related action and the new national coal-leasing program, an agency deals with specific action of known dimensions. With appropriate allowances for the inexactness of all predictive ventures, the agency can analyze the environmental consequences and describe alternatives as envisioned by §102(2)(C). Of course, since the kind of impact statement required depends upon the kind of "'federal action' being taken" the statement on a proposed mining plan or a lease application may bear little resemblance to the statement on the national coal-leasing program. Nevertheless, in each case the bounds of the analysis are defined, which is not the case with coal development in general in the region identified by respondents.

must begin a statement. The factors to be considered were identified as the likelihood and imminence of the program's coming to fruition, the extent to which information is available on the effects of implementing the expected program and on alternatives thereto, the extent to which irretrievable commitments are being made and options precluded "as refinement of the proposal progresses," and the severity of the environmental effects should the action be implemented.

. . .

The Court's reasoning and action find no support in the language or legislative history of NEPA. The statute clearly states when an impact statement is required, and mentions nothing about a balancing of factors. Rather, under the first sentence of §102(2)(C) the moment at which an agency must have a final statement ready "is the time at which it makes a recommendation or report on a proposal for federal action." The procedural duty imposed upon agencies by this section is quite precise, and the role of the courts in enforcing that duty is similarly precise. A court has no authority to depart from the statutory language and, by a balancing of court-devised factors, determine a point during the germination process of a potential proposal at which an impact statement *should be prepared.* Such an assertion of judicial authority would leave the agencies uncertain as to their procedural duties under NEPA, would invite judicial involvement in the day-to-day decisionmaking process of the agencies, and would invite litigation. As the contemplation of a project and the accompanying study thereof do not necessarily result in a proposal for major federal action, it may be assumed that the balancing process devised by the Court of Appeals also would result in the preparation of a good many unnecessary impact statements.[15]

. . .

V

. . . Respondents insist that, even without a comprehensive federal plan for the development of the Northern Great Plains, a "regional" impact statement nevertheless is required on all coal-related projects in the region because they are intimately related.

---

15. This is not to say that §102(2)(C) imposes no duties upon an agency prior to its making a report or recommendation on a proposal for action. The section states that prior to preparing the impact statement the responsible official "shall consult with and obtain the comments of any Federal agency which has jurisdiction by law or special expertise with respect to any environmental impact involved." Thus, the section contemplates a consideration of environmental factors by agencies during the evolution of a report or recommendation on a proposal. But the time at which a court enters the process is when the report or recommendation on the proposal is made, and someone protests either the absence or the adequacy of the final impact statement. This is the point at which an agency's action has reached sufficient maturity to assure that judicial intervention will not hazard unnecessary disruption.

There are two ways to view this contention. First, it amounts to an attack on the sufficiency of the impact statements already prepared by the petitioners on the coal-related projects that they have approved or stand ready to approve. As such, we cannot consider it in this proceeding, for the case was not brought as a challenge to a particular impact statement and there is no impact statement in the record. It also is possible to view the respondents' argument as an attack upon the decision of the petitioners not to prepare one comprehensive impact statement on all proposed projects in the region. This contention properly is before us, for the petitioners have made it clear they do not intend to prepare such a statement.

We begin by stating our general agreement with respondents' basic premise that §102(2)(C) may require a comprehensive impact statement in certain situations where several proposed actions are pending at the same time. NEPA announced a national policy of environmental protection and placed a responsibility upon the Federal Government to further specific environmental goals by "all practicable means, consistent with other essential considerations of national policy." §101(b), 42 U.S.C. §4331(b). Section 102(2)(C) is one of the "action-forcing" provisions intended as a directive to "all agencies to assure consideration of the environmental impact of their actions in decisionmaking." By requiring an impact statement Congress intended to assure such consideration during the development of a proposal or — as in this case — during the formulation of a position on a proposal submitted by private parties. A comprehensive impact statement may be necessary in some cases for an agency to meet this duty. Thus, when several proposals for coal-related actions that will have cumulative or synergistic environmental impact upon a region are pending concurrently before an agency, their environmental consequences must be considered. Only through comprehensive consideration of pending proposals can the agency evaluate different courses of action.

Agreement to this extent with respondents' premise, however, does not require acceptance of their conclusion that all proposed coal-related actions in the Northern Great Plains region are so "related" as to require their analysis in a single comprehensive impact statement. Respondents informed us that the Secretary recently adopted an approach to impact statements on coal-related actions that provides:

> "A. As a general proposition, and as determined by the Secretary, when action is proposed involving coal development such as issuing several coal leases or approving mining plans in the same region, such actions will be covered by a single EIS rather than by multiple statements. In such cases, the region covered will be determined by basin boundaries, drainage areas, areas of common reclamation problems, administrative boundaries, areas of economic interdependence, and other relevant factors."

. . . Thus, the Department has decided to prepare comprehensive impact statements of the type contemplated by §102(2)(C), although it has not deemed it appropriate to prepare such a statement on all proposed actions in the region identified by respondents.

Respondents conceded at oral argument that to prevail they must show that petitioners have acted arbitrarily in refusing to prepare one comprehensive statement on this entire region, and we agree. The determination of the region, if any, with respect to which a comprehensive statement is necessary requires the weighing of a number of relevant factors, including the extent of the interrelationship among proposed actions and practical considerations of feasibility. Resolving these issues requires a high level of technical expertise and is properly left to the informed discretion of the responsible federal agencies. Absent a showing of arbitrary action, we must assume that the agencies have exercised this discretion appropriately. Respondents have made no showing to the contrary.

. . .

In sum, respondents' contention as to the relationships between all proposed coal-related projects in the Northern Great Plains region does not require that petitioners prepare one comprehensive impact statement covering all before proceeding to approve specific pending applications. As we already have determined that there exists no proposal for regionwide action that could require a regional impact statement, the judgment of the Court of Appeals must be reversed, and the judgment of the District Court reinstated and affirmed. The case is remanded for proceedings consistent with this opinion. . . .

JUSTICE MARSHALL, with whom JUSTICE BRENNAN joins, concurring in part and dissenting in part.

While I agree with much of the Court's opinion, I must dissent from Part IV, which holds that the federal courts may not remedy violations of . . . NEPA[] — no matter how blatant — until it is too late for an adequate remedy to be formulated. As the Court today recognizes, NEPA contemplates agency consideration of environmental factors throughout the decisionmaking process.

Since NEPA's enactment, however, litigation has been brought primarily at the end of that process — challenging agency decisions to act made without adequate environmental impact statements or without any statements at all. In such situations, the courts have had to content themselves with the largely unsatisfactory remedy of enjoining the proposed federal action and ordering the preparation of an adequate impact statement. This remedy is insufficient because, except by deterrence, it does nothing to further early consideration of environmental factors. . . .

NOTES ON *KLEPPE*, CUMULATIVE IMPACTS, AND TIERING

1. *Cumulative impacts.* CEQ regulations generally require consideration of cumulative impacts. Mandelker, *supra,* at §10.42. In considering why such consideration might be important, consider Professor Houck's comments about wetland permitting decisions:

> Each of the some ten thousand permit applications processed each year is a localized event, taking one-half acre, three acres, twenty-one acres of wetlands, for this pier, that channel, a sand and gravel pit, or a building site. The indirect effects of even these individual takings — how much they will pollute, subside, or slowly asphyxiate their surroundings — are uncertain, and in any event will not be witnessed for years. The cumulative effects of these and similar activities — of one more marina on Galveston Bay, of one more logging road on the grizzly bear — may be far greater than the sum of the parts, and are even less susceptible to proof. Even those direct effects are disputable: The oysters may be able to survive a little more turbidity, the pelicans may relocate to another island. Or they may not.

Oliver A. Houck, *Hard Choices: The Analysis of Alternatives under Section 404 of the Clean Water Act and Similar Environmental Laws,* 60 U. Colo. L. Rev. 773, 776 (1989). *See also* 33 U.S.C. §1344(e) (authorizing issuance of "general permits" for activities dredging and filling wetlands, but only when the activities have "minimal cumulative adverse effect on the environment"). Logging, coal mining, oil drilling, and other activities can create serious cumulative impacts, even if each individual instance of the activity appears de minimis. Information will look different, depending on the scale of analysis.

2. *Evaluating Kleppe.* Is the Court's decision consistent with the requirement to consider cumulative impacts? Does the Department of Interior address concerns about regional impacts adequately through its planning process?

3. *No national EIS.* Suppose that the Department of the Interior had not prepared a national EIS. Should it then prepare an EIS like that requested here?

4. *When might a regional EIS be advisable?* The decision does not say a lot about the contents of any of the environmental analyses prepared so far by the Department. Suppose that the national EIS said very little about the particular environmental effects on rivers in the Northern Great Plains, and that the agency's remaining environmental analysis was site specific (*i.e.*, not regional), each considering the effect of a single coal lease in isolation. Should the agency then prepare a regional analysis?

5. *Agency action.* Suppose that the agency had sent copies of the NGPRP to each federal manager responsible for coal leasing in the Northern Great Plains with instructions to minimize the environmental impacts identified as serious in the statement where practicable. Should this communication trigger a requirement for a regional impact statement?

6. *Scale.* Should the Department of the Interior make a regional decision about how much coal mining to allow? If so, how large should the region be, and how should it be defined?

7. *Action forcing.* Under *Kleppe*, must an agency modify regional or national plans causing a serious cumulative impact?

8. *When should cumulative impacts be considered?* Section 404(e) of the Clean Water Act authorizes "general permits . . . for any category of activities involving discharges of dredged or fill material if the Secretary determines that the activities will cause only minimal adverse environmental effects when performed separately, and will have only minimal cumulative adverse effect on the environment. . . . " 42 U.S.C. §1344(e). The Army Corps of Engineers issued a nationwide permit for "Discharges of dredged or fill materials associated with coal mining." The Army Corps did not claim that this entire category of activities invariably had a minimal impact. But it imposed a general condition on the nationwide permit, requiring a determination by an Army Corps District Engineer that adverse environmental effects are minimal, both individually and cumulatively, before the permit could be used. Environmental groups opposing mountaintop removal as a coal-mining technique challenged this permit and a district court invalidated it:

> The fundamental problem with the Corps' approach is that NWP 21 defines a procedure instead of permitting a category of activities. Section 404(e) of the Clean Water Act directs the Corps to determine that certain activities will invariably have only minimal effects on the environment. The statute unambiguously requires determination of minimal impact before, not after, the issuance of a nationwide permit. The issuance of a nationwide permit thus functions as a guarantee *ab initio* that every instance of the permitted activity will meet the minimal impact standard. Congress intended for a potential discharger whose project fits into one of those categories to begin discharging with no further involvement from the Corps, no uncertainty, and no red tape. In issuing NWP 21, however, the Corps did not define activities that will invariably have only minimal effects; rather, NWP 21 provides for a *post hoc*, case-by-case evaluation of environmental impact. It therefore runs afoul of the statutory requirement of initial certainty. By combining features of both individual and general permitting in NWP 21, the Corps allows an activity with the potential to have significant effects on the environment to be permitted without being subject to public notice and comment or the other procedural hurdles to authorization pursuant to Section 404(a) [which governs individual permits].

Ohio Valley Environmental Coalition v. Bulen, 315 F. Supp. 2d 821 (S.D. W. Va. 2004) (granting a preliminary injunction), *aff'd*, 410 F. Supp. 2d 450 (S.D. W. Va. 2004), *vacated* 429 F.3d 493 (4th Cir. 2005). The District Court initially invalidated this "general permit" because the Corps circumvented public notice and comment requirements. But will there be any differences in the information considered if District Engineers assess cumulative impacts each time a permit is issued instead of doing it once on a nationwide basis? Do you expect headquarters or District Engineers to be better at assessing the impacts of the individual activity or cumulative impacts, respectively?

c. Mitigating Environmental Injustice and Cumulative Impacts

A grass roots environmental justice movement grew up in the 1980s to address the general problem of disproportionate pollution burdens in communities of color. *See* LUKE COLE AND SHEILA FOSTER, FROM THE GROUND UP: ENVIRONMENTAL RACISM AND THE RISE OF THE ENVIRONMENTAL JUSTICE MOVEMENT (2001). This movement led a number of scholars and institutions to study the siting of industrial facilities. A number of studies found that government officials often sited hazardous waste treatment facilities and other polluting plants in communities of color. *See* CLIFFORD RECHTSCHAFFEN AND EILEEN GUANA, ENVIRONMENTAL JUSTICE: LAW, POLICY, AND REGULATION 55-76 (2002) (reviewing this claim and critiques of it). The cumulative impacts of these facilities might well subject communities of color to disproportionate health impacts.

In 1994, President Clinton signed an Executive Order requiring federal agencies to take environmental justice concerns into account. E.O. 12898. Since then, federal agencies have struggled with the question of how to address these concerns. The environmental justice movement has a keen interest in public participation, so that efforts by agencies to enhance effective participation of people of color in decisions about facilities in their communities can address some of the movement's concerns. But this still leaves a question about how information about disproportionate cumulative impacts should influence siting decisions and other decisions going forward.

The Council on Environmental Quality issued guidance on incorporating environmental justice concerns into NEPA. The memorandum makes the following statements regarding mitigation and the consideration of alternatives:

Council of Environmental Quality, Guidance Under the National Environmental Policy Act
(December 10, 1997), available at http://www.whitehouse.gov/CEQ.

* * *

. . . Mitigation measures identified as part of an environmental assessment (EA), a finding of significant impact (FONSI), and environmental impact statement (EIS), or a record of decision (ROD) should, whenever feasible, address significant and adverse environmental effects of proposed federal actions on minority populations, and Indian tribes.
. . .

. . . When the agency has identified a disproportionately high and adverse human health or environmental effect on low-income populations, minority populations, or Indian tribes from either the proposed action or alternatives, the distribution as well as the magnitude of the disproportionate impacts in these communities should be a factor in determining the environmentally preferable alternative. In weighing this factor, the agency should consider the views it has received from the affected communities, and the magnitude of environmental impacts associated with alternatives that have a less disproportionate and adverse effect on low-income populations, minority populations, or Indian tribes.

. . .

_____

This memorandum also urges specific measures to enhance community participation and analysis of cumulative impacts on communities. *See id.* at 10-15.

Compare this approach to that of the Department of Transportation, which manages highway projects and other projects contributing air pollution to minority communities:

Department of Transportation (DOT) Order To Address Environmental Justice in Minority Populations and Low-Income Populations
62 Fed. Reg. 18377 (April 15, 1997)

* * *

8. Actions To Address Disproportionately High and Adverse Effects.

. . .

c. The Operating Administrators and other responsible DOT officials will ensure that any of their respective programs, policies or activities that will have a disproportionately high and adverse effect on minority populations or low-income populations will only be carried out if further mitigation measures or alternatives that would avoid or reduce the disproportionately high and adverse effect are not practicable. In determining whether a mitigation measure or an alternative is "practicable," the social, economic (including costs) and environmental effects of avoiding or mitigating the adverse effects will be taken into account.

d. Operating Administrators and other responsible DOT officials will also ensure that any of their respective programs, policies or activities that will have a disproportionately high and adverse effect on populations protected by Title VI ("protected populations") will only be carried out if:

(1) a substantial need for the program, policy or activity exists, based on the overall public interest; and

(2) alternatives that would have less adverse effects on protected populations (and that still satisfy the need identified in subparagraph (1) above), either (i) would have other adverse social, economic, environmental or human health impacts that are more severe, or (ii) would involve increased costs of extraordinary magnitude.

How do these two approaches differ? Which is better?

Section 3004(o)(7) of the Resources Conservation and Recovery Act requires EPA to "specify criteria for the acceptable location of new and existing treatment, storage, or disposal facilities, as necessary to protect human health and the environment." 42 U.S.C. §6924(o)(7). Should these criteria prohibit siting hazardous waste treatment facilities in communities of color suffering disproportionate cumulative impacts? *See generally* Richard J. Lazarus and Stephanie Tai, *Integrating Environmental Justice into EPA Permitting Authority*, 26 Ecology L.Q. 617, 642-47 (1999) (discussing various RCRA provisions, including section 3004(o)(7) and the potential to use them to address cumulative impacts raising justice concerns).

d. NEPA's Record

Scholars vary in their assessment of NEPA. A very detailed review of NEPA's impact on the Army Corps of Engineers and the United States Forest Service reached this conclusion:

Before the National Environmental Policy Act, most federal agencies paid scant attention to environmental values. . . . [W]hen []inside analysts are able to explore the possible environment–development trade-offs of a wide range of alternative designs, environmentally better decisions are likely to result: all projects benefitted from relatively inexpensive environmental mitigation. When, in addition, environmentally concerned outsiders pay attention to the EIS process, some of the worst projects — those projects with the great environmental costs and little political support within the agency and among its other constituencies — get eliminated.

SERGE TAYLOR, MAKING BUREAUCRACIES THINK: THE ENVIRONMENTAL IMPACT STATEMENT STRATEGY OF ADMINISTRATIVE REFORM 251 (1984). Other analysts have been more skeptical. One of NEPA's architects, Lynton Keith Caldwell, has criticized decisions like *Methow Valley* for having abandoned a serious effort to realize substantive environmental goals through NEPA. *See* LYNTON KEITH CALDWELL, THE NATIONAL ENVIRONMENTAL POLICY ACT (1998).

A 1997 assessment by the Council of Environmental Quality, which oversees NEPA implementation generally, reached the following conclusions:

> Overall, . . . NEPA is a success — it has made agencies take a hard look at the potential environmental consequences of their actions, and it has brought the public into the agency decision-making process like no other statute. . . .
>
> Despite these successes, however, NEPA's implementation at times has fallen short of its goals. For example, . . . agencies may sometimes confuse the purpose of NEPA. Some act as if the detailed statement called for in the statute is an end in itself, rather than a tool to enhance and improve decision-making. As a consequence, the exercise can be one of producing a document to no specific end. But NEPA is supposed to be about good decision-making — not endless documentation.
>
> The Study finds that agencies sometimes engage in consultation only after a decision has — for all practical purposes — been made. In such instances, other agencies and the public at large believe that their concerns have not been heard. As a result, they may find themselves opposing even worthy proposed actions. This may in turn lead to agencies seeking "litigation-proof" documents, increasing costs and time but not necessarily quality. In such cases, potential cost savings are also lost because a full range of alternatives has not been adequately examined. Other matters of concern to participants in the Study were the length of NEPA processes, the extensive detail of NEPA analyses, and the sometimes confusing overlay of other laws and regulations.

COUNCIL ON ENVIRONMENTAL QUALITY, THE NATIONAL ENVIRONMENTAL POLICY ACT: A STUDY OF ITS EFFECTIVENESS AFTER TWENTY-FIVE YEARS iii (1997).

2. TSCA Testing Requirements and Other Provisions Informing Pollution Control Decisions

You have seen that NEPA generates information about government decisions to take actions significantly affecting the environment, such as decisions about the management of federal lands. The Toxic Substances Control Act (TSCA) seeks information to guide government decisions about regulating pollution. As you read the information request below, ask yourself how the information requested might be useful in regulating PFOA and its salts:

*Perfluorooctanoic Acid (PFOA), Fluorinated
Telomers; Request for Comment, Solicitation of
Interested Parties for Enforceable Consent
Agreement Development, and Notice of Public
Meeting*
68 Fed. Reg. 18626, 18632 (April 16, 2003)

* * *

IV.   Specific Requests for Comments, Data, and Information

EPA specifically requests comments, data, and information on the following topics.

A.   *Use and Production Volume Information*

What are the specific chemical identities (by Ninth Collective Index name and CAS No., if available) of the telomer chemicals, including polymers derived from these telomers, and of the fluoropolymers and fluoroelastomers made with PFOA or related chemicals, currently in commerce? In what volumes and at what locations are these chemicals manufactured or imported? How and in what volumes are these chemicals used? What are the benefits of these chemicals and products in their specific uses, and what alternatives to these chemicals may be available for specific uses?

B.   *Exposure Information*

How are products containing the chemicals identified in Unit IV.A. used? How are these products disposed of? What environmental releases occur at manufacturing and processing facilities where these chemicals are used? What data are available on worker exposures to these chemicals? What data are available on exposures to the general population? What data are available on measured levels of these chemicals in humans and the environment, in all environmental media? What data are available on the biodegradation of these chemicals, on releases of these chemicals from consumer and industrial products, and on their breakdown during product biodegradation, incineration, and other disposal practices?

C.   *Monitoring and Related Information*

EPA specifically requests that any persons who have in their possession existing human or environmental monitoring data indicating or assessing the presence of PFOA and related fluorochemicals in humans, in wildlife, or in any environmental media, including studies conducted in other countries, provide those data to the Agency in response to the publication of this notice to enhance the understanding of PFOA presence in the environment and of the pathways leading to exposures. EPA includes in this request any existing data not otherwise provided to EPA concerning the toxicity, pharmacokinetics, and half-life of PFOA in organisms.

D.   Additional Data

Are there other pieces of information not addressed . . . that would help EPA more accurately assess the risks of these chemicals and determine appropriate further action, if warranted?

NOTES AND QUESTIONS ON THE PFOA
INFORMATION REQUEST

1. *Use under section 6.* How would EPA use the information requested to justify a rule limiting exposure to PFOA and its salts under section 6 of the Toxic Substances Control Act, which authorizes EPA to ban chemicals or take other actions reducing their environmental impact? (Recall *Corrosion Proof Fittings.*)

2. *Use to choose a media-specific statute.* Which, if any information requested here, might help EPA figure out whether to use TSCA section 6 or some other federal statute (*e.g.*, the Clean Air, Act or the Clean Water Act) to regulate this problem?

3. *Voluntary testing.* As the title of this Federal Register notice suggests, this notice does not propose a test rule, but instead seeks voluntary consent decrees about the development of additional information. *See id.* at 18628, 18632.

Section 4 of TSCA authorizes EPA to develop test rules, requiring companies to develop basic toxicity data about individual chemicals or mixtures. In promulgating TSCA in 1976, Congress declared a policy that chemical manufacturers and processors should develop "adequate data with respect to the effect of chemical substances and mixtures on health and the environment." 15 U.S.C. §2601(b)(1).

Information produced under section 4 can inform decisions about regulation of toxic chemicals under both section 6 of TSCA and under the media-specific statutes, such as the Clean Air Act, the Clean Water Act, the Resources Conservation and Recovery Act (land disposal primarily), and the Comprehensive Environmental Response, Compensation and Liability Act (clean-up of existing hazardous waste sites). Thus, section 4 can produce information to inform pollution control decisions, just as NEPA generates and organizes information useful in federal natural resources decision-making.

More than 20 years after TSCA's enactment, an industry study concluded that we lack even elementary toxicity screening data for the overwhelming majority of high volume chemicals in commerce in the United States. *See* ICF KAISER INTERNATIONAL, PUBLIC AVAILABILITY OF SIDS-RELATED TESTING DATA FOR

U.S. HIGH PRODUCTION CHEMICALS (1998). The National Academy of Sciences, EPA, and environmental groups have reached similar conclusions. *See* U.S. EPA, OFFICE OF POLLUTION PREVENTION AND TOXICS, CHEMICAL HAZARD DATA AVAILABILITY STUDY: WHAT DO WE REALLY KNOW ABOUT THE SAFETY OF HIGH PRODUCTION VOLUME CHEMICALS? 2 (1998) (no basic toxicity information is available for 43 percent of high volume chemicals and a full basic set of information exists for only 7 percent); ENVIRONMENTAL DEFENSE FUND, TOXIC IGNORANCE: THE CONTINUING ABSENCE OF BASIC HEALTH TESTING FOR TOP-SELLING CHEMICALS IN THE UNITED STATES 3 (1997) (basic toxicity results cannot be found in the public record for 75 percent of the top volume chemicals in commercial use); NATIONAL RESEARCH COUNCIL, TOXICITY TESTING: STRATEGIES TO DETERMINE NEEDS AND PRIORITIES 1 (1984).

EPA has not promulgated nearly enough test rules to realize the statutory objective of providing adequate information about health and environmental effects. As of early 2005, EPA had promulgated test rules addressing 120 chemicals and published decisions not to test another 250. Lynn L. Bergeson, Lisa M. Campbell, and Carla N. Hutton, *TSCA, Chemical Testing Issues*, 35 Envtl. L. Rep. (Envtl. L. Inst.) 10085, 10087 (2005). These rulemaking actions did not even consider test rules for most of the 2,800 high production chemicals in commercial use in the United States. *See* ENVIRONMENTAL DEFENSE, FACING THE CHALLENGE: A STATUS REPORT ON THE U.S. HPV CHALLENGE PROGRAM 2 (2003) (noting that industry has identified nearly 3,000 high volume chemicals, 90 percent of which lacked sufficient screening data). EPA officials have reported that the "lengthy and costly rule-making process" has led the agency to eschew greater reliance on test rules.

Industry has generally resisted test rules, and, often, the disclosure of information it possesses. EPA has made some limited progress through voluntary testing rules, often negotiated in lieu of a mandatory testing rule, like the PFOA request above. Why do you suppose that industry resists producing and generating information? Consider TSCA section 4(a):

(a) Testing requirements
If the Administrator finds that —
(1)(A)(i) the manufacture, distribution in commerce, processing, use, or disposal of a chemical substance or mixture, or that any combination of such activities, may present an unreasonable risk of injury to health or the environment,
(ii) there are insufficient data and experience upon which the effects of such manufacture, distribution in commerce, processing, use, or disposal of such substance or mixture or of any combination of such activities on health or the environment can reasonably be determined or predicted, and
(iii) testing of such substance or mixture with respect to such effects is necessary to develop such data; or

(B)(i) a chemical substance or mixture is or will be produced in substantial quantities, and (I) it enters or may reasonably be anticipated to enter the environment in substantial quantities or (II) there is or may be significant or substantial human exposure to such substance or mixture,

    (ii) there are insufficient data and experience upon which the effects of the manufacture, distribution in commerce, processing, use, or disposal of such substance or mixture or of any combination of such activities on health or the environment can reasonably be determined or predicted, and

    (iii) testing of such substance or mixture with respect to such effects is necessary to develop such data; . . .

the Administrator shall by rule require that testing be conducted on such substance or mixture to develop data with respect to the health and environmental effects for which there is an insufficiency of data and experience and which are relevant to a determination that the manufacture, distribution in commerce, processing, use, or disposal of such substance or mixture, or that any combination of such activities, does or does not present an unreasonable risk of injury to health or the environment.

15 U.S.C. §2603(a). Another provision of the statute authorizes judicial review and requires that the agency provide "substantial evidence" to support a testing rule. 15 U.S.C. §2628(c)(1)(B)(i). Given that the purpose of a testing rule is to require generation of data when data is either non-existent or inadequate, does this provision offer a sensible trigger to testing requirements? Would it be better to just require a finding that the chemical poses a significant risk, much like the NEPA finding that a proposed action will have a significant effect on the environment?

TSCA also requires "Premanufacture Notices" for new chemicals. But these notices have revealed very little toxicity data. Mary L. Lyndon, *Information Economics and Chemical Toxicity: Designing Laws to Produce and Use Data*, 87 Mich. L. Rev. 1795, 1823-24 (1989).

What legal reforms might address the failure to promulgate test rules? *See* John S. Applegate, *The Perils of Unreasonable Risk: Information, Regulatory Policy and Toxic Substances Control*, 91 Colum. L. Rev. 261, 318-30 (1991) (proposing amendments to TSCA). *See generally* Wendy A. Wagner, *Commons Ignorance: The Failure of Environmental Law to Produce Needed Information on Health and the Environment*, 53 Duke L.J. 1619 (2004). Other statutes also provide authority to gather information needed for regulatory processes. *See, e.g.,* 7 U.S.C. §136a(c)(1)(F) (authorizing testing requirements for new pesticides). A National Toxicology Program in the Department of Health and Human Services coordinates federal toxicity research. And the Comprehensive Environmental Response, Compensation, and Liability Act maintains a Toxic Substances Disease Registry to manage data related to hazardous waste sites.

Given the enormity of the challenge, failure should hardly be surprising. EPA estimates that approximately 87,000 chemicals should be tested for their potential to disrupt the endocrine system, which regulates the body through the production of hormones. *See* Valerie J. Watnick, *Our Toxics Regulatory System and Why Risk Assessment Does Not Work: Endocrine Disrupting Chemicals as a Case in Point,* 2004 Utah L. Rev. 1305, 1308-1310. And this is just one of the many health issues toxic chemicals raise. We develop new chemicals daily, thus compounding this problem. *Id.* Ideally, we should have comprehensive information about these chemicals' potential effects, including information about their potential to cause cancer, birth defects, immune system disorders, neurological problems, etc. But obtaining this information involves costly tests that can never fully resolve the uncertainties surrounding a chemical's likely effects on humans.

While EPA has authority to promulgate test rules and companies have the duty to submit pre-manufacturing notices for new chemicals, TSCA also requires companies to disclose the results of their own tests and other information. Section 8(e) provides:

> Any person who manufactures, processes, or distributes in commerce a chemical substance or mixture and who obtains information which reasonably supports the conclusion that such substance or mixture presents a substantial risk of injury to health or the environmental shall immediately inform [EPA]. . . .

15 U.S.C. §2607(e).

Imagine that you represent DuPont, a maker of PFOA. Your company decides to study the effects of PFOA on its pregnant workers. That study generates the following document, which reports the parts per million (PPM) of C-8 (which is another name for PFOA) found in the blood of pregnant workers at its plant, and in some cases, of their babies (see p.375).

Would you recommend that your client disclose this information to EPA under TSCA section 8(e)? Suppose that EPA asks DuPont to provide "known toxicological information" regarding PFOA to EPA. *See* Order Denying Motions for Accelerated Decision on Counts II and III, *In the matter of E.I. du Pont de Nemours and Company,* at 43, TSCA-HQ-2004-0016, RCRA-HQ-2004-0016, TSCA-HQ-2005-5001. Is the company obligated to disclose this document in response to this request, assuming that EPA has adequate statutory authority to make it?

The researcher who conducted this study proposed that DuPont do a detailed study to determine if exposure to C8 caused birth defects. DuPont officials declined to do so. *DuPont Proposed, Dropped '81 Study of C8, Birth Defects,* The Charleston Gazette (July 10, 2005), available at http://www.wvgazette.com/webtools/print/News/2005070930.

```
                          Personal & Confidential
                          C-8 Blood Sampling Results

     Births and Pregnancies

        Current (v)
     PPM C-8
     in Blood                                    Status
     (April 1981)

        0.45          Normal child - born June 1980.
                      Transferred out of Fluorocarbons 4/79.

        0.28          Normal child - born April 1981.

        0.078         Normal child - born April 1981.
                      Umbilical cord blood 0.055 ppm.

        1.5           Five months pregnant. On pregnancy leave

        0.013         Five months pregnant. Normal child - born August 1

        2.5*          Child - 2 plus years.
                      Unconfirmed eye and tear duct defect.

        0.048         Child - 4 months.
                      One nostril and eye defect.
                      Babies blood 0.012ppm

        <.007         Normal child - born July 1981

     *Current blood level - in fluorocarbons area only one month
      before pregnancy.
```

B. INFORMATION MOTIVATING PRIVATE ACTION

Just as information generated and disclosed under NEPA or TSCA can inform and motivate government action, information can sometimes motivate private parties to protect the environment. The following materials examine this use of information as a means of "regulation."

1. Community Right to Know

The Community Right to Know Act requires factories emitting large amount of certain hazardous pollutants to report their releases of certain hazardous chemicals to land, air, and, water. EPA compiles this information in a toxic release inventory (TRI), which is available to the public.

The media often uses this information to report on the releases of the most egregious polluters or to compare pollution levels in different regions.

This compilation, however, has some limitations. First, it only applies to very large industrial polluters, mostly chemical plants. Second, it only applies to a fraction of the chemicals that may pose risks of serious illness, like cancer. Third, it gives polluters great flexibility in choosing how they measure or estimate emissions. This flexibility has led to frequent revisions of pollution estimates and means that the data are not as reliable as data generated through carefully chosen protocols.

On the other hand, just creating this information had a much greater effect than some observers predicted. The large emissions many facilities discovered when they actually looked surprised the managers of the corporations owning the facilities and alarmed the public and regulators in some cases. These discoveries led many facilities to voluntarily reduce their emissions. *See* Bradley Karkkainen, *Information as Environmental Regulation: TRI and Performance Benchmarking, Precursor to a New Paradigm?*, 89 Georgetown L.J. 257, 297 (2001). This information also helped motivate state governments and the United States to regulate hazardous air pollutants more broadly.

Are reductions in response to TRI wholly voluntary? Consider the following allegations made by Citizens for a Better Environment in a case seeking penalties and injunctive relief for a company's failure to report TRI data:

The complaint contains claims "on behalf of both [respondent] itself and its members." It describes respondent as an organization that seeks, uses, and acquires data reported under. [The Emergency Planning and Community Right to Know Act] EPCRA. It says that respondent "reports to its members and the public about storage and releases of toxic chemicals into the environment, advocates changes in environmental regulations and statutes, prepares reports for its members and the public, seeks the reduction of toxic chemicals and further seeks to promote the effective enforcement of environmental laws." The complaint asserts that respondent's "right to know about [toxic chemical] releases and its interests in protecting and improving the environment and the health of its members have been, are being, and will be adversely affected by [petitioner's] actions in failing to provide timely and required information under EPCRA." The complaint also alleges that respondent's members, who live in or frequent the area near petitioner's facility, use the EPRCA-reported information "to learn about toxic chemical releases, the use of hazardous substances in their communities, to plan emergency preparedness in the event of accidents, and to attempt to reduce the toxic chemicals in areas in which they live, work and visit." The members' "safety, health, recreational, economic, aesthetic and environmental interests" in the information, it is claimed, "have been, are being, and will be adversely affected by [petitioner's] actions in failing to file timely and required reports under EPCRA."

Steel Company v. Citizens for a Better Environment, 523 U.S. 83, 104-05 (1998). How can the Citizens group use this information to "attempt to reduce" releases of "toxic chemicals"?

2. Proposition 65 and Labeling

California's voters passed an initiative, called Proposition 65, requiring producers to affix a warning label to products containing carcinogens or reproductive toxins. *See generally* Clifford Rechtschaffen, *The Warning Game: Evaluating Warnings Under California's Proposition 65*, 23 Ecology L.Q. 303 (1996). Many producers decided that they would prefer reformulating their products to announcing, in effect, that their products threatened to cause cancer or harm unborn children, or to paying fines for non-compliance with Proposition 65. *Id.* at 341-47.

3. Radon

Indoor air pollution can expose residents to radiation when radon is present. Several states have addressed this problem by requiring measurement and disclosure of radon levels prior to a real estate sale. Many sellers and purchasers act to reduce radon levels voluntarily when confronted with the information. Is this an example of an economic incentive program? Why would a seller reduce radon levels? Why would the buyer?

4. Green Lights

Many investments in energy efficiency pay for themselves over time. For example, one can reduce use of electricity in a building by using energy-efficient light bulbs and adding insulation. While the insulation and the light bulbs have a cost, installation reduces the electricity bill, so that, after a while, the cost savings more than make up for the cost of the installation. Reductions in energy use reduce the pollutants associated with electricity generation. EPA has a Green Lights program to show businesses how to improve their energy efficiency and to convince them that it pays to do so. This program has motivated measures to increase energy efficiency. The budget for the program, however, limits the amount of people EPA can hire to spread the word. Is there any need for a government program to show companies profitable opportunities to improve the environment? Why wouldn't companies just adopt these measures on their own?

5. Certification Regimes

Various private groups have created management standards of various kinds that may prompt environmental measures. The chemical industry runs a "Responsible Care" program, which encourages "best environmental management practices" aimed at "continuous improvement" in pollution prevention.

Karkkainen, *supra*, at 305-306. The International Organization for Standard-
ization's ISO 14000 environmental management program offers another
example of an obligation to establish certain management processes. Industry
runs these programs. The Forest Stewardship Council's Well-Managed Forests
Program, however, has some environmental representation. Environmentalists
have been eager to secure voluntary commitments to more sustainable forestry,
because they regard governments as ineffectual in protecting forests around
the world. These voluntary programs tend to impose fairly weak inchoate
obligations on their members. Fulfillment of these obligations entitles producers to put labels on their products advising consumers that they have met the
voluntary standards. These obligations, even though often weak, still have
some potential to lead to positive change. While some risk exists that firms will
duck even mild obligations when they prove inconvenient, purchasers of
products, including businesses, may demand compliance with these voluntary
standards, so that some improvements may result. In part because of some of
the possibilities of informal enforcement, one commentator has argued that
these programs "may amount to a form of non-governmental law making." *See*
Errol Meidinger, *"Private" Environmental Regulation, Human Rights, and
Community,* 7 Buff. Envtl. L.J. 123, 236 (2000).

6. Some Theoretical Perspectives on Information-Based Regimes

How much potential do these approaches have to motivate voluntary
action? Should we use voluntary information generation mechanisms to
supplement standard setting or as a substitute? While voluntary regimes have
sometimes motivated cost saving pollution prevention measures, they have not
generated a whole lot of changes that have significant costs associated with
them. Switches to low emission vehicles, significant efforts to limit power plant
emission rates, and phase-outs of ozone depleting chemicals all came about as
a result of regulation.

Notice that Proposition 65 works by playing on industry fears about
possible consumer responses to toxic substances. Douglas Kysar explicitly
defends the value of consumers taking environmental values into account in
making purchasing decisions, linking it with an old progressive tradition of
taking social values into account in making purchasing decisions. Douglas A.
Kysar, *Preferences for Processes: The Process/Product Distinction and the Regulation of Consumer Choice,* 118 Harv. L. Rev. 525, 579-640 (2004). On the
other hand, will consumers, acting as consumers, prove as socially conscious as
citizens acting through political processes? *See* Mark Sagoff, The Economy of
The Earth: Philosophy, Law, and The Environment (1988).

Consider the problem of agricultural use of pesticides. These pesticides
play a significant role in increasing water pollution and many of them are toxic.

Environmentalists have long argued that organic agriculture offers an environ-mentally attractive alternative. Should EPA consider the possibility of organic agriculture in deciding, as a regulatory matter, whether to ban a particular pesticide? What if organic agriculture is cleaner, but more expensive? Should that matter? Regardless of what EPA should do, we know that it has historically done very little to limit pesticide use under FIFRA.

The United States Department of Agriculture (USDA) recently issued a rule setting a standard for labeling food as "organic." At one point during the rule making, the USDA proposed standards that allowed food made with genetically modified ingredients to be labeled organic. This proposal elicited a storm of protest. The USDA ultimately issued a rule that conformed fairly closely to consumers' concepts of organic practice. Organic food has been a growth industry as of late. What does this say about the potential of informa-tion regimes?

Firms producing genetically modified organisms (GMOs) have argued that GMOs offer a good alternative to agricultural practices based on large doses of pesticides. It is possible to engineer the DNA of plants to produce strains that require less use of pesticides. Some believe that GMOs may threaten biological diversity, *i.e.*, that they might crowd out native species. They have also created some concerns regarding allergies. On the other hand, some analysts regard the use of GMOs as much safer than traditional pesticide-based agriculture. The USDA has taken the position that GMOs are indistin-guishable from ordinary crops from a food safety standpoint. For that reason, it has rejected labeling of food made with GMOs. Europe, on the other hand, has required labeling. Which approach is correct? *See* Kysar, *supra*, at 590 (arguing that the concept of consumer sovereignty should lead to the use of a label). Should government choose between GMOs, pesticide-based agricul-ture, and organic agriculture, or should it provide consumers with information as the predominant approach?

Consider the following:

> While the basic idea of informing consumers about environmental impacts is straightforward, the task of educating the public is daunting. The environmental impacts of consumer product choices are manifold and complex. Most signifi-cantly, consumers have little basis for assessing these impacts when choosing among the myriad products on retail shelves or making other daily choices. Even the most diligent consumer cannot accurately assess the environmental effects caused by the extraction of raw materials, production, and transportation of the product before it reaches the store shelf and any subsequent impacts from usage and ultimate disposal. Comparing these impacts across a range of products within a particular category multiplies the problem.

Peter Menell, *Environmental Federalism: Structuring a Market-Oriented Federal Eco-Information Policy*, 54 Md. L. Rev. 1435, 1436 (1995).

What about the potential to use information to investors as a strategy? An international Global Reporting Initiative is underway to create company

reports about sustainability. See http://www.globalreporting.org/about/
brief.asp. While the United Nations Environment Program has supported it, it
has evolved into a private multi-stakeholder effort to develop reporting guidelines and encourage their adoption. Will private investors use information
about carbon dioxide reductions, for example, to inform their decisions? What
about institutional investors, like pension funds and insurance companies? The
problem below explores issues associated with informing investors further as a
strategy.

PFOA PROBLEM: SEC DISCLOSURE

The Securities and Exchange Commission (SEC) requires companies to
report risks material to their finances to the SEC and to private investors. *See* 15
U.S.C. §§78l,78o(d). The following appeared in 3M Company's Form
10k disclosure form for fiscal year 2004:

Environmental Matters and Litigation . . .

Remediation: Under certain environmental laws, including the United
States Comprehensive Environmental Response, Compensation and Liability
Act of 1980 . . . , the Company may be jointly and severally liable, typically with
other companies, for the costs of environmental contamination it current or
former facilities . . . . The Company has identified numerous sites . . . at which it
may have some liability.

Regulatory Activities: The Company has been voluntarily cooperating
with ongoing reviews by local, state, national (primarily the . . . EPA), and
international agencies of possible environmental and health effects of perfluor-
coctanyl compounds (perfluorooctanic acid or "PFOA" and perfluorooctane
sulfonate or "PFOS"). As a result of its phase-out decision in May 2000, the
Company no longer manufactures perflurooctanyl compounds except that a
subsidiary recycles PFOA for its manufacturing operations.

The previously disclosed EPA consent order negotiating process to obtain
additional information to enable EPA to further develop a human health risk
assessment and identify routes of exposure concerning PFOA is in progress. The
EPA signed a Memorandum of Understanding with the Company and Dyneon
LLC, a subsidiary of the Company, on October 25, 2004, under which the
Company is monitoring at and around the Company's manufacturing facility in
Decatur, Alabama the potential presence of PFOA.

On January 12, 2005, the EPA issued a draft risk assessment for
PFOA and submitted it for review to a Science Advisory Board that the EPA
empaneled. The EPA document expresses the EPA's preliminary assessment in

terms of the margin of exposure between the levels of that compound that cause adverse health effects in laboratory animals and the levels found in human blood sera in the U.S. population. . . .

The Company, in cooperation with local and state agencies, tested ground-water beneath two former waste disposal sites in Washington County, Minnesota, used many years ago by the Company to dispose of waste containing perfluo-rooctanyl compounds. The test results show that water from municipal wells near the former disposal sites contain low levels of . . . PFOS and PFOA that the Minnesota Department of Health does not currently consider to pose a health risk. Additional testing will be conducted. . . .

Litigation: A purported class action lawsuit involving perfluorooctanyl chemistry that originally was filed in 2002 against the Company by a former employee remains pending. The lawsuit seeks unstated compensatory and puni-tive damages and alleges that plaintiffs suffered fear, increased risk, and sub clinical injuries from exposure to perfluorooctanyl chemistry at or near the Company's Decatur, Alabama, manufacturing facility. The complaint also alleges that the Company acted improperly with respect to disclosures to workers concerning such chemistry. The Company is awaiting a decision from the court on the Company's motion to dismiss the complaint. . . . On February 3, 2005, the judge granted the Company's motion to abate the case, effectively putting the case on hold pending the outcome of the class certification decision in the action. . . .

NOTES ABOUT 3M's FORM 10k DISCLOSURE

1. *Adequacy.* Do you believe that this statement adequately informs potential investors about 3M's potential financial risks from PFOA and PFOS? *See generally* Mitchell F. Crusto, *Endangered Green Reports: "Cumulative Materiality" in Corporate Environmental Disclosure After Sarbanes-Oxley,* 42 Harv.
J.Legis. 483, 493-500 (2005) (explaining that disclosure has not been robust, but that stakeholder demand for better environmental disclosure has in-creased); Gov't Accountability Office, Environmental Disclosure: SEC Should Explore Ways to Improve Tracking and Transparency of Information (GAO-04-808, July, 2004); Mitchell F. Crusto, *Green Business: Should We Revoke Corporate Charters for Environmental Violations,* 63 La. L. Rev. 175, 226-34 (2003) (reviewing the history of SEC guidance on environmental disclosures). If you were 3M's attorney, what, if any changes, would you recommend in the disclosure statement?

2. *Phase-out decision.* Note that 3M has decided to phase out manufacture and use of PFOA and PFOS. What motivations could explain this decision? Do you think that the requirement to disclose potential liability under the Securi-ties and Exchange Act of 1934 might have played a role?

3. *Buy?* Suppose that you were an investor satisfied that purchasing shares in 3M made sense, apart from its environmental liabilities. Would the company's decision to phase out PFOA and PFOS influence your decision about whether to invest? Would the environmental liabilities disclosed in this statement with respect to PFOA and PFOS dissuade you from purchasing the stock?

4. *Incentives provided.* While 3M decided to phase out PFOA and PFOS, Dupont still makes these compounds. Do the SEC disclosure requirements provide substantial incentives to improve environmental performance? Should the SEC require disclosure of general progress in reducing use of hazardous chemicals?

5. *Comparison with other information requirements.* Would requiring a label about the potential dangers of PFOA on teflon cookware prove more effective than SEC disclosure at encouraging measures reducing human exposure? Would such a disclosure be appropriate if PFOA is used to manufacture teflon, but is not present in the teflon coating itself? If a label is to be included, what should it say?

6. *Negotiated agreement on PFOA.* Dupont and seven other manufacturers have agreed to a 95 percent reduction in PFOA by 2010 and to work with EPA toward the "elimination" of PFOA by 2015. If the companies implement the agreement by substituting other chemicals for PFOA, that would constitute an example of "pollution prevention," a technique we consider in the next chapter.

11
Moving Upstream: Pollution Prevention and Recycling

Traditional regulation often, but not always, encouraged polluters to install end-of-the-pipe technologies, *i.e.*, devices that reduce pollution by treating a waste stream to change its chemical composition or to concentrate contaminants into a form that can be disposed of elsewhere. The performance standard encouraging use of scrubbers encountered in Chapter 9 offers an example of this sort of regulation. You have already seen several examples of how traditional regulation, emissions trading, and information-based approaches encourage pollution prevention, *i.e.*, changing the inputs into a process, the way something is produced, or the thing or service being produced to reduce or eliminate pollution. For example, EPA attempted to ban asbestos in order to avoid pollution in any other medium, but the judicial reversal in *Corrosion Proof Fittings* thwarted EPA's ban. EPA had, however, controlled asbestos pollution in particular media, as illustrated by the requirement to wet down asbestos in *Adamo Wrecking*. While performance standards limiting pollution in particular media often lead to end-of-the-pipe controls, polluters sometimes have responded with process changes designed to lower compliance costs or seize other benefits. *See* Kurt Strasser, *Cleaner Technology, Pollution Prevention, and Environmental Regulation*, 9 Fordham Envtl. L.J. 1, 28-32 (1997). The acid rain trading program encouraged electric utilities to burn low sulfur coal, which produces less sulfur dioxide emissions than burning high sulfur coal. And the TRI program encouraged a number of efforts to eliminate the use of some toxic substances in production processes.

Pollution prevention offers a number of advantages. It often proves cheaper than end-of-the-pipe controls. Indeed, sometimes pollution prevention measures save money, for example, when less toxic feedstocks cost less than the toxic feedstocks being replaced. Pollution prevention's cost-saving potential helps explain why polluters adopt pollution prevention measures voluntarily, *i.e.*, without extensive regulation. And pollution prevention can eliminate or reduce releases to all environmental media (air, land, water). By

387

contrast, end-of-the-pipe controls sometimes reduce pollution in one medium, but create additional pollution in another. *Cf.* City of Chicago v. Environmental Defense Fund, 511 U.S. 328, 330 (1994) (explaining that incineration of municipal waste produces an ash that may be hazardous, but was disposed of in landfills).

Congress specifically recognized the value of pollution prevention in the Pollution Prevention Act of 1990:

42 U.S.C. §13101. Findings and policy

(a) **Findings — The Congress finds that**:

(1) The United States of America annually produces millions of tons of pollution and spends tens of billions of dollars per year controlling this pollution.

(2) There are significant opportunities for industry to reduce or prevent pollution at the source through cost-effective changes in production, operation, and raw materials use. Such changes offer industry substantial savings in reduced raw material, pollution control, and liability costs as well as help protect the environment and reduce risks to worker health and safety.

(3) The opportunities for source reduction are often not realized because existing regulations, and the industrial resources they require for compliance, focus upon treatment and disposal, rather than source reduction; existing regulations do not emphasize multi-media management of pollution; and businesses need information and technical assistance to overcome institutional barriers to the adoption of source reduction practices.

(4) Source reduction is fundamentally different and more desirable than waste management and pollution control. The Environmental Protection Agency needs to address the historical lack of attention to source reduction.

(5) As a first step in preventing pollution through source reduction, the Environmental Protection Agency must establish a source reduction program which collects and disseminates information, provides financial assistance to States, and implements the other activities provided for in this chapter.

(b) **Policy** — The Congress hereby declares it to be the national policy of the United States that pollution should be prevented or reduced at the source whenever feasible; pollution that cannot be prevented should be recycled in an environmentally safe manner, whenever feasible; pollution that cannot be prevented or recycled should be treated in an environmentally safe manner whenever feasible; and disposal or other release into the environment should be employed only as a last resort and should be conducted in an environmentally safe manner.

§13102. Definitions

For purposes of this chapter —

. . .

(5)(A) The term "source reduction" means any practice which —

(i) reduces the amount of any hazardous substance, pollutant, or contaminant . . . prior to recycling, treatment, or disposal; and

(ii) reduces the hazards to public health and the environment associated associated with . . . such substances, pollutants, or contaminants. The term includes equipment or technology modifications, reformulation or redesign of products, substitution of raw materials, and improvements in housekeeping, maintenance, training, or inventory control.

(B) The term "source reduction" does not include any practice which alters the physical, chemical, or biological characteristics or the volume of a hazardous substance, pollutant, or contaminant through a process or activity which itself is not integral to and necessary for the production of a product or the providing of a service.

---

1. *Recycling and Prevention.* Suppose DuPont abandoned use of perfluorooctanic acid (PFOA) in making teflon coatings for its pans and substituted a less toxic substance. Would that involve pollution prevention or recycling? Suppose that Dupont offered to take back used pans and developed a process to reclaim teflon coatings. It then used the reclaimed material to coat new pans. Is this an example of pollution prevention or recycling?

2. *Hierarchy of Preferred Approaches.* What might justify the congressional preference for pollution prevention or reduction over recycling? What might justify the preference for recycling over treatment?

3. *How to Encourage Pollution Prevention.* While regulators often wish to promote pollution prevention, they face some difficulties in incorporating that approach into routine standard setting. While process changes can save money and create environmental benefits, mature industries worry that new approaches might compromise the performance or other characteristics of their products. Thus, California regulators ran into fierce industry resistance when they sought to require cars to meet emission limits that would require radical redesign of automobiles. It can be difficult for regulators to evaluate claims that significant changes in what is manufactured or how something is manufactured will compromise performance. Moreover, Congress has expressed a reluctance to allow federal bureaucrats to intrude too intensively into actual industrial production decisions, *i.e.*, to give them authority to dictate what will be produced, and how.

Pollution prevention advocates often suggest multimedia rulemaking. EPA has experimented with such rulemakings. For example, EPA considered air and water pollution regulatory requirements together in regulating the pulp and paper industry. In this case, there was a fairly obvious way of eliminating a significant water pollution problem and limiting most air pollutants of concern, by eliminating the use of chlorine in paper manufacturing. Chlorine bleaching makes paper whiter, but produces dioxins and other toxic pollutants. Some companies, however, have made paper without using chlorine. Industry argued that meeting effluent and air pollution limitations based on the capabilities of chlorine-free processing would prove infeasible, cost too much, and produce an inferior product. Does a multi-media rulemaking procedure provide any aid in evaluating these claims? Does it make adoption of a good pollution prevention option more likely (assuming that this option is good)?

We have already seen that information-based approaches encourage pollution prevention. These approaches do not require regulators to intrude deeply into industry decision-making, because the industry can voluntarily choose how to respond to the information. Regulation, however, can play a role in encouraging pollution prevention. The following materials consider how regulation of solid waste has addressed both pollution prevention and recycling.

A. THE RCRA SCHEME

As mentioned in Chapter 1, Americans produce more than 229 million tons of municipal solid waste per year, approximately 4.4 pounds per person per day. This waste includes paper (more than 35 percent of the total), yard trimmings, food scraps, plastics, metals, rubber, leather, textiles, glass, and wood. In addition, industrial facilities in 2001 generated more than 40 million tons of hazardous waste.

Congress passed the Resources Conservation and Recovery Act (RCRA), Pub. L. 94-580, 90 Stat. 2795, in 1976, amending the Solid Waste Disposal Act, codified currently at 42 U.S.C. §§6901-6992k, to address the problem of improper disposal of this vast river of waste. RCRA responded to prevalent practices of simply dumping wastes on the ground. Congress saw RCRA's regulation of land disposal as filling the gap left when it regulated air emissions through the Clean Air Act Amendments of 1970 and effluent discharges through the Federal Water Pollution Control Act of 1972. The end-of-pipe controls used to meet air and water pollution control requirements often resulted in waste "sludges," concentrated forms of the pollutants that formerly were emitted into air or water, which then might cause problems when disposed in or on land. RCRA generally authorizes EPA regulation of "solid waste," a broad term that includes both hazardous and non-hazardous waste (in solid, liquid, and even gaseous forms). See 42 U.S.C. §6903(27). Paper, for example, is considered non-hazardous solid waste. But many toxic chemicals are considered hazardous solid waste, at least when disposed of. RCRA establishes two core programs. Subtitle D of RCRA regulates municipal solid waste by establishing guidelines for municipal solid waste disposal programs, which primarily manage non-hazardous waste. *But see City of Chicago*, 511 U.S. at 332-334 (explaining that RCRA establishes a "household waste exclusion" that exempts hazardous waste generated by households from subtitle C, thereby allowing municipal treatment of some hazardous waste). This program, for example, did away with open dumping, requiring that municipalities line their landfills and conform to other practices designed to limit leaching of waste into groundwater and surface water. Subtitle C regulates industrial hazardous waste management. Both of these programs have an objective of encouraging source reduction and recycling. *See* 42 U.S.C. §6902(a)(6).

Subtitle C establishes a "cradle to grave" system to manage hazardous waste. Chemical Waste Management v. Hunt, 504 U.S. 334, 337 n.1 (1992). The Act employs a manifest system to track and assure proper disposal of hazardous waste. Generators and transporters of hazardous waste must employ a document called a manifest to track it and assure that it ends up at a proper treatment facility. *See* 42 U.S.C. §§6922(a)(5), 6923(a)(3). RCRA then imposes detailed obligations on facilities authorized to treat, store, or dispose of hazardous waste, called Treatment, Storage, and Disposal Facilities (TSDFs):

> TSDFs . . . are subject to much more stringent regulation than either generators or transporters, including a 4-to-5 year permitting process, burdensome financial assurance requirements, stringent design and location standards, and, perhaps most onerous of all, responsibility to take corrective action for releases of hazardous substances and to ensure safe closure of each facility, see 42 U.S.C. §6924; 40 CFR pt. 264 (1993).

City of Chicago, 511 U.S. at 332.

Notice that this system does not authorize EPA to require manufacturing facilities not engaged in treatment, storage, or disposal to engage in either source reduction or recycling. RCRA does, however, require generators of hazardous waste to certify in the manifest that they have a program to reduce the amount and toxicity of waste "to the degree determined by the generator to be economically practicable." *See* 42 U.S.C. §6922(b)(1). The tracking and treatment system creates some additional incentives for manufacturing facilities to practice source reduction. Because treatment at TSDF facilities can prove expensive and facilities generating waste must carefully track their hazardous waste, generators like to avoid having their waste designated as hazardous waste. RCRA has motivated significant pollution prevention. One of the easiest ways of avoiding TSDF treatment and the tracking obligation involves simply avoiding the generation of hazardous waste in the first place. *See* Mark H. Dorfman et al., Environmental Dividends: Cutting More Chemical Wastes, 44-45 (1992) (citing "problems and cost associated with waste disposal" as "the most frequently mentioned reason for implementing source reduction activities").

Some Key RCRA Provisions

Subtitle A	General Provisions	
	42 U.S.C. §6901	Congressional Findings
	42 U.S.C. §6902	Objectives and National Policy
	42 U.S.C. §6903	Definitions
	Subsection (3)	Disposal
	Subsection (5)	Hazardous Waste
	Subsection (27)	Solid Waste
	Subsection (34)	Treatment

Subtitle C[1]	Hazardous Waste Management	
	42 U.S.C. §6921	Listing and Identification of Hazardous Waste
	42 U.S.C. §6922	Manifest (and other) Requirements for Hazardous Waste Generators
	42 U.S.C. §6923	Manifest (and other) Requirements for Hazardous Waste Transporters
	42 U.S.C. §6924	TSDF Requirements
	Subsection (a)	Performance Standards[2]
	Subsections (d)-(m)	Land Ban
	Subsection (t)	Financial Assurance
	Subsections (u),(v)	Corrective Action
	42 U.S.C. §6925	TSDF Permits

Subtitle D	State or Regional Solid Waste Plans	
	42 U.S.C. §6944	Criteria for Sanitary Landfills
	42 U.S.C. §6945	Prohibition on Open Dumping

1. Practitioners use lettered subtitles to refer to parts of RCRA, which correspond to the divisions found in Pub. L. No. 94-580, 90 Stat. 2795 (1976). As codified in the United States Code, however, subtitle C becomes subchapter III and subtitle D becomes subchapter IV.

2. The term "performance standard" in this statutory context is broader than the term performance standard as a term of art distinguishing work practice from performance standards, including treatment standards, 42 U.S.C. §6924(a)(3), and recordkeeping and reporting requirements, 42 U.S.C. §6924 (a)(1), (2).

Does imposing stricter cleanup standards for municipal landfills provide comparable incentives for source reduction? Will homeowners carry cloth bags to grocery stores (thereby minimizing use of plastic bags), because landfill disposal costs have gone up? Does the answer to this question depend upon who pays the disposal costs? Would it matter whether the municipality funds disposal from municipal taxes, from dedicated fees that are assessed equally to every household, or from a fee that varied with the amount of trash put out by a household? A major question under RCRA involves how EPA should address recycling. EPA declined to mandate local solid waste management goals for particular materials. But EPA set a voluntary recycling and source reduction goal of 25 percent, which most states met by 1992. EPA, 25 YEARS OF RCRA: BUILDING ON OUR PAST TO PROTECT OUR FUTURE 8 (2001). Some municipalities have done better than 25 percent and some worse. If the agency is convinced that all municipalities can reduce waste by 30%, should it mandate such a goal through regulations? In practice, municipal policy has a big effect on recycling and source reduction. Local governments establish recycling programs. Germany, by contrast, requires manufacturers to take back packaging material or contract for its proper disposal. Does this provide a better incentive for pollution prevention? What about deposit/refund systems, where consumers get money back when they return bottles to the grocery store?

B. THE SOLID WASTE DEFINITION AND RECYCLING POLICY

EPA has used fine-grained regulatory definitions of solid waste to address recycling policy. These definitional choices have created a great deal of complexity and controversy. They determine the jurisdictional reach of RCRA's hazardous waste management program and profoundly influence the program's incentives for recycling and proper waste treatment. It is quite common for important policy issues to inform decisions about a program's jurisdictional reach and for interested parties to extensively lawyer these threshold questions.

To understand the recycling policy problem and how it might be addressed, consider a variant on our Teflon problem. Suppose that Dupont decides to avoid using PFOA in its production process by reclaiming and recycling Teflon coatings, rather than produce new coatings. Suppose that these coatings constitute a hazardous waste under RCRA. Suppose further that recycling is considered a form of treatment. It would follow that the Dupont plant reclaiming and recycling Teflon coatings would become a TSDF facility under RCRA. It would then face strict treatment standards and onerous corrective action requirements — requirements that it clean up any waste found on the site. Suppose DuPont did not want the trouble and expense of becoming a TSDF facility. Could it avoid the problem by simply using new PFOA on site, rather than recycling its Teflon products? Is using new PFOA preferrable to recycling Teflon products? What if the recycling process produced more on-site pollution than using new PFOA, because of the stripping process used to remove the coating?

Suppose that EPA wanted to encourage DuPont to recycle by relieving it of TSDF obligations. Read the statutory definition below to determine whether it has authority to do that:

> The term "treatment", when used in connection with hazardous waste, means any method, technique, or process, including neutralization, designed to change the physical, chemical, or biological character or composition of any hazardous waste so as to neutralize such waste or so as to render such waste nonhazardous, safer for transport, amenable for recovery, amenable for storage, or reduced in volume. Such term includes any activity or processing designed to change the physical form or chemical composition of hazardous waste so as to render it nonhazardous.

42 U.S.C. §6903(34).

Read the definition below to determine whether EPA could exempt PFOA from TSDF requirements by declaring it not to be a solid waste:

> The term "solid waste" means any garbage, refuse, sludge from a waste treatment plant, water supply treatment plant, or air pollution control facility and other discarded material, including solid, liquid, semisolid, or contained gaseous material resulting from industrial, commercial, mining, and agricultural operations, and from community activities. . . .

42 U.S.C. §6903(27). If EPA exempts PFOA from the definition of solid waste, then can EPA apply TSDF standards to a DuPont effort to treat this waste that does not involve recycling? Here is how the agency thought about the problem in an early Federal Register notice:

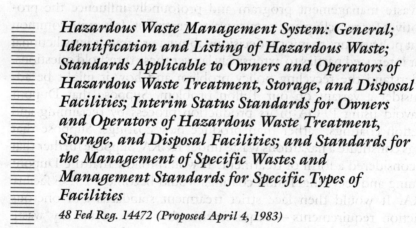

> ### Hazardous Waste Management System: General; Identification and Listing of Hazardous Waste; Standards Applicable to Owners and Operators of Hazardous Waste Treatment, Storage, and Disposal Facilities; Interim Status Standards for Owners and Operators of Hazardous Waste Treatment, Storage, and Disposal Facilities; and Standards for the Management of Specific Wastes and Management Standards for Specific Types of Facilities
>
> *48 Fed. Reg. 14472 (Proposed April 4, 1983)*

In implementing the hazardous waste management subtitle of RCRA, the Agency has found that "recycled" hazardous wastes pose a special problem.

(Throughout this preamble, "recycling" refers generally to using, reusing, or reclaiming a waste. . . . [)]

. . . On one hand, through RCRA, Congress authorized the Agency to regulate hazardous wastes that are being recycled. When improperly managed, such wastes have caused many damage incidents. On the other, RCRA is intended to encourage resource conservation and recovery, and any regulatory regime should take this goal into account to the extent that adequate control of hazardous waste management is not jeopardized. The interim final rules published on May 19, 1980, attempted to meet both of these often conflicting objectives (see 40 CFR 261.2 and 261.6). However, the Agency now believes that this attempt was not completely satisfactory, and accordingly is proposing the revision described in this preamble. . . .

. . .

PART 1: Determining which Materials are Hazardous Wastes when Recycled

I. EPA Has Authority Under RCRA To Regulate Hazardous Wastes That Are Recycled

Because no material can be a "hazardous waste" without first being a "solid waste" (Section 1004(5)), a definition of solid waste is the necessary starting point for the hazardous waste management system. Solid waste is defined in Section 1004(27) of RCRA as:

> any garbage, refuse, sludge from a waste treatment plant, water supply treatment plant, or air pollution control facility and other discarded material, including solid, liquid, semisolid, or contained gaseous material, resulting from industrial, commercial, mining, and agricultural operations, and from community activities

> * * *

This definition does not explicitly state that a material being recycled (or destined for recycling) is a solid waste and, if hazardous, a hazardous waste. However, reading the definition in conjunction with other parts of the statute and with the legislative history (as well as with subsequent expressions of congressional intent) makes it clear that Congress indeed intended that materials being recycled or held for recycling can be wastes and, if hazardous, hazardous wastes.

In this regard, the many statutory definitions dealing with resource recovery are particularly significant. These indicate unequivocally that recycling involves reclaiming material or energy from *"solid waste"*, demonstrating that a material being recycled can be a solid waste within the meaning of Section 1004(27). In addition to this express statutory language, there is already a body of judicial precedent that upholds RCRA hazardous waste jurisdiction over persons engaged in recycling activities (including seventeen cases to date where courts have exercised jurisdiction in actions instituted under Section 7003 of RCRA against recycling facilities). [Section 7003 authorizes abatement of imminent hazards, 42 U.S.C. §6973.]

Not only can materials destined for recycling or being recycled be solid and hazardous wastes, but the Agency clearly has the authority to regulate recycling activities as hazardous management. EPA possesses the authority to regulate under Subtitle C the storage, treatment, and disposal of hazardous waste. Hazardous waste recycling and ancillary activities are within the statutory meanings of these terms. RCRA's legislative history likewise shows that Congress specifically intended Subtitle C regulations to control unsafe recycling of hazardous waste. In any case, it would make little sense to allow that recycled materials can be hazardous wastes under RCRA (as shown in the paragraph above) but then to deny that Congress intended these wastes to be regulated under the Subtitle C regulations.[3]

. . .

Many commenters to the Agency's May 19, 1980 regulations argued that recycled materials cannot be wastes under RCRA, basing their claim largely on the phrase "other discarded material" in the statutory definition (a term nowhere defined in RCRA). They claim that this language means that a material must first be discarded, in the sense of thrown away or abandoned, before it can be a RCRA solid waste.

The Agency disagrees with this reading. It is quite clear from the text of other statutory provisions that recycled materials can be wastes. Perhaps the most pertinent provision is the definition of "hazardous waste management." This term (which is the title of Subtitle C) is defined as "the systematic control of the collection, source separation, storage, transportation, processing, treatment, recovery, and disposal of hazardous waste." (Section 1004(7).) The recycling activities of recovery, source separation (the selection of recyclable from nonrecyclable items), and collection thus can involve hazardous waste.

Equally clear, a whole series of statutory definitions dealing with resource recovery indicate that this activity involves reclaiming material or energy from solid waste, demonstrating again that a material being recycled can be a waste. "Resource recovery" itself means "the recovery of material or energy *from solid waste.*" (Section 1004(22) (emphasis added).) A "resource recovery facility" is "any facility at which solid waste is processed for the purpose of extracting, converting to energy, or otherwise separating and preparing *solid waste* for reuse." (Section 1004(24) (emphasis added).) A "resource recovery system" is a "solid waste management system which provides for collection, separation, recycling, and recovery *of solid wastes,* including disposal of non-recoverable waste residues." (Section 1004(23) (emphasis added).) A "recovered resource" is "material or energy recovered *from solid waste.*" (Section 1004(2)

---

3. [Editors' note: The following three paragraphs come from Appendix A in this proposed rule, 48 Fed. Reg. at 14502, elaborating the legal basis for the conclusions expressed at 48 Fed. Reg. at 14473.]

(emphasis added).) Section 6002(c)(2) speaks of "systems that have the technical capability of using energy or fuels *derived from solid waste.*" See also Sections 1004(18), (28), and (29) all of which likewise presuppose a solid waste from which resources can be recovered. There also are repeated references to resource recovery throughout the statute; these references would be meaningless if solid wastes were never reclaimed or otherwise recycled. *See, e.g.,* Section 1002(c)(2) and (3), 1003(1) and (5)-(8), 2003, 4002(c)(10), 4003(5) and (6), 4008 (a)(2)(A) and (d), 5001, 5002, and 6002 (c)-(g).[4]

. . .

We have concluded that recycled materials can be hazardous wastes under RCRA and can be regulated under the Subtitle C regulations. This conclusions fully agrees with the statute's paramount policy objective; to control the management of hazardous waste from its generation to its final disposition.

II. *The Agency's Strategy In Exercising Its Authority Over Hazardous Wastes That Are Recycled*

To determine that recycled materials can be solid and hazardous wastes does not answer the question of precisely which materials are wastes. Nor does it answer how we are to exercise our authority. We explain in this section the general considerations that shaped our thinking on this question. We also go on to refute the argument that hazardous wastes that are recycled do not require any regulation because they are inherently valuable and do not pose significant environmental risks.

The Agency is convinced that there is a compelling need to exercise the authority granted by Congress. The paramount policy objective of RCRA is to control the management of hazardous waste from point of generation to point of final disposition. Further, wastes destined for recycling can present the same potential for harm as wastes destined for treatment and disposal. That is, in many cases, the risk associated with transporting and storing wastes is unlikely to vary whether the waste ultimately is recycled, treated, or disposed of. Similarly, using or reusing wastes by placing them directly on the land or by burning them for energy recovery may present the same sorts of hazards as actually incinerating or disposing of them.

This is not to say that hazardous waste recycling always must be regulated in the same way as other types of hazardous wastes management. There are certain types of hazardous waste recycling that pose diminished environmental risks, for example, where recycled wastes — because they are valuable — are dealt with much like raw materials.

The Agency also acknowledges the strong statutory policy to encourage recycling, and believes this policy applies even when hazardous wastes are involved. This is especially true when a recycling activity provides a reduced potential for harm. In these situations, the Agency is proposing not to regulate

---

4. [Editors' note: This concludes the excerpt from Appendix A. The following paragraph comes from 48 Fed. Reg. at 14474 and states the position defended in Appendix A.]

particular recycling activities, but to conditionally exempt those recycling activities where existing commercial or marketing incentives appear sufficient to protect against substantial environmental harm. . . . In this way, we avoid regulations that could discourage recycling without significantly increasing overall environmental protection. At the same time, we believe these proposed regulations fulfill the overriding statutory mandate to regulate hazardous waste management as may be necessary to protect human health and the environment.

Some recycling activities pose a much greater potential for harm than others, and we are proposing regulations, or are developing regulatory controls, to guard against these risks. There are three such activities: (1) Those where wastes are recycled in a manner analogous to disposal or incineration; (2) those where wastes are overaccumulated before recycling; and (3) those where recyclers cannot guarantee an end market for their recycled materials — specifically where wastes are regenerated or recovered by reclaimers who did not generate the reclaimed material and are not themselves going to use it. The proposed regulations, for the most part, are targeted at these activities.

Some commenters, however, question whether the Agency should regulate any form of hazardous waste recycling. They maintain that recycled wastes are inherently valuable because they are not being thrown away, and so will not be mishandled. This argument goes much too far. In fact, recycling operations account for some of the most notorious hazardous waste damage incidents — including nearly one-third of the 61 imminent hazard actions filed to date under Section 7003 of RCRA, and 20 of the first 160 interim priority sites listed under the Comprehensive Environmental Response, Compensation, and Liability Act (Superfund). . . . It is important to note that these incidents did not involve sham operators who merely held themselves out as recyclers but in reality disposed of . . . the waste received. Rather, operators of these damage sites engaged in some recycling and meant to recycle the wastes they received.

Facilities that recycle hazardous wastes have caused serious health and environmental problems by directly placing the wastes on the land and by burning the wastes as fuels or burning waste-derived fuels. Improper storage, overaccumulation of inventory, and unsafe transport before recycling have also been recurring problems where the facilities are independent reclaimers — *i.e.,* reclaimers who do not generate the waste and do not use the reclaimed material. The resulting damages include contamination of soil, ground water, surface water, and air. In the case of indiscriminate storage of incompatible wastes (such as oxidizers and flammables, or acids and cyanides) before recycling, fires and explosions have also been a recurring circumstance. In addition, since many of these recyclers have failed to label or otherwise document their incoming materials, later cleanup efforts have been extremely difficult.

. . .

Perhaps the archetypal damage case involving an independent hazardous waste recycler is the incident involving the Chem-Dyne Corporation. Located in Hamilton, Ohio, Chem-Dyne was in the business of obtaining organic wastes and blending them to form "Chem-Fuel", a fuel substitute. Chem-Dyne also engaged in waste reclamation. The company overaccumulated huge amounts of these materials. The site constituted a dangerous fire hazard due to the improper storage of flammable organic materials, and there were in fact a number of fires at the plant. In addition, many of the accumulated drums leaked excessively. As a result, some of the chemical wastes present (including benzene, 1,2-dichloroethane, trichloroethane, and other toxic and carcinogenic wastes) contaminated both surrounding soils and the ground water. Volatilizing toxicants have polluted the air. Surface cleanup costs are estimated at $3.5 million; ground water cleanup costs have not yet been estimated. The company is in receivership.

The cleanup costs for other incidents also are very high. Although reliable cost estimates are not yet generally available for most of the sites, costs at a number of sites already have proven considerable: $30 million for cleanup of the Seymour site; over $1 million at the Midco site for surface cleanup, with an unknown amount needed to complete the cleanup; $2.9 million to date at the Silresim site; and $1.7 million to date at the Ottati and Goss/Great Lakes Container Corp. sites. At the Laskin Greenhouse site, approximately $1.7 million has already been spent; additional work is anticipated. Most of the recyclers involved in these incidents are either bankrupt or have insufficient funds to meet cleanup expenses.

We consequently have determined that some exercise of our authority is necessary to protect human health and the environment. Before explaining how we are proposing to craft these standards, however, we discuss briefly the Agency's current regulations defining which recycled materials are solid wastes, and how these materials are to be regulated.

III.   *The Agency's Existing Definition of Solid Waste*

The key feature of the existing definition of solid waste states that certain materials are always solid wastes, *irrespective of whether they are disposed of or are destined for recycling*. These materials are garbage, refuse, sludge, materials that have served their original intended use and "sometimes (are) discarded," and manufacturing or mining by-products that "sometimes (are) discarded." (See 40 CFR 261.2 (a) and (b); see also the preamble to Part 261, 45 FR, at 33093, May 19, 1980.)

Thus, the existing regulations establish broad jurisdiction over recycled materials and recycling operations, although this is tempered by regulating quite narrowly (see 40 CFR 261.6). There are several problems with this approach.

First, materials within the terms of the existing definition are considered to be solid waste, even if they are being recycled in a manner not ordinarily thought of as waste management. For example, bottom ash from utility boilers (a by-product) being used as an ingredient in concrete is considered to be a solid waste because it is "sometimes discarded". A sludge used similarly also would be a waste because all sludges are defined without exception as solid wastes.

Second, the "sometimes discarded" test sweeps many product-like materials into the solid waste net — unless the material is never thrown away. Although the Agency never intended to call these "legitimate by-products" solid wastes, a zealous but literal reading of the regulation yields this result.

. . .

Commenters . . . argued against regulating materials that are reused or reclaimed by their generator. The generator, they argued, can ensure that such materials are handled safely, because he will have a definite plan to use the materials productively, and can control their disposition. Unrelated parties, by contrast, cannot guarantee a final use or disposition for their reclaimed materials (such as a buyer for their reclaimed solvents) and so are more prone to overaccumulate or mishandle the wastes they take in. This argument finds empirical support in the damage cases, since most known incidents were caused by independent recyclers who accepted secondary materials for reuse or reclamation, rather than by generators accumulating secondary materials for their own reuse (although generators remain capable of overaccumulating these materials).

. . .

. . . [T]he Agency would like to amend the definition of solid waste. We wish to remove materials being reused as ingredients in production processes and product-like sludges and by-products from the solid waste category. We also wish to target the regulations more directly at the class of recycling operations that, so far as we know, present substantial environmental risks. . . .

IV.   *The Proposed Amendment To The Definition of Solid Waste.*

A.   **Changes in Overall Approach Between the Proposed and the Existing Definitions**

The proposed amendment would make several important changes in the definition [of] solid waste. First — and perhaps most fundamental — the amended definition would no longer base a material's status as solid waste on whether it is "sometimes discarded". Instead, a recycled material's regulatory status would depend upon both what the material is and how it actually is managed — and the status could vary with the means of recycling. For example, [an] electroplating wastewater treatment sludge used as an ingredient in a manufacturing process would not be a solid waste, whereas the same sludge being applied directly to the land for land reclamation would be. This change in regulatory approach meets one of the chief criticisms raised in the comments.

Second, we have tailored the accompanying management standards so as to regulate only those recycling activities — or those particular aspects of recycling activities — that pose a significant potential for environmental harm. The principal example is reclamation where this activity is conducted by the generator of the waste, or by a person who subsequently uses the reclaimed material in his own operation.

NOTES ON EPA'S DEFINITION

1. *Goals.* Consider the following goals that Congress established for RCRA:

Objectives and national policy

(a) **Objectives** The objectives of this chapter are to promote the protection of health and the environment and to conserve valuable material and energy resources by —

. . .

(4) assuring that hazardous waste management practices are conducted in a manner which protects human health and the environment;

(5) requiring that hazardous waste be properly managed in the first instance thereby reducing the need for corrective action at a future date;

(6) minimizing the generation of hazardous waste and the land disposal of hazardous waste by encouraging process substitution, materials recovery, properly conducted recycling and reuse, and treatment;

. . .

42 U.S.C. §6902(a)(4)-(6). Do these objectives conflict?

2. *Clarity.* EPA did not make a clear decision to either include or exclude recycled hazardous materials from the definition of solid waste. *See* Hazardous Waste Management System: Definition of Solid Waste, Final Rule, 50 Fed. Reg. 614, 617 (January 4, 1985). Instead, it ultimately adopted an extraordinarily complicated rule that made fine-grained distinctions based on the agency's assessment of the environmental hazards posed by particular types of waste and particular types of recycling treatments. *See id.* at 616, 617, 663-664, codified at 40 C.F.R. part 261. Do you agree with EPA's decision to vary the scope of the term "solid waste" with its estimate of hazard? The statutory

definition of solid waste includes materials "otherwise disposed of." Is recycling disposal or not? In any case, the foregoing materials should make clear that policy considerations have driven the regulatory decisions about the definition of solid waste.

3. *Sometimes discarded versus functional approach.* EPA notes that its first RCRA rules on this topic regulated any material that was "sometimes discarded." In the rule proposed in the above preamble, EPA announces that it will assess "what the material is and how it actually is managed" to determine whether it is solid waste. It explains that this means that a substance's status as solid waste may vary with the means of recycling employed. Which approach has the broadest regulatory reach? Which is clearer? Which best encourages recycling?

4. *Legal rationale.* Are you satisfied with EPA's legal rationale? Does EPA have authority to regulate recycled hazardous materials under subtitle C of RCRA as hazardous solid waste? Does EPA have discretion to decline to do so in instances where it does not see a great potential for environmental harm from the means of recycling employed?

5. *On-site versus off-site recycling.* The rule promulgated after this proposal clarified the status of a number of off-site recycling operations, often applying TSDF standards to waste shipped off-site. Yet, EPA had less success in clarifying the law relative to situations where a generator recycles its own waste, using a hazardous waste as an input into its own production process. In the proposed rule, it commented:

> In these situations, there appears to be a significantly reduced risk of waste mismanagement, because the generator or ultimate user has decided to retain control of the recycled waste and, thus, can assure a market for the recycled materials. Our investigation of hazardous waste recycling activities indicates that improper storage, overaccumulation, and subsequent damage have been associated with reclamation where the market for the recycled material is uncertain or where the recycling technology is unproven. Overaccumulation is a particular risk where reclaimers are paid to take wastes they don't intend to use themselves, since this creates an incentive to keep accepting wastes that may prove unsalable after recycling. The most severe damage incidents, such as Chem-Dyne and Silresim, all fit this pattern. These circumstances are least likely to be present when a generator or ultimate user reclaims because of the continued exercise of control and ability to assure the wastes' end disposition. We consequently are proposing conditional exemptions for these situations. The conditions are designed primarily to guard against overaccumulation which (based on existing data), is the chief danger in these operations.

Proposed Rule, 48 Fed. Reg. at 14477.

EPA ultimately adopted a rule exempting materials returned to the original manufacturing process if not reclaimed. Under this rule, however,

RCRA regulates reclaimed materials or materials stemming from one manufacturing process that are returned to a *different* manufacturing process at the same facility. Industry challenged this distinction in the following case:

American Mining Congress v. EPA
824 F.2d 1177 (D.C. Cir. 1987)

STARR, CIRCUIT JUDGE.

These consolidated cases arise out of EPA's regulation of hazardous wastes under the Resource Conservation and Recovery Act of 1976 ("RCRA"), as amended, 42 U.S.C. §§6901-6933 (1982 & Supp. III 1985). Petitioners, trade associations representing mining and oil refining interests, challenge regulations promulgated by EPA that amend the definition of "solid waste" to establish and define the agency's authority to regulate secondary materials reused within an industry's ongoing production process. In plain English, petitioners maintain that EPA has exceeded its regulatory authority in seeking to bring materials that are not discarded or otherwise disposed of within the compass of "waste."

RCRA is a comprehensive environmental statute under which EPA is granted authority to regulate solid and hazardous wastes. RCRA was enacted in 1976, and amended in 1978, 1980, and 1984.

Congress' "overriding concern" in enacting RCRA was to establish the framework for a national system to insure the safe management of hazardous waste. In passing RCRA, Congress expressed concern over the "rising tide" in scrap, discarded, and waste materials. 42 U.S.C. §6901(a)(2). As the statute itself puts it, Congress was concerned with the need "to reduce the amount of waste and unsalvageable materials and to provide for proper and economical solid waste disposal practices." *Id.* §6901(a)(4). Congress thus crafted RCRA "to promote the protection of health and the environment and to conserve valuable material and energy resources." *Id.* §6902.

RCRA includes two major parts: one deals with non-hazardous solid waste management and the other with hazardous waste management. Under the latter, EPA is directed to promulgate regulations establishing a comprehensive management system. *Id.* §6921. EPA's authority, however, extends only to the regulation of "hazardous waste." Because "hazardous waste" is defined as a subset of "solid waste," *id.* §6903(5), the scope of EPA's jurisdiction is limited to those materials that constitute "solid waste." That pivotal term is defined by RCRA

> as any garbage, refuse, sludge from a waste treatment plant, water supply treatment plant, or air pollution control facility *and other discarded material*, including solid, liquid, semisolid or contained gaseous material, resulting from industrial, commercial, mining, and agricultural operations, and from community activities.

42 U.S.C. §6903(27) (emphasis added). As will become evident, this case turns on the meaning of the phrase, "and other discarded material," contained in the statute's definitional provisions.

Under the final rule, if a material constitutes "solid waste," it is subject to RCRA regulation *unless* it is directly reused as an ingredient or as an effective substitute for a commercial product, or is returned as a raw material substitute to its original manufacturing process. In the jargon of the trade, the latter category is known as the "closed-loop" exception. In either case, the material must not first be "reclaimed" (processed to recover a usable product or regenerated). EPA exempts these activities "because they are like ordinary usage of commercial products."

II

Petitioners, American Mining Congress ("AMC") and American Petroleum Institute ("API"), challenge the scope of EPA's final rule. Relying upon the statutory definition of "solid waste," petitioners contend that EPA's authority under RCRA is limited to controlling materials that are *discarded* or *intended for discard*. They argue that EPA's reuse and recycle rules, as applied to in-process secondary materials, regulate materials that have not been discarded, and therefore exceed EPA's jurisdiction.

To understand petitioners' claims, a passing familiarity with the nature of their industrial processes is required.

Petroleum. Petroleum refineries vary greatly both in respect of their products and their processes. Most of their products, however, are complex mixtures of hydrocarbons produced through a number of interdependent and sometimes repetitious processing steps. In general, the refining process starts by "distilling" crude oil into various hydrocarbon streams or "fractions." The "fractions" are then subjected to a number of processing steps. Various hydrocarbon materials derived from virtually all stages of processing are combined or blended in order to produce products such as gasoline, fuel oil, and lubricating oils. Any hydrocarbons that are not usable in a particular form or state are returned to an appropriate stage in the refining process so they can eventually be used. Likewise, the hydrocarbons and materials which escape from a refinery's production vessels are gathered and, by a complex retrieval system, returned to appropriate parts of the refining process. Under EPA's final rule, this reuse and recycling of materials is subject to regulation under RCRA.

Against this factual backdrop, we now examine the legal issues presented by petitioners' challenge.

III

Congress, it will be recalled, granted EPA power to regulate "solid waste." Congress specifically defined "solid waste" as "discarded material." EPA then defined "discarded material" to include materials destined for reuse in an industry's *ongoing* production processes. The challenge to EPA's jurisdictional reach is founded, again, on the proposition that in-process secondary materials are outside the bounds of EPA's lawful authority. Nothing has been *discarded*, the argument goes, and thus RCRA jurisdiction remains untriggered.

Congress defined "solid waste" as "discarded material." The ordinary, plain-English meaning of the word "discarded" is "disposed of," "thrown away" or "abandoned." Encompassing materials retained for immediate reuse within the scope of "discarded material" strains, to say the least, the everyday usage of that term.

RCRA was enacted, as the Congressional objectives and findings make clear, in an effort to help States deal with the ever-increasing problem of solid waste *disposal* by encouraging the search for and use of alternatives to existing methods of disposal (including recycling) and protecting health and the environment by regulating hazardous wastes. To fulfill these purposes, it seems clear that EPA need not regulate "spent" materials that are recycled and reused in an *ongoing* manufacturing or industrial process. These materials have not yet become part of the waste disposal problem; rather, *they are destined for beneficial reuse or recycling in a continuous process by the generating industry itself.*

[T]he statutory definition of "solid waste" is quite specific. Although Congress well knows how to use broad terms and broad definitions, . . . the definition here is carefully crafted with specificity. It contains three specific terms and then sets forth the broader term, "other discarded material." That definitional structure brings to mind a long-standing canon of statutory construction, *ejusdem generis*. Under that familiar canon, where general words follow the enumeration of particular classes of things, the general words are most naturally construed as applying only to things of the same general class as those enumerated. Here, the three particular classes — garbage, refuse, and sludge from a waste treatment plant, water supply treatment plant, or air pollution control facility — contain materials that clearly fit within the ordinary, everyday sense of "discarded." It is most sensible to conclude that Congress, in adding the concluding phrase "other discarded material," meant to grant EPA authority over similar types of waste, but not to open up the federal regulatory reach of an entirely new category of materials, *i.e.*, materials neither disposed of nor abandoned, but passing in a continuous stream or flow from one production process to another.[18]

18. The dissent contends that RCRA's "functional" definition of the term "disposal" suggests that RCRA embodies a "functional approach to problems of waste disposal." Without quibbling over the propriety of characterizing the definition of "disposal" as "functional," we observe that Congress, in defining "disposal," was specific and precise:

The term "disposal" means the discharge, deposit, injection, dumping, spilling, leaking, or placing of any solid waste or hazardous waste into or on any land or water so that such solid waste or hazardous waste or any constituent thereof may enter the environment or be emitted into the air or discharged into any waters, including ground waters.

IV

We are constrained to conclude that Congress clearly and unambiguously expressed its intent that "solid waste" (and therefore EPA's regulatory authority) be limited to materials that are "discarded" by virtue of being disposed of, abandoned, or thrown away. While we do not lightly overturn an agency's reading of its own statute, we are persuaded that by regulating in-process secondary materials, EPA has acted in contravention of Congress' intent. Accordingly, the petition for review is *Granted*.

Mikva, Circuit Judge, dissenting:

The court today strains to overturn the Environmental Protection Agency's interpretation of the Resource Conservation and Recovery Act to authorize the regulation of certain recycled industrial materials. Under today's decision, the EPA is prohibited from regulating in-process secondary materials that contribute to the ominous problem that Congress sought to eradicate by passing the RCRA. In my opinion, the EPA has adequately demonstrated that its interpretation is a reasonable construction of an ambiguous term in a statute committed to the agency's administration. We therefore are obliged to defer to the agency's interpretation under the principles of Chevron U.S.A., Inc. v. NRDC. I dissent.

I

I agree with the majority that the case turns on the definition of solid waste as "discarded material" in RCRA. *See* 42 U.S.C. §6903(27).

In my opinion, the EPA's interpretation of solid waste is completely reasonable in light of the language, policies, and legislative history of RCRA. Congress had broad remedial objectives in mind when it enacted RCRA, most notably to "regulat[e] the treatment, storage, transportation, and disposal of hazardous wastes which have adverse effects on the environment." 42 U.S.C. §6902(4). The disposal problem Congress was combating encompassed more than just abandoned materials. RCRA makes this clear with its definition of the central statutory term "disposal":

> the discharge, deposit, injection, dumping, spilling, leaking, or placing of any solid waste or hazardous waste into or on any land or water so that such solid waste or hazardous waste or any constituent thereof may enter the environment or be emitted into the air or discharged into any waters, including ground waters.

---

42 U.S.C. §6903(3). Far from indicating that Congress intended that the language used in its definitions be "functionally" interpreted, Congress' care and precision suggests that it intended to give the potentially vague terms that it was defining, such as "solid waste" and "disposal," specific content.

42 U.S.C. §6903(3). This definition clearly encompasses more than the everyday meaning of disposal, which is a "discarding or throwing away." *Webster's Third International Dictionary* 654 (2d ed. 1981). The definition is *functional*: waste is disposed under this provision if it is put into contact with land or water in such a way as to pose the risks to health and environment that animated Congress to pass RCRA. Whether the manufacturer subjectively intends to put the material to additional use is irrelevant to this definition, as indeed it should be, because the manufacturer's state of mind bears no necessary relation to the hazards of the industrial processes he employs.

Faithful to RCRA's functional approach, EPA reasonably concluded that regulation of certain in-process secondary materials was necessary to carry out its mandate. The materials at issue in this case can pose the same risks as abandoned wastes, whether or not the manufacturer intends eventually to put them to further beneficial use. As the agency explained, "simply because a waste is likely to be recycled will not ensure that it will not be spilled or leaked before recycling occurs." The storage, transportation, and even recycling of in-process secondary materials can cause severe environmental harm. Indeed, the EPA documented environmental disasters caused by the handling or storage of such materials. It also pointed out the risk of damage from spills or leaks when certain in-process secondary materials are placed on land or in underground product storage.

Moreover, the agency's action is carefully aligned with Congress' functional approach to problems of waste disposal. The agency is not seeking to regulate all recycled materials. Rather, it has promulgated a complicated scheme of different categories so as to regulate materials only when they present the same types of environmental risks RCRA seeks to correct. EPA stressed that "to determine if a secondary material is a RCRA solid waste when recycled, one must examine both the material and the recycling activity involved. A consequence is that the same material can be a waste if it is recycled in certain ways, but would not be a waste if it is recycled in other ways." Thus, the agency has sought to regulate these materials only when they present the risks Congress was combating in RCRA.

[I]n this case the EPA has interpreted solid waste in a manner that seems to expand the everyday usage of the word "discarded." Its conclusion, however, is fully supportable in light of the statutory scheme and legislative history of RCRA. The agency concluded that certain on-site recycled materials constitute an integral part of the waste disposal problem. This judgment is grounded in the EPA's technical expertise and is adequately supported by evidence in the record. The majority nevertheless reverses the agency because it believes that the materials at issue "have not yet become part of the waste disposal problem." This declaration is nothing more than a substitution of the majority's own conclusions for the sound technical judgment of the EPA. The EPA's interpretation is a reasonable construction of an ambiguous statutory provision and should be upheld. . . .

I dissent.

NOTES ON *AMERICAN MINING CONGRESS*

1. *Holding.* Did the court find a particular provision of EPA's rule contrary to the statute? If so, which provision? Did the court hold that EPA may not regulate recycling under RCRA? Did it hold that EPA may not regulate on-site recycling under RCRA? Did it hold that EPA may not regulate certain sorts of on-site recycling?

2. *Literal versus functional approach.* The entire court, including the dissent, agrees that the core of this case involves the interpretation of the term "otherwise discarded" in the statutory definition of solid waste. Is the dissent correct to suggest that the statutory definition of "disposal" should control the definition of discarding? Suppose that the hydrocarbons are stored in a way that permits leakage pending recycling. Does the process still involve no discarding?

3. *Goals.* As we noted in Chapter 4, the goals of the statute can sometimes influence judicial interpretation of operational provisions, such as the definition of disposal at issue in this case. What two competing goals of RCRA are at issue in this case? If one main statutory goal is to promote the reuse and recycling of solid and hazardous waste to *prevent* waste disposal problems, does EPA discourage industry from engaging in recycling and reuse if it still must comply with stringent hazardous waste regulations when it does so?

4. *Destiny.* The majority distinguishes between materials that are part of the waste disposal problem and those that are "destined for beneficial for beneficial reuse or recycling in a continuous process by the generating industry itself." Does a material's destiny determine whether it is part of the waste disposal problem? What determines the destiny of hydrocarbons that remain after producing gasoline?

Note On *American Mining Congress'* Progeny

The D.C. Circuit interpreted *American Mining Congress* (*AMC I*) narrowly in several subsequent cases. In American Petroleum Institute v. EPA, 906 F.2d 729, 732, 741 (D.C. Cir. 1990), the court held that EPA may regulate slag residuals from a metals reclamation process from treatment standards. Because the slag inputs to the reclamation process were first disposed of before reclamation, the court held that they were solid wastes. *Id.* at 741. In American Mining Congress v. EPA, 907 F.2d 1179, 1186-87 (D.C. Cir. 1990) (American Mining Congress II), the court held that EPA may regulate sludges from wastewater that *may* be reclaimed in the future as solid waste. Both of these cases read *AMC I* as only exempting materials that were immediately reused in an ongoing manufacturing process. In Ass'n of Battery Recyclers, Inc. v. EPA, 208 F.3d 1047, 1053 (D.C. Cir. 2000), however, the court held that RCRA does not apply to materials stored temporarily prior to recycling, and suggested that the "immediate" reuse language in *AMC I* cannot be read literally. In

American Petroleum Institute v. EPA, 216 F.3d 50 (D.C. Cir. 2000), the court vacated an EPA rule regulating oil-bearing wastewater. *Id.* at 58. It applied a "primary purpose" test, under which wastewater treatment would prove subject to RCRA regulation only if the oil refiner's primary purpose was compliance with the Clean Water Act, rather than recovery of used oil. *Id.* at 57-58. At the same time, the court upheld a rule prohibiting sham recycling by treating non-refinable materials in used oil as hazardous waste and limiting "speculative accumulation" of used oil. *Id.* at 58-59. In another post-*AMC I* case, the court stated that materials reused in a different industry than that which generated them can fall outside of RCRA's definition of solid waste. Safe Food and Fertilizer v. EPA, 350 F.3d 1263, 1268 (D.C. Cir. 2003), *amended,* 365 F.3d 46 (D.C. Cir. 2004). This statement stands in some tension with the early post-*AMC I* cases, which relied heavily on the narrow *AMC I* language referring to recycling at the facility generating the waste. The *Safe Food and Fertilizer* court, however, remanded to the agency, because environmentalists showed that the fertilizer made with reclaimed metal had higher concentrations of chromium than fertilizer made from virgin materials. *Id.* at 1271. The court suggested that such higher limits were only acceptable if they did not change the environmental risk.

Thus, the line between solid wastes and materials outside of EPA's jurisdiction under RCRA has proven quite blurry. It is clear that RCRA regulates discarded materials and does not regulate material that is not part of the waste disposal problem. It is less clear when materials will be deemed discarded, at least when a recycling process is involved.

C. CERCLA AND POLLUTION PREVENTION

RCRA has a prospective orientation. It seeks to regulate the disposal of solid waste to limit future environmental problems, such as creation of sites filled with untreated hazardous waste. Unfortunately, quite a bit of dumping of hazardous waste occurred before RCRA's enactment.

Congress adopted RCRA in its modern form in 1976. Two years later, heavy rains washed mixtures of previously dumped hazardous chemicals into the basements of residents of a Buffalo suburb, which eventually led to the demolition of homes and the relocation of 1,000 families who lived at Love Canal, as this site is called. This incident and the realization that thousands of other sites around the nation contained potent brews of previously dumped toxic waste led, a few years later, to the enactment of a law to prompt cleanup of existing disposal sites, the Comprehensive Environmental Response, Compensation, and Liability Act (CERCLA), 42 U.S.C. §§9601-9675. CERCLA made a host of parties with existing or past links to existing disposal sites liable for cleanup costs. In the next chapter, we will discuss this liability scheme in more detail. But some discussion on the prospective effect of this imposition of retroactive liability has relevance to the question of pollution prevention. CERCLA liability has proven extremely onerous to potentially responsible parties (PRPs, *i.e.*, those within the liable class). Cleanup can prove expensive and agreement about the division of cost among PRPs and the degree of appropriate cleanup often requires years of negotiation and litigation. Superfund liability has proven extremely irksome to PRPs, because many parties can incur a potentially expensive inchoate financial obligation that can take years to clarify. Yet, this onerous approach to liability has provided powerful incentives to avoid the creation of future disposal sites. Those who might get saddled with liability for a cleanup acquire a strong desire to avoid dumping that might create future liability. One way of making sure that a site never becomes a Superfund site is to simply avoid generating hazardous waste in the first place.

One can think of the RCRA debate over recycling policy as but one example of a larger debate about the role of regulation and deregulation in encouraging pollution prevention and recycling. Does EPA encourage pollution prevention by exempting recycling processes from regulation? Would comprehensively regulating all recycling processes better encourage pollution prevention?

CERCLA liability applies to those associated with sites at which a "hazardous substance" is released, or where there is a threatened release. *See* 42 U.S.C. §9607(a). The definition of "hazardous substance" under CERCLA is broader than the definition of "hazardous waste" under RCRA. *See* 42 U.S.C. §9601(14). *Accord* THE RCRA PRACTICE MANUAL 26 (THEODORE L. GARRETT, ed., 2004). This means that a company that has fully complied with RCRA might still become a PRP under CERCLA. How does this disparity in definitions influence incentives for pollution prevention?

In Chapter 10, we noted that information strategies sometimes motivate voluntary pollution prevention. Do you think these approaches are likely to be more or less effective than the creation of liability for disposal costs? Is emissions trading likely to encourage pollution prevention? What factors might affect your answer about which approach(es) should work best?

PFOA AND SOURCE REDUCTION

3M Company discontinued its use of perflourooctyl sulfonate (PFOS), a chemical similar to PFOA, between 2000 and 2002. Suppose that EPA is convinced that PFOA poses a sufficient hazard to justify a source reduction approach. As you read EPA's description of how PFOA and its salts are used and produced, think about how EPA could best encourage reductions in PFOA's use and manufacture:

≡≡≡≡
≡≡≡≡   *Perfluorooctanoic Acid (PFOA), Fluorinated*
≡≡≡≡   *Telomers; Request for Comment, Solicitation of*
≡≡≡≡   *Interested Parties for Enforceable Consent*
≡≡≡≡   *Agreement Development, and Notice of Public*
≡≡≡≡   *Meeting*
≡≡≡≡   *68 Fed. Reg. 18626, 18628-9 (April 16, 2003)*

* * *

III.   Background

. . .

A.   PFOA Sources and Uses

PFOA and its salts are fully fluorinated organic compounds that can be produced synthetically and formed through the degradation or metabolism of certain other manmade fluorochemical products. . . .

PFOA is used primarily to produce its salts, which are used as essential processing aids in the production of fluoropolymers and fluoroelastomers. Although they are made using PFOA, finished fluoropolymer and fluoroelastomer products are not expected to contain PFOA. In recent years, less than 600 metric tons per year of PFOA and its salts have been manufactured or imported in the United States. The major fluoropolymers manufactured using PFOA salts are polytetrafluoroethylene (PTFE) and polyvinylidine fluoride (PVDF). PTFE has hundreds of uses in many industrial and consumer products, including soil, stain, grease, and water resistant coatings on textiles and carpet; uses in the automotive, mechanical, aerospace, chemical, electrical, medical, and building/construction industries; personal care products; and non-stick coatings on cookware. PVDF is used primarily in three major industrial sectors: Electrical/electronics, building/construction, and chemical processing.

. . .

. . . Releases from manufacturing processes are one source of PFOA in the environment. [Today] . . . domestic producers [use] the telomerization process exclusively [to produce PFOA].

. . .

. . . Commercial products manufactured through the telomerization process, sometimes known as telomers, are generally mixtures of perfluorinated compounds with even carbon numbers, although the process can also produce compounds with odd carbon numbers.

. . .

EPA has also received data which indicate that the 8-2 telomer alcohol (1-Decanol, 3,3,4,4,5,5,6,6,7,7,8,8,9,9,10,10,10-heptadecafluoro- (CAS No. 678-39-7)) although not itself made with PFOA, can be metabolized by living organisms or biodegrade under environmental conditions to produce PFOA. Other telomer chemicals have not been tested to determine whether they may also metabolize or degrade to form PFOA. Telomers are used widely in a range of commercial products, including some that are directly released into the environment, such as fire fighting foams, as well as soil, stain, and grease resistant coatings on carpets, textiles, paper, and leather. The extent to which these telomer-containing products might degrade to release PFOA is unknown. However, anecdotal evidence of the atmospheric presence of telomer alcohols in a multi-city North American survey suggests that telomers may be one source of environmental PFOA. Additional fate information is necessary to determine whether and the extent to which telomer product degradation may be a source of PFOA.

. . .

In addition to this information, an EPA fact sheet states that:

> Fluoropolymer manufacturers have indicated that there are no know alternatives. Some manufacturing processes can use different technologies that don't employ PFOA, but these processes could not currently be used to produce most fluoropolymer products. Nevertheless, the principal fluoropolymer manufacturers committed to a minimum 50 percent reduction in total global emissions by 2006.

See The Society of the Plastics Industry, PFOA-facts.com, available at http://www.pfoa-facts.com/?gclid=CMb_qqv-mYgCFU5xFQodLiHUXA (last visited October 26, 2006).

Subsequently, as we saw, many companies agreed to a 95 percent reduction and to work toward a phase-out. What explains the apparent discrepancy between the manufacturers' pessimistic statements to EPA and their subsequent willingness to promise substantial cuts?

This part has examined various means of regulation, including traditional regulation, economic incentives, information-based approaches, and, in this last chapter, pollution prevention and recycling. At this point, you should have some understanding of how regulators make decisions both about how much environmental protection to achieve and about some of the means available to achieve environmental goals. We now move to a discussion of who bears responsibility for environmental cleanup measures and decisions.

IV

ALLOCATION OF RESPONSIBILITY

This part addresses the question of who takes responsibility for environmental issues and problems. Chapter 12 addresses the distribution of private responsibility for cleanup, focusing primarily upon the CERCLA, the statute where these issues arise most often. Chapter 13 discusses the distribution of responsibility and authority for standard setting and enforcement among government units. Chapter 13 also emphasizes federalism considerations and explains some of the broad structural decisions found in major statutes. Chapter 14 explains responsibility and principles for making decisions about international environmental issues, including bilateral, regional, and global environmental problems.

12

Private Cleanup Responsibility

Generally, statutory regimes and the common law both make private parties responsible for environmental cleanups and other obligations that arise out of their own activities. Governments can also acquire comparable environmental cleanup responsibilities when they pollute while acting in a proprietary capacity. In international environmental law, this concept of responsibility to clean up one's own mess is known as the "polluter pays" principle. *See* Rio Declaration on Environment and Development, U.N. Conference on Environment and Development, U.N. Doc. A/CONF.151/5/Rev.1, 31 I.L.M. 874 (1992), Principle 16. This concept comports with our general sense of fairness, that people should be responsible for their own conduct and the implications of their actions, and should not be allowed to shift environmental or other liabilities to others. The "polluter pays" principle also makes sense under the basic economic justifications that underlie both common law liability and the rationale for government intervention into the free market. If someone is not required to bear the external costs of her activity, she reaps unfair profits at the expense of those who suffer health problems or live in a degraded environment as a result.

The statutes we have discussed thus far and the common law both typically address ongoing pollution. In principle, figuring out who has responsibility for cleanup for ongoing pollution under a polluter pays principle is not terribly difficult. The owner and operator of a facility causes the ongoing pollution, and that person or entity bears responsibility for cleanup. *See, e.g.*, 42 U.S.C. §7411(a)(5), (e) (requiring owners and operators of pollution sources to comply with new source performance standards). Not every polluter acquires a cleanup obligation. *See, e.g.*, 42 U.S.C. §§7412(c)(3) (requiring regulation of some, but not all, "area sources" emitting hazardous air pollution), 6921(b)(2)(A) (exempting certain wastes associated with oil and gas production from RCRA). But the polluter pays principle still furnishes a useful general rule explaining many statutory provisions establishing cleanup obligations and a central thrust of the common law.

415

With respect to hazardous waste dumps, the polluter pays principle does not always get one very far. Often, multiple polluters have contributed to the contamination of a single site. So the polluter pays principle requires some apportionment of liability amongst them. And in many cases, those who dumped hazardous waste have become insolvent or cannot be identified. That scenario raises a question of who should then be responsible for cleanup. The polluter pays principle in this context often does not answer the question of who should be held responsible.

This chapter discusses this question of who has responsibility for environmental harm in the context of the Comprehensive Environmental Response, Compensation, and Liability Act (CERCLA), 42 U.S.C. §§9601–9675, which addresses the difficult problem of who should pay for cleanup of hazardous waste disposal sites. Many of those sites have long, complicated, and obscure histories, making the assignment of responsibility a difficult endeavor. Section A focuses on the assignment of liability for cleanup. Section B discusses cleanup standards for hazardous waste sites, and the process CERCLA establishes for site-specific remedy selection. As a practical matter, both the cost of the remedy and apportionment of responsibility help determine the amount and scope of a party's liability under CERCLA.

A. APPORTIONING STATUTORY LIABILITY FOR ENVIRONMENTAL HARM

A number of federal and state environmental statutes embrace private liability as a principal method of environmental cleanup and protection. In Chapter 11, we discussed the use of liability under CERCLA as an incentive for pollution prevention. A co-equal goal of liability statutes is to promote prompt but effective cleanups of contaminated sites, and to ensure that cleanup costs are borne to the maximum extent possible by responsible private parties, rather than the general public. At the federal level, liability-based statutes include section 311 of the Clean Water Act, 33 U.S.C. §1321, the Oil Pollution Act of 1990, 33 U.S.C. §§2701–2761 (a statute enacted in the aftermath of the Exxon-Valdez oil spill), and most notably, CERCLA.[1] Simply stating the concept of private liability, however, obscures the difficulty of deciding *who* should be held liable for what kinds of contamination, under what circumstances, and how that liability should be allocated when there are multiple responsible parties. In this section, we explore the manner in which Congress and the courts have allocated liability under CERCLA.

1. A number of states have also passed state "Superfund" statutes modeled after CER-CLA. *See* Office of Emergency and Remedial Response, EPA Pub. No. EPA/540/8–91/002, An Analysis of State Superfund Programs: 50–State Study, 1990 Update.

At first blush, some principles and applications of CERCLA liability might seem unfair. Clearly, liability is appropriate for those who actually cause contamination of a site, such as "midnight dumpers" who illegally dispose of hazardous waste under cover of darkness. As you will see, however, CERCLA liability can extend to many other private parties as well, including those who arguably "did nothing wrong." As you read the following cases and materials, try to focus on whether the various principles of liability make sense in terms of CERCLA's main goals, and other aspects of public policy.

1. Strict Liability under CERCLA

State of New York v. Shore Realty
759 F.2d 1032 (2d Cir. 1985)

OAKES, CIRCUIT JUDGE.

This case involves several novel questions about the scope of the Comprehensive Environmental Response, Compensation, and Liability Act of 1980 ("CERCLA"). CERCLA — adopted in the waning hours of the Ninety-sixth Congress, and signed by President Carter on December 11, 1980 — was intended to provide means for cleaning up hazardous waste sites and spills, and may generally be known to the public as authorizing the so-called Superfund, the $1.6 billion Hazardous Substances Response Trust Fund.

On February 29, 1984, the State of New York brought suit against Shore Realty Corp. ("Shore") and Donald LeoGrande, its officer and stockholder, to clean up a hazardous waste disposal site at One Shore Road, Glenwood Landing, New York, which Shore had acquired for land development purposes. At the time of the acquisition, LeoGrande knew that hazardous waste was stored on the site and that cleanup would be expensive, though neither Shore nor LeoGrande had participated in the generation or transportation of the nearly 700,000 gallons of hazardous waste now on the premises. On October 15, 1984, the district court granted the State's motion for partial summary judgment. Apparently relying at least in part on CERCLA, it directed by permanent injunction that Shore and LeoGrande remove the hazardous waste stored on the property, subject to monitoring by the State, and held them liable for the State's "response costs."

We affirm, concluding that Shore is liable under CERCLA for the State's response costs. We hold that Shore properly was found to be a covered person under 42 U.S.C. § 9607(a); that the nonlisting by the Environmental Protection Agency ("EPA") of the site on the National Priorities List ("NPL"), is irrelevant to Shore's liability; that Shore cannot rely on any of CERCLA's affirmative defenses. Moreover, we hold LeoGrande jointly and severally liable under CERCLA.

FACTS

Some of the most heated arguments on this appeal involve whether certain material facts are undisputed. After careful scrutiny of the record and the district court's supplemental memorandum, we base our decision on the following facts.

LeoGrande incorporated Shore solely for the purpose of purchasing the Shore Road property. All corporate decisions and actions were made, directed, and controlled by him. By contract dated July 14, 1983, Shore agreed to purchase the 3.2 acre site, a small peninsula surrounded on three sides by the waters of Hempstead Harbor and Mott Cove, for condominium development. Five large tanks in a field in the center of the site hold most of some 700,000 gallons of hazardous chemicals located there, though there are six smaller tanks both above and below ground containing hazardous waste, as well as some empty tanks, on the property. And before June 15, 1984, one of the two dilapidated masonry warehouses on the site contained over 400 drums of chemicals and contaminated solids, many of which were corroded and leaking.[3] It is beyond dispute that the tanks and drums contain "hazardous substances" within the meaning of CERCLA. The substances involved — including benzene, dichlorobenzenes, ethyl benzene, tetrachloroethylene, trichloroethylene, 1,1,1–trichloroethene, chlordane, polychlorinated biphenyls (commonly known as PCBs), and bis (2-ethylhexyl) phthalate — are toxic, in some cases carcinogenic, and dangerous by way of contact, inhalation, or ingestion. These substances are present at the site in various combinations, some of which may cause the toxic effect to be synergistic.

The purchase agreement provided that it could be voided by Shore without penalty if after conducting an environmental study Shore had decided not to proceed. LeoGrande was fully aware that the tenants were then operating — illegally, it may be noted — a hazardous waste storage facility on the site. Shore's environmental consultant, WTM Management Corporation ("WTM"), prepared a detailed report in July, 1983. The report concluded that over the past several decades "the facility ha[d] received little if any preventive maintenance, the tanks (above ground and below ground), pipeline, loading rack, fire extinguishing system, and warehouse have deteriorated." WTM found that there had been several spills of hazardous waste at the site, including at least one large spill in 1978. Though there had been some attempts at cleanup, the WTM testing revealed that hazardous substances, such as benzene, were still leaching into the groundwater and the waters of the bay immediately adjacent to the bulkhead abutting Hempstead Harbor. After a site visit on July 18, 1983, WTM reported firsthand on the sorry state of the facility, observing, among other things, "seepage from the bulkhead," "corro-

---

3. When these drums concededly were "bursting and leaking," Shore employees asked the State to enter the site, inspect it, and take steps to mitigate the "life-threatening crisis situation." Pursuant to stipulation and order entered on June 15, 1984, Shore began removing the drums. Some may still remain at the site.

sion" on all the tanks, signs of possible leakage from some of the tanks, deterioration of the pipeline and loading rack, and fifty to one hundred fifty-five gallon drums containing contaminated earth in one of the warehouses. The report concluded that if the current tenants "close up the operation and leave the material at the site," the owners would be left with a "potential time bomb." WTM estimated that the cost of environmental cleanup and monitoring would range from $650,000 to over $1 million before development could begin. After receiving this report Shore sought a waiver from the State Department of Environmental Conservation ("DEC") of liability as landowners for the disposal of the hazardous waste stored at the site. Although the DEC denied the waiver, Shore took title on October 13, 1983, and obtained certain rights over against the tenants, whom it subsequently evicted on January 5, 1984. Nevertheless, between October 13, 1983, and January 5, 1984, nearly 90,000 gallons of hazardous chemicals were added to the tanks. And during a state inspection on January 3, 1984, it became evident that the deteriorating and leaking drums of chemicals referred to above had also been brought onto the site. Needless to say, the tenants did not clean up the site before they left. Thus, conditions when Shore employees first entered the site were as bad as or worse than those described in the WTM report. As LeoGrande admitted by affidavit, "the various storage tanks, pipe lines and connections between these storage facilities were in a bad state of repair." While Shore claims to have made some improvements, such as sealing all the pipes and valves and continuing the cleanup of the damage from earlier spills, Shore did nothing about the hundreds of thousands of gallons of hazardous waste standing in deteriorating tanks. In addition, although a growing number of drums were leaking hazardous substances, Shore essentially ignored the problem until June, 1984.

On September 19, 1984, a DEC inspector observed one of the large tanks, which held over 300,000 gallons of hazardous materials, with rusting floor plates and tank walls, a pinhole leak, and a four-foot line of corrosion along one of the weld lines. On three other tanks, flakes of corroded metal "up to the size and thickness of a dime" were visible at the floorplate level.

CERCLA

CERCLA was designed "to bring order to the array of partly redundant, partly inadequate federal hazardous substances cleanup and compensation laws."[6] It applies "primarily to the cleanup of leaking inactive or abandoned sites and to emergency responses to spills." And it distinguishes between two

6. In defining the term "hazardous substance," CERCLA incorporates by reference the substances designated as hazardous or toxic under the Clean Air Act, the Clean Water Act, the Resource Conservation and Recovery Act of 1976 ("RCRA"), the Toxic Substances Control Act, while authorizing EPA to designate additional substances that "may present substantial danger to the public health or welfare or the environment."

kinds of response: remedial actions — generally long-term or permanent containment or disposal programs — and removal efforts — typically short-term cleanup arrangements.

CERCLA authorizes the federal government to respond in several ways. EPA can use Superfund resources to clean up hazardous waste sites and spills. The National Contingency Plan ("NCP"), prepared by EPA pursuant to CERCLA, governs cleanup efforts by "establish[ing] procedures and standards for responding to releases of hazardous substances." At the same time, EPA can sue for reimbursement of cleanup costs from any responsible parties it can locate, allowing the federal government to respond immediately while later trying to shift financial responsibility to others. Thus, Superfund covers cleanup costs if the site has been abandoned, if the responsible parties elude detection, or if private resources are inadequate. In addition, CERCLA authorizes EPA to seek an injunction in federal district court to force a responsible party to clean up any site or spill that presents an imminent and substantial danger to public health or welfare or the environment. In sum, CERCLA is not a regulatory standard-setting statute such as the Clean Air Act. Rather, the government generally undertakes pollution abatement, and polluters pay for such abatement through tax and reimbursement liability.

Congress clearly did not intend, however, to leave cleanup under CERCLA solely in the hands of the federal government. A state or political subdivision may enter into a contract or cooperative agreement with EPA, whereby both may take action on a cost-sharing basis. And states, like EPA, can sue responsible parties for remedial and removal costs if such efforts are "not inconsistent with" the NCP. While CERCLA expressly does not preempt state law, it precludes "recovering compensation for the same removal costs or damages or claims" under both CERCLA and state or other federal laws, and prohibits states from requiring contributions to any fund "the purpose of which is to pay compensation for claims . . . which may be compensated under" CERCLA. Moreover, "any . . . person" who is acting consistently with the requirements of the NCP may recover "necessary costs of response." Finally, responsible parties are liable for "damages for injury to, destruction of, or loss of natural resources, including the reasonable costs of assessing such injury, destruction, or loss resulting from such a release."

Congress intended that responsible parties be held strictly liable, even though an explicit provision for strict liability was not included in the compromise. Section 9601(32) provides that "liability" under CERCLA "shall be construed to be the standard of liability" under section 311 of the Clean Water Act, which courts have held to be strict liability, and which Congress understood to impose such liability. Strict liability under CERCLA, however, is not absolute; there are defenses for causation solely by an act of God, an act of war, or acts or omissions of a third party other than an employee or agent of the defendant or one whose act or omission occurs in connection with a contractual relationship with the defendant.

DISCUSSION

A.   *Liability for Response Costs Under CERCLA*

We hold that the district court properly awarded the State response costs.

1. Covered Persons. CERCLA holds liable four classes of persons:

(1) the owner and operator of a vessel (otherwise subject to the jurisdiction of the United States) or a facility,[15] (2) any person who at the time of disposal of any hazardous substance owned or operated any facility at which such hazardous substances were disposed of, (3) any person who by contract, agreement, or otherwise arranged for disposal or treatment, or arranged with a transporter for transport for disposal or treatment, of hazardous substances owned or possessed by such person, by any other party or entity, at any facility owned or operated by another party or entity and containing such hazardous substances, and (4) any person who accepts or accepted any hazardous substances for transport to disposal or treatment facilities or sites selected by such person.

As noted above, section [107(a)] makes these persons liable, if "there is a release, or a threatened release which causes the incurrence of response costs, of a hazardous substance" from the facility, for, among other things, "all costs of removal or remedial action incurred by the United States Government or a State not inconsistent with the national contingency plan." Shore argues that it is not covered by section 9607(a)(1) because it neither owned the site at the time of disposal nor caused the presence or the release of the hazardous waste at the facility. While section 9607(a)(1) appears to cover Shore, Shore attempts to infuse ambiguity into the statutory scheme, claiming that section 9607(a)(1) could not have been intended to include all owners, because the word "owned" in section 9607(a)(2) would be unnecessary since an owner "at the time of disposal" would necessarily be included in section 9607(a)(1). Shore claims that Congress intended that the scope of section 9607(a)(1) be no greater than that of section 9607(a)(2) and that both should be limited by the "at the time of disposal" language. By extension, Shore argues that both provisions should be interpreted as requiring a showing of causation. We agree with the State, however, that section 9607(a)(1) unequivocally imposes strict liability on the current owner of a facility from which there is a release or threat of release, without regard to causation.

Shore's claims of ambiguity are illusory; section 9607(a)'s structure is clear. Congress intended to cover different classes of persons differently. Section 9607(a)(1) applies to all current owners and operators, while section 9607(a)(2) primarily covers prior owners and operators. Moreover, section 9607(a)(2)'s scope is more limited than that of section 9607(a)(1). Prior

---

15. CERCLA defines the term "facility" broadly to include any property at which hazardous substances have come to be located.

owners and operators are liable only if they owned or operated the facility "at the time of disposal of any hazardous substance"; this limitation does not apply to current owners, like Shore.

Shore's causation argument is also at odds with the structure of the statute. Interpreting section 9607(a)(1) as including a causation requirement makes superfluous the affirmative defenses provided in section 9607(b), each of which carves out from liability an exception based on causation. Without a clear congressional command otherwise, we will not construe a statute in any way that makes some of its provisions surplusage.

Furthermore, as the State points out, accepting Shore's arguments would open a huge loophole in CERCLA's coverage. It is quite clear that if the current owner of a site could avoid liability merely by having purchased the site after chemical dumping had ceased, waste sites certainly would be sold, following the cessation of dumping, to new owners who could avoid the liability otherwise required by CERCLA. Congress had well in mind that persons who dump or store hazardous waste sometimes cannot be located or may be deceased or judgment-proof. We will not interpret section 9607(a) in any way that apparently frustrates the statute's goals, in the absence of a specific congressional intention otherwise.

4. Affirmative defense. Shore also claims that it can assert an affirmative defense under CERCLA, which provides a limited exception to liability for a release or threat of release caused solely by an act or omission of a third party other than an employee or agent of the defendant, or than one whose act or omission occurs in connection with a contractual relationship, existing directly or indirectly, with the defendant (except where the sole contractual arrangement arises from a published tariff and acceptance for carriage by a common carrier by rail), if the defendant establishes by a preponderance of the evidence that (a) he exercised due care with respect to the hazardous substance concerned, taking into consideration the characteristics of such hazardous substance, in light of all relevant facts and circumstances, and (b) he took precautions against foreseeable acts or omissions of any such third party and the consequences that could foreseeably result from such acts or omissions. 42 U.S.C. §9607(b)(3). We disagree. Shore argues that it had nothing to do with the transportation of the hazardous substances and that it has exercised due care since taking control of the site. Who the "third part(ies)" Shore claims were responsible is difficult to fathom. It is doubtful that a prior owner could be such, especially the prior owner here, since the acts or omissions referred to in the statute are doubtless those occurring during the ownership or operation of the defendant.[23] Similarly, many of the acts and omissions of the prior tenants/operators fall outside the scope of section 9607(b)(3), because they

23. While we need not reach the issue, Shore appears to have a contractual relationship with the previous owners that also blocks the defense. The purchase agreement includes a provision by which Shore assumed at least some of the environmental liability of the previous owners.

occurred before Shore owned the property. In addition, we find that Shore cannot rely on the affirmative defense even with respect to the tenants' conduct during the period after Shore closed on the property and when Shore evicted the tenants. Shore was aware of the nature of the tenants' activities before the closing and could readily have foreseen that they would continue to dump hazardous waste at the site. In light of this knowledge, we cannot say that the releases and threats of release resulting of these activities were "caused solely" by the tenants or that Shore "took precautions against" these "foreseeable acts or omissions."

D. *LeoGrande's Personal Liability*

We hold LeoGrande liable as an "operator" under CERCLA for the State's response costs. Under CERCLA "owner or operator" is defined to mean "any person owning or operating" an onshore facility, and "person" includes individuals as well as corporations. More important, the definition of "owner or operator" excludes "a person, who, without participating in the management of a . . . facility, holds indicia of ownership primarily to protect his security interest in the facility." The use of this exception implies that an owning stockholder who manages the corporation, such as LeoGrande, is liable under CERCLA as an "owner or operator." That conclusion is consistent with that of other courts that have addressed the issue. In any event, LeoGrande is in charge of the operation of the facility in question, and as such is an "operator" within the meaning of CERCLA.

NOTES AND QUESTIONS ON *SHORE REALTY*

1. *Who is responsible for cleanup?* Under section 107(a) of CERCLA, a party potentially incurs liability when it falls within one of the four categories identified in section 107(a), *i.e.*, a current owner or operator of a vessel or facility, a past owner or operator at the time of disposal of hazardous substances, an "arranger" for disposal or treatment of hazardous substances, or a transporter of hazardous substances at a facility or site selected by that person. 42 U.S.C. §9607(a). We will discuss the boundaries of these categories of potentially responsible parties ("PRPs") in more detail later.

2. *Elements of liability for PRPs.* A party that falls within one of the four categories of PRPs is liable when there is a release or threatened release, from a facility, of a hazardous substance, which causes another person to incur response costs covered by the statute. As noted in the case, Congress defined the terms "facility" and "hazardous substances" very broadly. *Id.* §9601(9), (14). Likewise, the term "release" is defined broadly to include "any spilling, leaking, pumping, pouring, emitting, emptying, discharging, injecting, escaping, leaching, dumping, or disposing into the environment (including the abandonment or discarding of barrels, containers, and other closed receptacles containing any hazardous substance or pollutant or contaminant)," with some

relatively narrow exceptions we will address later. *Id.* §9601(22). *See, e.g.,* Vermont v. Staco, Inc., 684 F. Supp. 822 (D. Vt. 1988) (mercury on employee's clothes, washed into local sewer system when laundered at home, constituted a "release" of a hazardous substance).

3. *Strict and retroactive liability.* As noted by the *Shore Realty* court, nothing in section 107(a) or anywhere else in CERCLA uses the words "strict liability." Yet the courts have universally interpreted the law as such, based on the legislative history and other factors. As a result of strict liability, what elements of common law liability are omitted from the CERCLA cause of action? What is the rationale for strict liability, in terms of the law's policy goals?

Strict liability under CERCLA is particularly controversial because it is also retroactive, the constitutionality of which has been challenged unsuccessfully in several cases. *See, e.g.,* U.S. v. Olin Corp., 107 F.3d 1506 (11th Cir. 1997) (reversing district court finding that retroactive liability under CERCLA is unconstitutional); United States v. Northeastern Pharmaceutical & Chemical Co., 810 F.2d 726, 734–37 (8th Cir. 1986) (citing cases). The statute includes a limited exception to retroactive liability for natural resource damages, discussed *infra*.

4. *Facts.* The court held Shore Realty liable as a current owner even though Shore was not responsible for the disposal or release of hazardous substances on the site. Why did the court deem this fair or appropriate? To what extent does this fulfill CERCLA's twin goals of pollution prevention and expeditious site cleanup?

5. *Past owners and operators, and passive migration.* The second category of potentially responsible parties under CERCLA is "any person who at the time of disposal of any hazardous substance owned or operated any facility at which such hazardous substances were disposed of." 42 U.S.C. §9607(a)(2). The *Shore Realty* court held that current owners or operators are potentially liable regardless of the time of disposal of hazardous substances on the property. Past owners or operators are liable only if hazardous substances were "disposed of" on the site during the period of ownership of operation. Consider the following transactions:

> A owns and operates a PFOA manufacturing facility, which buries drums of waste with PFOA residuals and other hazardous substances out back. A sells the property to B, who merely holds the site for speculation. (No additional waste is added to the site during B's ownership). B sells the property to C, who converts the old manufacturing plant to luxury lofts (and who also does nothing to add to site contamination). During the site conversion, groundwater contamination is discovered.

Under these circumstances, who is potentially liable under the language of CERCLA section 107(a)(1) and (2)? Does this distinction make sense for CERCLA purposes?

The past owner and operator category has generated significant litigation over the meaning of the phrase "at the time of disposal of any hazardous substance." In the above hypothetical, does it matter whether the drums were leaking during the time of B's ownership? Does such a "passive" release, *i.e.*, one in which no affirmative activity leading to the release occurs (such as additional burial of drums), constitute "disposal" for purposes of potential liability? Some courts have found that liability should be imposed even for such "passive" disposal. *See, e.g.*, Nurad, Inc. v. William Hooper & Sons Co., 966 F.2d 837, 846 (4th Cir. 1992) (noting that §9607 "imposes liability not only for active involvement in the 'dumping' or 'placing' of hazardous waste at the facility, but for ownership of the facility at a time that hazardous wastes were 'spilling' or 'leaking'"); Carson Harbor Village v. Unocal Corp., 270 F.3d 863 (9th Cir. 2001) (en banc) (declining to find passive soil migration to be a "disposal" but holding that other passive migration events can serve as a predicate for CERCLA liability), *cert. denied*, 535 U.S. 971 (2002). Does this result make sense in terms of the CERCLA's goals?

Congress did not define "disposal" separately in CERCLA. Rather, the CERCLA definition, 42 U.S.C. §9601(29), adopts by reference the definition of "disposal" in RCRA:

the discharge, deposit, injection, dumping, spilling, leaking, or placing of any solid waste or hazardous waste into or on any land or water so that such solid waste or hazardous waste or any constituent thereof may enter the environment or be emitted into the air or discharged into any waters, including ground waters.

42 U.S.C. §6903(3). For purposes of RCRA, because of the use of word "leaking," some courts have found that this definition includes passive as well as active disposal. *E.g.*, United States v. Waste Industries, Inc., 734 F.2d 159 (4th Cir. 1984) (declining to adopt a "strained reading" of disposal under which CERCLA liability does not attach absent "active human conduct"). Some courts, as in the *Nurad* and *Carson Harbor* cases cited above, have followed this reasoning and found CERCLA liability for past owners or operators based on passive migration of wastes. How do you think this interpretation would affect the total number of potentially responsible parties under CERCLA? Other courts, however, have held that the word "leaking" in the RCRA definition takes its meaning from the other surrounding verbs, all of which require some active participation, *E.g.*, United States v. 150 Acres of Land, 204 F.3d 698 (6th Cir. 2000) (disposal under CERCLA cannot occur without "evidence that there was human activity involved in whatever movement of hazardous substances [that] occurred on the property"); United States v. CDMG Realty, 967 F.3d 706 (3d Cir. 1996) (passive migration does not constitute disposal). These courts note the distinction between the list of actions in the RCRA definition, all of which can be read to require active participation, and the CERCLA definition of "release," which includes entirely passive terms such as "escaping" and "leaching." *See* 42 U.S.C. §9601(22).

6. *Affirmative defenses and innocent landowners.* One of the most controversial aspects of strict liability under CERCLA is the notion that a party may
be liable for "someone else's mess," without having done anything "wrong"
themselves. Here, Shore purchased contaminated property, and perhaps
allowed contamination to continue unabated during its ownership, but it
dumped no wastes itself at the site. Should an "innocent" purchaser in this
situation be held liable for contamination caused by others?

Notwithstanding the background principle of strict liability, section
107(b) of CERCLA does allow potentially responsible parties a series of
potential affirmative defenses:

> There shall be no liability for a person otherwise liable who can
> establish by a preponderance of the evidence that the release or threat of
> release of a hazardous substance and the damages resulting therefrom were
> caused solely by —
>
> (1) an act of God;
> (2) an act of war;
> (3) an act or omission of a third party other than an employee or
> agent of the defendant, or than one whose act or omission occurs in
> connection with a contractual relationship, existing directly or indirectly,
> with the defendant if the defendant establishes by a preponderance of the
> evidence that (a) he exercised due care with respect to the hazardous
> substance concerned, taking into consideration the characteristics of such
> hazardous substances, in light of all relevant facts and circumstances, and
> (b) he took precautions against foreseeable acts or omissions of any such
> third party and the consequences that could foreseeably result from such
> acts or omissions; or
> (4) any combination of the foregoing paragraphs.

42 U.S.C. § 9607(b). Subsection (3), the act or omission of a third party, is by
far the most important of the three statutory affirmative defenses. Why could
Shore Realty not establish the elements of this defense?

If Shore had extensive knowledge of the contamination before it purchased the property, how might that have affected the purchase price? Should
the result change if Shore knew nothing about the past contamination at the
time of purchase? What if Shore made no inquiry whatsoever into the potential
presence of site contamination? If it conducted a reasonable inquiry but
learned nothing? In the 1986 amendments to CERCLA (known as the
Superfund Amendment and Reauthorization Act, or SARA, Pub. L. 99–499,
Oct. 17, 1986), Congress broadened the third party defense to account for
so-called "innocent landowners." It did so, however, through a somewhat
convoluted definitional back door. Congress added a lengthy definition of the
term "contractual relationship," which specifies by exception what a purchaser
must do to take advantage of the third party defense:

The term "contractual relationship" includes, but is not limited to, land contracts, deeds, easements, leases, or other instruments transferring title or possession, unless the real property on which the facility concerned is located was acquired by the defendant after the disposal or placement of the hazardous substance on, in, or at the facility, and one or more of the circumstances described in clause (i), (ii), or (iii) is also established by the defendant by a preponderance of the evidence:

(i) At the time the defendant acquired the facility the defendant did not know and had no reason to know that any hazardous substance which is the subject of the release or threatened release was disposed of on, in, or at the facility.

(ii) The defendant is a government entity which acquired the facility by escheat, or through any other involuntary transfer or acquisition, or through the exercise of eminent domain authority by purchase or condemnation.

(iii) The defendant acquired the facility by inheritance or bequest.

42 U.S.C. §9601(35)(A) (as amended). Subsection (B) provides that, in order to take advantage of the first of these exceptions (lack of knowledge), a purchaser must conduct "all appropriate inquiries" into the condition of the property, and take reasonable actions to mitigate and contain any contamination once it is discovered on the property. *Id.* §9601(35)(B). What is the effect of this statutory amendment on the theory of CERCLA liability? If the purchaser does not "know and had no reason to know" about contamination at the time of purchase, after "all appropriate inquiry," how would this affect the purchase price and other terms of sale in ways that might justify the departure from the CERCLA liability principle? Pursuant to a later statutory amendment, EPA[2] issued regulations further defining the steps a prospective buyer must take in order to meet the "all appropriate inquiries" requirements. 70 Fed. Reg. 66,070-01 (November 1, 2005) (Standards and Practices for All Appropriate Inquiries, 40 C.F.R. Part 312).

7. *Brownfields redevelopment and bona fide purchasers.* Another variation on the "innocent landowner" problem is that of prospective developers who want to purchase properties that they *know are contaminated* for purposes of redevelopment. Many former industrial areas are now prime property for urban renewal. In fact, such urban "infill" development is viewed as a potent antidote to the significant environmental problems caused by suburban sprawl, which include air pollution due to increased traffic, loss of open space and wildlife habitat, and storm water runoff pollution. *See* EPA, Smart Growth in Brownfield Communities, October 28, 2003, available at www.epa.gov/smartgrowth/brownfields.htm. Given the prospect of CERCLA liability,

---

2. While CERCLA itself requires decisions to be made by "the President," this authority was delegated to EPA shortly after the law was passed. *See* Exec. Order No. 12,316, 46 Fed. Reg. 42,237 (1981); Exec. Order No. 12,286, 46 Fed. Reg. 9901 (1981). For purposes of simplicity, we will substitute EPA for the statutory references to the President.

however, developers are likely to avoid potentially contaminated properties like the plague, which poses a barrier to redevelopment. Congress addressed this environmental paradox in the Brownfields Revitalization and Environmental Restoration Act of 2001, Pub. L. 107–118, Title II, 115 Stat. 2360, Jan. 11, 2002. Congress defined a "brownfield site" as "real property, the expansion, redevelopment, or reuse of which may be complicated by the presence or potential presence of hazardous substance, pollutant, or contaminant." 42 U.S.C. §9601(39)(A). It excludes, however, properties that are already the subject of remediation or enforcement actions under CERCLA or other environmental laws. *Id.* §9601(39)(B). Brownfield status renders a site eligible for federal grants or loans to communities, nonprofit organizations, or developers to assist in site assessment and remediation. *Id.* §9604(k). Federal funding is used as a carrot to encourage the purchase, remediation, and redevelopment of contaminated sites.

Moreover, in the Brownfields Act, Congress created an entirely prospective liability exemption distinct from that already available for innocent purchasers, and tailored to sites that the purchaser knows to be contaminated after making appropriate inquiries. A "bona fide prospective purchaser" is defined as someone who acquires ownership after passage of the brownfields provision, and who can show that all disposal of hazardous substances occurred prior to acquisition; she made all appropriate inquiries as defined for purposes of the innocent landowner exemption; she took reasonable steps to stop continuing releases, prevent future releases, and mitigate harm from past releases; she cooperates fully with those authorized to take response actions, and she meets other specified requirements. *Id.* §9601(40). Congress then provided that "a bona fide prospective purchaser whose potential liability for a release or threatened release is based solely on the purchaser's being considered to be an owner or operator of a facility shall not be liable so long as the bona fide prospective purchaser does not impede the performance of a response action or natural resource restoration." *Id.* §9607(r)(1). Does the same rationale that justified liability relief for innocent purchasers, who do not know about site contamination at the time of purchase, apply to purchasers who do have such knowledge?

8. *Federally permitted releases.* In spite of the exceptions mentioned so far, CERCLA establishes liability for a wide variety of parties where there is a release or threatened release from a facility or vessel. CERCLA, however, includes the following simple but potentially broad liability exemption: "Recovery by any person (including the United States or any State or Indian tribe) for response costs or damages resulting from a federally permitted release shall be pursuant to existing law in lieu of this section." 42 U.S.C. §9607(j). The statute defines "federally permitted release" to include discharges, emissions, and other releases to the environment covered by a range of federal laws, including the Clean Water Act, the Solid Waste Disposal Act (RCRA), the Ocean Dumping Act, the Safe Drinking Water Act, the Clean Air Act, the Atomic Energy Act, and certain state laws as well. *Id.* §9601(10).

2. Joint and Several Liability under CERCLA

≣ *O'Neil v. Picillo*
≣ *883 F.2d 176 (1st Cir. 1989)*

COFFIN, SENIOR CIRCUIT JUDGE.

In July of 1977, the Picillos agreed to allow part of their pig farm in Coventry, Rhode Island to be used as a disposal site for drummed and bulk waste. That decision proved to be disastrous. Thousands of barrels of hazardous waste were dumped on the farm, culminating later that year in a monstrous fire ripping through the site. In 1979, the state and the Environmental Protection Agency (EPA) jointly undertook to clean up the area. What they found, in the words of the district court, were massive trenches and pits "filled with free-flowing, multi-colored, pungent liquid wastes" and thousands of "dented and corroded drums containing a veritable potpourri of toxic fluids." *O'Neil v. Picillo*, 682 F.Supp. 706, 709, 725 (D.R.I.1988).

This case involves the State of Rhode Island's attempt to recover the clean-up costs it incurred between 1979 and 1982 and to hold responsible parties liable for all future costs associated with the site. The state's complaint originally named thirty-five defendants, all but five of whom eventually entered into settlements totaling $5.8 million, the money to be shared by the state and EPA. After a month-long bench trial, the district court, in a thorough and well reasoned opinion, found three of the remaining five companies jointly and severally liable under section 107 of the Comprehensive Environmental Response, Compensation, and Liability Act of 1980, ("CERCLA") for all of the State's past clean-up costs not covered by settlement agreements, as well as for all costs that may become necessary in the future. The other two defendants obtained judgments in their favor, the court concluding that the state had failed to prove that the waste attributed to those companies was "hazardous," as that term is defined under the Act. Two of the three companies held liable at trial, American Cyanamid and Rohm and Haas, have taken this appeal. Both are so-called "generators" of waste, as opposed to transporters or site owners. Neither takes issue with the district court's finding that some of their waste made its way to the Picillo site. Rather, they contend that their contribution to the disaster was insubstantial and that it was, therefore, unfair to hold them jointly and severally liable for all of the state's past expenses not covered by settlements. They further contend that it was error to hold them liable for all future remedial work because the state has not demonstrated that such work ever will be necessary. With far less vigor, they also raise a series of equitable defenses, claiming that their liability should be reduced, either in whole or part, because (1) much of the damage to the site resulted from the government's sloppy handling of barrels; (2) the government's clean-up procedures were not cost-efficient as required by the Act, and (3) their waste ended up at the site through the acts of wholly unrelated third parties. Finally, they argue that the Act should not be applied retroactively and that it was inappropriate for the district court to award the government prejudgment interest in this case. After a careful review of the record, we conclude that none of these arguments suffices to warrant reversal of the judgment below.

Joint and Several Liability

Statutory Background

It is by now well settled that Congress intended that the federal courts develop a uniform approach governing the use of joint and several liability in CERCLA actions. The rule adopted by the majority of courts, and the one we adopt, is based on the Restatement (Second) of Torts: damages should be apportioned only if the *defendant* can demonstrate that the harm is divisible.

The practical effect of placing the burden on defendants has been that responsible parties rarely escape joint and several liability, courts regularly finding that where wastes of varying (and unknown) degrees of toxicity and migratory potential commingle, it simply is impossible to determine the amount of environmental harm caused by each party. It has not gone unnoticed that holding defendants jointly and severally liable in such situations may often result in defendants paying for more than their share of the harm. Nevertheless, courts have continued to impose joint and several liability on a regular basis, reasoning that where all of the contributing causes cannot fairly be traced, Congress intended for those proven at least partially culpable to bear the cost of the uncertainty.

In enacting the Superfund Amendments and Reauthorization Act of 1986 ("SARA"), Congress had occasion to examine this case law. Rather than add a provision dealing explicitly with joint and several liability, it chose to leave the issue with the courts, to be resolved as it had been — on a case by case basis according to the predominant "divisibility" rule. Congress did, however, add two important provisions designed to mitigate the harshness of joint and several liability. First, the 1986 Amendments direct the EPA to offer early settlements to defendants who the Agency believes are responsible for only a small portion of the harm, so-called *de minimis* settlements.[3] Second, the Amendments provide for a statutory cause of action in contribution, codifying what most courts had concluded was implicit in the 1980 Act. Under this section, courts "may allocate response costs among liable parties using such equitable factors as the court determines are appropriate." We note that appellants already have initiated a contribution action against seven parties before the same district court judge who heard this case.

While a right of contribution undoubtedly softens the blow where parties cannot prove that the harm is divisible, it is not a complete panacea since it frequently will be difficult for defendants to locate a sufficient number of additional, solvent parties. Moreover, there are significant transaction costs

---

3. Appellants apparently were offered settlements, but chose instead to try this case.

involved in bringing other responsible parties to court. If it were possible to locate all responsible parties and to do so with little cost, the issue of joint and several liability obviously would be of only marginal significance. We, therefore, must examine carefully appellants' claim that they have met their burden of showing that the harm in this case is divisible.[4]

Even assuming that a strict application of the Restatement rule would allow appellants to escape joint and several liability in a situation such as this — something which is far from clear, appellants having provided us with no common law tort precedents to support their reading of the Restatement formulation — we would nonetheless decline to place this threshold burden on the government in CERCLA actions. As we noted earlier, Congress intended for the federal courts to develop a uniform approach to govern the use of joint and several liability. The Restatement is one source for us to consult. While courts generally have looked to the Restatement for guidance, they have declined to place the burden of showing that defendants are "substantial" contributors on the government, recognizing Congress' concern that cleanup efforts not be held hostage to the time-consuming and almost impossible task of tracing all of the waste found at a dump site. As we also noted earlier, in passing the 1986 Amendments Congress chose not to dismantle the existing approach, but instead, to add provisions dealing with *de minimis* settlements and contribution actions. It is at these stages, then, that the question of "substantiality" should be considered, and not at the point of determining liability to the government.

Divisibility

The district court issued two rulings on joint and several liability. First, the court held appellants jointly and severally liable for all of the state's past costs not covered by settlements, roughly $1.4 million including prejudgment interest. According to appellants, this money was spent exclusively on "removal" costs or "surface cleanup" (e.g., sampling the waste, contacting responsible parties, and ultimately, *removing* the barrels and contaminated soil), and not on remedying the alleged damage to groundwater and other natural resources ("remedial" costs). Second, the district court held appellants jointly and severally liable for all future removal costs to be incurred by the state, as well as for all cost-efficient remedial action the state (and EPA) may deem necessary after conducting further tests. The parties discuss the two holdings separately and we shall do likewise.

---

4. Before we can turn to the divisibility issue, however, we must first resolve a threshold question raised by appellants. Citing the Restatement (Second) of Torts § 433B, appellants contend that before joint and several liability may be imposed, the *government* has the initial burden of showing that the defendants were a "substantial" cause of the harm. If the government cannot prove that the defendants were substantial contributors, then joint and several liability may not be imposed and the defendant's burden of demonstrating that the harm is divisible never arises. We reject this approach.

Past Costs

Appellants begin by stressing that the state's past costs involved only surface cleanup. They then argue that because it was possible to determine how many barrels of waste they contributed to the site, it is also possible to determine what proportion of the state's removal expenses are attributable to each of them simply by estimating the cost of excavating a single barrel. The EPA advances two reasons why this approach is incorrect. First, it claims that it was not possible to determine how many barrels were traceable to appellants, nor was it possible to determine how much of the contaminated soil removed by the state was attributable to each appellant, and therefore, that it is impossible to apportion the state's removal costs. Second, it argues that even if it were possible to determine what proportion of the state's removal costs are attributable to appellants, joint and several liability still would have been proper because the "harm to be apportioned is not the cost but the environmental contamination that prompts the response action." We shall discuss the EPA's two arguments in reverse order.

We state at the outset that we have some trouble with the EPA's second argument. Assuming the government ultimately undertakes remedial action to clean the groundwater in the area and then seeks to recover the costs of doing so, it will have in effect submitted two separate bills, one for the cost of removing the barrels and soil, and one for cleaning the water. We think it likely that the harm to the water will be indivisible, and therefore, that appellants could properly be held jointly and severally liable for the cost of this remedial action. But simply because the costs associated with cleaning the groundwater cannot be apportioned does not mean that we should decline to apportion the costs of removing the barrels and soil if those costs are in fact divisible. This would seem to follow from the basic common law principle that defendants not be held responsible for those costs traceable to others. We think that the EPA would have to accept as much. Nonetheless, the Agency adheres to the position that it is irrelevant whether or not the costs of *removal* can be apportioned.

The reason the Agency takes this position is not, then, because the environmental harm that *actually occurred* was indivisible, but because the additional environmental harm that the government *averted* would have been indivisible had it occurred. This argument gives us pause because it appears to contravene the basic tort law principle that one pays only for the harm that was, and not for the harm that might have been.

Assume that it costs the government $1 million to remove all of the barrels from a site, but of this million, only $300,000 were spent removing the defendant's barrels. Also assume that had the barrels not been removed, the additional damage to the environment would have been $5 million and that this five million would not have been divisible. The government certainly would not take the position that it could recover $5 million in such a situation. Instead, it would ask only for the $1 million that it actually spent. Yet when it comes to apportioning that million, the Agency argues that we should look to whether the $5 million of averted harm would be divisible.

If we were to accept the EPA's "averted harm" argument, it appears that apportionment would be appropriate only in the highly unlikely event that (1) all of the barrels were empty and no further environmental harm was possible; (2) the individual barrels were sufficiently far apart that even if further spillage occurred, there would be no commingling of wastes and thus no difficulty determining whose waste caused what damage; or (3) every barrel contained precisely the same type of waste so that even if there was further spillage and commingling, the environmental harm could be apportioned according to the volumetric contribution of each defendant. As the EPA undoubtedly recognizes, it rarely, if ever, will be the case that one of these three conditions is present. As a practical matter, then, joint and several liability will be imposed in *every* case.

Because we believe Congress did not intend for joint and several liability to be imposed without exception, we are troubled by the practical implications of the Agency's argument, the more so because it seems to find no support in common law tort principles, which were to be one of our benchmarks in developing a uniform approach to govern the imposition of joint and several liability. At oral argument, the Agency did not claim, however, that its theory fit within the common law framework of joint and several liability, but instead, took the position that these CERCLA cases are not standard tort suits. Although we recognize that Congress deviated from certain tort principles, we had thought that on the issue of joint and several liability we were to take our lead from evolving principles of common law. It would seem incumbent upon the Agency, then, to demonstrate that on this *particular* question of joint and several liability, Congress intended for us to abandon the common law.

Having said all that, we choose not to resolve the issue in this case. Had appellants met their burden of showing that the costs *actually incurred* by the state were capable of apportionment, we would have had no choice but to address the EPA's theory. But because we do not believe appellants have done so, we can, and do, choose to leave the question for another day. We turn now to the EPA's first contention that the state's removal costs are not capable of apportionment.

Removal Costs

The state's removal efforts proceeded in four phases (0-3), each phase corresponding roughly to the cleanup of a different trench. The trenches were located in different areas of the site, but neither party has told us the distance between trenches. Appellants contend that it is possible to apportion the state's removal costs because there was evidence detailing (1) the total number of barrels excavated in each phase, (2) the number of barrels in each phase attributable to them, and (3) the total cost associated with each phase. In support of their argument, they point us to a few portions of the record, but for the most part are content to rest on statements in the district court's opinion. Specifically, appellants point to the following two sentences in the opinion: (1) "I find that [American Cyanamid] is responsible for ten drums of toxic hazardous material found at the site;" and (2) as to Rohm and Haas, "I accept the state's estimate [of 49 drums and 303 five-gallon pails]." Appellants then add, without opposition from the government, that the ten barrels of American Cyanamid waste discussed by the district court were found exclusively in Phase II, and that the 303 pails and 49 drums of Rohm and Haas waste mentioned by the court were found exclusively in Phase III. They conclude, therefore, that American Cyanamid should bear only a minute percentage of the $995,697.30 expended by the state during Phase II in excavating approximately 4,500 barrels and no share of the other phases, and that Rohm and Haas should be accountable for only a small portion of the $58,237 spent during Phase III in removing roughly 3,300 barrels and no share of the other phases. We disagree.

The district court's statements concerning the waste attributable to each appellant were based on the testimony of John Leo, an engineer hired by the state to oversee the cleanup. We have reviewed Mr. Leo's testimony carefully. Having done so, we think it inescapably clear that the district court did not mean to suggest that appellants had contributed only 49 and 10 barrels respectively, but rather, that those amounts were all that could be *positively attributed* to appellants. Mr. Leo testified that out of the approximately 10,000 barrels that were excavated during the four phases, only "three to four hundred of the drums contained markings which could potentially be traced." This is not surprising considering that there had been an enormous fire at the site, that the barrels had been exposed to the elements for a number of years, and that a substantial amount of liquid waste had leaked and eaten away at the outsides of the barrels. Mr. Leo also testified that it was not simply the absence of legible markings that prevented the state from identifying the overwhelming majority of barrels, but also the danger involved in handling the barrels. Ironically, it was appellants themselves who, in an effort to induce Mr. Leo to lower his estimate of the number of barrels attributable to each defendant, elicited much of the testimony concerning the impossibility of accurately identifying all of the waste.

In light of the fact that most of the waste could not be identified, and that the appellants, and not the government, had the burden to account for all of this uncertainty, we think it plain that the district court did not err in holding them jointly and severally liable for the state's past removal costs. Perhaps in this situation the only way appellants could have demonstrated that they were limited contributors would have been to present specific evidence documenting the whereabouts of their waste at all times after it left their facilities. But far from doing so, appellants deny all knowledge of how their waste made its way to the site. Moreover, the government presented evidence that much of Rohm and Haas' waste found at the site came from its laboratory in Spring House, Pennsylvania and that during the relevant years, this lab generated over two thousand drums of waste, all of which were consigned to a single transporter. Under these circumstances, where Rohm and Haas was entrusting substantial amounts of waste to a single transporter who ultimately proved unreliable, we simply cannot conclude, absent evidence to the contrary, that only a handful of the 2,000 or more barrels reached the site.[11]

NOTES AND QUESTIONS ON *O'NEILL v. PICILLO*

1. *Fairness.* Joint and several liability can lead to what can seem to be highly inequitable results. While not likely in practice, a party that contributes a single barrel of waste to a large site contaminated by waste from numerous sources can be held liable for the entire cleanup, especially if other contributors are insolvent or cannot be identified or located. What is the justification for joint and several liability in terms of the pollution prevention and cleanup goals of CERCLA?

2. *Divisibility.* Joint and several liability is not an absolute rule in CERCLA cases. As discussed in the case, the courts leave open the possibility that a *defendant* can prove "divisibility" pursuant to section 433A of the Restatement (Second) of Torts, which provides:

> (1) Damages for harm are to be apportioned among two or more causes where
>> (a) there are distinct harms, or
>> (b) there is a reasonable basis for determining the contribution of each cause to a single harm.
> (2) Damages for any other harm cannot be apportioned among two or more causes.

In what way does this allocation of the burden of proof serve the statutory goals? What are the inherent difficulties in proving divisibility in hazardous waste cases?

In practice, courts have been very reluctant to find divisibility in cost recovery cases. Defendants must prove divisibility of *harm*, and not just the raw proportion of wastes they contributed to a contaminated site:

11. Even if it were possible to determine how many barrels each appellant contributed to the site, we still would have difficulty concluding that the state's removal costs were capable of apportionment. To apportion the cost of removing the over 10,000 barrels, we would have to know the cost of removing a single barrel. Appellants have proceeded on the assumption that the cost of removing barrels did not vary depending on their content. This assumption appears untenable given the fact that the state had to take added precautions in dealing with certain particularly dangerous substances, including those traceable to Rohm and Haas. Moreover, in addition to excavating barrels the state had to remove large amounts of soil. Because there was substantial commingling of wastes, we think that any attempt to apportion the costs incurred by the state in removing the contaminated soil would necessarily be arbitrary.

The generator defendants bore the burden of establishing a reasonable basis for apportioning liability among responsible parties. To meet this burden, the generator defendants had to establish that the environmental harm was divisible among responsible parties. They presented no evidence, however, showing a relationship between waste volume, the release of hazardous substances, and the harm at the site. Further, in light of the commingling of hazardous substances, the district court could not have reasonably apportioned liability without some evidence disclosing the individual and interactive qualities of the substances deposited there. Common sense counsels that a million gallons of certain substances could be mixed together without significant consequences, whereas a few pints of others improperly mixed could result in disastrous consequences. Under other circumstances proportionate volumes of hazardous substances may well be probative of contributory harm.

United States v. Monsanto Co., 858 F.2d 160, 172 (4th Cir. 1988). Courts have found divisibility in some cases, however, with a limited number of defendants, where the amounts contributed by individual defendants can be quantified easily, and where there are no issues involving the mixture of different wastes. *E.g.*, United States v. Hercules, Inc., 247 F.3d 706 (8th Cir. 2001) (discussing criteria that inform divisibility), *cert. denied*, 534 U.S. 1065 (2001); In re Bell Petroleum Services, Inc., 37 F.3d 889 (5th Cir. 1993) (finding divisibility where successive owners conducted the same activities, and proportionate activities could be documented).

3. *Incentives to settle.* The combination of strict liability, limited affirmative defenses, and the prospect of joint and several liability provide a huge incentive for defendants to settle for a known, fixed share of the total liability, which can temper the harshness of strict, joint and several liability. Note that 30 of the original 35 defendants entered into settlements with EPA and the state. Why, then, do you think that five of the defendants here chose to litigate and risk joint and several liability rather than accepting a liability-limiting settlement?

In the 1986 SARA amendments, Congress added section 122, which provides a wide range of potential kinds of settlement for various kinds of parties. 42 U.S.C. §9622. Congress added more settlement options and exemptions in the Small Business Liability Relief and Brownfields Revitalization Act of 2002, discussed above in the context of brownfields redevelopment. These include a "de microminimis exemption" from response costs for sites on the National Priorities List, for arrangers and transporters (not current or past owners or operators) who can demonstrate that they contributed extremely small quantities of waste to contaminated sites (less than 110 gallons of liquid materials or less than 200 pounds of solid materials), unless those materials "have contributed significantly or could contribute significantly, either individually or in the aggregate, to the cost of the response action or natural resource restoration with respect to the facility." 42 U.S.C. §9607(o). The arranger defendants in *Picillo* probably would not have met these quantity limitations, but if they had, how useful would this exemption have been?

4. *Contribution claims.* A second way liable parties can temper the harshness of joint and several liability, as noted by the court in *Picillo*, is the availability of contribution actions against other potentially responsible parties. Contribution claims were recognized by courts under the original version of CERCLA, but expressly ratified by Congress in the 1986 Amendments, when it added section 113(f). 42 U.S.C. §9613(f). The court in *Picillo*, however, notes that the right of contribution "is not a panacea since it frequently will be difficult for defendants to locate a sufficient number of additional, solvent parties." The Supreme Court also ruled recently that contribution claims under section 113(f) may only be brought "during or following" a civil action under section 106 or section 107. Cooper Indus., Inc. v. Aviall Services, Inc., 543 U.S. 157 (2004).

Unlike cost recovery claims under section 107(a), contribution claims under section 113(f) do not include joint and several liability: "In resolving contribution claims, the court may allocate response costs among liable parties using such equitable factors as the court determines are appropriate." 42 U.S.C. §9613(f)(1). While the statute itself does not identify the factors a court might consider in allocating liability among responsible parties in a contribution claim, some members of Congress identified a list of factors in the legislative process. Known as the "Gore factors" because then Congressman Al Gore endorsed them, these factors include:

- the ability of the parties to demonstrate that their contribution to releases can be distinguished;
- the degree of toxicity of the hazardous substances involved; the amount of hazardous substances involved;
- the parties' degree of involvement in generating, transporting, treating, storing, or disposing of the hazardous substances;
- the degree of care exercised by the parties; and the parties' cooperation with the government to prevent harm to health and the environment.

See, e.g., In re Bell Petroleum Services, Inc., 37 F.3d 889 (5th Cir. 1993) (applying Gore factors). Thus, absent settlements, the process of allocating liability among the various responsible parties is shifted from the initial cost recovery action to any subsequent contribution action. What purpose does this serve in fulfilling the statutory goals? Does it achieve one efficiency goal (expediting the initial cost recovery phase) at the expense of another (requiring a second phase of litigation)?

3. Categories of Responsible Parties

The true significance of strict liability and joint and several liability becomes clear when you focus on the breadth of parties who may fall within the four categories of statutory liability. In *Shore Realty*, the court found the company liable as a current owner of the contaminated property, even though it contributed no waste to the site. Its principal shareholder and official, LeoGrande, was liable not as an owner, but as a current operator of the property, even though he intended to operate a condominium development, not a hazardous waste site. In *Picillo*, American Cyanamid and Rohm & Haas purportedly transferred relatively small amounts of waste to disposal companies, and did not even know where their waste would be shipped. Yet the court found them jointly and severally liable for the entire cleanup at a site that handled wastes from many generators. This gives you a sense of the breadth of parties that might incur extensive CERCLA liability. But it does not even cover all categories of potentially responsible parties.

What acts, omissions, or circumstances justify liability under CERCLA? As you read in *Shore Realty*, to some extent, answers are simply a matter of statutory construction. Courts often construe the statute and answer these questions in light of the major goals of the statute. Some CERCLA liability issues, however, are addressed under principles of common law, in part as a matter of legislative intent, and in part because Congress did not address some issues in the statute. In the case that follows, the Supreme Court provided some guidance on how these issues should be addressed in general, and in the specific context of parent-subsidiary corporate relationships. It also will give you some sense of the potential intricacies of CERCLA litigation, which can involve hundreds of parties.

U.S. v. Bestfoods
524 U.S. 51 (1998)

JUSTICE SOUTER delivered the opinion of the Court.

The United States brought this action for the costs of cleaning up industrial waste generated by a chemical plant. The issue before us, under [CERCLA], is whether a parent corporation that actively participated in, and exercised control over, the operations of a subsidiary may, without more, be held liable as an operator of a polluting facility owned or operated by the subsidiary. We answer no, unless the corporate veil may be pierced. But a corporate parent that actively participated in, and exercised control over, the operations of the facility itself may be held directly liable in its own right as an operator of the facility.

I

In 1980, CERCLA was enacted in response to the serious environmental and health risks posed by industrial pollution. [Under CERCLA], those actually "responsible for any damage, environmental harm, or injury from chemical poisons [may be tagged with] the cost of their actions." The term "person" is defined in CERCLA to include corporations and other business organizations, and the term "facility" enjoys a broad and detailed definition as well. The phrase "owner or operator" is defined only by tautology, however, as "any person owning or operating" a facility, and it is this bit of circularity that prompts our review.

II

In 1957, Ott Chemical Co. (Ott I) began manufacturing chemicals at a plant near Muskegon, Michigan, and its intentional and unintentional dumping of hazardous substances significantly polluted the soil and ground water at the site. In 1965, respondent CPC International Inc.[3] incorporated a wholly owned subsidiary to buy Ott I's assets in exchange for CPC stock. The new company, also dubbed Ott Chemical Co. (Ott II), continued chemical manufacturing at the site, and continued to pollute its surroundings. CPC kept the managers of Ott I, including its founder, president, and principal shareholder, Arnold Ott, on board as officers of Ott II. Arnold Ott and several other Ott II officers and directors were also given positions at CPC, and they performed duties for both corporations.

In 1972, CPC sold Ott II to Story Chemical Company, which operated the Muskegon plant until its bankruptcy in 1977. Shortly thereafter, when respondent Michigan Department of Natural Resources (MDNR) examined the site for environmental damage, it found the land littered with thousands of leaking and even exploding drums of waste, and the soil and water saturated with noxious chemicals. MDNR sought a buyer for the property who would be willing to contribute toward its cleanup, and after extensive negotiations, respondent Aerojet-General Corp. arranged for transfer of the site from the Story bankruptcy trustee in 1977. Aerojet created a wholly owned California subsidiary, Cordova Chemical Company (Cordova/California), to purchase the property, and Cordova/California in turn created a wholly owned Michigan subsidiary, Cordova Chemical Company of Michigan (Cordova/Michigan), which manufactured chemicals at the site until 1986.

By 1981, the federal Environmental Protection Agency had undertaken to see the site cleaned up, and its long-term remedial plan called for expenditures well into the tens of millions of dollars. To recover some of that money, the United States filed this action under §107 in 1989, naming five defendants as responsible parties: CPC, Aerojet, Cordova/California, Cordova/Michigan, and Arnold Ott.[6] (By that time, Ott I and Ott II were defunct.) After the parties (and MDNR) had launched a flurry of contribution claims, counterclaims, and cross-claims, the District Court consolidated the cases for trial in three phases: liability, remedy, and insurance coverage. So far, only the first phase has been

---

3. CPC has recently changed its name to Bestfoods. Consistently with the briefs and the opinions below, we use the name CPC herein.

6. Arnold Ott settled out of court with the Government on the eve of trial.

completed; in 1991, the District Court held a 15-day bench trial on the issue of liability. Because the parties stipulated that the Muskegon plant was a "facility" . . . , that hazardous substances had been released at the facility, and that the United States had incurred reimbursable response costs to clean up the site, the trial focused on the issues of whether CPC and Aerojet, as the parent corporations of Ott II and the Cordova companies, had "owned or operated" the facility within the meaning of §107(a)(2).

[The Supreme Court explained the reasoning applied by the District Court, which held both parent corporations (CPC and Aerojet) liable as operators. It then quoted the Court of Appeals' reasoning for reversing the District Court in a 7 to 6 *en banc* opinion:]

> [W]here a parent corporation is sought to be held liable as an operator based upon the extent of its control of its subsidiary which owns the facility, the parent will be liable only when the requirements necessary to pierce the corporate veil [under state law] are met. In other words, whether the parent will be liable as an operator depends upon whether the degree to which it controls its subsidiary and the extent and manner of its involvement with the facility, amount to the abuse of the corporate form that will warrant piercing the corporate veil and disregarding the separate corporate entities of the parent and subsidiary.

Applying Michigan veil-piercing law, the Court of Appeals decided that neither CPC nor Aerojet was liable for controlling the actions of its subsidiaries, since the parent and subsidiary corporations maintained separate personalities and the parents did not utilize the subsidiary corporate form to perpetrate fraud or subvert justice.

We granted certiorari to resolve a conflict among the Circuits over the extent to which parent corporations may be held liable under CERCLA for operating facilities ostensibly under the control of their subsidiaries. We now vacate and remand.

III

It is a general principle of corporate law deeply "ingrained in our economic and legal systems" that a parent corporation (so-called because of control through ownership of another corporation's stock) is not liable for the acts of its subsidiaries. Thus it is hornbook law that "the exercise of the 'control' which stock ownership gives to the stockholders . . . will not create liability beyond the assets of the subsidiary. That 'control' includes the election of directors, the making of by-laws . . . and the doing of all other acts incident to the legal status of stockholders. Nor will a duplication of some or all of the directors or executive officers be fatal." Although this respect for corporate distinctions when the subsidiary is a polluter has been severely criticized in the literature, nothing in CERCLA purports to reject this bedrock principle, and against this venerable common-law backdrop, the congressional silence is audible. The Government has indeed made no claim that a corporate parent is liable as an owner or an operator under §107 simply because its subsidiary is subject to liability for owning or operating a polluting facility.

But there is an equally fundamental principle of corporate law, applicable to the parent-subsidiary relationship as well as generally, that the corporate veil may be pierced and the shareholder held liable for the corporation's conduct when, *inter alia,* the corporate form would otherwise be misused to accomplish certain wrongful purposes, most notably fraud, on the shareholder's behalf. Nothing in CERCLA purports to rewrite this well-settled rule, either. CERCLA is thus like many another congressional enactment in giving no indication that "the entire corpus of state corporation law is to be replaced simply because a plaintiff's cause of action is based upon a federal statute," and the failure of the statute to speak to a matter as fundamental as the liability implications of corporate ownership demands application of the rule that "[i]n order to abrogate a common-law principle, the statute must speak directly to the question addressed by the common law." The Court of Appeals was accordingly correct in holding that when (but only when) the corporate veil may be pierced,[7] may a parent corporation be charged with derivative CERCLA liability for its subsidiary's actions.[8]

IV

A.

If the Act rested liability entirely on ownership of a polluting facility, this opinion might end here; but CERCLA liability may turn on operation as well as ownership, and nothing in the statute's terms bars a parent corporation from direct liability for its own actions in operating a facility owned by its subsidiary. The fact that a corporate subsidiary happens to own a polluting facility operated by its parent does nothing, then, to displace the rule that the parent "corporation is [itself] responsible for the wrongs committed by its agents in the course of its business." It is this direct liability that is properly seen as being at issue here.

Under the plain language of the statute, any person who operates a polluting facility is directly liable for the costs of cleaning up the pollution. This

---

7. There is significant disagreement among courts and commentators over whether, in enforcing CERCLA's indirect liability, courts should borrow state law, or instead apply a federal common law of veil piercing. Since none of the parties challenges the Sixth Circuit's holding that CPC and Aerojet incurred no derivative liability, the question is not presented in this case, and we do not address it further.

8. Some courts and commentators have suggested that this indirect, veil-piercing approach can subject a parent corporation to liability only as an owner, and not as an operator. We think it is otherwise, however. If a subsidiary that operates, but does not own, a facility is so pervasively controlled by its parent for a sufficiently improper purpose to warrant veil piercing, the parent may be held derivatively liable for the subsidiary's acts as an operator.

is so regardless of whether that person is the facility's owner, the owner's parent corporation or business partner, or even a saboteur who sneaks into the facility at night to discharge its poisons out of malice. If any such act of operating a corporate subsidiary's facility is done on behalf of a parent corporation, the existence of the parent-subsidiary relationship under state corporate law is simply irrelevant to the issue of direct liability.

This much is easy to say: the difficulty comes in defining actions sufficient to constitute direct parental "operation." Here of course we may again rue the uselessness of CERCLA's definition of a facility's "operator" as "any person operating" the facility, which leaves us to do the best we can to give the term its "ordinary or natural meaning." And in the organizational sense more obviously intended by CERCLA, the word ordinarily means "[t]o conduct the affairs of; manage: *operate a business.*" So, under CERCLA, an operator is simply someone who directs the workings of, manages, or conducts the affairs of a facility. To sharpen the definition for purposes of CERCLA's concern with environmental contamination, an operator must manage, direct, or conduct operations specifically related to pollution, that is, operations having to do with the leakage or disposal of hazardous waste, or decisions about compliance with environmental regulations.

B.

With this understanding, we are satisfied that the Court of Appeals correctly rejected the District Court's analysis of direct liability. But we also think that the appeals court erred in limiting direct liability under the statute to a parent's sole or joint venture operation, so as to eliminate any possible finding that CPC is liable as an operator on the facts of this case.

1.

By emphasizing that "CPC is directly liable under section 107(a)(2) as an operator because CPC actively participated in and exerted significant control over Ott II's business and decision-making," the District Court applied the "actual control" test of whether the parent "actually operated the business of its subsidiary," as several Circuits have employed it.

The well-taken objection to the actual control test, however, is its fusion of direct and indirect liability; the test is administered by asking a question about the relationship between the two corporations (an issue going to indirect liability) instead of a question about the parent's interaction with the subsidiary's facility (the source of any direct liability). If, however, direct liability for the parent's operation of the facility is to be kept distinct from derivative liability for the subsidiary's own operation, the focus of the enquiry must necessarily be different under the two tests. "The question is not whether the parent operates the subsidiary, but rather whether it operates the facility, and that operation is evidenced by participation in the activities of the facility, not the subsidiary. Control of the subsidiary, if extensive enough, gives rise to indirect liability under piercing doctrine, not direct liability under the statutory language." The District Court was therefore mistaken to rest its analysis on CPC's relationship with Ott II, premising liability on little more than "CPC's 100-percent ownership of Ott II" and "CPC's active participation in, and at times majority control over, Ott II's board of directors." The analysis should instead have rested on the relationship between CPC and the Muskegon facility itself.

In sum, the District Court's focus on the relationship between parent and subsidiary (rather than parent and facility), combined with its automatic attribution of the actions of dual officers and directors to the corporate parent, erroneously, even if unintentionally, treated CERCLA as though it displaced or fundamentally altered common-law standards of limited liability. Indeed, if the evidence of common corporate personnel acting at management and directorial levels were enough to support a finding of a parent corporation's direct operator liability under CERCLA, then the possibility of resort to veil piercing to establish indirect, derivative liability for the subsidiary's violations would be academic. There would in essence be a relaxed, CERCLA-specific rule of derivative liability that would banish traditional standards and expectations from the law of CERCLA liability. But, as we have said, such a rule does not arise from congressional silence, and CERCLA's silence is dispositive.

2.

We accordingly agree with the Court of Appeals that a participation-and-control test looking to the parent's supervision over the subsidiary, especially one that assumes that dual officers always act on behalf of the parent, cannot be used to identify operation of a facility resulting in direct parental liability. Nonetheless, a return to the ordinary meaning of the word "operate" in the organizational sense will indicate why we think that the Sixth Circuit stopped short when it confined its examples of direct parental operation to exclusive or joint ventures, and declined to find at least the possibility of direct operation by CPC in this case.

In our enquiry into the meaning Congress presumably had in mind when it used the verb "to operate," we recognized that the statute obviously meant something more than mere mechanical activation of pumps and valves, and must be read to contemplate "operation" as including the exercise of direction over the facility's activities. The Court of Appeals recognized this by indicating that a parent can be held directly liable when the parent operates the facility in the stead of its subsidiary or alongside the subsidiary in some sort of a joint venture. We anticipated a further possibility above, however, when we observed that a dual officer or director might depart so far from the norms of parental influence exercised through dual officeholding as to serve the parent, even when ostensibly acting on behalf of the subsidiary in operating the facility. Yet another possibility, suggested by the facts of this case, is that an agent of the parent with no hat to wear but the parent's hat might manage or direct activities at the facility.

Identifying such an occurrence calls for line-drawing yet again, since the acts of direct operation that give rise to parental liability must necessarily be distinguished from the interference that stems from the normal relationship between parent and subsidiary. Again norms of corporate behavior (undisturbed by any CERCLA provision) are crucial reference points. Just as we may look to such norms in identifying the limits of the presumption that a dual officeholder acts in his ostensible capacity, so here we may refer to them in distinguishing a parental officer's oversight of a subsidiary from such an officer's control over the operation of the subsidiary's facility. "[A]ctivities that involve the facility but which are consistent with the parent's investor status, such as monitoring of the subsidiary's performance, supervision of the subsidiary's finance and capital budget decisions, and articulation of general policies and procedures, should not give rise to direct liability." The critical question is whether, in degree and detail, actions directed to the facility by an agent of the parent alone are eccentric under accepted norms of parental oversight of a subsidiary's facility.

There is, in fact, some evidence that CPC engaged in just this type and degree of activity at the Muskegon plant. The District Court's opinion speaks of an agent of CPC alone who played a conspicuous part in dealing with the toxic risks emanating from the operation of the plant. G.R.D. Williams worked only for CPC; he was not an employee, officer, or director of Ott II, and thus, his actions were of necessity taken only on behalf of CPC. The District Court found that "CPC became directly involved in environmental and regulatory matters through the work of . . . Williams, CPC's governmental and environmental affairs director. Williams . . . became heavily involved in environmental issues at Ott II." He "actively participated in and exerted control over a variety of Ott II environmental matters," and he "issued directives regarding Ott II's responses to regulatory inquiries."

We think that these findings are enough to raise an issue of CPC's operation of the facility through Williams's actions, though we would draw no ultimate conclusion from these findings at this point.

NOTES AND QUESTIONS ON *BESTFOODS*

1. *Holding.* What is the holding of the case? Are parent corporations ever liable under CERCLA? If so, when? Is Bestfoods liable?

2. *Statute versus common law.* According to the Supreme Court, how should courts decide when to apply common law principles in ruling on issues of CERCLA liability, and when should they ground decisions in the language and policy of the statute? Why shouldn't *all* issues of CERCLA liability be guided, at least in part, by the goals and policies underlying the statute?

3. *Successor corporations.* A similar issue about the applicability of common law as opposed to CERCLA-specific liability rules affects the liability of successor corporations under CERCLA. CERCLA does not speak directly to what legal standard applies to gauge the appropriateness of imposing successor liability. Under traditional successor liability analysis, there is no liability for successor corporations unless (1) the purchaser expressly or impliedly agrees to assume the liabilities; (2) the transaction is a de facto merger or consolidation; (3) the purchaser is a "mere continuation" of the seller; or (4) the transaction is an effort to fraudulently escape liability. FLETCHER, CYCLOPEDIA OF THE LAW OF PRIVATE CORPORATIONS §7122 (2004). Prior to *Bestfoods*, several circuits had embraced an expansive view of successor liability — the "substantial continuation" theory — that enlarged the "mere continuation" theory of liability beyond the boundaries of traditional federal common law and most states' corporate law. *See, e.g.,* U.S. v. Mexico Feed and Seed Co., 980 F.2d 478 (8th Cir. 1992) (upholding application of "substantial continuation" theory to effectuate remedial purposes of CERCLA); U.S. v. Carolina Transformer Co., 978 F.2d 832 (4th Cir. 1992) (same). The justification for such expansion was the broad liability net envisioned by Congress in enacting CERCLA. In *Bestfoods*, however, the Supreme Court found that CERCLA's "failure to speak to a matter as fundamental as the liability implications of corporate ownership demands application of the rule that 'in order to abrogate a common-law principle, the statute must speak directly to the question addressed by the common law.'" 524 U.S. at 64.

Courts addressing successor liability post-*Bestfoods* have ruled that judicially fashioned CERCLA-specific rules — such as the "substantial continuation" theory of successor liability — are not appropriate where an adequate body of applicable common law exists to resolve the issue at hand. *See, e.g.,* New York v. Nat'l Servs. Indus., Inc., 352 F.3d 682, 685 (2d Cir. 2003) ("[W]e take from *Bestfoods* the principle that when determining whether liability under CERCLA passes from one corporation to another, we must apply common law rules and not create CERCLA-specific rules."); United States v. Davis, 261 F.3d 1, 54 (1st Cir. 2001) (observing that after *Bestfoods* there is "little room for the creation of a federal rule of liability under [CERCLA]"); Atchison, Topeka & Santa Fe Ry. Co. v. Brown & Bryant, 159 F.3d 358, 364 (9th Cir. 1998) ("[W]e choose not to extend the 'mere continuation' exception to include the broader notion of a 'substantial continuation' recogniz[ing] that 'the traditional rules of successor liability in most states' should determine the limits of CERCLA liability.") (citations omitted).

4. *Owners and operators: reprise.* The *Bestfoods* decision sheds some light on the distinction between the terms "owner" and "operator" under section 107(a)(1) of CERCLA, terms that courts sometimes conflated in earlier CERCLA decisions. Whether a parent corporation is an "owner" of a facility otherwise held by a subsidiary corporation is, according to the Supreme Court, purely a matter of the pre-existing common law of corporate relationships. A parent will be held liable as an "owner" only where the corporate veil is pierced,

a rather difficult test to meet. Does this allow a parent corporation to use a poorly capitalized subsidiary to generate profits, but to shelter itself from potential CERCLA liability?

Whether a parent corporation can be held liable as an "operator," however, is a separate inquiry. To meet this test, a parent corporation (or one of its officials) "must manage, direct, or conduct operations specifically related to pollution, that is, operations having to do with the leakage or disposal of hazardous waste, or decisions about compliance with environmental regulations." Thus, officials from a parent corporation can "manage" a subsidiary corporation's fiscal and general business affairs, for purposes of protecting the parent corporation's general investment interests, without incurring CERCLA liability. Once they make decisions that affect environmental compliance and waste management issues, however, the door may be open to liability as an "operator" under CERCLA. What if the parent corporation decides to reduce the environmental compliance budget of the subsidiary to fund more product development work, with a goal of increasing profits?

5. *State or federal common law?* The Supreme Court leaves open the question of whether CERCLA liability should reflect the separate common law (or, where applicable, statutory law) of different states, or a unified body of federal common law. Should concerns about uniformity in application of CERCLA override concerns about uniformity in application of state business law?

6. *Management control.* In *Shore Realty*, recall that the court found LeoGrande liable as an operator of the Shore Road site, an issue we will explore further in the following case. It did not, however, find ownership liability based on the fact that LeoGrande was the sole shareholder of the company. Explain this result, using the reasoning of *Bestfoods.* For similar reasons, Congress created statutory exceptions for entities who have ownership interests purely to secure a loan, with a distinction between a pure ownership interest and management participation very similar to that articulated by the Supreme Court in *Bestfoods*:

> The term "owner or operator" does not include a person that is a lender that, without participation in the management of a vessel or facility, holds indicia of ownership primarily to protect the security interest of the person in the vessel or facility.

42 U.S.C. §9601(20)(E)(I). The legislative definition then identifies the kinds of decisions that constitute "participation in management" sufficient to confer liability. *Id.* §9601(20)(F). This includes such actions as exercising decision-making control over environmental compliance, or exercising control over day-to-day facility management in ways that affect environmental compliance. The definition clarifies, however, that the mere "capacity to influence, or the unexercised right to control" is not sufficient to confer liability, *cf.* U.S. v. Gurley, 43 F.3d 1188 (8th Cir. 1994), *cert. denied*, 516 U.S. 817 (1995)

(pre-*Bestfoods* decision finding operator liability based on mere authority to control), and includes a long list of actions that do not constitute "participation in management." 42 U.S.C. §9601(20)(F)(iv). Likewise, in the Asset Conservation Act of 1996, Congress limited the liability of a fiduciary to the value of the assets held, absent evidence of negligence on the part of the fiduciary that gave rise, in whole or in part, to the activities creating CERCLA liability. Asset Conservation, Lender Liability and Deposit Insurance Protection Act of 1996, 110 Stat. 3009 *et seq.*; *see* 42 U.S.C. §9607(n).

The court noted in *Picillo* that the arranger defendants (American Cyanamid and Rohm & Haas) had already filed contribution actions in an effort to avoid the full bite of joint and several liability. The companies brought these claims against various parties along the chain of waste management, including transporters, waste brokers, and others involved in the final disposal site. The continuing saga is reflected in the following decision:

American Cyanamid Co. v. Capuano
381 F.3d 6 (1st Cir. 2004)

TORRUELLA, CIRCUIT JUDGE.

In 1977, Warren Picillo, Sr. and his wife agreed to allow part of their pig farm in Coventry, Rhode Island ("Picillo site") to be used as a disposal site for drummed and bulk waste. Later that year, after thousands of barrels of hazardous waste replaced what pigs at one time called home, a monstrous explosion ripped through the Picillo site. The towering flames, lasting several days, brought the waste site to the attention of the Rhode Island environmental authorities. Rhode Island investigators "discovered large trenches and pits filled with free-flowing, multi-colored, pungent liquid wastes." Recognizing the environmental disaster it had discovered, Rhode Island closed the pig farm and, with the federal government, began the cleanup process.

In a nutshell, this case involves an action under [CERCLA], brought by a company whose hazardous waste was deposited at the Picillo site against a group of people who were involved with the site.

I. Background

A. CERCLA

CERCLA is a statutory scheme that provides specific procedures for the remediation of a hazardous site. To understand this appeal, it is necessary to mention some of these procedures and define certain terms.

The remediation process at a hazardous site is called a response action. A response action involves removal actions, which "means the cleanup or removal of released hazardous substances from the environment," and remedial actions, which "means those actions consistent with permanent remedy taken instead of or in addition to removal actions in the event of a release or threatened release of a hazardous substance into the environment."

When the government performs a response action, it can bring "a cost recovery action under §9607 for the costs of the cleanup [against] a party found to be an owner or operator, past operator, transporter, or arranger." "A party found liable under §9607 may in turn bring an action for contribution" against potentially responsible parties ("PRPs") under §9613(f).

B. The Parties

Defendants-appellants, Daniel Capuano, Jr.; Jack Capuano; United Sanitation, Inc.; A. Capuano Brothers, Inc.; and Capuano Enterprises, Inc. (hereinafter referred to as "the Capuanos"), were in the business of hauling hazardous waste. Jack Capuano was the president and sole shareholder of Sanitary Landfill, Inc., a landfill operation located in Cranston, Rhode Island. Jack Capuano and Daniel Capuano jointly owned United Sanitation, Inc., a waste hauling company. Jack Capuano was the president of United Sanitation and Daniel was the vice-president. In 1977, the Capuanos reached an agreement with Warren Picillo to dump hazardous waste on his pig farm.

In 1977, plaintiff-appellee, Rohm & Haas Company ("R & H") operated research facilities in Spring House and Bristol, Pennsylvania, which generated hazardous waste. Forty-nine of the 10,000 drums of waste at Picillo were generated by R & H.

These drums ended up at the Picillo site in a round-about way. R & H's Spring House facility contracted with Jonas Waste Removal ("Jonas") to dispose of its waste. Jonas sent the waste to the Chemical Control Corporation, which later contracted with Chemical Waste Removal to dispose of the waste. Chemical Waste Removal disposed of the waste at the Picillo site. R & H's Bristol facility contracted with Scientific Chemical Processing ("SCP") to dispose of its waste. SCP later contracted with Daniel Capuano and United Sanitation to dispose of the waste at the Picillo site.

C. The Soil Cleanup

In 1983, Rhode Island brought an enforcement action under CERCLA §107, for cleanup costs at the Picillo site. This initial action was brought against 35 defendants "who were either owner/operators of the site, parties who allegedly transported waste there, parties alleged to have arranged for their waste to be transported to the site, and parties alleged to have produced waste deposited at the site."

Rhode Island settled with twenty of the defendants, including the Capuanos. The Capuanos agreed to pay $500,000. Rhode Island went to trial against five of the remaining defendants, including R & H. After trial, the district court found R & H and two other companies jointly and severally liable for un-reimbursed past response costs of $991,937 and for "all future costs of removal or remedial action incurred by the state includ[ing] any costs associated with the removal of contaminated soil piles." We affirmed the district court's holdings. *O'Neil v. Picillo*, [*supra*].

The United States also sought reimbursement for its response costs associated with the soil cleanup at the Picillo site and settled with many parties, including the Capuanos. The Capuanos agreed to pay $1,500,000. The settling parties received contribution protection as part of the settlement agreement. *See* 42 U.S.C. §9613(f)(2) ("A person who has resolved its liability to the United States or a State in an administrative or judicially approved settlement shall not be liable for claims for contribution regarding matters addressed in the settlement."). In 1989, the United States filed a cost recovery action under §9607 against R & H and another company, American Cyanamid.

D. Groundwater Cleanup

In 1987, the United States began developing a Remedial Investigation and Feasibility Study ("RI/FS") with respect to the groundwater at the Picillo site. By September 1993, the United States called for a groundwater cleanup. On March 30, 1994, the United States issued a "special notice letter" to twenty PRPs, including the Capuanos and R & H, demanding they implement a groundwater remedy and reimburse the Environmental Protection Agency ("EPA") for the costs related to the RI/FS and enforcement costs. In response to the United States's letter, two groups of PRPs made settlement offers. The Capuanos joined neither group. R & H joined one of the groups making a settlement offer. As a result, R & H began incurring cleanup costs in late 1994. R & H was expelled from the settlement group, however, in March 1995 because it could not agree with the group regarding R & H's contribution. Without R & H, a group of PRPs settled with the United States and agreed to implement a groundwater remedy.

In 1998, R & H entered a consent decree with the United States to pay $4,350,000 to compensate the United States for direct response costs related to groundwater cleanup, plus $110,000 towards oversight costs, and $69,000 towards natural resource damage. The consent decree was approved in October 1998.

E. R & H's Contribution Action

In April 1995, R & H instituted a contribution action to recover past and future response costs related to groundwater cleanup. The suit named 52 PRPs, including the Capuanos.

II.   Part One: Affirmative defenses

C.   *Contribution Immunity*

In 1988, the Capuanos entered settlement agreements with the United States and Rhode Island. In return for contribution immunity, the Capuanos paid $1,500,000 to the United States and $500,000 to Rhode Island. The Capuanos argue that their Consent Decree provides contribution immunity against R & H's contribution claims. The Capuanos' settlement agreement provided immunity for "future liability" for past response costs, but it did not provide immunity for claims related to "groundwater protection or remediation." The Capuanos argue that R & H failed to prove that the money R & H paid to the United States, and for which R & H now seeks contribution, was for groundwater protection or remediation. We disagree. The Capuanos' argument is nothing more than creative word play. According to the Capuanos, R & H settled with the government for "past response costs." R & H's "past response costs" are costs incurred by the United States through October 25, 1995. Thus, R & H's "past response costs" would be "future liability" for past response costs as it pertains to the Capuanos and the Capuanos have contribution protection for future liability for past response costs.

Regardless of how the Capuanos choose to phrase the costs incurred, it is undisputed that the four corners of the Capuanos Consent Decree does not provide contribution immunity for costs relating to groundwater protection or remediation. At trial, R & H introduced documents detailing the work performed by the United States in regard to the groundwater remediation and introduced the testimony of an expert that the cost of the groundwater Remedial Investigation ("RI") and Feasibility Study ("FS") exceeded $4.7 million. The expert testified that the groundwater RI/FS was different from the soil RI/FS and the $4.7 million did not include any costs dealing with the soil remediation. R & H ultimately settled with the United States for $4.35 million and is seeking contribution for a portion of that amount. The evidence showed, therefore, that the costs R & H paid to the United States, for which it now seeks contribution, were for groundwater protection and remediation, and the Capuanos do not have contribution immunity for costs relating to groundwater protection or remediation.

In the alternative, the Capuanos argue that even if there was proof showing that R & H is seeking contribution for the RI/FS relating to the groundwater, a RI/FS is part of a "removal action" and is not "groundwater protection or remediation" and thus it is not a cost that was excluded from the Capuanos' Consent Decree.

The RI/FS is part of the groundwater protection and remediation process. "The purpose of the . . . (RI/FS) is to assess site conditions and evaluate alternatives to the extent necessary to select a remedy. Developing and conducting an RI/FS generally includes the following activities: project scoping,

data collection, risk assessment, treatability studies, and analysis of alternatives." Since the RI/FS is the first step in groundwater protection and
remediation, the RI/FS is not a cost excluded by this Consent Decree.

III. Issues Relating to the Trial

E. Transporter Liability

The Capuanos appeal the district court's conclusion that the Capuanos
transported hazardous waste to the Picillo site. CERCLA imposes transporter
liability on "any person who accepts or accepted any hazardous substances for
transport to disposal or treatment facilities, incineration vessels or sites selected
by such person" from which there is a release of hazardous substances. The
district court concluded that United Sanitation and its officers, Jack and Daniel
Capuano, were liable as transporters for 7.94% of the waste delivered to the
Picillo site since Jack and Daniel selected the Picillo site and United Sanitation
transported 960 55-gallon drums of hazardous waste to the site.

The Capuanos argue that the district court's finding was clearly erroneous
because (1) United Sanitation did not transport hazardous waste; (2) United
Sanitation and the Capuanos had no trucks capable of transporting hazardous
waste; and (3) the only Capuano remotely identified with hazardous waste
disposal was Anthony Capuano. After examining the record, we find that the
district court's conclusion that the Capuanos were "transporters" was not
clearly erroneous.

First, Picillo testified that "the Capuanos themselves brought their own
waste down [to the Picillo site] on their own trucks" and that some of the
barrels "came from Danny Capuano's place." Although this testimony supports the finding that the Capuanos physically transported some of the waste,
we have interpreted CERCLA not to impose liability on a transporter who
merely follows the directives of a generator. Rather, for CERCLA liability to
attach, a transporter must "actively participate in the selection decision or have
substantial input in that decision." In this case, the Capuanos had substantial
input in the decision, often making the final determination whether to allow
waste to be dumped at their own land fill or to send it on to the Picillo site.
Further, the Capuanos arranged for employees of the Scientific Chemical
Corporation to visit the Picillo site as a possible waste dumping location. After
viewing the site, the visitors concluded "this would be an ideal spot."

Second, according to deposition and trial testimony, trucks carrying
hazardous waste would arrive at the Capuanos place of business only to be
redirected by the Capuanos, or their employee Louie Falcone, to the Picillo
site. Indeed, since the Picillo site was difficult to find, the Capuanos would
come to the Picillo site "in a pick-up truck in front of the big trucks and show
them where the farm was and show them where the dump was, to dump" the
hazardous waste.

Third, when the drivers arrived at the Picillo site, they would give Picillo, Sr. a bill of lading. At the end of the week, Picillo, Sr. would take the bills of lading to the Capuanos to get paid. The record confirms that Mr. Picillo received United Sanitation checks signed by Jack Capuano and Dan Capuano. Although these payments do not, in and of themselves, prove that the Capuanos transported the waste, the payments do support the inference that the Capuanos were involved with the transportation of waste to the Picillo site.

F. Operator Liability

The Capuanos appeal the district court's conclusion that the Capuanos were liable as operators of the Picillo site. [The court summarized the *Bestfoods* standard for operator liability.]

The district court's conclusion that the Capuanos were operators of the site was not clearly erroneous. First, the Capuanos approached Warren Picillo with the idea of dumping on his pig farm. Once Warren agreed, he gave the Capuanos exclusive disposal rights at the site and the Capuanos hired a bulldozer to clear the trees and "dig a big, big hole." The Capuanos walked the operator of the bulldozer to the site and "showed him what to do and how to do it." Such actions are consistent with those of an operator of a facility "who directs the workings of, manages, or conducts the affairs of a facility" [quoting *Bestfoods*].

Second, as discussed earlier, the Capuanos directed the hazardous waste to the Picillo site. If the drivers of the waste did not know how to reach the site, the Capuanos would drive them to the site so they could dump the waste. Further, the Capuanos managed and conducted the affairs of the Picillo site by organizing and implementing its payment structure. The waste generators paid the Capuanos to dispose of their waste and then the Capuanos would give Warren Picillo a share of the money. "[O]perator liability requires an ultimate finding of involvement with operations having to do with the leakage or disposal of hazardous waste." The fact that the Capuanos developed the idea for using the site, prepared the site for dumping, arranged for waste to be dumped at the site, showed transporters where to dump on the site, and collected payment and transmitted a share to Warren Picillo for dumping at the site demonstrates that the district court's conclusion that the Capuanos were liable as operators of the site was not clearly erroneous.

G. Arranger Liability

The Capuanos appeal the district court's conclusion that the Capuanos were liable as arrangers. The district court concluded that the Capuanos were arrangers because their conduct "constituted active participation as a broker in the disposal of their customer's waste." The Capuanos argue that arranger liability can only be imposed on a party that owned or possessed hazardous materials, not on a party that brokered the disposal of hazardous material.

An arranger is defined as:

any person who by contract, agreement, or otherwise arranged for disposal or treatment, or arranged with a transporter for transport for disposal or treatment, of hazardous substances owned or possessed by such person, *by any other party or entity,* at any facility owned or operated by another party or entity and containing such hazardous substances.

42 U.S.C. § 9607(a)(3) (emphasis added). We begin our inquiry by examining the plain language of the statute. This [language] can be read two ways, depending on which words the clause "by any other party or entity" modifies. First, this clause can be read to modify the preceding words "owned or possessed by such person," which would make liable any person who arranged for the disposal of a hazardous substance "owned or possessed by such person [or] by any other party or entity." Or, second, the clause can be read to modify the words "disposal or treatment," which would make the sentence read "any person who arranged for disposal or treatment by any other party or entity." The sentence structure makes it clear that the latter interpretation is the correct one. The clause "by any other party or entity" clarifies that, for arranger liability to attach, the disposal or treatment must be performed by another party or entity, as was the case here.

Some courts have held parties liable as arrangers even if they did not actually own or physically possess the hazardous waste so long as they had the authority to control the handling and disposal of the hazardous substances. Most of these cases involved a corporate officer of a generator of hazardous waste claiming he could not be liable as an arranger because he did not personally own or possess the waste. Thus, these holdings reflect the idea that a corporate officer can be liable as an arranger if he controls the decision to dispose of the waste on behalf of his company that owns the waste. These cases are distinguishable from the case at hand because this case does not involve corporate officers; rather it involves a party that does not own the waste and that arranges for the disposal of others' waste.

When a broker arranges for the disposal of hazardous waste and it does so by exercising control over the waste, such control can amount to constructive possession of the waste. Were we to interpret CERCLA not to impose liability on a party that constructively possessed hazardous waste and arranged for its illegal disposal, then the statute would be subject to a loophole through which brokers and middlemen could escape liability by arranging to have hazardous waste picked up and deposited at an illegal site. In addition to escaping liability, the broker would also profit by charging a fee for his services. Indeed, the Capuanos earned most of their profits in this manner. The Capuanos found a site, the Picillo pig farm, where hazardous waste could be dumped illegally. They then arranged for the waste to be picked up from various waste generators across New England and dumped on the illegal site. A broker should not be able to profit from such activity, much less escape liability. We therefore hold that a broker can be liable as an arranger if the broker controls the disposal of the waste.

Since the Capuanos, as discussed above, selected, secured, and directed the waste to the Picillo site, all for a fee, it was not clearly erroneous for the district court to conclude that the Capuanos were liable as arrangers given our interpretation of the statute.

NOTES AND QUESTIONS ON *AMERICAN CYANAMID*

1. *Scope of settlements.* Following the *Picillo* case, we discussed the powerful settlement-inducing nature of CERCLA liability, and the resulting frequency and importance of settlements in CERCLA practice. This case underscores the equally important corollary issue of the scope and meaning of CERCLA settlements. Section 113(f)(2) of CERCLA provides:

A person who has resolved his liability to the United States or a State in an administrative or judicially approved settlement shall not be liable for claims for contribution *regarding matters addressed in the settlement.* Such settlement does not discharge any other potentially liable persons unless its terms so provide, but it reduces the potential liability of the others by the amount of the settlement.

42 U.S.C. §9613(f)(2) (emphasis added). The following subsection preserves the right of the United States or a state to bring cost recovery actions against non-settling parties, as well as the right of settling private parties to bring contribution claims. As between the two kinds of claims, however, contribution claims by private parties remain subordinate to cost recovery claims brought by the governments. *Id.* §9613(f)(3). Section 122 includes more detailed provisions regarding the effect of particular kinds of CERCLA settlements, but embodies the same general principles. *See id.* §9622(c), (f), (g)(5). What was the significance of the language in section 113(f)(2) italicized above in the *Picillo/American Cyanamid* matter?

2. *Other PRP categories.* The *American Cyanamid* case also sheds more light on the breadth of other categories of potentially liable parties:

A. *Transporters.* The Capuanos were held liable under section 107(a)(4) because they not only physically transported waste to the Picillo pig farm site, but also "had substantial input in the decision" about *where* the waste would go. Why did Congress assign CERCLA liability to transporters who bring wastes to "sites selected by such person," but not to those who simply transport waste to sites selected by the waste generator or someone else? How might the business arrangements differ between waste generators and transporters who select the disposal site and those who do not, and why should that make a difference in terms of CERCLA liability?

    Why does the court interpret the statutory words "sites selected by such person" to require only "substantial input into the decision?" *See* U.S. v. Davis, 261 F.3d 1 (1st Cir. 2001) (discussing the proper interpretation of "sites selected by such person" in determining transporter liability under CERCLA); Tippins, Inc. v. USX Corp., 37 F.3d 87 (3d Cir. 1994) (distinguishing between the propriety of imposing CERCLA liability on a transporter who plays an active role in selecting a disposal site and a transporter who acts as "no more than a conduit of the waste"), *cert. denied*, 519 U.S. 808 (1996).

B. *Operators.* In *Shore Realty*, the court found LeoGrande liable as an operator because of his direct managerial role in making decisions at the site that affected the ongoing release of hazardous substances. In *Bestfoods*, however, the Supreme Court made clear that general management control is not sufficient to confer operator liability. Rather, "an operator must manage, direct, or conduct operations specifically related to pollution, that is, operations having to do with the leakage or disposal of hazardous waste, or decisions about compliance with environmental regulations." 524 U.S. at 66-67. Does this standard allow someone to effectively "manage" the environmental result at a site without making decisions "specifically" related to pollution? What did the Capuanos do that led the court to hold that they were "operators" of the disposal site for CERCLA purposes?

C. *Arrangers.* Rohm & Haas and American Cyanamid are the prototypical "arrangers" in the CERCLA liability scheme. The theory of arranger liability contemplates only that the potentially liable party "owned" or "possessed" the relevant hazardous material(s), and that the party arranged for the disposal of such materials, whether by contract, agreement or otherwise. Raytheon Constructors, Inc. v. Asarco, Inc., 368 F.3d 1214, 1219 (10th Cir. 2003). General intent to dispose of waste is sufficient for liability; specific site or method selection is not necessary. GenCorp, Inc. v. Olin Corp., 390 F.3d 433, 446 (6th Cir. 2004). The Capuanos clearly were not the original generators of the hazardous substances released from the pig farm site, as were Rohm & Haas, American Cyanamid, and others. However, the court still found the Capuanos liable as "arrangers," because of their role as "brokers and middlemen." What purpose does this interpretation serve beyond the liability that already attaches to transporters who choose the disposal site (and for which the Capuanos were already found liable)?

The concept of "arranger" liability has also generated a series of cases in which courts have scrutinized business relationships that led to the generation of hazardous substances in connection with subcontracting of manufacturing processes and product licensing. In U.S. v. Aceto Agricultural Chemical Corporation, 872 F.2d 1373 (8th Cir. 1989), for example, the Eighth Circuit used a "business surrogate" theory to find pesticide manufacturers liable under CERCLA for releases of hazardous substances at the site of a defunct formulator. In the business arrangement at issue in that case, the manufacturers of pesticide active ingredients (PAIs) shipped their products to formulators who mixed the PAIs with inert ingredients and packaged them for sale, with contemporaneous disposal of waste materials. The manufacturers retained ownership of the hazardous products. What is the basis for finding "arranger" liability under these circumstances? Was it the fact that the manufacturers continued to "own" the hazardous substances that led to the release? What if the manufacturer sold the formulator the materials and then bought them back in their reprocessed form?

What if a company sells a used product, with hazardous substances that must be disposed of before the remainder can be reused or recycled? *See, e.g.,* Catellus Development Corp. v. U.S., 34 F.3d 748 (9th Cir. 1994) (sale of spent auto batteries requiring lead disposal before casings can be resued); Cadillac Fairview v. U.S., 41 F.3d 562 (9th Cir. 1999) (sale of contaminated styrene for reprocessing). In those cases, the sellers were found liable because the transactions had a significant waste disposal component.

B. THE SCOPE OF THE CLEANUP OBLIGATION

Thus far, we have focused on the apportionment of CERCLA liability among PRPs. The second major factor that affects how much a party must pay is the nature and cost of the cleanup. A third factor is which costs parties must pay for.

Section 107(a) imposes liability for:

(A) all costs of removal or remedial action incurred by the United States Government or a State or an Indian tribe not inconsistent with the national contingency plan;

(B) any other necessary costs of response incurred by any other person consistent with the national contingency plan;

(C) damages for injury to, destruction of, or loss of natural resources, including the reasonable costs of assessing such injury, destruction, or loss resulting from such a release; and

(D) the costs of any health assessment or health effects study carried out under section 9604(I) of this title.

42 U.S.C. §9607(a). Note first what is *not* included in this list, which is toxic tort-type liability to private parties for damages other than those listed above, although the statute does expressly preserve the availability of common law or other statutory claims for those injuries. *Id.* §9607(j). (The "health assessment or health effects" liability in subsection (D) only covers the costs of the study,

conducted by the Agency for Toxic Substances and Disease Registry (ATSDR) within the Centers for Disease Control (CDC), and not actual damages from adverse health effects caused by the release.)

Natural resource damages may be recovered by federal, state, or tribal natural resource trustees, pursuant to a detailed set of regulations promulgated by a group of federal agencies. *See* 42 U.S.C. §9607(f); State of Ohio v. Department of the Interior, 880 F.2d 432 (D.C. Cir. 1989); 59 Fed. Reg. 14,265 (March 25, 1994). Unlike the other categories of recoverable damages under CERCLA, however, natural resource damages include a limited exception from the principle of retroactive liability. Damages may not be recovered "where such damages and the release of a hazardous substance from which such damages resulted" occurred "wholly before December 11, 1980." 42 U.S.C. §9607(f)(1). This provision of the statute has been used sparingly. *See* U.S. General Accounting Office, Status of Selected Federal Natural Resource Damage Settlements (November 1999); U.S. General Accounting Office, Superfund: Outlook and Experience with Natural Resource Settlements (April 1999).

Reference to the "national contingency plan" hints at, but does not come close to explicating, the significant quasi-regulatory role played by the federal and state governments in dictating the nature, cost and environmental adequacy of CERCLA cleanups. Thus, Judge Oakes' statement in *Shore Realty* that "CERCLA is not a regulatory standard-setting statute such as the Clean Air Act," 759 F.2d at 1041, is only partially correct, and belies the significant government role in establishing cleanup methods, standards and procedures both generally and for individual sites. Because these governmental decisions significantly affect the nature and costs of CERCLA cleanups, and because they will help you to understand better how the overall statutory scheme works, the following is a brief primer on the "regulatory side" of CERCLA.

The National Contingency Plan, or NCP, is a lengthy set of EPA regulations outlining "procedures and standards for responding to releases of hazardous substances, pollutants, and contaminants." 42 U.S.C. §9605(a). The NCP is published at 40 CFR §300 (2004). EPA originally developed the NCP to address oil spills and hazardous substance spills under section 311 of the Clean Water Act, 33 U.S.C. §1321, but Congress directed EPA to revise and republish the plan to address the much broader circumstances and responsibilities encompassed in CERCLA. The NCP thus addresses both the handling of emergency spills and leaks, and longer-term responses to the release of hazardous substances at a range of contaminated sites. Compliance with the NCP is particularly important to the CERCLA liability scheme, because liability is contingent on the response being "not inconsistent with" the plan for government cost recovery actions, and "consistent with" the plan for private cost recovery actions. *See* Washington State Dept. of Transp. v. Washington Natural Gas Co., 36 E.R.C. 1045 (W.D. Wash. 1992), *aff'd*, 51 F.3d 1489 (9th Cir. 1994), *amended and superseded by* 59 F.3d 793 (9th Cir. 1995) (disallowing recovery due to noncompliance with NCP).

For contaminated sites that are on the National Priorities List (NPL), and that undergo an intensive government cleanup process, the nature of the cleanup is also dictated by a somewhat complex "remedy selection" process. (A private owner of a contaminated site can avoid this process, of course, by conducting its own cleanup, and recover its costs from PRPs if they can be located and are solvent, and if the cleanup is conducted consistent with the NCP.) The major steps in a government-led process, all of which must be conducted pursuant to the NCP, are outlined in the following table:

Stage	Activity
Site identification.	The site is placed on CERCLIS, a national EPA database that includes over 10,000 sites. An updated list is available at http://www.epa.gov/superfund/sites.
Preliminary assessment.	Agency officials conduct a brief analysis of site conditions based on readily available information.
Site inspection.	On-site visit is used, along with the preliminary assessment (jointly known as a "PA/SI") to determine what additional action is needed.
Removal action.	The federal government is authorized to take immediate action to respond to a release or substantial threat of release of a hazardous substance into the environment, or a release or substantial threat of release of any other pollutant or contaminant into the environment that "may present an imminent and substantial danger to the public health or welfare." Removal actions are designed to reduce or eliminate immediate threats from releases or threatened releases, and may include actions such as the removal of the materials themselves, monitoring, placement of fencing or other containment structures, replacement of contaminated water supply, temporary evacuation and housing of threatened people, and similar emergency assistance.
Hazard ranking/listing.	The hazard ranking system is a process by which EPA determines the degree of risk to human health and the environment posed by a site compared to others around the country. While the NPL is used to determine EPA's cleanup priorities and the use of federal cleanup funds, it is not a prerequisite to liability or other statutory abatement authority.
Remedial investigation and feasibility study ("RI/FS") and remedy selection.	EPA conducts a more detailed evaluation of the site to determine what contaminants are present, the degree of contamination, and to evaluate feasible alternative remedies based on efficacy, cost, and other factors. Based on this investigation and other considerations discussed below, EPA issues a proposed plan for public comment, followed by a record of decision regarding the appropriate cleanup remedy and methods.

CERCLA section 121 sets forth a somewhat confusing and complex set of substantive standards used by EPA to determine the appropriate remedy at particular sites. Section 121(a) requires EPA to select "cost-effective" responses, taking into account both short- and long-term costs and operation and maintenance costs. Presumably, this favors permanent solutions over those that require ongoing treatment or maintenance. Section 121(b) establishes a hierarchy in which "treatment which permanently and significantly reduces the volume, toxicity or mobility of the hazardous substances, pollutants, or contaminants" is preferred over other cleanup methods, and in which offsite transport and disposal of contaminants without treatment is "the least favored alternative remedial action where practicable treatment technologies are available." The provision includes a list of factors EPA should consider in choosing among options, followed by the following:

> The President shall select a remedial action that is protective of human health and the environment, that is cost-effective, and that utilizes permanent solutions and alternative treatment technologies or resource recovery technologies to the maximum extent practicable.

42 U.S.C. §9621(b)(1). Section 121(d) adds to this set of standards a list of requirements under other federal or state environmental laws and regulations that must be met in CERCLA cleanups if they are "legally applicable or relevant and appropriate" standards (known from this language as "ARARs").

Finally, section 113(h) of the statute precludes "pre-enforcement review" of EPA's remedy selection decisions. That provision prohibits a federal court from reviewing EPA's remedy selection decision, except in connection with a list of cost recovery or enforcement actions under the statute, and then limits judicial relief to an order limiting cost recovery to those costs consistent with the NCP, and "such other relief as is consistent with" the NCP. Stated more succinctly, a party may not simply challenge a remedy selection when it is made, as is commonly true for review of EPA regulatory decisions, but only when it is implemented. Then, the presumptive relief is not reversal of EPA's remedy decision, but rather an assurance that responsible parties will be held liable not for the successfully challenged gold-plated Rolls Royce cleanup, but for the Honda Civic cleanup that would have been found consistent with the NCP.

NOTES AND QUESTIONS ON THE CLEANUP PROCESS

1. *Authority for cleanup decisions.* While the CERCLA approach is based primarily on "polluter pay" concepts of liability, Congress combined those principles with quasi-regulatory decisions left in the hands of EPA and the states. How does this combination of responsibility and authority serve the statutory goals? Suppose that a PRP decided to voluntarily clean up a site in hopes of avoiding protracted litigation under the Superfund. Would you advise the PRP to comply with the NCP? Why or why not?

2. *Consistency with the NCP.* Congress allowed cost recovery actions by governmental parties for costs "not inconsistent with" the NCP, while to be eligible for recovery, private costs must be "consistent with" the NCP. What practical significance does that difference have in CERCLA litigation?

3. *Nature of cleanup standards.* In part to review the concepts you learned in Parts II and III of this book, how would you characterize the cleanup standards included in section 121, quoted and explained above? Does the reference to "cost-effectiveness" make this a cost-benefit standard? Does the requirement that remedies be "protective of human health and the environment" make it an effects-based standard? Or does the preference for particular kinds of permanent treatment remedies make it a technology-based design standard?

PFOA SUPERFUND LIABILITY AND COUNSELING PROBLEM

For many years, Plastics, Inc. (PI) manufactured PFOA at one of its facilities. Recently, it announced that it would discontinue PFOA production. What possible reasons might have caused PI to reach this decision? What role do you think PI's lawyers played in this decision, *i.e.,* what kind of information and advice do you think they provided company executives to inform the decision? What can or should lawyers do if a client decides not to take their advice regarding this kind of decision? What about a decision regarding compliance with mandatory environmental laws and regulations (as opposed to the decision about what products to manufacture)?

The following additional facts are purely hypothetical. Also assume for purposes of this problem that PFOA, along with other wastes created during PFOA production, are "hazardous substances" for purposes of CERCLA.

Part 1 — The manufacturing site

After PI discontinues PFOA production, it decides that the remaining chemicals produced at that facility are not profitable enough to justify keeping the plant open. It is also a desirable location for a new high-density housing project for the rapidly growing nearby city, just a few blocks from the new station on the light commuter rail to downtown. A local developer (Greenbuilders) is interested in purchasing the property for an "eco-friendly" planned community. The developer proposes to tear down the chemical plant and build a mixed density, mixed use, transit-oriented development that would allow residents to walk to schools, most shopping, and amenities, and commute downtown by train. It would also preserve significant open space on PI's former grounds around the facility.

For decades before PI knew of any dangers from PFOA or related waste products, it disposed of some of its PFOA production wastes on site. Workers dumped large volumes of very dilute wastes (from equipment rinsing and such) on open fields behind the plant. PI was proud of its beautiful grounds, and the wastewater actually irrigated fields of wildflowers. While this wastewater contained very low concentrations of any particular chemical, over the long period of PFOA production, and because of the high volumes of wastewater, contaminant levels in the soil built up to fairly high levels. When it rains, some of these chemicals leach into nearby drinking water wells, and into local streams near the property. Recently, PFOA has been detected in drinking water from these wells, and in local streams, at levels that exceed the state's recently issued drinking water standards and surface water quality standards for PFOA, respectively.

1. If PI sells the property to Greenbuilders, will PI retain potential CERCLA liability after the sale? Why? Didn't PI do the "right thing" by discontinuing PFOA production? Is it being penalized for making that decision, and then for selling the site to a company that will redevelop it in an environmentally beneficial way?

2. If you were PI's lawyer, what advice would you give it regarding the proposed property sale? Are there any ways in which PI can avoid potentially uncertain CERCLA liability? What steps should it take to avoid or minimize potential liability?

3. What if PI sold the property to a real estate investment trust (REIT), an investment vehicle some people use to defer taxes on retirement income investments. The REIT purchases the property from PI several years before the light rail line is built. It knows about the PFOA contamination and uses that fact to reduce the purchase price, but does nothing to the land, and holds the property until its value skyrockets because of the new rail station. Then it sells the property to Greenbuilders for a significant profit. Is the REIT a PRP under CERCLA after it sells the property? Why or why not?

4. What advice would you give Greenbuilders before it purchases the property? What options does it have to avoid or minimize liability? Assuming that the PFOA contamination has been publicized widely in the local news media, can Greenbuilders take advantage of the "innocent landowner" provisions of CERCLA? What other options does it have under the statute?

5. Assume that PFOA leaches from the PI site, through groundwater on an adjacent property, and into the local stream. Is the adjacent landowner a PRP? Why or why not? What should the adjacent landowner do if it is a defendant in a later cost recovery action?

Part 2 — The landfill

Over the years, PI sent its more concentrated PFOA wastes in barrels to local industrial landfills. In the early years, PI simply contracted with a waste hauling company (Trashco) to collect PFOA wastes along with all of the other waste from the plant (from regular "garbage" to industrial wastes). Trashco decided where it would bring these wastes, choosing from local landfills and other disposal sites depending on costs, capacity, and other factors. Later, Waste Disposal Inc. (WDI), a national leader in solid and hazardous waste disposal services, purchased Trashco, along with all of its trucks and other equipment, and took over all of Trashco's existing customers. WDI stopped sending PI's PFOA wastes to Ernie's Landfill, Inc., choosing instead to bring all chemical and other industrial wastes to a new hazardous waste treatment and disposal facility designed, permitted, and operated in full compliance with RCRA and other applicable laws.

The most frequent destination for PI's PFOA wastes was Ernie's Landfill, Inc., an unlined facility sited on an abandoned gravel mine, with very porous soils. The state environmental agency closed this landfill shortly after enactment of RCRA, and the original company (Ernie's) went bankrupt. The company was wholly-owned and managed by Ernie Ernest. The property, however, is owned by Ernie's brother, Bert. Bert leased the property to Ernie's Landfill, Inc., but otherwise had no involvement in the operation or management of the landfill.

Needless to say, leachate from the landfill now causes serious groundwater contamination, and an expensive cleanup is needed. Test data shows PFOA and other chemicals related to PFOA production in the contaminated groundwater, along with a chemical soup of other contaminants from many other sources. EPA takes charge of the CERCLA cleanup.

1. After incurring significant costs for the initial removal action, and anticipating significant costs for the later remedial action, EPA wants to initiate a cost recovery action. Which of the following parties are potentially liable for these costs, and why or why not: (1) PI; (2) WDI; (3) Ernie; (4) Bert?

2. What advice would you give PI regarding the cost recovery action? Should it defend in court, or settle with EPA? If it settles, what issues should it address in the settlement? What else should it do to make sure that the settlement costs are reasonable? Assuming that PI incurs significant liability even via settlement, what other steps might it take to recover some of those costs after the settlement?

13

Allocation of Government Responsibility

A. INTRODUCTION

In the last chapter, we discussed allocation of private responsibility for environmental cleanup. Throughout the book, however, you have seen how much responsibility for environmental protection lies in the hands of government. An equally important set of decisions involves where within government various decisions should be made. In Chapter 3, we addressed one aspect of this allocation: which branches of government (legislative, executive, and judicial) make, and review, environmental policy and regulatory decisions. We did not, however, discuss the circumstances that might prompt Congress to adopt specific environmental standards itself, or to delegate those decisions to agencies. A second key allocation choice is which *level* of government — federal, state, or local — should make various kinds of environmental decisions. We address both of these choices in this chapter, and explain how allocation of responsibility and authority affects the manner in which Congress designs statutory schemes as a whole. A range of legal and policy factors, some of constitutional dimensions, influence these allocation decisions. Because our main purpose is to teach environmental law and policy, in this chapter we focus on factors grounded in environmental policy, but explain secondarily how issues of constitutional law may affect or constrain those policy considerations.

AN OPENING THOUGHT EXERCISE

Let's return to our focus on PFOA, and ask which governmental entities are most appropriate to address various aspects of the PFOA problem. Recall the various ways in which PFOA contamination might affect human health and the environment. PFOA has been detected in a local water supply in the small community of Little Hocking, Ohio. PFOA has also been found in the Ohio River, an interstate water body that runs along the Ohio and West Virginia

---

border. (Water pollution in the Ohio River is also addressed in part by an interstate commission called the Ohio River Sanitary Commission, or OR-SANCO.) PFOA has also been detected in the blood of factory workers, and of the general public, on a national level, possibly from exposure to various consumer products. Before we take up the relevant law, consider the following issues as a matter of policy.

1. *Congress or agencies?* Should Congress tackle the PFOA problem by itself, setting its own conditions or standards for PFOA manufacturing, use, and releases? Or should Congress delegate responsibility for addressing various aspects of the PFOA problem to other governmental entities? What arguments favor direct legislative control over environmental issues? *See* David Schoenbrod, *The Delegation Doctrine: Could the Court Give it Substance?*, 83 Mich. L. Rev. 1223 (1984). What arguments favor delegation of authority to administrative agencies? *See* Mistretta v. United States, 488 U.S. 361, 371-2 (1989) (explaining the Court's "practical understanding that in our increasingly complex society, replete with ever changing and more technical problems, Congress simply cannot do its job absent an ability to delegate power under broad general directives"); Howard Latin, *Ideal Versus Real Regulatory Efficiency: Implementation of Uniform Standards and "Fine-Tuning" Regulatory Reforms*, 27 Stan. L. Rev. 1267 (1985).

2. *Federal, state, or local?* If Congress chooses to delegate responsibility for addressing PFOA, which issues should it delegate to EPA or other agencies within the federal government, which might be addressed better by state or local governments, and why? Can Congress force state or local governments to regulate PFOA, and if so, how? What other methods might Congress use to encourage or induce other levels of government to address PFOA problems? What arguments favor federal control over environmental problems? What arguments favor state control? This debate has generated significant commentary for many years. *See, e.g.,* Richard Stewart, *Pyramids of Sacrifice? Problems of Federalism in Mandating State Implementation of National Environmental Policy*, 86 Yale L.J. 1196 (1977); Richard L. Revesz, *Rehabilitating Interstate Competition: Rethinking the "Race-to-the-Bottom" Rationale for Federal Environmental Regulation*, 67 N.Y.U. L. Rev. 1210 (1992); Richard L. Revesz, *Federalism and Environmental Regulation: A Public Choice Analysis*, 115 Harv. L. Rev. 553 (2001); Kirsten H. Engel, *State Environmental Standard-Setting: Is There a "Race" and is it "To the Bottom"?*, 48 Hastings L.J. 271 (1997); Peter P. Swire, *The Race to Laxity and the Race to Undesirability: Explaining Failures in Competition Among Jurisdictions in Environmental Law*, 14 Yale L. & Pol'y L. Rev. 67 (1996); David L. Markell, *The Role of Local Governments in Environmental Regulation: Shoring Up Our Federal System*, 44 Syracuse L. Rev. 885 (1993).

B. THE CONGRESSIONAL ROLE: TO DELEGATE OR NOT TO DELEGATE

Most of the environmental standards and regulations you have learned about in this book involve substantial delegation of authority to administrative agencies. Examples include both (1) the effects-based standards discussed in Chapter 5, in which Congress articulated the general goals of regulation (protecting health and the environment to varying degrees), but delegated the task of setting actual standards to federal or state agencies; and (2) technology-based standards discussed in Chapter 6, in which Congress outlined the general rules for considering what technologies are considered "available" to treat pollution under various circumstances, but assigned to agencies the job of translating those rules into numeric standards for releases of specific pollutants from particular factories under varying circumstances. In some cases, such as the ban on "takings" in the ESA or the prohibition against major federal actions that may significantly affect the environment absent preparation of an EIS, Congress established non-numeric rules of conduct, but nevertheless delegated to agencies the task of applying those rules to specific projects and circumstances.

Even where Congress delegates significant authority to administrative agencies, Congress clearly retains some role in the process. To avoid running afoul of the constitutional non-delegation doctrine discussed in Chapter 3, Congress always must articulate some "intelligible principle" to guide the agency sufficiently in delegated functions. While the courts have applied this test quite leniently, only rejecting non-delegation challenges based on extremely vague statutory standards, in practice, Congress has adopted widely varying approaches to how much detail it provides and how many conditions and limitations it establishes when it delegates authority. For example, in delegating authority to EPA to promulgate National Ambient Air Quality Standards (NAAQS), Congress articulated an extremely succinct governing standard of "requisite to protect the public health," 42 U.S.C. §7409(b)(1), and left it largely to EPA to determine which pollutants to regulate under the NAAQS program, *id*. §7408. *See* Whitman v. American Trucking Associations, Inc., 531 U.S. 457 (2001) (upholding the "requisite to protect the public health" standard against non-delegation challenge).

Compare this relatively bare-bones delegation with the level of detail Congress included in the 1990 amendments to section 112 of the Clean Air Act, regarding hazardous air pollutants. 42 U.S.C. §7412. In that provision, which consumes 29 pages in the United States Code, Congress (1) included a set of definitions specific to regulation of hazardous air pollutants, *id*. §7412(a); (2) identified a long list of pollutants that must be regulated, *id*. §7412(b); (3) established detailed rules for identifying sources to be regulated, *id*. §7412(c), and emissions standards for those sources, *id*. §7412(d), in some cases with instructions as to technology to be evaluated for particular sources, *id.* §7412(d)(8) (coke ovens); (4) mandated schedules and deadlines for issuance of certain numbers of standards, *id.* §7412(e); and (5) legislated requirements for residual risk standards, articulating, *inter alia*, a specific cancer risk standard, *id.* §7412(f). What factors might lead Congress to delegate with only the faintest indication of an "intelligible principle," and when do you think it might use more detailed and fine-tuned guidance?

In rare cases, Congress adopted specific environmental standards in the statute. Why do you suppose it might do so? Consider the following examples, both from the Clean Air Act.

1. Tailpipe Emission Standards

In Title II of the Clean Air Act, added in 1970, Congress adopted specific tailpipe emissions standards for particular pollutants and kinds of vehicles, along with mechanisms and deadlines for attainment of those standards. *See* 42 U.S.C. §7521 (emissions standards for new motor vehicles and engines). As an example of the level of detail with which Congress has adopted actual vehicle emissions standards, consider the following provision, which established standards for light duty trucks and other light duty vehicles:

> (g) Light-duty trucks up to 6,000 lbs. GVWR and light-duty vehicles; standards for model years after 1993
>
> (1) NMHC, CO, and NO$_x$
>
> Effective with respect to the model year 1994 and thereafter, the regulations under subsection (a) of this section applicable to emissions of nonmethane hydrocarbons (NMHC), carbon monoxide (CO), and oxides of nitrogen (NO$_x$) from light-duty trucks (LDTs) of up to 6,000 lbs. gross vehicle weight rating (GVWR) and light-duty vehicles (LDVs) shall contain standards which provide that emissions from a percentage of each manufacturer's sales volume of such vehicles and trucks shall comply with the levels specified in table G. The percentage shall be as specified in the implementation schedule below:

TABLE G
Emission Standards for NMHC, CO, and NO$_x$ From Light-Duty Trucks
of up to 6,000 Lbs. GVWR and Light-Duty
Vehicles

Vehicle Type	Column A (5 yrs/50,000 mi) NMHC	CO	NOx	Column B (10 yrs/100,000 mi) NMHC	CO	NOx
LDTs (0–,750 lbs. LVW) and light-duty vehicles	0.25	3.4	0.4*	0.31	4.2	0.6*
LDTs (3,751–,750 lbs. LVW)	0.3	24.4	0.7**	0.40	5.5	0.97

Standards are expressed in grams per mile (gpm).

For standards under column A, for purposes of certification under section 7525 of this title, the applicable useful life shall be 5 years or 50,000 miles (or the equivalent), whichever first occurs.

For standards under column B, for purposes of certification under section 7525 of this title, the applicable useful life shall be 10 years or 100,000 miles (or the equivalent), whichever first occurs.

* In the case of diesel-fueled LDTs (0–,750 lvw) and light-duty vehicles, before the model year 2004, in lieu of the 0.4 and 0.6 standards for NOx, the applicable standards for NO_x shall be 1.0 gpm for a useful life of 5 years or 50,000 miles (or the equivalent), whichever first occurs, and 1.25 gpm for a useful life of 10 years or 100,000 miles (or the equivalent), whichever first occurs.

** This standard does not apply to diesel-fueled LDTs (3,751–,750 lbs.LVW).

Implementation Schedule for Table G Standards

Model year	Percentage *
1994	40
1995	80
After 1995	100

(2) PM Standard

Effective with respect to model year 1994 and thereafter in the case of light-duty vehicles, and effective with respect to the model year 1995 and thereafter in the case of light-duty trucks (LDTs) of up to 6,000 lbs. gross vehicle weight rating (GVWR), the regulations under subsection (a) of this section applicable to emissions of particulate matter (PM) from such vehicles and trucks shall contain standards which provide that such emissions from a percentage of each manufacturer's sales volume of such vehicles and trucks shall not exceed the levels specified in the table below. The percentage shall be as specified in the Implementation Schedule below.

PM Standard for LDTS of up to 6,000 Lbs. GVWR

Useful life period	Standard
5/50,000	0.80 gpm
10/100,000	0.10 gpm

The applicable useful life, for purposes of certification under section 7525 of this title and for purposes of in-use compliance under section 7541 of this title, shall be 5 years or 50,000 miles (or the equivalent), whichever first occurs, in the case of the 5/50,000 standard.

The applicable useful life, for purposes of certification under section 7525 of this title and for purposes of in-use compliance under section 7541 of this title, shall be 10 years or 100,000 miles (or the equivalent), whichever first occurs in the case of the 10/100,000 standard.

Implementation Schedule for PM Standards

Model year	Light-duty vehicles	LDTs
1994	40%*	—
1995	80%*	40%*
1996	100%*	80%*
after 1996	100%*	100%*

*Percentages in the table refer to a percentage of each manufacturer's sales volume.

42 U.S.C. §7521(g).

However, congressional specification of these standards does not eliminate the agency role in implementing and enforcing those standards. Recall that, in Chapter 6, we identified these tailpipe emissions standards as a prime example of technology-forcing in environmental law, because at the time of enactment, Congress did not know whether automobile manufacturers could meet these standards. What would happen if the standards turned out to be impossible to meet? Should entire model years of automobiles be prohibited? Would that make air pollution better or worse? More important for our current inquiry, *who* should decide what relief is appropriate if Congress' initial standards turned out to be infeasible? Should Congress have to amend the law, or might it delegate variances or other relief mechanisms to EPA? Here is how an early court decision explained the relationship between the statutory standards set by Congress, and EPA's role in implementing and providing relief from the statutory standards:

On December 31, 1970, Congress amended the Clean Air Act to set a statutory standard for required reductions in levels of hydrocarbons (HC) and carbon monoxide (CO), which must be achieved for 1975 models of light duty vehicles. Section 202(b) of the Act, added by the Clean Air Amendments of 1970, provides that, beginning with the 1975 model year, exhaust emission of hydrocarbons and carbon monoxide from "light duty vehicles" must be reduced at least 90 per cent from the permissible emission levels in the 1970 model year. In accordance with the Congressional directives, the Administrator on June 23, 1971, promulgated regulations limiting HC and CO emissions from 1975 model light duty vehicles to .41 and 3.4 grams per vehicle mile respectively. At the same time, as required by section 202(b)(2) of the Act, he prescribed the test procedures by which compliance with these standards is measured.

Congress was aware that these 1975 standards were "drastic medicine," designed to "force the state of the art." There was, naturally, concern whether the manufacturers would be able to achieve this goal. Therefore, Congress provided, in Senator Baker's phrase, a "realistic escape hatch": the manufacturers could petition the Administrator of the EPA for a one-year suspension of the 1975 requirements, and Congress took the precaution of directing the National

Academy of Sciences to undertake an ongoing study of the feasibility of compliance with the emission standards. The "escape hatch" provision addressed itself to the possibility that the NAS study or other evidence might indicate that the standards would be unachievable despite all good faith efforts at compliance. This provision was limited to a one-year suspension, which would defer compliance with the 90% reduction requirement until 1976. Under section 202(b)(5)(D) of the Act, the Administrator is authorized to grant a one-year suspension only if he determines that (i) such suspension is essential to the public interest or the public health and welfare of the United States, (ii) all good faith efforts have been made to meet the standards established by this subsection, (iii) the applicant has established that effective control technology, processes, operating methods, or other alternatives are not available or have not been available for a sufficient period of time to achieve compliance prior to the effective date of such standards, and (iv) the study and investigation of the National Academy of Sciences conducted pursuant to subsection (c) of this section and other information available to him has not indicated that technology, processes, or other alternatives are available to meet such standards.

International Harvester v. Ruckelshaus, 478 F.2d 615, 623-24 (D.C. Cir. 1973) (remanding EPA's denial of suspension of statutory standards). *See also* Natural Resources Defense Council, Inc. v. U.S. Environmental Protection Agency, 655 F.2d 318 (D.C. Cir. 1981) (excerpted in Chapter 6, regarding EPA's implementation of tailpipe emission standards for diesel vehicles); National Petrochemical & Refiners Ass'n v. E.P.A., 287 F.3d 1130 (D.C. Cir. 2002) (upholding EPA regulation regarding diesel emissions and fuels).

2. Acid Rain Controls

In the 1990 Clean Air Act Amendments, Congress adopted a similar approach with respect to the acid rain program, embodied in a new Title IV of the statute. It included specific environmental standards directly in the statute, but also left many implementation details to EPA. Congress set specific emissions reduction goals for sulphur dioxide and nitrogen oxide, directing that sulphur dioxide emissions were to be reduced by 10 million tons below 1980 levels and nitrogen oxide emissions were to be reduced by 2 million tons by the year 2000. The acid rain program employs a market-based approach to achieving these statutory targets, in which Congress allocates "allowances" (each allowance permits sulphur dioxide emissions of one ton annually) to units at regulated facilities, which the facilities are in turn permitted to buy, sell or bank. Even here, however, Congress adopted specific numeric standards in the statute itself. The acid rain program incorporated two phases of emissions reductions. In 1995, the program targeted specific generating units with larger facilities and, then, in 2000, imposed additional restrictions on the Phase I facilities and imposed restrictions on additional, smaller Phase II facilities. Facilities with units that emit in excess of their allowances must pay penalties for each ton of excess emissions. Under the program, a certain number of statutorily-specified allowances (corresponding to annual tonnage of sulphur dioxide emissions) were retired at the end of each year. Upon implementation of Phase II of the acid rain program, the total number of allowances was permanently capped at 8.95 million allowances.

NOTES AND QUESTIONS ABOUT DIRECT CONGRESSIONAL ADOPTION OF ENVIRONMENTAL STANDARDS

1. *Rationale.* What is it about the motor vehicle emissions and acid rain issues that might have prompted Congress to adopt numerical statutory standards, rather than delegating that task to EPA or another agency?

2. *Complexity, expertise, and process.* One main reason Congress delegates standard-setting authority to agencies is the tremendous complexity involved in that process for virtually every approach to standard setting (effects-based, technology-based, cost-benefit, etc.). As you learned in Chapter 3, when promulgating standards, agencies first develop an administrative record, on which interested members of the public may comment, and then base their decisions on information identified or developed by the agency, as well as information submitted by others. When Congress sets standards directly in the statute, on what information does it base its decisions? What opportunity does the interested public have to submit its own information, or to question or challenge other information being considered by Congress? Which process (direct legislative standard-setting or administrative rulemaking) do you think is likely to produce better standards, and why?

3. *Judicial review.* When Congress delegates to agencies the task of setting specific environmental regulations, those rules are subject to judicial review under the relevant provisions of the substantive statute and the APA. Are requirements adopted directly in the statute similarly subject to judicial review? Under what standards of review and on what substantive grounds? How might this affect the nature of the rules that are actually implemented?

4. *Flexibility.* The science and other information on which environmental standards are based sometimes changes frequently, and sometimes dramatically. How easy do you think it is for Congress to amend a statute to change standards it adopts, relative to the ability of agencies to change administrative regulations? Which is more desirable, as a matter of environmental policy, stable rules that stay in place a long time and are hard to change, or flexible rules that can be changed as new or different information surfaces?

C. FEDERAL VERSUS STATE AND LOCAL CONTROL

Where Congress delegates standard setting or other environmental responsibility or authority, it also must choose which level (or levels) of government are most appropriate to perform those functions. Some statutes delegate most or all responsibility to federal agencies. In the Toxic Substances Control Act (TSCA), for example, Congress delegated all of the principal implementing authority to the federal EPA. The same is true in the Federal Insecticide, Fungicide, and Rodenticide Act (FIFRA), the statute that delegates to EPA the task of regulating pesticides and herbicides. The following chart summarizes some of the key authorities Congress delegated to EPA in these laws. What is it about the regulation of toxic chemicals and pesticides that might explain Congress' judgment that a national approach is appropriate?

Principal Federal Authorities Under TSCA and FIFRA

FIFRA		*7 U.S.C. §§136-136y*
	7 U.S.C. §136a(a)	Generally prohibits sale of unregistered pesticides.
	7 U.S.C. §136a(c)(2)	EPA may collect information about pesticides to inform registration decisions.
	7 U.S.C. §136a(c)(5), (6)	EPA may refuse to register pesticides with "unreasonable" environmental effects.[1]
		EPA may refuse to register mislabeled or ineffective pesticides.
	7 U.S.C. §136a	EPA must reregister certain older pesticides
	7 U.S.C. §136d	EPA may cancel pesticide registrations.
TSCA		*15 U.S.C. §§2601–2692*
	15 U.S.C. §2603	EPA generally must require testing of toxic substances that "may present an unreasonable risk of injury to health or the environment" when needed to fill data gaps.

Continued

TSCA		*15 U.S.C. §§2601–2692*
	15 U.S.C. §2604(a)(2)	EPA may determine which uses of a chemical are significant new uses requiring submission of data.
	15 U.S.C. §2605	EPA must ban or regulate toxic substances that it finds pose an "unreasonable risk of injury to health or the environment."[2]

1. The courts have generally interpreted this requirement as imposing a cost-benefit test on pesticide registration. *See, e.g.,* Envtl. Def. Fund, Inc. v. EPA, 548 F.2d 998, 1012-18 (D.C. Cir. 1976) (proponent of a pesticide must show that its benefits outweigh its risks).

2. The courts have generally interpreted this section as imposing a cost-benefit test on TSCA regulatory decisions. *See* Corrosion Proof Fittings v. EPA, 947 F.2d 1201 (5th Cir. 1991).

In other statutes, including the Clean Air Act, the Clean Water Act, and RCRA, Congress chose a strategy of "cooperative federalism" in which the federal and state governments share responsibility in various ways. Congress delegated some functions to the federal government, and others to the states. In some programs, Congress provided for federal regulation with an option for states to assume program authority, subject to EPA oversight. In the following survey, we explain how Congress allocated various kinds of environmental decisions among different levels of government. This review will also give you a better sense of how each of these statutes operates as a whole.

1. Setting Effects-Based Standards

Who should be responsible for setting basic environmental standards of the type studied in Part II of this book? Should one set of standards apply nationally, or should individual states adopt different standards to reflect different circumstances? Consider the following case, explaining the allocation of authority for effects-based standards under the Clean Water Act:

 ### *Mississippi Commission on Natural Resources v. Costle*
625 F.2d 1269 (5th Cir. 1980)

FAY, CIRCUIT JUDGE.

The Mississippi Commission on Natural Resources (Commission) challenges the authority of the United States Environmental Protection Agency (EPA) to promulgate a water quality standard on dissolved oxygen for Mississippi . . . .

I.   Statutory Framework

Prior to 1972, the Federal Water Pollution Control Act (FWPCA) relied primarily upon state-promulgated water quality standards as the means for reaching its goal of enhancing the quality of the nation's waters. A water quality standard has two components. The first is the use for the water in an area. Possible uses are for industry, agriculture, propagation and protection of fish and wildlife, recreation, and public water supply. The second component is the water quality criteria necessary to meet the designated use. For most pollutants, criteria are expressed as specific numerical concentration limits. For example, a state might set the water quality standard for a certain creek by designating it as a fishing area and requiring that the chloride concentration be no greater than 250 milligrams per liter of water.

In 1965, Congress considered whether the states or a federal administrator should establish water quality standards. Concerned that federal promulgation would discourage state plans for water quality and "would place in the hands of a single Federal official the power to establish zoning measures to control the use of land within watershed areas" throughout the nation, Congress gave the states primary authority to set water quality standards. The state standards and plans were submitted to the federal administrator, who determined whether they were consistent with the Act's requirements. If the state did not adopt complying standards, the administrator promulgated water quality uses and criteria.

As the Act was passed, states promulgate water quality standards, which are submitted to EPA for approval. EPA can promulgate standards if the state does not set standards consistent with the Act or whenever EPA determines that another "standard is necessary to meet the requirements of (the Act)." State standards are reviewed every three years. 33 U.S.C. §1313 (1976). NPDES permits must contain not only any [technology-based] effluent limitations set by EPA and the states, but also any more stringent limits necessary to reach the water quality standards. Id. §1311(b). In addition, EPA must develop and publish "criteria for water quality accurately reflecting the latest scientific knowledge." Id. §1314.

II.   Facts

The dispute in this case arises from EPA's refusal to approve the Mississippi water quality standard for dissolved oxygen (DO) and EPA's subsequent promulgation of a DO standard. Dissolved oxygen is necessary for the protection and propagation of fish and aquatic life, and is generally measured in milligrams per liter (mg/l).

VI.   Disapproval of Mississippi's Standard

A.   *Scope of Authority*

The Commission contends that EPA exceeded its statutory authority by tipping the balance of federal and state power created by Congress in the FWPCA. The Commission argues that EPA may substitute its judgment only if a state fails to act or acts irresponsibly. Furthermore, the Commission asserts that EPA misconstrues its authority as allowing disapprovals of standards that do not meet the requirements of EPA policy instead of those not meeting the requirements of the Act.

Congress did place primary authority for establishing water quality standards with the states. Furthermore,

> it is the policy of the Congress to recognize, preserve, and protect the primary responsibilities and rights of States to prevent, reduce, and eliminate pollution, to plan the development and use (including restoration, preservation, and enhancement) of land and water resources, and to consult with the Administrator in the exercise of his authority under this chapter.

33 U.S.C. §1251(b) (1976). As noted above, the legislative history reflects congressional concern that the Act not place in the hands of a federal administrator absolute power over zoning watershed areas. The varied topographies and climates in the country call for varied water quality solutions.

Despite this primary allocation of power, the states are not given unreviewable discretion to set water quality standards. All water quality standards must be submitted to the federal Administrator. 33 U.S.C. §1313(c)(2) (1976). The state must review its standards at least once every three years and make the results of the review available to the Administrator. Id. §1313(c)(1). EPA is given the final voice on the standard's adequacy:

> If the Administrator determines that any such revised or new standard is not consistent with the applicable requirements of this chapter, he shall not later than the ninetieth day after the date of submission of such standard notify the State and specify the changes to meet such requirements. If such changes are not adopted by the State within ninety days after the date of notification, the Administrator shall promulgate such standard pursuant to paragraph (4) of this subsection.

Id. §1313(c)(3). EPA's role also is more dominant when water quality criteria are in question. Although the designation of uses and the setting of criteria are interrelating chores, the specification of a waterway as one for fishing, swimming, or public water supply is closely tied to the zoning power Congress wanted left with the states. The criteria set for a specific use are more amenable to uniformity. Congress recognized this distinction by placing with EPA the duty to develop and publish water quality criteria reflecting the latest scientific knowledge shortly after the amendment's passage and periodically thereafter. Id. §1314(a)(1). EPA correctly points out that by leaving intact the Mississippi use designations it has acted in the manner least intrusive of state prerogatives. Nothing indicates a congressional intent to restrict EPA's review of state standards to the issue of whether the state acted arbitrarily or capriciously. The FWPCA requires EPA to determine whether the standard is "consistent with" the Act's requirements. The Commission argues that the Administrator has improperly construed his power as authorizing disapproval of state standards that do not meet EPA policy as embodied in the Red Book.

The statute enumerates the following requirements for water quality standards:

> Such standards shall be such as to protect the public health or welfare, enhance the quality of water and serve the purposes of this chapter. Such standards shall be established taking into consideration their use and value for public water supplies, propagation of fish and wildlife, recreational purposes, and agricultural, industrial, and other purposes, and also taking into consideration their use and value for navigation.

33 U.S.C. §1313(c)(2) (1976). One purpose of the Act is

> the national goal that wherever attainable, an interim goal of water quality which provides for the protection and propagation of fish, shellfish, and wildlife and provides for recreation in and on the water be achieved by July 1, 1983.

Id. §1251(a)(2). The EPA administrator did not improperly construe his authority by interpreting the FWPCA as allowing him to translate these broad statutory guidelines and goals into specifics that could be used to evaluate a state's standard. One "requirement of the Act" is that EPA formulate these policies for water quality criteria. Id. §1314(a)(1). It was not unreasonable for the EPA Administrator to interpret the Act as allowing him to require states to justify standards not in conformance with the criteria policy.

NOTES AND QUESTIONS ON *MISSISSIPPI COMMISSION*

1. *Holding.* What is the holding of *Mississippi Commission*? Are water quality standards set by EPA, the states, or both? If both, how is authority divided, and why?

2. *EPA oversight.* How much leeway can or should EPA give states in adopting environmental standards that are subject to EPA oversight? Should states only be allowed to adopt different standards on the basis of varying environmental conditions, or may they adopt standards that provide different levels of protection (for example, different cancer risk levels)? Recall from the PFOA example in Chapter 5 the extreme degree of difference in possible water

quality criteria for toxics, depending on plausible differences in variables and assumptions plugged into the risk assessment equation. *See* NRDC v. EPA, 16 F.3d 1395 (4th Cir. 1993) (upholding EPA approval of state water quality criteria for dioxin significantly weaker than recommended by EPA and using a less protective cancer risk level).

3. *Air quality versus water quality standards.* Ambient air quality standards are promulgated by EPA, and apply uniformly nationwide. Why did Congress instruct EPA to adopt uniform national air quality standards, but delegate the authority for water quality standards to individual states (subject to EPA review)? Does the distinction make sense?

2. Output Standards and State Planning

Regardless of who establishes ambient standards, significant environmental policy decisions remain even after those standards are in place. Ambient health-based standards do not in themselves dictate which pollution sources must reduce pollution, and by how much, such that the ambient standards will be attained. Congress must choose which levels of government are most appropriate to create output standards either in aid of meeting ambient standards or to reduce pollution not addressed by ambient standards. Congress delegated to EPA the responsibility for setting most of the technology-based standards under the Clean Water Act, *e.g.*, 33 U.S.C. §§1311, 1314 (effluent limitations for existing sources), 1316 (new source performance standards), 1317 (pretreatment standards for indirect dischargers); and some of those under the Clean Air Act, *e.g.*, 42 U.S.C. §§7412(d) (emissions standards for hazardous air pollutants), 7411 (new source performance standards). In the Clean Water Act, states adopt technology-based standards for individual facilities based on "best professional judgment" for those sources for which EPA has not yet issued national standards, and when the state implements the NPDES permit program. *See* 33 U.S.C. §§1342(a)(1)(B), (b). (EPA adopts such standards for individual sources when EPA runs the permit program for a particular state.) What are the arguments for and against setting technology-based standards at a national level? The state level?

a. Attaining Ambient Environmental Standards: SIPs and TMDLs

As you learned in Chapter 5, ambient effects-based environmental standards (most notably, the NAAQS and water quality standards) dictate how clean the air, water, or other environmental media must be where we use them, in the external environment. They do not, however, automatically define the obligations of particular pollution sources to control pollution sufficiently such that, when all reductions are combined, the ambient standards are met.

Congress first addressed this difficult allocation task in the 1970 Clean Air Act Amendments. While assigning EPA the job of issuing the NAAQS, Congress delegated to the states the task of developing and implementing output standards in air quality control regions throughout the country in order to meet the ambient standards, subject to minimum statutory requirements and EPA oversight. The Act contemplates substantial state technology-based standard setting in the service of the Act's goal of meeting the NAAQS. The Supreme Court described how this process is designed, and how it compared to the relative federal and state roles under earlier versions of the statute, in an early case:

> Congress initially responded to the problem of air pollution by offering encouragement and assistance to the States. In 1955 the Surgeon General was authorized to study the problem of air pollution, to support research, training, and demonstration projects, and to provide technical assistance to state and local governments attempting to abate pollution. In 1960 Congress directed the Surgeon General to focus his attention on the health hazards resulting from motor vehicle emissions. The Clean Air Act of 1963 authorized federal authorities to expand their research efforts, to make grants to state air pollution control agencies, and also to intervene directly to abate interstate pollution in limited circumstances. Amendments in 1965 broadened federal authority to control motor vehicle emissions and to make grants to state pollution control agencies.
>
> The focus shifted somewhat in the Air Quality Act of 1967. It reiterated the premise of the earlier Clean Air Act 'that the prevention and control of air pollution at its source is the primary responsibility of States and local governments.' Its provisions, however, increased the federal role in the prevention of air pollution, by according federal authorities certain powers of supervision and enforcement. But the States generally retained wide latitude to determine both the air quality standards which they would meet and the period of time in which they would do so.
>
> The response of the States to these manifestations of increasing congressional concern with air pollution was disappointing. Even by 1970, state planning and implementation under the Air Quality Act of 1967 had made little progress. Congress reacted by taking a stick to the States in the form of the Clean Air Amendments of 1970. These Amendments sharply increased federal authority and responsibility in the continuing effort to combat air pollution. Nonetheless, the Amendments explicitly preserved the principle: 'Each State shall have the primary responsibility for assuring air quality within the entire geographic area comprising such State.' The difference under the Amendments was that the States were no longer given any choice as to whether they would meet this responsibility. For the first time they were required to attain air quality of specified standards, and to do so within a specified period of time.
>
> The Amendments directed that within 30 days of their enactment the Environmental Protection Agency should publish proposed regulations describing national quality standards for the 'ambient air,' which is the statute's term for the outdoor air used by the general public. After allowing 90 days for comments on the proposed standards, the Agency was then obliged to promulgate such standards. The standards were to be of two general types: 'primary' standards,

which in the judgment of the Agency were 'requisite to protect the public health,' and 'secondary' standards, those that in the judgment of the Agency were 'requisite to protect the public welfare from any known or anticipated adverse effects associated with the presence of such air pollutant in the ambient air.'

Within nine months after the Agency's promulgation of primary and secondary air quality standards, each of the 50 States was required to submit to the Agency a plan designed to implement and maintain such standards within its boundaries. The Agency was in turn required to approve each State's plan within four months of the deadline for submission, if it had been adopted after public hearings and if it satisfied eight general conditions set forth in §110(a)(2).[2]

2. Section 110(a)(2), 42 U.S.C. §1857c–(a)(2), reads as follows:

'The Administrator shall, within four months after the date required for submission of a plan under paragraph (1), approve or disapprove such plan, or each portion thereof. The Administrator shall approve such plan, or any portion thereof, if he determines that it was adopted after reasonable notice and hearing and that—

"(A) (i) in the case of a plan implementing a national primary ambient air quality standard, it provides for the attainment of such primary standard as expeditiously as practicable but (subject to subsection (e) of this Section) in no case later than three years from the date of approval of such plan (or any revision thereof to take account of a revised primary standard); and (ii) in the case of a plan implementing a national secondary ambient air quality standard, it specifies a reasonable time at which such secondary standard will be attained;

"(B) it includes emission limitations, schedules, and timetables for compliance with such limitations, and such other measures as may be necessary to insure attainment and maintenance of such primary or secondary standard, including, but not limited to, land-use and transportation controls;

"(C) it includes provision for establishment and operation of appropriate devices, methods, systems, and procedures necessary to (i) monitor, compile, and analyze data on ambient air quality and, (ii) upon request, make such data available to the Administrator;

"(D) It includes a procedure, meeting the requirements of paragraph (4), for review (prior to construction or modification) of the location of new sources to which a standard of performance will apply;

"(E) it contains adequate provisions for intergovernmental cooperation, including measures necessary to insure that emissions of air pollutants from sources located in any air quality control region will not interfere with the attainment or maintenance of such primary or secondary standard in any portion of such region outside of such State or in any other air quality control region;

"(F) it provides (i) necessary assurances that the State will have adequate personnel, funding, and authority to carry out such implementation plan, (ii) requirements for installation of equipment by owners or operators of stationary sources to monitor emissions from such sources, (iii) for periodic reports on the nature and amounts of such emissions; (iv) that such reports shall be correlated by the State agency with any emission limitations or standards established pursuant to this Act, which reports shall be available at reasonable times for public inspection; and (v) for authority comparable to that in section 303, and adequate contingency plans to implement such authority;

"(G) it provides, to the extent necessary and practicable, for periodic inspection and testing of motor vehicles to enforce compliance with applicable emission standards; and

"(H) it provides for revision, after public hearings, of such plan (i) from time to time as may be necessary to take account of revisions of such national primary or secondary ambient air quality standard or the availability of improved or more expeditious methods of achieving such primary or secondary standard; or (ii) whenever the Administrator finds on

Probably the principal of these conditions, and the heart of the 1970 Amendments, is that the plan provide for the attainment of the national primary ambient
air quality standards in the particular State 'as expeditiously as practicable but
. . . in no case later than three years from the date of approval of such plan.' In
providing for such attainment, a State's plan must include 'emission limitations,
schedules, and timetables for compliance with such limitations'; it must also
contain such other measures as may be necessary to insure both timely attainment and subsequent maintenance of national ambient air standards.

Train v. Natural Resources Defense Council, Inc., 421 U.S. 60, 63-67 (1975).

A year later, the Court addressed the degree of flexibility states have in
deciding how to attain the NAAQS in air quality control regions within their
states:

Union Electric Co. v. Environmental Protection Agency
427 U.S. 246 (1976)

JUSTICE MARSHALL delivered the opinion of the Court.

After the Administrator of the Environmental Protection Agency (EPA)
approves a state implementation plan under the Clean Air Act, the plan may be
challenged in a court of appeals within 30 days, or after 30 days have run if
newly discovered or available information justifies subsequent review. We must
decide whether the operator of a regulated emission source, in a petition for
review of an EPA-approved state plan filed after the original 30-day appeal
period, can raise the claim that it is economically or technologically infeasible to
comply with the plan.

I

[The Court summarized the history and explanation of the 1970 Amendments provided in *Train*, set forth above.]

On April 30, 1971, the Administrator promulgated national primary and
secondary standards for six air pollutants he found to have an adverse effect on
the public health and welfare. Included among them was sulfur dioxide, at issue
here. After the promulgation of the national standards, the State of Missouri
formulated its implementation plan and submitted it for approval. Since sulfur
dioxide levels exceeded national primary standards in only one of the State's
five air quality regions the Metropolitan St. Louis Interstate region, the
Missouri plan concentrated on a control strategy and regulations to lower

---

the basis of information available to him that the plan is substantially inadequate to achieve
the national ambient air quality primary or secondary standard which it implements."

emissions in that area. The plan's emission limitations were effective at once, but the State retained authority to grant variances to particular sources that could not immediately comply. The Administrator approved the plan on May 31, 1972.

Petitioner is an electric utility company servicing the St. Louis metropolitan area, large portions of Missouri, and parts of Illinois and Iowa. Its three coal-fired generating plants in the metropolitan St. Louis area are subject to the sulfur dioxide restrictions in the Missouri implementation plan. Petitioner did not seek review of the Administrator's approval of the plan within 30 days, as it was entitled to do under §307(b)(1) of the Act, but rather applied to the appropriate state and county agencies for variances from the emission limitations affecting its three plants. Petitioner received one-year variances, which could be extended upon reapplication. The variances on two of petitioner's three plants had expired and petitioner was applying for extensions when, on May 31, 1974, the Administrator notified petitioner that sulfur dioxide emissions from its plants violated the emission limitations contained in the Missouri plan. Shortly thereafter petitioner filed a petition in the Court of Appeals for the Eighth Circuit for review of the Administrator's 1972 approval of the Missouri implementation plan. . . .

Since a reviewing court regardless of when the petition for review is filed may consider claims of economic and technological infeasibility only if the Administrator may consider such claims in approving or rejecting a state implementation plan, we must address ourselves to the scope of the Administrator's responsibility. The Administrator's position is that he has no power whatsoever to reject a state implementation plan on the ground that it is economically or technologically infeasible, and we have previously accorded great deference to the Administrator's construction of the Clean Air Act. After surveying the relevant provisions of the Clean Air Amendments of 1970 and their legislative history, we agree that Congress intended claims of economic and technological infeasibility to be wholly foreign to the Administrator's consideration of a state implementation plan.

As we have previously recognized, the 1970 Amendments to the Clean Air Act were a drastic remedy to what was perceived as a serious and otherwise uncheckable problem of air pollution. The Amendments place the primary responsibility for formulating pollution control strategies on the States, but nonetheless subject the States to strict minimum compliance requirements. These requirements are of a "technology-forcing character," and are expressly designed to force regulated sources to develop pollution control devices that might at the time appear to be economically or technologically infeasible.

This approach is apparent on the face of 110(a)(2). The provision sets out eight criteria that an implementation plan must satisfy, and provides that if these criteria are met and if the plan was adopted after reasonable notice and hearing, the Administrator "shall approve" the proposed state plan. The mandatory "shall" makes it quite clear that the Administrator is not to be concerned with factors other than those specified, and none of the eight factors appears to permit consideration of technological or economic infeasibility. Nonetheless, if a basis is to be found for allowing the Administrator to consider such claims, it must be among the eight criteria, and so it is here that the argument is focused.

It is suggested that consideration of claims of technological and economic infeasibility is required by the first criterion that the primary air quality standards be met "as expeditiously as practicable but in no case later than three years," and that the secondary air quality standards be met within a "reasonable time." The argument is that what is "practicable" or "reasonable" cannot be determined without assessing whether what is proposed is possible. This argument does not survive analysis.

Section 110(a)(2)(A)'s three-year deadline for achieving primary air quality standards is central to the Amendments' regulatory scheme and, as both the language and the legislative history of the requirement make clear, it leaves no room for claims of technological or economic infeasibility. The 1970 congressional debate on the Amendments centered on whether technology forcing was necessary and desirable in framing and attaining air quality standards sufficient to protect the public health, standards later termed primary standards. . . .

It is argued that when such a state plan calls for proceeding more rapidly than economics and the available technology appear to allow, the plan must be rejected as not "practicable." Whether this is a correct reading of §110(a)(2)(A) depends on how that section's "as expeditiously as practicable" phrase is characterized. The Administrator's position is that §110(a)(2)(A) sets only a minimum standard that the States may exceed in their discretion, so that he has no power to reject an infeasible state plan that surpasses the minimum federal requirements — a plan that reflects a state decision to engage in technology forcing on its own and to proceed more expeditiously than is practicable. On the other hand, petitioner and Amici supporting its position argue that §110(a)(2)(A) sets a mandatory standard that the States must meet precisely and conclude that the Administrator may reject a plan for being too strict as well as for being too lax.

We read the "as may be necessary" requirement of §110(a)(2)(B) to demand only that the implementation plan submitted by the State meet the "minimum conditions" of the Amendments.[13] Beyond that, if a State makes the legislative determination that it desires a particular air quality by a certain date and that it is willing to force technology to attain it — or lose a certain industry if attainment is not possible — such a determination is fully consistent with the structure and purpose of the Amendments, and §110(a)(2)(B)

13. Economic and technological factors may be relevant in determining whether the minimum conditions are met. Thus, the Administrator may consider whether it is economically or technologically possible for the state plan to require more rapid progress than it does. If he determines that it is, he may reject the plan as not meeting the requirement that primary standards be achieved "as expeditiously as practicable" or as failing to provide for attaining secondary standards within "a reasonable time."

provides no basis for the EPA Administrator to object to the determination on the ground of infeasibility.

In sum, we have concluded that claims of economic or technological infeasibility may not be considered by the Administrator in evaluating a state requirement that primary ambient air quality standards be met in the mandatory three years. And, since we further conclude that the States may submit implementation plans more stringent than federal law requires and that the Administrator must approve such plans if they meet the minimum requirements of §110(a)(2), it follows that the language of §110(a)(2)(B) provides no basis for the Administrator ever to reject a state implementation plan on the ground that it is economically or technologically infeasible. Accordingly, a court of appeals reviewing an approved plan under §307(b)(1) cannot set it aside on those grounds, no matter when they are raised.

III

Our conclusion is bolstered by recognition that the Amendments do allow claims of technological and economic infeasibility to be raised in situations where consideration of such claims will not substantially interfere with the primary congressional purpose of prompt attainment of the national air quality standards. Thus, we do not hold that claims of infeasibility are never of relevance in the formulation of an implementation plan or that sources unable to comply with emission limitations must inevitably be shut down.

Perhaps the most important forum for consideration of claims of economic and technological infeasibility is before the state agency formulating the implementation plan. So long as the national standards are met, the State may select whatever mix of control devices it desires, and industries with particular economic or technological problems may seek special treatment in the plan itself. Moreover, if the industry is not exempted from, or accommodated by, the original plan, it may obtain a variance, as petitioner did in this case; and the variance, if granted after notice and a hearing, may be submitted to the EPA as a revision of the plan. Lastly, an industry denied an exemption from the implementation plan, or denied a subsequent variance, may be able to take its claims of economic or technological infeasibility to the state courts.

NOTES AND QUESTIONS ON
UNION ELECTRIC AND SIPS

1. *Holding.* According to this decision, how much flexibility do states have in implementing the NAAQS? Can they be stricter than the statute demands in order to achieve the NAAQS more quickly, or with a higher degree of confidence? Does it matter whether a state chooses to shut down a particular facility in order to meet the standards? Conversely, can a state adopt a weaker SIP in order to keep a particular facility open, for example to save jobs, if it

decides that preventing unemployment is more important than meeting the standards quickly?

2. *Zero sum game.* If a state weakens air pollution controls for a particular source or category of sources in a SIP or a SIP amendment, to save jobs or otherwise, what must it then do to compensate for the resulting increase in emissions? Assume that serious air pollution in a city results partly from the local steel industry, which employs a large percentage of the workforce and provides significant secondary economic stimulus. A large portion of the air pollution, however, comes from automobiles. The state could tighten controls on the steel mills, at the risk of plant closures and economic dislocation. Or, it could try to reduce the amount people drive through devices such as land use controls, higher parking fees, increased mass transit, and public education. How should it decide which approach to take?

3. *The federalism rationale.* Congress assigned EPA the task of promulgating the NAAQS, while requiring the states to adopt the necessary implementing plans, with EPA oversight of that process. Does this strike the proper balance between federal and state needs and interests?

4. *EPA oversight and SIP enforceability.* Under what circumstances can EPA disapprove a SIP? Should EPA approve a SIP in which a state decides that it can obtain adequate emissions reductions to meet the NAAQS through largely voluntary efforts, such as "no drive days" encouraged through public education, rather than enforceable emissions limits on stationary sources?

5. *EPA and state and local land use.* If EPA believes that more transit, denser land use patterns, and higher parking fees are the keys to reducing automotive pollution sufficiently to meet the standards, can it impose those solutions on a state? In 1990, Congress eliminated much of EPA's authority to address such issues as parking fees, tolls, or certain other aspects of land use and transportation planning. *See* 42 U.S.C. §7410(c); Penny Mintz, *Transportation Alternatives Within the Clean Air Act: A History of Congressional Failure to Effectuate and Recommendations for the Future,* 3 N.Y.U. Envtl. L.J. 156 (1994). Why is federal control over such issues so controversial?

6. *Federal Implementation Plans (FIPs).* Ultimately, if EPA disapproves a SIP or a SIP revision and the state fails to adopt adequate changes, EPA is required, at least in theory, to adopt a federal implementation plan (FIP) to replace the defective SIP. What are the federalism implications of such an action? How likely is it politically to occur? (In practice, EPA has drafted but never imposed a FIP.) Would EPA adoption of a FIP violate states' rights under the Tenth Amendment? *See* Commonwealth of Virginia v. Browner, 80 F.3d 869, 882-23 (4th Cir. 1996), *cert. denied,* 519 U.S. 1090 (1997) (holding that CAA's highway sanction, offset sanction, and requirement for federal implementation plan (FIP) in absence of adequate SIP did not violate spending power or Tenth Amendment).

7. *Process and uncertainty.* To get some sense of what is involved in developing, tracking, and, if necessary, revising a SIP, think through what minimum steps states must go through to comply with section 110. You begin

with EPA's NAAQS, which themselves can be stated in quite simple terms. The standard for sulphur dioxide at issue in *Union Electric*, for example, was .03 parts per million (p.p.m.) (annual level) and 0.14 p.p.m. (maximum 24-hour concentration not to be exceeded more than once a year). 40 C.F.R. §§50.4-50.5 (1975). After that, however, the process can get rather complicated and infused with uncertainty. What must a state do to ascertain with adequate certainty whether the air in a particular region violates the NAAQS, and if so, by how much? What real-world variables might affect whether particular levels of emissions will cause NAAQS violations in a given region? Assuming there is a violation, how then does the state determine the source of all emissions of the pollutant in question, or at least a high enough percentage of those emissions to develop a workable plan? Next, how does the state decide what emissions reductions are possible, from which sources, and with what costs and other considerations that may be relevant to its decision? Only then is the state prepared to make the difficult decision of "whose ox gets gored," *i.e.*, which sources must reduce emissions by how much, such that the standard is likely to be met in a timely way. Finally, once the state establishes (and EPA approves) pollution control obligations in the SIP, what must the state do to assure compliance with those obligations and attainment of the NAAQS?

8. *Complexity.* The above discussion gives only a sketch of the SIP process. Already complex in the 1970 statute, Congress added many layers of detail in the 1990 Clean Air Act Amendments, in part in response to persistent nonattainment problems around the country nearly two decades after the initial round of SIPs. Different statutory requirements now apply to different pollutants. *See, e.g.*, 42 U.S.C. §§7511 *et seq.* (ozone); 7512 *et seq.* (carbon monoxide); 7513 *et seq.* (particulate matter); 7514 *et seq.* (sulfur oxides, nitrogen dioxide and lead). Requirements also vary between attainment areas, nonattainment areas, and "maintenance" areas that formerly violated but now meet the NAAQS. *See, e.g., id.* §§7502 (general nonattainment plan provisions); 7507 (motor vehicle emission standards in nonattainment areas); 7511-7511f (additional provisions for ozone nonattainment areas); 7512-7512a (additional provisions for carbon monoxide nonattainment areas); 7513-7513b (additional provisions for particulate matter nonattainment areas); 7514-7514a (additional provisions for nonattainment areas for sulfur oxides, nitrogen dioxide, and lead); 7505a (provisions for maintenance areas). In general, the 1990 requirements are far more prescriptive than those included in the 1970 law, and leave states with less flexibility in planning and implementing SIPs. Is this trend toward increased congressional prescription consistent with the general philosophy of the Act described in the above cases regarding allocation of authority between the federal and state governments? Do you think it will help or hurt attainment of the statutory goals? We leave most of the details to your own study or practice, or to upper level courses in air pollution law.

9. *Implementation.* Under section 110 of the Clean Air Act, SIPs must include enforceable emissions limitations and other requirements sufficient to

ensure that targeted emissions reductions are achieved. That task is relatively easy for small numbers of stationary sources that can be identified and regulated individually. What happens, however, when a significant portion of air pollution responsible for NAAQS violations comes from a large number of very diffuse sources? In heavily polluted urban areas in Southern California, for example, violation of the ozone NAAQS cannot be met without reductions in emissions from such sources as lawnmowers, lighter fluid from barbeque grills, and spray paints. How can states prove to EPA that control requirements for those sources are sufficiently "enforceable" to pass muster?

b. Assessment of the SIP Process

The following table provides a highly simplified summary of the relative federal and state roles under the CAA, and how they fit together:

Principal Federal and State Clean Air Act Roles

Federal Roles	*State Roles*
Issue National Ambient Air Quality Standards	Designate Air Quality Control Regions
Approve SIPs and SIP Amendments or issue Federal Implementation Plans (FIPs)	Adopt State Implementation Plans (SIPs) and SIP Amendments (different requirements for attainment, non-attainment, and maintenance areas)
Adopt national technology-based standards (*e.g.*, new sources, hazardous air pollutants)	Adopt technology-based standards for individual sources
Adopt national mobile source standards	Adopt land use and transportation controls
Enforce SIP provisions	Enforce SIP provisions

The SIP process has a checkered history of successes and failures. While some regions have come into compliance with the NAAQS, there has also been a significant history of delays, missed deadlines, litigation, SIP revisions, political haggling between EPA and the states, congressional fine-tuning or mass overhauls, and yet more revisions to respond to statutory changes and judicial remands. After describing the history and complexity of the SIP process in overwhelming detail, Professor Arnold Reitze, who has been one of the leading students of CAA law and policy for many years, writes his sobering assessment of the SIP program's failure, and why he thinks it has failed, with equally notable brevity:

Arnold W. Reitze, Jr., Air Quality Protection Using
State Implementation Plans — Thirty-Seven Years
of Increasing Complexity
15 Vill. Envt. L.J. 209 (2004)

§7.   The Failure Of The SIP Approach

The Air Quality Act of 1967 began an air pollution control program based on reaching ambient air quality goals through an implementation plan that imposed specific requirements on air pollution sources. The 1970 CAA Amendments greatly expanded federal authority. National Ambient Air Quality Standards (NAAQS) would be established by EPA to be reached pursuant to a state implementation plan. An attainment date of 1975 was specified, with a few exceptions. The pervasive failure to achieve these goals led to the 1977 CAA Amendments, which extended the compliance date to 1982, or 1987 for areas that could not meet ozone or carbon monoxide NAAQS due to transportation related emissions. This effort also failed, although substantial progress was made in reducing the air pollution emissions from stationary sources per unit of production and from motor vehicles based on an emission per vehicle mile traveled. When the 1990 CAA Amendments were enacted, 100 areas exceeded the ozone standard, fifty-one exceeded the SO_2 standard and twelve exceeded the lead standard. The 1990 Amendments provided more time for meeting NAAQS. For ozone, the most difficult pollutant to control, extensions as late as November 15, 2010 were provided for the most polluted areas. For the areas with marginal violations, compliance was to be achieved by November 15, 1993. Other areas compliance dates ranged between 1993 and 2010, but milestones are specified that must be met. Carbon monoxide nonattainment areas had an attainment date as late as December 31, 2000, for seriously polluted areas.

Despite the twenty-five percent reduction in aggregate emissions of the six criteria pollutants since 1970, approximately 133 million people in 2001 lived in counties that violated one or more NAAQS. This number would be considerably lower if the $PM_{2.5}$ and eight-hour ozone standards had not been promulgated July 18, 1997. Under the pre-1997 regulations, 40.2 million people live in counties that have ozone NAAQS violations and 11.1 million people live in counties with PM_{10} NAAQS violations. About 3.4 million people live in areas violating any of the other four NAAQS. In 1990 there were 230 nonattainment areas; in 2001 there were 130 nonattainment areas. In 2002, forty-one states and the District of Columbia exceeded the ozone standard nearly 9,000 times, a ninety percent increase from 2001. Solving the nation's air pollution problem turned out to be more difficult than expected in 1967, but progress is being made. Some of the reasons for the failure of many SIPs to meet the NAAQS are listed, and briefly discussed below.

(1) The air quality problems the CAA has been attempting to correct are exacerbated by increases in population and consumption. The 1970 U.S. resident population of 203.984 million grew to 249.464 million by 1990, and grew to 275.130 million in 2000. U.S. energy use, which is responsible for most air pollution, went from 66.43 quadrillion Btus in 1970 to 84.2 quads in 1990. Electric power generation, the most significant stationary source of air pollution, grew from 1532 billion kilowatt hours (KWh) in 1970 to 2795 billion KWh in 1990. Energy consumed by the highway transportation sector grew from 15.32 quads in 1970 to 21.66 quads in 1990 to 26.52 quads in 2000. The size of the motor vehicle fleet in the U.S. grew from 108 million vehicles in 1970 to 189 million vehicles in 1980 and to 220.5 million vehicles in 2000. The effect of this growth was to nullify much of the progress made under the Clean Air Act.

The ability of the SIP program to comply with the NAAQS will continue to be challenged by growth in the population and in energy use. President Bush's National Energy Policy Development Group estimates that in the next twenty years U.S. oil consumption will increase thirty-three percent and electricity demand will increase forty-five percent. The Bush Administration projects a need for an additional 393,000 MW of generating capacity in the next twenty years, which will require between 1,300 and 1,900 new power plants to be constructed or about sixty to ninety plants per year. This projection is unlikely to occur, but the use of energy is expected to grow substantially. Much of the increase in electric power baseload generation capacity will be fueled by coal with the attendant air pollutant emissions. Petroleum consumption is expected to rise from 19.5 million barrels per day in 2000 to 25.8 million barrels per day in 2020, primarily because of the demand for fuel for transportation. Thus, SIPs can be expected to be periodically revised to continue the trend of increased stringency and higher costs.

(2) Although Congress passed the CAA Amendments and the President signed them into law, those concerned with the costs of air pollution control are working to control the costs of implementing the CAA. Some sources are seriously burdened because the CAA imposes its costs unevenly. Economic growth in some areas of the nation is restricted more than in other areas. Some industries faced huge compliance costs while dealing with stiff foreign competition. This leads to political opposition to new air pollution controls. The various administrations, acting through the Office of Management and Budget have slowed or stopped regulations or required that they be rewritten to lower costs to the private sector. The appropriation process is used by Congress to limit the money needed to implement the CAA. The Congressional oversight process has

sometimes been used to limit EPA's aggressive pursuit of the CAA goals.

(3) The 1970 CAA demanded a ninety percent reduction in motor vehicle emissions. This anticipated reduction from motor vehicles was programmed into SIPs through the modeling assumptions that states used to develop an air program and led to underpredicting of overall emissions. The mobile source air pollution program is very successful when compared to other pollution control programs, but achieving a ninety percent reduction in emissions has been difficult. Further, both vehicle miles traveled (VMT) and the energy consumed by transportation were increasing more rapidly than projected by the emission inventories used to implement the 1970 CAA. This helped create nonattainment status for much of the urbanized United States. Moreover, the mix of vehicles changed dramatically as the number of trucks grew from 18.8 million in 1970 to 54.47 in 1990, to 87.1 million in 2000, which increased fuel consumption. The shift in the mix of vehicles resulted in a greater portion of VMT in an area is driven by light truck and SUVs, which usually have higher emissions. Heavy duty trucks are an even more serious problem. In the Metropolitan Washington D.C. area, for example, heavy-duty diesel vehicles account for less than three percent of the VMT, but produce about thirty percent of the NO_x emissions. Diesel engines are not subject to more stringent regulations until 2007.

(4) From 1982 to 1997, developed land increased by forty-seven percent, but the population increased by only seventeen percent. This dispersion of the population contributed to VMT growth that for the last thirty years has increased roughly at a rate four times faster than the population. Most air quality planning occurs with little concern for the impact of land use. Transportation air quality plans are based on projections of growth in VMTs with little concern for utilizing land use planning that will be more protective of air quality. Sprawl is more strongly correlated to peaks levels of ozone than is per capita income or employment levels.

(5) The mathematical models used to develop the SIPs projected overly optimistic reductions because:

(a) incorrect data was used as inputs in many models;

(b) linear rollback models that initially were used did not work well, especially for ozone because its atmospheric formation is complex, and more sophisticated models subsequently used also had significant limitations; and

(c) unjustified assumptions concerning the effectiveness of various control strategies were used in SIPs.

A report of EPA's Inspector General reported that air pollution control strategies are threatened by unreliable emission factors used to estimate releases from stationary sources. Emission factors are used to estimate air releases when more reliable data is unavailable. In 1985, EPA used 2073 emission factors; in 1996 it used more than 16,000. Almost half were not rated for reliability, and thousands were considered to have below average or poor reliability. The problem, according to EPA's Inspector General, was the result of EPA alliance with industry in developing emission factors. While the validity of models continues to improve, their costs have become significant. In 2002, the Washington D.C. region spent over $400,000 in four months to model and test the air quality conformity of its proposed long-range transportation plan and its transportation improvement plan. Maintaining and applying the models in this region requires about thirty-six percent of the transportation planning budget, or about $2.9 million per year.

(6)   The CAA regulated new sources much more stringently than existing sources. The expectation was that over time air quality would improve as existing sources were replaced. The costs of complying with the CAA, however, led industry to maintain existing facilities beyond their expected useful life. Thus, the imposition of new source standards moved more slowly than originally expected. The New Source Review (NSR) program has been very controversial, and the adverse impact on air quality of old electric power plants is an ongoing controversy.

(7)   Control measures were not implemented because:
   (a)   technology was not available or was too costly to use; or
   (b)   local opposition prevented the quick and effective implementation of strategies such as I/M and Stage II vapor recovery.

(8)   Gasoline volatility was increased by the refiners, in part to compensate for the effects of not using lead additives in gasoline because more "light ends such as butane, benzene and zylene were in the fuel." This resulted in increases in VOC emissions in the 1980s that led to new provisions in the CAA to control Reed Vapor Pressure (RVP), which is the measure of gasoline volatility.

(9)   Control measures and other requirements of the CAA were not always adequately enforced. EPA's civil judicial settlements numbered 215 in FY 1999, 219 in FY 2000, 221 in FY 2001 and 216 in FY 2002. In FY 2002, EPA issued about 1,300 administrative orders, and 250 criminal cases were referred to the Department of Justice.

(10) Ozone transport from upwind states has not been effectively controlled by the CAA's programs. This means that downwind areas are held hostage to regulatory and enforcement efforts made by upwind states. Moreover, EPA has been willing to grant extensions due to

ozone transport to areas that have not implemented the applicable rate of progress requirements.

(11) There is no punishment imposed on a state or its elected officials for a failure to achieve the goals of the SIP. The development and implementation of a stringent SIP-based program, however, could lead to the subsequent defeat of an elected official. Thus, there is little incentive for an elected official to aggressively pursue CAA compliance. Moreover, the probability that EPA will promulgate a FIP is small.

(12) EPA threatens to impose sanctions, but it virtually never imposes them. In 1997, the Congressional Research Service reported that the only area in the nation that was subject to an EPA-imposed sanction was a small area in East Helena, Montana.

(13) In 1990, Congress in section 182(g) provided for milestones to be used to measure progress in meeting the NAAQS for ozone. If appropriate progress is not made, EPA can force the state to have the area reclassified or require implementing additional measures. EPA, however, has been criticized for the collapse of the milestone program, which prevents state failures from being identified and remedied.

§8. Conclusion

The SIP program may have largely outlived its usefulness, but after more than thirty years of evolution, drastic change may be more harmful than beneficial. Most likely, SIPs will continue to become both more complex and irrelevant. The weakness of the SIP process is not due to a failure to accomplish its goals. Since 1970 the gross domestic product has increased by 164 percent and energy consumption in up forty-two percent, yet the aggregate emissions of the six criteria pollutants is down forty-eight percent.

The SIP's failure is related to the premise that air pollution is a localized phenomenon that is best handled as a state program with minimum federal involvement. That changed over the years as federal mandated measures became an increasing portion of the emission reduction demanded by the SIP. The CAA's subchapter II program for mobile sources and their fuels have, since 1970, played an important role in determining the effectiveness of the SIP program. The inspection and maintenance program for in-use motor vehicles, the use of reformulated gasoline and conformity planning that are discussed in the body of this article are examples of the SIP process being federalized in order to obtain the reductions necessary to have a SIP that projects attainment. The sulfur dioxide control program under CAA subchapter IV has become the most important program for sulfur emissions control, yet it operates largely outside of the SIP program. In the future, federally mandated measures will be the major cause of the additional emissions reductions that are needed if progress is to be made. The heavy-duty diesel rule and the associated sulfur reduction from diesel fuel will provide significant air quality improvement. Additional control on nonroad vehicles and more stringent Tier 2 requirements for motor vehicles also will be important. The eight-hour ozone standard and the $PM_{2.5}$ standard will require more effort to be made to control interstate transport of pollution if these air quality standards are to be met. The pending Clear Skies legislation, or some variant, will add additional federal limitations on emissions. Finally, the continued promulgation and implementation of MACT standards to control air toxics impose federally-based limitations on emissions from major sources. The effect of these legislative and regulatory requirements will be to continue the trend of reducing the importance of state SIP implementation.

NOTES AND QUESTIONS ON REITZE CRITIQUE

1. *Reasons for nonattainment.* While Professor Reitze describes the problems with the current SIP process in some detail, in general, which of his suggested reasons for continued nonattainment do you think are most significant? Which do you think are easiest and hardest to fix, and why?

2. *Drastic change.* Despite his detailed critique of the existing system, Professor Reitze concludes that "drastic change may be more harmful than beneficial." Do you agree? Why or why not?

c. The Clean Water Act Planning Process

The Clean Water Act includes a series of planning provisions that similarly assign states the job of ensuring that aggregate pollution controls on numerous and diverse sources suffice to attain state water quality standards. However, while EPA implemented the SIP process as the centerpiece of the Clean Air Act program shortly after the 1970 amendments, it relegated the water quality planning provisions to the back seat for many years. Since the early 1990s, however, in the face of significant pressure from citizen suits, EPA began to take the Clean Water Act planning requirements more seriously, with increased focus on the "total maximum daily load" (TMDL) process that serves in the CWA as the functional analogy to SIPs. *See generally* OLIVER HOUCK, THE CLEAN WATER ACT TMDL PROGRAM: LAW, POLICY, AND IMPLEMENTATION (2d ed. 2002).

In the CAA, the SIP process is complicated by the fact that so much air pollution can come from large numbers of automobiles, and from dispersed "area sources," as well as smaller numbers of larger stationary sources. Similarly, TMDLs and other aspects of comprehensive water pollution planning are complicated by potentially large numbers of pollution sources and types of sources, and the fact that Congress tackled two categories of water pollution in very different ways. *See* Robert W. Adler, *Integrated Approaches to Water Pollution: Lessons from the Clean Air Act*, 23 Harv. Envtl. L. Rev. 203 (1999). "Point sources," defined as "any discernable, confined, and discrete conveyance," 33 U.S.C. §1362(14), may not discharge pollutants into "waters of the United States" without a permit that imposes enforceable effluent limitations dictated by EPA, the states, or both, pursuant to the mandatory requirements of the Act and applicable EPA regulations. *See id.* §§1311, 1313, 1314, 1341, 1342, 1344. Congress left control of pollution from so-called "nonpoint sources," however, largely to the states. *See id.* §§1288 (comprehensive state water quality planning program included in the 1972 statute), 1329 (specific nonpoint source pollution planning program added in 1987). Nonpoint sources include a somewhat nebulous category of activities that might best be characterized as "anything but point sources," and can include dispersed pollution from farms, logging operations, and any other land disturbance or other activities that contaminate runoff, as well as structures such as dams that alter the "chemical, physical, or biological, and radiological integrity of water." *See id.* §1362(19) (definition of "pollution"). To the extent that this distinction was not clear in the 1972 law, in 1977, Congress added the following exception to the statutory definition of point source: "This term does not include agricultural stormwater discharges and return flows from irrigated agriculture." 33 U.S.C. §1362(14).

In the following case, the Ninth Circuit describes the differences between point source and nonpoint source pollution, and how it relates to the TMDL planning process.

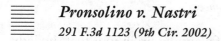

Pronsolino v. Nastri
291 F.3d 1123 (9th Cir. 2002)

BERZON, CIRCUIT JUDGE.

The United States Environmental Protection Agency ("EPA") required California to identify the Garcia River as a water body with insufficient pollution controls and, as required for waters so identified, to set so-called "total maximum daily loads" ("TMDLs") — the significance of which we explain later — for pollution entering the river. Appellants challenge the EPA's authority under the Clean Water Act ("CWA" or the "Act") § 303(d), to apply the pertinent identification and TMDL requirements to the Garcia River. The district court rejected this challenge, and we do as well.

CWA § 303(d) requires the states to identify and compile a list of waters for which certain "effluent limitations" "are not stringent enough" to implement the applicable water quality standards for such waters. Effluent limitations pertain only to point sources of pollution; point sources of pollution are those from a discrete conveyance, such as a pipe or tunnel. Nonpoint sources of pollution are non-discrete sources; sediment run-off from timber harvesting, for example, derives from a nonpoint source. The Garcia River is polluted only by nonpoint sources. Therefore, neither the effluent limitations referenced in §303(d) nor any other effluent limitations apply to the pollutants entering the Garcia River.

The precise statutory question before us is whether the phrase "are not stringent enough" triggers the identification requirement both for waters as to which effluent limitations apply but do not suffice to attain water quality standards and for waters as to which effluent limitations do not apply at all to the pollution sources impairing the water. We answer this question in the affirmative, a conclusion which triggers the application of the statutory TMDL requirement to waters such as the Garcia River.

Congress enacted the CWA in 1972, amending earlier federal water pollution laws that had proven ineffective. Prior to 1972, federal water pollution laws relied on "water quality standards specifying the acceptable levels of pollution in a State's interstate navigable waters as the primary mechanism for the control of water pollution." The pre-1972 laws did not, however, provide concrete direction concerning how those standards were to be met in the foreseeable future.

In enacting sweeping revisions to the nation's water pollution laws in 1972, Congress began from the premise that the focus "on the tolerable effects rather than the preventable causes of pollution" constituted a major shortcoming in the pre 1972 laws. The 1972 Act therefore sought to target primarily "the preventable causes of pollution," by emphasizing the use of technological controls.

At the same time, Congress decidedly did not in 1972 give up on the broader goal of attaining acceptable water quality. Rather, the new statute recognized that even with the application of the mandated technological controls on point source discharges, water bodies still might not meet state-set water quality standards. The 1972 statute therefore put in place mechanisms other than direct federal regulation of point sources, designed to "restore and maintain the chemical, physical, and biological integrity of the Nation's waters." §101(a).

In so doing, the CWA uses distinctly different methods to control pollution released from point sources and that traceable to nonpoint sources. The Act directly mandates technological controls to limit the pollution point sources may discharge into a body of water. On the other hand, the Act "provides no direct mechanism to control nonpoint source pollution but rather uses the 'threat and promise' of federal grants to the states to accomplish this task," thereby "recogniz[ing], preserv[ing], and protect[ing] the primary responsibilities and rights of States to prevent, reduce, and eliminate pollution, [and] to plan the development and use of land and water resources" §101(b).

Section 303 is central to the Act's carrot-and-stick approach to attaining acceptable water quality without direct federal regulation of nonpoint sources of pollution. Entitled "Water Quality Standards and Implementation Plans," the provision begins by spelling out the statutory requirements for water quality standards: "Water quality standards" specify a water body's "designated uses" and "water quality criteria," taking into account the water's "use and value for public water supplies, propagation of fish and wildlife, recreational purposes, and agricultural, industrial, and other purposes" §303(c)(2). The states are required to set water quality standards for all waters within their boundaries regardless of the sources of the pollution entering the waters. If a state does not set water quality standards, or if the EPA determines that the state's standards do not meet the requirements of the Act, the EPA promulgates standards for the state. §§303(b), (c)(3)–4).

2. Section 303(d): "Identification of Areas with Insufficient Controls; Maximum Daily Load"[1]

Section 303(d)(1)(A) requires each state to identify as "areas with insufficient controls" "those waters within its boundaries for which the effluent limitations required by section [301(b)(1)(A)] and section [301(b)(1)(B)] of this title are not stringent enough to implement any water quality standard applicable to such waters." The CWA defines "effluent limitations" as restrictions on pollutants "discharged from point sources." CWA §502(11). Section 301(b)(1)(A) mandates application of the "best practicable control technology" effluent limitations for most point source discharges, while §301(b)(1)(B) mandates application of effluent limitations adopted specifically for secondary treatment at publicly owned treatment works.

For waters identified pursuant to §303(d)(1)(A) (the "§303(d)(1) list"), the states must establish the "total maximum daily load" ("TMDL") for pollutants identified by the EPA as suitable for TMDL calculation.[2] "A TMDL defines the specified maximum amount of a pollutant which can be discharged or 'loaded' into the waters at issue from all combined sources." The TMDL "shall be established at a level necessary to implement the applicable water quality standards. . . ." §303(d)(1)(c).

---

1. The complete text of sections 303(d)(1)(A) and (C) reads:

(A) Each State shall identify those waters within its boundaries for which the effluent limitations required by section 1311(b)(1)(A) and section 1311(b)(1)(B) of this title are not stringent enough to implement any water quality standard applicable to such waters. The State shall establish a priority ranking for such waters, taking into account the severity of the pollution and the uses to be made of such waters.

(C) Each State shall establish for the waters identified in paragraph (1)(A) of this subsection, and in accordance with the priority ranking, the total maximum daily load, for those pollutants which the Administrator identifies under section 1314(a)(2) of this title as suitable for such calculation. Such load shall be established at a level necessary to implement the applicable water quality standards with seasonal variations and a margin of safety which takes into account any lack of knowledge concerning the relationship between effluent limitations and water quality.

2. The EPA has identified all pollutants, under proper technical conditions, as suitable for TMDL calculation. 43 Fed. Reg. 60662 (Dec. 28, 1978).

Section 303(d)(2), in turn, requires each state to submit its §303(d)(1) list and TMDLs to the EPA for its approval or disapproval. If the EPA approves the list and TMDLs, the state must incorporate the list and TMDLs into its "continuing planning process," the requirements for which are set forth in §303(e). If the EPA disapproves either the §303(d)(1) list or any TMDLs, the EPA must itself put together the missing document or documents. The state then incorporates any EPA-set list or TMDL into the state's continuing planning process.

Each state must also identify all waters not placed on its §303(d)(1) list (the "§303(d)(3) list") and "estimate" TMDLs for pollutants in those waters. §303(d)(3). There is no requirement that the EPA approve the §303(d)(3) lists or the TMDLs estimated for those waters.

The EPA in regulations has made more concrete the statutory requirements. Those regulations, in summary, define "water quality limited segment[s]" — those waters that must be included on the §303(d)(1) list — as "[a]ny segment where it is known that water quality does not meet applicable water quality standards, and/or is not expected to meet applicable water quality standards, even after the application of the technology-based effluent limitations required by sections 301(b) and 306." 40 C.F.R. §130.2(j) (2000). The regulations then divide TMDLs into two types: "load allocations," for nonpoint source pollution, and "wasteload allocations," for point source pollution. Under the regulations, states must identify those waters on the §303(d)(1) lists as "still requiring TMDLs" if any required effluent limitation or other pollution control requirement (including those for nonpoint source pollution) will not bring the water into compliance with water quality standards.

Continuing Planning Process

The final pertinent section of §303, §303(e), requiring each state to have a "continuing planning process," gives some operational force to the prior information-gathering provisions. The EPA may approve a state's continuing planning process only if it "will result in plans for all navigable waters within such State" that include, inter alia, effluent limitations, TMDLs, areawide waste management plans for nonpoint sources of pollution, and plans for "adequate implementation, including schedules of compliance, for revised or new water quality standards." The upshot of this intricate scheme is that the CWA leaves to the states the responsibility of developing plans to achieve water quality standards if the statutorily-mandated point source controls will not alone suffice, while providing federal funding to aid in the implementation of the state plans. TMDLs are primarily informational tools that allow the states to proceed from the identification of waters requiring additional planning to the required plans. As such, TMDLs serve as a link in an implementation chain that includes federally-regulated point source controls, state or local plans for point and nonpoint source pollution reduction, and assessment of the impact of such measures on water quality, all to the end of attaining water quality goals for the nation's waters.

The Garcia River TMDL for sediment is 552 tons per square mile per year, a sixty percent reduction from historical loadings. The TMDL allocates portions of the total yearly load among the following categories of nonpoint source pollution: a) "mass wasting" associated with roads; b) "mass wasting" associated with timber-harvesting; c) erosion related to road surfaces; and d) erosion related to road and skid trail crossings. [EPA adopted the Garcia River TMDL.]

[The Court first explained why EPA's interpretation of the statute was more consistent with the precise language and structure of section 303(d), and then proceeded to address the overall statutory scheme and issues of federalism:]

The Statutory Scheme as a Whole

The Pronsolinos' objection is, in essence, that the CWA as a whole distinguishes between the regulatory schemes applicable to point and nonpoint sources, so we must assume such a distinction in applying §§303(d)(1)(A) and (c). We would hesitate in any case to read into a discrete statutory provision something that is not there because it is contained elsewhere in the statute. But here, the premise is wrong: There is no such general division throughout the CWA.

Point sources are treated differently from nonpoint sources for many purposes under the statute, but not all. In particular, there is no such distinction with regard to the basic purpose for which the §303(d) list and TMDLs are compiled, the eventual attainment of state-defined water quality standards. Water quality standards reflect a state's designated uses for a water body and do not depend in any way upon the source of pollution.

Nor is there any other basis for inferring from the structure of the Act an implicit limitation in §§303(d)(1)(A) and (C). The statutory subsection requiring water quality segment identification and TMDLs appears in the section entitled "Water Quality Standards and Implementation Plans," not in the immediately preceding section, entitled "Water Quality Related Effluent Limitations." So the section heading does not suggest any limitation to waters subject to effluent limitations.

Additionally, §303(d) follows the subsections setting forth the requirements for water quality standards, §303(a)–c) — which, as noted above, apply without regard to the source of pollution — and precedes the "continuing planning process" subsection, §303(e), which applies broadly as well. Thus, §303(d) is structurally part of a set of provisions governing an interrelated goal-setting, information-gathering, and planning process that, unlike many other aspects of the CWA, applies without regard to the source of pollution.

True, there are, as the Pronsolinos point out, two sections of the statute as amended, §208 and §319, that set requirements exclusively for nonpoint sources of pollution. But the structural inference we are asked to draw from those specialized sections — that no other provisions of the Act set requirements for waters polluted by nonpoint sources — simply does not follow. Absent some irreconcilable contradiction between the requirements contained in §§208 and 319, on the one hand, and the listing and TMDL requirements of §303(d), on the other, both apply.

There is no such contradiction. Section 208 provides for federal grants to encourage the development of state "areawide waste treatment management plans" for areas with substantial water quality problems, and requires that those plans include a process for identifying and controlling nonpoint source pollution "to the extent feasible." Section 319, added to the CWA in 1987, directs states to adopt "nonpoint source management programs"; provides grants for nonpoint source pollution reduction; and requires states to submit a report to the EPA that "identifies those navigable waters within the State which, without additional action to control nonpoint sources of pollution, cannot reasonably be expected to attain or maintain applicable water quality standards or the goals and requirements of this chapter." This report must also describe state programs for reducing nonpoint source pollution and the process "to reduce, to the maximum extent practicable, the level of pollution" resulting from particular categories of nonpoint source pollution. §319(a)(1)(C), (D).

The CWA is replete with multiple listing and planning requirements applicable to the same waterways (quite confusingly so, indeed), so no inference can be drawn from the overlap alone.

Nor are we willing to draw the more discrete inference that the §303(d) listing and TMDL requirements cannot apply to nonpoint source pollutants because the planning requirements imposed by §208 and §319 are qualified ones — "to the extent feasible" and "to the maximum extent practicable" — while the §303(d) requirements are unbending. For one thing, the water quality standards set under §303 are functional and may permit more pollution than it is "feasible" or "practicable" to eliminate, depending upon the intended use of a particular waterway. For another, with or without TMDLs, the §303(e) plans for attaining water quality standards must, without qualification, account for elimination of nonpoint source pollution to the extent necessary to meet those standards.

The various reporting requirements that apply to nonpoint source pollution are no more impermissibly redundant than are the planning requirements. . . .

Essentially, §319 encourages the states to institute an approach to the elimination of nonpoint source pollution similar to the federally-mandated effluent controls contained in the CWA, while §303 encompasses a water quality based approach applicable to all sources of water pollution. As various sections of the Act encourage different, and complementary, state schemes for cleaning up nonpoint source pollution in the nation's waterways, there is no basis for reading any of those sections — including §303(d) — out of the statute.

There is one final aspect of the Act's structure that bears consideration because it supports the EPA's interpretation of §303(d): The list required by §303(d)(1)(A) requires that waters be listed if they are impaired by a combination of point sources and nonpoint sources; the language admits of no other reading. Section 303(d)(1)(C), in turn, directs that TMDLs "shall be established at a level necessary to implement the applicable water quality standards. . . ." So, at least in blended waters, TMDLs must be calculated with regard to nonpoint sources of pollution; otherwise, it would be impossible "to implement the applicable water quality standards," which do not differentiate sources of pollution . . . .

Nothing in the statutory structure — or purpose — suggests that Congress meant to distinguish, as to §303(d)(1) lists and TMDLs, between waters with one insignificant point source and substantial nonpoint source pollution and waters with only nonpoint source pollution. Such a distinction would, for no apparent reason, require the states or the EPA to monitor waters to determine whether a point source had been added or removed, and to adjust the §303(d)(1) list and establish TMDLs accordingly. There is no statutory basis for concluding that Congress intended such an irrational regime.

Looking at the statute as a whole, we conclude that the EPA's interpretation of §303(d) is not only entirely reasonable but considerably more convincing than the one offered by the plaintiffs in this case.

Federalism Concerns

The Pronsolinos finally contend that, by establishing TMDLs for waters impaired only by nonpoint source pollution, the EPA has upset the balance of federal-state control established in the CWA by intruding into the states' traditional control over land use. That is not the case.

The Garcia River TMDL identifies the maximum load of pollutants that can enter the Garcia River from certain broad categories of nonpoint sources if the river is to attain water quality standards. It does not specify the load of pollutants that may be received from particular parcels of land or describe what measures the state should take to implement the TMDL. Instead, the TMDL expressly recognizes that "implementation and monitoring" "are state responsibilities" and notes that, for this reason, the EPA did not include implementation or monitoring plans within the TMDL.

Moreover, §303(e) requires — separately from the §303(d)(1) listing and TMDL requirements — that each state include in its continuing planning process "adequate implementation, including schedules of compliance, for revised or new water quality standards" "for all navigable waters within such State." The Garcia River TMDL thus serves as an informational tool for the creation of the state's implementation plan, independently—and explicitly — required by Congress.

California chose both if and how it would implement the Garcia River TMDL. States must implement TMDLs only to the extent that they seek to avoid losing federal grant money; there is no pertinent statutory provision otherwise requiring implementation of §303 plans or providing for their enforcement.

Finally, it is worth noting that the arguments that the Pronsolinos raise here would apply equally to nonpoint source pollution controls for blended waters. Yet, as discussed above, Congress definitely required that the states or the EPA establish TMDLs for all pollutants in waters on §303(d)(1) lists, including blended waters.

NOTES AND QUESTIONS ON *PRONSOLINO* AND TMDLs

1. *Point versus nonpoint sources.* Why do you think Congress imposed strict, mandatory federal obligations on point sources, but relegated the control of nonpoint source pollution to individual state discretion? Is it explained by the policy articulated by Congress in section 101(b) of the Act, "to recognize, preserve, and protect the primary responsibilities and rights of States to prevent, reduce, and eliminate pollution [and] *to plan the development and use of land and water resources.*" *Id.* §1251(b) (emphasis added)?

2. *TMDLs versus SIPs.* What similarities are there between TMDLs and SIPs? What differences? There seemed to be no question that SIPs should account for all kinds of sources of air pollution, from stationary sources to areawide sources to the ubiquitous automobile. Why would Congress, as the *Pronsolino* plaintiffs argued, exclude nonpoint sources from the analogous TMDL process?

3. *The stakes.* The Court seems clear that even where EPA writes a TMDL, the states are in charge of implementation under the continuing planning process in section 303(e), including decisions about whether, and how, to regulate nonpoint sources. If so, why did the plaintiffs care whether TMDLs apply to nonpoint sources? The Association of Metropolitan Sewerage Agencies (AMSA), which represents point source public dischargers from the largest cities in the country, intervened on EPA's side of this case. Why did this representative of large point source dischargers care about the results of this case?

4. *Complexity and uncertainty.* As is true for SIPs, what may seem like a simple process in concept can get complicated very quickly. The same general sequence of analysis is needed for TMDLs as for SIPs. States first must monitor waters to determine where water quality standards are violated, and by how much. Then, they must identify and quantify the sources of the pertinent kind

of pollution, ascertain what controls are potentially achievable, allocate pollution reduction obligations among those sources, decide on implementing methods, and then continue to monitor to determine whether standards are attained. Consider, however, the following examples of the kinds of complexities and uncertainties inherent in this process:

    a.   *Nonpoint sources.* Some uncertainty exists for any kind of environmental monitoring. For point sources, discharges may vary over time in volume, concentration of pollutants, and other factors. However, at least we know where the outlet source is, and can sample effluent directly. It is considerably more difficult to measure, or even estimate, pollution from nonpoint sources, such as how much pollution runs off thousands of acres of farm fields within a watershed.

    b.   *Pollutant variability, fate and transport.* Measuring and predicting water quality would be much easier in a "closed system," in which everything we put into the water remains and everything we take out is gone, and in which conditions remain relatively constant. What variables in real water bodies will affect concentrations of pollutants in the water, and, hence, the degree to which water quality standards are attained or violated? In what ways might concentrations of different kinds of pollutants change once they enter a real waterway, and how would those factors affect the degree to which water quality standards are met?

    c.   *Different forms of water quality criteria.* Recall from Chapter 5 that, unlike the NAAQS which are expressed entirely in numerical terms, water quality criteria come in different forms: narrative, numeric, toxicity-based, and biological. TMDLs are required for all violations of water quality criteria, whatever the format. How would you write TMDLs for narrative water quality criteria, such as waters free from noxious odors? Toxicity-based criteria, such as no more than 1 percent mortality of test organisms exposed to a given level of water quality? Biocriteria, such as 75 percent of species diversity, compared to an unimpaired reference stream? What would implementation plans for those kinds of TMDLs look like?

    5. *Implementation.* Section 301(b)(1)(C) of the Clean Water Act (in conjunction with the section 402 permitting requirement and other provisions) requires that point sources achieve effluent limitations sufficient to ensure the attainment of water quality standards, if those limits are stricter than imposed by any applicable technology-based requirements. As you learned in *Pronsolino*, no such firm requirement exists for nonpoint sources, in section 303(d) or (e) of the Clean Water Act or elsewhere. In the face of litigation and political pressure, EPA ultimately withdrew the proposed regulations identified by the court, which would have imposed a mandatory implementation

plan requirement for all TMDLs. In the face of this implementation gap, is the requirement to prepare TMDLs somewhat akin to pushing on a loose string?

8. *Assessment.* As noted above, EPA began to implement the SIP program immediately after Congress adopted the 1970 CAA Amendments. As Professor Houck explains in detail, however, EPA focused primarily on implementing the technology-based requirements of the CWA as implemented through the NPDES permitting program, largely to the exclusion of the TMDL process, until forced to implement TMDLs by a rash of citizen suits. Therefore, EPA did not begin to implement the TMDL program seriously until more than two decades after the 1972 amendments. *See* OLIVER HOUCK, THE CLEAN WATER ACT TMDL PROGRAM: LAW, POLICY, AND IMPLEMENTATION (2d ed. 2002). The following is a simplified depiction of the major federal and state roles under the CWA:

Principal Federal and State Clean Water Act Roles

Federal Roles	*State Roles*
Issue national technology-based effluent limitations standards	
Review state-issued point source permits; authority to veto inadequate permits	Apply technology-based standards in individual point source permits
Issue water quality criteria guidance; review and approve state water quality standards, or issue federal water quality standards	Adopt water quality standards (WQS)
Review and approve state TMDLs, or issue federal TMDLs	Adopt "total maximum daily loads" (TMDLs) for water bodies that do not meet WQS; revise point source permits as necessary to implement TMDLs
No authority to issue federal nonpoint source control plans or water quality implementation plans (remedies limited to withholding grants)	Adopt nonpoint source control plans and water quality implementation plans

Whether for this or for other reasons, one of us has noted that the nation faces failures in achieving water quality standards similar to the CAA nonattainment problems identified by Professor Reitze: "More than a third of the nation's rivers and almost half of its lakes do not meet designated water quality uses in whole or in part — trends that have not changed significantly over the past decade — because of a combination of chemical pollution and other factors." Robert W. Adler, *The Two Lost Books in the Water Quality Trilogy: The Elusive Objectives of Physical and Biological Integrity*, 33 Envtl. L. 29, 49-50 (2003). Once the TMDL program is implemented more fully, do you think it has any better chance of success than the SIP process? Why or why not? What are the major impediments to the success of the TMDL program? How might they be fixed?

PROBLEM: A PFOA TMDL

Where a water body is impaired by numerous and diverse sources, TMDLs (like SIPs) can become extremely complex. Among the many thorny implementation problems are uncertainties in measurement, modeling, environmental variability, and other factors similar to those identified by Professor Reitze in the SIP process. Consider the following, relatively simple hypothetical scenario for PFOA. (Actual TMDL calculations are considerably more complex.)

One of the factories that produces PFOA wastes is located on the banks of the Blue River. In the past, the factory dumped PFOA wastes onto adjacent fields, and PFOA has now seeped into the groundwater. Some PFOA regularly leaches from the groundwater into the adjacent river. Current PFOA wastes from the factory are treated as part of the facility's overall waste stream, but some PFOA residuals remain in the waste water released into the Blue River. Finally, some highly concentrated PFOA wastes were sent in barrels to a nearby industrial waste landfill. Due to improper handling and storage of those barrels, some PFOA has leaked into the ground beneath the landfill. However, the landfill has a leachate collection and treatment system, through which some PFOA residuals are discharged into the Blue River.

Thus, there are at least three existing sources of PFOA discharge into the Blue River (the groundwater, the factory discharge, and the landfill discharge). The state department of environmental quality (DEQ) determines that PFOA levels in the Blue River exceed the applicable state water quality criterion. To use easy, rather than realistic, numbers for now, the state determines that total PFOA releases into the river must be reduced by 10 micrograms of PFOA per day in order to meet the standards.

1. On what basis should the state "allocate" the required load reductions among the three existing sources? What principles can you think of that a state might use in deciding how to allocate pollution reduction allocations among various parties in a TMDL process?

2. Once the state makes that determination, how will it implement and enforce those required reductions? How will it enforce reductions for the factory and landfill discharges? What about the groundwater seepage? Is that a point or a nonpoint source? Should it be included in the TMDL under the *Pronsolino* case? If so, how can any reductions be implemented and enforced? How can compliance with any required reduction be monitored?

3. Now, assume that the flow of the Blue River varies over time. During the spring, mountain snowmelt or heavy spring rains cause the river to swell to high levels, but by the end of September, the river is a fraction of what it is in May. Why does this matter in writing a TMDL? What flow assumption should the state use in writing the TMDL?

4. Next, assume that a new factory wants to locate to the Blue River upstream of the existing discharges. The factory will make high-tech waterproof fabrics and clothing, but will involve additional PFOA releases to the Blue River as a result. The Governor wants to encourage the new facility because it will create many new jobs and stimulate the economy. Can the state allow the new discharge, even when the PFOA water quality standard is already violated? See Arkansas v. Oklahoma,

503 U.S. 91 (1992) (holding that the CWA does not "mandate a complete ban on discharges into a waterway that is in violation of [state] water quality standards"); Trustees for Alaska v. EPA, 749 F.2d 549 (9th Cir. 1984) (remanding and directing EPA to develop and include in NPDES permits for mining operations specific effluent limitations and monitoring standards necessary to achieve state water quality standards); 40 C.F.R. §§122.4(d), 122.4(i). If so, what must the state do to allow the new discharge?

Note on the Scope and Coverage of Federal Regulation

Federal environmental regulation can extend to a wide range of activities that otherwise might seem quite local in scope and impact. Under section 404 of the Clean Water Act, for example, the Army Corps of Engineers regulates construction of new homes or shopping centers if construction involves the discharge of dredge or fill material into wetlands or other waters of the United States. See, e.g., Bersani v. EPA, 850 F.2d 36 (1st Cir. 1988), cert. denied, 489 U.S. 1089 (1989) (shopping mall); Buttrey v. United States, 690 F.2d 1170 (5th Cir. 1982), cert. denied, 461 U.S. 927 (1983) (housing development). Similarly, Section 7 of the ESA requires the Fish and Wildlife Service to determine whether otherwise local projects might jeopardize the continued existence of a threatened or endangered species, and whether the project may proceed or must implement reasonable and prudent alternatives. See, e.g., Rancho Viejo v. Norton, 323 F.3d 1062 (D.C. Cir. 2003), rehearing and rehearing en banc denied 334 F.3d 1158 (D.C. Cir. July 22, 2003), cert. denied, 540 U.S. 1218 (2004) (upholding applicability to ESA to toad species limited to small habitats entirely within Southern California); National Association of Homebuilders v. Babbitt, 130 F.3d 1041 (D.C. Cir. 1997) (upholding ESA as applied to fly restricted to an eight-mile radius in two California counties).

The reach of federal environmental laws theoretically might be limited by the scope of federal power under the Commerce Clause, especially under the Supreme Court's rulings in U.S. v. Lopez, 514 U.S. 549 (1995), and U.S. v. Morrison, 529 U.S. 598 (2000), which invalidated, as beyond the scope of federal commerce power, aspects of federal gun control legislation and the civil remedy provisions of legislation designed to protect women against violent crimes, respectively. To date, however, courts have either rejected or avoided Commerce Clause challenges to a range of federal environmental statutes. See, e.g., U.S. v. Olin Corp., 107 F.3d 1506 (11th Cir. 1997) (CERCLA); Gibbs v. Babbitt, 214 F.3d 483 (4th Cir. 2000) (ESA); State of Nebraska v. EPA, 331 F.3d 995 (D.C. Cir. 2003), rehearing en banc denied (D.C. Cir. Aug. 22, 2003) (Safe Drinking Water Act); Solid Waste Agency of Northern Cook County v. U.S. Army Corps of Engineers, 531 U.S. 159 (2001) (Clean Water Act; Commerce Clause issue avoided).

Congress might find, as a matter of policy, however, that federal regulation of activities of some kinds, in some places, or with impacts that fall below a certain threshold, should be governed by states and localities, rather than the federal government. Those line-drawing exercises, in turn, might affect the manner in which comprehensive statutory schemes work (or do not work), as suggested by the problems of controlling air pollution from diffuse sources and water pollution from nonpoint sources.

As one prime example, you have seen that courts can interpret the manner in which Congress allocated water pollution control authority under the CWA in light of stated statutory goals or policies regarding states' rights. In *PUD No. 1 of Jefferson County*, for example, studied in Chapter 5, the Supreme Court considered the proper scope of state authority to use its water quality standards to control water flows through a federally-licensed dam in light of Congress' stated policy that "the authority of each State to allocate quantities of water within its jurisdiction shall not be superseded, abrogated or otherwise impaired" by the CWA. 33 U.S.C. §1251(g). Similarly, the court in *Mississippi Commission on Natural Resources, supra*, interpreted state power to determine the appropriate designated uses of water bodies in light of Congress' policy to recognize and preserve state authority over land and water uses. *See* 33 U.S.C. §1251(b).

Several key issues remain hotly disputed regarding the relative scope of federal and state regulation under the CWA, all of which are governed by specific statutory text and definitions, but guided by policy factors and constitutional overtones. In section 301 of the CWA, Congress prohibited "the discharge of any pollutant by any person," 33 U.S.C. §1311(a), absent a valid permit under section 402 of the Act. *Id.* §1342 (providing for National Pollutant Discharge Elimination System (NPDES) permits). "Discharge of a pollutant" is defined as "any addition of any pollutant to navigable waters from any point source." *Id.* §1362(12). Parties continue to litigate the meaning of all three of the key terms included in this definition — "addition," "navigable waters," and "point source" — to determine which activities are governed by federal law, and which are left to the states:

1. *Addition.* In National Wildlife Federation v. Gorsuch, 693 F.2d 156 (D.C. Cir. 1982), the D.C. Circuit upheld EPA's decision not to require NPDES permits for discharges of water through dams, because those discharges move pollutants from one part of a river to another, and thus do not constitute an "addition" of pollutants to navigable waters. While the court based its decision in part on the statutory text, it was also influenced by indications in the statute and in the legislative history that Congress "did not want to interfere any more than necessary with state water management." *Id.* at 178-79. *See also* National Wildlife Federation v. Consumers Power Co., 862 F.2d 580 (6th Cir. 1988) (upholding EPA decision that NPDES permit was not required for discharges of dead fish through pumped storage hydropower facility). More recently, however, three appellate courts have found that an NPDES permit is required for discharges for water that transfers pollutants from one water body to another. Catskill Mountains Chapter of Trout Unlimited v. City of New York, 273 F.3d 481 (2d Cir. 2001) (holding that water

pumped from a reservoir, through a tunnel, into a creek required a permit); Dubois v. U.S. Department of Agriculture, 102 F.3d 1273 (1st Cir. 1996) (requiring permit for water pumped from a river to a mountain pond for purposes of snowmaking at ski resort); Miccosukee Tribe v. South Florida Water Management District, 280 F.3d 1364 (11th Cir. 2002) (requiring permit for stormwater runoff from canal pumped through levee into undeveloped water conservation area).

The Supreme Court reviewed the Eleventh Circuit's decision in the *Miccosukee* case, remanding to the district court for a determination of whether the pumping source and the discharge location were "meaningfully distinct water bodies." South Florida Water Management District v. Miccosukee Tribe of Indians, 541 U.S. 95, 112 (2005). While not reaching the issue of whether Congress excluded these activities from the NPDES program as a matter of federalism, Justice O'Connor explained the competing federalism implications of the issue:

> If we read the Act to require an NPDES permit for every engineered diversion of one navigable water into another, thousands of new permits might have to be issued, particularly by western States, whose water supply networks often rely on engineered transfers among various natural water bodies. Many of those diversions might also require expensive treatment to meet water quality criteria. It may be that construing the NPDES program to cover such transfers would therefore raise the costs of water distribution prohibitively, and violate Congress' specific instruction that "the authority of each State to allocate quantities of water within its jurisdiction shall not be superseded, abrogated or otherwise impaired" by the Act. §1251(g). On the other hand, it may be that such permitting authority is necessary to protect water quality, and that the States or EPA could control regulatory costs by issuing general permits to point sources associated with water distribution programs.

Id. at 108. Should the decision in this case be governed by the congressional policy of preserving state authority over water allocation, or by the statutory objective of controlling water pollution?

In S.D. Warren v. Maine Board of Environmental Protection, 126 S. Ct. 1843 (2006), the Supreme Court distinguished section 401 of the CWA from section 402, and held that an addition of a pollutant was not required to meet the definition of discharge (triggering the need for state water quality certification under section 401, *see PUD No. 1 of Jefferson County*, Chapter 5), as it is to constitute the "discharge of a pollutant" for purposes of section 402 (triggering the need for an NPDES permit). Ironically, however, by establishing a broader definition of discharge for purposes of section 401, the Supreme Court expanded state authority to control water pollution from federally licensed facilities.

2. *Navigable waters.* The term "navigable waters" is defined in the Act as "waters of the United States, including the territorial seas," and has been the subject of much dispute regarding the geographic scope of federal regulation

of water pollution. In United States v. Riverside Bayview Homes, 474 U.S. 121 (1985), the Supreme Court upheld the Corps of Engineers' interpretation of "navigable waters" as including wetlands that are "adjacent to" navigable bodies of water. In upholding the federal regulation, Justice White focused on the statutory goal of restoring and maintaining aquatic ecosystem integrity on a broad, systematic basis:

> [The Act] constituted a comprehensive legislative attempt "to restore and maintain the chemical, physical, and biological integrity of the Nation's waters." This objective incorporated a broad, systematic view of the goal of maintaining and improving water quality: as the House Report on the legislation put it, "the word 'integrity' . . . refers to a condition in which the natural structure and function of ecosystems [are] maintained." Protection of aquatic ecosystems, Congress recognized, demanded broad federal authority to control pollution, for "[w]ater moves in hydrologic cycles and it is essential that discharge of pollutants be controlled at the source."

Id. at 132.

In *Riverside Bayview Homes*, however, the Court left open the question of whether the statute applied to so-called "isolated waters" that are not adjacent to waters that are traditionally navigable. In *Solid Waste Agency of Northern Cook County, supra* (*SWANCC*), the Court rejected Clean Water Act jurisdiction based on use of an isolated series of ponds by migratory birds, and implicitly found that discharges to isolated waters cannot be regulated under the Act. Rather than focusing primarily on the statutory goal of restoring the integrity of the Nation's waters, Chief Justice Rehnquist argued that the statutory language must be read narrowly to avoid an unnecessary constitutional decision, especially where federalism concerns are at stake:

> Where an administrative interpretation of a statute invokes the outer limits of Congress' power, we expect a clear indication that Congress intended that result. This requirement stems from our prudential desire not to needlessly reach constitutional issues and our assumption that Congress does not casually authorize administrative agencies to interpret a statute to push the limit of congressional authority. *This concern is heightened where the administrative interpretation alters the federal-state framework by permitting federal encroachment upon a traditional state power.*

531 U.S. at 172-73 (emphasis added).

Following *SWANCC*, lower courts have decided numerous cases trying to draw the line between "adjacent" waters governed by the Act under *Riverside Bayview Homes*, and "isolated" waters excluded from that coverage under *SWANCC*. *See, e.g.*, United States v. Rapanos, 339 F.3d 447 (6th Cir. 2003), *cert. denied*, 124 S. Ct. 1874 (2004) (concluding that *SWANCC* was relevant only to jurisdiction asserted under the Migratory Bird Rule and did not preclude jurisdiction under the CWA over a roadside ditch and the adjacent wetlands); United States v. Deaton, 332 F.3d 698 (4th Cir. 2003), *cert. denied*, 124 S. Ct. 1874 (2004) (reading *SWANCC* narrowly and determining that the CWA provides for jurisdiction over inland waters, provided that those waters have a hydrological connection to navigable waters); Headwaters, Inc. v. Talent Irrigation District, 243 F.3d 526 (9th Cir. 2001) (concluding that polluted irrigation canals which received water from natural streams and lakes were not isolated waters and were properly subject to jurisdiction under the CWA); *but see* In re Needham, 354 F.3d 340 (5th Cir. 2003) (deciding that *SWANCC* limits jurisdiction under the CWA to navigable waters and water bodies directly abutting navigable waters). In deciding these cases, should courts be influenced more by the aquatic ecosystem restoration and protection goal emphasized by Justice White in *Riverside Bayview Homes*, or by the federalism concerns raised by Chief Justice Rehnquist in *SWANCC*?

The Supreme Court revisited this issue in 2006 in two cases involving wetlands connected to navigable waters by ditches or other man-made conveyances. Rapanos v. United States, 126 S. Ct. 2208 (2006). Writing for a four-member plurality, Justice Scalia would impose two limiting conditions to the exercise of CWA jurisdiction. His first proposed condition relates to the nature of the water body:

> In sum, on its only plausible interpretation, the phrase "the waters of the United States" include only those relatively permanent, standing or continuously flowing bodies of water "forming geographic features" that are described in ordinary parlance as "streams[,] . . . ocean, rivers, [and] lakes." See Webster's Second 2882. The phrase does not include channels through which water flows intermittently or ephemerally, or channels that periodically provide drainage for rainfall.

Id. at 2225. Justice Scalia's second suggested condition relates to the degree of connection between the water body to be regulated and a traditional navigable water:

> Therefore, *only* those wetlands with a continuous surface water connection to bodies that are "waters of the United States" in their own right, so that there is no clear demarcation between "waters" and wetlands, are "adjacent to" such waters and covered by the Act. Wetlands with only an intermittent, physically remote hydrologic connection to "waters of the United States" do not implicate the boundary-drawing problem in *Riverside Bayview*, and thus lack the necessary connection to covered waters that we described as a "significant nexus" in *SWANCC*.

Id. at 2226 (emphasis in original). A prominent theme in Justice Scalia's opinion was that a broader interpretation of the Act's scope was not consistent with Congress' expressed goal, in section 101(b) of the Act, to recognize the primary role of the states in water pollution control. *See id.* at 2215, 2223-2224.

Justice Kennedy, concurring in the judgment, would require only an adequate showing, on the record, that the water or wetland to be regulated has a "'significant nexus' to waters that are or were navigable in fact or that could reasonably be so made." *Id.* at 2236. Justices Stevens, Souter, Ginsberg and Breyer dissented, and would have upheld the agencies' exercise of jurisdiction based on the principles articulated in *Riverside Bayview Homes. Id.* at 2253 *et seq.* Those opinions focused more heavily on Congress' intent to control water pollution and to protect aquatic ecosystems on a national scale, without as much attention to states' rights. (Chief Justice Roberts penned a separate concurring opinion, and Justice Breyer a separate dissent.) Given the fractured nature of the opinions, lower courts have differed on what rules to apply to cases involving various bodies of water. The Ninth Circuit and the Seventh Circuit have decided to apply Justice Kennedy's opinion as the narrowest ground on which the judgment was based. No. Cal. River Watch v. City of Healdsburg, 457 F.3d 1023 (9th Cir. 2006); United States v. Gerke Excavating, Inc., 2006 WL 2707971 (7th Cir. 2006). The First Circuit and one lower court adopted Justice Stevens' suggestion that courts uphold applicability of the CWA to any water that meets either Justice Scalia's or Justice Kennedy's proposed tests. *See* United States v. Johnson, No. 05-1444 (1st Cir. Oct. 31, 2006); United States v. Evans, 2006 WL 2221629 (M.D. Fla. 2006). Another district court, however, applied prior Fifth Circuit precedent because of the absence of a clear majority in *Rapanos.* United States v. Chevron Pipeline Co., 437 F. Supp. 2d 605 (N.D. Tex. 2006). Unless and until Congress steps in and clarifies the reach of the Act, it appears that confusion will remain about which waters are covered by the national statutory scheme, and which are left entirely to state regulation and control.

3. *Point sources.* In *Pronsolino*, you saw that Congress included point sources within the federal regulatory scheme while leaving nonpoint source controls largely to individual states, in large part because of a concern about the degree to which federal regulation of nonpoint sources would intrude on state authority over land and water use. The stakes here are very high. Point sources require NPDES permits that may bring hefty permit application and compliance costs, and subject the discharger to significant potential enforcement liability for any violations. State non-point source controls typically are weak to nonexistent. As a result, parties have litigated intensively whether various activities are covered by the definition of point source. *See, e.g.,* Concerned Area Residents for the Environment v. Southview Farm, 34 F.3d 114 (2d Cir. 1994) (manure spreading and spraying); Natural Resources Defense Council, Inc. v. Train, 510 F.2d 692 (D.C. Cir. 1974) (storm water); The Avoyelles Sportsmen's League, Inc. v. Marsh, 715 F.2d 897 (5th Cir. 1983) (construction equipment); U.S. v. Earth Sciences, Inc., 599 F.2d 368 (10th Cir. 1979) (mining ponds); Dague v. City of Burlington, 935 F.2d 1343 (2d Cir. 1991) (landfill). The statute defines a "point source" as:

> any discernible, confined and discrete conveyance, including but not limited to any pipe, ditch, channel, tunnel, conduit, well, discrete fissure, container, rolling stock, concentrated animal feeding operation, or vessel or other floating craft,

from which pollutants are or may be discharged. This term does not include agricultural stormwater discharges and return flows from irrigated agriculture.

33 U.S.C. §1362(14). In deciding where the point/nonpoint source line should be drawn, should courts focus more on the functional issues suggested in the definition, *i.e.*, whether the discharge is amenable to regulation in a permit because it is "discernible, confined and discrete," or federalism concerns of whether the *activity* to be regulated affects state authority over land and water use?

3. Delegating Federal Programs to States

In some cases, rather than delegating responsibility either to the federal government or to states, Congress took a middle ground in which programs are implemented by federal agencies unless they are delegated to willing states and subject to federal approval and oversight. Key examples include 33 U.S.C. §1342 (CWA NPDES permits); *id.* §1344 (CWA dredge and fill permits); 42 U.S.C. §7661 (CAA permits); 42 U.S.C. §6926 (RCRA hazardous waste planning); *id.* §6933 (RCRA hazardous waste management); 30 U.S.C. §§1253-1254 (Surface Mining Conservation and Reclamation Act (SMCRA) program). This form of cooperative federalism, however, raises additional issues regarding the degree to which the federal government should oversee delegated state programs. Consider the following case, which explains the balance Congress struck in allowing EPA to delegate the NPDES program to states, but with significant ongoing EPA oversight:

Save the Bay v. Administrator, EPA
556 F.2d 1282 (5th Cir. 1977)

GOLDBERG, CIRCUIT JUDGE.

The 1972 amendments to the Federal Water Pollution Control Act joined the Environmental Protection Agency and the fifty states in a delicate partnership charged with controlling and eventually eliminating water pollution throughout the United States. . . .

The Mississippi Air and Water Pollution Control Commission is a member of this pollution battling alliance. In 1975 the Commission granted to E. I. DuPont de Nemours & Co. a permit to operate a titanium dioxide plant at Bay St. Louis, Mississippi. EPA acquiesced in this action by its partner; petitioner here challenges that acquiescence. Petitioner specifically claims, first, that the Commission so mishandled DuPont's permit application that the EPA should have revoked the Commission's authority to grant such permits. Second, petitioner would have this court review EPA's failure to block the DuPont permit.

EPA strenuously urges that this court is without jurisdiction to consider either of petitioner's contentions. We conclude that this court has both the authority and obligation to review EPA decisions to withdraw or not to withdraw a state's delegated permit authority. Certain preconditions to that review are here missing, however, and preclude our determination of the merits of petitioner's first claim. Second, we conclude that this court lacks jurisdiction to review EPA's failure to veto the permit. To the extent EPA's action in this regard is reviewable, original jurisdiction must lie in the district courts.

I. Legislative and Factual Background

The Federal Water Pollution Control Act Amendments of 1972, (hereinafter "Amendments") substantially overhauled the nation's system of water quality control, declaring "the national goal that the discharge of pollutants into the navigable waters be eliminated by 1985." Toward that end the Amendments introduced a system of "effluent limitations" on "point sources" of pollutants. Formerly federal water pollution control efforts centered on standards of water quality specifying acceptable levels of pollution in interstate navigable waters. Through the shift in the 1972 Amendments to strict limitations applicable to each individual point of discharge, Congress intended to "facilitate enforcement by making it unnecessary to work backward from an overpolluted body of water to determine which point sources are responsible and which must be abated."

To enforce the effluent limitations, the Amendments created the National Pollution Discharge Elimination System (NPDES), a scheme for issuing permits to individual dischargers of pollutants. Without an NPDES permit, one may not lawfully discharge a pollutant. Discharge in compliance with the terms of an NPDES permit, on the other hand, is with few exceptions deemed compliance with the Amendments for enforcement purposes. Thus the terms of individual NPDES permits provide the chief means of implementing the strict national standards mandated by the Amendments.

Congress vested this all-important permit issuing authority in EPA as an original matter. In keeping with congressional desire "to recognize, preserve, and protect the primary responsibilities and rights of States to prevent, reduce, and eliminate pollution," the 1972 legislation also offered states the opportunity to obtain permit issuing authority. Under §402(b), a state may submit to EPA a proposed permit program governing discharges into navigable waters within its borders. The state must demonstrate that it will apply the effluent limitations and the Amendments' other requirements in the permits it grants and that it will monitor and enforce the terms of those permits.[3] Unless the

---

3. The Amendments set out the full list of requirements a state program must meet at §402(b). Under §304(h)(2), EPA sets procedural, monitoring, and enforcement guidelines to which state proposals must conform.

Administrator of EPA determines that the proposed state program does not meet these requirements, he must approve the proposal.

Upon approval of a state program, EPA must suspend its own issuance of permits covering those navigable waters subject to the program. Although its role as issuer of NPDES permits thereupon ceases, the federal agency retains review authority and responsibility over an approved state program. The two aspects of this supervisory role form the subjects of the case at bar.

First, EPA may withdraw its approval of a state program upon determining, after notice and an opportunity to respond, that the program is not being administered in compliance with the requirements of §402. See §402(c)(3). Second, EPA may veto individual permits issued under approved state programs. Section 402(d)(1) requires a state to send EPA a copy of each permit application it receives and to notify EPA of every action related to the application, including any proposed permit. Section 402(d)(2)(B) provides that no permit shall issue

> if the Administrator within ninety days of the date of transmittal of the proposed permit by the State objects in writing to the issuance of such permit as being outside the guidelines and requirements of this chapter.

The Administrator may waive his right to object to any individual permit application. §402(d)(3). Additionally, at the time he approves a state program the administrator may waive as to any category of point sources the requirement that the state transmit proposed permit applications and related action as well as his veto power over permits within the category. §402(e). The Administrator may also promulgate regulations, applicable to every approved state program, designating categories of point sources within which the transmittal requirements and veto power will not apply. §402(f) . . .

Mississippi submitted a proposed NPDES program for EPA approval in August 1973. The federal agency gave its approval on May 1, 1974, transferring authority to issue NPDES permits for dischargers in Mississippi to the Mississippi Air and Water Pollution Control Commission (hereinafter "Commission").

On August 28, 1974, the Commission sent EPA a copy of DuPont's application for a permit to discharge from a proposed titanium dioxide manufacturing plant to be located on St. Louis Bay. The company proposed one discharge point into the Bay and two into a deep well injection system. EPA did not waive its authority to review the DuPont proposal. Rather the agency undertook consideration of the matter in consultation with the Commission's staff. EPA suggested certain changes in the Commission's proposed permit, including increased monitoring requirements of the deep well discharges and a requirement that DuPont conduct a study to determine the present levels of various elements in the Bay.

On January 17, 1975, the Commission sent EPA a final draft permit, incorporating the requested changes. EPA informed the Commission it would not veto the permit as drafted, but requested further changes. On February 3, 1975, the Commission issued the DuPont permit, which again incorporated all EPA's requests.

Save the Bay, Inc., an incorporated association concerned with environmental protection, filed its petition in this court on March 11, 1975. Petitioner presses two claims. First, it asserts that the Commission so violated federal guidelines in handling the DuPont permit that EPA should have revoked the state's NPDES authority pursuant to §402(c)(3). Second, petitioner claims EPA should have vetoed the permit as "outside the guidelines and other requirements" of the Amendments. EPA vigorously responds that this court lacks jurisdiction over either of petitioner's claims.

[The Court concluded it lacked jurisdiction over the claims as presented. It held that EPA had not yet taken a final agency action on the request to withdraw Mississippi's NPDES program, and that EPA decisions on whether to veto individual permits could not be reviewed by the Court of Appeals under CWA section 509. It did find that the district courts could review EPA's decisions regarding individual permit vetoes under a very limited standards, as explained below:]

The Administrator may veto proposed permits on the grounds that they are "outside the guidelines and requirements" of the Amendments. §402(d)(2). The reference to guidelines and requirements includes at least the effluent limitation regulations promulgated under §301, the more general effluent limitations guidelines issued under §304(b), and the guidelines governing the procedure for issuing NPDES permits, promulgated under §304(h).

While these guidelines and regulations could provide "law to apply" in reviewing a decision not to veto a permit, the legislative history makes very clear that Congress intended EPA to retain discretion to decline to veto a permit even after the agency found some violation of applicable guidelines. That legislative history, more explicit and unequivocal than generally found, leans in almost every expression toward a minimal federal intervention when a state plan has been approved. First, there was a significant shift in the language of the veto provision during the legislative process. The original Senate version provided that, unless the Administrator affirmatively waived his review of a specific permit, it could not issue "until the Administrator is satisfied that the conditions meet the requirements of this Act." The conference compromise, in addition to retaining the waiver provisions, allows the state permit to issue unless the Administrator affirmatively objects, which the statute authorizes, but does not expressly require, upon a finding of departure from the guidelines. While the use of permissive language is of little persuasive effect itself, the shift from the original Senate version does suggest that not every permit out of compliance with the guidelines need be vetoed.

The post-conference floor debates also disclose intent to confer such discretion. The House had originally rejected any permit-by-permit veto power. The floor managers set out to mollify opponents of that power by explaining the nature of the veto prerogative inserted at conference. Representative Jones emphasized that the Administrator was not intended to veto a permit except upon a "clear showing" of noncompliance with the guidelines. Congressman Wright noted that the Administrator "may stop" the issuance of an unlawful permit and further explained:

> I must give added emphasis to this point. The managers expect the Administrator to use this authority judiciously; it is their intent that the Act be administered in such a manner that the abilities of the States to control their permit programs will be developed and strengthened.

The primacy of state and local enforcement of water pollution controls is a theme that resounds throughout the legislative history of the Amendments. In light of the pervasiveness of this theme, the specific references to the veto power above, and the conferral of broad discretion to waive review of individual permits, we conclude that Congress intended to allow the Administrator to consider the significance of any guideline violations in terms of the overall goal of the Amendments, the elimination of all discharge of pollutants into the nation's navigable waters by 1985. Federal refractions are to be very limited, and 20/20 vision by the states is not to be expected or exacted. To conclude otherwise would contravene the spirit of the federal-state partnership created by the Amendments and establish an undue incentive for the EPA to waive review of proposed permits.

Given discretion to weigh the substantiality of any violations of the guidelines and requirements of the Amendments as well as a mandate to determine the presence of such violations, EPA's decision not to veto a particular permit takes on a breadth that in our judgment renders the bottom line of that decision unreviewable in the federal courts. Once the relevant factors are before the agency, it can weigh them within this broad mandate with an expertise to which the restraining powers of judicial review could add little. Given such a mandate, a judge's judgment on the significance in terms of water quality of the provisions of a permit is not likely to be sounder or fairer to the challenger, whether environmentalist or industrialist, than that of the EPA.

Accordingly, we hold that the Administrator's conclusion not to veto an individual permit is itself immune to judicial review. However, this observation does not mean that the Administrator is completely beyond the scrutiny of the federal courts in performing the supervisory role over state permits that Congress, after exhaustive debate on the specific subject, saw fit to establish.

While Congress in considering the Amendments articulated a definite commitment to a hands-off policy toward the states, equally clearly it did not intend the hands of the federal government completely to be tied. In light of the precedent for partial review of administrative action, we must be loathe totally to eradicate judicial review from a legislative framework in which the federal government has not wholly abdicated its role. From that perspective we find that judicial review may appropriately confine EPA's discretion along two very narrow lines. First, nothing in the statute or its history suggest any basis for allowing EPA in reviewing the merits of a permit totally to omit consideration of a particular violation of the guidelines and requirements of the Amendments. When all the relevant factors are before the agency, there is such insufficient likelihood of improving the decision that the presumption for judicial review falls. Judicial review, however, can quite easily be effective to assure that all those factors receive the agency's attention. Accordingly, an aggrieved person must be able to present a claim in district court that a proposed permit contains a violation of applicable federal guidelines that the agency has failed to consider. Upon sufficient showing of a violation, the agency, if it claims to have attended to the factor during its review, will have to explain in a manner that cannot be labeled arbitrary how it concluded the violation did not warrant veto. Failing that, it will have to reconsider its decision in light of the new factor.

The other available avenue of review runs in precisely the opposite direction. There is no suggestion anywhere in the Amendments' history that EPA may base a decision not to veto on factors other than a specific permit's consistency with the guidelines or the insignificance of any departures. There must accordingly be room for claims that unlawful factors have tainted the agency's exercise of its discretion. For example, there is no room for consideration of the political popularity of a decision to veto a permit and, thereby, some local project. Nor could EPA let pass a permit it would otherwise veto on acknowledgment of the fact that the state agency involved had generally drawn up lawful permits. Once EPA explained or removed the alleged illegitimate factor, of course, the final decision not to veto would be within its unreviewable discretion.

With only that minimal intrusion, the partial review outlined will help assure that potentially serious violations of law in proposed permits that threaten individuals or businesses will not go unattended as EPA carries out the supervisory responsibility Congress unequivocally placed within its walls. The limited scope of the reviewable issues and the nonreviewability of EPA's final determination offer sufficient sanctuary from any imagined onslaught of frivolous petitions. The courts may easily supply this limited review. To do less would be to ignore the limited but important federal side of the partnership created by the Amendments; moreover, it would be unnecessarily to denigrate the role of private citizens of all persuasions in the administrative process and to abrogate the strong presumption in favor of judicial review of administrative action.

V. Conclusion

We have been called upon to examine a statutory scheme that has the potential for the optimum of federalism. The legislation contains problems of accommodation that will require additional interstitial interpretation and environmental exploration as the partners pirouette. The success of their federalist venture will depend not only upon the grace, but also the substance of movement by both partners in the ballet. We have endeavored to ink a most self-effacing role for the federal judiciary, one which should foster a harmonious background to the dance and necessitate intervention only when a point of unmelodious discord seriously threatens the contrapuntal balance.

NOTES AND QUESTIONS ON *SAVE THE BAY*

1. *Holding.* Because the court never reached the merits of Save the Bay's claims, technically it does not tell us how much discretion EPA has in reviewing state permit decisions and broader requests to review state program implementation. How much deference does the court *suggest* EPA should afford state permit decisions? How much deference does the court suggest a reviewing court (the district court) should afford EPA's decisions in reviewing state permits or programs? What message does this send to states about how much scrutiny their programs will receive? Is it justified by the federalism rationale of state program delegation?

2. *Clean Air Act.* Congress used a similar approach to federalism in the Clean Air Act and the Clean Water Act. In the 1990 Amendments to the Clean Air Act, Congress adopted Title V, which embodies a similar permitting program to the NPDES, and a similar relationship between EPA and the states. Under section 502, EPA adopted regulations specifying the minimum requirements for CAA permitting programs. Congress directed the states to submit to EPA programs complying with those rules. After a state misses several opportunities to correct any deficiencies, EPA is required to adopt and implement a program for the deficient state. When presented with citizen suits challenging the stringency of EPA oversight of Title V programs, courts have taken an approach similar to that adopted in *Save the Bay*, finding EPA's decisions subject to wide discretion and therefore not subject to meaningful judicial review. *See* Ohio Public Interest Research Group, Inc. v. Whitman, 386 F.3d 792 (6th Cir. 2004) (holding that EPA non-enforcement decision under CAA Title V was a matter of agency discretion and thus left no avenue for judicial review); Public Citizen, Inc. v. U.S. E.P.A., 343 F.3d 449 (5th Cir. 2003) (upholding EPA's approval of Texas' Title V program despite ongoing resolution of program deficiencies because EPA's action was entitled to substantial deference and holding that related EPA non-enforcement decisions were immune from judicial review). EPA may also use other statutory "sanctions" against states, as discussed in the last section of this chapter.

With respect to individual permit decisions, however, the Supreme Court upheld an EPA action disapproving a state permit which EPA believed did not properly implement one of the technology-based provisions of the statute ("best available control technology" (BACT)) for new or modified sources in attainment areas subject to the "prevention of significant deterioration" (PSD) provisions of the Act). While upholding EPA's action, however, the Court was mindful of the balance to be struck between flexibility to account for variations in local conditions and circumstances, and the need to uphold the basic statutory requirements:

> Understandably, Congress entrusted state permitting authorities with initial responsibility to make BACT determinations "case-by-case." A state agency, no doubt, is best positioned to adjust for local differences in raw materials or plant configurations, differences that might make a technology "unavailable" in a particular area. But the fact that the relevant statutory guides — "maximum" pollution reduction, considerations of energy, environmental, and economic impacts — may not yield a "single, objectively 'correct' BACT determination," surely does not signify that there can be no *unreasonable* determinations. Nor does Congress' sensitivity to site-specific factors necessarily imply a design to preclude in this context meaningful EPA oversight. EPA claims no prerogative to designate the correct BACT; the Agency asserts only the authority to guard against unreasonable designations.

Alaska Dept. of Envt'l Conservation v. EPA, 540 U.S. 461, 488-89 (2004).

4. *RCRA.* In RCRA, Congress adopted a somewhat similar program of cooperative federalism, but with an interesting twist. Congress divided the universe of solid waste into two broad categories: hazardous solid waste and nonhazardous solid waste (although certain specified categories of wastes may fall somewhere in between, *see* 42 U.S.C. §3001(b)(3)). Generally speaking, hazardous wastes are subject to more federal control than nonhazardous wastes. EPA promulgates regulations governing which materials are deemed hazardous, *id.* §3001; and standards applicable to hazardous waste generators, transporters, and "treatment, storage and disposal facilities" (TSDFs), including detailed treatment standards for particular kinds of wastes, *id.* §§3002-3004. EPA also issues permit requirements for TSDFs. *Id.* §6925. However, Congress authorized states to adopt hazardous waste management programs pursuant to EPA guidelines, in which case the state may assume hazardous waste permitting responsibility. *Id.* §6926.

Congress also established provisions for state nonhazardous solid waste plans subject to EPA guidelines, review, and approval, as well as federal funding assistance. 42 U.S.C. §§6942–6948. Federal requirements for approval of nonhazardous solid waste plans and programs, however, are far less prescriptive than those for hazardous waste. In essence, states must commit to two main substantive requirements: (1) all existing open dumps in the state must be closed or upgraded to sanitary landfills meeting federal guidelines, and new open dumps must be prohibited; and (2) and solid waste in the state either must be used for resource recovery (reused or recycled) or disposed of in approved sanitary landfills. *Id.* §6943(a).

5. *One-tiered preemption and the motor vehicle exception.* A common theme in the environmental statutes with optional delegated programs is that states may adopt and enforce pollution standards that are stricter, but not

weaker, than those specified in the federal statute or regulations. One example is in the hazardous waste title of RCRA, which provides:

> Upon the effective date of regulations under this subchapter no State or political subdivision may impose any requirements less stringent than those authorized under this subchapter respecting the same matter as governed by such regulations . . . . Nothing in this chapter shall be construed to prohibit any State or political subdivision thereof from imposing any requirements, including those for site selection, which are more stringent than those imposed by such regulations.

42 U.S.C. §6929. *See also id.* §7416 (CAA); 33 U.S.C. §1370 (CWA). What is the justification for allowing states the authority to strengthen, but not to weaken, federal environmental requirements?

One notable exception to the one-tiered preemption principle is that, with limited exceptions, section 209 of the CAA prohibits states from adopting emissions requirements for motor vehicles that are stricter *or* weaker than those set by Congress and EPA pursuant to Title II of the CAA. *See* 42 U.S.C. §7543. *See also id.* §§7574(c)(4) (motor vehicle fuels), 7573 (airplane emissions). Why do you think Congress generally preempted state regulation of motor vehicle emissions and fuels (aside from the exceptions discussed below), regardless of how much vehicle emissions may contribute to nonattainment in any given state or region within a state, and despite the fact that states are free to adopt standards stricter than required by federal law for other major sources of pollution that contribute to nonattainment? *See* Motor Vehicle Mfrs. Assn. of U.S. v. New York State Dept. Of Environmental Conservation, 810 F. Supp. 1331 (N.D.N.Y. 1993), *modified on reconsideration*, 831 F. Supp. 57, *affirmed in part, reversed in part on other grounds*, 17 F.3d 521 (2d Cir. 1994).

Congress, however, provided a limited exception for California, which faces particularly difficulty vehicle-related emissions problems, to adopt and maintain vehicle emissions standards stricter than those required by federal law. *See* 42 U.S.C. §7543(b); Ford Motor Co. v. Environmental Protection Agency, 606 F.2d 1293 (D.C. Cir. 1979). Moreover, other states may adopt vehicle emissions standards identical to (*i.e.,* no stricter than) those adopted by California, in order to control emissions in nonattainment areas. *See* 42 U.S.C. §7507. Some states have tested the breadth of this set of preemption requirements, for example, by requiring auto manufacturers to produce and offer for sale in the state a particular number of "zero emission vehicles" (ZEVs), or that ZEVs comprise a certain percentage of vehicle sales in a particular state. Do such requirements constitute a "standard relating to the control of emissions from any new motor vehicle" prohibited by section 209 of the CAA? *See, e.g.,* Assn. Of Int'l Auto. Mfrs., Inc. v. Commissioner, Mass. Dept. of Environmental Protection, 208 F.3d 1 (1st Cir. 2000) (finding Massachusetts' ZEV sales mandates to be standards, and thus preempted by CAA section 209)); American Auto. Mfrs. Assn. v. Cahill, 152 F.3d 196 (2d Cir. 1998) (holding New

York ZEV requirement to be "standard relating to the control of emissions" that was preempted by CAA section 209).

D. ENFORCING STATE OBLIGATIONS

The above survey identified a number of ways in which Congress — based on various policy considerations — allocates environmental authority and responsibility among the federal and state governments. As you know from your knowledge of constitutional law, however, Congress is not simply free to assume any possible authority for the federal government, or to delegate obligations to states and localities without limit. The Constitution, as interpreted by the courts, identifies those areas in which Congress may act, and the methods by which it may permissibly assign responsibilities to the states. As you read the following case, think about how the principles articulated by the Supreme Court would apply to the various allocations of environmental authority described above:

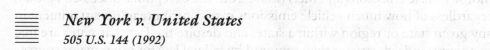

New York v. United States
505 U.S. 144 (1992)

JUSTICE O'CONNOR delivered the opinion of the Court.

These cases implicate one of our Nation's newest problems of public policy and perhaps our oldest question of constitutional law. The public policy issue involves the disposal of radioactive waste: In these cases, we address the constitutionality of three provisions of the Low-Level Radioactive Waste Policy Amendments Act of 1985. The constitutional question is as old as the Constitution: It consists of discerning the proper division of authority between the Federal Government and the States. We conclude that while Congress has substantial power under the Constitution to encourage the States to provide for the disposal of the radioactive waste generated within their borders, the Constitution does not confer upon Congress the ability simply to compel the States to do so. We therefore find that only two of the Act's three provisions at issue are consistent with the Constitution's allocation of power to the Federal Government.

I

We live in a world full of low level radioactive waste. Radioactive material is present in luminous watch dials, smoke alarms, measurement devices, medical fluids, research materials, and the protective gear and construction materials used by workers at nuclear power plants. Low level radioactive waste is generated by the Government, by hospitals, by research institutions, and by various industries. The waste must be isolated from humans for long periods of time, often for hundreds of years. Millions of cubic feet of low level radioactive waste must be disposed of each year.

Our Nation's first site for the land disposal of commercial low level radioactive waste opened in 1962 in Beatty, Nevada. Five more sites opened in the following decade. [The Court described the sequential closure of these sites.]

Faced with the possibility that the Nation would be left with no disposal sites for low level radioactive waste, Congress responded by enacting the Low-Level Radioactive Waste Policy Act. Relying largely on a report submitted by the National Governors' Association, Congress declared a federal policy of holding each State "responsible for providing for the availability of capacity either within or outside the State for the disposal of low-level radioactive waste generated within its borders," and found that such waste could be disposed of "most safely and efficiently . . . on a regional basis." The 1980 Act authorized States to enter into regional compacts that, once ratified by Congress, would have the authority beginning in 1986 to restrict the use of their disposal facilities to waste generated within member States. The 1980 Act included no penalties for States that failed to participate in this plan.

By 1985, only three approved regional compacts had operational disposal facilities; not surprisingly, these were the compacts formed around South Carolina, Nevada, and Washington, the three sited States. The following year, the 1980 Act would have given these three compacts the ability to exclude waste from nonmembers, and the remaining 31 States would have had no assured outlet for their low level radioactive waste. With this prospect looming, Congress once again took up the issue of waste disposal. The result was the legislation challenged here, the Low-Level Radioactive Waste Policy Amendments Act of 1985.

The 1985 Act was again based largely on a proposal submitted by the National Governors' Association. In broad outline, the Act embodies a compromise among the sited and unsited States. The sited States agreed to extend for seven years the period in which they would accept low level radioactive waste from other States. In exchange, the unsited States agreed to end their reliance on the sited States by 1992.

The mechanics of this compromise are intricate. The Act directs: "Each State shall be responsible for providing, either by itself or in cooperation with other States, for the disposal of . . . low-level radioactive waste generated within the State," with the exception of certain waste generated by the Federal Government. The Act authorizes States to "enter into such [interstate] compacts as may be necessary to provide for the establishment and operation of regional disposal facilities for low-level radioactive waste." For an additional seven years beyond the period contemplated by the 1980 Act, from the beginning of 1986 through the end of 1992, the three existing disposal sites "shall make disposal capacity available for low-level radioactive waste generated by any source," with certain exceptions not relevant here. But the three States in which the disposal sites are located are permitted to exact a graduated surcharge for waste arriving from outside the regional compact in 1986–1987, $10 per cubic foot; in 1988–1989, $20 per cubic foot; and in 1990–1992, $40 per cubic foot. After the 7-year transition period expires, approved regional compacts may exclude radioactive waste generated outside the region. The Act provides three types of incentives to encourage the States to comply with their statutory obligation to provide for the disposal of waste generated within their borders.

1. *Monetary incentives.* One quarter of the surcharges collected by the sited States must be transferred to an escrow account held by the Secretary of Energy. The Secretary then makes payments from this account to each State that has complied with a series of deadlines. By July 1, 1986, each State was to have ratified legislation either joining a regional compact or indicating an intent to develop a disposal facility within the State. By January 1, 1988, each unsited compact was to have identified the State in which its facility would be located, and each compact or stand-alone State was to have developed a siting plan and taken other identified steps. By January 1, 1990, each State or compact was to have filed a complete application for a license to operate a disposal facility, or the Governor of any State that had not filed an application was to have certified that the State would be capable of disposing of all waste generated in the State after 1992. The rest of the account is to be paid out to those States or compacts able to dispose of all low level radioactive waste generated within their borders by January 1, 1993. Each State that has not met the 1993 deadline must either take title to the waste generated within its borders or forfeit to the waste generators the incentive payments it has received.

2. *Access incentives.* The second type of incentive involves the denial of access to disposal sites. States that fail to meet the July 1986 deadline may be charged twice the ordinary surcharge for the remainder of 1986 and may be denied access to disposal facilities thereafter. States that fail to meet the 1988 deadline may be charged double surcharges for the first half of 1988 and quadruple surcharges for the second half of 1988, and may be denied access thereafter. States that fail to meet the 1990 deadline may be denied access. Finally, States that have not filed complete applications by January 1, 1992, for a license to operate a disposal facility, or States belonging to compacts that have not filed such applications, may be charged triple surcharges.

3. *The take title provision.* The third type of incentive is the most severe. The Act provides: "If a State (or, where applicable, a compact region) in which low-level radioactive waste is generated is unable to provide

for the disposal of all such waste generated within such State or compact region by January 1, 1996, each State in which such waste is generated, upon the request of the generator or owner of the waste, shall take title to the waste, be obligated to take possession of the waste, and shall be liable for all damages directly or indirectly incurred by such generator or owner as a consequence of the failure of the State to take possession of the waste as soon after January 1, 1996, as the generator or owner notifies the State that the waste is available for shipment."

These three incentives are the focus of petitioners' constitutional challenge.

In the seven years since the Act took effect, Congress has approved nine regional compacts, encompassing 42 of the States. All six unsited compacts and four of the unaffiliated States have met the first three statutory milestones. New York, a State whose residents generate a relatively large share of the Nation's low level radioactive waste, did not join a regional compact. Instead, the State complied with the Act's requirements by enacting legislation providing for the siting and financing of a disposal facility in New York. The State has identified five potential sites, three in Allegany County and two in Cortland County. Residents of the two counties oppose the State's choice of location.

Petitioners — the State of New York and the two counties — filed this suit against the United States in 1990. They sought a declaratory judgment that the Act is inconsistent with the Tenth and Eleventh Amendments to the Constitution, with the Due Process Clause of the Fifth Amendment, and with the Guarantee Clause of Article IV of the Constitution. The States of Washington, Nevada, and South Carolina intervened as defendants. The District Court dismissed the complaint. The Court of Appeals affirmed. Petitioners have abandoned their due process and Eleventh Amendment claims on their way up the appellate ladder; as the cases stand before us, petitioners claim only that the Act is inconsistent with the Tenth Amendment and the Guarantee Clause.

II

A

While no one disputes the proposition that "[t]he Constitution created a Federal Government of limited powers;" and while the Tenth Amendment makes explicit that "[t]he powers not delegated to the United States by the Constitution, nor prohibited by it to the States, are reserved to the States respectively, or to the people"; the task of ascertaining the constitutional line between federal and state power has given rise to many of the Court's most difficult and celebrated cases.

These questions can be viewed in either of two ways. In some cases the Court has inquired whether an Act of Congress is authorized by one of the powers delegated to Congress in Article I of the Constitution. In other cases the Court has sought to determine whether an Act of Congress invades the province of state sovereignty reserved by the Tenth Amendment. In a case like these, involving the division of authority between federal and state governments, the two inquiries are mirror images of each other. If a power is delegated to Congress in the Constitution, the Tenth Amendment expressly disclaims any reservation of that power to the States; if a power is an attribute of state sovereignty reserved by the Tenth Amendment, it is necessarily a power the Constitution has not conferred on Congress.

It is in this sense that the Tenth Amendment "states but a truism that all is retained which has not been surrendered." This has been the Court's consistent understanding: "The States unquestionably do retai[n] a significant measure of sovereign authority to the extent that the Constitution has not divested them of their original powers and transferred those powers to the Federal Government."

Congress exercises its conferred powers subject to the limitations contained in the Constitution. Thus, for example, under the Commerce Clause Congress may regulate publishers engaged in interstate commerce, but Congress is constrained in the exercise of that power by the First Amendment. The Tenth Amendment likewise restrains the power of Congress, but this limit is not derived from the text of the Tenth Amendment itself, which, as we have discussed, is essentially a tautology. Instead, the Tenth Amendment confirms that the power of the Federal Government is subject to limits that may, in a given instance, reserve power to the States. The Tenth Amendment thus directs us to determine, as in this case, whether an incident of state sovereignty is protected by a limitation on an Article I power.

This framework has been sufficiently flexible over the past two centuries to allow for enormous changes in the nature of government. The Federal Government undertakes activities today that would have been unimaginable to the Framers in two senses; first, because the Framers would not have conceived that *any* government would conduct such activities; and second, because the Framers would not have believed that the *Federal* Government, rather than the States, would assume such responsibilities. Yet the powers conferred upon the Federal Government by the Constitution were phrased in language broad enough to allow for the expansion of the Federal Government's role. Among the provisions of the Constitution that have been particularly important in this regard, three concern us here.

First, the Constitution allocates to Congress the power "[t]o regulate Commerce among the several States." Art. I, §8, cl. 3. Interstate commerce was an established feature of life in the late 18th century. The volume of interstate commerce and the range of commonly accepted objects of government regulation have, however, expanded considerably in the last 200 years, and the regulatory authority of Congress has expanded along with them. As interstate commerce has become ubiquitous, activities once considered purely local have come to have effects on the national economy, and have accordingly come within the scope of Congress' commerce power.

Second, the Constitution authorizes Congress "to pay the Debts and provide for the general Welfare of the United States." Art. I, §8, cl. 1. As conventional notions of the proper objects of government spending have changed over the years, so has the ability of Congress to "fix the terms on which it shall disburse federal money to the States. While the spending power is "subject to several general restrictions articulated in our cases," these restrictions have not been so severe as to prevent the regulatory authority of Congress from generally keeping up with the growth of the federal budget.

The Court's broad construction of Congress' power under the Commerce and Spending Clauses has of course been guided, as it has with respect to Congress' power generally, by the Constitution's Necessary and Proper Clause, which authorizes Congress "[t]o make all Laws which shall be necessary and proper for carrying into Execution the foregoing Powers."

Finally, the Constitution provides that "the Laws of the United States shall be the supreme Law of the Land any Thing in the Constitution or Laws of any State to the Contrary notwithstanding." U.S. Const., Art. VI, cl. 2. As the Federal Government's willingness to exercise power within the confines of the Constitution has grown, the authority of the States has correspondingly diminished to the extent that federal and state policies have conflicted. We have observed that the Supremacy Clause gives the Federal Government "a decided advantage in th[e] delicate balance" the Constitution strikes between state and federal power.

The actual scope of the Federal Government's authority with respect to the States has changed over the years, therefore, but the constitutional structure underlying and limiting that authority has not. In the end, just as a cup may be half empty or half full, it makes no difference whether one views the question at issue in these cases as one of ascertaining the limits of the power delegated to the Federal Government under the affirmative provisions of the Constitution or one of discerning the core of sovereignty retained by the States under the Tenth Amendment. Either way, we must determine whether any of the three challenged provisions oversteps the boundary between federal and state authority.

B

Petitioners do not contend that Congress lacks the power to regulate the disposal of low level radioactive waste. Space in radioactive waste disposal sites is frequently sold by residents of one State to residents of another. Regulation of the resulting interstate market in waste disposal is therefore well within Congress' authority under the Commerce Clause. Petitioners likewise do not dispute that under the Supremacy Clause Congress could, if it wished, preempt state radioactive waste regulation. Petitioners contend only that the

Tenth Amendment limits the power of Congress to regulate in the way it has chosen. Rather than addressing the problem of waste disposal by directly regulating the generators and disposers of waste, petitioners argue, Congress has impermissibly directed the States to regulate in this field.

Most of our recent cases interpreting the Tenth Amendment have concerned the authority of Congress to subject state governments to generally applicable laws.

This litigation instead concerns the circumstances under which Congress may use the States as implements of regulation; that is, whether Congress may direct or otherwise motivate the States to regulate in a particular field or a particular way. Our cases have established a few principles that guide our resolution of the issue.

1

As an initial matter, Congress may not simply "commandee[r] the legislative processes of the States by directly compelling them to enact and enforce a federal regulatory program." Hodel v. Virginia Surface Mining & Reclamation Assn., Inc. In *Hodel,* the Court upheld the Surface Mining Control and Reclamation Act of 1977 precisely because it did *not* "commandeer" the States into regulating mining. The Court found that "the States are not compelled to enforce the steep-slope standards, to expend any state funds, or to participate in the federal regulatory program in any manner whatsoever. If a State does not wish to submit a proposed permanent program that complies with the Act and implementing regulations, the full regulatory burden will be borne by the Federal Government."

The Court reached the same conclusion the following year in *FERC v. Mississippi.* At issue in *FERC* was the Public Utility Regulatory Policies Act of 1978, a federal statute encouraging the States in various ways to develop programs to combat the Nation's energy crisis. We observed that "this Court never has sanctioned explicitly a federal command to the States to promulgate and enforce laws and regulations." As in *Hodel,* the Court upheld the statute at issue because it did not view the statute as such a command.

These statements in *FERC* and *Hodel* were not innovations. While Congress has substantial powers to govern the Nation directly, including in areas of intimate concern to the States, the Constitution has never been understood to confer upon Congress the ability to require the States to govern according to Congress' instructions.

In providing for a stronger central government the Framers explicitly chose a Constitution that confers upon Congress the power to regulate individuals, not States. As we have seen, the Court has consistently respected this choice. We have always understood that even where Congress has the authority under the Constitution to pass laws requiring or prohibiting certain acts, it lacks the power directly to compel the States to require or prohibit those acts. The allocation of power contained in the Commerce Clause, for example, authorizes Congress to regulate interstate commerce directly; it does not authorize Congress to regulate state governments' regulation of interstate commerce.

2

This is not to say that Congress lacks the ability to encourage a State to regulate in a particular way, or that Congress may not hold out incentives to the States as a method of influencing a State's policy choices. Our cases have identified a variety of methods, short of outright coercion, by which Congress may urge a State to adopt a legislative program consistent with federal interests. Two of these methods are of particular relevance here.

First, under Congress' spending power, "Congress may attach conditions on the receipt of federal funds." Such conditions must (among other requirements) bear some relationship to the purpose of the federal spending; otherwise, of course, the spending power could render academic the Constitution's other grants and limits of federal authority. Where the recipient of federal funds is a State, as is not unusual today, the conditions attached to the funds by Congress may influence a State's legislative choices . . . .

Second, where Congress has the authority to regulate private activity under the Commerce Clause, we have recognized Congress' power to offer States the choice of regulating that activity according to federal standards or having state law pre-empted by federal regulation. This arrangement, which has been termed "a program of cooperative federalism," is replicated in numerous federal statutory schemes. These include the Clean Water Act, the Occupational Safety and Health Act of 1970, the Resource Conservation and Recovery Act of 1976, and the Alaska National Interest Lands Conservation Act.

By either of these methods, as by any other permissible method of encouraging a State to conform to federal policy choices, the residents of the State retain the ultimate decision as to whether or not the State will comply. If a State's citizens view federal policy as sufficiently contrary to local interests, they may elect to decline a federal grant. If state residents would prefer their government to devote its attention and resources to problems other than those deemed important by Congress, they may choose to have the Federal Government rather than the State bear the expense of a federally mandated regulatory program, and they may continue to supplement that program to the extent state law is not pre-empted. Where Congress encourages state regulation rather than compelling it, state governments remain responsive to the local electorate's preferences; state officials remain accountable to the people.

By contrast, where the Federal Government compels States to regulate, the accountability of both state and federal officials is diminished. If the citizens of New York, for example, do not consider that making provision for the disposal of radioactive waste is in their best interest, they may elect state officials who share their view. That view can always be pre-empted under the

Supremacy Clause if it is contrary to the national view, but in such a case it is the Federal Government that makes the decision in full view of the public, and it will be federal officials that suffer the consequences if the decision turns out to be detrimental or unpopular. But where the Federal Government directs the States to regulate, it may be state officials who will bear the brunt of public disapproval, while the federal officials who devised the regulatory program may remain insulated from the electoral ramifications of their decision. Accountability is thus diminished when, due to federal coercion, elected state officials cannot regulate in accordance with the views of the local electorate in matters not pre-empted by federal regulation.

With these principles in mind, we turn to the three challenged provisions.

III

The parties in these cases advance two quite different views of the Act. As petitioners see it, the Act imposes a requirement directly upon the States that they regulate in the field of radioactive waste disposal in order to meet Congress' mandate that "[e]ach State shall be responsible for providing for the disposal of low-level radioactive waste." Petitioners understand this provision as a direct command from Congress, enforceable independent of the three sets of incentives provided by the Act. Respondents, on the other hand, read this provision together with the incentives, and see the Act as affording the States three sets of choices. According to respondents, the Act permits a State to choose first between regulating pursuant to federal standards and losing the right to a share of the Secretary of Energy's escrow account; to choose second between regulating pursuant to federal standards and progressively losing access to disposal sites in other States; and to choose third between regulating pursuant to federal standards and taking title to the waste generated within the State.

The Act could plausibly be understood either as a mandate to regulate or as a series of incentives. Under petitioners' view, however the Act would clearly "commandee[r] the legislative processes of the States by directly compelling them to enact and enforce a federal regulatory program." We must reject this interpretation of the provision for two reasons. First, such an outcome would, to say the least, "upset the usual constitutional balance of federal and state powers." "[I]t is incumbent upon the federal courts to be certain of Congress' intent before finding that federal law overrides this balance," but the Act's amenability to an equally plausible alternative construction prevents us from possessing such certainty. Second, "where an otherwise acceptable construction of a statute would raise serious constitutional problems, the Court will construe the statute to avoid such problems unless such construction is plainly contrary to the intent of Congress. This rule of statutory construction pushes us away from petitioners' understanding of the Act, under which it compels the States to regulate according to Congress' instructions.

Construed as a whole, the Act comprises three sets of "incentives" for the States to provide for the disposal of low level radioactive waste generated within their borders. We consider each in turn.

A

The first set of incentives works in three steps. First, Congress has authorized States with disposal sites to impose a surcharge on radioactive waste received from other States. Second, the Secretary of Energy collects a portion of this surcharge and places the money in an escrow account. Third, States achieving a series of milestones receive portions of this fund.

The first of these steps is an unexceptionable exercise of Congress' power to authorize the States to burden interstate commerce. While the Commerce Clause has long been understood to limit the States' ability to discriminate against interstate commerce, that limit may be lifted, as it has been here, by an expression of the "unambiguous intent" of Congress. Whether or not the States would be permitted to burden the interstate transport of low level radioactive waste in the absence of Congress' approval, the States can clearly do so *with* Congress' approval, which is what the Act gives them.

The second step, the Secretary's collection of a percentage of the surcharge, is no more than a federal tax on interstate commerce, which petitioners do not claim to be an invalid exercise of either Congress' commerce or taxing power. The third step is a conditional exercise of Congress' authority under the Spending Clause: Congress has placed conditions — the achievement of the milestones — on the receipt of federal funds. Petitioners do not contend that Congress has exceeded its authority in any of the four respects our cases have identified. The expenditure is for the general welfare; the States are required to use the money they receive for the purpose of assuring the safe disposal of radioactive waste. The conditions imposed are unambiguous; the Act informs the States exactly what they must do and by when they must do it in order to obtain a share of the escrow account. The conditions imposed are reasonably related to the purpose of the expenditure; both the conditions and the payments embody Congress' efforts to address the pressing problem of radioactive waste disposal. Finally, petitioners do not claim that the conditions imposed by the Act violate any independent constitutional prohibition.

Petitioners contend nevertheless that the *form* of these expenditures removes them from the scope of Congress' spending power. Petitioners emphasize the Act's instruction to the Secretary of Energy to "deposit all funds received in a special escrow account. The funds so deposited shall not be the property of the United States." Petitioners argue that because the money collected and redisbursed to the States is kept in an account separate from the general treasury, because the Secretary holds the funds only as a trustee, and because the States themselves are largely able to control whether they will pay into the escrow account or receive a share, the Act "in no manner calls for the spending of federal funds."

The Constitution's grant to Congress of the authority to "pay the Debts and provide for the general Welfare" has never, however, been thought to mandate a particular form of accounting. That the States are able to choose whether they will receive federal funds does not make the resulting expenditures any less federal; indeed, the location of such choice in the States is an inherent element in any conditional exercise of Congress' spending power.

The Act's first set of incentives, in which Congress has conditioned grants to the States upon the States' attainment of a series of milestones, is thus well within the authority of Congress under the Commerce and Spending Clauses. Because the first set of incentives is supported by affirmative constitutional grants of power to Congress, it is not inconsistent with the Tenth Amendment.

B

In the second set of incentives, Congress has authorized States and regional compacts with disposal sites gradually to increase the cost of access to the sites, and then to deny access altogether, to radioactive waste generated in States that do not meet federal deadlines. As a simple regulation, this provision would be within the power of Congress to authorize the States to discriminate against interstate commerce. Where federal regulation of private activity is within the scope of the Commerce Clause, we have recognized the ability of Congress to offer States the choice of regulating that activity according to federal standards or having state law pre-empted by federal regulation.

This is the choice presented to nonsited States by the Act's second set of incentives: States may either regulate the disposal of radioactive waste according to federal standards by attaining local or regional self-sufficiency, or their residents who produce radioactive waste will be subject to federal regulation authorizing sited States and regions to deny access to their disposal sites. The affected States are not compelled by Congress to regulate, because any burden caused by a State's refusal to regulate will fall on those who generate waste and find no outlet for its disposal, rather than on the State as a sovereign. A State whose citizens do not wish it to attain the Act's milestones may devote its attention and its resources to issues its citizens deem more worthy; the choice remains at all times with the residents of the State, not with Congress. The State need not expend any funds, or participate in any federal program, if local residents do not view such expenditures or participation as worthwhile. Nor must the State abandon the field if it does not accede to federal direction; the State may continue to regulate the generation and disposal of radioactive waste in any manner its citizens see fit.

The Act's second set of incentives thus represents a conditional exercise of Congress' commerce power, along the lines of those we have held to be within Congress' authority. As a result, the second set of incentives does not intrude on the sovereignty reserved to the States by the Tenth Amendment.

C

The take title provision is of a different character. This third so-called "incentive" offers States, as an alternative to regulating pursuant to Congress' direction, the option of taking title to and possession of the low level radioactive waste generated within their borders and becoming liable for all damages waste generators suffer as a result of the States' failure to do so promptly. In this provision, Congress has crossed the line distinguishing encouragement from coercion.

The take title provision offers state governments a "choice" of either accepting ownership of waste or regulating according to the instructions of Congress. Respondents do not claim that the Constitution would authorize Congress to impose either option as a freestanding requirement. On one hand, the Constitution would not permit Congress simply to transfer radioactive waste from generators to state governments. Such a forced transfer, standing alone, would in principle be no different than a congressionally compelled subsidy from state governments to radioactive waste producers. The same is true of the provision requiring the States to become liable for the generators' damages. Standing alone, this provision would be indistinguishable from an Act of Congress directing the States to assume the liabilities of certain state residents. Either type of federal action would "commandeer" state governments into the service of federal regulatory purposes, and would for this reason be inconsistent with the Constitution's division of authority between federal and state governments. On the other hand, the second alternative held out to state governments — regulating pursuant to Congress' direction — would, standing alone, present a simple command to state governments to implement legislation enacted by Congress. As we have seen, the Constitution does not empower Congress to subject state governments to this type of instruction.

Because an instruction to state governments to take title to waste, standing alone, would be beyond the authority of Congress, and because a direct order to regulate, standing alone, would also be beyond the authority of Congress, it follows that Congress lacks the power to offer the States a choice between the two. Unlike the first two sets of incentives, the take title incentive does not represent the conditional exercise of any congressional power enumerated in the Constitution. In this provision, Congress has not held out the threat of exercising its spending power or its commerce power; it has instead held out the threat, should the States not regulate according to one federal instruction, of simply forcing the States to submit to another federal instruction. A choice between two unconstitutionally coercive regulatory techniques is no choice at all. Either way, "the Act commandeers the legislative processes of the States by directly compelling them to enact and enforce a federal regulatory program," an outcome that has never been understood to lie within the authority conferred upon Congress by the Constitution.

Respondents emphasize the latitude given to the States to implement Congress' plan. The Act enables the States to regulate pursuant to Congress' instructions in any number of different ways. States may avoid taking title by contracting with sited regional compacts, by building a disposal site alone or as part of a compact, or by permitting private parties to build a disposal site. States that host sites may employ a wide range of designs and disposal methods, subject only to broad federal regulatory limits. This line of reasoning, however, only underscores the critical alternative a State lacks: A State may not decline to administer the federal program. No matter which path the State chooses, it must follow the direction of Congress.

The take title provision appears to be unique. No other federal statute has been cited which offers a state government no option other than that of implementing legislation enacted by Congress. Whether one views the take title provision as lying outside Congress' enumerated powers, or as infringing upon the core of state sovereignty reserved by the Tenth Amendment, the provision is inconsistent with the federal structure of our Government established by the Constitution.

NOTES AND QUESTIONS ON *NEW YORK*

1. *Holding.* How would you characterize the dividing line the Court established between permissible congressional incentives to states and impermissible coercion? What is fundamentally different about the "take title" provisions of the Low Level Radioactive Waste Act and the provisions upheld by the Court?

2. *Direct preemption.* Why did the state plaintiffs in *New York* concede that the federal government has the power to regulate low level radioactive waste directly? As we noted at the beginning of this chapter, to date, most federal environmental statutes have survived challenges based on Commerce Clause and other constitutional limits. In *SWANCC*, however, the majority indicated that the Clean Water Act, as applied to the facts of that case, at least approaches the limits of the Commerce Clause, but declined to rule on those grounds in favor of a more limiting interpretation of the statute.

3. *Conditional preemption.* Congress uses conditional preemption when it regulates a field directly but provides an option for states to assume program responsibility. In essence, Congress gives each state the choice of regulating a particular activity itself, or allowing the federal government to regulate the state's economic or other resources directly, something states often fear. How much less coercive do you think that is than the "take title" provisions the Court found unconstitutional in *New York*? What factors would you expect states to consider in deciding whether to assume program responsibility?

4. *Spending power.* The Court explains that Congress can use federal tax dollars as an incentive to state action, so long as the spending promotes the general welfare and any strings attached are reasonably related to the purpose of the spending. Congress provides significant amounts of funding to states and localities to implement environmental programs.

5. *Sanctions.* Congress armed EPA with a set of particularly onerous *potential* sanctions to redress state violations of the SIP obligations of the CAA, including the ability to prevent the Secretary of Transportation from awarding grants for state highway projects. 42 U.S.C. §7509(b). *See* William J. Klein, *Pressure or Compulsion? Federal Highway Fund Sanctions of the Clean Air Act Amendments of 1990*, 26 Rutgers L.J. 855 (1995). Is this a legitimate use of Congress' spending power authority? *See* Commonwealth of Virginia. v. Browner, 80 F.3d 869 (4th Cir 1996), *cert. denied*, 519 U.S. 1090 (1997) (upholding highway sanctions and offset sanctions under the CAA as legitimate exercise of congressional spending power). For political reasons, EPA has been quite reluctant to exercise its sanction authority.

6. *Federal regulation of states and localities.* State and local governments often are regulated directly under various environmental statutes. Local sewage treatment plants that discharge to waters of the United States, for example, must obtain NPDES permits and comply with applicable treatment and discharge standards. Municipal solid waste incinerators must comply with regulations under both the Clean Air Act and RCRA. Governments can be liable for hazardous substance releases under CERCLA. Why can Congress "mandate" that states and localities act under those provisions, but not under the kinds of provisions that the Court invalidated in *New York*?

7. *Unfunded federal mandates.* Does it matter how much money it costs the cities to comply with federal mandates, or whether the federal government provides any financial assistance? The Supreme Court has rejected constitutional challenges to such "unfunded federal mandates," so long as the underlying statute is otherwise lawful. *See* Printz v. United States, 521 U.S. 898 (1997) (invalidating portions of the Brady Bill (federal handgun control) because they "commandeered" the local regulatory apparatus, but not because they were unfunded federal mandates). However, Congress provided some relief to states and localities in the Unfunded Mandates Reform Act. While the Act does not prohibit unfunded mandates, it does require analysis and consideration of the impacts of new mandates imposed by Congress or federal agencies. For a critique of the statute and the unfunded mandates issue generally, *see* Robert W. Adler, *Unfunded Mandates and Fiscal Federalism: A Critique*, 50 Vand. L. Rev. 1137 (1997).

Federalism and PFOA Revisited

1. Could Congress pass a law requiring each state to allow, condition, or prohibit the sale of any consumer product that might expose the public in that state to significant amounts of PFOA residuals, based on the state's own assessment of the potential risks and benefits from those products?

2. Is there any question that Congress could regulate PFOA directly? For example, could it direct EPA to decide whether PFOA use should be allowed, prohibited, or regulated, based on its own assessment of risks and other factors?

3. Could Congress direct EPA to regulate PFOA, but provide each state with a choice to do so itself?

4. Could Congress provide direct, unconditional grants to states to address the health and environmental effects of PFOA? Can it condition those grants on state regulation of some aspects of the PFOA problem? Can it condition those grants on a requirement that the state "take title" to any PFOA wastes for which no responsible party can be identified?

5. If municipalities use products with PFOA to protect components of their transit systems, can Congress hold those cities liable for any resulting health and environmental impacts? *See* Garcia v. San Antonio Metropolitan Transit Authority, 469 U.S. 528 (1985) (holding state employers subject to the Fair Labor Standards Act).

14

Decision-Making for International Problems

Some environmental problems concern more than one country. When this occurs, a question arises as to who has the authority and ability to effectively address the problem. Thus, international environmental law raises some institutional issues, similar to the institutional issues you confronted in the chapters addressing administrative law and federalism. Who addressed the environmental problem set out in the case below?

Trail Smelter Arbitral Tribunal Decision
3 R. Int'l Arb. Awards 1909 (Trail Smelter Arb. Trib. April 16, 1938)

Reported on April 16, 1938, to the Government of the United States of America and to the Government of the Dominion of Canada Under the Convention Signed April 15, 1935.

This Tribunal is constituted under, and its powers are derived from and limited by, the Convention between the United States of America and the Dominion of Canada signed at Ottawa, April 15, 1935, duly ratified by the two parties, and ratifications exchanged at Ottawa, August 3, 1935 (herein-after termed "the Convention").

By Article II of the Convention, each Government was to choose one member of the Tribunal, "a jurist of repute", and the two Governments were to choose jointly a Chairman who should be a "jurist of repute and neither a British subject nor a citizen of the United States". . . .

The duty imposed upon the Tribunal by the Convention was to "finally decide" the following questions:

1. Whether damage caused by the Trail Smelter in the State of Washington has occurred since the first day of January, 1932, and, if so, what indemnity should be paid therefor?

2. In the event of the answer to the first part of the preceding question being in the affirmative, whether the Trail Smelter should be required to refrain from causing damage in the State of Washington in the future and, if so, to what extent?

3. In the light of the answer to the preceding question, what measures or régime, if any, should be adopted or maintained by the Trail Smelter?

4. What indemnity or compensation, if any, should be paid on account of any decision or decisions rendered by the Tribunal pursuant to the next two preceding questions?

. . .

The Tribunal is prepared now to decide finally Question No. 1, propounded to it in Article III of the Convention; and it hereby reports its final decision on Question No. 1, its temporary decision on Questions No. 2 and No. 3, and provides for a temporary régime thereunder and for a final decision on these questions and on Question No. 4, within three months from October 1, 1940.

Wherever, in this decision, the Tribunal has referred to decisions of American courts or has followed American law, it has acted pursuant to Article IV as follows: "The Tribunal shall apply the law and practice followed in dealing with cognate questions in the United States of America. . . . "

In all the consideration which the Tribunal has given to the problems presented to it, and in all the conclusions which it has reached, it has been guided by that primary purpose of the Convention expressed in the words of Article IV, that the Tribunal "shall give consideration to the desire of the high contracting parties to reach a solution just to all parties concerned", and further expressed in the opening paragraph of the Convention as to the "desirability and necessity of effecting a permanent settlement" of the controversy.

The controversy is between two Governments involving damage occurring in the territory of one of them (the United States of America) and alleged to be due to an agency situated in the territory of the other (the Dominion of Canada), for which damage the latter has assumed by the Convention an international responsibility. In this controversy, the Tribunal is not sitting to pass upon claims presented by individuals or on behalf of one or more individuals by their Government, although individuals may come within the meaning of "parties concerned", in Article IV and of "interested parties", in Article VIII of the Convention and although the damage suffered by individuals may, in part, "afford a convenient scale for the calculation of the reparation due to the State" (see Jugdment No. 13, Permanent Court of International Justice, Series A, No. 17, pp. 27, 28).

. . .

PART ONE.

... In December, 1927, the United States Government proposed to the Canadian Government that problems growing out of the operation of the Smelter at Trail should be referred to the International Joint Commission, United States and Canada, for investigation and report, pursuant to Article IX of the Convention of January 11, 1909, between the United States and Great Britain. Following an extensive correspondence between the two Governments, they joined in a reference of the matter to that Commission under date of August 7, 1928. It may be noted that Article IX of the Convention of January 11, 1909, provides that the high contracting parties might agree that "any other question or matters of difference arising between them involving the rights, obligations or interests of either in relation to the other, or to the inhabitants of the other, along the common frontier between the United States and the Dominion of Canada shall be referred from time to time to the International Joint Commission for examination and report. . . . Such reports shall not be regarded as decisions of the question or matters so submitted either on the facts or on the law, and shall not, in any way, have the character of an arbitral award."

The questions referred to the International Joint Commission were five in number, the first two of which may be noted: First, the extent to which property in the State of Washington has been damaged by fumes from Smelter at Trail, B.C.; second, the amount of indemnity which would compensate United States interests in the State of Washington for past damages. . . .

On February 28, 1931, the Report of the Commission was signed and delivered to the proper authorities. The report was unanimous and need not be considered in detail.

Paragraph 2 of the report, in part, reads as follows:

> In view of the anticipated reduction in sulphur fumes discharged from the Smelter at Trail during the present year, as hereinafter referred to, the Commission therefore has deemed it advisable to determine the amount of indemnity that will compensate United States interests in respect of such fumes, up to and including the first day of January, 1932. The Commission finds and determines that all past damages and all damages up to and including the first day of January next, is the sum of $350,000. Said sum, however, shall not include any damage occurring after January 1, 1932.

In paragraph 4 of the report, the Commission recommended a method of indemnifying persons in Washington State for damage which might be caused by operations of the Trail Smelter after the first of January, 1932, as follows:

> Upon the complaint of any persons claiming to have suffered damage by the operations of the company after the first of January, 1932, it is recommended by the Commission that in the event of any such claim not being adjusted by the company within a reasonable time, the Governments of the United States and

Canada shall determine the amount of such damage, if any, and the amount so fixed shall be paid by the company forthwith.

This recommendation, apparently, did not commend itself to the interested parties. In any event, it does not appear that any claims were made after the first of January, 1932, as contemplated in paragraph 4 of the report.

In paragraph 5 of the report, the Commission recommended that the Consolidated Mining and Smelting Company of Canada, Limited, should proceed to erect and put in operation certain sulphuric acid units for the purpose of reducing the amount of sulphur discharged from the stacks. It appears, from the evidence in the present case, that the General Manager of the company had made certain representations before the Commission as to the intentions of the company in this respect. There is a conflict of testimony as to the exact scope of these representations, but it is unnecessary now to consider the matter further, since, whatever they were, the company proceeded after 1930 to make certain changes and additions. With the intention and purpose of lessening the sulphur contents in the smoke emissions at the stacks, the following installations (amongst others) have been made in the plant since 1931; three 112 tons sulphuric acid plants in 1931; ammonia and ammonium sulphate plant in 1931; two units for reduction and absorption of sulphur in the zinc smelter, in 1936 and 1937, and an absorption plant for gases from the lead roasters in June, 1937. In addition, in an attempt to lessen injurious fumigations, a new system of control over the emission of fumes during the crop-growing season has been in operation, particularly since May, 1934. It is to be noted that the chief sulphur contents are in the gases from the lead smelter, but that there is still a certain amount of sulphur content in the fumes from the zinc smelter. As a result of the above, as well as of depressed business conditions, the tons of sulphur emitted into the air from the plants fell from about 10,000 tons per month in 1930 to about 7,200 tons in 1931, and to 3,400 tons in 1932. The emission of sulphur rose in 1933 to 4,000 tons, and in 1934 to nearly 6,300 tons, and in 1935 to 6,800 tons. In 1936, it fell to 5,600 tons; and in January to July, 1937 inclusive, it was 4,750 tons.

Two years after the signing of the International Joint Commission's Report of February 28, 1931, the United States Government on February 17, 1933, made representations to the Canadian Government that existing conditions were entirely unsatisfactory and that damage was still occurring, and diplomatic negotiations were renewed. Correspondence was exchanged between the two countries, and although that correspondence has its importance, it is sufficient here to say, that it resulted in the signing of the present Convention.

Consideration of the terms of that Convention is given more in detail in the later parts of the Tribunal's decision.

PART TWO.

The first question under Article III of the Convention which the Tribunal is required to decide is as follows:

(1) Whether damage caused by the Trail Smelter in the State of Washington has occurred since the first day of January, 1932, and, if so, what indemnity should be paid therefor.

In the determination of the first part of this question, the Tribunal has been obliged to consider three points, viz., the existence of injury, the cause of the injury, and the damage due to the injury. . . .

. . . [T]he Tribunal answers Question 1 in Article III, as follows: Damage caused by the Trail Smelter in the State of Washington has occurred since the first day of January, 1932, and up to October 1, 1937, and the indemnity to be paid therefor is seventy-eight thousand dollars ($78,000), and is to be complete and final indemnity and compensation for all damage which occurred between such dates. Interest at the rate of six per centum per year will be allowed on the above sum of seventy-eight thousand dollars ($78,000) from the date of the filing of this report and decision until date of payment. This decision is not subject to alteration or modification by the Tribunal hereafter.

The fact of existence of damage, if any, occurring after October 1, 1937, and the indemnity to be paid therefor, if any, the Tribunal will determine in its final decision.

PART THREE.

As to Question No. 2, in Article III of the Convention, which is as follows:

(2) In the event of the answer to the first part of the preceding question being in the affirmative, whether the Trail Smelter should be required to refrain from causing damage in the State of Washington in the future and, if so, to what extent?

the Tribunal decides that until the date of the final decision provided for in Part Four of this present decision, the Trail Smelter shall refrain from causing damage in the State of Washington in the future to the extent set forth in such Part Four until October 1, 1940, and thereafter to such extent as the Tribunal shall require in the final decision provided for in Part Four.

PART FOUR.

As to Question No. 3, in Article III of the Convention, which is as follows:

(3) In the light of the answer to the preceding question, what measures or régime, if any, should be adopted or maintained by the Trail Smelter?

the Tribunal is unable at the present time, with the information that has been placed before it, to determine upon a permanent régime, for the operation of the Trail Smelter. . . .

. . . [T]he Tribunal directs that the Trail Smelter shall be operated with the following limitations on the sulphur emissions — it being understood that the Tribunal is not at present ready to make such limitations permanent, but feels that they will for the present probably reduce the chance or possibility of injury in the area of probable damage.

(a) For the periods April 25 to May 10 and June 22 to July 6, which are periods of greater sensitivity to sulphur dioxide for certain crops and trees in that area, not more than 100 tons per day of sulphur shall be emitted from the stacks of the Trail Smelter.

(b) As a further precaution, and for the entire period until October 1, 1938, the sulphur dioxide recorder at Columbia Gardens and the sulphur dioxide recorder at the Stroh farm (or any other point approved by the Technical Consultants) shall be continuously operated, and observations of relative humidity shall also be taken at both recorder stations. When, between the hours of sunrise and sunset, the sulphur dioxide concentration at Columbia Gardens exceeds one part per million for three consecutive 20-minute periods, and the relative humidity is 60 per cent or higher, the Trail Smelter shall be notified immediately; and the sulphur emission from the stacks of the plant maintained at 5 tons of sulphur per hour or less until the sulphur dioxide concentration at the Columbia Gardens recorder station falls to 0.5 part per million. . . .

The Trail Smelter Arbitral Tribunal made the preliminary decision excerpted above in 1938. In a part of the decision omitted from this excerpt, the Tribunal appointed expert consultants to further study the Trail Smelter and gave it detailed instructions on what to study. The Tribunal used this data to reach its final decision, excerpted below, in 1941.

Trail Smelter Arbitral Decision
3 R. Int'l Arb. Awards 1938 (Trail Smelter Arb. Trib. March 11, 1941)

Reported on March 11, 1941, to the Government of the United States of America and to the Government of the Dominion of Canada, Under the Convention Signed April 15, 1935.

. . . As between the two countries involved, each has an equal interest that if a nuisance is proved, the indemnity to damaged parties for proven damage shall be just and adequate and each has also an equal interest that unproven or unwarranted claims shall not be allowed. For, while the United States' interests may now be claimed to be injured by the operations of a Canadian corporation, it is equally possible that at some time in the future Canadian interests might be claimed to be injured by an American corporation. As has well been said: "It would not be to the advantage of the two countries concerned that industrial effort should be prevented by exaggerating the interests of the agricultural community. Equally, it would not be to the advantage of the two countries that the agricultural community should be oppressed to advance the interest of industry."

Considerations like the above are reflected in the provisions of the Convention in Article IV, that "the desire of the high contracting parties" is "to reach a solution just to all parties concerned". And the phraseology of the questions submitted to the Tribunal clearly evinces a desire and an intention that, to some extent, in making its answers to the questions, the Tribunal should endeavor to adjust the conflicting interests by some "just solution" which would allow the continuance of the operation of the Trail Smelter but under such restrictions and limitations as would, as far as foreseeable, prevent damage in the United States, and as would enable indemnity to be obtained, if in spite of such restrictions and limitations, damage should occur in the future in the United States.

In arriving at its decision, the Tribunal has had always to bear in mind the further fact that in the preamble to the Convention, it is stated that it is concluded with the recognition of "the desirability and necessity of effecting a permanent settlement". . . .

In conclusion (end of Part Two of the previous decision), the Tribunal answered Question No. 1 as follows:

> Damage caused by the Trail Smelter in the State of Washington has occurred since the first day of January, 1932, and up to October 1,1937, and the indemnity to be paid therefor is seventy-eight thousand dollars ($78,000), and is to be complete and final indemnity and compensation for all damage which occurred between such dates. Interest at the rate of six per centum per year will be allowed on the above sum of seventy-eight thousand dollars ($78,000) from the date of the filing of this report and decision until date of payment. This decision is not subject to alteration or modification by the Tribunal hereafter. The fact of existence of damage, if any, occurring after October 1, 1937, and the indemnity to be paid therefor, if any, the Tribunal will determine in its final decision.

Answering Questions No. 2 and No. 3, the Tribunal decided that, until a final decision should be made, the Trail Smelter should be subject to a temporary régime (described more in detail in Part Four of the present decision) and a trial period was established to a date not later than October 1, 1940, in order to enable the Tribunal to establish a permanent régime based on a "more adequate and intensive study", since the Tribunal felt that the information that had been placed before it did not enable it to determine at that time with sufficient certainty upon a permanent régime. . . .

II (a).

The Tribunal is requested to say that damage has occurred in the State of Washington since October 1, 1937, as a consequence of the emission of sulphur dioxide by the smelters of the Consolidated Mining and Smelting Company at Trail, B.C., and that an indemnity in the sum of $34,807 should be paid therefor. . . .

. . . No damage caused by the Trail Smelter in the State of Washington has occurred since the first day of October, 1937, and prior to the first day of October, 1940, and hence no indemnity shall be paid therefor.

PART THREE.

The second question under Article III of the Convention is as follows:

> In the event of the answer to the first part of the preceding question being in the affirmative, whether the Trail Smelter should be required to refrain from causing damage in the State of Washington in the future and, if so, to what extent?

Damage has occurred since January 1, 1932, as fully set forth in the previous decision. To that extent, the first part of the preceding question has thus been answered in the affirmative. . . .

The first problem which arises is whether the question should be answered on the basis of the law followed in the United States or on the basis of international law. The Tribunal, however, finds that this problem need not be solved here as the law followed in the United States in dealing with the quasi-sovereign rights of the States of the Union, in the matter of air pollution, whilst more definite, is in conformity with the general rules of international law.

Particularly in reaching its conclusions as regards this question as well as the next, the Tribunal has given consideration to the desire of the high contracting parties "to reach a solution just to all parties concerned".

As Professor Eagleton puts in (*Responsibility of States in International Law,* 1928, p. 80): "A State owes at all times a duty to protect other States against injurious acts by individuals from within its jurisdiction." A great number of such general pronouncements by leading authorities concerning the duty of a State to respect other States and their territory have been presented to the Tribunal. These and many others have been carefully examined. International decisions, in various matters, from the Alabama case onward, and also earlier ones, are based on the same general principle, and, indeed, this principle, as such, has not been questioned by Canada. But the real difficulty often arises rather when it comes to determine what, *pro subjecta materie,* is deemed to constitute an injurious act.

A case concerning, as the present one does, territorial relations, decided by the Federal Court of Switzerland between the Cantons of Soleure and Argovia, may serve to illustrate the relativity of the rule. Soleure brought a suit against her sister State to enjoin use of a shooting establishment which endangered her territory. The court, in granting the injunction, said: "This right (sovereignty) excludes. . . . not only the usurpation and exercise of sovereign rights (of another State). . . . but also an actual encroachment which might prejudice the natural use of the territory and the free movement of its inhabitants." As a result of the decision, Argovia made plans for the improvement of the existing installations. These, however, were considered as insufficient protection by Soleure. The Canton of Argovia then moved the Federal Court to decree that the shooting be again permitted after completion of the projected improvements. This motion was granted. "The demand of the Government of Soleure", said the court, "that all endangerment be absolutely abolished apparently goes too far." The court found that all risk whatever had not been eliminated, as the region was flat and absolutely safe shooting ranges were only found in mountain valleys; that there was a federal duty for the communes to provide facilities for military target practice and that "no more precautions may be demanded for shooting ranges near the boundaries of two Cantons than are required for shooting ranges in the interior of a Canton". (R. O. 26 I, p. 450, 451; R. O. 41, I, p. 137; see D. Schindler, "The Administration of Justice in the Swiss Federal Court in Intercantonal Disputes", *American Journal of International Law*, Vol. 15 (1921), pp. 172-174.)

No case of air pollution dealt with by an international tribunal has been brought to the attention of the Tribunal nor does the Tribunal know of any such case. The nearest analogy is that of water pollution. But, here also, no decision of an international tribunal has been cited or has been found.

There are, however, as regards both air pollution and water pollution, certain decisions of the Supreme Court of the United States which may legitimately be taken as a guide in this field of international law, for it is reasonable to follow by analogy, in international cases, precedents established by that court in dealing with controversies between States of the Union or with other controversies concerning the quasi-sovereign rights of such States, where no contrary rule prevails in international law and no reason for rejecting such precedents can be adduced from the limitations of sovereignty inherent in the Constitution of the United States.

In the suit of the State of Missouri *v.* the State of Illinois (200 U.S. 496, 521) concerning the pollution, within the boundaries of Illinois, of the Illinois River, an affluent, of the Mississippi flowing into the latter where it forms the boundary between that State and Missouri, an injunction was refused. "Before this court ought to intervene", said the court, "the case should be of serious magnitude, clearly and fully proved, and the principle to be applied should be one which the court is prepared deliberately to maintain against all considerations on the other side. (See Kansas *v.* Colorado, 185 U.S. 125.)" The court found that the practice complained of was general along the shores of the Mississippi River at that time, that it was followed by Missouri itself and that thus a standard was set up by the defendant which the claimant was entitled to invoke.

As the claims of public health became more exacting and methods for removing impurities from the water were perfected, complaints ceased. It is significant that Missouri sided with Illinois when the other riparians of the Great Lakes' system sought to enjoin it to desist from diverting the waters of that system into that of the Illinois and Mississippi for the very purpose of disposing of the Chicago sewage.

In the more recent suit of the State of New York against the State of New Jersey (256 U.S. 296, 309), concerning the pollution of New York Bay, the injunction was also refused for lack of proof, some experts believing that the plans which were in dispute would result in the presence of "offensive odors and unsightly deposits", other equally reliable experts testifying that they were confidently of the opinion that the waters would be sufficiently purified. The court, referring to Missouri v. Illinois, said: ". . . . the burden upon the State of New York of sustaining the allegations of its bill is much greater than that imposed upon a complainant in an ordinary suit between private parties. Before this court can be moved to exercise its extraordinary power under the Constitution to control the conduct of one State at the suit of another, the threatened invasion of rights must be of serious magnitude and it must be established by clear and convincing evidence."

What the Supreme Court says there of its power under the Constitution equally applies to the extraordinary power granted this Tribunal under the Convention. What is true between States of the Union is, at least, equally true concerning the relations between the United States and the Dominion of Canada.

In another recent case concerning water pollution (283 U.S. 473), the complainant was successful. The City of New York was enjoined, at the request of the State of New Jersey, to desist, within a reasonable time limit, from the practice of disposing of sewage by dumping it into the sea, a practice which was injurious to the coastal waters of New Jersey in the vicinity of her bathing resorts.

In the matter of air pollution itself, the leading decisions are those of the Supreme Court in the State of Georgia v. Tennessee Copper Company and Ducktown Sulphur, Copper and Iron Company, Limited. Although dealing with a suit against private companies, the decisions were on questions cognate to those here at issue. Georgia stated that it had in vain sought relief from the State of Tennessee, on whose territory the smelters were located, and the court defined the nature of the suit by saying: "This is a suit by a State for an injury to it in its capacity of quasi-sovereign. In that capacity, the State has an interest independent of and behind the titles of its citizens, in all the earth and air within its domain."

On the question whether an injunction should be granted or not, the court said (206 U.S. 230):

> It (the State) has the last word as to whether its mountains shall be stripped of their forests and its inhabitants shall breathe pure air. . . . It is not lightly to be presumed to give up quasi-sovereign rights for pay and. . . . if that be its choice, it may insist that an infraction of them shall be stopped. This court has not quite the same freedom to balance the harm that will be done by an injunction against that of which the plaintiff complains, that it would have in deciding between two subjects of a single political power. Without excluding the considerations that

equity always takes into account. . . . it is a fair and reasonable demand on the part of a sovereign that the air over its territory should not be polluted on a great scale by sulphurous acid gas, that the forests on its mountains, be they better or worse, and whatever domestic destruction they may have suffered, should not be further destroyed or threatened by the act of persons beyond its control, that the crops and orchards on its hills should not be endangered from the same source. . . . Whether Georgia, by insisting upon this claim, is doing more harm than good to her own citizens, is for her to determine. The possible disaster to those outside the State must be accepted as a consequence of her standing upon her extreme rights.

Later on, however, when the court actually framed an injunction, in the case of the Ducktown Company (237 U.S. 474, 477) (an agreement on the basis of an annual compensation was reached with the most important of the two smelters, the Tennessee Copper Company), they did not go beyond a decree "adequate to diminish materially the present probability of damage to its (Georgia's) citizens".

Great progress in the control of fumes has been made by science in the last few years and this progress should be taken into account.

The Tribunal, therefore, finds that the above decisions, taken as a whole, constitute an adequate basis for its conclusions, namely, that, under the principles of international law, as well as of the law of the United States, no State has the right to use or permit the use of its territory in such a manner as to cause injury by fumes in or to the territory of another or the properties or persons therein, when the case is of serious consequence and the injury is established by clear and convincing evidence.

The decisions of the Supreme Court of the United States which are the basis of these conclusions are decisions in equity and a solution inspired by them, together with the régime hereinafter prescribed, will, in the opinion of the Tribunal, be "just to all parties concerned", as long, at least, as the present conditions in the Columbia River Valley continue to prevail.

Considering the circumstances of the case, the Tribunal holds that the Dominion of Canada is responsible in international law for the conduct of the Trail Smelter. Apart from the undertakings in the Convention, it is, therefore, the duty of the Government of the Dominion of Canada to see to it that this conduct should be in conformity with the obligation of the Dominion under international law as herein determined.

The Tribunal, therefore, answers Question No. 2 as follows: (2) So long as the present conditions in the Columbia River Valley prevail, the Trail Smelter shall be required to refrain from causing any damage through fumes in the State of Washington; the damage herein referred to and its extent being such as would be recoverable under the decisions of the courts of the United States in suits between private individuals. The indemnity for such damage should be fixed in such manner as the Governments, acting under Article XI of the Convention, should agree upon.

PART FOUR.

The third question under Article III of the Convention is as follows: "In the light of the answer to the preceding question, what measures or régime, if any, should be adopted and maintained by the Trail Smelter?"

Answering this question in the light of the preceding one, since the Tribunal has, in its previous decision, found that damage caused by the Trail Smelter has occurred in the State of Washington since January 1, 1932, and since the Tribunal is of opinion that damage may occur in the future unless the operations of the Smelter shall be subject to some control, in order to avoid damage occurring, the Tribunal now decides that a régime or measure of control shall be applied to the operations of the Smelter and shall remain in full force unless and until modified in accordance with the provisions hereinafter set forth in Section 3, Paragraph VI of the present part of this decision.
. . .

IV. Maximum Permissible Sulphur Emission.

The following two tables and general restrictions give the maximum hourly permissible emission of sulphur dioxide expressed as tons per hour of contained sulphur.

Growing Season

	Turbulence Bad		Turbulence Fair		Turbulence Good		Turbulence Excellent
	(1)	(2)	(3)	(4)	(5)	(6)	(7)
	Wind not favorable	Wind favorable	Wind not favorable	Wind favorable	Wind not favorable	Wind favorable	Wind not favorable and favorable
Midnight to 3 a.m . . .	2	6	6	9	9	11	11
3 a.m. to 3 hrs. after sunrise	0	2	4	4	4	6	6
3 hrs. after sunrise to 3 hrs. before sunset	2	6	6	9	9	11	11
3 hrs. before sunset to sunset	2	5	5	7	7	9	9
Sunset to Midnight . . .	3	7	6	9	9	11	11

Non-Growing Season

	Turbulence Bad		Turbulence Fair		Turbulence Good		Turbulence Excellent
	(1)	(2)	(3)	(4)	(5)	(6)	(7)
	Wind not favorable	Wind favorable	Wind not favorable	Wind favorable	Wind not favorable	Wind favorable	Wind not favorable and favorable
Midnight to 3 a.m . . .	2	8	6	11	9	11	11

	Turbulence Bad		Turbulence Fair		Turbulence Good		Turbulence Excellent
	(1) Wind not favorable	(2) Wind favorable	(3) Wind not favorable	(4) Wind favorable	(5) Wind not favorable	(6) Wind favorable	(7) Wind not favorable and favorable
3 a.m. to 3 hrs. after sunrise	0	4	4	6	4	6	6
3 hrs. after sunrise to 3 hrs. before sunset	2	8	6	11	9	11	11
3 hrs. before sunset to sunset	2	7	5	9	7	9	9
Sunset to Midnight ..	3	9	6	11	9	11	11

General Restrictions and Provisions.

(a) If the Columbia Gardens recorder indicates 0.3 part per million or more of sulphur dioxide for two consecutive twenty minute periods during the growing season, and the wind direction is not favorable, emission shall be reduced by four tons of sulphur per hour or shut down completely when the turbulence is bad, until the recorder shows 0.2 part per million or less of sulphur dioxide for three consecutive twenty minute periods.

   If the Columbia Gardens recorder indicates 0.5 part per million or more of sulphur dioxide for three consecutive twenty minute periods during the non-growing season and the wind direction is not favorable, emission shall be reduced by four tons of sulphur per hour or shut down completely when the turbulence is bad, until the recorder shows 0.2 part per million or less of sulphur dioxide for three consecutive twenty minute periods.

(b) In case of rain or snow, the emission of sulphur shall be reduced by two (2) tons per hour. This regulation shall be put into effect immediately when precipitation can be observed from the Smelter and shall be continued in effect for twenty (20) minutes after such precipitation has ceased.

(c) If the slag retreatment furnace is not in operation the emission of sulphur shall be reduced by two (2) tons per hour.

(d) If the instrumental reading shows turbulence excellent, good or fair, but visual observations made by trained observers clearly indicate that there is poor diffusion, the emission of sulphur shall be reduced to the figures given in column (1) if wind is not favorable, or column (2) if wind is favorable.

(e) When more than one of the restricting conditions provided for in (a), (b), (c), and (d) occur simultaneously, the highest reduction shall apply.

(f) If, during the non-growing season, the instrumental reading shows turbulence fair and wind not favorable but visual observations by trained observers clearly indicate that there is excellent diffusion, the maximum permissible emission of sulphur may be increased to the figures in column (5). The general restrictions under (*a*), (*b*), (*c*) and (*e*), however, shall be applicable.

. . .

PART FIVE.

The fourth question under Article III of the Convention is as follows:

What indemnity or compensation, if any, should be paid on account of any decision or decisions rendered by the Tribunal pursuant to the next two preceding Questions?

The Tribunal is of opinion that the prescribed régime will probably remove the causes of the present controversy and, as said before, will probably result in preventing any damage of a material nature occurring in the State of Washington in the future.

But since the desirable and expected result of the régime or measure of control hereby required to be adopted and maintained by the Smelter may not occur, and since in its answer to Question No. 2, the Tribunal has required the Smelter to refrain from causing damage in the State of Washington in the future, as set forth therein, the Tribunal answers Question No. 4 and decides that on account of decisions rendered by the Tribunal in its answers to Question No. 2 and Question No. 3 there shall be paid as follows: (*a*) if any damage as defined under Question No. 2 shall have occurred since October 1, 1940, or shall occur in the future, whether through failure on the part of the Smelter to comply with the regulations herein prescribed or notwithstanding the maintenance of the régime, an indemnity shall be paid for such damage but only when and if the two Governments shall make arrangements for the disposition of claims for indemnity under the provisions of Article XI of the Convention. . . .

NOTES AND QUESTIONS ON THE *TRAIL SMELTER* CASE

1. *Who decides?* What decision-makers tried to make decisions about the *Trail Smelter* during the history of this matter? Who makes up this Tribunal? How did this dispute get to this Tribunal?

2. *Opinio juris.* Notice that the arbitrators drew upon common law United States Supreme Court cases, including some featured at the beginning of this book. Why are these internal United States cases relevant to an international dispute? In general, *opinio juris* (judicial opinion), if relevant, constitutes a source of international law.

3. *Customary law.* If a legal norm commands sufficient international support, the international community will deem it a "customary law" and treat the norm as a binding legal obligation. In identifying customary norms, international tribunals evaluate state practice to determine whether the international community accepts a norm as binding. A large number of states acting as if bound by a particular principle constitutes evidence that the principle is a binding customary norm. Most commentators agree that international law establishes a customary norm of avoiding significantly damaging the neighboring states' environment. Does this norm apply when the damage occurs on private property?

4. *The Great Lakes.* The Great Lakes lie between the United States and Canada. Numerous enterprises, including farms and factories of various kinds on both sides of the border, contribute to pollution in the Great Lakes. Would an agreement to allow courts to arbitrate disputes about particular pollution sources contributing to Great Lakes pollution provide an effective approach to addressing Great Lakes water quality concerns? If not, who should address this concern? Notice that these questions raise issues on the international level similar to the questions we posed earlier about American common law's adequacy.

A. REGIONAL ENVIRONMENTAL PROBLEMS

Most international law addressing pollution of waters flowing between or abutting several countries uses some sort of regional approach. One example that has served as a prototype for many regional efforts comes from the treaties between the United States and Canada to address water quality issues in the Great Lakes. This treaty regime has established the International Joint Commission (IJC), which studies Great Lakes pollution and seeks to establish cooperative agreements between the United States and Canada on how to address pollution problems. This is the same body to which the United States and Canada referred the Trail Smelter problem before it went to arbitration.

Jack P. Manno, Advocacy and Diplomacy: NGOs and the Great Lakes Water Quality Agreement, in Environmental NGOs
World Politics: Linking the Local and the Global (Thomas Princen and Matthias Finger, eds. 1994)

Background of Canada–US Great Lakes Water Quality Agreement

The negotiating history leading to the GLWQA dates to the late nineteenth century, when significant advances were made in waterworks engineering and economic development. Along with advances in technology came plans for constructing major works with the potential for altering parts of the Great Lakes hydrological system. Proposed canals and dams raised concerns about water resource rights. . . . A proposal for a Chicago drainage canal to divert Lake Michigan water into the Mississippi Rover basin, and another for a dam at the outlet of Lake Erie, were two of the most controversial. Both were initiated on the US side, with little consideration given to the possible impact on Canadian rights and resources.

Dominion representatives pressed for a treaty that would protect Canadian interests, which they felt were constantly being pitted against US economic might. Canada sought a strong treaty enforced by a commission with wide ranging authority. The United States, however, preferred measures that would not impinge on national sovereignty rights. The Boundary Waters Treaty of 1909 was the compromise result. It established a body, the International Joint Commission (IJC), empowered to act only upon those cases jointly referred to it by the parties. It held no authoritative powers over the two participating states to ensure compliance with its recommendations. Still, its structure did offer a unique approach to international problem solving. The six commissioners, three Canadian and three American, were expected to represent the commission, not their home countries. Decisions were to be made by consensus and, to insulate commissioners from political pressure, no record was kept of the decision-making process itself.

Great Lakes Water Pollution: A Catalyst for Change

Interest in water pollution antedated the 1909 Boundary Waters Treaty. At that time, typhoid fever was a major health problem in the United States and Canada, and a clear link had been established between polluted water and the spread of typhoid. Investigative studies of Lake Michigan and Lake Erie suggested the need for federal public health legislation. As a result, the Boundary Waters Treaty addressed water pollution in Article IV: 'It is hereby agreed that the waters herein defined as boundary waters and waters flowing across the boundary shall not be polluted on either side to the injury of health or property on the other.'

This article has grown immensely in importance since 1909. It has provided the basis for IJC investigations into water pollution and water quality issues, and eventually provided the rationale for the GLWQA. The IJC received its first reference to investigate water pollution in 1913. Following investigative studies in the connecting channels, both the US and Canadian commissioners issued preliminary reports that were dramatic in their urgency. The language expressed deep concern: 'The situation along the frontier which is generally chaotic, everywhere perilous and in some cases disgraceful [and the conditions] imperil the health and welfare of the citizens in substantial contravention of the spirit of the Treaty.' . . .

By the time the general public took serious notice in the 1960s the momentum of large system modification had already caused considerable damage. Scientific concern for the health of the lakes and public demand for action led the governments of Canada and the United States to ask the IJC in 1964 for a study of water pollution problems in the lower lakes, Lakes Erie and Ontario, and the St Lawrence. The study took six years to complete, but the IJC's response of 1970 called for an international clean-up effort, urging the governments to develop programmes to reduce phosphorous inputs and to agree on controls and/or regulations on several pollution sources. Those six years also saw a dramatic outpouring of public concern about the environment. Negotiations leading to the Great Lakes Water Quality Agreement of 1972 began almost immediately after the governments received the report. By that time major fish die-offs, beach closings, mounds of rotting seaweed, and river surfaces that actually had caught fire had had their effects. The visible outcome of sewage and fertilizer pollution and the resulting eutrophication of the lakes served as the motivating backdrop for the GLWQA negotiations, and the control of phosphorous inputs was its primary remedial strategy.

The 1972 Great Lakes Water Quality Agreement

In the 1972 GLWQA the parties expressed their determination to 'restore and maintain the chemical, physical and biological integrity of the Great Lakes'. The agreement also gave the IJC additional responsibilities for:

(1) collecting, analysing, and disseminating information on the operations and effectiveness of government programmes to improve water quality of the Great Lakes;
(2) tendering advice and recommendations to federal, state, or provincial governments for dealing with water quality problems;
(3) assisting in the coordination of joint efforts to control pollution, including the discharge of phosphorus into the lakes.

These new powers, in effect, constituted a permanent reference. The commission was no longer required to wait for the parties to refer specific questions to it before commenting, criticizing, and offering advice. To carry out its new functions under the GLWQA, two new binational IJC boards were established: the Water Quality Board and the Great Lakes Science Advisory Board. The Water Quality Board serves as the principal advisor to the IJC on all matters pertaining to the GLWQA. The Science Advisory Board serves a broader, less-focused purpose, advising the commissioners on research and scientific matters and calling attention to new and emerging issues.

The new boards made available to the commission a source of technical and managerial expertise, allowing the commissioners to comment broadly in the biennial reports they issued under the GLWQA. The boards' research and reports did several things besides informing the commission. They clarified and documented the causes of water pollution, recommended government action, and alerted the public. The boards also stimulated and became part of a new complex of working relationships among US and Canadian natural scientists, ecologists, bureaucrats, and policy scholars with links to both governments and the new environmental NGOs of the 1970s. . . .

The agreement's remedial strategies grew principally out of the recommendations of the two reference groups constituted in 1964 to study the lower Great Lakes and the St Lawrence River where the pollution was most conspicuous. To expand on the previously completed studies the GLWQA called for two major follow-up studies: one on the upper lakes and the other on the diffuse sources known as 'nonpoint pollution'. Two IJC study groups were formed: the Upper Lakes Reference Group and the Pollution from Land Use Activities Reference Group (PLUARG). The Upper Lakes Reference Group played a key role in the evolution of public participation in IJC reference studies. The group set up to carry out the studies in Support of the Upper Lakes reference decided to hold a series of public workshops to explain the issues and solicit opinions. The group contracted with Great Lakes Tomorrow, the first binational Great Lakes citizens group that had been set up to educate the public and facilitate public involvement in Great Lakes decisions. This experience provided the basis for future citizen involvement in IJC activities.

The advances the Upper Lakes Reference Group made in public participation were taken to new levels in the massive ecological study known as the Pollution from Land-Use Activities Reference. PLUARG consisted of more than one hundred investigators in a five-year study of pollution from agriculture, forestry, and other land uses. As the first IJC reference dealing with the entire Great Lakes basin and involving public consultation panels from throughout the basin, it proved to be very important not only in expanding scientific understanding of multiple sources of pollution but also in laying the groundwork for an ecosystemic approach and expanding public participation in IJC activities. . . .

The 1972 GLWQA was in force for five years, after which it was to be revisited by the parties. In the years between 1972 and 1978 progress was made in reducing phosphorous inputs, through sewage treatment and the gradual elimination of phosphorus from laundry detergents. The eutrophication problem was on its way to being resolved. With this success, the problem of toxic industrial chemicals and pesticides present in the flesh of fish and other animals, previously masked by the more visible problems of eutrophication, re-emerged as the focus of concern in the Great Lakes.

As early as 1963, studies of herring gull eggs in Lake Michigan concluded that thinning shells and poor reproductive success was probably associated with concentrations of DDT and its toxic metabolite, DDE, that the birds received from their diets of Lake Michigan fish. In 1968 mercury from the chlor-alkali wastes being dumped into the lakes and tributaries was measured in the sediment and fish of Lake Ontario. In 1971, common terns in Hamilton

Harbor were discovered with deformed cross bills, an apparent result of the chemical stew of PCB, DDT, and hexachlorobenzene found in the eggs. Mirex, an organic chemical fire retardant and pesticide, was discovered in fish in the early 1970s. By the mid-1970s, states and provinces were routinely issuing warnings about eating the fish from the lakes, and several commercial fisheries were closed.

The chemicals of primary concern are synthetic organic chemicals produced directly or as by-products of industrial processes. Sources include industrial and municipal outfalls; contaminated air and rain; leaking landfills; previously contaminated sediment resuspended by currents, dredging, and storms; agricultural practices; and the widespread household use of solvents and pesticides. They represent a source of biochemical stress new to the industrial era that Great Lakes creatures had never encountered, and for which they had evolved few mechanisms to cope. The most serious threat came from chemicals that did not break down through metabolic action and those that were insoluble in water and concentrated in fat. Their resulting environmental persistence means they circulate and recirculate unchanged through the eco-system's physical and biological pathways, gradually becoming ubiquitous throughout the system. Because they are stored in fatty tissues and accumulate, they concentrate as they rise up the stages of the food chain. For instance, PCBs are bioaccumulated 25,000,000-fold in Great Lakes food webs from water to bald eagles' eggs. Hence, minute amounts of certain chemicals can become large problems throughout the whole system.

The toxics problem was significantly more complicated than the primary problem addressed by the 1972 agreement — nutrient pollution — which could be traced comparatively easily to municipal sewage systems and phos-phorus in detergents. The solutions to nutrient pollution — sewage treatment plants and detergent phosphorus bans — although expensive, were manage-able with the participation and coordination of existing state and provincial governments. By contrast, the problem emphasized in the 1978 agreement, toxic contamination, could not be solved by a single jurisdiction nor without substantial changes in industry and consumer practices. The agreement needed, therefore, to break new ground in international cooperation and institutional arrangments.

The revision of the GLWQA signed in 1978 greatly expanded the definition of the problem, as reflected in the agreement's area of purview. After recognizing that the problems of toxics in the Great Lakes water could not be resolved by actions focused on the lakes alone the 1978 revisions extended the scope of the GLWQA to the entire Great Lakes ecosystem, including the land surrounding the lakes and the inflowing streams. In addition to extending the physical boundaries, they expanded the concept of water quality and acknowl-edged the interdependence of all components of the ecosystem, including humans. The 1978 GLWQA defined the Great Lakes ecosystem as 'the interacting components of air, land, water and living organisms, including humans, within the drainage basin of the St Lawrence River' (Art. I, g).

The 1978 agreement expressed several additional concerns in response to the findings of PLUARG, nonpoint source pollution, and the effects of air pollution on water quality. The US and Canadian governments also agreed that

> the discharge of toxic substances in toxic amounts be prohibited and the discharge of any or all persistent toxic substances be virtually eliminated (Art II, a) that the philosophy adopted for control of inputs of persistent toxic substances shall be zero discharge (Annex 12).

These two aspects of the GLWQA — the ecosystem approach to environmental protection and zero discharge of persistent toxics — derived from the growing awareness of ecology and the nature of the toxics problems. The adoption of these concepts within a binational agreement is of major international importance. The challenge facing the governments in the region is how to translate an ecosystem approach and zero discharge into meaningful action feasible within the constraints presented by each nation's federal structures and political cultures.

Important Provision of the 1972 Great Lakes Agreement

Article I — Definitions

Article II — General Water Quality Objectives. These objectives provide narrative objectives agreed to by the two countries, such as committing to ensure that the waters are free from substances in concentrations that are toxic for human, animal, or aquatic life. Other objectives deal with putrescent sludge material, floating debris, materials that may cause a nuisance, and nutrients.

Article III — Specific Water Quality Objectives. These provisions commit to meeting specific numeric objectives for levels of reduction of pollutants as set out in Annex 1 to the agreement.

Article IV — Standards and Other Regulatory Requirements. This article commits the governments to have their domestic standards consistent with the agreement.

Article V — Programs and Other Measures. These provisions commit the governments to the development of programs directed toward the achievement of the water-quality objectives. These include programs for pollution controls from municipal and industrial sources and eutrophication from agricultural, forestry and other land-use activities; and pollution from shipping, dredging, and onshore and offshore facilities, among others.

Article VI — Powers, Responsibilities and Functions of the IJC. These provisions outline powers and responsibilities of the commission, including two references, one with respect to pollution from agricultural, forestry, and other land-use activities, and one pertaining to the quality of the waters of Lake Huron and Lake Superior.

Article VII — Joint Institutions. This provision mandates the establishment of a Water Quality Board and a Research Advisory Board, as well as a regional office located in the Great Lakes basin.

Article VIII — Submission and Exchange of Information. This article outlines requirements between the governments and the IJC concerning data and other information relating to water quality.

Article IX — Consultation and Review. This article requires consultation among the IJC and the governments. It commits to a comprehensive review of the agreement after five years.

Article X — Implementation. This article commits the governments to appropriating adequate funds to implement the agreement, and to enacting any necessary legislation to implement the agreement.

LEE BOTTS AND PAUL MULDOON, EVOLUTION OF THE GREAT LAKES WATER QUALITY AGREEMENT 16 (2005).

NOTES AND QUESTIONS ON THE GREAT LAKES
WATER QUALITY AGREEMENT

1. *IJC powers.* What powers does the IJC have? Do these powers suffice to address water pollution in the Great Lakes? What other entities have power to address Great Lakes water quality issues?

2. *Objectives.* Articles II and III of the 1972 Great Lakes Water Quality Agreement spell out water quality objectives and Article IV commits the governments to make their standards and regulatory requirements consistent with the agreement. Given these agreements, is the IJC necessary? Why or why not?

3. *NGOs.* Professor Manno's chapter emphasizes the growing role of non-governmental organizations in the Great Lakes regime. What roles should NGOs perform in resolving regional international problems?

4. *International EPA.* Should governments delegate decision-making authority over standards to the IJC, much like Congress delegates authority to EPA? Who must establish specific standards for pollution sources discharging into the Great Lakes?

B. GLOBAL ENVIRONMENTAL PROBLEMS

As the Boundary Waters Treaty and the *Trail Smelter* case illustrate, international environmental law has existed for some time. But the field really took off in the 1970s with the the proliferation of international environmental treaties and, not coincidentally, the growth of domestic environmental law in the United States and abroad. While most of these new treaties addressed regional problems (including the Great Lakes Water Quality Agreement), some addressed global environmental problems. The table below lists some prominent treaties addressing global issues and their dates. You can see the breadth of the problems addressed by looking carefully at the treaties' names in most cases.

Selected Global Environmental Treaties Post-1970

Treaty	Citations
Convention on International Trade in Endangered Species	26 U.S.T. 1087, T.I.A.S. No. 8249 (1973)
International Convention on Pollution From Ships	17 I.L.M. 546 (1978)

Continued

Treaty	Citations
United Nations Convention on the Law of the Sea	21 I.L.M. 1261 (1982)
Montreal Protocol on Substances that Deplete the Ozone Layer	26 I.L.M. 1550 (1987)
Basel Convention on the Control of Transboundary Movements of Hazardous Wastes and Their Disposal	28 I.L.M. 649 (1989)
Convention on Biological Diversity	31 I.L.M. 818 (1992)
Kyoto Protocol to the Framework Convention on Climate Change	37 I.L.M. 22 (1998)
Stockholm Convention on Persistent Organic Pollutants	entered into force 2004

You can see that this subject merits a course in its own right. The article below addresses only one international environmental problem, that of climate change, as a means of introducing the question of who should make decisions in addressing global environmental problems. We chose this problem because of the prominence and importance of the issue, but other global environmental problems raise similar issues of where to locate decision-making authority.

1. The United Nations Framework Convention on Climate Change

The excerpt below addresses the first international agreement addressing global warming:

Daniel Bodansky, *The United Nations Framework Convention on Climate Change: A Commentary*
18 Yale J. Int'l L. 451 (1993)

I. Introduction

Each year, mankind injects approximately six billion tons of carbon into the atmosphere from the burning of fossil fuels, as well as a substantial (although still uncertain) amount from deforestation. Since the advent of the industrial revolution, atmospheric concentrations of carbon dioxide have risen by more than twenty-five percent, from 280 to more than 350 parts per million (ppm). Scientists estimate that if current patterns of emissions continue unchecked, the increasing concentrations of carbon dioxide, together with parallel increases in other trace gases such as methane and nitrous oxide, will cause an average global warming in the range of 0.2 to 0.5 [degrees] C per decade, or 2 to 5 [degrees] C (3.6 to 9 [degrees] F) by the end of the next century. Such a temperature rise, more rapid than at any time in human history, could have severe effects on coastal areas, agriculture, forests, and human health.

In response to this threat, the U.N. General Assembly established the Intergovernmental Negotiating Committee for a Framework Convention on Climate Change (INC) in December 1990, with the mandate to negotiate a convention containing "appropriate commitments" in time for signature at the U.N. Conference on Environment and Development (UNCED) in June 1992. The INC met six times between February 1991 and May 1992, and adopted the U.N. Framework Convention on Climate Change (Climate Change Convention, or Convention) on May 9, 1992. The Convention was opened for signature at UNCED, where it was signed by 154 states and the European Community. It requires fifty ratifications for entry into force.

To many, the Convention was a disappointment. Despite early hopes that it would seek to stabilize or even reduce emissions of greenhouse gases by developed countries, the Convention contains only the vaguest of commitments regarding stabilization and no commitment at all on reductions. It fails to include innovative proposals to establish a financial and technology clearinghouse or an insurance fund, or to use market mechanisms such as tradeable emissions rights. Furthermore, it not only contains significant qualifications on the obligations of developing countries, but gives special consideration to the situation of fossil-fuel producing states.

Nevertheless, given the complexity both of the negotiations, which involved more than 140 states with very different interests and ideologies, and of the causes, effects, and policy implications of global warming, reaching agreement at all in such a limited period of time was a considerable achievement. In fact, the final text is significantly more substantive than either the bare-bones convention advocated by some delegations or previous framework conventions dealing with transboundary air pollution and depletion of the ozone layer. While the Convention does not commit states to specific limitations on greenhouse gas emissions, it recognizes climate change as a serious threat and establishes a basis for future action. First, it defines as a common long-term objective the stabilization of atmospheric concentrations of greenhouse gases "at a level that would prevent dangerous anthropogenic interference with the climate system." Second, to guide future work, it sets forth principles relating to inter- and intra-generational equity, the needs of developing countries, precaution, cost-effectiveness, sustainable development, and the international economy. More importantly, it establishes a process designed to improve our information base and reduce uncertainties, to encourage national planning, and to produce more substantive international standards should scientific evidence continue to mount that human activities are changing the Earth's climate.

NOTES AND QUESTIONS ON THE FRAMEWORK CONVENTION ON CLIMATE CHANGE

1. *Why international?* Why does addressing climate change require an international effort? Why not just leave individual nations to take action as they see fit?

2. *State consent.* The European Union favored firm reduction commitments, but the United States opposed them. Notice that the final agreement reflects what the countries of the world could agree to, since no international dictator or legislature exists to force countries to comply with treaties they do not approve of.

3. *Equity.* Professor Bodansky mentions early hopes for developed country commitments to emission reductions. Developing countries were unwilling to adopt reduction commitments, because the developed countries have historically emitted most of the pollution creating global warming. Because the developed countries recognized that they have better technological capabilities to reduce greenhouse gas emissions than developing countries, they agreed to a principle of "common but differentiated responsibilities" for addressing climate change.

4. *Principles.* Does the act of agreeing to a set of principles in the Framework Convention materially advance efforts to subsequently adopt a Protocol committing nation states to reductions of greenhouse gas emissions?

5. *Secretariat.* The Convention establishes a secretariat to facilitate exchange of information and further negotiation. *See* United Nations Framework Convention on Climate Change, Art. 8, 31 I.L.M. 1849 (1992). Are these two powers sufficient to allow the secretariat to solve the climate change problem?

2. The Kyoto Protocol to the Framework Convention on Climate Change

Developed countries did not meet the Framework Convention's "aim" of stabilizing emissions at 1990 levels, and scientific evidence mounted that this goal was inadequate anyway. In the years following adoption of the Framework Convention, many developed countries actively sought agreement on a set of binding reduction targets cutting emissions substantially below 1990 levels, at least for developed countries. The United States opposed cuts below 1990 baseline emission levels, but sought to incorporate international environmental benefit trading into the agreement. Under such an approach, one country could forego compliance with its target, if it purchased a corresponding climate change benefit from elsewhere.

In 1997, the Conference of the Parties, the governing body for the climate change treaty regime, adopted a compromise in which the United States signed on to an agreement for modest cuts below 1990 levels in exchange for incorporation of environmental benefit trading in the agreement.

The Kyoto Protocol contemplates a 5 percent reduction in developed country emissions below 1990 levels. It seeks to accomplish this by assigning varying emission reduction obligations to different countries. *See* Kyoto Protocol to the Framework Convention on Climate Change, Annex B, 37 I.L.M. 22 (1998). Thus, the agreement generally requires Japan, the United States, and the European Union to cut emissions by 6, 7, and 8 percent, respectively, but authorizes limited increases above 1990 levels for some developed countries. See *id.*

The treaty's environmental benefit trading, of course, means that countries need not meet their assigned reduction targets, if they purchase credits for surplus reductions from other countries. (Recall the material on emissions trading in Chapter 9.) The agreement also contemplates the possibility of countries assigning greenhouse gas emission reduction obligations to their polluters, but allowing them to meet some of these obligations through purchases of credits abroad.

One of the most controversial trading provisions creates a "Clean Development Mechanism," an authority for developed countries to meet their targets, at least in part, through purchases of reductions earned in developing countries. Kyoto Protocol, *supra*, Art. 12. Developing countries are not themselves subject to any binding targets under the Kyoto Protocol. This creates accounting and measurement difficulties.

The United States Senate never ratified the Kyoto Protocol. And President George W. Bush repudiated it as too costly and ineffective because of its failure to assign reduction obligations to developing countries. In spite of this, the agreement entered into force in 2005 without the United States as a party.

NOTES ON THE KYOTO PROTOCOL

1. *Recalcitrants.* Many developed country officials believe that the United States, the world's leading greenhouse gas emitter, should ratify and implement the Kyoto Protocol. Does anybody have the power to force the United States to comply? If you were the Prime Minister of a country threatened with serious damage from climate change, what actions might you take to try and bring about United States compliance?

2. *Means.* We have seen that environmental policy requires choices about not only the goals of environmental regulation, but also the means of meeting those goals. For example, countries may choose between traditional regulation, emissions trading, or pollution taxes as an approach to meeting environmental goals. Who should control the choice of means to meeting internationally chosen targets? See *generally* David M. Driesen, *Choosing Environmental Instruments in a Transnational Context*, 27 Ecology L.Q. 1 (2000).

3. *National choices.* The Kyoto Protocol requires parties to "individually or jointly" meet their greenhouse gas reduction targets. Kyoto Protocol, *supra*, Art. 3. It authorizes countries to acquire credits from other parties as a means

of compliance. *Id.*, Arts. 6, 12. Prior to the adoption of the Kyoto Protocol, many European countries favored use of carbon taxes to meet their targets. After signing the Protocol, however, the European Parliament adopted a directive creating an emissions trading scheme for major industrial sources in the European Union. Council Directive 2003/87(EC), 2003 O.J. (L 275). A subsequent directive allowed the European pollution sources to use credits purchased from developing country project developers under the Clean Development Mechanism to fulfill some of their reduction obligations. Council Directive 2004/101/(EC), amending Directive 2003/87/EC, establishing a scheme for greenhouse gas emission allowance trading within the Community, in respect of [sic] the Kyoto Protocol's project mechanisms, 2004 O.J. (L 338) 18 (EC). This about face may reflect the influence of international law on regional choices about the means of environmental protection.

4. *State and local action.* In spite of federal repudiation of the Kyoto Protocol in the United States, a large number of states and municipalities have committed themselves to meeting Kyoto targets or adopting programs aimed at ameliorating global warming. *See* Kirsten H. Engel, *Mitigating Global Climate Change in the United States: A Regional Approach,* 14 N.Y.U. Envtl. L.J. 54 (2005-2006). To what extent can municipal or state governments address international environmental problems?

5. *Framework and Protocol approach.* The approach of adopting a Framework Convention and then adopting Protocols or other kinds of subsequent agreements with more specific obligations has become very common in international environmental law. For example, the Convention on International Trade in Endangered Species of Wild Fauna and Flora (CITES), 12 I.L.M. 1085 (1973), contains an agreement to limit imports and exports of endangered species and their parts. But the Conference of the Parties names the actual species getting protection in subsequent listing decisions. Typically, every international environmental treaty establishes its own problem-specific secretariat and provides for regular meetings of the parties to the particular agreement for major policy decisions. Is this a good approach? What problems might it create?

C. COMPLIANCE AND ENFORCEMENT

Who should enforce international environmental law and how? Consider the following view:

Abram Chayes, Antonia Handler Chayes, and Ronald B. Mitchell, *Managing Compliance: A Comparative Perspective*

Engaging Countries: Strengthening Compliance with International Environmental Accords (Edith Brown Weiss and Harold K. Jacobson eds., 1998)

Approaches to Compliance: "Enforcement" or "Management"

. . . Although an enforcement model of compliance rests on the availability and use of sanctions to deter violations, systemic features of international society severely constrain the use of sanctions. Only two treaties, the United Nations Charter and the Organization of American States Charter, authorize the use of concerted military or economic measures, and these have been invoked in only a dozen or so cases. More frequently, economic sanctions have been used unilaterally to advance particular foreign policy goals, not to enforce treaty obligations. Only powerful states or coalitions of states can use them, and only against weaker states. . . .

In contrast, a managerial model of compliance suggests that regimes usually keep noncompliance at acceptable levels by an iterative process of discourse among the parties, the treaty organization, and the wider public. Most states enter agreements intending to comply. Compliance often serves the state interests that led to, and were shaped by, the negotiation process. Treaties legally bind the member states and carry a presumptive obligation to comply. Moreover, compliance reduces decision costs and conforms to bureaucratic modes of action. . . .

We believe that effective compliance management requires establishing and maintaining a transparent information system and a response system. The information system must produce adequate and accurate information about actors' behaviors under the treaty. The managerial response system must then produce discriminating responses to different types of noncompliance, using both multilateral, treaty-based and unilateral actions to induce behavioral change.

Norms: The Foundation for Compliance

Norms provide the foundation for this compliance process. Here we use "norms" to refer generally to "prescriptions for action in situations of choice, carrying a sense of obligation, a sense that they ought to be followed"(Chayes and Chayes 1995:113) . . .

If a normative consensus on an issue area exits, then much initial compliance may be motivated by this consensus rather than by treaty compliance mechanisms. The international norm of *pacta sunt servanda,* "treaties must be obeyed," and the voluntariness of treaty signature provide further pressures for compliance. Even with the deep inequities in the distribution of power, countries accept agreements that discriminate in favor of powerful states as legitimate, when they have participated in the negotiation, because those agreements may be preferable to available alternatives. For example, the Nuclear Non-proliferation Treaty is viewed as binding on nonnuclear signatory states even though it allows five major powers to remain nuclear "haves" while prohibiting the "have-nots" from attaining such status.

Treaties do not simply reflect norms, however, but can create and strengthen norms that did not previously exist. Treaties banning deployment of nuclear weapons on the seabed, in outer space, and in Antarctica created new international norms. It is easy to imagine that arms races would have developed in these areas had the treaties not generated expectations that others would abide by the norm. Treaties also can widen a norm's scope, as is evident in the human-rights arena, where nations may initially sign a treaty because of public and diplomatic pressures, but over time internalize the norms embodied in the treaty. The almost universal signature of the Chemical Weapons Convention and the United Nations Conference on Environment and Development agreements suggests powerful public international pressures to sign treaties that establish new norms, with the costs of compliance playing a minor role in most countries' calculus regarding signature. Nevertheless, the treaty norms are likely to constrain future behavior.

. . .

The treaty and treaty secretariat need not rely exclusively on norms to alter behavior, however. Several more active means are available to them. The two key components of successful efforts at eliciting compliance are a transparent information system and a managerial strategy of responses to induce compliance.

Developing a Transparent Information System

To manage compliance effectively, the treaty regime must have a transparent information system. We use "transparency" to mean the adequacy, accuracy, availability, and accessibility of knowledge and information about the policies and activities of parties to the treaty, and of the central organizations established by it on matters relevant to compliance and effectiveness, and about the operation of the norms, rules, and procedures established by the treaty.

An information system's transparency can be evaluated against several standards. First, does the system collect a wide range of relevant information on compliance and effectiveness? Second, is the available information perceived as accurate, reliable, and legitimate? Third, does information available to the secretariat get analyzed and processed effectively? Fourth, is the information available to the sectretariat made available to industry, NGOs, and publics as well as governments?

The Functions of Transparency

Transparency fosters compliance by permitting actors to coordinate their behavior, reassuring actors who desire to cooperate but fear being "suckered," and deterring actors contemplating noncompliance. In many instances, the actor's independent responses to these forces will assure compliance. Where strategic interaction is insufficient, transparency allows other parties to observe deviations from prescribed conduct and to require that those deviations be accounted for and justified.

Coordination.   In simple cases where actors care more that a single rule govern the activity, than which rule governs it, treaties facilitate cooperation by creating and publicizing an agreed-upon rule. Some rules are literally rules of the road, such as rules established for air transport, marine navigation, and satellite communication allocation. Once the parties understand the rules, no actors have incentives to violate them. In other cases, regimes produce collective information that participating states would find it impossible, or prohibitively expensive, to assemble on their own. Various commodity agreements and the International Monetary Fund (IMF) have produced industrial, financial, and economic databases that facilitate numerous loans and private economic transactions. Periodic reporting on SO_2 emissions under the Long-Range Trans-Boundary Air Pollution (LRTAP) Convention led most parties to limit their emissions by some 30 percent unilaterally; only subsequently was a protocol to that effect negotiated. The credible, integrated database that was essential to common scientific judgment and coordinated action would not have emerged in the absence of the regime (Ausubel and Victor 1992).

Reassurance.   Transparency also reassures parties that others are meeting their obligations; and if they are not, it permits a timely response. Reassurance is needed when actors otherwise inclined to comply are concerned that they will be placed at a disadvantage if their compliance is not matched by others. To preserve a common pool resource, actors must adopt a "contingent strategy" of committing to follow the rules as long as others do so, but such actors must have "information about the rates of rule conformance adopted by others" (Ostrom 1990: 187). Treaties banning deployment of nuclear weapons in certain environments worked by reassuring each side: since each side had incentives to place weapons in these areas only if the other side did, ordinary surveillance reassured each side of the other's compliance.

Regimes for confidence-building measures in Europe required states to give notice of military maneuvers to assure all Europeans that neither the North Atlantic Treaty Organization nor the Warsaw Pact was preparing a surprise attack. If the conditions of an assurance problem hold — that is, if the benefits to a state exceed its costs of contribution so long as others also comply — transparency supplies the reassurance needed for parties to make safe, advantageous, and credible commitments to follow the rules.

Deterrence.   Deterrence is the obverse of reassurance. A party disposed to comply needs reassurance. A party contemplating violation needs to be deterred. Transparency supplies both. The probability that conduct departing from treaty requirements will be discovered operates to reassure the first and to deter the second, and that probability increases with the transparency of the treaty regime. Deterrence succeeds if discovery entails penalties that increase the costs of defection enough to exceed the expected gains. Penalties can involve loss of the anticipated benefits of the regime. Even when direct retaliation seems unlikely, exposure alone can cause behavior to change.

. . .

In a multilateral setting, the delinquent may suffer more diffuse negative reactions from states and other groups with a stake in the treaty regime. Some of the country studies demonstrate that even fear of negative reputational impacts and diffuse reciprocity may be adequate to deter (Charny 1990; Keohane 1986).

Assembling the Database

Creating a successful transparent information system crucially depends on the types of behavior the treaty seeks to regulate, the way the treaty defines those behaviors, and the available means for identifying whether a proscribed action has occurred.

The framing of the treaty's rules has at least three implications for regime transparency. First, it determines the number of actors whose behavior must be verified. For example, treaties regulating habitat destruction seek to restrain relatively large numbers of actors whose behaviors face little if any regulation, whereas those regulating chlorofluorocarbon (CFC) manufacturing need monitor only a few chemical plants that already face considerable regulation of their activities for other reasons. Second, information regarding certain actors that is already available through other regulatory infrastructures reinforces and facilitates transparency. The International Labor Organization's (ILO) Committee of Experts uses a variety of existing informational sources to identify violations of the many conventions it administers. Third, the type and level of standards must match the capacities of existing monitoring technologies. Transparency regarding compliance increased dramatically in treaties regulating intentional oil pollution when rules limiting discharges at sea were replaced with rules requiring installation of specific equipment to prevent such discharges (Mitchell 1994).

Once the rules are established, transparency requires developing data on the behavior of the parties with respect to the principal treaty norms. Independent data collection by a central organization is rare, and most regulatory treaties contain provisions for some kind of voluntary reporting by the parties, exchange of information, or joint research and data collection (Ausubel and Victor 1992; Chayes and Chayes 1995). Indeed, establishing a database is often the primary initial objective of a framework-type agreement.

Self-reporting

Self-reporting on measures taken to implement the treaty is often central to efforts to create a transparent information system and assure compliance. Examples of requirements for self-reporting are ubiquitous in international regimes of all stripes, from early agreements on slavery to almost all recent environmental accords. However, such requirements do not equate with actual reporting (General Accounting Office 1992; Mitchell 1994). . . .

The principal problems with respect to self-reporting seem to be less the deliberate flouting of reporting requirements than limitations of capacity and of the bureaucratic setting in which reports are generated. . . .

Why would a state report information that shows it to be out of compliance? We assume that countries usually prepare reports to represent the facts as known, although some nations face difficulties in collecting and analyzing complete and accurate data sets. For most functional agreements, middle- or lower-level officials within relevant ministries prepare reports that are reviewed by officials concerned about their international "audience." This bureaucratic setting provides some insulation against deliberate misreporting. Day-to-day policy-making and administration require reliable statistical data. Indeed, nations often report to international secretariats only data that they already collect for other reasons. This circumstance undoubtedly means that much information frequently remains unreported, but it also makes it somewhat more difficult to "cook the books."

On the other hand, incentives exist to make performance look good. The Soviet Union systematically exceeded international quotas on important whale species, and deliberately misreported kills to the International Whaling Commission. In more open societies, bureaucrats will generally face more checks, and even direct challenges to the accuracy and completeness of their reports. . . .

Independent Reporting and Verification

Although environmental treaties usually require only national self-reporting, ways of skirting the "self-incrimination" problems inherent in such systems are increasingly being recognized and put to use. Agreements regulating trade in coffee, endangered species, and weapons require both the exporting and the importing party to report on each transaction (Chayes and Chayes 1994; Trexler 1989). . . . Environmental NGOs have made it their business to collect information on treaty related behavior and to sponsor scientific measurements of atmospheric conditions, ozone depletion, and species populations, thus providing information independent from that provided by their governments.

The Commission on Sustainable Development explicitly created a legitimate channel for NGOs to provide reports to secretariats in order to facilitate evaluation of compliance and noncompliance. Even industry may provide independent information on compliance. The International Chamber of Shipping, a private consortium of shipping companies, has regularly identified ports that have not provided reception facilities as required by MARPOL, and much CFC production information is provided directly by industry (Mitchell 1994).

The availability of other sources for the same data sometimes facilitates verification of national data. Data from one country can be compared with those from other countries and validated against information available on highly correlated independent statistics. The LRTAP Secretariat develops, and to an extent verifies, emissions reports by comparing them with fuel consumption statistics converted into sulfur emission estimates (Levy 1993). A similar procedure may prove useful for verifying parts of the Framework Convention on Climate Change. Scientific monitoring devices are available and of increasing utility in measuring emissions both directly and indirectly (Ausubel and Victor 1992).

Finally, a secretariat can provide independent verification by direct inquiries. . . .

The 1971 Convention on Wetlands of International Importance (Ramsar Convention) established on-site monitoring procedures that have been used dozens of times to verify noncompliance and assist countries in identifying strategies to encourage compliance (Ramsar Convention Bureau 1990).

Analysis, Evaluation, and Dissemination

Collected data contribute to compliance management only if the regime provides analysis, evaluation, interpretation, and dissemination of the information acquired. Some regimes make extensive use of the data they collect.... The Convention on International Trade in Endangered Species (CITES) makes extensive use of the reports of TRAFFIC, an NGO, to attempt to identify trends in wildlife trade.

However, several factors inhibit secretariats' analysis of the data available to them. First, they lack resources. . . .

Second, the secretariat may lack the incentives to conduct certain types of analyses, and may even be directed by member states not to do so. For example, although the European marine enforcement regime requires each state to inspect 25 percent of the ships entering its ports, the annual reports do not analyze inspections on a country-by-country basis because of a desire by signatories to avoid being subject to "shaming" for failing to meet the requirements. Even when such analyses are conducted, they may not be disseminated beyond the governments of the member states because of diplomatic deference and each party's willingness not to publicize another's noncompliance in exchange for not having its own noncompliance identified.

A Managerial Model of Compliance

Most regulatory regimes should be regarded as instruments to manage an issue area over time, rather than as sets of prohibitory rules. Just as private companies and public bureaucracies commonly produce and review information about past performance in order to measure and manage their own progress, so creating transparency in international treaties generates information for assessing compliance of individual parties as well as evaluating overall regime effectiveness.

Essentially, the tasks of managing compliance are threefold:

1. Reviewing and assessing the performance of the parties in order to identify problems with the regime itself and to distinguish intentional violations from other types of noncompliance.
2. Ensuring that appropriate responses to noncompliance and violations produce and maintain a level of compliance "acceptable" to the regime parties.
3. Adjusting the rules to improve regime performance.

As in other managerial settings, the approach is not primarily accusatory or adversarial. In fact, regime management frequently starts with education and building a public constituency and awareness. Although effective regime management requires distinguishing willful violation from unintentional noncompliance, the process starts with the assumption that all regime members are engaged in a common enterprise. Initially, assessments seek to discover how to improve individual and system performance. Secretariats and other parties give states ample — sometimes, it seems, excessive — opportunities to explain and justify their conduct. Technical or financial assistance may be provided. Promises of improvement contain increasingly concrete, detailed, and measurable undertakings. If resistance persists, however, states and the secretariat may take more confrontational stances and intensify pressures for compliance. This process creates pressures to correct suspect conduct attributable to inadvertence, misunderstanding, or inattention while identifying, exposing, and isolating deliberate offenders.

Regime management usually involves three different levels of treaty evaluation. The first, review and assessment, evaluates each member state's performance and seeks to improve it while holding the regime rules relatively constant. The second, dispute resolution and interpretation, helps to clarify those areas of regulation and behavior that, at least initially, pose ambiguities. The third, adaptation and revision, entails the less frequent reappraisal of whether alternative rules would prove more effective at inducing compliance and achieving treaty goals.

. . .

Capacity-Building

As traditionally conceived, treaties govern the actions of states. Treaty compliance involves making state behavior conform with treaty rules. However, environmental treaties also seek to change the actions of private actors. The problem of incapacity presents itself at several steps in such a compliance process. (On the importance of capacity-building in improving environmental treaty effectiveness, see Levy, Keohane, and Haas 1993.) First, compliance may require a state to enact legislation regulating the conduct of its corporate and individual citizens in accordance with the stipulations of the treaty. That capability may be deficient in some states, particularly those in transition to democracy. Technical assistance and advice from other states can help to develop workable and appropriate legislation, as shown in experience with the ILO, IMF, and CITES agreements (International Labor Conference 1982; Strange 1974). (The International Union for the Conservation of Nature's Environmental Law Center in Bonn, Germany, catalogs existing legislation and promotes the adoption of model legislation for CITES. [Burhenne-Guilmin 1992].)

The next step is harder. The state must mobilize an effective administrative and political effort to translate the legislation on the books into the reality of changing the behavior of private parties in accordance with treaty norms. Environmenral treaties implicate the capacity of the state to govern — to enforce its own rules in significant ways. . . .

Economic instruments, such as taxes and charges, will place new strains on existing infrastructures. Tax collection requires public discipline and a well-functioning bureaucracy. Despite the widely touted efficiency of taxes as a regulatory instrument, economists cannot accurately forecast the exact magnitude of behavioral response to a tax, a situation creating the possibility that a well-planned tax may fail to achieve an emissions target (Epstein and Gupta 1990).

Similarly, compliance with CITES requires customs officers to make fine distinctions among species while simultaneously preventing imports of drugs and other contraband, and moving legitimate shipments rapidly through the customs process. Even customs officials in countries strongly committed to CITES, like the United States, may lack the necessary abilities and training.

In developing countries, the problem of enforcement capacity is often particularly acute. Inadequacies may exist in the administrative structures, available man power, procedures for statistical record-keeping, the priority given to enforcement, and financial resources. . . .

Environmental treaties increasingly make assistance conditional on improving compliance. The Montreal Protocol multilateral fund, the Climate Fund of the Framework Convention on Climate Change, and the Global Environmental Facility proceed on the premise that developing countries need technical and financial assistance to facilitate compliance. All these mechanisms are designed to finance the "incremental costs" of compliance, including not only operating projects but also education, training of national enforcement officials, improvement of scientific facilities, assistance to plannig departments, enhancement of data systems, and the like.

. . .

Finally, the capacity to elicit compliance from domestic actors depends on the nature of treaty rules. Revising treaty rules to match existing monitoring and enforcement capabilities can sometimes prove to be the easiest and cheapest means of "increasing" capacity. MARPOL's discharge requirements proved difficult to enforce because, although aerial observation could detect oil slicks that violated treaty provisions, authorities often could not make the links to particular ships that are necessary for prosecution. Later agreement to require construction of tankers with separate tanks for oil and water ballast allowed much easier verification of compliance through inspection in port. The easing of the enforcement burden has boosted compliance to figures approaching 100 percent (Mitchell 1994).

. . .

Dispute Resolution and Interpretation

Many analysts regard dispute settlement as a side track to, rather than an integral part of, a compliance strategy. But, as we have stated, treaties, like most other legal instruments, are rarely self-defining. When differences over meaning arise in the concrete circumstances of a particular case, whether or not they take the form of a "legal dispute," their resolution serves a dual function. It clarifies the meaning of the norm for all parties, and specifies the performance required of the disputants in the particular circumstances.

As in all legal systems, parties settle most treaty disputes by negotiation without recourse to available formal processes. The question is, What happens when negotiation fails? The United Nations Charter rehearses a familiar sequence of settlement methods: negotiation, inquiry, mediation, conciliation, arbitration, and judicial settlement. Yet the Charter does not require states to invoke any of these, apart from a generalized obligation of peaceful settlement. International lawyers make claims for the value of binding adjudication, either in the International Court of Justice or through a specialized tribunal or arbitral panel. Despite their alleged virtues, the Court and binding arbitration have played a minor role in treaty compliance to date, and seem unlikely to do more in the future. Besides being costly, contentious, cumbersome, and slow — the usual defects of litigation — they have the additional unattractive features of raising the political visibility of the problem and failing to be subject to party control.

Most treaty regimes turn to a variety of relatively informal meditative processes if the disputants cannot resolve the issues themselves. . . .

Conclusion: Toward an Active Integrated Management Strategy

. . .

These approaches merge in a process of "jawboning" — an effort to persuade a state to change its ways that is the characteristic form for eliciting international compliance. Jawboning exploits the de facto necessity for alleged violators to explain and justify suspect conduct. These justifications are evaluated in many forums, both public and private, formal and informal, domestic and international. This process distinguishes justifiable or inadvertent noncompliance — those instances that comport with a good-faith compliance standard — from those relatively rare cases of willful violation. Most compliance problems yield to this process. For those that do not, the process confronts the offending state with the stark choice between conforming to the rule as defined and applied in the particular case, or openly and explicitly flouting its obligation. The discomfort of such a position proves sufficient in most circumstances to get the transgressor to bring its behavior in line with its obligations.

NOTES AND QUESTIONS ON COMPLIANCE AND ENFORCEMENT

1. *Who complies?* Who must comply with international environmental law? Only states? Or private actors as well? See THE IMPLEMENTATION AND EFFECTIVENESS OF INTERNATIONAL ENVIRONMENTAL COMMITMENTS: THEORY AND PRACTICE 5–6 (DAVID G. VICTOR, KAL RAUSTIALA AND EUGENE B. SKOLNIKOFF eds., 1998) (discussing the implementation process and noting that treaties ultimately aim to influence the behavior of "targets," those who cause the environmental problem giving rise to a treaty).

2. *Who enforces?* Who should enforce international environmental law and why? Individual states? Non-governmental organizations? Judicial panels? International bodies?

3. *Sanctions.* The excerpt above describes a managerial compliance model, and expresses some doubt about the utility of sanctions in the international context. What sorts of sanctions could one employ? How would they be enforced? Will they work?

The authors' statement that only two treaties (neither environmental) authorize "concerted military or economic measures" must be read narrowly to be accurate. The Montreal Protocol on Substances that Deplete the Ozone Layer, 26 I.L.M. 1541 (1987), prohibits importing of ozone-depleting substances from countries not complying with the treaty. Similarly, CITES, *supra*, bans imports of endangered species and their parts. This raises the question of the extent to which international environmental law should rely upon limitations of trade as an enforcement technique.

Countries have often employed trade sanctions unilaterally to encourage development of international standards or compliance with existing international standards. *See* Steve Charnovitz, *Environmental Trade Sanctions and the GATT: An Analysis of the Pelly Amendments on Foreign Environmental Practices*, 9 Am. U. J. Int'l L. & Pol'y, 751, 772-75 (1994) (evaluating the effectiveness of U.S. law prohibiting importation of fish caught in violation of international fishing quotas); Steve Charnovitz, *Free Trade, Fair Trade, Green Trade: Defogging the Debate*, 27 Cornell Int'l L. J. 459, 493 (1994) (noting that trade sanctions frequently precede the creation of many international environmental regimes). *See, e.g.*, David M. Driesen, *The Congressional Role in International Environmental Law and its Implications for Statutory Interpretation*, 19 B.C. Envtl. Aff. L. Rev. 287, 303–05 (1991) (discussing the role of threats of unilateral action in encouraging development of pollution standards for ships); Japan Whaling Ass'n v. American Cetacean Soc'y, 478 U.S. 221, 225 (1986) (stating that each threat of sanctions for violations of fishery agreements secured compliance commitments from offending countries).

4. *Jawboning.* The authors of this excerpt support the managerial model of enforcement, which has proven quite prevalent in international environmental law. Some commentators, however, have expressed some dismay about compliance with international environmental law. *See, e.g.*, David A. Wirth, *The International Trade Regime and the Municipal Law of Federal States: How Close a Fit?*, 49 Wash. & Lee L. Rev. 1389, 1391 (1992) (stating that the current international law system "invites the proliferation of holdouts, free-riders, laggards, scofflaws, and defectors"). Yet, devising practical alternatives to the managerial model poses challenges.

The editors of the book from which the excerpt above comes detect a general trend toward strengthened treaty compliance, but note that in some cases compliance was weak and had declined. Weiss & Jacobson, *supra*, at 512. Victor and Raustiala find that almost all countries comply with almost all of their binding international commitments. Victor, Raustalia, & Skolnikoff, *supra*, at 661. But they note that compliance is often difficult and that countries often negotiate weak treaties to avoid compliance difficulties. *Id.* at 662.

D. TRADE AND THE ENVIRONMENT

Trade sanctions raise issues under international trade law. The World Trade Organization (WTO) now administers several global trade agreements, including the General Agreement on Tariffs and Trade (GATT), 55 U.N.T.S. 194 (1947). These agreements generally obligate members to comply with various "trade disciplines" that prohibit, among other things, discriminating against the exports of WTO members and quantitatively limiting imports from WTO member states. These agreements, however, include defenses that permit transgression of the trade disciplines under some circumstances to advance non-trade-related values.

The members of the WTO have agreed to binding adjudication of disputes arising under GATT and other trade agreements. Some disputes have arisen under WTO-administered free trade agreements when countries have unilaterally restricted imports as a means of enforcing domestic laws protecting public health or of persuading other countries to solve international environmental problems. Is it appropriate for trade panels to decide disputes about the legality of environmental measures? *See* David M. Driesen, *What is Free Trade?: The Real Issue Lurking Behind the Trade and Environment Debate*, 41 Va. J. Int'l L. 279, 313-329 (2001) (questioning the legitimacy of WTO decision-making under a broad understanding of free trade). If not, who should decide these issues? *See* Lakshman D. Guruswamy, *Should UNCLOS or GATT/WTO Decide Trade and Environment Disputes?*, 7 Minn. J. Global Trade 287 (1998); Jeffrey L. Dunoff, *Institutional Misfits: The GATT, the ICJ & Trade-Environment Disputes*, 15 Mich. J. Int'l L. 1043 (1994).

The Tuna/Dolphin case below addressed an allegation that a United States effort to use trade restrictions on tuna imports to get other countries to fish for tuna in a way that would not harm dolphins violated GATT. Notice what the language of GATT says and how the trade panel interprets the agreement in resolving this case. Consider the issue of whether the WTO should decide trade disputes involving environmental measures in the context of this case, which created a furor:

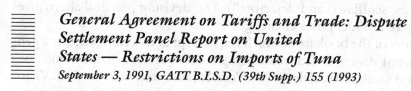

General Agreement on Tariffs and Trade: Dispute Settlement Panel Report on United States — Restrictions on Imports of Tuna
September 3, 1991, GATT B.I.S.D. (39th Supp.) 155 (1993)

[The Panel Report has not yet been adopted; on November 29, 1991, the Report was derestricted at the joint request of Mexico and the United States.]

2. Fatual Aspects

Purse-seine fishing of tuna

2.1   The last three decades have seen the deployment of tuna fishing technology based on the "purse-seine" net in many areas of the world. A fishing vessel using this technique locates a school of fish and sends out a motorboat (a "seine skiff") to hold one end of the purse-seine net. The vessel motors around the perimeter of the school of fish, unfurling the net and encircling the fish, and the seine skiff then attaches its end of the net to the fishing vessel. The fishing vessel then purses the net by winching in a cable at the bottom edge of the net, and draws in the top cables of the net to gather its entire contents.

2.2   Studies monitoring direct and indirect catch levels have shown that fish and dolphins are found together in a number of areas around the world and that this may lead to incidental taking of dolphins during fishing operations. . . . When dolphins and tuna together have been surrounded by purse-seine nets, it is possible to reduce or eliminate the catch of dolphins through using certain procedures.

. . .

2.3   The Marine Mammal Protection Act of 1972, as revised (MMPA) requires a general prohibition of "taking" (harassment, hunting, capture, killing or attempt thereof) and importation into the United States of marine mammals, except where an exception is explicitly authorized. Its stated goal is that the incidental kill or serious injury of marine mammals in the course of commercial fishing be reduced to insignificant levels approaching zero. . . .

2.5   Section 101(a)(2) of the MMPA . . . states that "The Secretary of Treasury shall ban the importation of commercial fish or products from fish which have been caught with commercial fishing technology which results in the incidental kill or incidental serious injury of ocean mammals in excess of United States standards."

. . .

2.7   On 28 August 1990, the United States Government imposed an embargo, pursuant to a court order, on imports of commercial yellowfin tuna and yellowfin tuna products harvested with purse-seine nets in the [Eastern Tropical Pacific Ocean] ETP until the Secretary of Commerce made positive findings based on documentary evidence of compliance with the MMPA standards. . . .

5.   Findings. . . .

B.   Prohibition of Imports of Certain Yellowfin Tuna and Certain Yellowfin Tuna Products from Mexico. . . .

Categorization as Internal Regulations (Article III) or Quantitative Restrictions (Article XI)

5.8   The Panel noted that Mexico had argued that the measures prohibiting imports of certain yellowfin tuna and yellowfin tuna products from Mexico imposed by the United States were quantitative restrictions on importation under Article XI, while the United States had argued that these measures were internal regulations enforced at the time or point of importation under Article III:4 and the Note Ad Article III, namely that the prohibition of imports of tuna and tuna products from Mexico constituted an enforcement of the regulations of the MMPA relating to the harvesting of domestic tuna.

5.9   The Panel examined the distinction between quantitative restrictions on importation and internal measures applied at the time or point of importation, and noted the following. While restrictions on importation are prohibited by Article XI:1, contracting parties are permitted by Article III:4 and the Note Ad Article III to impose an internal regulation on products imported from other contracting parties provided that it: does not discriminate between products of other countries in violation of the most-favoured-nation principle of Article I:1; is not applied so as to afford protection to domestic production, in violation of the national treatment principle of Article III:1; and accords to imported products treatment no less favourable than that accorded to like products of national origin, consistent with Article III:4. The relevant text of Article III:4 provides:

> "The products of the territory of any contracting party imported into the territory of any other contracting party shall be accorded treatment no less favourable than that accorded to like products of national origin in respect of all laws, regulations and requirements affecting their internal sale, offering for sale, purchase, transportation, distribution or use."

> The Note Ad Article III provides that:

> "Any internal tax or other internal charge, or any law, regulation or requirement of the kind referred to in [Article III:1] which applies to an imported product and the like domestic product and is collected or enforced in the case of the imported product at the time or point of importation, is nevertheless to be regarded as an internal tax or other internal charge, or a law, regulation or requirement of the kind referred to in [Article III:1], and is accordingly subject to the provisions of Article III."

5.10   The Panel noted that the United States had claimed that the direct import embargo on certain yellowfin tuna and certain yellowfin tuna products of Mexico constituted an enforcement at the time or point of importation of the requirements of the MMPA that yellowfin tuna in the ETP be harvested with fishing techniques designed to reduce the incidental taking of dolphins. The MMPA did not regulate tuna products as such, and in particular did not regulate the sale of tuna or tuna products. Nor did it prescribe fishing techniques that could have an effect on tuna as a product. This raised in the Panel's view the question of whether the tuna harvesting regulations could be regarded as a measure that "applies to" imported and domestic tuna within the meaning of the Note Ad Article III and consequently as a measure which the United States could enforce consistently with that Note in the case of imported tuna at the time or point of importation. The Panel examined this question in detail and found the following.

5.11 The text of Article III:1 refers to the application to imported or domestic products of "laws, regulations and requirements affecting the internal sale . . . of *products*" and "internal quantitative regulations requiring the mixture, processing or use of *products*"; it sets forth the principle that such regulations on *products* not be applied so as to afford protection to domestic production. Article III:4 refers solely to laws, regulations and requirements affecting the internal sale, etc. of *products*. This suggests that Article III covers only measures affecting products as such. . . .

5.14 The Panel concluded . . . that the Note Ad Article III covers only those measures that are applied to the product as such. The Panel noted that the MMPA regulates the domestic harvesting of yellowfin tuna to reduce the incidental taking of dolphin, but that these regulations could not be regarded as being applied to tuna products as such because they would not directly regulate the sale of tuna and could not possibly affect tuna as a product. Therefore, the Panel found that the import prohibition on certain yellowfin tuna and certain yellowfin tuna products of Mexico and the provisions of the MMPA under which it is imposed did not constitute internal regulations covered by the Note Ad Article III.

5.15 The Panel further concluded that, even if the provisions of the MMPA enforcing the tuna harvesting regulations (in particular those providing for the seizure of cargo as a penalty for violation of the Act) were regarded as regulating the sale of tuna as a product, the United States import prohibition would not meet the requirements of Article III. . . . Article III:4 calls for a comparison of the treatment of imported tuna as a *product* with that of domestic tuna as a *product*. Regulations governing the taking of dolphins incidental to the taking of tuna could not possibly affect tuna as a product. Article III:4 therefore obliges the United States to accord treatment to Mexican tuna no less favourable than that accorded to United States tuna, whether or not the incidental taking of dolphins by Mexican vessels corresponds to that of United States vessels. . . .

Articles XI and XIII

1. The Panel noted that under the General Agreement, quantitative restrictions on imports are forbidden by Article XI:1, the relevant part of which reads:

> "No prohibitions or restrictions . . . whether made effective through quotas, import or export licenses or other measures, shall be instituted or maintained by any contracting party on the importation of any product of the territory of any other contracting party . . . ."

The Panel therefore found that the direct import prohibition on certain yellowfin tuna and certain yellowfin tuna products from Mexico and the provisions of the MMPA under which it is imposed were inconsistent with Article XI:1. The United States did not present to the Panel any arguments to support a different legal conclusion regarding Article XI. . . .

Article XX

General. . . .

5.23 The Panel proceeded to examine whether Article XX(b) or Article XX(g) could justify the MMPA provisions on imports of certain yellowfin tuna and yellowfin tuna products, and the import ban imposed under these provisions. The Panel noted that Article XX provides that:

> "Subject to the requirement that such measures are not applied in a manner which would constitute a means of arbitrary or unjustifiable discrimination between countries where the same conditions prevail, or a disguised restriction on international trade, nothing in this Agreement shall be construed to prevent the adoption or enforcement by any contracting party of measures . . .
> (b) necessary to protect human, animal or plant life or health; . . .
> (g) relating to the conservation of exhaustible natural resources if such measures are made effective in conjunction with restrictions on domestic production or consumption; . . . ."

Article XX(b)

5.25 The Panel noted that the basic question raised by these arguments, namely whether Article XX(b) covers measures necessary to protect human, animal or plant life or health outside the jurisdiction of the contracting party taking the measure, is not clearly answered by the text of that provision. It refers to life and health protection generally without expressly limiting that protection to the jurisdiction of the contracting party concerned. The Panel therefore decided to analyze this issue in the light of the drafting history of Article XX(b), the purpose of this provision, and the consequences that the interpretations proposed by the parties would have for the operation of the General Agreement as a whole.

5.26   The Panel noted that the proposal for Article XX(b) dated from the Draft Charter of the International Trade Organization (ITO) proposed by the United States, which stated in Article 32, "Nothing in Chapter IV [on commercial policy] of this Charter shall be construed to prevent the adoption or enforcement by any Member of measures: . . . (b) necessary to protect human, animal or plant life or health". In the New York Draft of the ITO Charter, the preamble had been revised to read as it does at present, and exception (b) read: "For the purpose of protecting human, animal or plant life or health, if corresponding domestic safeguards under similar conditions exist in the importing country." This added proviso reflected concerns regarding the abuse of sanitary regulations by importing countries. Later, Commission A of the Second Session of the Preparatory Committee in Geneva agreed to drop this proviso as unnecessary. Thus, the record indicates that the concerns of the drafters of Article XX(b) focused on the use of sanitary measures to safeguard life or health of humans, animals or plants within the jurisdiction of the importing country.

5.27   The Panel further noted that Article XX(b) allows each contracting party to set its human, animal or plant life or health standards. The conditions set out in Article XX(b) which limit resort to this exception, namely that the measure taken must be "necessary" and not "constitute a means of arbitrary or unjustifiable discrimination or a disguised restriction on international trade", refer to the trade measure requiring justification under Article XX(b), not however to the life or health standard chosen by the contracting party. The Panel recalled the finding of a previous panel that this paragraph of Article XX was intended to allow contracting parties to impose trade restrictive measures inconsistent with the General Agreement to pursue overriding public policy goals to the extent that such inconsistencies were unavoidable. The Panel considered that if the broad interpretation of Article XX(b) suggested by the United States were accepted, each contracting party could unilaterally determine the life or health protection policies from which other contracting parties could not deviate without jeopardizing their rights under the General Agreement. The General Agreement would then no longer constitute a multilateral framework for trade among all contracting parties but would provide legal security only in respect of trade between a limited number of contracting parties with identical internal regulations.

5.28   The Panel considered that the United States' measures, even if Article XX(b) were interpreted to permit extrajurisdictional protection of life and health, would not meet the requirement of necessity set out in that provision. The United States had not demonstrated to the Panel — as required of the party invoking an Article XX exception — that it had exhausted all options reasonably available to it to pursue its dolphin protection objectives through measures consistent with the General Agreement, in particular through the negotiation of international cooperative arrangements, which would seem to be desirable in view of the fact that dolphins roam the waters of many states and the high seas. Moreover, even assuming that an import prohibition were the only resort reasonably available to the United States, the particular measure chosen by the United States could in the Panel's view not be considered to be necessary within the meaning of Article XX(b). The United States linked the maximum incidental dolphin taking rate which Mexico had to meet during a particular period in order to be able to export tuna to the United States to the taking rate actually recorded for United States fishermen during the same period. Consequently, the Mexican authorities could not know whether, at a given point of time, their policies conformed to the United States' dolphin protection standards. The Panel considered that a limitation on trade based on such unpredictable conditions could not be regarded as necessary to protect the health or life of dolphins.

5.29   On the basis of the above considerations, the Panel found that the United States' direct import prohibition imposed on certain yellowfin tuna and certain yellowfin tuna products of Mexico and the provisions of the MMPA under which it is imposed could not be justified under the exception in Article XX(b).

Article XX(g)

5.31   The Panel noted that Article XX(g) required that the measures relating to the conservation of exhaustible natural resources be taken "in conjunction with restrictions on domestic production or consumption." A previous panel had found that a measure could only be considered to have been taken "in conjunction with" production restrictions "if it was primarily aimed at rendering effective these restrictions." A country can effectively control the production or consumption of an exhaustible natural resource only to the extent that the production or consumption is under its jurisdiction. This suggests that Article XX(g) was intended to permit contracting parties to take trade measures primarily aimed at rendering effective restrictions on production or consumption within their jurisdiction.

5.32   The Panel further noted that Article XX(g) allows each contracting party to adopt its own conservation policies. The conditions set out in Article XX(g) which limit resort to this exception, namely that the measures taken must be related to the conservation of exhaustible natural resources, and that they not "constitute a means of arbitrary or unjustifiable discrimination . . . or a disguised restriction on international trade" refer to the trade measure requiring justification under Article XX(g), not however to the conservation policies adopted by the contracting party. The Panel considered that if the extrajurisdictional interpretation of Article XX(g) suggested by the United States were accepted, each contracting party could unilaterally determine the conservation policies from which other contracting parties could not deviate without jeopardizing their rights under the General Agreement. The considerations that led the Panel to reject an extrajurisdictional application of Article XX(b) therefore apply also to Article XX(g).

5.33 The Panel did not consider that the United States measures, even if Article XX(g) could be applied extrajurisdictionally, would meet the conditions set out in that provision. A previous panel found that a measure could be considered as "relating to the conservation of exhaustible natural resources" within the meaning of Article XX(g) only if it was primarily aimed at such conservation. The Panel recalled that the United States linked the maximum incidental dolphin-taking rate which Mexico had to meet during a particular period in order to be able to export tuna to the United States to the taking rate actually recorded for United States fishermen during the same period. Consequently, the Mexican authorities could not know whether, at a given point of time, their conservation policies conformed to the United States conservation standards. The Panel considered that a limitation on trade based on such unpredictable conditions could not be regarded as being primarily aimed at the conservation of dolphins.

5.34 On the basis of the above considerations, the Panel found that the United States direct import prohibition on certain yellowfin tuna and certain yellowfin tuna products of Mexico directly imported from Mexico, and the provisions of the MMPA under which it is imposed, could not be justified under Article XX(g). . . .

NOTES AND QUESTIONS ON *TUNA/DOLPHIN*

1. *Tuna/Dolphin II*. In a subsequent case reaffirming this holding, the United States argued that the trade panel should consider various international agreements authorizing trade restrictions to protect the environment in addressing the legality of the United States' application of the MMPA. The panel responded that its sole duty was to construe the GATT and found environmental treaties irrelevant to that task. GATT Dispute Settlement Panel Report on United States-Restrictions on the Imports of Tuna, July 1994, 33 I.L.M. 839, 892 (1994) (Tuna-Dolphin II). Is this appropriate? Or should differing

bodies of law be considered together? The Vienna Convention on the Law of Treaties provides that "any relevant rules of international law applicable in the relations between the parties" shall be taken into account in construing a treaty. If international environmental law should be considered along with GATT, should a trade panel adjudicate the case?

2. *Quantitative restrictions.* The panel characterizes the prohibition on importing tuna caught in purse-seine nets as a quantitative restriction on trade, rather than border enforcement of a product regulation. Since GATT generally prohibits quantitative restrictions on trade, this characterization places this work practice standard in jeopardy. In reaching this result, the Panel relied on a distinction between a product regulation under GATT Article III and the regulation of a production process. Had the GATT panel characterized this work practice standard as a non-discriminatory regulation of a product, it probably would have been upheld as not violating any trade discipline. Trade panels consist of trade experts. The trade panelists' background may have influenced their decision to treat the restriction on importing tuna caught with purse-seine nets as a quantitative restriction on trade, rather than as the enforcement of a product regulation at the border.

3. *Article XX.* The panel rejected a defense available under Article XX(b) for non-discriminatory measures "necessary to protect . . . animal . . . health." It construed this provision quite narrowly, rejecting the rights of parties to "unilaterally determine . . . life or health protection policies." It worried that a broad interpretation would undermine the multilateral trade regime.

A Note on Subsequent Trade and Environment Cases

Distress regarding Tuna/Dolphin I and II contributed to street demonstrations at a WTO meeting in Seattle. In the Shrimp/Turtle decision, a WTO panel held an import restriction aimed at protecting endangered sea turtles contrary to GATT. WTO Appellate Body Report on United States-Import Prohibition of Certain Shrimp and Shrimp Products, Oct. 12, 1998, 38 I.L.M. 118 (1999). This raised concerns about the validity of a regulation under the Marine Mammal Protection Act that precluded importation of shrimp, unless the shrimpers used a turtle excluder device to protect endangered sea turtles from entrapment. In the Shrimp/Turtle decision, however, the WTO recognized that a general prohibition against unilateral measures could eviscerate the Article XX defenses in GATT. This suggests recognition of the fact that enforcement of domestic environmental law might regularly require unilateral restrictions. For example, if the United States wants to clean up the air by requiring cleaner reformulations of gasoline, it must unilaterally limit imports of gasoline that does not comply with its standards in order to effectively enforce its regulation. The Panel's recognition of problems with a general prohibition of unilateral measures led it to rely more heavily on the perceived unfairness and rigidity of the U.S. approach, which generally imposed a blanket rule forbidding imports of shrimp caught without turtle excluder devices. Before Shrimp/Turtle, a WTO Panel struck down discriminatory enforcement measures in the Clean Air Act rule governing reformulated gasoline. WTO Appellate Body Report on United States — Standards for Reformulated and Conventional Gasoline, May 20, 1996, 35 I.L.M. 603 (1996).

A WTO panel also held a European ban on the sale of beef injected with growth hormones contrary to the Agreement on Sanitary and Phytosanitary Measures (SPS Agreement). WTO Appellate Body Report on E.C. — Measures Concerning Meat and Meat Products (Hormones), 1998 WL 25520 (Jan. 16 1998). This case interpreted the SPS Agreement as requiring a risk assessment and found that the European Community had not carried one out, in spite of the use of some scientific opinion in informing the EU decision. You may recall that qualitative risk assessment serves as a regulatory trigger in for many kinds of standard setting (recall the *Ethyl* case) and plays a role in U.S. effects-based standard setting as well. This decision's interpretation of the SPS agreement as potentially requiring rather robust risk assessment raised some concerns about trade panels interfering with science policy decisions, because often sufficient information for robust risk assessment is lacking. See Vern R. Walker, *Keeping the WTO from Becoming the "World Trans-science Organization": Scientific Uncertainty, Science Policy, and Fact-finding in the Growth Hormones Dispute*, 31 Cornell Int'l L. J. 251 (1998). *See generally* David A. Wirth, *The Role of Science in the Uruguay Round and NAFTA Trade Disciplines*, 27 Cornell Int'l L.J. 817 (1994). In particular, WTO panels have not employed the kind of deference to administrative science policy decisions that United States federal courts, and courts in many other countries, espouse.

More recently, a WTO panel, for the first time in the WTO's history, upheld an environmental measure, a ban on asbestos. WTO Dispute Settlement Panel Report on European Communities — Measures Affecting Asbestos and Asbestos-Containing Products, 2000 WL 1449942 (Sept. 18, 2000) (upholding European asbestos ban under Article XX).

Just as the WTO began to show signs of increasing acceptance of environmental measures, international panels arbitrating disputes under the North American Free Trade Agreement (NAFTA) began to articulate new legal principles providing a greater potential threat to environmental law than the WTO decisions. In the Metalclad case, a NAFTA panel held that a Mexican municipality's denial of a permit to dispose of hazardous waste constituted an expropriation in violation of NAFTA. This amounts to treating a permit denial, a regulatory decision, as a taking of private property. Under the United States Constitution and the constitutions of many countries, a government taking of private property requires compensation. Most countries, however, to do not consider permit denials or other regulatory decisions to constitute takings, requiring compensation only when the government actually takes land or other property away from an owner. The United States, however, has developed a regulatory takings doctrine that in some situations considers very restrictive regulatory decisions to constitute a taking if they go "too far." The Metalclad decision incorporated an expansive concept of regulatory takings into NAFTA and ultimately created a $15.6 million liability for the Mexican government. United Mexican States v. Metalclad Corp., 2001 British Columbia Supreme Court 664 (May 2, 2001). Even though neither United States nor Mexico have any regulatory takings doctrine, the NAFTA decision in Metalclad went far beyond even the most property protective conceptions of regulatory takings doctrine found in U.S. law. Vicki Been & Joel Beauvais, *The Global Fifth Amendment? NAFTA's Investment Protections and the Misguided Quest for an International "Regulatory Takings" Doctrine*, 78 N.Y.U. L. Rev. 30 (2003).

This existence of this expansive regulatory takings doctrine on the international level put quite a bit of pressure on governments. Ethyl Corporation filed an expropriation claim against Canada over its ban of MMT, a toxic gasoline additive containing manganese, seeking $250 million in damages. Canada withdrew its ban in response, paid $13 million in legal fees and damages, and issued a statement that "current scientific information did not demonstrate MMT's toxicity." Public Citizen, NAFTA's Threat to Sovereignty and Democracy: The Record of NAFTA Chapter 11 Investor-State Cases 1994–2005, at 21–22 (2005), available at http://www.citizen.org/documents/Chapter%2011%20Report%20Final.pdf. EPA and California had both previously banned this additive in spite of a paucity of direct information about MMT, because health data linked manganese (an ingredient of MMT) to neurological impairment.

In another case, S.D. Myers sought $20 million from Canada to cover lost profits during a 16-month Canadian ban on shipment of PCBs to the United States. The United States had long ago banned PCB production and importation, but had temporarily allowed for PCB's transport into the United States for disposal purposes. The NAFTA panel rejected S.D. Myers regulatory takings claim, but held that Canada had not afforded S.D. Myers "national treatment" as required by NAFTA, awarding $4.8 million in damages. Partial Award, in a NAFTA Arbitration under the UNCITRAL Arbitration Rules, S.D. Myers, Inc. v. Government of Canada, November 13, 2000. NAFTA's "national treatment" obligation requires that NAFTA members afford imports from other countries the same regulatory treatment that they offer domestic actors. Similar obligations exist in the GATT and other trade agreements.

In 2002, however, a NAFTA panel declined jurisdiction over a regulatory takings claim emanating from a California decision to ban MTBE, a gasoline additive that had contaminated California drinking water. Preliminary Award on Jurisdiction and Admissibility, In the Arbitration Under Chapter 11 of the North America Free Trade Agreement and the UNCITRAL Arbitration Rules Between Methanex Corporation and the United States of America, United Nations Commission on International Trade Law, Aug. 7, 2002. But NAFTA panels have adjudicated several claims of expropriation stemming from disputes arising under Mexican municipal waste management contracts with foreign companies in Metalclad's wake, with conflicting results. See International Centre for the Settlement of Investment Disputes: Tecnicas Medioambientales Tecmed S.A. v. United Mexican States (additional facility), 43 I.L.M. 133, 186 (2004) (awarding $5.5 million); International Centre for the Settlement of Investment Disputes: Waste Management, Inc. v. United Mexican States, 43 I.L.M. 967, 1003 (2004) (dismissing expropriation claim).

Companies have also filed NAFTA claims seeking recompense for a U.S. border closure to guard against the spread of mad cow disease, the impacts of California restrictions on mining conducted on federal land in California, and financial losses stemming from settlements of suits addressing the health impacts of cigarettes. Public Citizen, *supra*, at 48–58.

Is it appropriate for trade tribunals to decide regulatory takings claims under NAFTA? Only member countries can bring claims to the WTO. But private companies can bring NAFTA claims to a trade tribunal. Does this difference have any impact?

International environmental problems create extraordinary governance challenges. While trade and environment cases have raised concerns among environmental advocates, some scholars see in the WTO a potential model for improving environmental governance. *See* C. Ford Runge, *A Global Environmental Organization (GEO) and the World Trading System*, 35 J. World Trade 399 (2001); Daniel Esty, *The Value of Creating a Global Environmental Organization*, 6 Env't Matters 13 (2000). *See also* Daniel C. Esty and Maria H. Ivanova, *Revitalizing Global Environmental Goverance: A Function Drive Approach, in* GLOBAL ENVIRONMENTAL GOVERNANCE: OPTIONS AND OPPORTUNITIES 181 (DANIEL C. ESTY AND MARIA H. IVANOVA, eds. 2002); DAVID M. DRIESEN, THE ECONOMIC DYNAMICS OF ENVIRONMENTAL LAW 178–80 (2003) (proposing establishing a general legal rule, enforceable against private parties, requiring them to avoid contributing to unnecessary international environmental harms even in the absence of a treaty). While international environmental law uses problem-specific treaties for each new environmental problem, the WTO imposes a set of broad trade disciplines upon its members, which cover all kinds of products (and increasingly services). Can you envision any ways of redistributing authority to better address international environmental harms?

PFOA AND THE POPS TREATY

Suppose that evidence mounts that PFOA is entering the blood stream of people in many countries. The international community has adopted the Stockholm Convention on Persistent Organic Pollutants (POPs), 40 I.L.M. 532 (2001) (POPs Treaty). Persistent organic pollutants (POPs) are chemical substances that persist in the environment, bioaccumulate through the food web, and pose a risk of causing adverse effects to human health and the environment. The POPs treaty, which entered into force in 2004, provides for the elimination of nine POPs in Annex A, with specific exemptions for some kinds of uses. It also provides for the restriction of DDT, which is listed in Annex B. None of the Annexes triggering regulatory obligations under the POPs treaty, however, list PFOA. Suppose that you wish to use the POPs treaty to encourage reduction or elimination of PFOA. What decision-makers would you appeal to and what arguments would you make? What steps would have to occur for the POPs treaty to lead to any progress on reducing environmental risks from PFOA? Some of the POP's treaty's key provisions follow:

Article 1

Objective

Mindful of the precautionary approach as set forth in Principle 15 of the Rio Declaration on Environment and Developoment, the objective of the Convention is to protect human health and the environment from persistent organic pollutants. . . . .

Article 3

Measures to Reduce or Eliminate Releases from Intentional Production and Use

1. Each Party shall:

(a) Prohibit and/or take the legal and administrative measures necessary to eliminate:

(i) Its production and use of the chemicals listed in Annex A subject to the provisions of that Annex; and

(ii) Its import and export of the chemicals listed in Annex A in accordance with the provisions of paragraph 2; and

(b) Restrict its production and use of the chemicals listed in Annex B in accordance with the provisions of that Annex.

2. Each Party shall take measures to ensure:

(a) That a chemical listed in Annex A or Annex B is imported only:

(i) For the purpose of environmentally sound disposal as set forth in paragraph 1(d) of Article 6; or

(ii) For a use or purpose which is permitted for that Party under Annex A or Annex B; . . . .

4. Each Party that has one or more regulatory and assessment schemes for pesticides or industrial chemicals shall, where appropriate, take into consideration within these schemes the criteria in paragraph 1 of Annex D when conducting assessments of pesticides or industrial chemicals currently in use. . . .

Article 5

Measures to Reduce or Eliminate Releases from
Unintentional Production

Each Party shall at a minimum take the following measures to reduce the total releases derived from anthropogenic sources of each of the chemicals listed in Annex C, with the goal of their continuing minimization and, where feasible, ultimate elimination:

(a) Develop an action plan . . .

(b) Promote the application of available, feasible and practical measures that can expeditiously achieve a realistic and meaningful level of release reduction or source elimination;

(c) Promote the development and, where it deems appropriate, require the use of substitute or modified materials, products and processes to prevent the formation and release of the chemicals listed in Annex C . . . .

Article 8

Listing of Chemicals in Annexes A, B and C

1. A Party may submit a proposal to the Secretariat for listing a chemical in Annexes A, B and/or C. The proposal shall contain the information specified in Annex D. In developing a proposal, a Party may be assisted by other Parties and/or by the Secretariat.

2. The Secretariat shall verify whether the proposal contains the information specified in Annex D. If the Secretariat is satisfied that the proposal contains the information so specified, it shall forward the proposal to the Persistent Organic Pollutants Review Committee.

3. The Committee shall examine the proposal and apply the screening criteria specified in Annex D in a flexible and transparent way, taking all information provided into account in an integrative and balanced manner.

4. If the Committee decides that:

(a) It is satisfied that the screening criteria have been fulfilled, it shall, through the Secretariat, make the proposal and the evaluation of the Committee available to all Parties and observers and invite them to submit the information specified in Annex E; or

(b) It is not satisfied that the screening criteria have been fulfilled, it shall, through the Secretariat, inform all Parties and observers and make the proposal and the evaluation of the Committee available to all Parties and the proposal shall be set aside.

5. Any Party may resubmit a proposal to the Committee that has been set aside by the Committee pursuant to paragraph 4. The resubmission may include any concerns of the Party as well as a justification for additional consideration by the Committee. If, following this procedure, the Committee again sets the proposal aside, the Party may challenge the decision of the Committee and the Conference of the Parties shall consider the matter at its next session. The Conference of the Parties may decide, based on the

screening criteria in Annex D and taking into account the evaluation of the Committee and any additional information provided by any Party or observer, that the proposal should proceed.

6. Where the Committee has decided that the screening criteria have been fulfilled, or the Conference of the Parties has decided that the proposal should proceed, the Committee shall further review the proposal, taking into account any relevant additional information received, and shall prepare a draft risk profile in accordance with Annex E. It shall, through the Secretariat, make that draft available to all Parties and observers, collect technical comments from them and, taking those comments into account, complete the risk profile.

7. If, on the basis of the risk profile conducted in accordance with Annex E, the Committee decides:

(a) That the chemical is likely as a result of its long-range environmental transport to lead to significant adverse human health and/or environmental effects such that global action is warranted, the proposal shall proceed. Lack of full scientific certainty shall not prevent the proposal from proceeding. The Committee shall, through the Secretariat, invite information from all Parties and observers relating to the considerations specified in Annex F. It shall then prepare a risk management evaluation that includes an analysis of possible control measures for the chemical in accordance with that Annex; or

(b) That the proposal should not proceed, it shall, through the Secretariat, make the risk profile available to all Parties and observers and set the proposal aside.

8. For any proposal set aside pursuant to paragraph 7(b), a Party may request the Conference of the Parties to consider instructing the Committee to invite additional information from the proposing Party and other Parties during a period not to exceed one year. After that period and on the basis of any information received, the Committee shall reconsider the proposal pursuant to paragraph 6 with a priority to be decided by the Conference of the Parties. If, following this procedure, the Committee again sets the proposal aside, the Party may challenge the decision of the Committee and the Conference of the Parties shall consider the matter at its next session. The Conference of the Parties may decide, based on the risk profile prepared in accordance with Annex E and taking into account the evaluation of the Committee and any additional information provided by any Party or observer, that the proposal should proceed. If the Conference of the Parties decides that the proposal shall proceed, the Committee shall then prepare the risk management evaluation.

9. The Committee shall, based on the risk profile referred to in paragraph 6 and the risk management evaluation referred to in paragraph 7(a) or paragraph 8, recommend whether the chemical should be considered by the Conference of the Parties for listing in Annexes A, B and/or C. The Conference of the Parties, taking due account of the recommendations of the Committee, including any scientific uncertainty, shall decide, in a precautionary manner, whether to list the chemical, and specify its related control measures, in Annexes A, B and/or C.

Annex D

Information Requirements and Screening Criteria

1. A Party submitting a proposal to list a chemical in Annexes A, B and/or C shall identify the chemical in the manner described in subparagraph (a) and provide the information on the chemical, and its transformation products where relevant, relating to othe screening criteria set out in subparagraphs (b) to (e):

(a) Chemical identity:

(i) Names, including trade name or names, commercial name or names and synonyms, Chemical Abstracts Service (CAS) Registry number, International Union of Pure and Applied Chemistry (IUPAC) name; and

(ii) Structure, including specification of isomers, where applicable, and the structure of the chemical class;

(b) Persistence:

(i) Evidence that the half-life of the chemical in water is greater than two months, or that its half-life in soil is greater than six months, or that its half-life in sediment is greater than six months; or

(ii) Evidence that the chemical is otherwise sufficiently persistent to justify its consideration within the scope of this Convention;

(c) Bio-accumulation:

(i) Evidence that the bio-concentration factor or bio-accumulation factor in aquatic species for the chemical is greater than 5,000 or, in the absence of such data, that the log Kow is greater than 5;

(ii) Evidence that a chemical presents other reasons for concern, such as high bio-accumulation in other species, high toxicity or ecotoxicity; or

(iii) Monitoring data in biota indicating that the bio-accumulation potential of the chemical is sufficient to justify its consideration within the scope of this Convention;

(d) Potential for long-range environmental transport:

(i) Measured levels of the chemical in locations distant from the sources of its release that are of potential concern;

(ii) Monitoring data showing that long-range environmental transport of the chemical, with the potential for transfer to a receiving environment, may have occurred via air, water or migratory species; or

(iii) Environmental fate properties and/or model results that demonstrate that the chemical has a potential for long-range environmental transport through air, water or migratory species, with the potential for transfer to a receiving environment in locations distant from the sources of its release. For a chemical that migrates significantly through the air, its half-life in air should be greater than two days; and

(e) Adverse effects:

(i) Evidence of adverse effects to human health or to the environment that justifies consideration of the chemical within the scope of this Convention; or

(ii) Toxicity or ecotoxicity data that indicate the potential for damage to human health or to the environment.

2. The proposing Party shall provide a statement of the reasons for concern including, where possible, a comparison of toxicity or ecotoxicity data with detected or predicted levels of a chemical resulting or anticipated from its long-range environmental transport, and a short statement indicating the need for global control.

3. The proposing Party shall, to the extent possible and taking into account its capabilities, provide additional information to support the review of the proposal referred to in paragraph 6 of Article 8. In developing such a proposal, a Party may draw on technical expertise from any source.

If a country does succeed in getting a listing, ultimately the effectiveness of any measures to address PFOA will depend on national environmental enforcement. Indeed, international environmental law generally depends on effective national enforcement of national implementing legislation regulating private parties. We address the United States' approach to environmental enforcement in the next part.

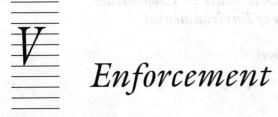

V

Enforcement

Standard-setting decisions appear in the Federal Register (or sometimes in statutes themselves) as mere pieces of paper. These papers only reduce pollution if polluters comply with the standards that government officials create. Accordingly, enforcement plays a critical role in government efforts to address environmental problems.

Chapter 15 discusses the problem of detecting violations by describing mechanisms to enable enforcers (and polluting companies) to discover violations. Chapter 16 provides an overview of government enforcement, focusing primarily upon policies governing the use of civil and criminal penalties. Chapter 17 focuses upon citizen enforcement.

Traditionally, environmental law has relied upon a deterrence model of enforcement, *i.e.*, on the idea that threats of substantial penalties should deter would-be-violators. Understanding that concept will prove crucial to making sense of the materials presented in this part. In recent years, however, government has placed increasing reliance on a model that relies more on cooperative relationships between government and the parties it regulates. As you learn the particulars of how environmental law is enforced, you should think about how it fits in with the deterrence model and about emerging critiques of that model. Accordingly, we provide below a presentation and critique of these models, which will serve as an introduction to these chapters on detection of violations, government enforcement, and citizen enforcement.

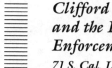

Clifford Rechtschaffen, Deterrence vs. Cooperation and the Evolving Theory of Environmental Enforcement

71 S. Cal. L. Rev. 1181 (1997-1998)

* * *

II. The Current System

The traditional practice of environmental enforcement is grounded in theory on a deterrence-based model of enforcement. It assumes that most regulated entities are rational economic actors that act to maximize profits. As such, decisions regarding compliance are based on self-interest. In short, businesses comply where the costs of noncompliance outweigh the benefits of noncompliance. The benefits of noncompliance consist of money saved by not purchasing pollution control equipment or taking other required measures. The costs of noncompliance include the costs of implementing control measures once a violation is detected, plus any additional penalties imposed for being found in violation, multiplied (discounted) by the probability that the violations will be detected. The task for enforcement agencies is to make penalties high enough and the probability of detection great enough that it becomes economically irrational for facilities to violate environmental requirements. The speed and the certainty with which sanctions are imposed are also important factors in obtaining compliance.

Deterrence may be achieved through civil or criminal sanctions. Criminal sanctions may be more appropriate where the amount of civil penalties needed to constitute an economic deterrent is unrealistic. Many also believe that the unique moral stigma and threat of jail time from criminal enforcement constitute the most powerful incentives to obey the law. But whether the penalty is civil or criminal, the essential inquiry turns on the same pleasure-pain calculus: Make the penalty sufficiently painful so that rational actors will be deterred despite the benefits of noncompliance. . . .

. . .

By contrast, a "compliance" or cooperative system emphasizes securing compliance rather than sanctioning wrongdoing. Penalties are seen as threats rather than sanctions, and sanctions are typically withdrawn if compliance is achieved. Levying penalties is seen as a mark of the system's failure (to otherwise obtain compliance); compliance systems rely far more on rewards and incentives than penalties. Enforcement is primarily prospective, oriented toward inducing conditions that lead to conformity. The system focuses more on the underlying conditions or violations than on the violator.

Deterrence-based enforcement is the prevailing societal approach for controlling unlawful individual and corporate conduct. This theory underlies the EPA's current enforcement system. The agency's enforcement approach is legalistic, and its extensive enforcement policies stress the use of formal enforcement actions. Since the mid-1980s, one of its guiding principles has been ensuring "timely and appropriate responses" to observed violations, which involves applying a series of escalating actions once noncompliance is detected. The agency has traditionally measured the success of its program by the number of inspections conducted, the number of enforcement actions initiated, and the number and size of penalties assessed — all indicators that some type of formal enforcement action has been taken. . . .

Although the theoretical underpinning of the current enforcement system relies largely on deterrence, in practice the process is much more flexible. Most enforcers use a hybrid strategy that includes elements of both coercion and cooperation; few rely on a strictly legalistic model. Most enforcement activity, particularly state enforcement, is aimed at bringing violators back into compliance rather than punishing or deterring. . . .

III. The Push for Reform. . . .

A. *Changed Corporate Attitudes and Practices*

One of the most vigorously asserted arguments is that the current enforcement system is based on an outdated model of corporate attitudes and behavior. The argument has several related components: (1) Most businesses try to comply with environmental laws because of a sense of social responsibility, and adherence to social and moral norms; (2) businesses are highly motivated to comply voluntarily because of external factors such as market forces, potential reputational harm, and third-party liability claims; and (3) many businesses have implemented sophisticated internal regulatory systems that parallel or exceed governmental requirements. As a result, a punitive enforcement approach is largely unnecessary. . . .

B. *The Complexity of Environmental Regulation*

Another motivation underlying current reform efforts is the complexity of environmental law. . . .

. . . One local prosecutor's guide candidly acknowledges that "[n]o facility of moderate complexity which handles hazardous materials or wastes . . . can be expected to be in full compliance at all times." Likewise, a survey of general corporate counsel at major firms found that two-thirds believed their businesses had operated, at least some time in the prior year, in violation of environmental laws. Nearly seventy percent indicated that they did not believe absolute compliance was achievable because of the law's complexity, varying interpretations by regulators, the role of human error, and cost considerations. Numerous other observers have likewise noted the difficulty of maintaining perfect, continuous compliance with all environmental rules. Small businesses face particularly great challenges in dealing with complicated environmental regulations. . . .

The complexity of environmental law suggests a number of things. It points out the need for agencies to spend considerably more resources on education and compliance promotion, particularly with smaller businesses. It highlights the need for agencies to be flexible and pragmatic in their enforcement of many requirements, which is how most environmental agencies operate in practice. It also indicates the need to re-examine the very liberal *mens rea* requirements of criminal environmental statutes. . . . But the law's complexity is not a justification for a wholesale dismantling of the enforcement system. . . .

C. *The Deterrence-Is-Counterproductive Argument*

Critics charge that a cooperative approach to enforcement is the best way to achieve compliance and that sanction-oriented enforcement is counterproductive. The basic argument proceeds from the assumption that corporations have a generalized commitment to abiding by the law. Under this mind-set, persuasion works better than punishment; essentially, carrots are superior to sticks. . . .

On the other hand, a host of studies, most notably a series of reports by the General Accounting Office and EPA's Inspector General, demonstrate considerable levels of noncompliance by regulated entities. In one recent report, for instance, the GAO found that one in six major facilities was in "significant noncompliance" of the discharge limits in their NPDES permits, and that the actual number could be twice as high. Moreover, during fiscal year 1994, fifty percent of major dischargers violated their permits at some time during the year (including both lesser infractions and significant violations). Other observers have reached similar conclusions. These latter studies do not tell us, however, whether noncompliance resulted from flaws in the deterrence-based model, or, as others argue, from a *lack of* meaningful deterrence-based enforcement.

The limited empirical data actually comparing deterrence and cooperative-oriented strategies is mixed. . . .

D. *The Inefficiency Argument Against Deterrence*

. . . Many critics note that government agencies lack the resources necessary to enforce environmental law according to the traditional model. The traditional model requires agencies to monitor and detect violations, inspect facilities, and timely and appropriately respond to each observed violation. Responses range from informal warnings to civil or administrative penalty actions. This is a highly resource-intensive approach. By contrast, a system that places greater reliance on self-policing and self-enforcement would allow a government to concentrate its limited resources on the most serious instances of noncompliance. It would also allow increased government spending on outreach and education efforts that commentators suggest can reach a larger audience and educate regulated entities at a lower cost to enforcement agencies. . . .

A cooperative approach, however, may or may not save agencies money, depending on its structure. Agencies will be spared some of the costs of monitoring, detecting, and proving violations, which will shift to private corporations. On the other hand, agencies will have to devote considerably more resources to providing technical advice and cooperative assistance to regulated facilities. In addition, the government oversight of regulated firms in a cooperative scheme may be just as costly as the traditional inspection model it is replacing. For example, inspectors in Cal/OSHA's Cooperative Compliance Program stopped most routine compliance inspections and were assigned to assist the joint labor-management safety committee in improving safety at construction sites. This new role for OSHA staff was expensive as inspectors spent up to ten times more time inspecting these sites than they did at other facilities. Likewise, as the General Accounting Office recently reported, measuring the results of cooperative enforcement strategies can be quite expensive. . . .

IV.   The Benefits of Deterrence-Based Enforcement

While the rush to dismantle traditional environmental enforcement may seem a welcome shift in some sectors, a heavy axe approach is short-sighted and detrimental to the country's long-term interest in effective environmental enforcement. A deterrence-based system contains many positive attributes that are essential to an effective system of enforcement. . . .

A.   The Expressive Function of Environmental Enforcement

Environmental regulation, like other areas of law, serves important expressive functions. . . .

. . . Deterrence-based enforcement, with its reliance on sanctions and enforcement orders, conveys a set of meanings about environmental violations that is very different from that communicated by a cooperative-oriented approach, with its emphasis on negotiation and conciliation. The message imparted by deterrence reaffirms for the public that environmental statutes are important and that transgressions are to be taken very seriously. This message is consistent with the public's expressed strong disapproval of noncompliance with environmental requirements — a desire evidenced by the harsh sweeping penalties for noncompliance and the potent enforcement tools contained in all of the major environmental statutes.

B. The Dangers of Agency Capture and Inconsistent Treatment

1. Agency Capture

A fundamental tenet of a cooperative-based system is that regulators work closely and in alliance with regulated facilities; they act more as educators and consultants than inspectors or punishers, seeking to solve problems jointly and bring facilities into compliance. While this approach can be highly beneficial, it raises an important countervailing concern: Regulators who become so cozy and closely identified with regulated entities will overlook important violations and bend over too far in the direction of lenient treatment. In short, the agency staff will be captured by those they are ostensibly regulating. . . .

2. Inconsistent Treatment

One of the most desired features of any enforcement system is consistency — similarly situated enterprises should be treated consistently. Such consistency is essential to ensuring the credibility of an enforcement program and widespread voluntary compliance. An oft-quoted and sagacious maxim of enforcement practice coined by Chester Bowles, a member of the 1941 wartime Office of Price Administration, holds that "20 percent of the regulated population will automatically comply with any regulation, 5 percent will attempt to evade it, and the remaining 75 percent will comply as long as they think that the 5 percent will be caught and punished." . . .

C. A Strong, Credible Threat of Enforcement

Environmental enforcement, like other areas of regulatory enforcement, is highly "leveraged." Because regulators lack the resources to systematically inspect and monitor every entity, their enforcement actions must provide a big bang for their buck. The actions must send a credible signal to other regulated entities that their noncompliance will also result in meaningful and certain penalties, including recovery of any economic gain realized from noncompliance. Without this general deterrent effect, widespread voluntary compliance is unlikely.

The perception of enforcement consequences is as important as the reality in achieving compliance. . . .

A fundamental problem with relying primarily on cooperative enforcement is that it threatens to significantly weaken the general deterrent effect of individual enforcement actions. Punitive enforcement may remain as a backstop for noncompliance, but it is likely to be used far less frequently, which regulated entities will understand. The public message will be that noncompliance is far more likely to be met with conciliation than sanctions, at least for most first-time violations. Experience has demonstrated that efforts to promote compliance are often ineffective alone. Moreover, having the opportunity to remedy noncompliance without the threat of penalty greatly reduces the incentive to comply. As one analyst explains:

> [I]t is now generally recognized that if the polluter expects no consequence from noncompliance (except having to meet with government officials to agree to do what was required in the first place), he has little incentive to undertake any costs of compliance before getting caught. This has proven to be true even when it is broadly understood that clean-up costs will increase substantially if violations are not corrected early and where actual cost savings from compliance activities has been realized.

Likewise, the General Accounting Office has concluded that penalties

> play a key role in environmental enforcement by deterring violators and by ensuring that regulated entities are treated fairly and consistently so that no one gains a competitive advantage. . . . [T]he Clean Water Act and other environmental statutes have been violated repeatedly when penalties have not been applied.

. . .

D. *A Strong System of Citizen Enforcement*

Currently, citizen enforcement is a feature in all the major federal environmental statutes. As a general matter, these statutes allow citizens to sue companies for violations when the government fails to do so and various, often strict, procedural conditions are met. Traditionally, Congress has viewed citizen enforcement as an important supplement to agency enforcement and an important prod to agency regulators. Congress therefore has repeatedly sought to strengthen it.

. . .

Citizen enforcement has played an extremely valuable role in achieving compliance with environmental law, including spurring EPA and state agency enforcement efforts. . . . Citizen action thus provides an important deterrent to noncompliance when government agencies fail to act either because of lack of resources or political will. . . .

V. How to Reform Environmental Enforcement

As discussed in Part III, the evidence is mixed about the best way to achieve compliance with environmental laws; it does not decidedly show the superiority of either deterrence or cooperative-oriented enforcement. Each approach has its strengths and weaknesses, and elements of both systems are desirable. . . .

A. Agencies Should Provide More Consultation and Cooperative Assistance

Enforcement agencies have always considered compliance promotion and education necessary to enforcement programs. Until recently, these efforts have often been overlooked and underfunded. One positive element in current reforms has been a push to expand cooperative assistance efforts significantly, particularly those directed at small businesses. . . .

B. Policies Automatically Precluding Sanctions and Eliminating Enforcement Discretion Are Undesirable

One very popular strand of current reform efforts seeks to preclude or greatly mitigate penalties for certain classes of violations or against small businesses. While in many circumstances this type of enforcement response is entirely appropriate, it is unwise public policy to negate agency discretion totally and mandate that sanctions are impermissible.

The most notable example of this type of initiative is the [Small Business Regulatory Enforcement Fairness Act] . . . , enacted by Congress in 1996. The statute requires federal agencies to develop policies that provide for the reduction *and waiver* of minor violations by small businesses in certain instances, such as when the violation is corrected within a reasonable period or is discovered in a compliance-assistance program. . . .

On the one hand, the notion of excusing first-time minor violations seems quite reasonable, particularly if limited in scope and tied to proactive measures by regulated facilities, such as requesting agency assistance or making good-faith efforts to comply. This allows agencies to devote their resources to serious cases and minimizes resentment by businesses when they are penalized for insignificant violations.

On the other hand, it is poor policy either to *mandate* that all minor violations be forgiven, or that they be forgiven simply because they are corrected. Such a policy is unnecessary since repeated empirical studies show that environmental requirements are enforced in a pragmatic way, with little likelihood of penalties being imposed rigidly or arbitrarily. More importantly, this approach removes *any* incentive for entities to comply before they are found in violation, since being caught has essentially no consequence other than perhaps a warning. . . . [T]his approach "often signals to the regulated community that it need not comply until enforcement begins." . . .

C. Greater Self-Regulation Should Be Encouraged to Supplement, Not Replace Enforcement

The environmental enforcement reforms advanced with the greatest vigor and currently attracting the most intense controversy concern internal environmental audits and environmental management systems. Businesses and other reformers aggressively have pushed to substitute these self-regulatory systems for traditional enforcement activities. Twenty-three states have adopted environmental audit privilege or immunity laws that provide qualified immunity from penalties for violations disclosed and corrected as a result of voluntary internal audits. Reformers propose to afford similar treatment to the self-policing efforts of management systems.

The expansion of internal regulatory systems is a positive development that should be encouraged. In fact, audits should be made mandatory for publicly traded corporations. Non-publicly traded firms that implement audits or management systems should receive enforcement benefits such as reduced penalties and inspections. But audit privilege and immunity laws, promoted by some businesses as a strategy to curtail government enforcement, should be resisted. These laws undermine incentives for preventative compliance measures and conceal important environmental information. More generally, self-policing systems should supplement, but not replace, traditional enforcement activities. . . .

[P]rivilege/immunity measures . . . seriously undermine the incentives for facilities to take preventative steps to achieve compliance. To varying degrees, they permit firms to sit back and wait until an audit is conducted before coming into compliance. . . . Second, privilege laws are highly objectionable because, as described above, they keep a category of public environmental information pertaining to the facility's compliance with environmental requirements secret and out of the public's reach. . . .

VI. Conclusion

The movement to transform environmental enforcement is being advanced with exceptional ardor. Before the old system is discarded however, it is critical for policymakers to engage in a careful and sober assessment of the calls for reform. If the system is flawed, will the proposed changes improve it? In particular, is there a sufficient basis on which to conclude that the new approaches will be superior to the ones being reformed?

The materials that follow will show how the deterrence-based model has influenced particular legal rules on enforcement, and present some information about the cooperative model reforms Professor Rechtschaffen mentions. As you read these materials, think about which model makes sense and what policy measures would best serve the goals of effective enforcement.

15

Detecting Violations: Permitting, Monitoring, Record-Keeping and Reporting

A. PERMITTING

Facilities that release a variety of pollutants may need to read and interpret numerous regulations and statutory provisions to understand their legal obligations. In order to make sure that each facility's operator knows and understands its legal obligations and to facilitate enforcement, the environmental statutes often require facility-specific permits. These permits are media-specific. Thus, a facility that releases pollution into both the air and water may need both an air and water permit. The air permit will collect the legal obligations restricting its air emissions and the water permit will collect the legal obligations limiting its effluent discharges. *Cf.* EPA Office of the Inspector General, *Substantial Changes Needed in Implementation and Oversight of Title V Permits if Program Goals are to be Fully Realized*, Report No. 2005-P-00010, at 5 (2005), available at http://www.epa.gov/oig/reports/2005/20050309-2005-P-00010.pdf (discussing failures to clearly state the obligations of sources in permits).

Generally, government officials and citizens can only enforce specifically defined legal obligations. This raises a fundamental question of the relationship between pollution control standards and enforcement. Should the basic rule be that firms cannot release pollutants without explicit government permission? Or, instead, should the rule be that firms may pollute freely except to the extent government has adopted specific requirements limiting releases of particular pollutants?

≣≣   *Atlantic States Legal Found. v. Eastman Kodak Co.*
≣≣   *12 F.3d 353 (2d Cir. 1993)*

WINTER, CIRCUIT JUDGE.

This appeal raises the issue of whether private groups may bring a citizen suit pursuant to Section 505 of the Federal Water Pollution Control Act (commonly known as the Clean Water Act), to stop the discharge of pollutants not listed in a valid permit issued pursuant to the Clean Water Act ("CWA" or "The Act"). We hold that the discharge of unlisted pollutants is not unlawful under the CWA. We also hold that private groups may not bring such a suit to enforce New York State environmental regulations.

Background

Appellee Eastman Kodak Company ("Kodak") operates an industrial facility in Rochester, New York that discharges wastewater into the Genesee River and Paddy Hill Creek under a State Pollutant Discharge Elimination System ("SPDES") permit issued pursuant to 33 U.S.C. §1342. Appellant Atlantic States Legal Foundation, Inc. ("Atlantic States") is a not-for-profit environmental group based in Syracuse, New York. . . .

On November 14, 1991, Atlantic States filed the complaint in the instant matter. The complaint alleged that Kodak had violated Sections 301 and 402 of the Clean Water Act, by discharging large quantities of pollutants not listed in its SPDES permit. . . .

Discussion

Atlantic States brought the present action under the citizen suit provision of Section 505, which permits private suits to enforce a CWA "effluent standard or limitation." Section 505 defines such an enforceable standard or limitation as, inter alia, "an unlawful act under section 1311," [section 301] and "a permit or condition thereof issued under . . . section 1342 of this title, which is in effect under this chapter." The question then is whether Atlantic States' action seeks to enforce an "effluent standard or limitation" imposed by the Act or by Kodak's SPDES permit issued by the [New York State Department of Environmental Conservation] DEC.

A.   *"Standards and Limitations" of the Clean Water Act*

Atlantic States argues first that the plain language of Section 301 of the CWA prohibits the discharge of any pollutants not expressly permitted. With regard to this claim, therefore, Atlantic States' standing to bring this action turns on the merits of the action itself.

Section 301(a) reads: "Except as in compliance with this section and sections 1312, 1316, 1317, 1328, 1342, and 1344 of this title, the discharge of any pollutant by any person shall be unlawful." This prohibition is tempered, however, by a self-referential host of exceptions that allow the discharge of many pollutants once a polluter has complied with the regulatory program of the CWA. The exception relevant to the instant matter is contained in Section 402, which outlines the NPDES, and specifies the requirements for suspending the national system with the submission of an approved state program. Section 402(k) contains the so-called "shield provision," which defines compliance with a NPDES or SPDES permit as compliance with Section 301 for the purposes of the CWA's enforcement provisions. The Supreme Court has noted that "The purpose of [Section 402(k)] seems to be . . . to relieve [permit holders] of having to litigate in an enforcement action the question whether their permits are sufficiently strict."

Atlantic States' view of the regulatory framework stands that scheme on its head. Atlantic States treats permits as establishing limited permission for the discharge of identified pollutants and a prohibition on the discharge of unidentified pollutants. Viewing the regulatory scheme as a whole, however, it is clear that the permit is intended to identify and limit the most harmful pollutants while leaving the control of the vast number of other pollutants to disclosure requirements. Once within the NPDES or SPDES scheme, therefore, polluters may discharge pollutants not specifically listed in their permits so long as they comply with the appropriate reporting requirements and abide by any new limitations when imposed on such pollutants.

The EPA lists tens of thousands of different chemical substances in the Toxic Substances Control Act Chemical Substance Inventory. . . . However, the EPA does not demand even information regarding each of the many thousand chemical substances potentially present in a manufacturer's wastewater because "it is impossible to identify and rationally limit every chemical or compound present in a discharge of pollutants." "Compliance with such a permit would be impossible and anybody seeking to harass a permittee need only analyze that permittee's discharge until determining the presence of a substance not identified in the permit." Indeed, Atlantic States could provide no principled reason why water itself, which is conceded to be a chemical, would not be considered a "pollutant" under its view of the Act.

The EPA has never acted in any way to suggest that Atlantic States' absolutist and wholly impractical view of the legal effect of a permit is valid. In fact, the EPA's actions and policy statements have frequently contemplated discharges of pollutants not listed under a NPDES or SPDES permit. It has addressed such discharges by amending the permit to list and limit a pollutant when necessary to safeguard the environment without considering pre-amendment discharges to be violations calling for enforcement under the CWA. . . .

The EPA is the federal agency entrusted with administration and enforcement of the CWA. As such, EPA's reasonable interpretations of the Act are due deferential treatment in the courts. . . . Because the EPA's implementation of the CWA is entirely reasonable, we defer to it.

B. New York Environmental "Standards and Limitations"

Atlantic States argues alternatively that the permit itself provides grounds for enforcement of New York State's regulations. States may enact stricter standards for wastewater effluents than mandated by the CWA and federal EPA regulations. These states' standards may be enforced under the CWA by the states or the EPA, but private citizens have no standing to do so. New York chose to implement its own environmental policies through its DEC's issuance of SPDES permits pursuant to N.Y. Envtl. Conserv. Law §17-0815 (McKinney 1984). However, state regulations, including the provisions of SPDES permits, which mandate "a greater scope of coverage than that required" by the federal CWA and its implementing regulations are not enforceable through a citizen suit under 33 U.S.C. §1365.

Atlantic States relies heavily on General Provision 1(b) of the SPDES permit to show a violation of the CWA. In particular, Atlantic States points to the final clause of that provision that requires, pursuant to N.Y. Envtl. Conserv. Law §17-0815(3), that

> the discharge of any pollutant not identified and authorized or the discharge of any pollutant more frequently than or at a level in excess of that identified and authorized by this permit shall constitute a violation of the terms and conditions of this permit.

However, General Provision 1(b) itself contemplates "new, increased or decreased discharges" that do not "violate the effluent limitations specified in this permit."[10] Moreover, Special Reporting Requirement 2(a) of the SPDES permit specifically contemplates discharges of pollutants not identified by the permit. It states, in relevant part:

---

10. General Provision 1(b) reads:

b. All discharges authorized by this permit shall be consistent with the terms and conditions of this permit; facility expansions, production increases, or process modifications which result in new, increased or decreased discharges of pollutants must be reported by submission of a new SPDES application or, if such new, increased, or decreased discharge does not violate the effluent limitations specified in this permit, by submission to the permit issuing authority of notice of such new or increased discharges of pollutants (in which case the permit may be modified to specify effluent limitations or any pollutants not identified and limited herein); the discharge of any pollutant not identified and authorized or the discharge of any pollutant more frequently than or at a level in excess of that identified and authorized by this permit shall constitute a violation of the terms and conditions of this permit.

All existing manufacturing . . . dischargers must notify the [DEC] as soon as they know or have reason to believe . . . [t]hat they have begun or expect to begin to use or manufacture as an intermediate or final product or byproduct any toxic pollutant which was not reported in the permit application. . . .

Like the SPDES permit, the DEC itself contemplates the discharge of unlisted pollutants. In September 1988, DEC notified Kodak that it was aware of 45 substances "reported to have releases to the Genesee River" out of which only 23 were "specifically limited or monitored by the SPDES permit." DEC advised Kodak that although the bulk of these 23 substances either did not appear to be a major concern, or at least did not "appear to be acutely toxic to aquatic life at the levels of discharge indicated," the remaining four should receive "additional attention."

It thus appears that the DEC's view of the SPDES permit is the same as the EPA's. If so, Atlantic States' action fails for reasons stated in Point A above. We need not resolve the issue, however, for, even if Atlantic States is right about New York law, the action would fail because New York would be implementing a regulatory scheme broader than the CWA, and such broader state schemes are unenforceable through Section 505 citizen suits. A citizen's suit under Section 505 is thus barred either because Section 17-0815(3) and the final clause of General Provision 1(b) implement a program with broader scope than that promulgated under the CWA and EPA regulations or because the permit more narrowly interpreted shields Kodak from such an action.

Conclusion

For the reasons stated above, we affirm the order of the district court granting summary judgment to Kodak.

NOTES ON *ATLANTIC STATES*

1. *Rationale.* Section 301(a) prohibits "the discharge of any pollutant" except as in compliance with various sections of the Act. So why exactly does the court not allow Atlantic States to enforce the restriction on discharge of pollutants not listed in its permit? Do you agree with the court's rationale? In thinking about this, study sections 301 and 402(k) carefully. Could New York State prosecute Eastman Kodak for discharging a non-listed pollutant? The Eleventh Circuit disagreed with the *Atlantic States* court's holding that citizens may not enforce state law provisions in an NPDES permit in Parker v. Scrap Metal Processors, Inc., 386 F.3d 993, 1006 n.15 (11th Cir. 2004). Could Atlantic States enforce an identical permit in the Eleventh Circuit?

2. *What is a pollutant?* *Atlantic States* argued that plain water might be a pollutant. Could *Atlantic States* have taken a narrower view of the definition of a pollutant without compromising its case against Eastman Kodak? Should it

have? Suppose that New York State seeks to prosecute a manufacturer for discharging a pollutant listed in the Clean Water Act, but not listed in the relevant permit. Could a district court within the Second Circuit hold that the discharger has violated section 301?

3. *Policy.* Should the law proceed on the premise that pollution is prohibited unless authorized or the premise that is authorized unless prohibited? If you were the lawyer for a polluting company and the law prohibits discharges unless authorized, would you seek to delay the promulgation of effluent limitations? What if the law allows discharges until prohibited?

4. *Permit shields.* The permit shield provision mentioned in *Atlantic States* is one of several requirements in environmental statutes that seek to assure, at a minimum, that uncertainty about the legality and interpretation of regulations is resolved prior to an enforcement proceeding whenever possible. As noted in Adamo Wrecking Co. v. United States, 434 U.S. 275, 285 (1978), the Clean Air Act contains a provision, 42 U.S.C. §7607(b)(2), forbidding litigation about the validity of a regulation in an enforcement proceeding. Similar requirements exist in other statutes. Often, however, the precise implications of a regulation for a facility require some interpretation of the regulation. Because regulatory requirements often are imprecise and permit a variety of compliance alternatives, specific requirements in permits can vary, even when the underlying regulation is the same nationwide. The permitting provisions of the statutes aim to resolve these questions in the permitting proceeding, rather than in the enforcement proceeding. Permit shield provisions like that set out in section 402(k) of the Clean Water Act protect operators, at a minimum, from government departures from interpretations of regulations arrived at in permitting proceedings. *See, e.g.,* 33 U.S.C. §1342(k), 42 U.S.C. §7661c(f).

5. *Information disclosure.* In answering the question of whether polluters should be liable for discharges not expressly limited in a permit, should it matter whether the discharger disclosed the presence (or potential presence) of the pollutant in its permit application?

As you read the following case, think about whether it's consistent with *Atlantic States.*

Northwest Envtl. Advocates v. City of Portland
56 F.3d 979 (9th Cir. 1995)

PREGERSON, CIRCUIT JUDGE.

Northwest Environmental Advocates and Nina Bell ("NWEA") appeal the district court's judgment in favor of Portland on their claims that the City is violating the Clean Water Act ("CWA"). On April 16, 1991, NWEA filed suit in the district court alleging that Portland's practice of discharging raw sewage during times of precipitation from 54 outfall points was not covered by a permit and that the practice had caused and was continuing to cause violations of Oregon's water quality standards. After a trial on the written record, the district court held that (1) the contested discharge points were covered by Portland's pollution permit, and (2) the court lacked jurisdiction to consider NWEA's water quality violation claims.

In *Northwest Environmental Advocates v. City of Portland* (*Northwest*), we affirmed. We held that the contested discharge points were covered by Portland's pollution permit and we held that *Northwest Environmental Advocates* lacked standing to bring a citizen suit under §505(a)(1) of the Clean Water Act to enforce water quality standards contained in Portland's permit. On December 28, 1993, NWEA filed a petition for rehearing with suggestion for rehearing en banc. While this petition was still pending, the Supreme Court decided *PUD No. 1 of Jefferson County v. Washington Department of Ecology*, [511] U.S. [700] (1994) (*Jefferson County*).

Jefferson County cast into considerable doubt our holding in *Northwest* that citizens do not have standing under the Clean Water Act to enforce water quality standards unless they have been translated into end-of-pipe effluent limitations. In light of *Jefferson County* and upon reconsideration of our prior opinion in *Northwest*, we now vacate that opinion and issue the following opinion.

II. . . .

B. Does NWEA Have a Cause of Action for Water Quality Violations?

NWEA argues that the district court erred in finding that it did not have jurisdiction over a citizen suit for the enforcement of the water quality maintenance provision of the NPDES permit.

. . . Specifically, NWEA alleged that Portland's [combined sewer overflow] CSO events violated a permit condition prohibiting any discharges that would violate Oregon water quality standards. The 1984 permit held, as a condition in Schedule A, that "notwithstanding the effluent limitations established by this permit, no wastes shall be discharged and no activities shall be conducted which will violate Water Quality Standards["]. . . .

The district court never reached the question of Portland's liability for violations of this permit condition. Instead, the district court held that §505 of the Clean Water Act did not grant federal jurisdiction for the citizen enforcement of water quality violations, "because water quality standards do not equal 'effluent standards or limitations under this chapter.'" The court concluded that violations of water quality standards may be actionable "only if they are incorporated into an NPDES permit through effluent limitations." Because the plain language of CWA §505, the legislative history, and case law support a finding of citizen suit jurisdiction in this case, we reverse on this issue.

The plain language of CWA §505 authorizes citizens to enforce *all* permit conditions. That section provides: "[A]ny citizen may commence a civil action . . . (1) against any person . . . who is alleged to be in violation of (A) an effluent standard or limitation under [the Clean Water Act]. . . ." An effluent standard or limitation includes "(2) an effluent limitation or other limitation under section 1311 . . . *or* (6) a permit or condition thereof. . . ." This language clearly contemplates citizen suits to enforce "a permit or condition thereof." Portland holds a National Pollutant Discharge Elimination System (NPDES) permit. . . .

Portland argues that §505 allows citizens to enforce only those water quality standards that are translated into effluent limitations. To support this argument, Portland reasons that the effluent limitations, which were imposed by the 1972 amendments to the CWA, effectively displaced water quality standards as the primary means of regulating pollution. Portland explains that Congress retained water quality standards as the ultimate goal of pollution control, but sought to achieve this goal through end-of-the-pipe limitations. . . .

By introducing effluent limitations into the CWA scheme, Congress intended to improve enforcement, not to supplant the old system.

Ample case law supports our view that Congress intended to confer citizens standing to enforce water quality standards. Most notably, in *Jefferson County*, the Supreme Court held that the Clean Water Act allows States to enforce the broad narrative criteria contained in water quality standards. In *Jefferson County*, a county which proposed to build an electricity-generating facility on a river challenged a minimum stream flow condition established by the State. Although the county did not contest the State's authority to set limitations designed to ensure compliance with state water quality standards adopted under CWA §303, the county argued that §303 requires the State to protect water quality standards solely through implementation of "specific numerical criteria." The county contended that the State may not require it to operate the dam in a manner consistent with a "designated use," which is a *qualitative* requirement of the §303 water quality standards.

The Court rejected the county's argument, and held that the State may require a permit applicant to comply with the qualitative designated uses requirement. The Court explained that under the literal terms of CWA §303(c)(2), a water quality standard must "consist of the designated uses of the navigable waters involved *and* the water quality criteria for such waters based upon such uses." Thus, the Court concluded that a project that does not comply with a designated use of the water does not comply with the applicable water quality standards. The Court also explained that CWA §401(d), which provides for State certification of projects, explicitly authorizes "any . . . limitations . . . necessary to assure that [the applicant] will comply with any . . . limitations under . . . [CWA §303] . . . and any other appropriate requirement of state law."

By its holding, the Court expressly rejected the county's argument that designated use requirements are "too open-ended" to be enforceable and that the Clean Water Act only contemplates enforcement of the more "specific and objective" numerical criteria. . . .

The county's losing argument in *Jefferson County* is very similar to the argument advanced by Portland in the instant case. Portland argues that citizens may not enforce the broad narrative conditions of state water quality standards, but may enforce *only* those conditions that have been translated into numeric effluent limitations.

We disagree with Portland's contention that *Jefferson County* is inapposite to the issue before us. Even though *Jefferson County* involved a state's authority to impose conditions under CWA §401, whereas the present litigation involves citizen suit enforcement of CWA §402 conditions, both the §401 certification process and the §402 permit process require applicants to comply with CWA §301. As noted above, §301 incorporates by reference the water quality requirements of §303.

Moreover, although *Jefferson County* addressed the authority of States, not citizens, to enforce the narrative conditions of CWA §303 water quality standards, nothing in the language of the Clean Water Act, the legislative history, or the implementing regulations restricts citizens from enforcing the same conditions of a certificate or permit that a State may enforce. To the contrary, as demonstrated above, these sources uniformly support broad citizen enforcement authority, including the authority to enforce water quality standards. . . .

By interpreting §505 to exclude citizen suit enforcement of water quality standards that are not translated into quantitative limitations, Portland would have us immunize the entire body of qualitative regulations from an important enforcement tool. Such a result would be especially troubling in this case, because no effluent limitations cover the discharges from Portland's combined . . . CSOs. . . .

III. Conclusion

For the foregoing reasons, we AFFIRM the district court's holding that the 1984 permit covered the CSOs, and we REVERSE the district court's holding that CWA §505(a) does not confer jurisdiction for citizen suits to enforce water quality standards when they are conditions of a CWA permit. . . . KLEINFELD, CIRCUIT JUDGE, dissenting:

I respectfully dissent from Part II-B of the opinion. . . .

. . . The majority opinion suggests that *Jefferson County* has changed the law. . . . [I]t does not.

The question before us is whether citizens' suits may be brought to enforce water quality standards, as opposed to effluent limitations. *Jefferson County* says nothing about that. . . .

Nevertheless, we previously concluded on the basis of analysis of several additional provisions of the statute that it is not the permittee who must comply with the water quality standards, but rather the issuing authority, which has a "duty . . . to include in the permit end-of-pipe effluent limitations that will ensure that water quality standards are met." That makes sense in light of what the Supreme Court said in *Jefferson County*. Congress meant for the issuing authority to decide upon end-of-pipe effluent standards for the permit, which it could derive from water quality standards, when Congress allowed citizens' suits to enforce permit limitations. It did not mean for citizens' suits to proceed on the basis of permit violations, where the permittee complied with end-of-pipe discharge limitations but the water still wound up being too polluted. A water quality standard should be deemed to be not among those authorized by the statute for purposes of citizen suit enforcement. . . .

The majority argues that as a matter of policy, Congress meant to prevent pollution, and citizens' suits add power to anti-pollution enforcement mechanisms, so there is no reason to deny citizens' suits enforcement. The first two propositions do not imply the third. There can be too much of a good thing. There is too much of a good thing when its value is exceeded by the value of other good things available for the same or less cost.

Water quality standards are a useful device for government enforcement authorities (who decided not to prosecute this case against the City of Portland), because they provide standards for effluent limitations and goals toward which enforcement should be aimed. They are too uncertain and amorphous, however, for use against specific polluters. Suppose, hypothetically, that a water quality standard allows for 100 units of a pollutant, upstream and non-point source polluters discharge 50 units, and the downstream discharger is permitted to discharge 50 units. If the upstream and non-point source polluters increase their discharge to 80 units, it does not automatically follow that the downstream discharger should be limited to 20. The burdens of so severe a limitation may exceed the burdens of the extra pollution, or enforcement efforts might more appropriately be directed at the other polluters. In the case at bar, the majority concedes that the social costs of filling the streets and basements of Portland with sewage, or spending between a half billion and $1.2 billion dollars on renovation, are the practical alternatives to tolerating violations of the water quality standards. A public authority might rationally decide that filling the streets and basements with sewage is worse than polluting the river with it, and that the citizens of Portland need several years to raise and spend the money necessary to avoid running the sewage into the streets, the basements, and the river. . . .

NOTES ON *NORTHWEST ENVIRONMENTAL ADVOCATES*

1. *Consistency.* Is this case consistent with *Atlantic States, supra?*
2. *Ease of enforcement.* Which is easier to enforce, a prohibition on interference with water quality standards or a general prohibition of discharges of pollutants not listed in a permit?

3. *The dissent.* Under the dissent's view of the law, would the government be able to collect civil penalties for a plant's failure to meet water quality standards?

4. *A permit's function.* A permit, at a minimum should collect the requirements applicable to a pollution source and spell out how that source will comply with the requirements. This collection function matters, because, often, several different regulations will apply to a pollution source. By collecting the requirements in one place and spelling out how the requirements apply to a particular polluter, a permit clarifies the precise compliance obligations of a facility operator. This should aid the operator, making it clearer what she should be doing. The permit can aid the public in understanding the scope of requirements applicable to a facility. The permit also can facilitate enforcement, allowing both citizen and government enforcers to compare a facility's environmental performance to its legal obligations. But this last function requires the collection of information about a facility's performance.

B. MONITORING, RECORD-KEEPING, AND REPORTING

Enforcement requires some means of allowing potential enforcers to detect violations. You might think that government inspectors should simply monitor each plant to determine if violations have occurred. And the environmental statutes do authorize government agencies to inspect polluting facilities. Inspectors often detect some environmental violations. But inspections provide a very incomplete deterrent. Government could never hire a sufficient number of inspectors to regularly inspect each of the thousands of facilities regulated under the various pollution control laws. Furthermore, an inspector frequently cannot tell whether a polluter has violated a permit condition by just looking at the facility. Often one needs some way of measuring or estimating the amount of pollution being released.

For these reasons, regulatory enforcement relies heavily upon voluntary compliance and a self-monitoring system, where polluters themselves monitor their compliance status and have obligations to report violations to government officials. *See generally* Arnold W. Reitze, Jr. and Steven D. Schell, *Self-Monitoring and Self-Reporting of Routine Air Pollution Releases*, 24 Colum. J. Envtl. L. 63 (1999). These obligations include monitoring, record-keeping, and reporting (MRR) obligations. Why are all three essential?

The acid rain program experience suggests that stringent MRR obligations have the capacity to greatly deter non-compliance. The law governing this program requires continuous monitoring of emissions and frequent electronic reporting of emissions data to the government. The deterrent effect of these strict MRR obligations may explain the lack of violations of the acid rain regulations. Most regulatory programs, though, have much weaker MRR requirements and much weaker compliance records.

1. Monitoring

The key issue in monitoring is often what monitoring technology is feasible and how often monitoring is conducted. Generally, more frequent and stringent monitoring produces more reliable information about violations, but may impose higher cost than less frequent and stringent monitoring. We examine these issues, first through a rare example of a case actually discussing policy considerations that influence monitoring decisions, and then through a note on the Enhanced Monitoring Provisions in the 1990 Clean Air Act Amendments.

United States Steel Corp. v. Train
556 F.2d 822, 850-51 (7th Cir. 1977)

TONE, CIRCUIT JUDGE.

. . . U.S. Steel has two basic complaints regarding the monitoring required by the permit: it is to be done too often and at too many places.

The initial monitoring requirements contained in the permit correspond closely to U.S. Steel's present monitoring practices, as required by the Indiana Stream Pollution Control Board. The final requirements increase the monitoring at all process-water outfalls, requiring daily monitoring for several pollutants as well as temperature and continuous monitoring for flow and pH at several outfalls. Both the remaining process-water and all cooling-water outfalls will be monitored once a week for several pollutants and once a month for others. All the monitoring requirements exceed those proposed by U.S. Steel and present levels, both in the frequency of measurement and in the number of pollutants for which measurements must be taken.

Section 308 of the [Clean Water] Act grants the Administrator broad authority to require NPDES permittees to monitor "at such locations [and] at such intervals" as he shall prescribe, "whenever [it is] required to carry out the objective of [the Act]." Similarly, §402 vests him with authority to "prescribe conditions for [NPDES] permits . . . including conditions on data and information collection. . . ." We conclude that the monitoring requirements set forth in the permit are within this broad authority.

EPA considered four factors in determining the monitoring requirements, and set the requirements separately for each outfall. These factors were: the nature of the discharges and their impact on the receiving stream; the variability of the discharges; the volume of water discharged; and the present monitoring practices of U.S. Steel. These factors are proper, and the record establishes that they were given appropriate weight by EPA. For example, because of the higher concentrations and greater variety of pollutants present in process water, the permit appropriately requires more frequent monitoring of process-water discharges than of cooling-water discharges. Similarly, more frequent monitoring was required at those outfalls which tended to fluctuate in the amount and quality of their discharges.

The monitoring requirements — similar to or less stringent than those imposed in the approximately 50 other steel-plant permits issued in Region Five — will not work an unjustified economic hardship on U.S. Steel. The chief difference between U.S. Steel's present monitoring practices and the initial requirements is that compliance at nine of the outfalls will be based on a 24-hour composite sample rather than the 8-hour composite sample presently prepared. The use of the 24-hour composite sample is extended to all outfalls by the final monitoring requirements. These changes will more than triple the number of samples taken. The use of a 24-hour composite sample will doubtless be more expensive than present monitoring practices, but it will present a more complete picture of the discharges from the Gary Works, reflecting fluctuations over the course of an entire day of production. At the outfalls monitored on a daily basis, it will allow an almost continuous check on the performance of the treatment facilities at Gary Works.

By comparison, U.S. Steel's permit proposals call for monitoring only once a week, even at the seven outfalls now sampled five times in eight days, and would replace the monitoring for several pollutants now conducted at each outfall with monitoring at the Pennsylvania Railroad Bridge, four-and-one-half miles downstream. Monitoring at each outfall enables the permittee and EPA to pinpoint the source of any discharges that exceed the plant-wide limitations on particular pollutants. Furthermore, the U.S. Steel proposal would, in effect, allow it to use the four-and-one-half mile stretch of the river as an extended treatment facility, something hardly contemplated by either the Indiana water quality standards or the FWPCA.

We cannot say that EPA exceeded its authority or acted unreasonably when it determined that regular and frequent monitoring at each outfall is necessary to insure prompt detection and rectification of permit violations. Therefore, we affirm the initial and final monitoring requirements set forth in the permit.

NOTES ON *U.S. STEEL*

1. *Variability.* EPA states that it takes the "variability" of discharges into account in writing monitoring requirements. Do highly variable discharges suggest the need for more frequent monitoring or less frequent monitoring than very constant discharges? Why?

2. *Discharge's nature.* EPA also takes into account the "nature of the discharges and their impact on the receiving streams." This suggests that EPA would require more frequent monitoring of pollutants it considers especially damaging. Should the stringency of monitoring vary with the impact of the pollution?

3. *Consistency.* The court cites the consistency of EPA's monitoring requirements for U.S. Steel with the monitoring regime imposed on other steel plants in the region as evidence that the requirements impose no "unjustified economic hardship" on *U.S. Steel.* Does consistency prevent economic hardship or provide a justification for it? Suppose that *U.S. Steel* was losing money and that the additional monitoring would add $1 million a year to its compliance costs. Would the monitoring impose an economic hardship? Why would the consistency justify the hardship? Is taking into account the impact of discharges on receiving waters (as EPA does) an approach likely to lead to consistent monitoring requirements?

4. *Sources of monitoring requirements.* In this case, monitoring requirements seem to come from discretionary decisions in a permit proceeding. EPA generally writes monitoring, record-keeping, and reporting requirements into its regulations. But the regulations sometimes provide requirements too vague to determine precisely what monitoring an individual source will perform, often because EPA gives polluters a menu of monitoring options, instead of mandating a specific set of requirements.

Sometimes, agencies have failed to impose specific monitoring requirements on sources even in a permit proceeding. *See, e.g., Office of the EPA Inspector General, supra,* at 19. For nonpoint source pollution and fugitive air pollution, monitoring is frequently impossible, and agencies must content themselves with emission estimates. As you read section 308 of the Clean Water Act below (which is also cited in *U.S. Steel, supra*), ask yourself whether EPA may decline to require monitoring when monitoring is possible, as it frequently is for point sources of water pollution:

> Whenever required to carry out the objective of this chapter, including but not limited to
>
> > (1) developing or assisting in the development of any effluent limitation, or other limitation, prohibition, or effluent standard, pretreatment standard, or standard of performance under this chapter;
> >
> > (2) determining whether any person is in violation of any such effluent limitation, or other limitation, prohibition or effluent standard, pretreatment standard, or standard of performance;
> >
> > (3) any requirement established under this section; or
> >
> > (4) carrying out sections 1315, 1321, 1342, 1344 (relating to State permit programs), 1345, and 1364 of this title —
> >
> > > (A) the Administrator shall require the owner or operator of any point source to
> > >
> > > > (i) establish and maintain such records,
> > > >
> > > > (ii) make such reports,
> > > >
> > > > (iii) install, use, and maintain such monitoring equipment or methods (including where appropriate, biological monitoring methods),

(iv) sample such effluents (in accordance with such methods, at such locations, at such intervals, and in such manner as the Administrator shall prescribe), and

(v) provide such other information as he may reasonably require.

33 U.S.C. §1318(a). *See* Envtl. Def. Fund v. Costle, 439 F. Supp. 980, 1003-1004 (E.D.N.Y. 1977) (stating that EPA has a mandatory duty to require monitoring and reporting, but rejecting a claim that EPA violated this section by funding sewage treatment plants while requiring some monitoring by regulation).

NOTE ON THE 1990 CLEAN AIR ACT AMENDMENTS

While discharge monitoring reports under the Clean Water Act have often facilitated government and citizen enforcement, air pollution monitoring has often been limited to occasional stack tests, and has sometimes been absent altogether. These lax monitoring requirements, together with the lack of a general permit program, may have made enforcement far more complex and often ineffectual under the Clean Air Act than under the Clean Water Act. The 1990 Clean Air Act Amendments introduced a general operating permit program into the Clean Air Act for the first time. Section 114, introduced into the Act in 1990, also contains the following enhanced monitoring provision:

(3) The Administrator shall in the case of any person which is the owner or operator of a major stationary source, and may, in the case of any other person, require enhanced monitoring and submission of compliance certifications. Compliance certifications shall include

(A) identification of the applicable requirement that is the basis of the certification,

(B) the method used for determining the compliance status of the source,

(C) the compliance status,

(D) whether compliance is continuous or intermittent,

(E) such other facts as the Administrator may require.

42 U.S.C. §7414(c)(3). Does this subsection require improvement of monitoring for any group of sources? Does it require the use of continuous monitoring? *See* Natural Resources Defense Council v. EPA, 194 F.3d 130, 138 (D.C. Cir. 1999) (holding that EPA's enhanced monitoring rule violated requirement to certify "whether compliance is 'continuous or intermittent,'" but upholding "compliance assurance monitoring"). Consider section 504(b) of the Act, which authorizes EPA to prescribe monitoring requirements, but

states that "continuous emissions monitoring need not be required if alternative methods . . . provide sufficiently reliable . . . information for determining compliance." 42 U.S.C. §7661c(b). Does section 114, read together with this section, require continuous emissions monitoring for highly variable sources?

2. Reporting

In *U.S. Steel*, the monitoring seemed primarily aimed at enabling EPA to detect violations of effluent limits. In such cases, the reporting requirements inform enforcers about violations and facilitate enforcement. Obviously, honest reporting can aid in the detection of violations. But a system requiring self-reporting can fail if it does not provide adequate incentives to keep reporting honest.

Section 114(a)(3) of the Clean Air Act requires the owner or operator of major stationary sources to submit "compliance certifications," which "shall include the compliance status." 42 U.S.C. §7414(a)(3). Section 504(c) then requires "a responsible corporate official" to sign and "certify" the "accuracy" of any report "required . . . by a permit." 42 U.S.C. §7661c(c). Section 113(c)(1) of the Act makes knowing violation of this certification requirement a criminal offense. 42 U.S.C. §7413(c)(1). If an operator of a source signs a document certifying that the facility is in compliance when it is not in compliance, do criminal penalties apply? Under the Clean Water Act, a person who "knowingly makes any false material statement, representation, or certification" may receive fines of up to $10,000 and/or up to two years in prison. 33 U.S.C. §1319(c)(4). *Cf.* United States v. Kuhn, 345 F.3d 431, 433 (6th Cir. 2003) (reviewing criminal sentence for falsifying monitoring results in report submitted to the government); United States v. Sinskey, 119 F.3d 712, 718-720 (8th Cir. 1997) (upholding criminal conviction for falsifying reported monitoring results). Should the government require operators to certify whether or not the facility is in compliance and then punish false statements criminally? If you were a manager required to file the certification, would you simply rely on the reports submitted to you by your engineers, or would you take additional steps to assure the accuracy of the data? What additional steps would you take? If you were given numbers showing a violation, would you certify non-compliance with the Act's requirements? Requirements for operators to certify the compliance status of water dischargers and the possibility of severe penalties for false reporting led many operators to report discharges in excess of permit levels during the 1980s. This made enforcement relatively simple, since the reports themselves documented violations of discharge levels. *Cf.* United States v. Allegheny Ludlum Corp., 366 F.3d 164, 170-76 (3d Cir. 2004) (allowing a "laboratory error" defense, but noting a split of authority on the issue of whether a company should ever escape liability when its own reports document a violation).

EPA has required manufacturers to provide EPA with a list of "any toxic pollutant which the applicant currently uses or manufactures as an intermediate or final product or byproduct." Does such a requirement facilitate the enforcement of effluent standards? In justifying this reporting requirement, EPA claimed that this requirement would enable it to see if it needed to impose additional discharge limitations in a permit, provide guidance about what substances EPA should test for when it does inspections, and assist EPA in recommending best management practices to prevent spills. Are these purposes permissible justifications for reporting requirements under section 308? *See* Natural Resources Defense Council, Inc. v. EPA, 822 F.2d 104, 117-19 (D.C. Cir. 1987).

CERCLA requires the person in charge of a facility to report "any release" of a hazardous substance that exceeds quantity thresholds EPA establishes to the National Response Center. *See* 42 U.S.C. §§9602, 9603. An overlapping provision in the Emergency Planning and Community Right to Know Act (EPCRA) requires immediate notification of state and local emergency coordinators after release of an "extremely hazardous substance." 42 U.S.C. §11004(a)-(b). Why the discrepancy in who gets the reports? What purposes do you suppose these provisions serve? What do you expect the agencies getting the reports to do with this information?

Here's how one district court described the purposes of these reporting requirements:

> The purpose of [sic] CERCLA notice requirement is to provide the EPA and other regulatory agencies with the information they need to assess hazards and mitigate potential injury from releases. Similarly, EPCRA establishes a framework of agencies designed to inform the public about the presence of hazardous and toxic chemicals, and to provide emergency response in the event of health-threatening releases. Without the required notices of alleged releases, regulatory agencies are without knowledge of the releases; and are consequently impeded from adequately mitigating the releases.

Sierra Club, Inc. v. Tysons Foods, Inc. 299 F. Supp. 2d 693, 705 (W.D. Ky. 2003). Under CERCLA, liability can attach for releases at levels below the reportable quantities. *See* United States v. Alcan Aluminum Corp., 990 F.2d 711, 720-21 (2d Cir. 1993) (holding that liability attaches regardless of the quantity of pollution released). Notice that the Clean Water Act reporting requirements envision reporting use of toxic pollutants that would probably not violate the Act. In any case, many environmental statutes have reporting requirements that allow the agency to calibrate a regulatory response or cope with an emergency, rather than solely to enforce existing pollution control obligations. *See generally* Roger M. Klein, *The Continuing Nature of Notification Violations Under Environmental Statutes*, 26 Envtl. L. 565, 567 (1996) (stating that reporting allows EPA to minimize the effects of releases of toxic substances).

A Note on audit Privileges

Since the 1970s, firms have set up systems to audit themselves in order to make themselves aware of possible violations of environmental laws, to improve environmental management, and/or to evaluate potential risks that could affect the firm. *See* William L. Thomas, Bertram C. Frey, and Fern Fleischer Daves, *Using Auditing, Pollution Prevention, and Management Systems to Craft Superior Environmental Enforcement Solutions*, 30 Envtl. L. Rep. (Envtl. L. Inst.) 10299, 10300 (2000). These audits can go beyond specific monitoring duties established by specific regulation. EPA has generally encouraged these audits.

Questions have arisen about what role these audits should play in enforcement. On the one hand, audits might reveal useful information that could aid enforcement of environmental laws. On the other hand, if regulators routinely sought discovery of audits for enforcement purposes, this might discourage useful efforts by firms to self-police.

Consider the range of policies adopted respecting audits over time and in different jurisdictions. How do these policies differ? Which policy do you think best?

EPA's 1986 audit policy. EPA generally refrained from requesting audits routinely as a method for detecting possible violations. But EPA reserved the right to request audit reports once a facility became a target for an investigation of a possible violation. EPA did not promise any particular relief to parties conducting audits, but retained the discretion to reduce penalties for parties that promptly disclosed violations of environmental laws and took appropriate remedial action.

EPA's 1995 self-policing policy. EPA may eliminate "gravity-based" penalties (*i.e.*, those that go beyond recouping the economic benefit realized through non-compliance) when facility operators find, promptly disclose, and correct violations found through an audit.

State audit shield laws. Several states have enacted statutes that shield companies from prosecution for violations uncovered through an audit.

Of course, the question of which policy one prefers directly implicates the debate between cooperative and deterrence-based enforcement. Should EPA require audits instead of providing incentives to get voluntary audits?

A National Conference of State Legislatures study concluded that "state audit privilege and immunity laws do not encourage facilities to begin auditing, to increase the number of audits they perform, or to disclose more violations to regulators." *See* Nancy K. Stoner and Wendy J. Miller, *National Conference of State Legislatures Study Finds that State Environmental Audit Laws Have No Impact on*

Company Self-Auditing and Disclosure of Violations, 29 Envtl. L. Rep. (Envtl. L. Inst.) 10265, 10265 (1999). The same study found that "inspector presence" strongly motivates companies to audit. *Id.* If this study's conclusions are correct, what implications do these conclusions have for the choice of policy toward audits?

16
Government Enforcement

This chapter addresses what government does once it detects violations. It contains a section on civil penalties and one on criminal penalties. The deterrence/cooperative enforcement debate influences the sanctions imposed for violations of environmental law. As you learn about the civil and criminal penalty provisions in the statutes, think about how they serve (or fail to serve) the deterrence goal. And think about how some of the reforms in enforcement policy in recent years reflect an increased reliance on a cooperative enforcement model.

A. CIVIL PENALTIES

The Clean Water Act contains the following civil penalty provision:

33 U.S.C. §1319. Enforcement

(d) Civil penalties; factors considered in determining amount

Any person who violates [certain Federal Water Pollution Control Act requirements] shall be subject to a civil penalty not to exceed $25,000 per day for each violation. In determining the amount of a civil penalty the court shall consider the seriousness of the violation or violations, the economic benefit (if any) resulting from the violation, any history of such violations, any good-faith efforts to comply with the applicable requirements, the economic impact of the penalty on the violator, and such other matters as justice may require. For purposes of this subsection, a single operational upset which leads to simultaneous violations of more than one pollutant parameter shall be treated as a single violation.

1. Maximum Penalty.

This provision is similar to comparable provisions in other environmental statutes. *See, e.g.,* 42 U.S.C. §7413(e). Suppose that a discharger violates effluent limits for biological oxygen demand and for nutrient loadings for one day. What is the maximum penalty? Suppose that she violates one effluent limit for 40 days. What is the maximum penalty? Does EPA have discretion to ask for less than the maximum penalty?

The Clean Air Act also provides a maximum penalty of $25,000 per day of violation. 42 U.S.C. §7413(b). In 2003, a federal district court concluded that Ohio Edison Company failed to install state-of-the-art pollution control devices when it modified its facility on several occasions between 1984 and 1998, as required by the new source review provisions of the Clean Air Act. *See* United States v. Ohio Edison Co., 276 F. Supp. 2d 829 (S.D. Ohio 2003). Ohio Edison subsequently agreed to spend $1.1 billion on pollution control, $25 million for supplemental environmental projects (cleanup projects going beyond the polluters' existing legal obligations), and pay a civil penalty of $8.5 million. Why do you think Ohio Edison agreed to such an expensive settlement? Three oil refiners also settled new source review enforcement actions by agreeing to spend $1 billion on pollution control. *See Three Oil Refiners to Spend $1 Billion To Reduce Air Emissions, Pay Penalties,* 36 Envt'l Rep. (BNA) 1279 (June 24, 2005). *Cf. Trial to Begin July 6 in Enforcement Case Against American Electric Power in Ohio,* 36 Envt'l Rep. (BNA) 1281 (June 24, 2005).

2. Gravity-Based Penalty.

Notice that section 309 (and other similar provisions as well) requires courts to take into account the seriousness of the violation. EPA refers to penalties based on the serious of violations as gravity-based penalties. Do you think that gravity-based penalties advance deterrence? Or would deterrence be better served by having uniform penalties, regardless of the seriousness of the violation? Should courts assume that harm is very serious when releases greatly exceed permit limits, or only when concrete harms to human health from the release are proven in court?

3. Economic Benefit.

The Clean Water Act requires consideration of the economic benefits of non-compliance in assessing a civil penalty. In the following case, a district court explained how the economic benefit factor is taken into account, in part through a reference to a model known as "BEN" that EPA uses to calculate economic benefit:

The Defendant, as a holder of an NPDES discharge permit, should not profit from noncompliance with that permit. If [the South Carolina Department of Health and Environmental Control] DHEC assessed a penalty that was below the Defendant's economic benefit of noncompliance, DHEC would not have penalized the Defendant at all; instead, the Defendant would have been rewarded for noncompliance with its permit. Economic benefit is the after-tax present value of avoided or delayed expenditures on necessary pollution control measures. Economic benefit represents the opportunity a polluter had to earn a return on funds that should have been spent to purchase, operate, and maintain appropriate pollution control devices. To determine a company's economic benefit from noncompliance with its permit, one must compare the company's cash flows associated with the delayed permit compliance measures to what those cash flows would have been if the company had obtained the necessary pollution control equipment on time.

EPA describes the nature of the economic benefit enjoyed by a firm that delays compliance with pollution control laws as follows:

> An organization's decision to comply with environmental regulations usually implies a commitment of financial resources; both initially, in the form of a capital investment or one-time expenditure, and over time, in the form of annual, continuing expenses. These expenditures might result in better protection of public health or environmental quality; however, they are unlikely to yield any direct economic benefit (i.e., net gain) to the organization. If these financial resources were not used for compliance, they presumably would be invested in projects with an expected direct economic benefit to the organization. This concept of alternative investment; that is, the amount the violator would normally expect to make by not investing in pollution control, is the basis for calculating the economic benefit of noncompliance.
>
> As part of the Civil Penalty Policy, EPA uses the Agency's penalty authority to remove or neutralize the economic incentive to violate environmental regulations. In the absence of enforcement and appropriate penalties, it is usually in the organization's best economic interest to delay the commitment of funds for compliance with environmental regulations and to avoid certain other associated costs, such as operating and maintenance expenses.

Friends of the Earth v. Laidlaw Environmental Services, Inc., 890 F. Supp. 470, 481 (D.S.C. 1995), *vacated on other grounds*, 149 F.3d 303 (4th Cir. 1998), *reversed*, 528 U.S. 167 (2000) (quoting EPA, *BEN User's Manual* I-6 (July 1990)). Because DHEC had not recouped the economic benefit Laidlaw had realized for its non-compliance when it filed a collusive lawsuit, the *Laidlaw* court found that the state had not diligently prosecuted Laidlaw and allowed a citizen suit to proceed. 890 F. Supp. at 499. The court later resolved a battle of economic expert witnesses and concluded that Laidlaw's noncompliance saved it $1,092,581. Friends of the Earth v. Laidlaw Environmental Services, 956 F. Supp. 588, 603 (D.S.C. 1997). *See generally* United States v. Municipal Auth. of Union Township, 150 F.3d 259, 264–65 (3d Cir. 1998) (district court judgments of economic benefit need not be precise because of the difficulty of determining economic benefit). Nevertheless, the district court awarded a penalty of only $405,800, because Laidlaw had incurred substantial legal expenses and would have to pay the attorney fees of its opponents. *Laidlaw*, 956 F. Supp. at 610–11. Was that appropriate? Which do you think is more difficult, proving a violation of a discharge limitation when monitoring data is accurate and reasonably frequent, or proving the economic benefit realized by non-compliance? More generally, a deterrence model seems to require confiscation of economic benefits derived from avoiding pollution control requirements.

4. Collection.

Surprisingly often, the government fails to collect all, or even a substantial portion of the fine assessed in an enforcement action. *See* Martha Mendoza and Christopher Sullivan, *Billions Uncollected in Penalties for Wrongdoing: How Does it Happen?: The System Punishes Symbolically, Imposing Massive Fines*, Salt Lake Tribune, March 19, 2006, available at http://www.sltrib.com/nationworld/ci_3618149. Government officials defended the frequent practice of drastically reducing penalties, sometimes even after announcing them to the public, by explaining that the agency's goal is "compliance," not the collection of penalties. Does reduction of assessed penalties serve the compliance goal?

A Note on Supplemental Environmental Projects

Most cases, of course, produce settlements, not trials. The settlements usually involve some combination of penalties and an agreement to take specific steps to remedy the violations. Increasingly, however, EPA has become interested in including requirements for supplemental environmental projects (SEPs), projects that go beyond merely correcting violations to provide affirmative, but not legally required, environmental benefits. *See Final EPA Supplemental Environmental Projects Policy Issued*, 63 Fed. Reg. 24796 (May 5, 1998) [hereinafter *SEP Policy*]. Commentators have praised the inclusion of these projects as mechanisms to benefit communities damaged by pollution. *See, e.g.*, Kathleen Boergers, *The EPA's Supplemental Environmental Projects Policy*, 26 Ecology L.Q. 777 (1999); Jeff Ganguly, *Environmental Remediation Through Supplemental Environmental Projects and Creative Negotiation: Renewed Community Involvement in Federal Enforcement*, 26 B.C. Envtl. Aff. L. Rev. 189 (1998-99).

In order to obtain the benefit of a SEP, EPA will sometimes agree to decrease a gravity-based penalty. This poses a significant legal issue, since both the environmental statutes and the Miscellaneous Receipts Act generally require that civil penalties go to the United States treasury. 31 U.S.C. §3302(b) (2000); Gwaltney of Smithfield, Ltd. v. Chesapeake Bay Foundation, 484 U.S. 49, 53 (1987) (stating that if a citizen prevails in a citizen suit, the court may impose a civil penalty "payable to the U.S. Treasury"). *Cf.* 42 U.S.C. §7604(g)(2) (2000) (authorizing use of a portion of a civil penalty to fund certain "beneficial mitigation projects"). If violators of environmental statutes spend money that would otherwise have gone to the Treasury to fund a SEP, this raises a question of whether civil penalties have been illegally diverted. *See* Sierra Club v. Elec. Controls Design, 909 F.2d 1350, 1352–56 (9th Cir. 1990) (allowing payment to an environmental organization "for their efforts to . . . protect" Oregon water quality, because no liability has been found, so no civil penalty has been diverted); Public Interest Research Group of New Jersey v. Powell Duffryn Terminals, Inc., 913 F.2d 64, 81–82 (3d Cir. 1990) (stating that "once the court labeled the money as civil penalties it could only be paid to the Treasury").

Accordingly, EPA's 1998 policy on SEPs requires that the minimum penalty assessed must remain greater than the economic benefit the polluter realized by not complying with the law. *See SEP Policy*, 63 Fed. Reg. at 24,801. Should EPA reduce gravity-based penalties in exchange for SEPs? Should EPA collect less of a monetary penalty than required to deprive the violator of any economic benefit from the violation? EPA has suggested that it may reconsider the requirement of making penalties adequate to confiscate any economic benefit, while noting that the 1998 guidance "is based upon the premise that collection of at least economic benefit ensures that violators are not allowed to obtain an economic advantage over their competitors who complied with the law." Memorandum from John Peter Suarez, Assistant Adm'r, EPA, to Various Administrators and Staff, Expanding the Use of Supplemental Environmental Projects 3 (July 11, 2003), available at http://www.epa.gov/compliance/resources/policies/civil/seps/seps-expandinguse.pdf. Does this premise hold up? Is this the best rationale for the policy? Should EPA approve profitable SEPs? Would more liberal SEP policies better serve deterrence? Would they create a more cooperative atmosphere? Which is more important?

In Public Interest Research Group of New Jersey v. Powell Duffryn Terminals, Inc., 913 F.2d 64, 82 (3d Cir. 1990), the Third Circuit stated that payments to an environmental benefit fund could qualify as injunctive relief if there is a "nexus" between the harm and the remedy. To the extent SEP payments are regarded as injunctive relief, the monies spent upon them do not fall into the category of civil penalties, which must go the Treasury, rather than to community or industry environmental projects. In 1993, EPA settled a case involving mobile source emission reductions by accepting public relations expenditures in exchange for a reduction in civil penalties. The Comptroller General questioned the legality of this settlement under the Miscellaneous Receipts Act because of the lack of nexus between the public relation expenditures and the harm from violating pollution control requirements, notwithstanding language in the relevant section of the Clean Air Act, 42 U.S.C.§7524, authorizing EPA to "compromise" civil penalties "with conditions." Opinion of the Comptroller General of the United States, GAO No. B–247155.2, available at 1993 WL 798227 (March 1, 1993). *See also* Opinion of the Comptroller General of the United States, GAO No. B-247155.2, available at 1992 WL 726317 (July 7, 1992). Suppose that the public relations campaign touted the benefits of low emission vehicles for the environment. Do you think that expenditures for this purpose have an adequate nexus to the harms done by violating mobile source pollution control requirements to qualify as appropriate injunctive relief?

Should problems of potential sweetheart deals lead to the abandonment of the possible environmental gains from SEPs? Should EPA allow companies to "promote" compliance in their industry by holding seminars as a SEP? *See SEP Policy*, 63 Fed. Reg. at 24800. What about environmental audits? *Id.* at 24799-800. Funding of university environmental research? *Id.* at 24801.

The pollution control statutes generally authorize courts to award any "appropriate relief." *See, e.g.*, 42 U.S.C. §7413(b). Why not just ask the court to order a SEP in addition to penalties, rather than induce one through penalty reduction?

In any case, civil remedies include fines and injunctions. The SEPs provide, in principle, a means of trading off some of the fines for agreement to a broad form of injunctive relief. But, these are not the only potential consequences of violations of pollution control statutes.

B.   CRIMINAL PENALTIES

Several statutes now supplement civil penalties with criminal penalties for certain kinds of violations. These penalties certainly have galvanized the attention of the regulated community and serve deterrence. But they have raised fairness concerns. The cases that follow focus on the problem of defining the sorts of violations that trigger criminal penalties. Generally, criminal penalties properly apply to only a subset of all violations.

United States v. Weitzenhoff
35 F.3d 1275 (9th Cir. 1993) (en banc)

FLETCHER, CIRCUIT JUDGE.

Michael H. Weitzenhoff and Thomas W. Mariani, who managed the East Honolulu Community Services Sewage Treatment Plant, appeal their convictions for violations of the Clean Water Act ("CWA"), contending that the district court misconstrued the word "knowingly" under section 1319(c)(2) of the CWA.

We affirm the convictions.

Facts and Procedural History

In 1988 and 1989 Weitzenhoff was the manager and Mariani the assistant manager of the East Honolulu Community Services Sewage Treatment Plant ("the plant"), located not far from Sandy Beach, a popular swimming and surfing beach on Oahu. The plant is designed to treat some 4 million gallons of residential wastewater each day by removing the solids and other harmful pollutants from the sewage so that the resulting effluent can be safely discharged into the ocean. The plant operates under a permit issued pursuant to the National Pollution Discharge Elimination System ("NPDES"), which established the limits on the Total Suspended Solids ("TSS") and Biochemical Oxygen Demand ("BOD") indicators of the solid and organic matter, respectively, in the effluent discharged at Sandy Beach. During the period in question, the permit limited the discharge of both the TSS and BOD to an average of 976 pounds per day over a 30-day period. It also imposed monitoring and sampling requirements on the plant's management.

. . . [W]aste activated sludge ("WAS"), was pumped to WAS holding tanks. From the holding tanks, the WAS could either be returned to other phases of the treatment process or hauled away to a different sewage treatment facility.

From March 1987 through March 1988, the excess WAS generated by the plant was hauled away to another treatment plant. . . . In March 1988, certain improvements were made to the East Honolulu plant and the hauling was discontinued. Within a few weeks, however, the plant began experiencing a buildup of excess WAS. Rather than have the excess WAS hauled away as before, however, Weitzenhoff and Mariani instructed two employees at the plant to dispose of it on a regular basis by pumping it from the storage tanks directly into the outfall, that is, directly into the ocean. The WAS thereby bypassed the plant's effluent sampler so that the samples taken and reported to Hawaii's Department of Health ("DOH") and the EPA did not reflect its discharge.

The evidence produced by the government at trial showed that WAS was discharged directly into the ocean from the plant on about 40 separate occasions from April 1988 to June 1989, resulting in some 436,000 pounds of pollutant solids being discharged into the ocean, and that the discharges violated the plant's 30-day average effluent limit under the permit for most of the months during which they occurred. Most of the WAS discharges occurred during the night, and none was reported to the DOH or EPA. DOH inspectors contacted the plant on several occasions in 1988 in response to complaints by lifeguards at Sandy Beach that sewage was being emitted from the outfall, but Weitzenhoff and Mariani repeatedly denied that there was any problem at the plant. In one letter responding to a DOH inquiry in October 1988, Mariani stated that "the debris that was reported could not have been from the East Honolulu Wastewater Treatment facility, as our records of effluent quality up to this time will substantiate." One of the plant employees who participated in the dumping operation testified that Weitzenhoff instructed him not to say anything about the discharges, because if they all stuck together and did not reveal anything, "they [couldn't] do anything to us."

Following an FBI investigation, Weitzenhoff and Mariani were charged in a thirty-one-count indictment with conspiracy and substantive violations of the Clean Water Act ("CWA"). At trial, Weitzenhoff and Mariani admitted having authorized the discharges, but claimed that their actions were justified under their interpretation of the NPDES permit. The jury found them guilty of six of the thirty-one counts.

Weitzenhoff was sentenced to twenty-one months and Mariani thirty-three months imprisonment. Each filed a timely notice of appeal.

Discussion

A. *Intent Requirement*

Section 1311(a) of the CWA prohibits the discharge of pollutants into navigable waters without an NPDES permit. 33 U.S.C. §1311(a). Section 1319(c)(2) makes it a felony offense to "knowingly violate section 1311, 1312, 1316, 1317, 1318, 1321(b)(3), 1328, or 1345, or any permit condition or limitation implementing any of such sections in a permit issued under section 1342."

Prior to trial, the district court construed "knowingly" in section 1319(c)(2) as requiring only that Weitzenhoff and Mariani were aware that they were discharging the pollutants in question, not that they knew they were violating the terms of the statute or permit. According to appellants, the district court erred in its interpretation of the CWA and in instructing the jury that "the government is not required to prove that the defendant knew that his act or omissions were unlawful," as well as in rejecting their proposed instruction based on the defense that they mistakenly believed their conduct was authorized by the permit. Apparently, no court of appeals has confronted the issue raised by appellants.

As with certain other criminal statutes that employ the term "knowingly," it is not apparent from the face of the statute whether "knowingly" means a knowing violation of the law or simply knowing conduct that is violative of the law. We turn, then, to the legislative history of the provision at issue to ascertain what Congress intended.

In 1987, Congress substantially amended the CWA, elevating the penalties for violations of the Act. Increased penalties were considered necessary to deter would-be polluters. With the 1987 amendments, Congress substituted "knowingly" for the earlier intent requirement of "willfully" that appeared in the predecessor to section 1319(c)(2). The Senate report accompanying the legislation explains that the changes in the penalty provisions were to ensure that "criminal liability shall attach to any person who is not in compliance with all applicable Federal, State and local requirements and permits *and causes* a

POTW [publicly owned treatment works] to violate any effluent limitation or condition in any permit issued to the treatment works." Similarly, the report accompanying the House version of the bill, which contained parallel provisions for enhancement of penalties, states that the proposed amendments were to "provide penalties for dischargers or individuals who knowingly or negligently violate *or cause the violation of* certain of the Act's requirements." Because they speak in terms of "causing" a violation, the congressional explanations of the new penalty provisions strongly suggest that criminal sanctions are to be imposed on an individual who knowingly engages in conduct that results in a permit violation, regardless of whether the polluter is cognizant of the requirements or even the existence of the permit.

Our conclusion that "knowingly" does not refer to the legal violation is fortified by decisions interpreting analogous public welfare statutes. The leading case in this area is *United States v. International Minerals & Chem. Corp.*, 402 U.S. 558 (1971). In *International Minerals*, the Supreme Court construed a statute which made it a crime to "knowingly violate any regulation" promulgated by the [Interstate Commerce Commission] pursuant to 18 U.S.C. §834(a), a provision authorizing the agency to formulate regulations for the safe transport of corrosive liquids. The Court held that the term "knowingly" referred to the acts made criminal rather than a violation of the regulation, and that "regulation" was a shorthand designation for the specific acts or omissions contemplated by the act. "Where . . . dangerous or deleterious devices or products or obnoxious waste materials are involved, the probability of regulation is so great that anyone who is aware that he is in possession of them or dealing with them must be presumed to be aware of the regulation."

[The court discusses its own precedent and cases in other jurisdictions following *International Minerals* in various cases, including several environmental cases.]

Subsequent to the filing of the original opinion in this case, the Supreme Court decided two cases which Weitzenhoff contends call our analysis into question. *See Ratzlaf v. United States*, 510 U.S. 135 (1994); *Staples v. United States*, 511 U.S. 600 (1994). We disagree.

The statute in *Ratzlaf* does not deal with a public welfare offense, but rather with violations of the banking statutes. . . . In contrast, parties such as Weitzenhoff are closely regulated and are discharging waste materials that affect public health. The *International Minerals* rationale requires that we impute to these parties knowledge of their operating permit. This was recognized by the Court in *Staples*.

The specific holding in *Staples* was that the government is required to prove that a defendant charged with possession of a machine gun knew that the weapon he possessed had the characteristics that brought it within the statutory definition of a machine gun. But the Court took pains to contrast the gun laws to other regulatory regimes, specifically those regulations that govern the handling of "obnoxious waste materials." It noted that the mere innocent ownership of guns is not a public welfare offense. The Court focused on the long tradition of widespread gun ownership in this country and, recognizing that approximately 50% of American homes contain a firearm, acknowledged that mere ownership of a gun is not sufficient to place people on notice that the act of owning an unregistered firearm is not innocent under the law.

   Staples thus explicitly contrasted the mere possession of guns to public welfare offenses, which include statutes that regulate ["]dangerous or deleterious devices or products or obnoxious waste materials["], and confirmed the continued vitality of statutes covering public welfare offenses, which "regulate potentially harmful or injurious items" and place a defendant on notice that he is dealing with a device or a substance "that places him in 'responsible relation to a public danger.'" . . . "In such cases Congress intended to place the burden on the defendant to ascertain at his peril whether [his conduct] comes within the inhibition of the statute."

   Unlike "[g]uns [which] in general are not 'deleterious devices or products or obnoxious waste materials,' that put their owners on notice that they stand 'in responsible relation to a public danger[,]'" the dumping of sewage and other pollutants into our nation's waters is precisely the type of activity that puts the discharger on notice that his acts may pose a public danger. Like other public welfare offenses that regulate the discharge of pollutants into the air, the disposal of hazardous wastes, the undocumented shipping of acids, and the use of pesticides on our food, the improper and excessive discharge of sewage causes cholera, hepatitis, and other serious illnesses, and can have serious repercussions for public health and welfare.

   The criminal provisions of the CWA are clearly designed to protect the public at large from the potentially dire consequences of water pollution and as such fall within the category of public welfare legislation. *International Minerals* . . . controls the case at hand. The government did not need to prove that Weitzenhoff and Mariani knew that their acts violated the permit or the CWA. . . .

   We *AFFIRM both the convictions.*

KLEINFELD, CIRCUIT JUDGE, with whom CIRCUIT JUDGES REINHARDT, KOZINSKI, TROTT, AND THOMAS G. NELSON join, dissenting from the order rejecting the suggestion for rehearing en banc.

   I respectfully dissent from our decision to reject the suggestion for rehearing en banc.

   . . . In my view, this is a case of exceptional importance, for two reasons. First, it impairs a fundamental purpose of criminal justice, sorting out the innocent from the guilty before imposing punishment. Second, it does so in the context of the Clean Water Act. This statute has tremendous sweep. Most statutes permit anything except what is prohibited, but this one prohibits all regulated conduct involving waters and wetlands except what is permitted. Much more ordinary, innocent, productive activity is regulated by this law than people not versed in environmental law might imagine.

. . . If we use prison to achieve social goals regardless of the moral innocence of those we incarcerate, then imprisonment loses its moral opprobrium and our criminal law becomes morally arbitrary.

We have now made felons of a large number of innocent people doing socially valuable work. They are innocent, because the one thing which makes their conduct felonious is something they do not know. It is we, and not Congress, who have made them felons. The statute, read in an ordinary way, does not. If we are fortunate, sewer plant workers around the circuit will continue to perform their vitally important work despite our decision. If they knew they risk three years in prison, some might decide that their pay, though sufficient inducement for processing the public's wastes, is not enough to risk prison for doing their jobs. We have decided that they should go to prison if, unbeknownst to them, their plant discharges exceed permit limits. Likewise for power plant operators who discharge warm water into rivers near their plants, and for all sorts of other dischargers in public and private life. If they know they are discharging into water, have a permit for the discharges, think they are conforming to their permits, but unknowingly violate their permit conditions, into prison they go with the violent criminals.

The statute does not say that. The statute at issue makes it a felony, subject to three years of imprisonment, to "knowingly violate[] . . . any permit condition or limitation." 33 U.S.C. §1319(c)(2)(A). . . .

In this case, the defendants, sewage plant operators, had a permit to discharge sewage into the ocean, but exceeded the permit limitations. The legal issue for the panel was what knowledge would turn innocently or negligently violating a permit into "knowingly" violating a permit. Were the plant operators felons if they knew they were discharging sewage, but did not know that they were violating their permit? Or did they also have to know they were violating their permit? Ordinary English grammar, common sense, and precedent, all compel the latter construction.

. . . NPDES permits are often difficult to understand and obey. The EPA had licensed the defendants' plant to discharge 976 pounds of waste per day, or about 409,920 pounds over the fourteen months covered by the indictment, into the ocean. The wrongful conduct was not discharging waste into the ocean. That was socially desirable conduct by which the defendants protected the people of their city from sewage-borne disease and earned their pay. The wrongful conduct was violating the NPDES permit by discharging 26,000 more pounds of waste than the permit authorized during the fourteen months. Whether these defendants were innocent or not, in the sense of knowing that they were exceeding their permit limitation, the panel's holding will make innocence irrelevant in other permit violation cases where the defendants had no idea that they were exceeding permit limits. The only thing they have to know to be guilty is that they were dumping sewage into the ocean, yet that was a lawful activity expressly authorized by their federal permit.

The statute says "knowingly violates . . . any permit condition or limitation." "Knowingly" is an adverb. It modifies the verb "violates." The object of the verb is "any permit condition or limitation." The word "knowingly" is placed before "violates" to "explain its meaning in the case at hand more clearly." Congress has distinguished those who knowingly violate permit conditions, and are thereby felons, from those who unknowingly violate permit conditions, so are not. The panel reads the statute as though it says "knowingly discharges pollutants." It does not. If we read the statute on the assumption that Congress used the English language in an ordinary way, the state of mind required is knowledge that one is violating a permit condition.

This approach has the virtue of attributing common sense and a rational purpose to Congress. It is one thing to defy a permit limitation, but quite another to violate it without realizing that one is violating it. Congress promulgated a parallel statute making it a misdemeanor "negligently" to violate a permit condition or limitation. 33 U.S.C. §1319(c)(1)(A). If negligent violation is a misdemeanor, why would Congress want to make it a felony to violate the permit without negligence and without even knowing that the discharge exceeded the permit limit? . . .

. . . [F]or the sake of discussion, suppose that the statute is ambiguous, as the panel says. Then the rule of lenity requires that the construction allowing the defendant more liberty rather than less be applied by the courts. "Lenity principles demand resolution of ambiguities in criminal statutes in favor of the defendant." The reason is the need for "fair warning."

The panel . . . tries to bolster its construction by categorizing the offense as a "public welfare offense," as though that justified more aggressive criminalization without a plain statutory command. This category is a modernized version of "malum prohibitum." Traditionally the criminal law distinguishes between *malum* in se, conduct wrong upon principles of natural moral law, and *malum prohibitum*, conduct not inherently immoral but wrong because prohibited by law. To put this in plain, modern terms, any normal person knows murder, rape and robbery are wrong, and they would be wrong even in a place with no sovereign and no law. Discharging 6% more pollutants than one's permit allows is wrong only because the law says so. Substitution of the modern term "public welfare offense" for the traditional one, *malum prohibitum*, allows for confusion by rhetorical suggestion. The new term suggests that other offenses might merely be private in their impact, and therefore less serious. The older set of terms made it clear that murder was more vile than violating a federal regulation. The category of *malum prohibitum*, or public welfare offenses, makes the rule of lenity especially important, most particularly for felonies, because persons of good conscience may not recognize the wrongfulness of the conduct when they engage in it.

Staples v. United States reminds us that "offenses that require no *mens rea* generally are disfavored." *Mens rea* may be dispensed with in public welfare offenses, but the penalty is a "significant consideration in determining whether the statute should be construed as dispensing with *mens rea*."

The potentially harsh penalty attached to violation of §5861(d) — up to 10 years' imprisonment—confirms our reading of the Act. Historically, the penalty imposed under a statute has been a significant consideration in determining whether the statute should be construed as dispensing with *mens rea*. Certainly, the cases that first defined the concept of the public welfare offense almost uniformly involved statutes that provided for only light penalties such as fines or short jail sentences, not imprisonment in the state penitentiary. . . .

Precedent cuts strongly against the panel's decision. Two Supreme Court decisions came down this term which should have caused us to rehear the case.

Ratzlaf v. United States, reversing a decision of ours, holds that to commit the crime of "willfully violating" the law against structuring cash transactions to evade currency transaction reporting requirements, the defendant has to know that his conduct is unlawful. It is not enough that he is engaging in the cash transactions with a purpose of evading currency transaction reporting requirements. Ignorance of the law generally is no excuse, but "Congress may decree otherwise." The Court was concerned that a narrower reading of the mental element of the crime would criminalize conduct committed without the criminal motive with which Congress was concerned.

At issue in *Staples v. United States* was a statute which made it a felony to possess an unregistered "firearm." The statute defined "firearm" to include a fully automatic gun, which would fire more than one bullet on a single pull of the trigger, but not a semiautomatic. The defendant possessed a fully automatic gun, but testified that he did not know it would fire more than one bullet with a single trigger pull. The trial judge had instructed the jury that his ignorance did not matter, so long as the government proved he possessed "a dangerous device of a type as would alert one to the likelihood of regulation." The Supreme Court again rejected dilution of the mental element of the crime. The Court explained that unlike the hand grenades in *United States v. Freed*, 401 U.S. 601 (1971), semiautomatics are innocently possessed by many people. Nor was knowledge that guns are regulated enough to require the owner to ascertain compliance with the regulations at his peril. That might do for a misdemeanor, but the felony status of the offense suggested a more plainly criminal mental state. Nor would the dangerousness of guns suffice to weaken the *mens rea* requirement:

> If we were to accept as a general rule the Government's suggestion that dangerous and regulated items place their owners under an obligation to inquire at their peril into compliance with regulations, we would undoubtedly reach some untoward results. Automobiles, for example, might also be termed "dangerous" devices and are highly regulated at both the state and federal levels. Congress might see fit to criminalize the violation of certain regulations concerning automobiles, and thus might make it a crime to operate a vehicle without a properly functioning emission control system. But we probably would hesitate to conclude on the basis of silence that Congress intended a prison term to apply to a car owner whose vehicle's emissions levels, wholly unbeknownst to him, began to exceed legal limits between regular inspection dates.

The panel cites *United States v. International Minerals & Chem. Corp.* . . . in support of its reading. *International Minerals* was a pre-*Ratzlaf* misdemeanor case. Because of the syntactically similar statute at issue in that case, it is the strongest authority for the panel's decision and raises the most serious question for my own analysis. It held that a shipper of sulfuric acid could be convicted of violating a statute applying to those who "knowingly violate[ ]" regulations governing shipments of corrosive liquids, regardless of whether he had knowledge of the regulations. *International Minerals* expressly limits its holding to "dangerous or deleterious devices or products or obnoxious waste materials." The Court distinguished materials not obviously subject to regulation:

> Pencils, dental floss, paper clips may also be regulated. But they may be the type of products which might raise substantial due process questions if Congress did not require "*mens rea*" as to each ingredient of the offense. But where, as here, dangerous or deleterious devices or products or obnoxious waste materials are involved, the probability of regulation is so great that anyone who is aware that he is in possession of them or dealing with them must be presumed to be aware of the regulation.

International Minerals would have much persuasive force for Weitzenhoff, because of the grammatical similarity of the statute, if (1) the Clean Water Act limited pollutants to "dangerous or deleterious devices or products or obnoxious waste materials;" (2) the crime was only a misdemeanor; and (3) *Staples* had not come down this term. But all three of these conditions are contrary to fact. The pollutants to which the Clean Water Act felony statute applies include many in the "pencils, dental floss, paper clips" category. Hot water, rock, and sand are classified as "pollutants" by the Clean Water Act. *See* 33 U.S.C. §1362(6). Discharging silt from a stream back into the same stream may amount to discharge of a pollutant. For that matter, so may skipping a stone into a lake. So may a cafeteria worker's pouring hot, stale coffee down the drain. Making these acts a misdemeanor is one thing, but a felony is quite another, as *Staples* teaches.

Congress made it a serious felony "knowingly" to violate permit limitations on discharge of pollutants. The harsh penalty for this serious crime must be reserved for those who know they are, in fact, violating permit limitations.

NOTES ON KNOWING VIOLATIONS

1. *Majority versus dissent.* Do you agree with the majority or the dissent in *Weitzenhoff*? Why?

2. *Fairness.* Is it fair to hold defendants liable for discharges if they do not know that they violate a permit? The permit at issue in *Weitzenhoff* authorized operators to bypass treatment and discharge effluent directly into the ocean for "essential maintenance to assure efficient operation." *Weitzenhoff*, 35 F.3d at

1287. Consider the following hypothetical variant on the *Weitzenhoff* problem. Suppose that Weitzenhoff can prove that accumulating sludge threatened to impede efficient operation of the plant. He consults with legal counsel who affirms, in good faith, that Weitzenhoff may legally discharge directly into the ocean, which he then does openly without trying to deceive anybody. EPA, however, ultimately disagrees with Weitzenhoff's interpretation of the permit condition authorizing bypass. EPA does not consider the bypass "essential" maintenance, because Weitzenhoff could have stored the waste or treated it off-site. EPA charges Weitzenhoff with "knowingly" violating his plant's NPDES permit. The court agrees with EPA's interpretation of the permit condition, reasoning that EPA could reasonably interpret the permit to deem bypass unessential when any plausible alternative existed. Should Weitzenhoff be held criminally liable for the violation?

What if the bypass only violated the bypass provision of the permit, but the discharge did not exceed effluent limitations? This would still be a violation of the permit, because permits forbid bypass unless one falls within the authorizing clause. But should it be a criminal violation? If not, should the law prohibit criminal prosecution under these circumstances, or should prosecutors employ discretion to eschew legally authorized criminal charges in this situation? Do you think that EPA would charge Weitzenhoff criminally under these facts?

3. *The limits of a knowing violation.* Suppose that Weitzenhoff had dumped the sludge into a pipe that he thought conducted the sludge into the treatment system. In fact, however, unknown to him, maintenance workers had rerouted the pipe to discharge directly into the ocean. If the effluent so discharged exceeded permit limits would there be a violation of the Act? Would the violation trigger criminal sanctions?

4. *Similar provisions.* Similar provisions exist in many other environmental statutes. *See, e.g.,* 15 U.S.C. §2615(b) (criminalizing knowing or willful violations of several TSCA provisions); 42 U.S.C. §7413(c) (criminal penalties for knowing violations of the Clean Air Act); §9603(b)(3), (c) (CERCLA); §11045(b)(4) (criminal penalties for knowing violations of one Emergency Planning and Community Right to Know Act provision); §6928(d) (criminal penalties for knowing violations of RCRA). Notice that the courts frequently consider interpretation of enforcement provisions in other statutes in interpreting a particular statutory provision. *See generally* William W. Buzbee, *The One Congress Fiction in Statutory Interpretation,* 149 U. Pa. L. Rev. 171 (2000).

5. *Knowing endangerment.* RCRA authorizes prison sentences of up to 15 years if a person illegally and "knowingly transports, treats, stores, disposes of, or exports" hazardous waste if he "knows . . . that he thereby places another person in imminent danger of death or serious bodily injury." 42 U.S.C. §6928(e). RCRA also authorizes criminal sanctions for knowing violations of RCRA if the violator does not endanger anybody or does not know that she does. *See* 42 U.S.C. §6928(d). But the maximum prison terms for first-time violations not involving knowing endangerment are two years of imprisonment for most violations and five years for some of them. *See id.*

Should any criminal penalty apply if the violator does not know that the acts put another in imminent danger?

In United States v. Hansen, 262 F.3d 1217 (11th Cir. 2001), the Court of Appeals for the Eleventh Circuit upheld the conviction of two CEOs and a plant manager for conspiracy to violate a number of environmental statutes and for knowing endangerment under RCRA. The knowing endangerment conviction arose out of the storage of highly caustic wastewater in a basement. Employees coming into contact with this wastewater testified that they suffered serious skin and respiratory conditions as a result. *Id.* at 1243. Suppose that nobody had suffered any serious bodily harm, but that the wastewater had the capacity to cause serious bodily harm. Should the court uphold a conviction for knowing endangerment?

United States v. Ahmad
101 F.3d 386 (5th Cir. 1996)

SMITH, CIRCUIT JUDGE.
Attique Ahmad appeals his conviction of, and sentence for, criminal violations of the Clean Water Act ("CWA"). Concluding that the district court erred in its instructions to the jury, we reverse and remand.

I

This case arises from the discharge of a large quantity of gasoline into the sewers of Conroe, Texas, in January 1994. In 1992, Ahmad purchased the "Spin-N-Market No. 12," a combination convenience store and gas station. . . . Some time after Ahmad bought the station, he discovered that one of the tanks, which held high-octane gasoline, was leaking. This did not pose an immediate hazard, because the leak was at the top of the tank; gasoline could not seep out. The leak did, however, allow water to enter into the tank and contaminate the gas. . . .

In October 1993, Ahmad hired CTT Environmental Services ("CTT"), a tank testing company, to examine the tank. CTT determined that it contained approximately 800 gallons of water, and the rest [7200 gallons] mostly gasoline. Jewel McCoy, a CTT employee, testified that she told Ahmad that the leak could not be repaired until the tank was completely emptied, which CTT offered to do for 65 cents per gallon plus $65 per hour of labor. After McCoy gave Ahmad this estimate, he inquired whether he could empty the tank himself. She replied that it would be dangerous and illegal to do so. On her testimony, he responded, "Well, if I don't get caught, what then?"

On January 25, 1994, Ahmad rented a hand-held motorized water pump from a local hardware store, telling a hardware store employee that he was planning to use it to remove water from his backyard. [Ahmad pumped gasoline and water from his tank, whence it flowed into Possum Creek and into the city sewer system. As a result, city officials had to use several vacuum trucks to decontaminate the creek, a sewage treatment plant supervisor evacuated the plant and called a hazardous materials crew to the scene, and firefighters evacuated two schools because of a "tremendous explosion hazard."] . . .

Ahmad was indicted for three violations of the CWA: knowingly discharging a pollutant from a point source into a navigable water of the United States without a permit. . . , knowingly operating a source in violation of a pretreatment standard. . . , and knowingly placing another person in imminent danger of death or serious bodily injury by discharging a pollutant. . . . At trial, Ahmad did not dispute that he had discharged gasoline from the tank or that eventually it had found its way to Possum Creek and the sewage treatment plant. Instead, he contended that his discharge of the gasoline was not "knowing," because he had believed he was discharging water.

[Ahmad attempted unsuccessfully to introduce evidence to] show that Ahmad did not knowingly discharge gasoline himself, but rather only negligently left the pump in the hands of his employees. . . . The jury found Ahmad guilty on counts one and two and deadlocked on count three.

II

Ahmad argues that the district court improperly instructed the jury on the *mens rea* required for count[] one. . . . The instruction on count one stated in relevant part:

> For you to find Mr. Ahmad guilty of this crime, you must be convinced that the government has proved each of the following beyond a reasonable doubt:
>
> (1) That on or about the date set forth in the indictment,
> (2) the defendant knowingly discharged
> (3) a pollutant
> (4) from a point source
> (5) into the navigable waters of the United States
> (6) without a permit to do so.

Ahmad contends that the jury should have been instructed that the statutory *mens rea*—knowledge—was required as to each element of the offenses, rather than only with regard to discharge or the operation of a source. . . .

The language of the CWA is less than pellucid. Title 33 U.S.C. §1319(c)(2)(A) says that "any person who knowingly violates" any of a number of other sections of the CWA commits a felony. One of the provisions that §1319(c)(2)(A) makes it unlawful to violate is §1311(a), which, when read together with a series of definitions in §1362, prohibits the addition of any pollutant to navigable waters from a "point source." That was the crime charged in count one. . . .

The principal issue is to which elements of the offense the modifier "knowingly" applies. . . . Ahmad argues that . . . "knowingly violates" should be read to require him knowingly to have acted with regard to each element of the offenses. The government, in contrast, contends that "knowingly violates" requires it to prove only that Ahmad knew the nature of his acts and that he performed them intentionally. Particularly at issue is whether "knowingly" applies to the element of the discharge's being a pollutant, for Ahmad's main theory at trial was that he thought he was discharging water, not gasoline.

The Supreme Court has spoken to this issue in broad terms. In *United States v. X-Citement Video, Inc.*, 513 U.S. 64 (1994), the Court read "knowingly" to apply to each element of a child pornography offense, notwithstanding its conclusion that under the "most natural grammatical reading" of the statute it should apply only to the element of having transported, shipped, received, distributed, or reproduced the material at issue. The Court also reaffirmed the long-held view that "the presumption in favor of a scienter requirement should apply to each of the statutory elements which criminalize otherwise innocent conduct."
. . .

Our own precedents are in the same vein. In *United States v. Baytank (Houston), Inc.*, 934 F.2d 599, 613 (5th Cir. 1991), we concluded that a conviction for knowing and improper storage of hazardous wastes under 42 U.S.C. §6928(d)(2)(A) requires "that the defendant know[ ] factually what he is doing — storing, what is being stored, and that what is being stored factually has the potential for harm to others or the environment, and that he has no permit. . . ." This is directly analogous to the interpretation of the CWA that Ahmad urges upon us. Indeed, we find it eminently sensible that the phrase "knowingly violates" in §1319(c)(2)(A), when referring to other provisions that define the elements of the offenses §1319 creates, should uniformly require knowledge as to each of those elements rather than only one or two. . . .

In support of its interpretation of the CWA, the government cites cases from other circuits. We find these decisions both inapposite and unpersuasive on the point for which they are cited. In *United States v. Hopkins*, 53 F.3d 533, 537–41 (2d Cir. 1995), the court held that the government need not demonstrate that a §1319(c)(2)(A) defendant knew his acts were illegal. The illegality of the defendant's actions is not an element of the offense, however. In *United States v. Weitzenhoff*, 35 F.3d 1275 (9th Cir. 1994), the court similarly was concerned almost exclusively with whether the language of the CWA creates a mistake-of-law defense. Both cases are easily distinguishable, for neither directly addresses mistake-of-fact or the statutory construction issues raised by Ahmad.

The government also protests that CWA violations fall into the judicially-created exception for "public welfare offenses," under which some regulatory crimes have been held not to require a showing of *mens rea*. On its face, the CWA certainly does appear to implicate public welfare.

As recent cases have emphasized, however, the public welfare offense exception is narrow. The *Staples* Court, for example, held that the statute prohibiting the possession of machine guns fell outside the exception, notwithstanding the fact that "[t]ypically, our cases recognizing such offenses involve statutes that regulate potentially harmful or injurious items."

Though gasoline is a "potentially harmful or injurious item," it is certainly no more so than are machine guns. Rather, *Staples* held, the key to the public welfare offense analysis is whether "dispensing with *mens rea* would require the defendant to have knowledge only of traditionally lawful conduct." The CWA offenses of which Ahmad was convicted have precisely this characteristic, for if knowledge is not required as to the nature of the substance discharged, one who honestly and reasonably believes he is discharging water may find himself guilty of a felony if the substance turns out to be something else.

The fact that violations of §1319(c)(2)(A) are felonies punishable by years in federal prison confirms our view that they do not fall within the public welfare offense exception. As the *Staples* Court noted, public welfare offenses have virtually always been crimes punishable by relatively light penalties such as fines or short jail sentences, rather than substantial terms of imprisonment. Serious felonies, in contrast, should not fall within the exception "absent a clear statement from Congress that *mens rea* is not required." Following *Staples*, we hold that the offenses charged in counts one and two are not public welfare offenses and that the usual presumption of a *mens rea* requirement applies. With the exception of purely jurisdictional elements, the *mens rea* of knowledge applies to each element of the crimes.

. . . .

IV

Because we reverse Ahmad's convictions, we need not address his sentencing claims. The convictions are REVERSED and the case REMANDED.

ADDITIONAL NOTES ON THE "KNOWINGLY VIOLATED" STANDARD

1. *Consistency with* Weitzenhoff. Is *Ahmad* consistent with *Weitzenhoff*?

2. *Public welfare offense.* The *Ahmad* court held that Ahmad's Clean Water Act violation did not amount to a public welfare offense. What is the consequence of that holding? The *Ahmad* holding on that point seems to be a minority view. *See* United States v. Kelley Technical Coatings, Inc., 157 F.3d 432, 439 n.4 (6th Cir. 1998) (expressing the Sixth Circuit's agreement with the Second and Ninth Circuits that CWA violations constitute public welfare offenses). On the other hand, the Supreme Court has held (as both cases

noted) that illegal possession of a machine gun does not constitute a public welfare offense. Should violations of the Clean Water Act be deemed a public welfare offense if violations of regulations of machine guns are not?

3. *When is criminal enforcement appropriate?* An EPA working group concluded that criminal enforcement should apply to the "most serious forms of environmental misconduct." CONSENSUS WORK GROUP, EPA, MANAGEMENT REVIEW OF EPA's CRIMINAL ENFORCEMENT PROGRAM 2 (1986). The working group established three goals: (1) deterring intentional violations, (2) severely punishing egregious violators, and (3) assuring the integrity of all EPA regulatory programs. Do you think that jailing Ahmad is consistent with the philosophy? What about Weitzenhoff?

4. *The Exxon Valdez.* On March 24, 1989, the Exxon Valdez supertanker ran aground, dumping around 10.8 million gallons of crude oil into Alaska's pristine Prince William Sound. The captain of the vessel was drunk and had a history of drunkenness known to Exxon's management. The third mate at the helm at the time of the accident was not legally authorized to pilot the tanker in those waters. Exxon did not have an adequate contingency plan for the vessel, had not made adequate emergency response equipment available, and had laid off much of its emergency response team before the accident. Robert W. Adler and Charles Lord, *Environmental Crimes: Raising the Stakes,* 59 Geo. Wash. L. Rev. 781, 782, 822 (1990-91). Assuming that all of these factors led to a serious environmental disaster, should criminal penalties apply to Exxon? Should the CEO go to jail? What about the head of personnel? (Prosecutors only brought criminal charges against the ship's captain.)

5. *Willful violations.* The Safe Drinking Water Act and the Emergency Planning and Community Right to Know Act only apply criminal penalties for willful violations. *See* 42 U.S.C. §§300h-2(b)(2), 11045(b)(4). Should courts require knowledge that the acts deliberately undertaken violate the law when this language is employed? *Cf.* United States v. Wilson, 133 F.3d 251, 262 (4th Cir. 1997) (suggesting that when Congress changed the Clean Water Act's "willful" violation language to establish a "knowing" violation trigger for criminal penalties, it rejected requirement of knowledge of an act's illegality).

PFOA REPORTING VIOLATIONS

You are the counsel for DuPont. EPA has charged your client with various reporting violations under TSCA stemming from its failure to report data showing that a high percentage of its pregnant employees exposed to PFOA gave birth to children with birth defects and other information. Consider the Environmental Working Group's assessment of DuPont's potential liability for violations of TSCA reporting requirements with respect to PFOA. If you represented DuPont, what arguments would you make to reduce the liability?

EPA Count 1 against DuPont: EPA found that DuPont violated federal law, Section 8(e) of [TSCA], by failing to inform EPA about the company's Teflon ingredient polluting human cord blood. This provision of TSCA requires that a company notify the Administrator within 15 days of findings that support a reasonable conclusion of a substantial risk of injury to human health or the environment and carries a maximum penalty of $183.8 million. . . .

Calculations
Duration of Violation: June 15, 1981–March 6, 2001

Daily fine from June 15, 1981 through January 30, 1997	$25,000/day
Fine through Jan 30 1997 =(5708 days) × ($25,000/day)	$142.7 million
Daily fine from February 1, 1998 through March 6, 2001	$27,500/day
Fine from Feb 1 1998 through Mar 6 2001=(1496 days) x ($27,500/day)	$41.1 million
Total Count 1 fine	$183.8 million

EPA Count 2 against DuPont: EPA found that DuPont violated federal law, Section 8(e) of [TSCA], by failing to inform EPA about the company's Teflon ingredient polluting local drinking water supplies surrounding the company's Parkersburg, West Virginia plant. This finding carries a maximum penalty of $91.6 million . . . .

Calculations
Duration of violation: July 24, 1991—March 6, 2001

Daily fine from July 24, 1991 through January 30, 1997	$25,000/day
Fine through Jan 30 1997=(2,017days)×($25,000/day)	$50.4 million
Daily fine from February 1, 1998 through March 6, 2001	$27,500/day
Fine from Feb 1 1998 through Mar 6 2001=(149days)×($27,500/day)	$41.1 million
Total Count 2 fine	$91.6 million

EPA Count 3 against DuPont: EPA issued a Notice of Deficiency on May 5, 1997 in DuPont's efforts to renew a site permit, requesting that DuPont submit to the agency all known toxicological information on the Teflon ingredient PFOA (C8). DuPont failed to submit data from its birth defects study. EPA found that this constitutes a violation of reporting requirements under the Resource Conservation and Recovery Act. This finding carries a maximum penalty of $37.6 million. . . .

Calculations
Duration of violation: June 6, 1997–March 6, 2001 (1369 days)

Daily fine:	$27,500/day
Fine (1369 days)×($27,500/day):	$37.6 million
Total Count 3 fine:	$37.6 million

Environmental Working Group, *EPA finds DuPont guilty of withholding Teflon blood and water pollution studies: Company faces fines of up to*

$313 million, available at http://www.ewg.org/issues/PFCs/tsca8e_teflon/index.php.

1. *Continuing Violation.* Assume that DuPont has violated section 8(e) of TSCA, which states:

> Any person who manufactures . . . a chemical . . . who obtains information which reasonably supports the conclusion that such substance or mixture presents a substantial risk of injury to health or the environment shall immediately inform the Administrator [of EPA]. . . .

15 U.S.C. §2607(e). TSCA section 16(a) requires violators of various TSCA provisions, including the reporting provision, to pay a civil penalty not to exceed $25,000 for each violations and then states that "Each day of violation shall . . . constitute a separate violation . . . ." 15 U.S.C. §2615(a). Assume that the durations of violations the Environmental Working Group set out correspond to the time between DuPont becoming aware of the document subject to a disclosure obligation under TSCA section 8(e) and the date it sent the document to EPA. Was there a continuous violation, as suggested by the Environmental Working Group? Compare All Regions Chem. Labs, Inc. v. EPA, 932 F.2d 73, 77 (1st Cir. 1991) (upholding a penalty of $20,000 when company failed to report a release, but a state agency and private citizen informed EPA of the releases) *with* United States v. Trident Seafoods Corp., 60 F.3d 556, 558–59 (9th Cir. 1995) (declining to find a continuous violation when statute and implementing regulation do not clearly require one, but citing cases imposing penalties for every day covered by a reporting period).

2. *SEPs.* Suppose that EPA proposes that DuPont remedy its reporting violations by agreeing to phase out PFOA. Do you think that your client can obtain a substantial reduction of penalties in exchange for agreeing to this?

3. *Criminal Penalties.* DuPont received an order from EPA to report "known toxicological information" about PFOA under RCRA. Suppose that DuPont did not reveal the results of its survey of its pregnant employees because its counsel advised it that PFOA is not a hazardous waste under RCRA and, therefore, EPA did not have authority to demand information about PFOA. A court later determines that EPA does have authority to demand information about potentially hazardous waste that is not yet classified as such under RCRA. Do you think that your client may be found criminally liable?

4. *Outcome.* DuPont settled the lawsuit stemming from the alleged reporting violations, paying a fine of $16.5 million. *Going, Going, Trying to Go Green*, N. Y. Times at C5 (Oct. 14, 2006).

While only the government can seek criminal penalties under the environmental statutes, citizens can sometimes seek civil penalties on their own. We turn to this use of citizen suits in the next chapter.

17

Citizen Enforcement

Congress included citizen enforcement provisions in numerous environmental statutes. *See, e.g.*, 42 U.S.C. §§6972 (RCRA), 7604 (Clean Air Act); 33 U.S.C. §1365 (Clean Water Act). It did so in order to supplement government enforcement resources. These provisions also serve as a check on lax government enforcement. During the Reagan Administration, for example, citizen suit enforcement assumed a leading role when federal enforcement dwindled.

This chapter first discusses the relationship between citizen enforcement and government enforcement. It then presents materials governing statutory and constitutional standing to sue, which are heavily influenced by ideas about the legitimacy of citizen suits. It addresses a matter of great practical importance, attorney's fees. The chapter closes with a very brief review of enforcement's record and a final PFOA problem that challenges you to work out an enforcement strategy, taking into account a lot of what you've learned from previous chapters.

A. RELATIONSHIP TO GOVERNMENT ENFORCEMENT

Allowing citizens to sue may invigorate enforcement, but it means that government cannot shield violators from penalties by simply declining to enforce. This may enhance the deterrent effect of enforcement, because polluters cannot rely on political power to limit enforcement. But it raises issues for those who believe that enforcement should be subject to political constraints and reasonably direct democratic controls.

A typical citizen suit provision (from the Clean Water Act) follows. As you read it, try to think about how it addresses the relationship between government and citizen enforcement:

33 U.S.C. §1365. Citizen suits

(a) Authorization; jurisdiction

... [A]ny citizen[1] [having an interest which may be adversely affected] may commence a civil action on his own behalf—

(1) against any person ... who is alleged to be in violation of (A) an effluent standard or limitation under this chapter or (B) an order issued by the Administrator or a State with respect to such a standard or limitation. ...

The district courts shall have jurisdiction to enforce such an effluent standard or limitation, or such an order ... and to apply any appropriate civil penalties under section 1319(d) of this title.

(b) Notice

No action may be commenced—

(1) under subsection (a)(1) of this section—

(A) prior to sixty days after the plaintiff has given notice of the alleged violation (i) to the Administrator, (ii) to the State in which the alleged violation occurs, and (iii) to any alleged violator of the standard, limitation, or order, or

(B) if the Administrator or State has commenced and is diligently prosecuting a civil or criminal action in a court of the United States, or a State to require compliance with the standard, limitation, or order, but in any such action in a court of the United States any citizen may intervene as a matter of right. ...

(c) Venue; intervention by Administrator; United States interests protected

(1) Any action respecting a violation by a discharge source of an effluent standard or limitation or an order respecting such standard or limitation may be brought under this section only in the judicial district in which such source is located.

(2) In such action under this section, the Administrator, if not a party, may intervene as a matter of right.

(3) PROTECTION OF INTERESTS OF UNITED STATES — Whenever any action is brought under this section in a court of the United States, the plaintiff shall serve a copy of the complaint on the Attorney General and the Administrator. No consent judgment shall be entered in an action in which the United States is not a party prior to 45 days following the receipt of a copy of the proposed consent judgment by the Attorney General and the Administrator.

---

1. Another subsection of this section defines citizen as "a person ... having an interest which is or may be adversely affected." 42 U.S.C. §1365(g).

Which subsections of this citizen suit provision set out above seek to preserve government discretion? How do they do this? Do they strike an appropriate balance between the desire for political control of enforcement and the desire to have citizen suits as an effective deterrent?

Notice that the Clean Water Act's citizen suit provision (and similar provisions in other statutes) bars citizen suits when the state or federal government has commenced and is "diligently prosecuting" a violation. Should citizen suits be barred in this instance? Should citizen suits be barred only for "diligent" prosecution or for any prosecution? Why do you suppose Congress allowed citizen suits when a non-diligent prosecution is underway? What constitutes diligent prosecution?

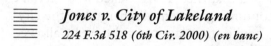

Jones v. City of Lakeland
224 F.3d 518 (6th Cir. 2000) (en banc)

KRUPANSKY, CIRCUIT JUDGE.

. . . Plaintiffs seek redress against the City for its ongoing practice of discharging contaminated sewage, sludge, and other toxic, noxious, and hazardous substances into Oliver Creek, in amounts exceeding those permitted by [its] National Pollutant Discharge Elimination System Permit (NPDES permit) . . . .

The City responded by asserting that federal court jurisdiction over citizen enforcement actions is denied by the Clean Water Act if the Administrator of the Environmental Protection Agency, or a state, had already commenced and was diligently prosecuting an action to require compliance with a standard, limitation, or order of the Agency or the state. The plaintiffs countered by stating that their complaint facially impugned the City's action of issuing, but not effectively enforcing, a series of compliance orders while concurrently permitting the City to continue to discharge increasing amounts of impermissible toxic, noxious, hazardous, and health-threatening sewage and other raw waste into Oliver Creek during the ten years preceding their legal action; and that the City's demonstrated lax enforcement did not constitute "diligent prosecution" mandated by the Clean Water Act that would preclude their suit. . . .

. . . [The Tennessee Department of Environment and Conservation's] TDEC's administrative enforcement action over a ten-year period was inadequate to address plaintiffs' concerns. During this inordinately long period of administrative enforcement, TDEC: (1) permitted the City to discharge impermissible volumes of contaminated raw human sewage, sludge, and other toxic, noxious substances into Oliver Creek on an ongoing basis thereby creating significant risks to human health and wildlife in, about, and along the water course; (2) permitted the City . . . to increase the impermissible volume of contaminated raw waste water discharging into the stabilizing lagoon that feeds Oliver Creek by allowing the City to continue to make connections

and/or line extensions to its wastewater collection system; (3) waived countless NPDES violation notices; (4) extended and waived the compliance deadlines of three, possibly four, of its sweetheart consent orders with the City; and
(5) imposed nominal token penalties in lieu of punitive compliance incentive
penalties of $10,000.00 per day authorized by the Clean Water Act, all of
which conduct contradicted a level of "diligent prosecution" demanded by 33
U.S.C. §1365(b), especially in light of the City's ongoing impermissible
pollution of Oliver Creek as late as September 30, 1996, the date this action
was commenced. The trial court's resolution to the contrary is not convincing
and clearly erroneous, and is REVERSED. . . .

NORRIS, CIRCUIT JUDGE, dissenting.

     . . . I respectfully dissent. . . .

     In their complaint, plaintiffs alleged that the "TDEC failed to undertake
any action to prevent or abate the continuing current discharge by [the city]
into Oliver Creek from the existing stabilization lagoon and thereby allowed
the wrongful discharge to increase." Plaintiffs' primary contention appears to
be not that the TDEC is doing nothing but, rather, that its prosecution cannot
be diligent if it continues to allow the city to dump impermissible amounts of
waste into Oliver Creek and if its attempts to remedy the problem are limited
to entering a series of ineffective administrative orders.

     I cannot agree with plaintiffs' view of the record. In concluding that the
state was in fact diligently prosecuting an action against the city, the district
court noted that four orders had been entered between the city (or its
predecessor in interest) and the TDEC, the last of which was on August 26,
1996, one month prior to plaintiffs' filing of this action. This latest order
required that the city be in full compliance with its National Pollutant
Discharge Elimination System ("NPDES") permit by July 1, 1997. The court
cited this fourth order as an example of the state's diligent prosecution of its
action against the city. The record before this court further reflects that the city
attempted to comply with the orders and that the TDEC extended deadlines in
response to practical difficulties the city encountered in reaching full compliance. The fourth order required the city to pay a fine and provided for
additional fines should the city fail to meet the full requirements of the order.
The district court recognized that an enforcing agency must be accorded the
latitude to respond to circumstances that delay remedial projects and warrant
reassessment of compliance target dates. In using the term "diligently prosecuting," Congress did not contemplate the rigidity plaintiffs would have us
visit upon the Clean Water Act's enforcement scheme. It is clear that the
TDEC is attempting to remedy the specific problems plaintiffs cite in their
complaint. Accordingly, I am unable to say that the district court erred when it
concluded that the TDEC's continued enforcement represents diligent prosecution as contemplated by the statute. . . .

NOTES ON *JONES*

1. *What is diligent prosecution?* Should the court find diligent prosecution under the facts of this case? Does a citizen suit in this context usefully supplement the state action or improperly interfere with state efforts to correct the violations? Assume that the state could intervene in the citizen suit (*i.e.*, secure a status where it has a right to participate in the court proceedings). Would the court tend to defer to the state when questions arose about what remedial orders and penalties were appropriate?

2. *Diligent administrative enforcement.* A number of courts have held that the diligent prosecution bar in section 505 only applies when a governmental entity has brought an action in state or federal court. *See* 33 U.S.C. §1365(b)(1)(B). Yet, many states, like the federal government, often use administrative, rather than judicial, proceedings as enforcement mechanisms. Section 309(g)(6)(A) establishes a diligent prosecution bar for federal administrative enforcement actions and for actions under state administrative enforcement provisions that are "comparable" to the federal administrative enforcement provisions. *See* 33 U.S.C. §1319(g)(6)(A)(i), (ii). Should courts hold state provisions comparable when they provide for smaller penalties than the federal statute? *Compare* North and South Rivers Watershed Ass'n v. Town of Scituate, 949 F.2d 552, 556 (1st Cir. 1991) (holding that a state statutory scheme authorizing the state to levy similar penalties to those provided by federal law is "comparable" even if the particular provision the state invoked does not authorize penalties) *with* Citizens for a Better Environment, California v. Union Oil Co. of California, 83 F.3d 1111, 1117-18 (9th Cir. 1996) (finding no comparability when California relied on a provision that did not authorize comparable civil penalties). What if a state statute provides identical penalties, but fails to offer citizens a right to participate in the crafting of a remedy, a right available in federal administrative proceedings? *Compare Jones*, 224 F.3d at 523–24 (holding that such state statutory provisions are not comparable to the federal provision); McAbee v. City of Fort Payne, 318 F.3d 1248, 1256–57 (11th Cir. 2003) (state law providing for only after-the-fact participation without adequate notice found not comparable to federal provision) *with* Arkansas Wildlife Federation v. ICI Americas, Inc., 29 F.3d 376, 381-82 (8th Cir. 1994) (finding comparability even though the state law only provided for after-the-fact citizen participation); Lockett v. EPA, 319 F.3d 678, 684–687 (5th Cir. 2003) (holding that state statute providing for public participation as of right for orders contested by the polluter and administrative discretion to offer the public an after-the-fact hearing for uncontested orders is comparable to federal provision).

B. STANDING AND THE GWALTNEY PROBLEM

The original citizen suit provisions in many statutes authorized "any person" to bring suit. *See, e.g.,* 42 U.S.C. §7604(a). *Cf.* 33 U.S.C. §1365(g) (defining a citizen who can bring suit as a person "having an interest which is or may be adversely affected"). This reflects an intention to allow an individual citizen to function as a private attorney general enforcing the law. Attitudes toward the legitimacy of such a role have influenced both the interpretation of the statutory citizen suit provisions and the judicial doctrine of standing, which limits who may sue.

In an early case in which the Sierra Club sought to challenge a United States Forest Service proposal to authorize a ski resort in the Mineral King Valley in California, the Supreme Court held:

> The injury alleged by the Sierra Club will be incurred entirely by reason of the change in the uses to which Mineral King will be put, and the attendant change in the aesthetics and ecology of the area. Thus, in referring to the road to be built through Sequoia National Park, the complaint alleged that the development "would destroy or otherwise adversely affect the scenery, natural and historic objects and wildlife of the park and would impair the enjoyment of the park for future generations." We do not question that this type of harm may amount to an "injury in fact" sufficient to lay the basis for standing under §10 of the [Administrative Procedure Act]. Aesthetic and environmental well-being, like economic well-being, are important ingredients of the quality of life in our society, and the fact that particular environmental interests are shared by the many rather than the few does not make them less deserving of legal protection through the judicial process. But the "injury in fact" test requires more than an injury to a cognizable interest. It requires that the party seeking review be himself among the injured.

Sierra Club v. Morton, 405 U.S. 727, 734-35 (1972). Thus, the Court accepted the idea that non-economic injury could create standing to sue. At the same time, it rejected a pure private attorney general theory that "any person" could be considered an aggrieved party entitled to judicial review under the Administrative Procedure Act (APA), the statute the Sierra Club relied upon to justify judicial review. The Court required the Sierra Club to show that it or some of its members would experience some of the environmental harms that the Mineral King development might bring. The early citizen suit provisions authorizing "any person" to sue thus offered broader statutory standing than that afforded by the APA.

In the following case, the court interpreted the Clean Water Act's citizen suit provision narrowly, thus denying an environmental group the right to litigate some kinds of violations.

Gwaltney of Smithfield, Ltd. v. Chesapeake Bay Foundation, Inc.
484 U.S. 49 (1987)

JUSTICE MARSHALL delivered the opinion of the Court.

In this case, we must decide whether §505(a) of the Clean Water Act, also known as the Federal Water Pollution Control Act . . . confers federal jurisdiction over citizen suits for wholly past violations.

I

. . . Between 1981 and 1984, petitioner repeatedly violated the conditions of [its] permit by exceeding effluent limitations on five of the seven pollutants covered. These violations are chronicled in the Discharge Monitoring Reports that the permit required petitioner to maintain. . . . Petitioner installed new equipment to improve its chlorination system in March 1982, and its last reported chlorine violation occurred in October 1982. The new chlorination system also helped to control the discharge of fecal coliform, and the last recorded fecal coliform violation occurred in February 1984. Petitioner installed an upgraded wastewater treatment system in October 1983, and its last reported TKN violation occurred on May 15, 1984.

Respondents Chesapeake Bay Foundation and Natural Resources Defense Council, two nonprofit corporations dedicated to the protection of natural resources, sent notice in February 1984 to Gwaltney, the Administrator of EPA, and the Virginia State Water Control Board, indicating respondents' intention to commence a citizen suit under the Act based on petitioner's violations of its permit conditions. Respondents proceeded to file this suit in June 1984, alleging that petitioner "has violated . . . [and] will continue to violate its NPDES permit." . . .

Before the District Court reached a decision, Gwaltney moved in May 1985 for dismissal of the action for want of subject-matter jurisdiction under the Act. Gwaltney argued that the language of §505(a), which permits private citizens to bring suit against any person "alleged to be in violation" of the Act,[1] requires that a defendant be violating the Act at the time of suit. . . .

---

1. In its entirety, §505(a), as codified, 33 U. S. C. § 1365(a), provides:

"Except as provided in subsection (b) of this section, any citizen may commence a civil action on his own behalf—

"(1) against any person (including (i) the United States, and (ii) any other governmental instrumentality or agency to the extent permitted by the eleventh amendment to the Constitution) who is alleged to be in violation of (A) an effluent standard or limitation under this chapter or (B) an order issued by the Administrator or a State with respect to such a standard or limitation, or

"(2) against the Administrator where there is alleged a failure of the Administrator to perform any act or duty under this chapter which is not discretionary with the Administrator.

We granted certiorari to resolve [a] three-way conflict in the Circuits. We now vacate the Fourth Circuit's opinion and remand the case.

II

A.

. . . The most natural reading of "to be in violation" is a requirement that citizen-plaintiffs allege a state of either continuous or intermittent violation that is, a reasonable likelihood that a past polluter will continue to pollute in the future. Congress could have phrased its requirement in language that looked to the past ("to have violated"), but it did not choose this readily available option.

Respondents urge that the choice of the phrase "to be in violation," rather than phrasing more clearly directed to the past, is a "careless accident," the result of a "debatable lapse of syntactical precision." But the prospective orientation of that phrase could not have escaped Congress' attention. Congress used identical language in the citizen suit provisions of several other environmental statutes that authorize only prospective relief. See, e. g., Clean Air Act, 42 U.S.C. §7604; Resource Conservation and Recovery Act of 1976, 42 U.S.C. §6972 (1982 ed. and Supp. III); Toxic Substances Control Act, 15 U.S.C. §2619 (1982 ed. and Supp. IV). Moreover, Congress has demonstrated in yet other statutory provisions that it knows how to avoid this prospective implication by using language that explicitly targets wholly past violations.

. . .

B.

Any other conclusion would render incomprehensible §505's notice provision, which requires citizens to give 60 days' notice of their intent to sue to the alleged violator as well as to the Administrator and the State. If the Administrator or the State commences enforcement action within that 60-day period, the citizen suit is barred, presumably because governmental action has rendered it unnecessary. It follows logically that the purpose of notice to the alleged violator is to give it an opportunity to bring itself into complete compliance with the Act and thus likewise render unnecessary a citizen suit. If we assume, as respondents urge, that citizen suits may target wholly past violations, the requirement of notice to the alleged violator becomes gratuitous. Indeed, respondents, in propounding their interpretation of the Act, can

---

"The district courts shall have jurisdiction, without regard to the amount in controversy or the citizenship of the parties, to enforce such an effluent standard or limitation, or such an order, or to order the Administrator to perform such act or duty, as the case may be, and to apply any appropriate civil penalties under section 1319(d) of this title."

think of no reason for Congress to require such notice other than that "it seemed right" to inform an alleged violator that it was about to be sued.

Adopting respondents' interpretation of §505's jurisdictional grant would create a second and even more disturbing anomaly. The bar on citizen suits when governmental enforcement action is under way suggests that the citizen suit is meant to supplement rather than to supplant governmental action. The legislative history of the Act reinforces this view of the role of the citizen suit. The Senate Report noted that "[t]he Committee intends the great volume of enforcement actions [to] be brought by the State," and that citizen suits are proper only "if the Federal, State, and local agencies fail to exercise their enforcement responsibility." Permitting citizen suits for wholly past violations of the Act could undermine the supplementary role envisioned for the citizen suit. This danger is best illustrated by an example. Suppose that the Administrator identified a violator of the Act and issued a compliance order under §309(a). Suppose further that the Administrator agreed not to assess or otherwise seek civil penalties on the condition that the violator take some extreme corrective action, such as to install particularly effective but expensive machinery, that it otherwise would not be obliged to take. If citizens could file suit, months or years later, in order to seek the civil penalties that the Administrator chose to forgo, then the Administrator's discretion to enforce the Act in the public interest would be curtailed considerably. The same might be said of the discretion of state enforcement authorities. Respondents' interpretation of the scope of the citizen suit would change the nature of the citizens' role from interstitial to potentially intrusive. We cannot agree that Congress intended such a result.

. . .

III

Our conclusion that §505 does not permit citizen suits for wholly past violations does not necessarily dispose of this lawsuit, as both lower courts recognized. The District Court found persuasive the fact that "[respondents'] allegation in the complaint, that Gwaltney was continuing to violate its NPDES permit when plaintiffs filed suit[,] appears to have been made fully in good faith." On this basis, the District Court explicitly held, albeit in a footnote, that "even if Gwaltney were correct that a district court has no jurisdiction over citizen suits based entirely on unlawful conduct that occurred entirely in the past, the Court would still have jurisdiction here." The Court of Appeals acknowledged, also in a footnote, that "[a] very sound argument can be made that [respondents'] allegations of continuing violations were made in good faith," but expressly declined to rule on this alternative holding. Because we agree that §505 confers jurisdiction over citizen suits when the citizen-plaintiffs make a good-faith allegation of continuous or intermittent violation, we remand the case to the Court of Appeals for further consideration.

Petitioner argues that citizen-plaintiffs must prove their allegations of ongoing noncompliance before jurisdiction attaches under §505. We cannot agree. The statute does not require that a defendant "be in violation" of the Act at the commencement of suit; rather, the statute requires that a defendant be "*alleged* to be in violation." Petitioner's construction of the Act reads the word "alleged" out of §505. . . . Our acknowledgment that Congress intended a good-faith allegation to suffice for jurisdictional purpose, however, does not give litigants license to flood the courts with suits premised on baseless allegations. Rule 11 of the Federal Rules of Civil Procedure, which requires pleadings to be based on a good-faith belief, formed after reasonable inquiry, that they are "well grounded in fact," adequately protects defendants from frivolous allegations.

. . .

Because the court below erroneously concluded that respondents could maintain an action based on wholly past violations of the Act, it declined to decide whether respondents' complaint contained a good-faith allegation of ongoing violation by petitioner. We therefore remand the case for consideration of this question. The judgment of the Court of Appeals is vacated, and the case is remanded for further proceedings consistent with this opinion.

NOTES ON *GWALTNEY*

1. *The verb tense.* Do you agree that the verb tense employed in the citizen suit provision justifies the holding that suits do not lie for "wholly past" violations?

2. *Notice.* The Court also supports its holding by positing that the 60-day-notice provision's purpose is to give the alleged violator "an opportunity to bring itself into complete compliance and therefore render" the suit unnecessary. Suppose that the Court (or Congress through a change of verb tense) authorizes citizen suits for wholly past violations. Does this wholly deprive the 60-day notice to violators of any purpose?

3. *Relationship to government enforcement.* Notice that the Court also relies on the diligent prosecution bar to support its holding, citing it as evidence that Congress intended the citizen suit "to supplement rather than to supplant government[ ]" enforcement. In light of the diligent prosecution bar, is there any need for a blanket prohibition on suits for past violations? Consider the Court's example. Suppose that the Administrator does not seek civil penalties but imposes "extreme corrective action" requirements. Would that constitute diligent enforcement barring the citizen suit? If not, would government intervention in the citizen suit (which is, remember, available as of right) prevent citizens from interfering with a fairly satisfactory remedy? After *Gwaltney*, suppose that the Administrator demands extremely lax corrective action in exchange for no penalties? Can the citizen sue? What if the Administrator demands that the violation be cured, but collects no penalties? Can the citizen sue? What if government does nothing, but the company cures the violation

before filing? Can the citizen sue? Should the law authorize a citizen suit in any or all of these situations?

4. *Complication of citizen enforcement.* Gwaltney has greatly complicated citizen enforcement. Recall that the Clean Water Act requires polluters to report their discharges and violations to state environmental agencies enforcing the Act. Prior to *Gwaltney*, a citizen could simply rely on the reported violations as an adequate basis for seeking and obtaining at least some relief in court. Suppose that a polluter claims that it has cured the violation under *Gwaltney*, what must citizens do to evaluate whether this claim is correct? Could a polluter shut down the particular unit causing a violation when the suit is filed (thus reducing effluent from that unit to zero), and just start up again after securing dismissal under *Gwaltney*?

5. *Pleading and ethics.* Notice that the Court does not order dismissal of the suit, because the environmental plaintiffs had alleged a continuing violation. Can environmental plaintiffs routinely avoid dismissal under *Gwaltney* by simply alleging continuing violations? *Cf.* Jones v. Dow Chemical Co., 885 F. Supp. 905, 910–11 (M.D. La. 1994) (dismissing citizen suit under Safe Drinking Water Act when citizens failed to allege a continuing violation). Suppose that the only information that the plaintiffs have at the time of filing are discharge reports showing frequent past violations. Would an allegation of a continuing violation be appropriate if the last discharge report was a month old at the time of filing? Recall that under Federal Rule of Civil Procedure 11, lawyers presenting pleadings to a federal court certify that:

> the allegations and other factual contentions have evidentiary support or, if specifically so identified, are likely to have evidentiary support after a reasonable opportunity for further investigation or discovery. . . .

FRCP 11(b)(3). *Cf.* Ohio Public Interest Research Group v. Laidlaw Environmental Services, 963 F. Supp. 635, 640–41 (S.D. Ohio 1996) (finding compliance with rule 11 when plaintiffs submit evidence of discharges after the complaint was filed).

6. *Deterrence.* Does this holding advance the statutory goal of deterrence?

7. *Implications for other statutes.* Notice that the Court's ruling rests on an interpretation of the Clean Water Act, not upon constitutional grounds. On the other hand, the Court stated that other citizen suit provisions had similar language.

Suppose that a chemical company has on several occasions in the past emitted more air pollution than its permit allows. A citizen group looks over the state records and discovers that the company has exceeded its permit limits again. The group sues under this citizen suit provision from the Clean Air Act:

> . . . Any person may commence a civil action . . . against any person . . . who constructs any new or modified major emitting facility without a permit. . . .

42 U.S.C. §7604(a)(3). This permit must impose a host of permanent pollution control obligations on the permit holder under the Act. The violator modified the facility a decade ago. Should the case be dismissed? *See* New York v. Niagara Mohawk Power Corp., 263 F. Supp. 2d 650, 658–60 (W.D.N.Y. 2003) (rejecting motion to dismiss claims alleging past violations of requirements for modified facilities).

At the time of *Sierra Club v. Morton*, the Court's standing jurisprudence represented primarily an interpretation of the APA. In subsequent years, however, the Court frequently stated that Article III of the United States Constitution, which authorizes the judiciary to adjudicate "cases or controversies," requires that litigants satisfy much of the Court's standing doctrine. The case below invalidating a citizen suit provision (at least in some applications), however, represented the first case where the Court actually invalidated an express statutory grant of standing as unconstitutional:

Lujan v. Defenders of Wildlife
504 U.S. 555 (1992)

JUSTICE SCALIA delivered the opinion of the Court with respect to Parts I, II, III–A, and IV, and an opinion with respect to Part III–B in which THE CHIEF JUSTICE, JUSTICE WHITE, and JUSTICE THOMAS join.

This case involves a challenge to a rule promulgated by the Secretary of the Interior interpreting §7 of the Endangered Species Act of 1973 in such fashion as to render it applicable only to actions within the United States or on the high seas. The preliminary issue, and the only one we reach, is whether the respondents here, plaintiffs below, have standing to seek judicial review of the rule.

I.

The ESA seeks to protect species of animals against threats to their continuing existence caused by man. The ESA instructs the Secretary of the Interior to promulgate by regulation a list of those species which are either endangered or threatened under enumerated criteria, and to define the critical habitat of these species. Section 7(a)(2) of the Act then provides, in pertinent part:

> Each Federal agency shall, in consultation with and with the assistance of the Secretary [of the Interior], insure that any action authorized, funded, or carried out by such agency is not likely to jeopardize the continued existence of any endangered species or threatened species or result in the destruction or adverse modification of habitat of such species which is determined by the Secretary, after consultation as appropriate with affected States, to be critical. 16 U.S.C. §1536(a)(2).

In 1978, the Fish and Wildlife Service (FWS) and the National Marine Fisheries Service (NMFS), on behalf of the Secretary of the Interior and the Secretary of Commerce respectively, promulgated a joint regulation stating that the obligations imposed by §7(a)(2) extend to actions taken in foreign nations. The next year, however, the Interior Department began to reexamine its position. A revised joint regulation, reinterpreting §7(a)(2) to require consultation only for actions taken in the United States or on the high seas, was . . . promulgated in 1986.

Shortly thereafter, respondents, organizations dedicated to wildlife conservation and other environmental causes, filed this action against the Secretary of the Interior, seeking a declaratory judgment that the new regulation is in error as to the geographic scope of §7(a)(2), and an injunction requiring the Secretary to promulgate a new regulation restoring the initial interpretation. The District Court granted the Secretary's motion to dismiss for lack of standing. The Court of Appeals for the Eighth Circuit reversed by a divided vote. On remand, the Secretary moved for summary judgment on the standing issue, and respondents moved for summary judgment on the merits. The District Court denied the Secretary's motion, on the ground that the Eighth Circuit had already determined the standing question in this case; it granted respondents' merits motion, and ordered the Secretary to publish a revised regulation. The Eighth Circuit affirmed. We granted certiorari.

II.

While the Constitution of the United States divides all power conferred upon the Federal Government into "legislative Powers," Art. I, §1, "[t]he executive Power," Art. II, §1, and "[t]he judicial Power," Art. III, §1, it does not attempt to define those terms. To be sure, it limits the jurisdiction of federal courts to "Cases and Controversies," but an executive inquiry can bear the name "case" (the Hoffa case) and a legislative dispute can bear the name "controversy" (the Smoot-Hawley controversy). Obviously, then, the Constitution's central mechanism of separation of powers depends largely upon common understanding of what activities are appropriate to legislatures, to executives, and to courts. . . . [A] landmark[] setting apart the "Cases" and "Controversies" that are of the justiciable sort referred to in Article III — "serv[ing] to identify those disputes which are appropriately resolved through the judicial process," — is the doctrine of standing. Though some of its elements express merely prudential considerations that are part of judicial self-government, the core component of standing is an essential and unchanging part of the case-or-controversy requirement of Article III.

Over the years, our cases have established that the irreducible constitutional minimum of standing contains three elements: First, the plaintiff must have suffered an "injury in fact" — an invasion of a legally-protected interest

which is (a) concrete and particularized,[1] and (b) "actual or imminent, not 'conjectural' or 'hypothetical.'" Second, there must be a causal connection between the injury and the conduct complained of — the injury has to be "fairly . . . trace[able] to the challenged action of the defendant, and not-O. . . th[e]
result [of] the independent action of some third party not before the court." Third, it must be "likely," as opposed to merely "speculative," that the injury will be "redressed by a favorable decision."

The party invoking federal jurisdiction bears the burden of establishing these elements. . . .

When the suit is one challenging the legality of government action or inaction, the nature and extent of facts that must be averred (at the summary judgment stage) or proved (at the trial stage) in order to establish standing depends considerably upon whether the plaintiff is himself an object of the action (or forgone action) at issue. If he is, there is ordinarily little question that the action or inaction has caused him injury, and that a judgment preventing or requiring the action will redress it. When, however, as in this case, a plaintiff's asserted injury arises from the government's allegedly unlawful regulation (or lack of regulation) of *someone else*, much more is needed. In that circumstance, causation and redressability ordinarily hinge on the response of the regulated (or regulable) third party to the government action or inaction — and perhaps on the response of others as well. The existence of one or more of the essential elements of standing "depends on the unfettered choices made by independent actors not before the courts and whose exercise of broad and legitimate discretion the courts cannot presume either to control or to predict," and it becomes the burden of the plaintiff to adduce facts showing that those choices have been or will be made in such manner as to produce causation and permit redressability of injury. Thus, when the plaintiff is not himself the object of the government action or inaction he challenges, standing is not precluded, but it is ordinarily "substantially more difficult" to establish.

III.

We think the Court of Appeals failed to apply the foregoing principles in denying the Secretary's motion for summary judgment. Respondents had not made the requisite demonstration of (at least) injury and redressability.

A.

Respondents' claim to injury is that the lack of consultation with respect to certain funded activities abroad "increas[es] the rate of extinction of endangered and threatened species." Of course, the desire to use or observe an animal species, even for purely esthetic purposes, is undeniably a cognizable

---

1. By particularized, we mean that the injury must affect the plaintiff in a personal and individual way.

interest for purpose of standing. *See, e. g.*, *Sierra Club v. Morton*, 405 U. S., at 734. "But the 'injury in fact' test requires more than an injury to a cognizable interest. It requires that the party seeking review be himself among the injured." *Id.* at 734–735. To survive the Secretary's summary judgment motion, respondents had to submit affidavits or other evidence showing, through specific facts, not only that listed species were in fact being threatened by funded activities abroad, but also that one or more of respondents' members would thereby be "directly" affected apart from their "'special interest' in th[e] subject."

With respect to this aspect of the case, the Court of Appeals focused on the affidavits of two Defenders' members — Joyce Kelly and Amy Skilbred. Ms. Kelly stated that she traveled to Egypt in 1986 and "observed the traditional habitat of the endangered nile crocodile there and intend[s] to do so again, and hope[s] to observe the crocodile directly," and that she "will suffer harm in fact as a result of [the] American . . . role . . . in overseeing the rehabilitation of the Aswan High Dam on the Nile . . . and [in] develop[ing] . . . Egypt's O. . .
Master Water Plan." Ms. Skilbred averred that she traveled to Sri Lanka in 1981 and "observed th[e] habitat" of "endangered species such as the Asian elephant and the leopard" at what is now the site of the Mahaweli project funded by the Agency for International Development (AID), although she "was unable to see any of the endangered species"; "this development project," she continued, "will seriously reduce endangered, threatened, and endemic species habitat including areas that I visited . . . [,which] may severely shorten the future of these species"; that threat, she concluded, harmed her because she "intend[s] to return to Sri Lanka in the future and hope[s] to be more fortunate in spotting at least the endangered elephant and leopard." When Ms. Skilbred was asked at a subsequent deposition if and when she had any plans to return to Sri Lanka, she reiterated that "I intend to go back to Sri Lanka," but confessed that she had no current plans: "I don't know [when]. There is a civil war going on right now. I don't know. Not next year, I will say. In the future."

We shall assume for the sake of argument that these affidavits contain facts showing that certain agency-funded projects threaten listed species — though that is questionable. They plainly contain no facts, however, showing how damage to the species will produce "imminent" injury to Mses. Kelly and Skilbred. That the women "had visited" the areas of the projects before the projects commenced proves nothing. As we have said in a related context, "'Past exposure to illegal conduct does not in itself show a present case or controversy regarding injunctive relief . . . if unaccompanied by any continuing, present adverse effects.'" And the affiants' profession of an "inten[t]" to return to the places they had visited before — where they will presumably, this time, be deprived of the opportunity to observe animals of the endangered species — is simply not enough. Such "some day" intentions — without any description of concrete plans, or indeed even any specification of *when* the some day will be — do not support a finding of the "actual or imminent" injury that our cases require.[2]

Besides relying upon the Kelly and Skilbred affidavits, respondents propose a series of novel standing theories. The first, inelegantly styled "ecosystem nexus," proposes that any person who uses *any part* of a "contiguous ecosystem" adversely affected by a funded activity has standing even if the activity is located a great distance away. This approach, as the Court of Appeals correctly observed, is inconsistent with our opinion in *National Wildlife Federation*, which held that a plaintiff claiming injury from environmental damage must use the area affected by the challenged activity and not an area roughly "in the vicinity" of it . . . .

Respondents' other theories are called, alas, the "animal nexus" approach, whereby anyone who has an interest in studying or seeing the endangered animals anywhere on the globe has standing; and the "vocational nexus" approach, under which anyone with a professional interest in such animals can sue. Under these theories, anyone who goes to see Asian elephants in the Bronx Zoo, and anyone who is a keeper of Asian elephants in the Bronx Zoo, has standing to sue because the Director of . . . AID did not consult with the Secretary regarding the AID-funded project in Sri Lanka. This is beyond all reason. Standing is not "an ingenious academic exercise in the conceivable,"

---

2. The dissent acknowledges the settled requirement that the injury complained of be, if not actual, then at least *imminent*, but it contends that respondents could get past summary judgment because "a reasonable finder of fact could conclude . . . that . . . Kelly or Skilbred will soon return to the project sites." This analysis suffers either from a factual or from a legal defect, depending on what the "soon" is supposed to mean. If "soon" refers to the standard mandated by our precedents — that the injury be "imminent" — we are at a loss to see how, as a factual matter, the standard can be met by respondents' mere profession of an intent, some day, to return. But if, as we suspect, "soon" means nothing more than "in this lifetime," then the dissent has undertaken quite a departure from our precedents. Although "imminence" is concededly a somewhat elastic concept, it cannot be stretched beyond its purpose, which is to insure that the alleged injury is not too speculative for Article III purposes — that the injury is "*certainly impending*". It has been stretched beyond the breaking point when, as here, the plaintiff alleges only an injury at some indefinite future time, and the acts necessary to make the injury happen are at least partly within the plaintiff's own control. In such circumstances we have insisted that the injury proceed with a high degree of immediacy, so as to reduce the possibility of deciding a case in which no injury would have occurred at all.

There is no substance to the dissent's suggestion that imminence is demanded only when the alleged harm depends upon "the affirmative actions of third parties beyond a plaintiff's control." Our cases *mention* third-party-caused contingency, naturally enough; but they also mention the plaintiff's failure to show that he will soon expose *himself* to the injury. And there is certainly no reason in principle to demand evidence that third persons will take the action exposing the plaintiff to harm, while *presuming* that the plaintiff himself will do so.

Our insistence upon these established requirements of standing does not mean that we would, as the dissent contends, "demand . . . detailed descriptions" of damages, such as a "nightly schedule of attempted activities" from plaintiffs alleging loss of consortium. That case and the others posited by the dissent all involve *actual* harm; the existence of standing is clear, though the precise extent of harm remains to be determined at trial. Where there is no actual harm, however, its imminence (though not its precise extent) must be established.

but as we have said requires, at the summary judgment stage, a factual showing of perceptible harm. It is clear that the person who observes or works with a particular animal threatened by a federal decision is facing perceptible harm, since the very subject of his interest will no longer exist. It is even plausible — though it goes to the outermost limit of plausibility — to think that a person who observes or works with animals of a particular species in the very area of the world where that species is threatened by a federal decision is facing such harm, since some animals that might have been the subject of his interest will no longer exist. It goes beyond the limit, however, and into pure speculation and fantasy, to say that anyone who observes or works with an endangered species, anywhere in the world, is appreciably harmed by a single project affecting some portion of that species with which he has no more specific connection.

B.

Besides failing to show injury, respondents failed to demonstrate redressability. Instead of attacking the separate decisions to fund particular projects allegedly causing them harm, the respondents chose to challenge a more generalized level of Government action (rules regarding consultation), the invalidation of which would affect all overseas projects. This programmatic approach has obvious practical advantages, but also obvious difficulties insofar as proof of causation or redressability is concerned. As we have said in another context, "suits challenging, not specifically identifiable Government violations of law, but the particular programs agencies establish to carry out their legal obligations . . . [are], even when premised on allegations of several instances of violations of law, . . . rarely if ever appropriate for federal-court adjudication."

The most obvious problem in the present case is redressability. Since the agencies funding the projects were not parties to the case, the District Court could accord relief only against the Secretary: He could be ordered to revise his regulation to require consultation for foreign projects. But this would not remedy respondents' alleged injury unless the funding agencies were bound by the Secretary's regulation, which is very much an open question. Whereas in other contexts the ESA is quite explicit as to the Secretary's controlling authority with respect to consultation the initiative, and hence arguably the initial responsibility for determining statutory necessity, lies with the agencies. When the Secretary promulgated the regulation at issue here, he thought it was binding on the agencies. The Solicitor General, however, has repudiated that position here, and the agencies themselves apparently deny the Secretary's authority. (During the period when the Secretary took the view that §7(a)(2) did apply abroad, AID and FWS engaged in a running controversy over whether consultation was required with respect to the Mahaweli project, AID insisting that consultation applied only to domestic actions.)

Respondents assert that this legal uncertainty did not affect redressability (and hence standing) because the District Court itself could resolve the issue of the Secretary's authority as a necessary part of its standing inquiry. Assuming that it is appropriate to resolve an issue of law such as this in connection with a threshold standing inquiry, resolution by the District Court would not have remedied respondents' alleged injury anyway, because it would not have been binding upon the agencies. They were not parties to the suit, and there is no reason they should be obliged to honor an incidental legal determination the suit produced. The Court of Appeals tried to finesse this problem by simply proclaiming that "[w]e are satisfied that an injunction requiring the Secretary to publish [respondents' desired] regulatio[n] . . . would result in consultation." We do not know what would justify that confidence, particularly when the Justice Department (presumably after consultation with the agencies) has taken the position that the regulation is not binding. The short of the matter is that redress of the only injury-in-fact respondents complain of requires action (termination of funding until consultation) by the individual funding agencies; and any relief the District Court could have provided in this suit against the Secretary was not likely to produce that action.

A further impediment to redressability is the fact that the agencies generally supply only a fraction of the funding for a foreign project. AID, for example, has provided less than 10% of the funding for the Mahaweli project. Respondents have produced nothing to indicate that the projects they have named will either be suspended, or do less harm to listed species, if that fraction is eliminated. As in *Simon*, it is entirely conjectural whether the nonagency activity that affects respondents will be altered or affected by the agency activity they seek to achieve. There is no standing.

IV.

The Court of Appeals found that respondents had standing for an additional reason: because they had suffered a "procedural injury." The so-called "citizen-suit" provision of the ESA provides, in pertinent part, that "any person may commence a civil suit on his own behalf (A) to enjoin any person, including the United States and any other governmental instrumentality or agency . . . who is alleged to be in violation of any provision of this chapter." 16 U.S.C. §1540(g). The court held that, because §7(a)(2) requires interagency consultation, the citizen-suit provision creates a "procedural righ[t]" to consultation in all "persons" — so that *anyone* can file suit in federal court to challenge the Secretary's (or presumably any other official's) failure to follow the assertedly correct consultative procedure, notwithstanding his or her inability to allege any discrete injury flowing from that failure. To understand the remarkable nature of this holding one must be clear about what it does *not* rest upon: This is not a case where plaintiffs are seeking to enforce a procedural requirement the disregard of which could impair a separate concrete interest of theirs (*e.g.*, the procedural requirement for a hearing prior to denial of their license application, or the procedural requirement for an environmental impact statement before a federal facility is constructed next door to them).[7] Nor is it simply a case where concrete injury has been suffered by many persons, as in mass fraud or mass tort situations. Nor, finally, is it the unusual case in which Congress has created a concrete private interest in the outcome of a suit against a private party for the government's benefit, by providing a cash bounty for the victorious plaintiff. Rather, the court held that the injury-in-fact requirement had been satisfied by congressional conferral upon *all* persons of an abstract, self-contained, noninstrumental "right" to have the Executive observe the procedures required by law. We reject this view.[8]

We have consistently held that a plaintiff raising only a generally available grievance about government — claiming only harm to his and every citizen's interest in proper application of the Constitution and laws, and seeking relief that no more directly and tangibly benefits him than it does the public at large — does not state an Article III case or controversy. . . .

We hold that respondents lack standing to bring this action and that the Court of Appeals erred in denying the summary judgment motion filed by the United States. The opinion of the Court of Appeals is hereby reversed, and the cause remanded for proceedings consistent with this opinion.

It is so ordered.

---

7. There is this much truth to the assertion that "procedural rights" are special: The person who has been accorded a procedural right to protect his concrete interests can assert that right without meeting all the normal standards for redressability and immediacy. Thus, under our case-law, one living adjacent to the site for proposed construction of a federally licensed dam has standing to challenge the licensing agency's failure to prepare an Environmental Impact Statement, even though he cannot establish with any certainty that the Statement will cause the license to be withheld or altered, and even though the dam will not be completed for many years. (That is why we do not rely, in the present case, upon the Government's argument that, *even if* the other agencies were obliged to consult with the Secretary, they might not have followed his advice.) What respondents' "procedural rights" argument seeks, however, is quite different from this: standing for persons who have no concrete interests affected — persons who live (and propose to live) at the other end of the country from the dam.

8. The dissent's discussion of this aspect of the case distorts our opinion. We do *not* hold that an individual cannot enforce procedural rights; he assuredly can, so long as the procedures in question are designed to protect some threatened concrete interest of his that is the ultimate basis of his standing. The dissent, however, asserts that there exist "classes of procedural duties . . . so enmeshed with the prevention of a substantive, concrete harm that an individual plaintiff may be able to demonstrate a sufficient likelihood of injury just through the breach of that procedural duty." If we understand this correctly, it means that the Government's violation of a certain (undescribed) class of procedural duty satisfies the concrete-injury requirement by itself, without any showing that the procedural violation endangers a concrete interest of the plaintiff (apart from his interest in having the procedure observed). We cannot agree. . . .

Justice Kennedy, with whom Justice Souter joins, concurring in part and concurring in the judgment.

. . .

I agree with the Court's conclusion in Part III-A that, on the record before us, respondents have failed to demonstrate that they themselves are "among the injured." . . .

While it may seem trivial to require that Mss. Kelly and Skilbred acquire airline tickets to the project sites or announce a date certain upon which they will return, this is not a case where it is reasonable to assume that the affiants will be using the sites on a regular basis, nor do the affiants claim to have visited the sites since the projects commenced. With respect to the Court's discussion of respondents' "ecosystem nexus," "animal nexus," and "vocational nexus" theories, I agree that on this record respondents' showing is insufficient to establish standing on any of these bases. I am not willing to foreclose the possibility, however, that in different circumstances a nexus theory similar to those proffered here might support a claim to standing.

In light of the conclusion that respondents have not demonstrated a concrete injury here sufficient to support standing under our precedents, I would not reach the issue of redressability that is discussed by the plurality in Part III-B.

I also join Part IV of the Court's opinion with the following observations. As government programs and policies become more complex and far-reaching, we must be sensitive to the articulation of new rights of action that do not have clear analogs in our common-law tradition. Modern litigation has progressed far from the paradigm of Marbury suing Madison to get his commission or Ogden seeking an injunction to halt Gibbons' steamboat operations. In my view, Congress has the power to define injuries and articulate chains of causation that will give rise to a case or controversy where none existed before, and I do not read the Court's opinion to suggest a contrary view. In exercising this power, however, Congress must at the very least identify the injury it seeks to vindicate and relate the injury to the class of persons entitled to bring suit. The citizen-suit provision of the Endangered Species Act does not meet these minimal requirements, because while the statute purports to confer a right on "any person . . . to enjoin the United States and any other governmental instrumentality or agency . . . who is alleged to be in violation of any provision of this chapter," it does not of its own force establish that there is an injury in "any person" by virtue of any "violation." 16 U.S.C. §1540(g)(1)(A).

The Court's holding that there is an outer limit to the power of Congress to confer rights of action is a direct and necessary consequence of the case and controversy limitations found in Article III. I agree that it would exceed those limitations if, at the behest of Congress and in the absence of any showing of concrete injury, we were to entertain citizen-suits to vindicate the public's nonconcrete interest in the proper administration of the laws. While it does not matter how many persons have been injured by the challenged action, the party bringing suit must show that the action injures him in a concrete and personal way. This requirement is not just an empty formality. It preserves the vitality of the adversarial process by assuring both that the parties before the court have an actual, as opposed to professed, stake in the outcome, and that "the legal questions presented . . . will be resolved, not in the rarefied atmosphere of a debating society, but in a concrete factual context conducive to a realistic appreciation of the consequences of judicial action." In addition, the requirement of concrete injury confines the Judicial Branch to its proper, limited role in the constitutional framework of Government.

An independent judiciary is held to account through its open proceedings and its reasoned judgments. In this process it is essential for the public to know what persons or groups are invoking the judicial power, the reasons that they have brought suit, and whether their claims are vindicated or denied. The concrete injury requirement helps assure that there can be an answer to these questions; and, as the Court's opinion is careful to show, that is part of the constitutional design.

With these observations, I concur in Parts I, II, III–A, and IV of the Court's opinion and in the judgment of the Court.

JUSTICE STEVENS, concurring in the judgment.

Because I am not persuaded that Congress intended the consultation requirement in §7(a)(2) of the Endangered Species Act of 1973 (ESA), 16 U.S.C. §1536(a)(2), to apply to activities in foreign countries, I concur in the judgment of reversal. I do not, however, agree with the Court's conclusion that respondents lack standing because the threatened injury to their interest in protecting the environment and studying endangered species is not "imminent." Nor do I agree with the plurality's additional conclusion that respondents' injury is not "redressable" in this litigation.

I.

In my opinion a person who has visited the critical habitat of an endangered species has a professional interest in preserving the species and its habitat, and intends to revisit them in the future has standing to challenge agency action that threatens their destruction.

. . . T]he "imminence" of such an injury should be measured by the timing and likelihood of the threatened environmental harm, rather than — as the Court seems to suggest — by the time that might elapse between the present and the time when the individuals would visit the area if no such injury should occur. . . .

The plurality also concludes that respondents' injuries are not redressable in this litigation. . . .

[But] [w]e must presume that if this Court holds that §7(a)(2) requires consultation, all affected agencies would abide by that interpretation and engage in the requisite consultations. Certainly the Executive Branch cannot be heard to argue that an authoritative construction of the governing statute by this Court may simply be ignored by any agency head. Moreover, if Congress has required consultation between agencies, we must presume that such consultation will have a serious purpose that is likely to produce tangible results. . . .

II.

Although I believe that respondents have standing, I nevertheless concur in the judgment of reversal because I am persuaded that the Government is correct in its submission that §7(a)(2) does not apply to activities in foreign countries.

JUSTICE BLACKMUN, with whom JUSTICE O'CONNOR joins, dissenting.

I part company with the Court in this case in two respects. First, I believe that respondents have raised genuine issues of fact — sufficient to survive summary judgment — both as to injury and as to redressability. Second, I question the Court's breadth of language in rejecting standing for "procedural" injuries. I fear the Court seeks to impose fresh limitations on the constitutional authority of Congress to allow citizen-suits in the federal courts for injuries deemed "procedural" in nature. I dissent.

I.

. . . To survive petitioner's motion for summary judgment on standing, respondents need not prove that they are actually or imminently harmed. They need show only a "genuine issue" of material fact as to standing. This is not a heavy burden. . . .

1.

Were the Court to apply the proper standard for summary judgment, I believe it would conclude that the sworn affidavits and deposition testimony of Joyce Kelly and Amy Skilbred advance sufficient facts to create a genuine issue for trial concerning whether one or both would be imminently harmed by the Aswan and Mahaweli projects. . . .

. . . [A] reasonable finder of fact could conclude from the information in the affidavits and deposition testimony that either Kelly or Skilbred will soon return to the project sites, thereby satisfying the "actual or imminent" injury standard. . . .

By requiring a "description of concrete plans" or "specification of *when* the some day [for a return visit] will be" the Court, in my view, demands what is likely an empty formality. No substantial barriers prevent Kelly or Skilbred from simply purchasing plane tickets to return to the Aswan and Mahaweli projects. . . .

I fear the Court's demand for detailed descriptions of future conduct will do little to weed out those who are genuinely harmed from those who are not. More likely, it will resurrect a code-pleading formalism in federal court summary judgment practice, as federal courts, newly doubting their jurisdiction, will demand more and more particularized showings of future harm. . . .

2.

The Court . . . rejects respondents' claim of vocational or professional injury. The Court says that it is "beyond all reason" that a zoo "keeper" of Asian elephants would have standing to contest his government's participation in the eradication of all the Asian elephants in another part of the world. I am unable to see how the distant location of the destruction *necessarily* (for purposes of ruling at summary judgment) mitigates the harm to the elephant keeper. If there is no more access to a future supply of the animal that sustains a keeper's livelihood, surely there is harm.

I have difficulty imagining this Court applying its rigid principles of geographic formalism anywhere outside the context of environmental claims. . . .

B.

A plurality of the Court suggests that respondents have not demonstrated redressability: a likelihood that a court ruling in their favor would remedy their injury. The plurality identifies two obstacles. The first is that the "action agencies" (*e.g.*, AID) cannot be required to undertake consultation with petitioner Secretary, because they are not directly bound as parties to the suit and are otherwise not indirectly bound by being subject to petitioner Secretary's regulation. Petitioner, however, officially and publicly has taken the position that his regulations regarding consultation under §7 of the Act are binding on action agencies. . . .

. . . I am not as willing as the plurality is to assume that agencies at least will not try to follow the law. . . . I believe respondents' injury would likely be redressed by a favorable decision.

The second redressability obstacle relied on by the plurality is that "the [action] agencies generally supply only a fraction of the funding for a foreign project." What this Court might "generally" take to be true does not eliminate the existence of a genuine issue of fact to withstand summary judgment. Even if the action agencies supply only a fraction of the funding for a particular foreign project, it remains at least a question for the finder of fact whether threatened withdrawal of that fraction would affect foreign government conduct sufficiently to avoid harm to listed species.

The plurality states that "AID, for example, has provided less than 10% of the funding for the Mahaweli project." The plurality neglects to mention that this "fraction" amounts to $170 million, not so paltry a sum for a country of only 16 million people with a gross national product of less than $6 billion in 1986 when respondents filed the complaint in this action.

. . .

. . . The plurality overlooks an Interior Department memorandum listing eight endangered or threatened species in the Mahaweli project area and recounting that "[t]he Sri Lankan government has requested the assistance of AID in mitigating the negative impacts to the wildlife involved." . . .

I do not share the plurality's astonishing confidence that, on the record here, a factfinder could only conclude that AID was powerless to ensure the protection of listed species at the Mahaweli project. . . .

I find myself unable to agree with the plurality's analysis of redressability, based as it is on its invitation of executive lawlessness . . . , unfounded assumptions about causation, and erroneous conclusions about what the record does not say. In my view, respondents have satisfactorily shown a genuine issue of fact as to whether their injury would likely be redressed by a decision in their favor.

II.

The Court concludes that any "procedural injury" suffered by respondents is insufficient to confer standing. . . .

Most governmental conduct can be classified as "procedural." . . .

The Court expresses concern that allowing judicial enforcement of "agencies' observance of a particular, statutorily prescribed procedure" would "transfer from the President to the courts the Chief Executive's most important constitutional duty, to 'take Care that the Laws be faithfully executed,' Art. II, sec. 3." In fact, the principal effect of foreclosing judicial enforcement of such procedures is to transfer power into the hands of the Executive at the expense — not of the courts — but of Congress, from which that power originates and emanates.

Under the Court's anachronistically formal view of the separation of powers, Congress legislates pure, substantive mandates and has no business structuring the procedural manner in which the Executive implements these mandates. . . .

Congress legislates in procedural shades of gray not to aggrandize its own power but to allow maximum Executive discretion in the attainment of Congress' legislative goals. . . . It is to be hoped that over time the Court will acknowledge that some classes of procedural duties are so enmeshed with the prevention of a substantive, concrete harm that an individual plaintiff may be able to demonstrate a sufficient likelihood of injury just through the breach of that procedural duty. For example, in the context of the NEPA requirement of environmental-impact statements, this Court has acknowledged "it is now well settled that NEPA itself does not mandate particular results [and] simply prescribes the necessary process," but "*these procedures are almost certain to affect the agency's substantive decision.*" Robertson v. Methow Valley Citizens Council, 490 U.S., 332, 350 (1989) (emphasis added). This acknowledgment of an inextricable link between procedural and substantive harm does not reflect improper appellate factfinding. It reflects nothing more than the proper deference owed to the judgment of a coordinate branch — Congress — that certain procedures are directly tied to protection against a substantive harm.

In short, determining "injury" for Article III standing purposes is a fact-specific inquiry. . . . There may be factual circumstances in which a congressionally imposed procedural requirement is so insubstantially connected to the prevention of a substantive harm that it cannot be said to work any conceivable injury to an individual litigant. But, as a general matter, the courts owe substantial deference to Congress' substantive purpose in imposing a certain procedural requirement. . . . There is no room for a *per se* rule or presumption excluding injuries labeled "procedural" in nature.

In conclusion, I cannot join the Court on what amounts to a slash-and-burn expedition through the law of environmental standing. In my view, "[t]he very essence of civil liberty certainly consists in the right of every individual to claim the protection of the laws, whenever he receives an injury." *Marbury v. Madison*, 1 Cranch 137, 163 (1803).

I dissent.

NOTES ON *DEFENDERS OF WILDLIFE*

1. *Injury-in-fact.* *Defenders* requires that the injury be "imminent." Suppose that Defenders submitted affidavits showing that one of their members planned to go to Sri Lanka in five years. Would that be sufficiently imminent? Do you agree that the member must go to the place whence the species may vanish to be harmed by the loss of a species? Is the dissent correct to assert that this decision demands more of a showing than is appropriate on a summary judgment motion with respect to injury? The concurrence supports the idea that Congress may create standing by defining injury and articulating chains of causation. Suppose that Congress passes a law granting any person the right to sue when an administrative action threatens a species they have observed in the wild or studied. Should the Court find that the Defenders of Wildlife affiants have standing?

2. *Procedural rights.* This case concerns the right to invoke a particular procedure, a consultation process for projects potentially affecting endangered species. Since procedures do not, by their nature, dictate outcomes, does it follow that claims of injuries from government failures to follow prescribed procedures cannot provide a sufficient basis for standing? *Cf.* Federal Election Commission v. Akins, 524 U.S. 11 (1998) (standing granted to seek information required to be disclosed).

3. *Causation.* Suppose that Defenders produced an affidavit showing a plan to go to the location of vanishing elephants within one year. Should the Court find that the causation requirement is met?

4. *Redressability.* Do Justice Scalia's views on redressability command a majority? Do you agree with him?

5. *Is Standing for environmental plaintiffs different?* Justice Scalia suggests that environmental plaintiffs should have more difficulty establishing standing than regulated parties. How does he justify this conclusion? Is it fair that standing doctrine not place both sides of a controversy on an equal footing? Is it appropriate under Article III?

6. *Implications.* Do you think that this case will seriously impair the ability of environmental groups to bring citizen suits? What effect do you expect it to have? What are the "obvious practical advantages" of challenging a rule, rather than individual applications of the rule? Do you expect citizens to eschew programmatic challenges in favor of challenging specific projects in light of the *Defenders* holding?

Defenders dealt with standing to try and avoid a potential future injury. The next two cases address standing to seek remedies for past violations of environmental statutes. As you read these cases, ask yourself if the Court converted the *Gwaltney* rule against citizen suits addressing wholly past violations from a statutory interpretation into a constitutional principle.

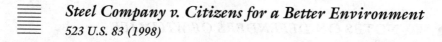

Steel Company v. Citizens for a Better Environment
523 U.S. 83 (1998)

JUSTICE SCALIA delivered the opinion of the Court.

This is a private enforcement action under the citizen-suit provision of the Emergency Planning and Community Right-To-Know Act of 1986 (EPCRA). . . .

I

Respondent, an association of individuals interested in environmental protection, sued petitioner, a small manufacturing company in Chicago, for past violations of EPCRA. EPCRA establishes a framework of state, regional and local agencies designed to inform the public about the presence of hazardous and toxic chemicals, and to provide for emergency response in the event of health-threatening release. Central to its operation are reporting requirements compelling users of specified toxic and hazardous chemicals to file annual "emergency and hazardous chemical inventory forms" and "toxic chemical release forms," which contain, *inter alia*, the name and location of the facility, the name and quantity of the chemical on hand, and, in the case of toxic chemicals, the waste-disposal method employed and the annual quantity released into each environmental medium. . . .

In 1995 respondent sent a notice to petitioner, the Administrator, and the relevant Illinois authorities, alleging — accurately, as it turns out — that petitioner had failed since 1988, the first year of EPCRA's filing deadlines, to complete and to submit the requisite hazardous-chemical inventory and toxic-chemical release forms. . . . Upon receiving the notice, petitioner filed all of the overdue forms with the relevant agencies. . . .

IV

. . .

The "irreducible constitutional minimum of standing" contains three requirements. First and foremost, there must be alleged (and ultimately proved) an "injury in fact" — a harm suffered by the plaintiff that is "concrete" and "actual or imminent, not 'conjectural' or 'hypothetical.'" Second, there must be causation — a fairly traceable connection between the plaintiff's injury and the complained-of conduct of the defendant. And third, there must be redressability — a likelihood that the requested relief will redress the alleged injury. This triad of injury in fact, causation, and redressability constitutes the core of Article III's case-or-controversy requirement, and the party invoking federal jurisdiction bears the burden of establishing its existence.

. . . The complaint contains claims "on behalf of both [respondent] itself and its members." It describes respondent as an organization that seeks, uses, and acquires data reported under EPCRA. It says that respondent "reports to its members and the public about storage and releases of toxic chemicals into the environment, advocates changes in environmental regulations and statutes, prepares reports for its members and the public, seeks the reduction of toxic chemicals and further seeks to promote the effective enforcement of environmental laws." The complaint asserts that respondent's "right to know about [toxic-chemical] releases and its interests in protecting and improving the environment and the health of its members have been, are being, and will be adversely affected by [petitioner's] actions in failing to provide timely and required information under EPCRA." The complaint also alleges that respondent's members, who live in or frequent the area near petitioner's facility, use the EPRCA-reported information "to learn about toxic chemical releases, the use of hazardous substances in their communities, to plan emergency preparedness in the event of accidents, and to attempt to reduce the toxic chemicals in areas in which they live, work and visit." The members' "safety, health, recreational, economic, aesthetic and environmental interests" in the information, it is claimed, "have been, are being, and will be adversely affected by [petitioner's] actions in failing to file timely and required reports under EPCRA."

As appears from the above, respondent asserts petitioner's failure to provide EPCRA information in a timely fashion, and the lingering effects of that failure, as the injury in fact to itself and its members. We have not had occasion to decide whether being deprived of information that is supposed to be disclosed under EPCRA — or at least being deprived of it when one has a particular plan for its use — is a concrete injury in fact that satisfies Article III.

And we need not reach that question in the present case because, assuming injury in fact, the complaint fails the third test of standing, redressability.

The complaint asks for (1) a declaratory judgment that petitioner violated EPCRA; (2) authorization to inspect periodically petitioner's facility and records (with costs borne by petitioner); (3) an order requiring petitioner to provide respondent copies of all compliance reports submitted to the EPA; (4) an order requiring petitioner to pay civil penalties of $25,000 per day for each violation of §§11022 and 11023; (5) an award of all respondent's "costs, in connection with the investigation and prosecution of this matter, including reasonable attorney and expert witness fees, as authorized by Section 326(f) of [EPCRA]"; and (6) any such further relief as the court deems appropriate. None of the specific items of relief sought, and none that we can envision as "appropriate" under the general request, would serve to reimburse respondent for losses caused by the late reporting, or to eliminate any effects of that late reporting upon respondent.

The first item, the request for a declaratory judgment that petitioner violated EPCRA, can be disposed of summarily. There being no controversy over whether petitioner failed to file reports, or over whether such a failure constitutes a violation, the declaratory judgment is not only worthless to respondent, it is seemingly worthless to all the world.

Item (4), the civil penalties authorized by the statute might be viewed as a sort of compensation or redress to respondent if they were payable to respondent. But they are not. These penalties — the only damages authorized by EPCRA — are payable to the United States Treasury. In requesting them, therefore, respondent seeks not remediation of its own injury — reimbursement for the costs it incurred as a result of the late filing — but vindication of the rule of law — the "undifferentiated public interest" in faithful execution of EPCRA. This does not suffice. Justice STEVENS thinks it is enough that respondent will be gratified by seeing petitioner punished for its infractions and that the punishment will deter the risk of future harm . . . . By the mere bringing of his suit, *every* plaintiff demonstrates his belief that a favorable judgment will make him happier. But although a suitor may derive great comfort and joy from the fact that the United States Treasury is not cheated, that a wrongdoer gets his just deserts, or that the Nation's laws are faithfully enforced, that psychic satisfaction is not an acceptable Article III remedy because it does not redress a cognizable Article III injury. Relief that does not remedy the injury suffered cannot bootstrap a plaintiff into federal court; that is the very essence of the redressability requirement.

[Justice Scalia states that the reimbursment for the cost of suing cannot constitute redressability for standing purposes.]

The remaining relief respondent seeks (item (2), giving respondent authority to inspect petitioner's facility and records, and item (3), compelling petitioner to provide respondent copies of EPA compliance reports) is injunctive in nature. It cannot conceivably remedy any past wrong but is aimed at deterring petitioner from violating EPCRA in the future. The latter objective can of course be "remedial" for Article III purposes, when threatened injury is one of the gravamens of the complaint. If respondent had alleged a continuing violation or the imminence of a future violation, the injunctive relief requested would remedy that alleged harm. But there is no such allegation here — and on the facts of the case, there seems no basis for it. Nothing supports the requested injunctive relief except respondent's generalized interest in deterrence, which is insufficient for purposes of Article III.

The United States, as *amicus curiae*, argues that the injunctive relief does constitute remediation because "there is a presumption of [future] injury when the defendant has voluntarily ceased its illegal activity in response to litigation," even if that occurs before a complaint is filed. This makes a sword out of a shield. The "presumption" the Government refers to has been applied to refute the assertion of mootness by a defendant who, when sued in a complaint that alleges present or threatened injury, ceases the complained-of activity. It is an immense and unacceptable stretch to call the presumption into service as a substitute for the allegation of present or threatened injury upon which initial standing must be based. To accept the Government's view would be to overrule our clear precedent requiring that the allegations of future injury be particular and concrete. "Past exposure to illegal conduct does not in itself show a present case or controversy regarding injunctive relief . . . if unaccompanied by any continuing, present adverse effects." Because respondent alleges only past infractions of EPRCA, and not a continuing violation or the likelihood of a future violation, injunctive relief will not redress its injury.

Having found that none of the relief sought by respondent would likely remedy its alleged injury in fact, we must conclude that respondent lacks standing to maintain this suit, and that we and the lower courts lack jurisdiction to entertain it. However desirable prompt resolution of the merits EPCRA question may be, it is not as important as observing the constitutional limits set upon courts in our system of separated powers. EPCRA will have to await another day.

The judgment is vacated and the case remanded with instructions to direct that the complaint be dismissed.

It is so ordered.

JUSTICE STEVENS, with whom JUSTICE SOUTER joins as to Parts I, III, and IV, and with whom JUSTICE GINSBURG joins as to Part III, concurring in the judgment.

* * *

II.

. . .

. . . The Court's conclusion that respondent does not have standing comes from a mechanistic application of the "redressability" aspect of our standing doctrine. "Redressability," of course, does not appear anywhere in the text of the Constitution. Instead, it is a judicial creation of the past 25 years. . . .

[T]he Court has never held — until today — that a plaintiff who is *directly injured* by a defendant lacks standing to sue because of a lack of redressability.

The Court acknowledges that respondent would have had standing if Congress had authorized some payment to respondent. Yet the Court fails to specify why payment to respondent — even if only a peppercorn — would redress respondent's injuries, while payment to the Treasury does not. Respondent clearly believes that the punishment of the Steel Company, along with future deterrence of the Steel Company and others, redresses its injury, and there is no basis in our previous standing holdings to suggest otherwise.

When one private party is injured by another, the injury can be redressed in at least two ways: by awarding compensatory damages or by imposing a sanction on the wrongdoer that will minimize the risk that the harm-causing conduct will be repeated. Thus, in some cases a tort is redressed by an award of punitive damages; even when such damages are payable to the sovereign, they provide a form of redress for the individual as well.

History supports the proposition that punishment or deterrence can redress an injury. In past centuries in England, in the American colonies, and in the United States, private persons regularly prosecuted criminal cases. The interest in punishing the defendant and deterring violations of law by the defendant and others was sufficient to support the "standing" of the private prosecutor even if the only remedy was the sentencing of the defendant to jail or to the gallows. Given this history, the Framers of Article III surely would have considered such proceedings to be "Cases" that would "redress" an injury even though the party bringing suit did not receive any monetary compensation.

The Court's expanded interpretation of the redressability requirement has another consequence. Under EPCRA, Congress gave enforcement power to state and local governments. Under the Court's reasoning, however, state and local governments would not have standing to sue for past violations, as a payment to the Treasury would no more "redress" the injury of these governments than it would redress respondent's injury. This would be true *even if Congress explicitly granted state and local governments this power.* Such a conclusion is unprecedented.

[The concurring Justices, however, would hold that the citizen suit provision does not authorize suits for wholly past violations.]

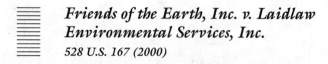

Friends of the Earth, Inc. v. Laidlaw Environmental Services, Inc.
528 U.S. 167 (2000)

JUSTICE GINSBURG delivered the opinion of the Court.

This case presents an important question concerning the operation of the citizen-suit provisions of the Clean Water Act. Congress authorized the federal district courts to entertain Clean Water Act suits initiated by "a person or persons having an interest which is or may be adversely affected." To impel future compliance with the Act, a district court may prescribe injunctive relief in such a suit; additionally or alternatively, the court may impose civil penalties payable to the United States Treasury. In the Clean Water Act citizen suit now before us, the District Court determined that injunctive relief was inappropriate because the defendant, after the institution of the litigation, achieved substantial compliance with the terms of its discharge permit. The court did, however, assess a civil penalty of $405,800. The "total deterrent effect" of the penalty would be adequate to forestall future violations, the court reasoned, taking into account that the defendant "will be required to reimburse plaintiffs for a significant amount of legal fees and has, itself, incurred significant legal expenses."

The Court of Appeals vacated the District Court's order. The case became moot, the appellate court declared, once the defendant fully complied with the terms of its permit and the plaintiff failed to appeal the denial of equitable relief. "Civil penalties payable to the government," the Court of Appeals stated, "would not redress any injury Plaintiffs have suffered." Nor were attorneys' fees in order, the Court of Appeals noted, because absent relief on the merits, plaintiffs could not qualify as prevailing parties.

We reverse the judgment of the Court of Appeals. The appellate court erred in concluding that a citizen suitor's claim for civil penalties must be dismissed as moot when the defendant, albeit after commencement of the litigation, has come into compliance. In directing dismissal of the suit on grounds of mootness, the Court of Appeals incorrectly conflated our case law on initial standing to bring suit with our case law on post-commencement mootness. A defendant's voluntary cessation of allegedly unlawful conduct ordinarily does not suffice to moot a case. The Court of Appeals also misperceived the remedial potential of civil penalties. Such penalties may serve, as an alternative to an injunction, to deter future violations and thereby redress the injuries that prompted a citizen suitor to commence litigation.

I

A

. . .

Under §505(a) of the Act, a suit to enforce any limitation in an [National Pollutant Discharge Elimination System] NPDES permit may be brought by any "citizen," defined as "a person or persons having an interest which is or may be adversely affected." Sixty days before initiating a citizen suit, however, the would-be plaintiff must give notice of the alleged violation to the EPA, the State in which the alleged violation occurred, and the alleged violator. "The purpose of notice to the alleged violator is to give it an opportunity to bring itself into complete compliance with the Act and thus render unnecessary a citizen suit." Accordingly, we have held that citizens lack statutory standing under §505(a) to sue for violations that have ceased by the time the complaint is filed. The Act also bars a citizen from suing if the EPA or the State has already commenced, and is "diligently prosecuting," an enforcement action.

B.

In 1986, defendant-respondent Laidlaw Environmental Services (TOC), Inc., bought a hazardous waste incinerator facility in Roebuck, South Carolina, that included a wastewater treatment plant. . . .

. . . [Laidlaw] received [an NPDES] permit, [and] began to discharge various pollutants into the waterway; repeatedly, Laidlaw's discharges exceeded the limits set by the permit . . . .

On April 10, 1992, plaintiff-petitioner Friends of the Earth (FOE) . . . sent a letter to Laidlaw notifying the company of their intention to file a citizen suit against it under §505(a) of the Act after the expiration of the requisite 60-day notice period. . . . Laidlaw's lawyer then contacted [the South Carolina Department of Health and Environmental Control] DHEC to ask whether DHEC would consider filing a lawsuit against Laidlaw. The District Court later found that Laidlaw's reason for requesting that DHEC file a lawsuit against it was to bar FOE's proposed citizen suit through the [statutory diligent prosecution bar]. DHEC agreed to file a lawsuit against Laidlaw; the company's lawyer then drafted the complaint for DHEC and paid the filing fee. On June 9, 1992, the last day before FOE's 60-day notice period expired, DHEC and Laidlaw reached a settlement requiring Laidlaw to pay $100,000 in civil penalties and to make "'every effort'" to comply with its permit obligations.

On June 12, 1992, FOE filed this citizen suit against Laidlaw under §505(a) of the Act, alleging noncompliance with the NPDES permit and seeking declaratory and injunctive relief and an award of civil penalties. Laidlaw moved for summary judgment on the ground that FOE had failed to present evidence demonstrating injury in fact, and therefore lacked Article III standing to bring the lawsuit. . . . [T]he District Court denied Laidlaw's summary judgment motion, finding that FOE had standing to bring the suit.

Laidlaw also moved to dismiss the action on the ground that the citizen suit was barred . . . by DHEC's prior action against the company. The . . . District Court held that DHEC's action against Laidlaw had not been "diligently prosecuted"; consequently, the court allowed FOE's citizen suit to proceed. The record indicates that after FOE initiated the suit, but before the District Court rendered judgment, Laidlaw violated the mercury discharge limitation in its permit 13 times. The District Court also found that Laidlaw had committed 13 monitoring and 10 reporting violations during this period. The last recorded mercury discharge violation occurred in January 1995, long after the complaint was filed but about two years before judgment was rendered.

On January 22, 1997, the District Court issued its judgment, . . . [awarding civil penalties, but declining injunctive relief on the ground that] "Laidlaw has been in substantial compliance with all parameters in its NPDES permit since at least August 1992."

FOE appealed the District Court's civil penalty judgment, arguing that the penalty was inadequate, but did not appeal the denial of declaratory or injunctive relief. Laidlaw cross-appealed, arguing, among other things, that FOE lacked standing to bring the suit. . . .

On July 16, 1998, the Court of Appeals for the Fourth Circuit issued its judgment. The Court of Appeals assumed without deciding that FOE initially had standing to bring the action, but went on to hold that the case had become moot. The appellate court stated, first, that the elements of Article III standing — injury, causation, and redressability — must persist at every stage of review, or else the action becomes moot. Citing our decision in *Steel Co.*, the Court of Appeals reasoned that the case had become moot because "the only remedy currently available to [FOE] — civil penalties payable to the government — would not redress any injury [FOE has] suffered." The court therefore vacated the District Court's order and remanded with instructions to dismiss the action. In a footnote, the Court of Appeals added that FOE's "failure to obtain relief on the merits of [its] claims precludes any recovery of attorneys' fees or other litigation costs because such an award is available only to a 'prevailing or substantially prevailing party.' "

According to Laidlaw, after the Court of Appeals issued its decision but before this Court granted certiorari, the entire incinerator facility in Roebuck was permanently closed, dismantled, and put up for sale, and all discharges from the facility permanently ceased.

We granted certiorari to resolve the inconsistency between the Fourth Circuit's decision in this case and the decisions of several other Courts of Appeals, which have held that a defendant's compliance with its permit after the commencement of litigation does not moot claims for civil penalties under the Act.

II

A. . . .

. . .

In *Lujan v. Defenders of Wildlife*, we held that, to satisfy Article III's standing requirements, a plaintiff must show (1) it has suffered an "injury in fact" that is (a) concrete and particularized and (b) actual or imminent, not conjectural or hypothetical; (2) the injury is fairly traceable to the challenged action of the defendant; and (3) it is likely, as opposed to merely speculative, that the injury will be redressed by a favorable decision. . . .

Laidlaw contends first that FOE lacked standing from the outset even to seek injunctive relief, because the plaintiff organizations failed to show that any of their members had sustained or faced the threat of any "injury in fact" from Laidlaw's activities. In support of this contention Laidlaw points to the District Court's finding, made in the course of setting the penalty amount, that there had been "no demonstrated proof of harm to the environment" from Laidlaw's mercury discharge violations.

The relevant showing for purposes of Article III standing, however, is not injury to the environment but injury to the plaintiff. To insist upon the former rather than the latter as part of the standing inquiry . . . is to raise the standing hurdle higher than the necessary showing for success on the merits in an action alleging noncompliance with an NPDES permit. Focusing properly on injury to the plaintiff, the District Court found that FOE had demonstrated sufficient injury to establish standing. For example, FOE member Kenneth Lee Curtis averred in affidavits that he lived a half-mile from Laidlaw's facility; that he occasionally drove over the North Tyger River, and that it looked and smelled polluted; and that he would like to fish, camp, swim, and picnic in and near the river between 3 and 15 miles downstream from the facility, as he did when he was a teenager, but would not do so because he was concerned that the water was polluted by Laidlaw's discharges. . . .

These sworn statements, as the District Court determined, adequately documented injury in fact. We have held that environmental plaintiffs adequately allege injury in fact when they aver that they use the affected area and are persons "for whom the aesthetic and recreational values of the area will be lessened" by the challenged activity.

. . .

Laidlaw argues next that even if FOE had standing to seek injunctive relief, it lacked standing to seek civil penalties. Here the asserted defect is not injury but redressability. Civil penalties offer no redress to private plaintiffs, Laidlaw argues, because they are paid to the government, and therefore a citizen plaintiff can never have standing to seek them.

. . .

We have recognized on numerous occasions that "all civil penalties have some deterrent effect." More specifically, Congress has found that civil penalties in Clean Water Act cases do more than promote immediate compliance by limiting the defendant's economic incentive to delay its attainment of permit limits; they also deter future violations. This congressional determination warrants judicial attention and respect. "The legislative history of the Act reveals that Congress wanted the district court to consider the need for retribution and deterrence, in addition to restitution, when it imposed civil penalties. . . . [The district court may] seek to deter future violations by basing the penalty on its economic impact."

It can scarcely be doubted that, for a plaintiff who is injured or faces the threat of future injury due to illegal conduct ongoing at the time of suit, a sanction that effectively abates that conduct and prevents its recurrence provides a form of redress. Civil penalties can fit that description. To the extent that they encourage defendants to discontinue current violations and deter them from committing future ones, they afford redress to citizen plaintiffs who are injured or threatened with injury as a consequence of ongoing unlawful conduct.

The dissent argues that it is the *availability* rather than the *imposition* of civil penalties that deters any particular polluter from continuing to pollute. This argument misses the mark in two ways. First, it overlooks the interdependence of the availability and the imposition; a threat has no deterrent value unless it is credible that it will be carried out. Second, it is reasonable for Congress to conclude that an actual award of civil penalties does in fact bring with it a significant quantum of deterrence over and above what is achieved by the mere prospect of such penalties. A would-be polluter may or may not be dissuaded by the existence of a remedy on the books, but a defendant once hit in its pocketbook will surely think twice before polluting again.
. . .

Laidlaw contends that the reasoning of our decision in *Steel Co.* directs the conclusion that citizen plaintiffs have no standing to seek civil penalties under the Act. We disagree. *Steel Co.* established that citizen suitors lack standing to seek civil penalties for violations that have abated by the time of suit. We specifically noted in that case that there was no allegation in the complaint of any continuing or imminent violation, and that no basis for such an allegation appeared to exist. In short, *Steel Co.* held that private plaintiffs, unlike the Federal Government, may not sue to assess penalties for wholly past violations, but our decision in that case did not reach the issue of standing to seek penalties for violations that are ongoing at the time of the complaint and that could continue into the future if undeterred.[4]

B

Satisfied that FOE had standing under Article III to bring this action, we turn to the question of mootness.

The only conceivable basis for a finding of mootness in this case is Laidlaw's voluntary conduct — either its achievement by August 1992 of

---

4. . . . [T]he dissent's broader charge that citizen suits for civil penalties under the Act carry "grave implications for democratic governance" seems to us overdrawn. Certainly the Federal Executive Branch does not share the dissent's view that such suits dissipate its authority to enforce the law. In fact, the Department of Justice has endorsed this citizen suit from the outset, submitting *amicus* briefs in support of FOE in the District Court, the Court of Appeals, and this Court. As we have already noted, the Federal Government retains the power to foreclose a citizen suit by undertaking its own action. And if the Executive Branch opposes a particular citizen suit, the statute allows the Administrator of the EPA to "intervene as a matter of right" and bring the Government's views to the attention of the court.

substantial compliance with its NPDES permit or its more recent shutdown of the Roebuck facility. It is well settled that "a defendant's voluntary cessation of a challenged practice does not deprive a federal court of its power to determine the legality of the practice." . . . In accordance with this principle, the standard we have announced for determining whether a case has been mooted by the defendant's voluntary conduct is stringent: "A case might become moot if subsequent events made it absolutely clear that the allegedly wrongful behavior could not reasonably be expected to recur." The "heavy burden of persuading" the court that the challenged conduct cannot reasonably be expected to start up again lies with the party asserting mootness.

The Court of Appeals justified its mootness disposition by reference to *Steel Co.*, which held that citizen plaintiffs lack standing to seek civil penalties for wholly past violations. In relying on *Steel Co.*, the Court of Appeals confused mootness with standing. The confusion is understandable, given this Court's repeated statements that the doctrine of mootness can be described as "the doctrine of standing set in a time frame: The requisite personal interest that must exist at the commencement of the litigation (standing) must continue throughout its existence (mootness)."
. . .

Standing doctrine functions to ensure, among other things, that the scarce resources of the federal courts are devoted to those disputes in which the parties have a concrete stake. In contrast, by the time mootness is an issue, the case has been brought and litigated, often (as here) for years. To abandon the case at an advanced stage may prove more wasteful than frugal. . . .

Laidlaw . . . asserts . . . that the closure of its Roebuck facility, which took place after the Court of Appeals issued its decision, mooted the case. The facility closure, like Laidlaw's earlier achievement of substantial compliance with its permit requirements, might moot the case, but — we once more reiterate — only if one or the other of these events made it absolutely clear that Laidlaw's permit violations could not reasonably be expected to recur. The effect of both Laidlaw's compliance and the facility closure on the prospect of future violations is a disputed factual matter. FOE points out, for example and Laidlaw does not appear to contest — that Laidlaw retains its NPDES permit. These issues have not been aired in the lower courts; they remain open for consideration on remand.
. . .

For the reasons stated, the judgment of the United States Court of Appeals for the Fourth Circuit is reversed, and the case is remanded for further proceedings consistent with this opinion.

It is so ordered.

Justice SCALIA, with whom Justice THOMAS joins, dissenting.

The Court begins its analysis by finding injury in fact on the basis of vague affidavits that are undermined by the District Court's express finding that Laidlaw's discharges caused no demonstrable harm to the environment. It then proceeds to marry private wrong with public remedy in a union that violates traditional principles of federal standing — thereby permitting law enforcement to be placed in the hands of private individuals. Finally, the Court suggests that to avoid mootness one needs even less of a stake in the outcome than the Court's watered-down requirements for initial standing. I dissent from all of this.

I

Plaintiffs, as the parties invoking federal jurisdiction, have the burden of proof and persuasion as to the existence of standing. The plaintiffs in this case fell far short of carrying their burden of demonstrating injury in fact . . . .

Typically, an environmental plaintiff claiming injury due to discharges in violation of the Clean Water Act argues that the discharges harm the environment, and that the harm to the environment injures him. This route to injury is barred in the present case, however, since the District Court concluded after considering all the evidence that there had been "no demonstrated proof of harm to the environment," that the "permit violations at issue in this citizen suit did not result in any health risk or environmental harm," that "all available data . . . fail to show that Laidlaw's *actual* discharges have resulted in harm to the North Tyger River," and that "the overall quality of the river exceeds levels necessary to support . . . recreation in and on the water."

The Court finds these conclusions unproblematic for standing, because "the relevant showing for purposes of Article III standing . . . is not injury to the environment but injury to the plaintiff." This statement is correct, as far as it goes. We have certainly held that a demonstration of harm to the environment is not *enough* to satisfy the injury-in-fact requirement unless the plaintiff can demonstrate how he personally was harmed. In the normal course, however, a lack of demonstrable harm to the environment will translate, as it plainly does here, into a lack of demonstrable harm to citizen plaintiffs. . . .

. . . By accepting plaintiffs' vague, contradictory, and unsubstantiated allegations of "concern" about the environment as adequate to prove injury in fact, and accepting them even in the face of a finding that the environment was not demonstrably harmed, the Court makes the injury-in-fact requirement a sham. If there are permit violations, and a member of a plaintiff environmental organization lives near the offending plant, it would be difficult not to satisfy today's lenient standard.

II

The Court's treatment of the redressability requirement — which would have been unnecessary if it resolved the injury-in-fact question correctly — is equally cavalier. . . . Only last Term, we held that penalties [paid to the U.S. treasury] do not redress any injury a citizen plaintiff has suffered from past violations. The Court nonetheless finds the redressability requirement satisfied here, distinguishing *Steel Co.* on the ground that in this case the petitioners allege ongoing violations; payment of the penalties, it says, will remedy petitioners' injury by deterring future violations by Laidlaw. It holds that a penalty payable to the public "remedies" a threatened private harm, and suffices to sustain a private suit.

That holding has no precedent in our jurisprudence, and takes this Court beyond the "cases and controversies" that Article III of the Constitution has entrusted to its resolution. Even if it were appropriate, moreover, to allow Article III's remediation requirement to be satisfied by the indirect private consequences of a public penalty, those consequences are entirely too speculative in the present case. The new standing law that the Court makes — like all expansions of standing beyond the traditional constitutional limits — has grave implications for democratic governance. . . .

A. . . .

. . . [R]elief against prospective harm is traditionally afforded by way of an injunction, the scope of which is limited by the scope of the threatened injury. In seeking to overturn that tradition by giving an individual plaintiff the power to invoke a public remedy, Congress has done precisely what we have said it cannot do: convert an "undifferentiated public interest" into an "individual right" vindicable in the courts. The sort of scattershot redress approved today makes nonsense of our statement . . . that the requirement of injury in fact "insures the framing of relief no broader than required by the precise facts." A claim of particularized future injury has today been made the vehicle for pursuing generalized penalties for past violations, and a threshold showing of injury in fact has become a lever that will move the world.

B

As I have just discussed, it is my view that a plaintiff's desire to benefit from the deterrent effect of a public penalty for past conduct can never suffice to establish a case or controversy of the sort known to our law. Such deterrent effect is, so to speak, "speculative as a matter of law." Even if that were not so, however, the deterrent effect in the present case would surely be speculative as a matter of fact.

The Court recognizes, of course, that to satisfy Article III, it must be "likely," as opposed to "merely speculative," that a favorable decision will redress plaintiffs' injury. Further, the Court recognizes that not *all* deterrent effects of *all* civil penalties will meet this standard — though it declines to "explore the outer limits" of adequate deterrence. It concludes, however, that in the present case "the civil penalties sought by FOE carried with them a deterrent effect" that satisfied the "likely [rather than] speculative" standard. There is little in the Court's opinion to explain why it believes this is so.

The Court cites the District Court's conclusion that the penalties imposed, along with anticipated fee awards, provided "adequate deterrence."

There is absolutely no reason to believe, however, that this meant "deterrence adequate to prevent an injury to these plaintiffs that would otherwise occur."
. . .

If the Court had undertaken the necessary inquiry into whether significant deterrence of the plaintiffs' feared injury was "likely," it would have had to reason something like this: Strictly speaking, no polluter is deterred by a penalty for past pollution; he is deterred by the *fear* of a penalty for *future* pollution. That fear will be virtually nonexistent if the prospective polluter knows that all emissions violators are given a free pass; it will be substantial under an emissions program such as the federal scheme here, which is regularly and notoriously enforced; it will be even higher when a prospective polluter subject to such a regularly enforced program has, as here, been the object of public charges of pollution and a suit for injunction; and it will surely be near the top of the graph when, as here, the prospective polluter has already been subjected to *state* penalties for the past pollution. The deterrence on which the plaintiffs must rely for standing in the present case is the marginal increase in Laidlaw's fear of future penalties that will be achieved by adding federal penalties for Laidlaw's past conduct.

I cannot say for certain that this marginal increase is zero; but I can say for certain that it is entirely speculative whether it will make the difference between these plaintiffs' suffering injury in the future and these plaintiffs' going unharmed. In fact, the assertion that it will "likely" do so is entirely far-fetched. . . .

In sum, if this case is, as the Court suggests, within the central core of "deterrence" standing, it is impossible to imagine what the "outer limits" could possibly be. The Court's expressed reluctance to define those "outer limits" serves only to disguise the fact that it has promulgated a revolutionary new doctrine of standing that will permit the entire body of public civil penalties to be handed over to enforcement by private interests.

C

Article II of the Constitution commits it to the President to "take Care that the Laws be faithfully executed," Art. II, §3, and provides specific methods by which all persons exercising significant executive power are to be appointed, Art. II, §2. As JUSTICE KENNEDY's concurrence correctly observes, the question of the conformity of this legislation with Article II has not been argued — and I, like the Court, do not address it. But Article III, no less than Article II, has consequences for the structure of our government, and it is worth noting the changes in that structure which today's decision allows.

By permitting citizens to pursue civil penalties payable to the Federal Treasury, the Act does not provide a mechanism for individual relief in any traditional sense, but turns over to private citizens the function of enforcing the law. A Clean Water Act plaintiff pursuing civil penalties acts as a self-appointed mini-EPA. Where, as is often the case, the plaintiff is a national association, it has significant discretion in choosing enforcement targets. Once the association is aware of a reported violation, it need not look long for an injured member, at least under the theory of injury the Court applies today. And once the target is chosen, the suit goes forward without meaningful public control. The availability of civil penalties vastly disproportionate to the individual injury gives citizen plaintiffs massive bargaining power — which is often used to achieve settlements requiring the defendant to support environmental projects of the plaintiffs' choosing. Thus is a public fine diverted to a private interest.

To be sure, the EPA may foreclose the citizen suit by itself bringing suit. This allows public authorities to avoid private enforcement only by accepting private direction as to when enforcement should be undertaken — which is no less constitutionally bizarre. Elected officials are entirely deprived of their discretion to decide that a given violation should not be the object of suit at all, or that the enforcement decision should be postponed. This is the predictable and inevitable consequence of the Court's allowing the use of public remedies for private wrongs.

III

. . .

By uncritically accepting vague claims of injury, the Court has turned the Article III requirement of injury in fact into a "mere pleading requirement"; and by approving the novel theory that public penalties can redress anticipated private wrongs, it has come close to "making the redressability requirement vanish." The undesirable and unconstitutional consequence of today's decision is to place the immense power of suing to enforce the public laws in private hands. I respectfully dissent.

NOTES ON LAIDLAW AND STEEL COMPANY

1. *Consistency.* Are *Laidlaw* and *Steel Co.* consistent? How does the *Laidlaw* Court seek to distinguish *Steel Co.*? Do you find the distinction drawn persuasive? Do penalties redress an injury or not? Would an injury alleged in the *Steel Co.* be redressable if Congress allowed plaintiffs to keep some or all of the penalties, instead of directing that they go the federal treasury?

2. *Injury-in-fact.* The *Laidlaw* majority relies upon injury to the plaintiff as opposed to injury to the environment. This distinction helps justify the Court's acceptance of Friends of the Earth's (FOE) allegations that the discharges at issue here limits its members' use of the North Tyger river. Justice Scalia, however, would require citizen enforcers to prove that the particular discharge prompting the citizen suit damaged the environment the plaintiffs would like to use. Suppose that Justice Scalia's approach had become the law. Would this greatly damage the capacity of citizen suits to serve as an effective deterrent? Why does the majority claim that requiring proof of environmental

harm "raises the standing bar higher than necessary for success on the merits"? What must plaintiffs prove to show an NPDES violation?

On the other hand, does acceptance of plaintiffs' allegations without proof of environmental harm mean that the court has accepted purely psychological harms as the basis for an injury-in-fact allegation? If so, is that appropriate?

3. *The legitimacy of citizen suits.* Justice Scalia expresses grave doubts about the legitimacy of citizen suits in his *Laidlaw* dissent:

> By permitting citizens to pursue civil penalties payable to the Federal Treasury, the Act does not provide a mechanism for individual relief in any traditional sense, but turns over to private citizens the function of enforcing the law. A Clean Water Act plaintiff pursuing civil penalties acts as a self-appointed mini-EPA. Where, as is often the case, the plaintiff is a national association, it has significant discretion in choosing enforcement targets. Once the association is aware of a reported violation, it need not look long for an injured member, at least under the theory of injury the Court applies today. And once the target is chosen, the suit goes forward without meaningful public control. The availability of civil penalties vastly disproportionate to the individual injury gives citizen plaintiffs massive bargaining power which is often used to achieve settlements requiring the defendant to support environmental projects of the plaintiffs' choosing. Thus is a public fine diverted to a private interest.

Laidlaw, 528 U.S. at 209-210. Do you agree that a settlement creating an environmental project chosen by an environmental organization diverts "a public fine to a private interest"? Does the lack of public control over an environmental organization's choice of enforcement targets interfere with the Executive Branch's duty to "take care the law is faithfully executed"? *See* William W. Buzbee, *Standing and the Statutory Universe,* 11 Duke Envt'l L. & Pol'y Forum 247, 276-279 (2001) (arguing that citizen suits vindicate several layers of political judgment employed in setting standards).

C. ATTORNEY'S FEES

While citizen enforcement may supplement government enforcement of environmental law, few attorneys can afford to bring citizen suits frequently, unless there is some prospect of reimbursement for the costs involved in bringing suit, including attorney's fees. In Aleyeska Pipeline Service Co. v. Wilderness Society, 421 U.S. 240 (1975), the Supreme Court reversed a decision employing a court's equitable discretion to award attorney's fees to an environmental group suing to force the Department of Interior to comply with the Mineral Leasing Act of 1920 and the National Environmental Policy Act of 1969. The Supreme Court held that the use of attorney's fees to reward successful private attorney generals conflicted with the traditional "American Rule," which generally requires each side to bear its own costs.

In order to encourage citizen enforcement, Congress ordered a departure from the American Rule in several environmental statutes. But the Court construed these departures narrowly. In Ruckelshaus v. Sierra Club, 463 U.S. 680 (1983), the Court interpreted a Clean Air Act provision authorizing attorney's fees "whenever [the court] determines that such award is appropriate." Although the provision on its face seemed to offer district courts wide latitude in deciding whether to award a fee, the Court in a 5-4 decision, reversed a ruling awarding a fee to an environmental group that had, in the court's judgment, helped EPA ward off some industry challenges, but had not prevailed on any of its own claims. The Court insisted that fee awards were only appropriate if the citizen suing was a prevailing party.

The courts have generally defined a "prevailing party" as one that succeeds on any significant issue in litigation that achieves some of the benefits the party sought in bringing suit. See Hensley v. Eckerhart, 461 U.S. 424, 433 (1983). An issue often arises as to whether citizens can collect attorney's fees when the government (or other defendant) voluntarily complies with the law to avoid suit. The courts have generally allowed plaintiffs to collect fees on a "catalyst" theory, when its suit seemed to cause the defendant to conform its conduct to the law. See, e.g., Environmental Defense Fund v. EPA, 716 F.2d 916, 919 (D.C. Cir. 1983) (allowing fees in a RCRA case on a catalyst theory). In Buckhannon Board and Care Home, Inc. v. West Virginia Dep't of Health and Human Resources, 532 U.S. 598, 605 (2001), however, the Supreme Court interpreted provisions in federal civil rights statutes awarding fees to prevailing parties as not embracing a catalyst theory. The lower courts, however, have continued to adhere to the catalyst theory in citizen suits under provisions offering fees where "appropriate," see, e.g., Association of California Water Agencies v. Evans, 386 F.3d 879, 885 (9th Cir. 2004) (Endangered Species Act); Sierra Club v. EPA, 322 F.3d 718, 721–26 (D.C. Cir. 2003) (Clean Air Act); Loggerhead Turtle v. County Council of Volusia County, 307 F.3d 1318, 1325-27 (11th Cir. 2002) (Endangered Species Act); Center for Biological Diversity v. Norton, 262 F.3d 1077, 1080 n.2 (10th Cir. 2001) (assuming that a catalyst theory applies), but not under provisions offering fees to "substantially prevailing parties," see Sierra Club v. City of Little Rock, 351 F.3d 840, 845-46 (8th Cir. 2004) (reversing an attorney's fee award predicated upon a catalyst theory under the Clean Water Act). The courts continuing to grant fees in catalyst cases relied on the citizen suit provisions' language authorizing an award of fees "whenever appropriate" and upon legislative history suggesting congressional support for liberal granting of fees to encourage citizen suits.

Often, plaintiffs prevail on some of their claims, but not others. The courts often award a full fee award in such cases, because it is difficult to apportion fees between interrelated claims. See Hensley, 461 U.S. at 435–38 (declining to divide up a fee award in a civil rights case, but suggesting that division may sometimes be appropriate).

The Court trimmed fees in City of Burlington v. Dague, 505 U.S. 557 (1992). Generally, courts calculate a "lodestar" attorney's fee by multiplying the reasonable hours invested in litigation by a "reasonable" hourly rate, typically determined by the prevailing rates for attorneys with comparable experience in the relevant community. In *Dague*, however, the lower court had increased the fee to reflect the risk that the plaintiff might get no fees at all, since he had accepted the case on a contingency basis (*i.e.*, no victory, no payment). The Court held that trial courts should not augment attorney's fees in citizen suits to reflect the difficulty of the case and the risks involved. Justice Scalia, writing for the majority, expressed a concern that providing a risk premium would "provide attorneys with the same incentive to bring relatively meritless claims as relatively meritorious ones." Do you think that providing a risk premium (raising fee awards for especially complex or risky cases) would have this effect? *See* David M. Driesen, The Economic Dynamics of Environmental Law 143 (2003). How much does the attorney collect if he loses his client's case?

Does the current approach to attorney's fees provide an adequate incentive to bring citizen suits? Does it provide an incentive for too much litigation? *See* Michael S. Greve, *The Private Enforcement of Environmental Law*, 65 Tulane L. Rev. 339 (1990) (arguing that the citizen suit provisions create overdeterrence). What, if any reforms should Congress enact to improve the incentives provided for citizen suits?

D.   ENFORCEMENT: A GENERAL ASSESSMENT

In spite of the array of statutory provisions aimed at enforcement, non-compliance remains widespread. *See, e.g.,* Robert W. Adler & Charles Lord, *Environmental Crimes: Raising the Stakes*, 59 Geo. Wash. L. Rev. 781, 789 (1990–91) (discussing reports by the General Accounting Office and various environmental organizations).

ONE LAST LOOK AT PFOA

Recall that EPA has received commitments from DuPont and other manufacturers to reduce PFOA releases into the environment and to work toward elimination of the chemical. Suppose that EPA issues a rule under the Clean Water Act requiring reporting of discharges into water under the voluntary agreement. The Environmental Working Group (EWG) finds that no reports have been filed during the previous six months, even though the rule requires monthly reports, and hires you to advise them on how to proceed. Would you recommend that EWG sue DuPont under TSCA's citizen suit provisions? Would you instead recommend that it urge EPA to prosecute the alleged violations? Or would you recommend some third course of action? Why?

Table of Cases

Index